Great Britain, Royal Commission on Historical Manuscripts

The Manuscripts of the Duke of Leeds

The Bridgewater Trust, Reading Corporation, the Inner Temple etc.

Great Britain, Royal Commission on Historical Manuscripts

The Manuscripts of the Duke of Leeds
The Bridgewater Trust, Reading Corporation, the Inner Temple etc.

ISBN/EAN: 9783337143084

Printed in Europe, USA, Canada, Australia, Japan

Cover: Foto ©ninafisch / pixelio.de

More available books at **www.hansebooks.com**

HISTORICAL MANUSCRIPTS COMMISSION.

ELEVENTH REPORT, APPENDIX, PART VII.

THE

MANUSCRIPTS

OF THE

DUKE OF LEEDS, THE BRIDGEWATER TRUST,
READING CORPORATION, THE INNER TEMPLE, &c.

𝔓𝔯𝔢𝔰𝔢𝔫𝔱𝔢𝔡 𝔱𝔬 𝔟𝔬𝔱𝔥 𝔥𝔬𝔲𝔰𝔢𝔰 𝔬𝔣 𝔓𝔞𝔯𔩁𔦀𔦀𔦀𔦀𔦀 𝔟𝔶 𝔠𝔬𝔪𝔪𝔞𝔫𝔡 𝔬𝔣 𝔥𝔢𝔯 𝔐𝔞𝔧𝔢𝔰𝔱𝔶.

LONDON:
PRINTED FOR HER MAJESTY'S STATIONERY OFFICE,
BY EYRE AND SPOTTISWOODE,
PRINTERS TO THE QUEEN'S MOST EXCELLENT MAJESTY.

And to be purchased, either directly or through any Bookseller, from
EYRE AND SPOTTISWOODE, EAST HARDING STREET, FLEET STREET, E.C. and
32, ABINGDON STREET, WESTMINSTER, S.W.; or
ADAM AND CHARLES BLACK, 6, NORTH BRIDGE, EDINBURGH; or
HODGES, FIGGIS, & Co., 104, GRAFTON STREET, DUBLIN.

1888.

[C.—5060.]—VII. *Price 2s.*

CONTENTS.

	PAGE.
THE MANUSCRIPTS OF THE DUKE OF LEEDS; BY THE REV. W. D. MACRAY, M.A.	1
THE MANUSCRIPTS OF LOUISA, MARCHIONESS OF WATERFORD; BY THE REV. JOS. STEVENSON, M.A.	85
THE MANUSCRIPTS OF LORD HOTHFIELD; BY WILLIAM O. HEWLETT	81
THE MANUSCRIPTS OF FRANCIS DARWIN, ESQ., OF CRESKELD; BY J. J. CARTWRIGHT, M.A.	90
CALENDAR OF THE PAPERS AT HUNSTANTON HALL; BY HAMON LE STRANGE	93
THE MANUSCRIPTS OF THE LATE AUGUSTUS W. SAVILE, ESQ., OF RUFFORD ABBEY; BY J. J. CARTWRIGHT, M.A.	119
THE MANUSCRIPTS AT THE BRIDGWATER TRUST OFFICE, WALKDEN; BY THE REV. W. D. MACRAY, M.A.	126
THE MANUSCRIPTS OF READING CORPORATION; BY THE REV. W. D. MACRAY, M.A.	167
THE MANUSCRIPTS IN THE INNER TEMPLE LIBRARY; BY THE REV. W. D. MACRAY, M.A.	227

U 24952. Wt. 6696.

HISTORICAL MANUSCRIPTS COMMISSION.

THE MANUSCRIPTS OF THE DUKE OF LEEDS AT HORNBY CASTLE, YORKSHIRE.

The manuscripts preserved at Hornby Castle, Yorkshire, consist firstly of the papers of Thomas Osborne, created Viscount Dunblaine in 1673, Earl of Danby in 1674, and Duke of Leeds 20 years later. From 1673 to 1679 he held the office of Lord High Treasurer, and he was one of the active promoters of the Revolution of 1688. Amongst his papers, a collection of Tower warrants, in 1660-65, a return of non-conformist meetings in London, and of Roman Catholic priests (with whom are strangely mingled Socinian preachers), and some Scottish letters intercepted in 1688, may be specially noticed. The Tower warrants furnish various particulars about some of the regicides, which possibly are not otherwise known; the inquests on Simon Mayne and Isaac Pennington, the transportation of Sir Henry Vane, Sir Hardress Waller, Colonels Harvey and Lilburne, &c.: while of other prominent names we meet with those of Haselrig, Lenthall, Antrim, Argyle, Praise God Barebone, Barkstead, Corbet, Okey, James Harrington, and George Wither. The order in 1663 that Margaret Johnston, the daughter of Archibald Johnston, Lord Warriston, should be admitted upon her own petition to live with her father in close confinement, records a touching instance of filial affection. And an isolated warrant of the year 1668 gives us another famous name, in an order for the admission of one Francis Cooke to see his master, William Penn, then in close confinement. A letter from Catherine Green, the mother of that son of Charles II. who at first was known by the name of *Don Carlos*, and was afterwards created Earl of Plymouth, possesses some interest; as does also a letter of Frampton, the non-juring Bishop of Gloucester.

The second portion consists of the papers of Robert D'Arcy, fourth and last Earl of Holdernesse, who was Secretary of State from July 1751 to March 1761, and governor to the sons of King George III. from 1771 to 1776, when he resigned his office (two years before his death) much to the regret of the King, who appears to have held him in the highest respect and esteem. His papers came, with the Castle in which they are preserved (which still bears on its sculptured doorways the name of William first Lord Conyers, who in the time of Henry VII. enlarged or rebuilt an older structure), into the possession of the Dukes of Leeds by the marriage of the only daughter of the Earl of Holdernesse to Francis, fifth Duke. Amongst them are specially to be noted the papers relating to Scotland, with the anonymous letters of a treacherous Jacobite in France offering, for sufficient remuneration, to furnish information of the agents employed by Prince Charles Edward; and the letters of George III. respecting the Prince of Wales and the Duke of York.

An idea has been prevalent that amongst these papers there would be found some clue to the authorship of the *Letters of Junius*. The reason for this is not known; but it is an idea which has been entertained for some years. But, unfortunately, after the examination of every box of family deeds and papers now existing at Hornby Castle, in which there was any chance of the discovery of the " missing link," nothing has been found which bears any reference to the letters or their writer. In 1850, the late well-known bookseller, Mr. H. G. Bohn, saw (as he relates in

MSS. OF THE DUKE OF LEEDS.

MSS. OF THE DUKE OF LEEDS. his edition of Lowndes' *Bibliographer's Manual*) in the family mansion in London, two parcels of papers marked " Secret," which he hoped might contain the desired information, but which he was not then permitted to examine. Many of the letters addressed to the Earl of Holdernesse are marked " Secret " and " Private " ; and if the parcels in question are now included among the papers at Hornby, it may well be the case that they comprehended all the letters and papers relating to the royal princes. It is noticeable that for the period from 1760 to the Earl's death in 1778 there is scarcely anything now existing besides the papers relating to his office in the royal family. To examine particularly every one of the letters in the mass of correspondence has been, of course, impossible ; but the fact that the above-mentioned period exhibits almost an entire dearth of correspondence enables me to say, with a tolerable degree of certainty, that the desired clue to the mystery is not to be found in this collection.

The last part of the papers comprises a portion of the political correspondence of the sixth Duke of Leeds, in 1784–5, and 1787–90, while, as Marquess of Carmarthen, holding office under Pitt as Foreign Secretary. The letters of Pitt, and the correspondence of the ambassador in France and his Secretary, which form the largest part of these papers, contribute to make this portion but little inferior in value to the others.

I.—DANBY PAPERS.

1660–1665.

1660. A series of warrants to Sir John Robinson, the Lieut. of the Tower, for committal and discharge of prisoners, &c. :—

1660. 13 Oct.—Acknowledgment by the Sheriffs of the receipt of the body of William Hewlett by writ of *Habeas Corpus*.

3 Nov.—Warrant by Sir Will. Morice for the discharge of John Thomson, esq.

30 Nov.—Order by the King for the delivery of the Marq. of Argyle in safe custody to the Earl of Middleton.

1661. 1661. 5 Jan.—Certificate by Judge Foster to the Lieut. that John Lenthall, esq. has put in security for his appearance next term.

12 Jan.—Order by Sir Edw. Nicholas for delivery of the corpse of Sir Arth. Haselrig, dead in the Tower, to his son for interment.

8 March.—Orders in Council for the bailing of Col. Rob. Phaire and John Rede, gent.

28 March.—Order in Council for the discharge of Francis Corker.

29 March.—Order in Council for the liberation, on bail for £20,000, of Randolph, Marquis of Antrim, for examination in Ireland.

16 Apr.—Warrant by Sir E. Nicholas for delivery of the corpse of Simon Mayne to his wife, for interment in the country without ostentation :—

Enclosed, the return of the coroner's inquest on 14 Apr., that Mayne died on 13 Apr. from gout, with fever and convulsion-fits, and that he was attended by Dr. Cox.

30 July.—Order by the King for the discharge of Joseph Bamfeild who is not to come within the verge of the Court.

18 Aug.—Warrants by Sir W. Morice for the imprisonment of Sir Rob. Howard, knt., James and Philip Howard, esqs., Sir Rob. Killegrew, knt., and Henry Killegrew, esq.

MSS. OF THE DUKE OF LEEDS.
1661.

21 Aug.—Warrant from the same for the discharge of the said five prisoners.

3 Sept.—Privy Council order for the discharge of Col. Hercules Hunks, or Huncks, on binding him over to give evidence at the trial of Col. Francis Hacker.

25 Oct.—Letter from Sir E. Nicholas to the Lieut. sending a warrant for the delivery of Sir Henry Vane to Capt. Thomas Allen on board the Foresight to be transported; together with the three warrants following. "You shall doe well not to be knowne whither Sir H. Vane is sent untill his Majestie give you leave to speake of it."

25 Oct.—Orders by the King for the delivery of Col. John Lambert, Sir Hardress Waller, and Col. Cobbet, to Hugh Hyde, Capt. of H.M.S. *The Adventure*, to be transported; with letter of 26 Oct., enclosing the orders, from Sir E. Nicholas, and acknowledgment by Capt. Hyde on 27 Oct. of the receipt of the prisoners.

31 Oct.—Orders by the King for the delivery of Col. Rob. Lilbourne and Col. Harvey to Capt. John Fletcher of H.M.S. *Eagle*, to be transported, with letter from Sir E. Nicholas of 1 Nov., and acknowledgment by Capt. Fletcher of 4 Nov.

8 Nov.—Order by the King for delivery of Col. Rob. Overton to the Duke of Albemarle as a prisoner; with warrant from the Duke on 11 Nov. for his delivery to Lieut. John Arundell, and acknowledgment by the latter of receipt on 12 Oct.

25 Nov.—Warrants by Sir E. Nicholas for the close imprisonment of Mr. Praisegod Barebone and Mr. Sam. Moyer for treasonable designs and practices.

Same date.—Warrant by the same for the close imprisonment of James Harrington for high treason in conspiring to change the government, "and for that purpose contriveing and designeing to meet and assemble att sett and appointed times and places, and meeting and assembling accordingly."

26 Nov.—Warrants by the same for the close imprisonment of Mr. John Wildeman and of James Harrington, lately called Sir Jas. Harrington, Mr. Ireton, lately called Alderman Ireton, and Major Haynes, for treasonable designs and practices.

27 Nov.—Council-warrant for imprisonment of Capt. Rob. Holmes, late commander of H.M.S. *Charles*, for "letting passe one of the King of Sweden's shipps, wherein the Swedish ambassador was, without striking his flagg, and doing the homage due and accustomed to his Majestie's shipps in his own seas."

29 Nov.—Warrant by Sir E. Nicholas for close imprisonment of Col. Samon for treasonable designs and practices.

2 Dec.—Warrant by the same for the release of Capt. Rob. Holmes.

5 Dec.—Warrant by the same for the close imprisonment of John Portman for seditious practices committed or justly suspected.

19 Dec.—Warrant by the same for delivery of the corpse of Isaac Pennington to his friends for burial; with return of the inquest on 17 Dec. that he died on the night of the 16th, merely from age, being about 80 years old.

30 Dec.—Warrant by the same for delivery of the corpse of Owen Roe; with return of the inquest that he died a natural death, of the spleen, on 25 Dec., aged 73.

MSS. OF THE DUKE OF LEEDS.
1662.

1662, 25 Jan.—Copy of order of the House of Commons for delivery to the Lieut. of such persons now in custody of the House as are by Act of Parliament to be carried on sleds from the Tower to Tyborne.

Same date.—Order by the King for delivery to the Sheriffs of Will. Mounson, Henry Mildmay, and Rob. Wallop, for the inflicting, on 27 Jan., of the pains and penalties ordered by Act of Parliament.

27 Jan.—Special order to the same effect by the King for the delivery of William, late Lord Mounson.

27 Jan.—Acknowledgment by the Sheriffs of the receipt of the body of Will. Mounson to be returned to the prison of the Fleet.

5 Feb.—Order by the Lords for the bringing to the bar of the House of the bodies of Owen Rowe, Aug. Garland, Henry Smith, Henry Martin, Rob. Tichborn, James Temple, Thos. Wayt, Will. Heveningham, Isaac Pennington, Peter Temple, Gilb. Millington, Vinc. Potter, and Tho. Wogan, mentioned in a bill sent up from the Commons, and also of Edm. Harvey, Sir Hardres Waller, Rob. Lilbourne, Symon Mayne, John Downes, and George Fleetwood.

16 March.—Order by the King for the sending a barge to Gravesend to receive the bodies of John Barkstead, Miles Corbet and John Okey, lately attainted of high treason, and now on board the *Blackemoore* frigate, in custody of Nich. Armerer, esq.

24 March.—Order of House of Commons for the committal of Geo. Withers to close custody, to be denied pen, ink, and paper, and debarred from having company; with appointment of a committee to peruse the seditious infamous libel by him composed,[1] and draw up an impeachment.

5 July.—Orders by the King for the delivery of Major Creede, John Ireton, lately called Alderman Ireton, and John Wildeman, to Capt. James Lambert, Capt. of the Duke of York's yacht, to be transported; with acknowledgment by Capt. Lambert of receipt on 7 July.

14 July.—Order by the King for the discharge of Zachary Crofton, clerk.

25 July.—Orders by the King for the delivery of Col. John Lambert, Col. Edward Salmon, James Harrington, Robert Tichburne, lately called Alderman Tichburne, John Portman, John Rye, Col. James Berry, and Rich. Goodgroome, to Capt. Jas. Lambert, commander of "our" yacht the *Anne*, to be transported; with acknowledgment by Lambert of the receipt of Lambert, Harrington and Salmon on 2 Aug., and of the others, together with Henry Martin, on 14 Aug.

8 Sept.—Order by the King for discharge of Sir Rob. Leech, committed for affronting the Earl of Peterborough.

10 Sept.—Order in Council, on the petition of Anne Middleton, wife of Thomas Middleton, a prisoner in the Gatehouse, for his release on being bound over to appear to answer to informations against him.

17 Sept.—Order in Council referring the petition of John Parker, Abell West, Mich. Cole, William Wigfall, John Gosnell, and Francis Lee, prisoners in the Gatehouse, to the Duke of Albemarle.

---

[1] This "seditious libel" was really an inoffensive appeal to the Parliament for more moderation in its new course of ardent loyalty. It was printed for the first time, from Withers' own first rough draft, by the writer of this report, in 1880. The poem is entitled "*Vox Populi*," and the original is preserved amongst the Clarendon MSS. in the Bodleian Library.

17 Sept.—Order of the Duke of Albemarle on a petition from Francis Lee, of Southwark, a prisoner in the Gatehouse by the Duke's warrant, for his release on taking the oaths and giving security.

MSS. OF THE DUKE OF LEEDS.

1662.

26 Sept.—Orders in Council upon petitions from William Angell, scrivener, and Jeremy Baynes, that the Duke of Albemarle give directions for their discharge, on their giving security and taking the oaths.

13 Nov.—Warrant by Sir W. Morice for the transfer to the Gatehouse of Rich. Pilgrim.

14 Nov.—Warrant by the same for the release, upon bail and taking the oaths, of — Robottom, —Plater, and — Turner, and of — Bolt upon taking the oaths only because he is a stranger in these parts.

Same date.—Warrant by the same for the discharge of Lieut. Harrison, Serjeant Sprigg, John Philipps, Thos. Roberts, — Horseman, and — Temple, lately apprehended on suspicion.

18 Nov.—Warrant by the same for continuance of the bail of John Bradley for ten days longer.

20 Nov.—Order of the Lieut. for the bringing before him from the Gatehouse of Mich. Cole, Abell Westcote, and John Gosnall, upon a petition from them to the Duke of Albemarle.

22 Nov.—Warrant by Sir W. Morice for the taking bail of John Lewis.

28 Nov.—Warrant by the same for continuance of bail of John Bradley for ten days longer, and on 8 Dec. for ten days again.

5 Dec.—Order in Council for the release of Philip Twistleton, esq., on his taking the oaths and giving bail in £1,000.

11 Dec.—Indenture (on parchment) signed and sealed by the Sheriffs that they have received the following prisoners from the Lieut., Thos. Tong, Francis Stubbs, James Hind, John Sellers, Nathaniel Gibbs, Rich. Tyler, and Edward Riggs.

18 Dec.—Warrant by Sir W. Morice for the discharge of John Bradley.

19 Dec.—Order in Council for the discharge of Thos. Fleete, mariner, (imprisoned for saying that he would draw his sword to prevent the Papists cutting his throat) on taking the oaths, and giving bond in £300.

31 Dec.—Order in Council for the discharge of Richard Sanford, a victualler in Moorfields, on taking the oaths and giving bond in £500.

1663, 24 Jan.—Warrant by Sir W. Morice for the discharge of John Sponge, on taking the oaths, and giving security in £1,000, and paying fees at a low rate; with a letter from Sir Edw. Walker, asking for his discharge without any fees, he being a poor man.

1663.

31 Jan.—Warrant by Sir H. Bennet for the close imprisonment of Andrew Kennedy "for being a complice and concealour of high treason," to be kept apart from Lord Warriston.

19 Feb.—Indenture by the Sheriffs of the receipt of Edw. Riggs and Rich. Tyler in pursuance of a writ of *Habeas corpus.*

25 Feb.—Order in Council for the discharge of Robert Swallow, on his taking the oaths, and giving security in £3,000.

4 March.—Warrant by Sir H. Bennet for the delivery of the body of James Johnson, lately deceased, to his friends to be buried.

MSS. OF THE DUKE OF LEEDS.
1663.

15 March.—Order in Council that Margaret Johnston be, upon her petition, admitted to live in the Tower with her father, Archibald Johnston, in close confinement.

18 March.—Order in Council referring the petition of Christian, wife of Michael Lunne, for her husband's release, to Sir Rich. Browne, Major-Gen. of the city of London.

2 Apr.—Warrant by Sir H. Bennet for the imprisonment of Abraham Goodman for attempting to murder the Duke of Bucks.

18 Apr.—Warrant by the same for removing Goodman from the dungeon where he now is to some other fit room.

19 May.—Warrant by the same for the imprisonment of Rich. White for treasonable practices.

26 May.—Warrant by Sir W. Morice for the imprisonment of Col. Rob. Overton, suspected of seditious practices, and refusing to take the oaths or give security.

29 May.—Warrant by Sir W. Morice for the imprisonment of Daniel Collingwood, esq., cornet to the King's troop of guards, for sending a challenge to the Duke of Richmond.

12 June.—Order by the Lords for the imprisonment of the Earl of Middlesex.

6 July.—Warrant by Sir H. Bennet for the imprisonment of George Elton for treasonable designs and practices.

8 July.—Warrant by the same for Elton's being detained close prisoner in the dungeon without admitting any to speak with him.

11 July.—Warrant by the same for the imprisonment of John Dodington, esq., for treasonable speeches and practices.

21 July.—Warrant by the same for giving Rich. White the liberty of the Tower, and allowing him to send for a physician, he being much indisposed.

20 Aug.—Warrant by the same for the close imprisonment of Paul Hobson for seditious and treasonable designs and practices.

Aug. 20.—Warrant by the same for removal of Elton from the dungeon to some other convenient place of safety.

1 Sept.—Letter from the Lord Chief Justice Bridgeman for sending Rich. Oliver to his chamber for examination concerning further discoveries; he desires to be sent with warders and not soldiers, pretending he would not have it made too public, but it must be so ordered that it may not be in his power to escape, "for I looke upon him as a very dangerous person."

21 Oct.—Warrant by Sir H. Bennet for Paul Hobson's having the liberty of the Tower.

25 Oct.—Orders by the King for the close imprisonment of John Hutchinson and Henry Nevill for treasonable practices.

2 Nov.—Warrant by Sir H. Bennet for the close imprisonment of Rich. Salway (formerly Major Salway) for treasonable and dangerous designs.

12 Nov.—Warrant by Sir H. Bennet for the close imprisonment of Rob. Walters and Charles Carr for treasonable practices.

26 Dec.—Warrant by Sir W. Morice for the strict custody of Capt. Martin Bokman, committed for a traitorous design to betray one of his Majesty's garrisons.

1664.

1664, 4 Jan.—Order by the King withdrawing the liberty of the Tower from all the prisoners to whom it was granted, they having frequently abused it.

9 Jan.—Order from the Duke of Albemarle for the custody of Capt. John Downing, sent by the King's command, but desiring that he may be civilly used, with such accommodation as can be given.
MSS. OF THE DUKE OF LEEDS.
1664.

21 Jan.—Warrant by Sir H. Bennet for the close imprisonment of Charles Bayly for seditious practices.

3 Feb.—Warrant by the same for the putting of Mr. Edw. Bagshaw in the dungeon.

Same date.—Warrant by the same for making Mr. Dodington a close prisoner, not to be allowed pen, ink or paper.

6 Feb.—Warrant by the same for removing Mr. Edw. Bagshaw from the dungeon, and keeping him only in safe custody.

8 April.—Warrant by the same for the close imprisonment of Rob. Atkinson for treasonable and seditious practices.

24 May.—Order by the King for the close imprisonment of Will. Leveing for treasonable designs and practices.

31 May.—Warrant by Sir H. Bennet for the restraining Rob. Atkinson from the liberty of conversing with any person, heretofore indulged him.

5 Sept.—Warrant by the same for custody of Mr. James Hamilton, for fighting in his Majesty's presence.

26 Sept.—Warrant by the same for imprisonment of Robert Walters for treasonable practices.

14 Dec.—Warrant by the same for imprisonment of — Greene, for treasonable designs and practices.

22 Dec.—Order by the King for imprisonment of Richard Talbot, esq., committed for high misdemeanours.

1665, 8 Jan.—Warrant by Sir H. Bennet for imprisonment of Major Robert Holmes.
1665.

12 Jan.—Order by the King for the imprisonment of Paul Hobson. (*Endorsed,* "Brought 23 Feb.")

14 Feb.—Warrant by Sir H. Bennet for imprisonment of Capt. (*sic*) Robert Holmes. (*Endorsed,* "Major Holmes' second committment.")

18 March.—Warrant by the same for imprisonment of John Atkinson, "commonly called The Stockener," for treasonable designs and practices.

1661-1666.—A few papers, chiefly consisting of letters from Sir Thos. Osborne to his wife, with notices of general public affairs. In one of 29 Sept., 1666, he says, with reference to the Fire of London, "for your satisfaction how the King beares itt, I assure you there is no appearance of the least alteration either in his mind or countenance." Letters from John Lewys, 30 Oct. 1661 ; William Hayes, York, 5 Dec. 1663 ; Duke of Albemarle, 26 March 1664 ; Sir P. Warwick, 22 Apr. 1665 ; Henry Thompson, York, Oct.—Dec. 1665 ; farmers of the Excise at Rotherham, Nov. 1664—Apr. 1655 ; the Mayor and Corp. of York, about exemption from the assessment for the militia, 22 May 1665; Peregrine Bertie to his sister, Lady Osborne, Dec. 1664—March 1665.

1668.—A few papers relating to the Navy, the Council of Trade, and the Irish Accounts, with the following warrant from Lord Arlington to Sir John Robinson, Lieut. of the Tower, dated at Whitehall, 24 Dec. "It is his Majesty's pleasure that you permitt the bearer, Francis Cooke, to have access to his master Mr. William Penne, now close prisoner under your custody, and to speake with him in the presence of his keeper; for which this shall be your warrant."

1669.—Report (in a bound volume) to the Duke of York, on the duties of the various officers of the Navy-yards, &c., signed by the Commissioners of the Navy (Lord Brouncker, Sir Jo. Mennes, T. Middleton, S. Pepys, and Jo. Cox) and dated 17 Apr. 1669.

1670.—Two letters to Sir Thomas Osborne from his brother, Charles Bertie, attending the English Ambassador, Copenhagen and Hamburgh, 4 May—2 Aug.[1]

Richard Blanshard, about the election of a High Steward at Hull; York, 20 Apr.

Sir John Hotham, Scarborough, 11 Aug., about a report that he will be deprived of his place as Custos Rotulorum for the East Riding, &c.

Sir Sam Morland, with a petition to the King for a pension; 9 Feb.

Three letters from the Earl of Orrery; Charleville, Aug.—Oct.

Proposal by William Rayer for the improvement of the excise.

Two printed papers respecting the merchants, the distillers, and the farmers of the excise, with regard to brandy and strong waters.

Narrative presented to the King by Sir Thomas Modyford, bart., "setting forth the reasons of the attempt of the privateers of Jamaica on the Spaniard in 1670, and why he could not then forbid them the Spanish shore," with a brief of his case, &c.

1672.—Attestation by Sir Edw. Walker of the swearing-in of Sir Thomas Osborne, Treasurer of the Navy, as one of the Privy Council, 3 May.

Warrants signed by the King and Lord Arlington for the discharge of prisoners from the Tower, viz., Sir George Downing, 19 March; Samuel Hartlibb, 28 March; Philip Holland, 13 June; William Howard, esq., 13 Nov.; and a warrant for removing Edward Purcell, a prisoner for threatening the life of the Duke of Ormonde, from the Tower to Bethlehem Hospital, as being insane, 8 Nov.

Warrant for increasing the number of messengers in ordinary from thirty to forty, as formerly; 5 Sept.

A long list of ships making fishing voyages to Newfoundland, with particulars of places, crews, &c.

Seven letters from the Earl of Orrery, May 1672—Feb. 1672-3, from Ballymartir and Charleville, on Irish affairs; astonishment at the great offence taken at a letter of his to the Earl of Anglesey; defence of the Presidency Court [of Munster]; arrest of Capt. Thomas Walcot.

Letters to Sir T. Osborne from Sir Orl. Bridgeman, Sir Rob. Southwell, Chas. Bertie (3), Sir Thos. Wentworth, Fras. Bridgeman (for the reversion of the Pipe Office), Sir G. Copley, Sir J. Harman, the Master and Fellows of Queen's College, Cambridge (thanking him for favouring them in an election to a fellowship), Lord Ogle, Edw. Christian; and four letters from his brother, Charles Osborne. Unsigned letter of news, dated 3 Aug.: "On Thursday the 1st inst. a marriage was solemnized at Goring-house between the Dutchess of Cleveland's 2d son

---

[1] In one of these letters he mentions a curious superstitious belief in charms in Denmark. Finding that a lad who carried his portmanteau was lame, he was told, on asking the cause, that the toes had dropped off from frost-bite, and was shown the dried portions which the boy carried with him in a box. Mr. Bertie very much wished to buy them, but the boy firmly refused to sell, saying that in such cases (which were common) the lost parts were carried about as a preservative from pain in the mutilated members; if once parted with, pain would immediately follow.

Henry, and the Earle of Arlington's onely daughter, both their Majesties and most of the nobility being present. . . . . . Mad^lle Kyroüel [Quérouaille] was brought to bed of a son last Monday night. A new gentleman begins to appeare, one Mr. Green, who hath been bred some years in Flanders. The King hath not seen him yet, much less owned him." Two news letters signed P. B. [P. Bertie?]
Order relative to the keeping the corpse of the Earl of Sandwich in the Navy Office at Deptford until the day of the funeral ; 24 June.
Letter from Sir T. Frescheville, at the Manor at York, 22 Feb. 1672-3, to Sir Henry Thompson at Escrigg.
A few papers of Treasury business.

MSS. OF THE DUKE OF LEEDS.
1672.

1674 and 1674-5.—Letters from the Earl of Essex, Lord Lieut. of Ireland (8) ; Lord Keeper Finch (2) ; Sir Ch. Harbord (3) ; the Earl's son, Lord Latimer; Lord Vaughan, from the Downs when sailing for Jamaica; the Earl of Orrery (2) ; Earl of Yarmouth ; F. de Reede, at London and the Hague (2); Lady Ka. Ross ; Earl of Plymouth ; Sir Conyers D'Arcy; Sir W. Temple, at the Hague (4) ; Sir Will. Killegrew, on his various proposals for encreasing the revenue (2) ; Sir H. Coventry, at Newmarket (2, with a letter from Sir Gabriel Sylvius); Earl of Lindsey, at Newmarket, Apr. 8 ; (a slight hurt in the King's knee. : " hee imputes it to a blow formerly received by a rackett in a tennis court, but Tom Elliott, who discourses freely, thinks it rather occasion'd by an amorous encounter. . . . . . The Duke of Monmouth seems still to gain ground with the King, the King supping this night with him, accompanied with most of the nobility. His Majestie's topping horse, Blewcapp, was beaten this day by a horse of my L. Suffolk's call'd Cripple, which hath emptied my purse of twenty guineas. To-morrow is the plate runn for, and Tom Elliott hath desired mee to bee his jockey "; Earl of Strafford, about a case to be heard before the Council of a scuffle between his wife's servants and some men in Smithfield ; Sir Will. Lockhart at Paris (2) ; Duke of Buckingham, with reference to complaints against him as Master of the Horse, and suspected intercepting of some of his letters, &c. (2); two letters from Arthur Fleetwood and Sir Rob. Vyner, about a case against Mr. Edlyn and Mr. John Brandling, a minister, for a pretended marriage at Boovington, near Berkhampstead; the Corporation of Lynn, about the election of Mr. Rob. Coke for Parliament; from the Heads of Houses at Cambridge, congratulating the Earl of Danby on his appointment as Lord Treasurer, and asking for payment of arrears due to Dr. Glisson, the Professor of Medicine, with eleven signatures, including Cudworth and Barrow) ; T. Street, desiring to be made a serjeant-at-law ; Jo. Jowett, about a prize-ship seized at Plymouth ; Edw. Backwell, at the Hague (4); Rob. Stockdale, about his stopping attempted enlistment at Dover of men for an Ostend privateer ; Richard Wyseman, about Excise proposals ; R. Thomas; Charles Bates; Charles Strode, on the condition of the New Forest, with suggestions for the management of the Royal forests. Copies of two letters from the Earl to the Prince of Orange, and of a letter to Van Reede. P. B[ertie] to his sister Lady Bridget Osborne, from the camp before Arras ; Lord Ogle to the Countess ; Lucy, Countess of Huntingdon, to Charles Bertie; R. Maddockes to Rev. Matthew Hopkins, recommending a person for employment in the Earl's family. Petition from James Herbert to the King about his right of fishing for oysters in the manor of Milton, Kent. Appointment, under the King's sign manual, of Col. Hercules Lowe to be a searcher in the port of London. Account of a battle between allied forces and the

1674.

MSS. OF THE DUKE OF LEEDS.
1674.

French under Turenne at Marle, near Strasbourg. Papers from Sir H. Cholmeley respecting Tangier. "A narrative of the most remarkable actions, civil and military, during both the late warrs betwixt Sueden and Denmarck, before and after the Roschild treatie"; by Sir Philip Meadowe (see additions to this under the next year) : with a dedicationletter to the Earl of Bristol, dated at Parham, Suffolk, Oct. 20, 1674; 42 pp., folio. A series of "foreign advices" from Cologne, Brussels, the Hague, and Frankfort, Nov. 1674—Jan. 1674-5.

1675.

1675 and 1675-6.—Letters from the Prince of Orange, 20 Feb. 1675, (and copy of a letter to him); John, Lord Berkeley, at Paris; Lord Vaughan, governor of Jamaica (5); William Berkeley, governor of Virginia, against a patent granted to Lord Culpeper; (the colony and the revenue are so much encreased that "to my knowledge there is not one laborer here that does not pay the king five pounds sterling yearly "); Lord Arlington ; Earl of Orrery (4); Sir W. Temple, at the Hague (11); Earl of Bristol; Earl of Winchilsea ; the Earl of Strafford (3) about his debts; (on his father's death "I was left with a debt of above a hundred thousand pounds "); Lord Inchiquin, at Tangier (3), with an account of the condition of the place; Earl of Ogle; Earl of Plymouth ; R. Arundell of Trerise; Ed. Cooke, recommending the case of a kinsman, Col. Cary Dillon ; Matthew Smallwood, at Holkham, on Mr. Coke's affairs (3); the seven members of Parliament for Staffordshire, for an allowance to the Clerk of the Peace; James Kennedy, at Brussels; Edward Wood, at Stockholm, with notice of an alleged plot against the King of Sweden; Robert Holt, M.P., on his necessitous condition; John Southcott; Rob. Coke, at Holkham; Corporation of Lynn Regis; H. Puckering; Edward Backwell, at Amsterdam; J. Atkins, at Barbadoes; Martin Headley; Edward Ourd, at Newcastle; Miles Bull.

Letters from Ireland, and on Irish affairs. Ten from the Earl of Essex, with one to the King about a grant from him of £13,000 for the purchase of Essex House; (nomination of Dean Ward to be Provost of Trinity College, Dublin). Two from Lord Conway; " since Mr. Harbord arrived my Lord Lieutenant hath been cruelly persecuted by him for accepting your Lordship's favour about Essex-house," which Lord Arlington is said to look upon "as an eternal disobligation"; insincerity and "juggling tricks" of Harbord. From William Harbord ; the Lord Lieut. is full of acknowledgment for the favour about Essex House. Mich. [Boyle] archbishop of Dublin. Art. Fortese.

Petition from Thomas Wyndham to the King.

Letters to the Countess of Danby from the Earl; from her brothers, the Earl of Lindsey, and Peregrine and Charles Bertie; the Earl of Northampton ; Robert Chapman; M. Hopkins ; Samuel Maydwell..

Col. John Butler (Monk's Quarter-master-general) to Peregrine Bertie in vindication of himself against speeches reported by Sir Anth. Irby. Letters to Rob. Bertie from his nephew and niece W. and E. Widdrington. Benj. Herne, at the Hague, to Sir W. Temple, about treasonous speeches made by one Major James. Sir Will. Killegrew to Pereg. Bertie, about his proposals for increasing the revenue. W. Candish to Sir Robert Thomas. J.B., at Paris, to Sir Ellis Leighton. Humphrey Garland, of Gray's Inn, to George Evans, about appointment as steward of the House to the Earl of Danby. H.A., at Cleonger, Heref., to Madam Wardour, in praise of the Earl.

Notes of speeches relative to the impeachment of the Earl on the hearing of the case. [1078 ?]

Proposal of Sir John James, knt. and Rob. Huntington, esq., to undertake the office of Receiver Gen. of Excise for £800 per an.

"Some additions made to a little treaty [*l.* treatise] made by Sir Phillip Medows entituled, a view of the Swedish and other affairs &c. 1675."

MSS. OF THE DUKE OF LEEDS.

1675.

1676.—Letters from the Prince of Orange (2); Lord Belasyse; W. Maynard, at Easton; the Earl of Winchilsea, at Florence, asking either for the governorship of Tangier or the Embassy to Spain, or some similar reward for his services; ("a great senatour of Venice speaking to me of the Lord Chancellour Clarendon's maxime, That the King should buy and reward his enemies, and do little for his friends because they are his allready, he sayd it was contrary to all pollicy to enrich their enemies who could never be made friends, and to make their old friends first despayr of all good, and then turne to be new enemies"); the Earl of Plymouth, at Saumur, on hearing "that the King had some designe of sending me to make a campagne this summer;" he hopes "with such an equipage as shal become one he is pleased to owne"; Lord Essex, at Dublin (2); Lord Orrery; Col. Cary Dillon, with papers relating to a grant made to him of lands in reprisal in Ireland, and a bond from Hugh, Earl of Mount Alexander, and letters from Jos. Allen at Dublin and Lord Conway; John Monson, asking for some reward for old loyal services (2); N. P. warning the Earl against a pensioner in his house, one Mr. Dunbarr, who reveals many deep secrets to an eminent member of the House of Commons, and against a servant who talks very intimately with one of Lord Shaftesbury's servants : Ed. Randolph, from Boston, New England, after delivering to the Governor and Council there a letter from the King with petitions from Mr. Mason and Mr. Gorge, giving an account of trade, army, &c. (the clergy generally "proud, ignorant, and imperious" holding "Owen and others *ejusdem farinæ*" in great veneration; "Goff the old rebell is still in this country . . . in those southerne parts, where he and others are harboured by their anti-monarchicall proselites"); Rob. Mason, previous to Randolph's departure for New England, about his petition; the Earl of Strafford, on his necessitous condition; R. Bulstrode at Brussels (2); John, Lord Berkeley, at Paris, to the Earl, the King, and Mr. Coventry, for payment of salary and expenses as ambassador, strongly representing his urgent case after fifty years' faithful service; George Evans, informing the Earl that all letters marked N.P. and directed to Mr. Langwith are to be conveyed to his (the Earl's) hands ; (two anonymous letters so addressed follow, speaking in mysterious terms about elections for parliament); Viscount Fitzharding, at Dublin, asking for preferment soon, "for I have an incurable disease upon me"; W. Darcy, complaining that in 16 years he has had no return for his loyalty and sufferings; Rich. Wyseman, about some business of Sir John Shaw and some country corporation, &c. (2); Honora Harding, about her pension of £300, which is five years in arrear; the Earl of Chesterfield; the Earl of Carlisle, recommending one Mr. Christian; Lord Vaughan[1], at Jamaica (2); Edw. Noel, about the New Forest, petition from Edw. Fenn, of the Navy Office, with order thereupon signed by the Duke of Monmouth, &c.; Thos. Wilson; the Earl of "Marleburgh," for a warrant for his annuity; the Earl of Yarmouth, on affairs of the county of

1676.

---

[1] The signature is always written " V: aubnn."

MSS. OF THE DUKE OF LEEDS.
1676.

Norfolk (2); the Earl of Northampton, Constable of the Tower, desiring the King's consent for the removal of Sir John Robinson, the Lieutenant, with an account of his irregularities and neglect of duty (Tichbourne, one of the regicides, "a very dangerous person" for a long time had no particular warder in charge of him); R. Robartes, proposing marriage for his son, who will have upwards of £7,000 a year, with Lady Marthe Osborne; George Neale, at Leeds, on behalf of his brother, an indigent officer, who spent a good estate and endured long imprisonment, in his service of Charles I.; the Corporation of Berwick, thanking the Earl for removing restraint on the importation of corn from Scotland custom free; Sir Robert Vyner; Edward Lord Mountagu, at Boughton, with thanks for the King's disafforesting Gedington woods (2); Rob. Thomas, asking the loan of £200; Jo. Ramsey, at Cambridge, asking for the living of Bramfield in Suffolk for Mr. Smallwood; J. Brisbane, at Paris; the Earl of Bath, with account of the King's going to Banstead Downs on Sept. 13 with Prince Rupert to see the Surrey Militia, dined at Sir Rich. Mason's at "Worster" park, and the next morning on going into his barge at Putney fell, and hurt his shin-bone very much so that it swelled and pained him greatly; he would be his own doctor, "and only would make use of Mons. Rabell's water, with which he washed the wound at night, and the next morning it took away the swelling and payne, and this [Sept. 16] being now but the third daye his Majestie sayes that he is perfectly well, which addes great fame to this new remedy, especially being now experimented by the King himselfe, to the great displeasure of our doctors and surgeons"; Col. Edw. Cooke [or Coke] (2); Sir H. Shere, at Tangier; Lord Chancellor Finch; Sir W. Temple, at the Hague (4, and two to Sir J. Williamson); Mich. [Boyle] Archbp. of Dublin, asking that his salary as Chancellor may be encreased to £2,000, as formerly, instead of £1,000; Sir John Trevor; Marq. of Winchester, for payment to him of 1,0.0 gnineas as Warden of the New Forest; James Kennedy, at Brussels; Lord Ranelagh, two long letters, in vindication of himself, and complaint of wrongs, with counter representations from the Council of Ireland; F. de Reede, at the Hague; Charles Osborne, the Earl's brother; — Kingdon, relating a conversation with Lord Shaftesbury, who declared he had no anger with the Earl but wished him well, but that Lord Ormond and Sir Will. Coventry were in counsel together against him, with Lords Halifax and Winchester, his professed enemies, to bring in Coventry and his party, and that Shaftesbury dreaded nothing more than Coventry's becoming Lord Treasurer; H., Duke of Newcastle, about the proposed election of the Earl's son, Lord Dunblane, as member for Berwick, and letters from Sir Rich. Stote and Luke Ogle, at Berwick, to the Duke; Sir R. Stote to the Earl, with account of his son's election there, the votes of those who were excommunicate for not repairing to church and receiving the Sacrament having been struck off; Girolamo Alberti de Conti, for a lease from the Crown of the manor of Appleby; G[uy Carleton], Bishop of Bristol, with a complaint by Sir Robert Yeomans of Bristol of some seditious words spoken by one Ellis, an Oliverian captain, in an ill-affected assembly; Sir Gabriel Sylvius, at the Hague; Bernard Howard to the Earl and to Mr. Will. Longueville; Sir Patience Ward; Bernard Grenville, at Genoa.

Letters to the Countess of Danby, from Sir Bernard Gascon, at Florence (is coming to England with his daughter who "has some good talent in the musike," who shall sing and play to her and the earl); the Earl of Nottingham, about arrears of his pensions; Lady Ogle, soon

afterwards Duchess of Newcastle, on their necessitous condition ; her
husband's father, " God knows, thinkes what is due to his sonn and his
children better beestowed of any then on them " ; William Fryer ; Rev.
M. Hopkins, her chaplain, about postponing the administration of Holy
Communion to Easter day, and about his parish in Lincolnshire to
which he is just presented ; Joseph Shirburne, at Paris, about a debt
due from the King ; George Evans ; Elizabeth Derham, at West Derham ; Jane Fleete ; J. Ramsey ; T. King ; Lord Yarmouth.

MSS. OF THE
DUKE OF LEEDS.
167f.

Secretary Williamson to the Duke of Lauderdale, with a letter from
Mr. Meredith, Sir W. Temple's secretary, at the Hague ; Sir Henry
Bedingfeld to the Duchess of Lauderdale ; Rich. Franklin to the Lord
Chamberlain ; J. Knight, at Rycot, to Mr. Maulyverer, fellow of Magd.
Coll. Cambridge (Lord Dunblane's tutor) ; J. Wright to Visc. Yarmouth ;
Will. Courtenay, at Ford, to Samuel Peacock, about the election at
Oakhampton ; Abr. Barrington to G. Evans ; J. Halliley to John
Ramsey, offering 100 guineas for a searcher's place at the Custom
House for Thomas Smith ; Thos. Carnaby to Major Dan. Collingwood,
M.P., about the election of [Peregrine] Lord Dunblane at Berwick ;
Charles Pratt to the same, on the same matter ; Eliz. Widdrington to
Mr. Watson, the mayor of Berwick, for the election of Lord Latimer
[*al.* Dunblane] ; (Mrs. ?) A Constable, at Everingham, to Mrs. Wise,
about a copy of her aunt Osborne's picture, which is desired by Lady
Danby ; J. Wivell to Peregrine Bertie.

Three letters from the Earl, at Wytham and Rycot, to his wife ;
one to his son Lord Latimer ; one to the Lord Chancellor, from Newmarket, 4 Apr., about various proposed preferments ; on the death of the
Bishop of Norwich the King will translate the Bishop of Exeter thither ;
the King is pleased with the observations of the L. C. Justice on his
circuit, "his resolutions being every day more fixt to shew his
steadinesse to the Church of England and his perseverance in the
councills he has taken . . . . . . Here is not one word of any thing
but horse matches."

Account of £20,000 paid to the King's privy purse from the revenue
of Ireland (of which £4,700 went to redeem Lady Portsmouth's jewels,
under a bill of sale).

Information by Philip Browne, a merchant of London, concerning
" practices " against the Earl, in preparing articles of impeachment
against him, with a letter requesting a loan from the King of £1,200.

Copies of letters of news from Paris to Secretary Coventry.

Petition to the King from Robert Bertie for the place of secretary
to the Commissioners of Customs.

Information respecting a club frequented by Lord Shaftesbury's
friends, at which it was agreed that the best way for Jenks was to
petition the King that he might be bailed ; dated 19 July.

Declarations by Will. Ellesdon of the seditious discourses (partly with
reference to Jenks) of John Harrington, of Weymouth, a kinsman of
Lord Shaftesbury, 15 July—30 Nov.

Admiralty proceedings at Jamaica in the trial of John Deane for
piracy, condemned to death for robbing a ship called the *John's
Adventure ;* with depositions in which Sir Henry Morgan is represented
as endeavouring to hush the matter up, saying " the privateers were
honest poore fellows," to which the plundered captain replied " that he
had not found them soe."

Deposition by Sir William D'Oyly, of Westminster, that what he
has informed the Earl of Danby concerning Sir Robert Howard is true.

MSS. OF THE DUKE OF LEEDS. 1676.

Copy of the writ issued by Sir Will. Berkeley, Governor of Virginia, for the electing a new Assembly; with notes of memorials on the condition of Virginia.

Statement of the arrears of pay due to the garrison at Tangier, signed by S. Pepys; with a paper of proposals respecting the revenue there.

Copy of a return of the numbers of deer in the New Forest in the years 1671–1676.

The following four papers are selected from those of this year for transcription at length.

LETTER of BISHOP MORLEY to the EARL OF DANBY.

" My Lord, I remember your lordship was pleased to think it fit an enquirie should be made in all the severall dioceses of this kingdome by theyr respective Bishops, what proportion or disproportion of number there is betwixt Papists and not Papists, as likewise betwixt other Non-conformists and Conformists, in order (as your Lordship was then pleased to tell me) to the obviating or answering of an objection the King seemed to have against his declaring his resolution to suppresse conventicles, namely, his Majestye's haveing bin informed that the number of those that were to be suppressed did very much exceed the number of those that were to suppresse them, and consequently, as the effecting of it would be impossible, soe the attempting of it would be dangerous, especially if it should (as probably it would) unite the Papists and all other the severall sects of Non-conformists together against us. I have, therefore, for his Majestye's and your lordship's satisfaction presumed to send you the enclosed abstract of the account I have received from my archdeacons of Hampshire and Surrey, and which they, in theyr late visitation of theyr severall provinces, received from the severall ministers and churchwardens of the severall respective deaneries and parishes in the aforesayd counties, whereby your lordship may see that the odds of number is very much more for us then the King was informed it was against us, at least if the returns from other dioceses be answerable to this of mine, as generally I verily beleeve they will be. And then I hope the King and the Lawes and the cheif Ministers of State together, with soe considerable an advantage of number, being on our side, there will appeare to be neither danger in attempting, nor any great difficulty in effecting, this great woork, which is absolutely necessary for the securing of the legally established goverment of the Church, and consequently as absolutely necessary for the securing of the legally established goverment in the State allso; and therefore I doubt not but all wise statesmen as well as all orthodox churchmen will be for the effectuall prosecution of it; at least I think soe, and think soe the rather because your lordship seemed to me to be of the same opinion.

Your Lordship's very humble servant,
Farnham Castle, June 10 [16]76. GEORG. WINTON.

" Of the number of Papists set down in the enclosed abstract, there are but few above an 100 in Surrey, all the rest are in Hampshire, as appears by the book I have sent to my lord of London (and which I presume he will shew unto your lordship) conteyning a particular account of the severall sorts that were to be numbred, from the ministers and churchwardens of all the severall parishes in the whole diocese. The persons numbered in the account are all of both sexes from 16 year-old upwards, that being the age at which men and women are required by the canon to receive the Communion." The abstract gives these numbers: inhabitants, 150,937; conformists, 142,065;

all dissenters, 8,872, of which, Popish recusants, 968. Enclosed in a small paper, written on two playing cards, is an abstract of the total number of Papists in the dioceses of the province of Canterbury above the age of 16, amounting to 11,870.

MSS. OF THE DUKE OF LEEDS.
1676.

PARTICULARS of CONVENTICLES, &c., in LONDON and WESTMINSTER.[1]

"In Westminster.—1. In the great Almry, Mr. Cotton *alias* Turner, a silenced Presbyterian; frequented by Sir William Walker and his lady, Mr. Henningham, the Lady Catharine More, Lady Clare, Clinton and Tircony, Mr. Blood and his two sons, with several other midling people. 2. In Tuttle street, in widow Brome's house, a Fifth Monarchy meeting, but considerable neither for quality nor number, and not constant. 3. In the little Almry a Quakers' meeting. 4. At a strong-water distiller's shop in Long-ditch, Mr. Nest, an Independent, frequented by some people of quality.

In Piccadilly.—In Swallow-street, one Mayo, an Anabaptist, in a place they call the Chappel, constant Sundayes and Wednesdayes in the afternoon, assisted by one Knowles.

In Covent Garden.—1. In Bridges street at Orange Mal's Mr. Manton, frequented by the Lord Wharton and his family, the Lady Manchester, Lady Bedford, Lady Clare, Lady Clinton, Wortland, Scarsdale, Seymer, and Trevors, the Lady Baker, Earl of Angleseye's sister, Sir William Lockier, Esq. Scrope, Esq. Creed, Mr. Baldwin a merchant, little Murray.

2. At the old play-house in Vere street, Farrington, a silk-weaver, a fellow of a notorious loud conversation, preaches Sundayes and most commonly Thursdayes, to near 1,000 auditors.

About Holborn.—1. In Great Russel-street in New Southampton Buildings, Mr. Baxter, assisted by Mr. Reason his kinsman ; Sir James Langham and his lady auditors, Lady Renalow, Countesses Bedford and Exeter, Lady Hollis, Lockier, Fitzjames, Lumley, Esq. New, Esq. Pim, Major Win, Stanley a merchant, Lord Limborow and his lady Swedes. 2. In Short's Gardens, Mr. Case, a Presbyterian, assisted by one formerly the Lord of Anglesey's chaplain.

In Southwark.—1. In Firefoot lane, Mr. Eager, an Anabaptist, teaches in his own house near 200 souls. 2. In New lane, near Newstairs, at Shad Tame's near 150 Anabaptists meet. 3. At Mr. Collet's house in Longlane Southwark, one Mr. Kentish, a Presbyterian, has every Munday a meeting. 4. In Salisbury Street, Mr. Roswell, a Presbyterian, about 300 persons present. 5. In Fan Street, a great Quakers' meeting, about 400 people of good quality, preach't to by 3 several men. 6. In Winchester Park a dangerous meeting, Mr. Slaton, an Anabaptist, their teacher. 7. In the same park Jasper Batto, John Norton and Stephen Draper, dangerous persons, teach at a Quakers' meeting. 8. In Maid lane, Mr. Chester, a Presbyterian. 9. In Globe alley, Mr. Parsons, a Presbyterian. 10. Mr. Frackman, an Anabaptist, by St. Savoryes Mill, near 250 men of some sort. 11. Mr. Chatch, an Anabaptist, in Goat yard, Horsy-down, about 200. 12. Mr. Tedmans, Presbyterian, in the close near St. Mary Overs, near 200. 13. Mr. Rasswel,[2] a Presbyterian, in St. Mary Magdalen parish, 200 of good condition. 14. Jones, a taylor, in the Mase at Southwark, Anabaptist,

---

[1] Of the first part of this paper there is a duplicate copy.
[2] In the second copy " Basswell."

MSS OF THE DUKE OF LEEDS. 1676.

and a dangerous fellow, near 200. 15. In Farthing Alley, in St. Toolyes parish, at Mr. Vincent's, one Love, a Presbyterian, near 600, some of good condition. 16. Mr. Turner, a haberdasher in the park, an Anabaptist, 300. 17. An Anabaptist in Lambeth, a rope-maker, much follow'd. 18. Mr. Vincent, in the Mayes, near 1,000. One Line preaches at the same place. 19. Slaton, Hole and Heath, Anabaptists, as likewise Norton and Jones, in Southwark, dangerous men against the Government, and one Davies, a brewer's servant.

For the city of London. — Without Bishopsgate. 1. Mr. Anslow, Presbyterian, in Spittlefields, near 600. 2. Mr. Mayo, a Presbyterian, in Winford street, in Angel alley near Spittlefields, 300. 3. Kiffin, at Devonshire House. 4. Mr. Watson, a Presbyterian, in Chequer Yard at Dowgate Hill, near 300. 5. Mr. Coal, a Presbyterian, at Cutlers' Hall, about 400. 6. Mr. Vincent the elder, a Presbyterian, in Hand alley in Bishopsgate street, 800. 7. At Glovers' Hall in Beech lane Cripplegate, a Fifth Monarchy meeting. 8. Mr. Harcostell, an Anabaptist, in Devonshire House, Bishopsgate, with Mr. Kiffin. 9. Mr. Cross, in New street near Fetter lane. 10. Peter Anslow, a meeting in Spittlefields. 11. An Anabaptist meeting in Bell lane Spittlefields.

Without Algate.—1. Barret, an Anabaptist, at Stratford Langthorn and in the parish of Westham, a mealman of Reddriff. 2. The constant teachers in the parish of Westham are Benjamin Dennis and Barret, Sundayes and Wednesdayes. Mr. Rich. Quintin and Mr. Will. Turpin auditors, Anabaptists, Mr. Bird and Mr. Hughes. 3. Mr. Laurence preaches at Mr. Mead's meeting-house in Stepny. The teachers are Mr. Matthew Dyer, Mead and Laurence, Thomas King. Auditors amongst others, William Northy of Old Ford, esq., in Bow parish, Mr. John Preston, sen. and jun. of Mile-end, Mr. Robert Nacklin, living in Dalby, of Upper Shadwell, butcher, Grey, a wollen-draper in Ratcliff, Mr. Graves at Limehouse. They meet Sundayes and Thursdayes at 2 in the afternoon. 4. Quakers' meeting-houses, 3 : 1. bought at Wansted in Eping Forest : 2. at Plaistow in the parish of Westham, at the house of Solomon Eagle: 3. bought at Barkin. Meet Sundayes and Fridayes, at 3 in the afternoon. The chief, Will. Pen, living in Hampshire, John Howard, living in London, William Gibson, in Gracechurch street, Major Chamberlain, of Bednal green, Gibbs of Walthamstow, Shippy of Wansted, Nichols of the same, John Haward, living near Devonshire House, a drysalter, Joshua Cobham of Westham, James Mathews, John Rushen, all of Westham parish, Luke Herbert, of Whitechappel, weaver. At Barkin, Benjamin Antrobus, at the Golden Harrow without Bishopsgate, linnendraper. At Plaistow, Clement Plumsted, ironmonger in Minories, John Haward by Devonshire House, drysalter, Ezekiel Woolly and Will. Fleetwood, in Spittlefields. At Wansted, Will. Pen, esq., Abraham Lowther, of Dedford, ship-carpenter, Will. Gibson of Grations street, Rich. Haward at the 3 Cranes in Thames street, coalmerchant. At Barkin, Thomas Bagley, of Lothbury, clockmaker, Rich. Whitepan, of Little Eastcheap, butcher, Will. Mead, of Cornhill, draper. At Plaistow, Christopher Taylor of Waltham Abbey, schoolmaster. 5. Samuel Loveday, of Leadenhall street, coat-seller, Anabaptist, preaches in Star alley in East Smithfield. 6. Isaac Lamb, of Bedlam, shoemaker, Anabaptist, has a conventicle at 7 Star alley in East Smithfield. 7. Will. Taylor of Barkin has a conventicle of Presbyterians at his own house. 8. In Booby lane in Wappin, near the Hermitage, two meetings, Mr. Knowles and Mr. Kentish. (H.W. and his companion discovered Jones and the Quaker for treason. *Interlined here by another hand.*)

Justices Pitfield of Hogsden and Wood of Wappin act upon information, and Underwood has promised to do so too. Several conventicles have been inform'd against and suppress'd in and about the city. Turner, a Popish bookseller, all his books seized. Two Papists sued for their 100 marks for being at mass at Sommerset House. Sir William Poultney sued for his £100 for not acting.

MSS. OF THE DUKE OF LEEDS.
1676.

Papists.

1. A little priest with black hair sayes mass at Tart Hall, the Lord Stafford's.
2. At my Lord Bellasis's his steward sayes mass.
3. At signior Brunetti's, factor for her Higness the Dutchess York, in York Garden, is mass sayd.
4. Mr. Rose, a Flemmin, perverted by Father James of Somerset House, has several priests lodge at his house, and lives not far from sig. Brunetti.
5. Signior Simone, an Italian that serves the King with snush (*sic*), a great factor of Mr. Coleman's, lives in the Hay-market.
6. In Duke Street next Lincoln's Inn Fields, on the left hand, at a widow's, lives Father Harcourt, that sayes mass there every holy-day.
7. In King's Street by Long Acre, at the sign of St. Paul, at Salvator Winter's a mountebank, diet a great many renagado priests and friers, that say mass there, and help him to write a book about monarchy.
8. Mr. Coleman lives in Dean's Yard.
9. Mrs. Stutsky, a Polander's wife, whose husband is no wiser than he should be, entertains young Crellius and his wife, and other Socinians, and has meetings there upon set dayes.
10. Price over against the Sun tavern in Portugal Street lodges several priests.
11. In Warwick Street, 3 doors from the King's Armes, one Betts, an Irishman, keeps a house where lodge priests and monks.
12. At a strong-water shop in the Hay-market mass is sayd every Sunday.
13. In St. Alban's Street, it being a joyner's, near the sign of the Wheel, lives a Popish bookseller, that prints or sells Popish books. (His name Dates ; *added by another hand.*)
14. Signior Fabio, who pretends to be banisht from Italy, but is rather an emissary from Rome, is an Abbot, and lives at Knightsbridge, trades in raw silk by his servants, and says mass.
15. In Drury lane, at an apothecary's, over against the Whitehorse tavern, lodge several priests and fryars.
16. Turner, a Popish bookseller, four doors from St. John Baptist's Head, near Turnstyle, Holborn.
17. Abbot Balletti lived four years in the house with Lord Arlington, and lives now in the city.
18. Signior Tarressi, a merchant near the Old Exchange, receives all Mr. Coleman's letters from abroade, and transports converts, &c.; it is he Monsieur Lusancy should have been transported by.
19. Signior David, a merchant at Charing Cross, near the King's coffee-house, transports all the priests and fryars.
20. In Coleman Street is a linnendraper's, over against the church, where the Socinians meet.
21. At Fauxhall lives a rich lady and others with her after the manner of nuns, and keep a priest to say mass.
22. At Battersey is such another.
23. At the Red Posts behind Drury Lane, over against the Spanish Ambassadour, is a great meeting of priests and fryars.

MSS. OF THE
DUKE OF LEEDS.
1676.

24. In the Hay-market, at the Blew Balconies, two doors from the King's Head, is another meeting.

25. In Bell alley, in Coleman Street, a Socinian congregation.

26. Langhorn, a Papist, a Counselour of the Temple, is Pen the Quaker's counsel.

27. In Smythfield, near the White Hare in Bartholomew court, is a press that prints all sorts of unlicensed bookes. (*Added by another hand.*)"

Short abstract, signed by SETH [WARD] BISHOP of SALISBURY. of the numbers and proportion of inhabitants, Conformists, and Dissenters in the diocese of Sarum.

Inhabitants, 108,294; Dissenters, 4,623; (Popish, 548; Separatists, 4075.) Conformists, 103,671.

Letter to LORD DANBY, from Mrs. GREEN, the mother of Lord Plymouth, called Don Carlos.

"My Lord, The disorder that Don Carlos is in and all his concerns I hope will bee a sufficient appologie for the troble I give your Lordship, not doubting your kindness to him will put a speedy stop to the inconveniencies are like to arise, for want of some fitt person that will be carefull of him and derect him better than I fear hitherto he hath been. I understand the Duke of Buckingham recommended Mr. Skelton to your Lordship, whose caracter I am so well sattisfied with that I should be rejoyced a person so fitt for such a trust, and one the child hath a perticular esteeme for, were by your Lordship alsoo approved on, and recomended to the King, that those errors hee some times comits might be corrected, and I dare promise a short time will produce a change in him much to his advantage. As to what relates to his establishment, of which there is great need, I shall not troble your Lordship, hopeing that when you see a convenient time for it you will move the King in his behalfe, your Lordship beeing now the only person whose patronage he relyes on. Nothing could give me a greater satisfaction than to see him putt into the hands of one whose kindness to the child will not neglect him, and whose principalls will not allow anything that is ill in him; therefore I most earnestly beg of your Lordship, it beeing the only concerne of my life, to see him well educated, knoweing his nature perfectly good, but easyly drawne to liberties pleasing to youth if he have not a constraint put upon him by one he valwes—that you would perswade the King to lay his comands upon Mr. Skelton before he goes to Windsor. In doeing this your Lordship will oblige me more and make me hapier than I can realy express and nothing but a mother's hart can be capable of resenting; and I doe ashwer your Lordship I will never importune the King or you in any other concerne, but rest intierly satisfied, to see him put into a way to regain what I am very sensible to much libertie and ill company has made him loose, who will eternaly be,

Your Lordship's most humble servant,
J.[1] GREEN.

(*Endorsed*, "Mrs Green's letter about Lord Plymouth in 1676.")

---

[1] Her Christian name is always given as Catharine.

1677.—Letters from the Earl of Essex, Lord-Lieut. of Ireland; Lord Ranelagh, about his accounts as Treasurer of Ireland (3); Lord Lauderdale (2), with eight from the Countess of Lauderdale to the Countess of Danby; Lords Conway (2), Plymouth, Marlborough, Campden, Salisbury (2), Roos, and Rutland (2); Sir W. Temple (5); R. Bulstrode (two news letters from Brussels); Philip Browne (2, with a declaration that he never said, as reported by Mr. Joseph Young, that he gave £1000 to the Countess of Danby for the farm of the law tax); George Evans (recommending Sir R. Filmer's *Grand Inquest of England*, which is in the hands of his son, as a book which may do good to the public peace); Rich. Stote; Thomas Salter; Charles Osborne (about the burgess-ship of East Looe); Charles Bertie; G. Copley; J. Brisbane; Christian Albrecht, Duke of Sleswig-Holstein; the Prince of Orange (about to come to England, in pursuance of the permission given by the King); W. Bentinck (2); Don Bernardo de Salinas (2); Don Carlos Ronquillos; the States General; Franç Egon, Prince of Strasburg (thanking him for attention to his brother's affairs); —— d'Este, in Spanish, on coming as envoy extraordinary; the Duque de Villa Hermosa.

The Commissioners of Virginia (Herb. Jeffreys, John Berry, and Francis Moryson), dated from Swan's Point, James River, 27 March, forwarding petitions, &c.

"Mémoire présente au Roy par l'envoyé de mons. le Duc de Holstein."

Draft of a treaty between Charles II., the Emperor, the King of Spain, and the States General; endorsed, "This treaty not perfected, by reason of the delays on the Spanish side, and more by the States Ambassador refuseing to have the word *consent* in the 5th Article."

Letter from the Earl of Danby to his wife, and one to the Countess of Salisbury; with a letter from the latter to the Countess of Danby.

Copy of a letter from the Earl to Mr. Montague, together with a letter to the same from the Countess of Northumberland about the intention of the Duchess of Cleveland to retire to Port Royal, in accordance with the King's wish.

Herald-painter's bill of charges at the installation of the Earl as K.G. at Windsor, 19 Apr. 1677.

Certificate of his taking the oaths in Parliament, 23 May 1678.

Letter of thanks from the Wardens of the Weavers' Company, 29 March 1677.

Two letters to Lord Latimer from Sir Robert Walsh and Eliz. Chesshire, about a book which Mr. King of the Middle Temple had, who died on Christmas Day 1676, and important writings "touching a discovery" which he made.

Reports of proceedings in the House of Commons, with notes of the speeches made, 21-29 March, 10-13 Apr., 21, 23, 25 May 1677.

1677-88.—Papers relating to the office of the Master of the Rolls, and the right of appointment of the Six Clerks; with several warrants signed by James II.

1678.—Nineteen letters from the Earl of Sunderland to the Earl of Danby, in Aug.—Oct., from Paris and Fontainebleau, about his negotiations, with copies of a few replies, with a letter from Arnauld de Pomponne.

Twenty-five letters from R. Montagu at Paris, Jan.—July, with intelligence about the coming of M. de Ruvigny to England, &c.; with one after Montagu's return to England. Copies of some replies are included.

MSS. OF THE
DUKE OF LEEDS.
1678.

Four letters from J. Brisbane at Paris, May—July.
Fourteen letters from Laurence Hyde, Jan.—Sept., and six from Sidney Godolphin, March—June, on their negotiations in Holland, with the Instructions for the latter, and copies of replies.

Sixteen letters from Sir W. Temple, at the Hague, on the negotiations, Jan—Dec., with replies.

Nine from the Prince of Orange, with the replies, Feb.—Nov.

From the Duke of Newcastle (6) ; Duke of Albemarle, about the election for Malden ; Lord Conway ; Earl of Lindsey ; Earl of Northampton ; Earl of Ossory (2) ; Douglas Lord Dunbarton ; the Earl of Carlisle (2), on his arrival at Jamaica as Governor ; Anne Countess of Sussex ; J. D. Lord Gerard (4) ; Edw. Wood at Stockholm ; Sir S. Morland ; Sir Godfrey Copley ; Jo. Temple ; Roger Meredith ; Thomas King ; R. Bulstrode ; Thos. Neale ; Bernard Howard (2) ; Jo. Willoughby ; Martin Headley ; Will. Rider ; John Shale ; Sir Rob. Vyner, with statement of Navy accounts due to him ; John Sansom. Some of these letters relate to elections for Parliament, as do also letters from Sir Ralph Knight to Charles Osborne, and from John Rushworth (the historian of Parliament) to Thomas Jones on Oct. 27, desisting "upon the earnest entreaty of my wife" and the advice of friends from standing for Berwick.

Letter about the election for Queenborough.

Eight letters from the Duke of Ormonde as Lord Lieut. of Ireland, Feb. — Sept., about the farmers of the revenue, excise on beer, the calling of Parliament, the bill for settlement of estates, Kinsale harbour, and recommending Dr. John Topham to be a Commissioner of Accounts.

Letter from Lord Conway (Portmore, 7 Sept.) on the meeting of the Irish Parliament, and in favour of Lord Ranelagh in the matter of his accounts. Lord Ormonde, the Lord Chancellor, and Col. Fitz-Patrick "are the sole cabinett that governes affaires heere"; recommends the sending "a person of worth out of England" to be the new primate.

Two letters from Thomas Sheridan, 14 Oct. 1678—25 Jan. 167$\frac{8}{9}$, applying for appointment as a Commissioner of Customs in Ireland, for the improvement of the revenue, and sending a memorial on behalf of his brother the Dean of Connor for an Irish bishopric.

Letter from H. Compton, Bishop of London, in June, about an intended meeting of all the Anabaptists and Fifth-monarchy men the next day in "Fauchurch" Street; it will probably last from 8 in the morning till 4 in the afternoon. Col. Danvers is to begin the holding forth ; suggests that four or five persons should be employed to take notes. Encloses a copy of a news letter he shewed the Earl ; a worse has come out since, "concerning the instrument for commissioner of Scotland ;" they are delivered out by a little tapster boy at Will's coffee house in Russel Street next Drury Lane ; several noblemen and others give £10 a year for them, and "any man that is cunning may have them at that price."

Letters from several foreign ministers: J. H. Bülow, of Brunswick and Lünebourg (3) ; Griffenfeld, at Copenhagen ; A. Ulcken, of Slesvig-Holstein ; W. Bentinck, at the Hague ; Joh. Paulin Olivekrans, Swedish envoy at Nimeguen (5).

One from the Prince of Orange, 19 Jan.

Engagement by Mr. Peregrine Bertie to endeavour to procure the reversion of the mastership of the Mint for Thos. Neale.

Letters about the Yorkshire Militia, with a return of arms found in the houses of Papists in the wapentake of Skirack.

1682-3.—Various papers relating to Lord Danby's applications for release from the Tower upon bail; notes taken "by Mr. Digby, called Long Digby," of what the Earl said in the King's Bench, 27 May; notes, in book-form, by Mr. — Blany, of what was said by the Earl and the Judges, on the hearing on 29 June; circular letter to the Lords to subscribe his petition to the King for a consultation of the judges, with a copy bearing the autograph signatures of Albemarle, Newcastle, Lindsey, Rutland, Bath, Ailesbury, Conyers, Berkeley, Oxford, Denbigh, Yarmouth, Sussex, Thanet, Norreys, Feversham, Campden, Maynard, Arundell, and Lumley; letters to the King, and petition to be allowed to visit his wife supposed to be dying from hurts by a fall from her coach, with letter to Lord Conway, memoranda, and draft order thereupon; letters to the Lord Chancellor and L. C. J. North; draft order for the King's approval for the bailing of the Earl, with a declaration of the King's conviction of his innocence, that he has granted him his pardon, and will grant it ten times over if it be defective in matter or form, 23 May. Ten letters from the Earl to his son. The following letter from the latter (Lord Latimer) to his father, written from Windsor in August is endorsed by the Earl as being "of moment."

MSS. OF THE DUKE OF LEEDS. 1682.

"My Lord, I have according to your commands delivered your letter to the King, which I had the better opportunity to do, my Lord Sunderland, Mr. Hyde, and Godolphin being gone to Altrop. Hee read your letter, and when hee had done hee talked with mee about itt. I tould him that most people had very much altered theire opinions as to your Lordship, and that now they pitied you as much as they had heretofore rejoyced att your sufferings, and that of the members of Parliament themselves (if itt were not those that were your professed enemies) I found none but would bee well enough content that you were out of the way rather then you should bee found where you are att theire meeting, and they be obliged to fall upon theire old differences of questioning his power to pardon, and the Bishops' sitting in capitall causes, which rights if his Majesty will defend, itt must certainly breake them, and so they shall neither bee able to try the Popish Lords, or do any other businesse. Hee gave me this answer, that hee had a good while been considering with himselfe, and adviseing with others of your friends, what way hee might do itt best and safest both to himselfe and you, for that hee was resolved to do itt, but that hee could nott sattisfie himselfe of the best way as yett, and therefore must advise with some that were your friends what was to bee done in itt; but that this hee was sure of, itt would bee convenient you should go abroad for some time. Hee bid, A pox take the Chancelor for a cowardly sneaking fellow, for had itt not been for him itt had not come to this; and that all the judges were cowards, for else itt might have been done before now; but hee say'd, hee would find out a way to do itt with all convenient speed hee could, and say'd hee should bee glad to speak with some of your counsell who you could best trust about itt.

I tould him farther that your Lordship had reason to think, by all those that were your friends that you had discoursed with, that though perhaps the Parliament might att first mention itt, yett they would, yts thought, bee willing enough after a smale time to lett itt fall rather then give a stop to all publick businesse. Hee tould mee, that whenever a Parliament mett, hee did believe that would bee the first thing they would medle with, but that hee did not believe they would passe itt over so easily; and that as hee must defend his power, so hee ought to do itt the safest way. Hee commanded mee to remember him very kindly to your Lordship, and assure you itt should be done as soon as possible, and that hee would send you a farther answer by mee, which I tould him I would stay for."

MSS. OF THE DUKE OF LEEDS. 1682.

Five other letters to the Earl of Danby from his son; one narrating a conversation with the Lord Chief Justice North in April, on delivering the Earl's letter mentioned above, who "seemed very obstinate," and others referring to marriage proposals made to him, one being by the Duke [of Newcastle], whose daughter he hears "is sickly and peevish;" one to the Countess on the same subject, in which he says he finds "welth and beauty will come together in the match;" with a copy of a letter in Nov. to the Duke, expressing sorrow in finding that two of his daughters are engaged, and the third resolved not to marry; with other letters to Charles Bertie and others.

Letters to the Earl from :—The Earl of Lindsey (3: Ministers run great hazards, being always hated by the people, if they have not the constant esteem of their master; more statesmen ruined in England than elsewhere, the Prince not being absolute; sorrow at the Bishop of Peterborough's opposing Lord Dunblane, from obligations to Ormond and Williamson, but dares positively affirm that "where things are plaine, hee will go according to his conscience as an honest and religious man "); Earl of Rutland (2); Countess of Rutland (2); Duke of Newcastle (7 : in one, of 16 March, 1682–3, he says: "I saw when my daughter Albemarle was here she was not madd, but there was a great consternation upon her, I sopose caused by her own folley and pride, and mallis of others, who noe doubt has indevored her ruen a long time ; and sure never woman has been so deafe to good councell as she has been, nor did ever parents doe soe much for a daughter as we have don for her, considering our condition; nor did ever any father doe soe much for a soun as I did for mine, and now waunt a great part of my esstate by it ; our fondness to our childeren brought us into this messery;") the Earl of Bath (4); Lord Lansdowne ; Lord Conway (3); William [Lloyd] Bishop of Peterborough (2: in the first, of 20 July, he says, "its fitt that your lady should be well secured from all assaults ; Dr. Trumbull can tell your Lordship of one Cuffe, who was hired to sease her while shee was att Sir Robert Viner's, and of all the intreagues of that conspiracy ;") Sir George Jeffreys (afterwards Lord Chancellor), on 21 and 22 June, about his interviews with A. (L. C. J. North) and B. [Judge Jones] about bailing the Earl ; unsigned (2); Charles Bertie (3); Henry Bertie ; George Johnson, at Bowden Park ; Earl of Ailesbury (2); Earl of Chesterfield ; Sir Humphrey Monouse, at Wotton ; John Brydall, advising the Earl, if the judges do not consent to his being bailed, to apply to the King for a warrant to the Lieut. of the Tower ; Thomas Lord Culpeper, a long letter on a dispute about the right to reversions in the Rolls' Office; Sir Edw. Northey, one of the Earl's counsel ; Martin Folkes ; John Ramsey, 7 Apr., enclosing a copy of a declaration by John Richardson, clerk to Mr. Thomas Langhorne who was executed, that he wrote out for circulation copies of the paper afterwards printed by Turner, a Roman Catholic bookseller in Holborn, under the title of " Some reflections upon the Earl of Danby in relation to the murther of Sir Edmund Bury Godfrey, in a letter to a friend," that the original was in the handwriting of Lord Powis, that Langhorne was employed in the business by Lady Powis and Mrs. Cellier, and that the copies were circulated by Mr. William Woodman, the Jesuit ; John Bury, a prisoner in the King's Bench for 18 months, about enquiry by the Council into the evil practices of Sarah Harwood, who had endeavoured to suborn him to swear against the Earl and the Duke of York ; information by Mrs. Edlin (mother of the Earl's page) that one Haynes told her he was offered £300 a year for life by the Duke of Buckingham to swear the murder of Sir E. Godfrey against the Earl, with notes by the Earl of his conversation with her in his room in the Tower, where he had concealed two persons in a closet to overhear what was said ; H. "Colleppyr" (son of Lord Culpeper); Lord Frescheville, 12 Jan. 1681-2 (shortly before his death); Lord O'Brien, the Earl's son-in-law ; C. Hanses, at Gray's Inn, enclosing some "foolish little scrible" as a testimony of duty, and recommending one Stivers in Southwark as the best shorthand writer he can hear of.

"A dialogue betwixt two jurists concerning equity "; folio tract, pp. 20.

MSS. OF THE DUKE OF LEEDS.

1682.

1688.

I. A parcel of Scottish letters endorsed as having been "taken at York," most of them without signatures.

1. To the Earl of Melfort, at London, not dated. "I am ready for evrything you will think for the King's service or to shew my kindnes and friendship to you and your brother."

2. The Earl of Perth to Sir Thomas Haggarston, Lieut.-Gov. of Berwick, Edinb., 20 Nov. "I doubt not but that you have heard of my Lord Cornbury's base action. I hear that my Lord Abbington is gone to the P. of O. The King is hopefull that few of his troups will follow Lord Cornbury's unworthy example. God preserve his Majesty from his ennimies and from his pretended friends."

3. To the Earl and Countess of Drumlangrig, at London, addressed as "Dst. son" and "My dear Hart" (from his mother, the Duchess of Queensberry ?), on the prospect of affairs ; Edinb., 20 Nov. Seal of arms.

4. To the "Vicount of Dundie, Maior-General, London," addressed inside as "My dear Colonel," in the same hand as the above letter to the Earl of Melfort; not dated. All think there will not be much fighting, but that things will be compounded. "Our forses here will doe use noe good, not that they are not better leit thean could be expected, but their hearts are not with use, and wee have noe offisers." The Duke of Queensberry "swears he will stick to the King to the last man : hee is verry consearned att preasent, and I belive hatred and fear of D. Hamlton maks him wish use weal att preasent, at least hee apears to bee furr honester thean meany you would hav expected better things from."

5. To the same, from another writer. "Signior, I alwyse fortold that the King and his ministers wold ruine themselvs for hoping to gaine a securitie which was worth the trusting to. . . . . . For God's sake entreat L. Melfort at last to know his friends from his enimies, at least from neuters. I wonder wee trust our militia or gentry, for both will faile us and turn in great numbers, and the countrey is so picqut at the expence and trouble that they will reveng themselvs that way. I wish all privat letters and papers wer burnt, for they may fall in ill hands, and they will wrong the seekers as much as the givers, and more. If I were a minister of stat ther, I would support the honour of my friends ; presse this, and assure Melfort I will be firm to my King and friends. I wish hee knew how litle the fanatiks here hav deserv'd his brothers friendship and his."

6. To Sir John Gordon "att the Barbars pools, Litel Suffulck Street, London," 30 Nov. The writer is to be a Lieut.-Gov. ; it was resolved in Council to-night to send "five of our number" to the King. Encloses a short note to the Duchess of Gordon.

1688.

MSS. OF THE
DUKE OF LEEDS.
1688.

7. To the Earl [of Seaforth or Melfort?], 22 Nov. "My dear Earl, This is not a tyme for papists to expect to meet with complements; doe not take it ill when I tell yow that at present wee are most contemptible. Yesterday I dined with D. L., and delivered my commission, who told me that Sir Patrick Hume had a tack of Brunstoun, and that it was not unknowne to her cousin"; to which the writer replied that had the Earl known it, he would not have applied for it. "Its true Sir Patrick is her advocat, councellour and grand trustie, and I supposed manadged that affaire of the oath which made so great a noise: he has some little tricks which gives him not such ane entire repute in the world, but I fancy for all the influence he has upon her if my Lord Seafort two years agoe, when her process was depending and Catholicks a little more respected, had demanded such a thing, he had not been refused. . . . . The son of D. was receaved yesterday, I was advertised (but came a little too late) by Mr. Leslie; he had neare done reading the profession of faith when I came in; his freend A. was there but not C. Yesterday D. L. told me (who is alwayes upon her intrigues) there is a designe to bend up a plea against yow for the lands of the Lews by your friend who is come in to us, pretending it belonged formerlie to his predecessors by a daughter which was ane airess. . . . If it be true (as I hope its but a lye and malice) his conversion must not be pure conviction; if interest be at the bottome, fye upon it: he must have allowance for that he has done, and the pretended differences betwixt him and his father are but shams. After I came from D. L. I went to L. E.; there was with her a verrie good churchman, one Mr. Burnet, and L. L.; so her favourite began to extoll that your freend had done, declairing himselfe at such a tyme as this. Sayes the father, Let us once see how he behaves before wee commend him too much, and whither or not there be designe in it: perhaps it may be with them as it is with the familie of Argyle, a knave and ane honest man: the father a knave, and the son ane honest man; if the King carried and have the victory, the father will make his court be the son, and if the Prince have (as God forbid) the better of it, the father secures the fortune. So I told what I did heare, but gave no author. I said if he had such a designe, God let him never have success, and I hoped there was no Catholick in this place but wou'd owne my Lord Seafort before him. Indeed L. E., to doe her justice, had verrie worthy and kynd expressions of yow; she said she wou'd owne none of that name that had the least shaddow or pretence of a plea with you. . . . . . So that our new convert has put us to a little demurr, but I hope its a lye. D. L. at this time is pro and con, and cunning to a miracle: but for Jesus' sake keep it to yourselfe, and let it never more be heard off. I confess nothing in the world I can conceale from yow; all that I know yow know, for my soul cleaves to my dear Earle, and so shall ever be your faithfull Tax . . (?).

As to that I have write, let it never more be heard tell off, and burne my letter."

8. To the Duke of Hamilton at London, from Holyrood house, 20 Nov. About receipt of letters from him. Lord Belcarras "is the great ruler in this place."

9. Copies of Orders in Council at Edinburgh, 29 Oct. and 28 Nov.

10. To Mr. David Craufurd, attending the Duke of Hamilton at London, Edinb., 20 Nov. General surprise at a report that the Duke is at such a time about to leave London. Reported that 10,000 men are being embarked at Rotterdam; a rendezvous of the militia to be at Leith links to-morrow; 500 Highland men came to Cramond this night.

11. Sir Patrick Home to the Duke of [Hamilton or Lauderdale?], Edinb., 1 Dec. Deputation from the Council appointed to go to the King on the affairs of this kingdom.

MSS. OF THE DUKE OF LEEDS.
1688.

12. To Mr. David Lyndsay, secretary to the Earl of Melfort, Edinb., 20 Nov. Necessary to concert with Mr. Rigby and Mr. Ashton to prorogue at this time the design of trading with Mr. Ernault; no such thing "can be caryed on without eminent danger, especially seing correspondence is so frequently cutt of by intercepting the packetts." The writer's "good friend" has so acted that they have made a town talk of it, and Lord Belcarras "has vented himself at his pleasure publickly and privatly in such terms as wes very unproper, and with which he has no concerne, which obleidged me roundly to reason the matter with him." Seal of initials, "A. A." interlaced.

The same to "Estienne Ernault, marchand, a Rowen." Received his letter of 23 Oct. from Paris. Considering the unjust and unnatural invasion, whereby correspondence is in a manner almost cut off, their " proceeding in a trade on such a nature as wes agreed upon cannot bot meet with great discouradgment and apparently great danger"; proposes therefore the postponement of their affair. "As to your concern with the town of Edinburgh, I will use all my endeavours for your satisfaction assoon as may be." Apparently signed, "Magnus Prince."

13. J. Slezer to Lieut.-Gen. Douglas, Master-Gen. of the Ordnance in Scotland, Edinburgh, 20 Nov. Wrote this day senight with account of his arrival with the train of artillery. Account of his march to Edinburgh: delayed at Aylisson bank by reports of the rebels. Need of additional men, and of instructions about precedence of officers and the writer's authority.

14. "A. A." to "Peter Middelton, Esq., att Killvinton, by the postmaster Northallerton," 22 Nov. The militia have taken the arms from the old company at York, and turned them adrift; strict watch kept at the bars, and none allowed to pass without strict examination; Capt. Wytham knocked down and his sword taken.

15. "Anna Adam" (not the writer of the preceding letters of A. A.) to some one at London, enclosing a letter for the Duke of Hamilton, 1 Dec. "My dear dear Cossent, ther cam no letters to me this post. It is said the black box was taken in Yorkshire, but the marchands letters to others in them have been delivered, tho' they weare oppend." Deputation appointed at the Council last night to go to the King.

II.—Miscellaneous Letters, to the Earl of Danby where not otherwise specified.

1. Lord Nottingham, about the presentation of Mr. Hutchins to the church at Hatton Garden; 15 March.

2. Two letters from Christopher Tanckred, of Whixley, about Papists in Yorkshire, and commissions for deputy lieutenants; Mr. Ingram keeps several Papists' horses in his stables; K. James' Declarations are as common as ballads; the insolence of Papists and other dissatisfied persons is insufferable; June 25, 29.

3. Letter of news from P. B. (Peregrine Bertie) at London, 25 Sept. Reports of the Dutch preparations, &c.; "to me itt seemes incredible that soe late in the year any wise peple should thinke of an invasion."

4. To the Countess of Danby from her daughter Lady Plymouth. The Prince of Orange is expected to land next week; but volunteers are said to be enlisted faster than at first, "which looks as if the people began to consider both their duty and their safety"; Oct. 11.

5. Order from the Office of Ordnance to Mr. Edw. Baldock at York to receive arms from Lord Fauconberg; 13 Oct.

MSS. OF THE
DUKE OF LEEDS.
1688.

6. From Sir H. Goodricke; York, 20 Oct. Assembling of the militia of Yorkshire by the Duke of Newcastle, and appointment of commanders.

7. Charles Osborne to Lord Latimer; the Earl has been sent for for some great matter; 20 Oct.

8. The Mayor and Corporation of Lichfield to the Earl, requesting him to re-assume the place of Recorder on the restoration of their Charter; 20 Oct.

9. Charles Bertie; Lond., 1 Nov. The Dutch fleet is under sail.

10. Ral. Hansby to Sir Walter Vavasour at York; 4 Nov. "God sende the King mayo finde who hee is to trust too." Had a bad fall from his horse yesterday.

11. Commission from the King to Francis Nicholls to be Lieutenant in the regiment of foot commanded by the Duke of Newcastle; countersigned by Lord Preston; Whitehall, 15 Nov.

12. Rowland Tempest to the Duke of Newcastle sending the above commission, he having disposed of his lieutenant's place to Mr. Nicholls; Whitehall, 20 Nov.

13. N. Colston, apparently a Roman Catholic priest, at a Mrs. Hammond's, to his aunt, Mrs. Bridget Foster, in New Elvet, Durham: "I hope with God's assistance our gracious King will teach the Hollanders a French dance, and ashure yourselfe there partners our unfortunate countrymen will suffer sharply (O loyall Church of England!) . . . . . You have mentioned nothing concerning the last things I sent for, to witt; my cap and crucifix . . . . When you have perus'd these, burn them." Towton, 20 Nov.

14. Ric. Hast to Sir Walter Vavasour at York; a letter of news. The bishops have petitioned for a free Parliament; the Prince of Orange fortifies himself at Exeter, "but I hope he will quickly be unkeneld;" many have enlisted as volunteers to guard the Queen, Lord Stafford being colonel; Lord Cornbury was not welcome to Schomberg, who told him he had done the King more service by going than if he had stayed; 13 companies, all Catholic officers, raised in Lancashire; 20 Nov.

15. Notes from the Duke of Newcastle to Patricius Crow, esq. and Lieut. Jennison; Tadcaster, 21 Nov.

16. [Capt. Wytham] to his sister Mrs. Wytham at Rokeby, from York, 22 Nov. "All is heare in an uproare;" Lord Fairfax has this day seized on the main-guard, has taken the keys from the governor, and seized him in his own house; "I expect to be next."

17. Jer. Mahony to Thomas Ratcliffe, Lieut. Col. of the Duke of Newcastle's regiment at Newcastle; York, 22 Nov. "His Grace went out of Yorck two hours before wee arrived heare. The reason of the sudden departure of his Grace was that all the militia of the controy came to towne without orders, and theire confounded ringleaders had the impudence to speake to his Grace for joyning with them for a free Parliament; and thereupon his Grace went away in the greatest pet and discontentment of the world; he was extreamly disatisfied that wee came through this confounded city . . . . The Scotch battalion is not marcht as yet from Hull . . . . . There is nothing to be expected from this diabolicall rabell but confusion, rebellion, disorder and disloyalty."

18. Thomas Errington to the same, "at Dilston;" York, 22 Nov., with a similar account; Lord Danby one of those who desired the Duke to join with them for a free Parliament; is ordered to march to Hull to-morrow.

19. Jacob Rookeby to William Grimston, esq.; York, 22 Nov. This day Lord Dunblane, Lord Danby, Lord Lumley and Sir H. Goodrick, seized the town, disarmed the soldiers, and took the governor, Sir John Reresby, prisoner.

MSS. OF THE DUKE OF LEEDS.

1688.

20. R. Midford, at Dilston, 22 Nov., to Hon. Francis Radcliffe, in London, about raising men for the latter's troop.

21. Da. Foulis to the Duke of Newcastle, about movements of troops at Whitby and Scarborough ; 24 Nov.

22. The Earl of Danby to Sir John Hanmer, bart., governor of Hull, urging him to surrender Hull, and join with the Prince of Orange, and offering £5,000 for compliance ; answer to be sent within six hours; York, Nov. 30.

23. Arbitration by six gentlemen in a dispute between Lord Lumley and Lord Willoughby, that the former shall ask pardon of the latter for striking him in the garrison of York ; 1 Dec.

24. Letter from John and Rich. Lowther, Christ. Dalston, and Andrew Hudleston, as to precautions taken (although opposed by Sir Christ. Musgrave and Sir George Fletcher) for securing Carlisle, and issuing a declaration of the gentlemen of Westmoreland and Cumberland for a free Parliament ; Lowther, 2 Dec.

25. The Earl of Devonshire, two letters from Nottingham, 3 Dec., and "Tuesday," (4 Dec.). Expects every hour to hear of the surrender of Hull ; the Princess (Anne) being here, great numbers come in every day. (There is also a short note from him on 1 Oct.).

26. Lord Danby to the Bishop of London, York, 4 Dec. ; joy at hearing of the Princess's arrival at Nottingham, "safe out of their hands by your Lordship's prudent conduct ; " wishes she were at York.

27. Lord Danby to the same and Lord Devonshire ; same date. Scarborough Castle being secured and garrisoned, the Princess can be kept there safe from all danger.

28. The Bishop of London ; Nottingham, 5 Dec. They want officers ; have sent an express to the Prince.

29. Duke of Newcastle to Lord Latimer ; Welbeck, Dec. 4. The deputations (*i.e.*, commissions for deputy-lieutenants) were not worth his acceptance.

30. Lord Devonshire ; Nottingham, Dec. 5. Communicated Lord Danby's letter (No. 27.) to the Princess ; no resolution can be taken till the express returns from the Prince of Orange.

31. Lord Lumley ; Durham, 5 Dec. Some nobility coming from Scotland desire security in passing through these parts.

32. John Lowther ; 5 Dec. Proposes the summoning the garrison at Carlisle to surrender ; the governor is so afraid of the town's-people that he has carried all their spits, pitchforks, and hatchets into the castle, and turned some of the guns upon the town ; one of the captains, Capt. Bub, is a mortal enemy to the Papists, and has fought a duel with the lieut.-gov., Capt. Crofts.

33. Lord Devonshire ; Nottingham, 8 Dec. The Princess determines to go to-morrow towards Oxford, the Prince being on his march towards Reading, "where the King's horse are quarter'd, if they think fitt to stay for him." "We" are about 1500 horse and two companies of foot. News that the garrison of Hull have seized the governor, and declared for the Prince of Orange.

34. The Bishop of London, to the same effect ; 8 Dec.

35. Declaration signed by the Mayor, Corporation, Officers, &c., of Newcastle for a free Parliament.

36. Warrant from Ph. Frowde, of the General Post Office, London, for the passage of John Roberts to York ; 11 Dec.

MSS. OF THE
DUKE OF LEEDS.
1688.

37. Earl of Lindsey; 11 Dec. A meeting of gentry appointed at Sleaford; if Sir Thos. Hussey weds the cause, his interest will do much to make this country unanimous.

38. John Lowther; 12 Dec. Has seized at Workington a quantity of arms going to Ireland, but has no ammunition; desires that Sir Christopher Musgrave and Sir George Fletcher may be threatened if they do not raise the militia, or that troops may be sent to take Carlisle. (A long letter.)

39. Thomas Love, at Tynemouth Castle, 14 Dec., about the condition of the castle and garrison, and the procuring its surrender by Lieut.-Gov. Villiers.

40. Francis Dodsworth, Mayor of Chesterfield, 14 Dec., desiring immediate help, as news has come that 7000 Papists and Irish have burned Birmingham, and are to come to Derby, &c., to-night.

41. Lord Danby to the Countess, York, 14 Dec. 6.30 a.m. News has just come that the King, Queen and Prince of Wales, have all gone beyond seas; consequent changes in London, &c., which "will make me march with coaches instead of troops." (A long letter.)

42. Philip Bertie; Grimsthorp, 14 Dec. "We are alarm'd by a body of fifteen hundred horse; they fire all, and put everie one to the sword. Yesterday they wear as far as Northampton. We shall make here as good a stand as we can."

43. Hasting Sayle, Mayor of Pomfret; Sunday (16 Dec.). News from Chester of sudden danger (from the Irish); they have therefore secured all the Papists, and are equipping themselves as well as they can.

44. Jo. Ellerker, Mayor of Doncaster, &c., 15 Dec., 1.30 p.m., repeating the news sent by the Mayor of Chesterfield, as above.

45. Philip Bickerstaffe, Cherton, 15 Dec., recommending Capt. Thomas Love; the garrison of Berwick Castle is ready to declare for the Prince of Orange, and Captains Villiers and Tempest at Tynemouth.

46. News-letter from London to Francis Howard esq., at Corby Castle; 15 Dec.

47. The Mayor and Corporation of Leeds, desiring that Sir Tho. Gower's troop of horse may stay there (on the alarm of the Irish); 15 Dec., 4 p.m.

48. Sir Thomas Gower; 15 Dec. Remains at Leeds by desire of the Mayor and Aldermen until he receives further orders.

49. Summons from Lord Danby to Lord Widdrington, governor of Berwick, to surrender; York, 15 Dec.

50. L. Copley to Capt. Wolseley at York; Hull, 16 Dec. Is sorry the news of massacres has stopped Wolseley's going to the Prince; heard yesterday of massacres at Grantham and Newark, but the news is contradicted to-day.

51. The Mayor and Corporation of Leeds to the Lords at York, praying for immediate help to defend them from the enemy's force, they being not far off; 16 Dec., 6 a.m.

52. Ralph Assheton, Jas. Holte and Alex. Butterworth, at Middleton, 16 Dec., to the Dep. Lieuts. of Yorkshire, "or the commanders who are on their march into Lancashire," thanking them for "notice of some danger from an Irish party, tho' fleeing."

53. Col. Rupert Billingsley to Sir Charles Porter at the Middle Temple, London; Berwick, 16 Dec. "This day as soon as morninge service was ended, I consulted the officers of the regiment in church, and told them I was resolved imeadiatly before I dismissed the regiment to declare for the preservation of the King's person and Protestant

religion and a free Parliament, and to assist the Prince of Orange in theise affayres, to which the officers all concurred. The Major of the towne being present, I ordered him to call togather his bretherne, and doe the same, which was alsoe don. I ordered Lord Widdrington, our late governor, to depart, soe that nowe I have the sole government of this place, at the Prince's service."

MSS. OF THE DUKE OF LEEDS.
1688.

54. L. Copley, Hull, 16 Dec., to the same effect as his letter above to Wolseley.

55. W. Belasyse ; Wakefield, Monday, 3 p.m. (17 Dec.). Sends a letter just received from Sir Thomas Gower, to stop the Earl's journey to Leeds ; concludes there is now no occasion for raising more regiments. One Hammerton, a Jesuit, who taught school at Pomfret, has been seized in disguise.

56. Letter from Sheffield, 17 Dec., with information that scouts had been sent out for many miles from Derby and Coventry as far as Birmingham, but nothing was heard of any party of Irish as reported.

57. Sir Miles Stapylton: his house was beset last night by 60 or 80 men of his neighbours armed with guns and pitchforks, who searched severely for arms, and this morning brought him prisoner thus far on his way to Pomfret, where meeting with Capt. Tankard, "the worthy captaine was pleas'd to take my word for my quiet liveing at home, which I hope your lordship will allowe me." Ferry Bridge, 17 Dec.

58. Sir Christopher Musgrave ; Carlisle, 17 Dec. On Saturday (15 Dec.) at 12 p.m. Mr. Howard, the governor of Carlisle, delivered into his possession the keys and government of the town.

59. The same, on 18 Dec., with a fuller account of the surrender, through his interest with Captains Bubb and Fielding. On 16 Dec. Mr. Howard and some Popish officers took passes to go to their several habitations, leaving their arms. Sir Geo. Fletcher came on Sunday. On Monday he turned the Popish soldiers out of the town.

60. Capt. Jer. Bubb, with an account of the surrender of Carlisle, similar to that in the preceding letter ; 18 Dec.

61. Sir Henry Villiers ; Tynemouth Castle, 18 Dec. There is not a Roman Catholic in the garrison ; they are for protecting the Protestant religion, and for a free Parliament: he has sent a messenger to London to the Prince.

62. Copy of summons to the governor of Tynemouth Castle ; York, 19 Dec.

63. Sir Henry Goodricke, about the surrender of Berwick, Carlisle, and Tynemouth, "so that nothing now remains in the North out of the Prince's hands." Reported by two expresses that Ripon was fired this morning by a strong party of Irish, "and not one word of truth in the report ;" York, 19 Dec.

64. The same to the Mayor of Newcastle ordering him as governor of Tynemouth to take up so much of the customs' revenue as shall be necessary for keeping the troops there ; and also for Berwick ; 19 Dec.

65. The same to Lord Danby, complaining that Capt. Bubb has recognised Sir Christ. Musgrave as governor of Carlisle, and that Sir Geo. Fletcher is called in to assist, and that Sir John Lowther, who deserved so very much, and was so little assisted by them, is excluded ; begs that he will give orders thereupon, or else represent Sir J. Lowther's merit to the Prince ; York, 20 Dec.

66. Short note in Dutch from two merchants at Rotterdam, J. and T. Weymans, to Lord Willoughby D'Eresby at the Hague ; 24 Dec.

67. Certificate by five deputy-lieuts. that William Walmesley, of Lower Hall, Samlesbury, Lanc., esq., lives peaceably, and keeps a horse and arms for the service of the present government ; and is therefore to be

MSS. OF THE
DUKE OF LEEDS.
1688.

allowed to live without molestation and to pass and re-pass freely; 24 Dec.

68. Sir H. Goodricke to Lord Danby. Has assured Capt. Villiers that Lord Danby removed him from the government of Tynemouth only because he (Lord Danby) gave such commands to such civil magistrates as deserved the Prince's favour; encloses "some letters intercepted here for Scotland;" York, 29 Dec.

69. Sir Geo. Mackenzie to Lord Danby, thanking him for a pass, and asking for one by the bearer (Sir Alex. Bruce of Broomhall) for the Earl of Marr to go to London, "one of our most ancient nobility, and who was layd asyd in our last parliament, and who has ever since own'd his religion with great zeal." Not dated, but endorsed "Dec."

70. Will. Andrewes to Lord Latimer, asking for employment for his son, as compensation for £2,000 advanced by his wife (deceased, a near kinswoman to Lord Latimer's father-in-law, Esquire Bennett), for the use of the King's army at Dublin at the beginning of the Irish rebellion, and for which she formerly petitioned Charles II.; 7 Jan. 1688–9.

71. Stephen Godfrey to Lord Danby; has, as ordered, kept possession of the manor, and secured the Popish chapel in it from the rabble, "but the other day Capt. Lawson (who is nephew to father Lawson) came to view the roomes and ground, and then demanded possession of them, affirmeing he has a grant of them for a terme to come, and that he onely let his uncle have the use of them;" desires instructions hereon; York, 26 Feb. 1688–9.

III.—Miscellaneous Papers.

1. Queries put by the Bishop of Durham to his clergy in April 1688, about compliance with the King's commands.

2. Two copies of the Bishop of Rochester's letter to the Ecclesiastical Commissioners, 16 Aug. 1688, resigning his place amongst them.

3. Memoranda by Lord Danby for a representation to the Prince of Orange of their need of help in the North, and of constant correspondence; resolved by divers lords and gentlemen that on 21 Nov. they will secure York, and seize the Duke of Newcastle and the governor; and that others on the same day would meet at Nottingham and issue a declaration "to tell my lord Shrewsbury (whose counterfeit name is Stephens) that I rely cheifely upon him and Mr. Russell (whose counterfeit name is Adams) to gett a despatch of these things as they ought to be." "The cipher of names is :—

The Prince	- Barebones.
Shrewsbury	- Stephens.
Abingdon	- Richards.
Mr. Russell	- Adams.
Mr. Sydney	- Lloyd.
Mr. Bentinck	- Wilson.
Northampton	- Cary.
Humphreys	- The messenger to be credited."

4. Copy of the order by the Lords, 24 Dec., for the committal to the Tower of the Earls of Salisbury and Peterborough.

5. Draft of an address from the Lord Mayor and Commonalty of York to the Prince of Orange. 14 Dec.

6. Argument in answer in the negative to "The grand question whether the King can . . . call such as he pleaseth to give their assent or dissent as Peers in the House of Peers *pro hac vice tantum*."

7. "The interregnum, or the proceedings of the Lords of the Council and others from the withdrawing of K. James to the meeting of the Convention." 66 pp.   MSS. OF THE DUKE OF LEEDS. 1688.
8. Printed broadsides. I. Petition of the Lords for a free Parliament and the King's answer, 17 Nov. II. The King's Proclamation of pardon to such as quit the Prince of Orange; Salisbury, 22 Nov. III. Order of Peers at London against pulling down of houses, especially those of Foreign Ministers ; 12 Dec. IV. Letter of the Peers to the Prince of Orange for the election of the Convention, &c. and his reply ; 25 Dec. V. Letter of the Prince summoning the Convention ; 29 Dec. VI. Declaration of the Prince authorising sheriffs, &c. to act ; 31 Dec.
9. Five letters from Lord Danby to his wife and son ; Feb.-Nov.
10. Extract from a Memorial of the Dissenters in New England presented to the King by Increase Mather, Sam. Newel and Eliz. Hutchinson, and read before him in July 1688.
11. News from Fort St. George, 30 Sept.

A series of muster-rolls of regiments at Chester, and returns about troops at York.

1689 and 1689-90.   1689.

Letters from [1]—

Abbott, Thomas, to Lord Willoughby, Boston 11 Jan. 1688-9, informing him that he and Sir Will. Yorke are elected the Boston members for the Convention.

Abingdon, Earl of, Rycott, 20 Sept., enclosing a copy of one from Rob. Pawling, one of the Corporation of Oxford, to the Mayor of Oxford, in answer to a summons to attend meetings ; in consequence of which he has been expelled.

Armytage, Thomas, Kirklees, 30 Sept.

Atholl, Marq. of, Edinb. 13 Apr. Account of proceedings in connection with the meeting of the Convention of Estates ; extravagant proposals of some hot-headed men who came over with the King from Holland. Reasons why he could not agree to saying that K. James had forfeited the government, or to the abolition of episcopacy, to which " considering my education and principles and zeale for the Church of England and our happie unione, being in one and the same isleand and under on King . . I could not give my consent.'" Last Friday they passed an Act that none should be absent from the diets under pain of imprisonment ; " this Act is mainly aimed at me ; " he therefore desires the King's leave (at whose proclamation at the Cross in Edinburgh he assisted) to go to London for his justification.

Atkyns, Edward ; Serjeants' Inn, 9 June.

Barrington, Abraham, April. Two letters, complaining of arrest.

Beaufort, Duke of, 19 Feb. 1689-90, against an order in Council relating to Malmesbury.

Beaumont, Col. John, 13 Apr.

Bertie, P., 12 Feb. 1689-90. Proposes the taking up idle seamen, skulking in villages on the east coast, to supply the navy.

Bolton, Lord, Basing, 27 Aug.

---

[1] Where not otherwise noted the letters are to the Earl of Danby, created in this year Marquis of Carmarthen.

MSS. OF THE
DUKE OF LEEDS.
1689.

Bradshaw, James, to the Company of Carpenters at Hull, denying, with reference to his proposed election for Parliament, that he was ever in favour of taking off the penal laws ; Risby, 24 Feb. 1689-90.

Breval, D., 23 July, introducing M. Tourville with reference to some proposal about concealed Crown lands. *French.*

Browne, John, Mayor of Boston, to Lord Willoughby d'Eresby, announcing his election, with Sir W. Yorke, for that town. 11 Jan. 1689-90.

Bury, Thos., to Sir Christ. Neville ; Linc. 19 Feb.

Butler, Sir N. (?) with proffers of service to the Prince ; 16 Jan.

Byndlos, J. (brother in-law to Sir Henry Morgan) enclosing a letter from Jamaica from Sir Rich. Derham (whom he highly commends), complaining that after the return to England of a Romish priest, father Churchill, who had been sent out to Jamaica by James II., he had been put out of all commissions; Portsmouth, 2 Sept.

Carter, Will., 27 Jan. ; address carefully torn off. The gentleman left for Flanders a week ago ; the house that sheltered him has been searched since his departure ; he said he had no safety here, but still hopes by means of the person addressed, " through your father's mediation to obtaine favour when time should serve, and the present storme was somewhat blowne over."

Comber, Dr. Thomas : three letters, 4 March, 19 Apr., 22 May, Lond. and York. Proposing Lord Danby's election to the Chancellorship of Cambridge, in place of the archbishop of Canterbury, resigned ; asking for preferment, *e.g.* the deanery of Lincoln, the dean having the disease of a very great age ; suggesting that the Earl should get a grant of the manor of York, and then that the writer may be allowed to pasture a cow and a horse there.

Cooke, Sir John, Secretary of State, enclosing the proposed preamble to Danby's patent as Marq. of Carmarthen ; 16 Apr.

Crompton, Rob., Hull, 8 May. The Corporation have denied Col. Alured his freedom.

Cunningham, John, Liverpool, 17 March, about the transport of troops from thence.

Dashwood, Sir Samuel, 2 May, 4 July ; two letters to Hon. Charles Bertie, about bills of exchange.

Effingham, Earl of, 28 Feb. 1689-90, about his commission and departure for Virginia.

[Evans, Rev. —, Uffington, near Stamford], 10 Apr. A long letter to Chas. Bertie on Church affairs, against the Comprehension bill, asserting the impossibility of satisfying the Presbyterians by concessions in ceremonies, and protesting against the lukewarmness of members of Parliament in not constantly attending to defend the Church. "You acquaint me with a design to expunge Athanasius' Creed, and make severall other alterations in our Liturgy. Good God ! how will this look to the Reformed Churches abroad, to thousands heer at home, and to future ages ? That a Parliament should reforme our Liturgie, expunge Creeds, tell us what wee must not beleeve and what wee must, without advising with a Convocation, or with ecclesiasticall men in ecclesiasticall affairs, what shall wee reply if this should happen (which God forbid) to our old adversaries at Rome, when they affirme that our religion is meerly parliamentary, that our Church hath noe power nor authority but what is derived from the law of the land ? "

Fairfax, Lord, 1 May, York. The country is much alarmed at the conduct of Sir John Lanere's regiment.

——, 12, 19, 23 Nov., Hull. Three letters about the landing of Danish troops at Hull (6,000 foot and 1,000 horse), and the arrival of the Duke of Wirtemberg. With these are letters (in French) to K. William from Ferd. Guill., Duke of Wirtemberg and — Vontoïsien, informing him of their fleet being driven by contrary winds to Hull, instead of pursuing their course to Edinburgh; from the Mayor, &c.; and from Geo. Barrett. Also, particulars of the regiments, and memoranda of orders that they should go to Chester.

MSS. OF THE DUKE OF LEEDS.
1689.

Fish, Rev. Robert, Little Bytham, 27 March, asking for preferment either for himself or for his son.

Frampton, Robert, the Bishop of Gloucester, 24 Dec. Copy of a letter from him. This letter is so interesting in reference to the early days of the non-jurors, and so honourable to the writer, that, although long, I cannot but copy it in full.[1]

"My good Lord, By my suspension, which is almost expired, and by my deprivation, which is hard at hand, you see that the water is come up unto my lips, and that, as wee use to say on publishing the banns of matrimony, I must now speake or else hereafter for ever hold my peace.

"Not that I have much to speake, nor anything at all in order to mine own indemnity. For who am I that I alone should escape, or hope to escape? And on that silly hope goe about progging for my single deliverance, when as so many better men than I are under the same condemnation, and, without some timely and friendly interposall, are likely to fall together. Who, tho' they are but few in respect to the whole English clergy, yet, if I may speake it without offence, are too many to be thrown away all at once, considering their inoffensiveness in all cases (but this alone) their great parts and their as great virtues, what they have done already for the good of the Church and State, and what they are further able and certain to do, if God spare their lives, and the Law be not so extreme as to dash them all in pieces like a potter's vessel.

It will therefore be no grief of heart to you, my good Lord, nor to any else, I hope, that are of your high station, if you, with the assistance of your friends, should move their Majesties and both the Houses that those good men may be at all at ease, yea confident I am (because I know your generous temper) that it will be the joy of your heart that you have been the first mover in it, tho' it should not succeed; how much more if, by God's blessing (which is all in all) you should come to accomplish it.

"Or if the Law, under which they are for not swearing, be so extreme, that it must have some atonement made, and the honour of the legislators cannot be salved otherwise, be pleased to endeavour that those atonements may be as few as possible : provided that I may be one of those few ; and happy, thrice happy, shall I deeme myself if my single suffering, be it what it will (undoing, banishment, imprisonment, or death itselfe) may be accepted for all the rest, at leest for those that are of mine own order.

"Not that I am so foolhardy as causelessly to engrosse the displeasure of my superiours, and draw it wholly on myselfe ; for I know the weight of it. I am sure it will crush me, and therefore if I could, would most certainly avoid it. Neither do I arrogate anything to myselfe upon this offer, as if it were my peculiar; for there is none (as I am persuaded) of all those for whom I plead but would leap into the gulph, for the safety

---

[1] It is mentioned in the anonymous contemporary Life of Bp. Frampton, published by Rev. T. S. Evans in 1876 (p. 202), as a letter that was written "to a great man as one that should have had more power than he had."

MSS. OF THE DUKE OF LEEDS.
1689.

of all the rest, as boldly and as willingly as I doe. I only hope that I have prevented them, and am the earlyest to offer it.

"Now, if you would know my reason for all this, St. Paul will give it; for one good man—soe he (for the number is singular), and I add for many; for soe many, and for soe many very good men (as I take them to be)—some one would even dare to dye; and that some one am I; for besides that the action is a good one, I have the farther inducement for it, that when I fall, it will be without the hurt, the losse, and the grief, of any, at most of but very few, whereas they cannot fall without the hurt, the losse, and the griefe, of very many.

"In all governments whatsoever, especially in newly erected ones (which therefore ought to aim at popularity, and for the most part doe so) those punishments are the least offensive which are the least severe; and those favours the most taking which are the most free and generous; for why should I not speake of some favour to be extended to those good men who have of late so well deserved of Church and State; if it may be, and is, extended, as I hear, to Quakers, who have deserved nothing at all of either, or very little, that I know of.

"Your Lordship needs not to be told what good effects are likely, yea certain, to ensue on such a temper, viz., the uniteing of all our minds in those things to which we have attained, which is a great happiness to Church and State, and our bearing with one another in what we have not or cannot attain unto. As little need have you to be told what bad effects are likely, yea certain, to be prevented by it, viz., those heartburnings and animosities which have so often endangered both, and noe where can do otherwise wheresoever they prevail: never did, nor ever will, for it is their very nature to destroy.

"Nor is it a small inducement to such a generous temper as yours is that our Rachel by your means will be fully comforted: I mean our good mother the Church of England, the best Christian Church that I know of in the world; when shee shall see so many of her children, and (without offence be it spoken) some of the choicest that shee hath, all safe, and no one of them cast out or cut off, but my selfe, who can best be spared, and will never repine at it.

"These things I write to you, my good Lord, and to noe man else alive: if all or any of them move you, trye what you can doe, and God blesse you in it. If you cannot, will not, or dare not, attempt it, for its impossibility, or any other smaller cause, burn this letter, and let it goe for nothing, though written by, my good Lord,

Your Lordship's much obliged and most affectionate servant, that will love you for ever,

ROBERT GLOUCESTER,
Dec. 24 [16]89."

Francklin, William, to Lord Shrewsbury, being sent from the associated gentlemen in the north of Ireland; Chester, 18 March. Begs that three frigates may go to Carrickfergus, and that instead of sending relief direct to Derry (a course so extremely destructive that the whole province of Ulster may be lost while that relief is going about for that place) help should be sent by way of Belfast to Hillsborough, where the Provincial Council was sitting on Wednesday when the writer left, and whither all their forces are being drawn.

Fryth, Charles; Chester, 14 Oct.

Goodricke, Sir H., York, 5 Jan., about elections for the Convention, &c.

Hamilton, James, on landing at Belfast, 12 Sept. Great want of horses, many having been lost on the passage. The Papists burned the town of Newry on quitting it. The fort of Charlemont is the only place remaining to them in Ulster.

MSS. OF THE DUKE OF LEEDS.
1689.

Hewley, John, York, 19 Feb. 1689-90, about the election of the Earl's son for York.

Jackson, —, to Lord Latimer, informing him of his election for Knaresborough; the cost of the election was 80*l.* ; should there be a new election, hopes it will be obtained at less charge.

Lancashire. Complaint signed by 15 justices of the ill-ordering of affairs by the sheriff; the complaints against him are so many that they know not where to begin, and pray that a better successor may be appointed; Lancaster sessions, 9 Oct.

Leighton, B. Shrewsbury, 7 Aug.; bitterly complaining that his loyal services have not been rewarded; it is beneath him to accept of less than a regiment or lieut. col. of horse ; will accept of any civil employment.

Lindsey, Earl of, Chelsea, 28 July, complaining of the King's rejection of his claim for certain fees at the coronation.

——, Grimsthorp, 10 March 1689-90, enclosing depositions taken at Grimsby 27 Feb. against Lord Lexington, Mr. Matthew Lister, and Mr. Hilliard for swearing at King William, and drinking to King James, &c.; suggests that it will be best to hush the matter up.

——, to his sister, the Marchioness of Carmarthen, upon the death of her daughter: a letter of Christian comfort ; Grimsthorp, 22 Sept.

Lister, Matthew, Burwell, 7 March, to Lord Willoughby, asking him to solicit Lord Danby for a place for him.

Mount Alexander, Earl of, to the Earl of Shrewsbury; Hillsborough, 6 March. The King and Queen were proclaimed on 5 March; state of affairs; want of ammunition and money.

Newcomen, George, Chester, 29 May, to Sir Oliver St. George at his house in Barkly Street, London. The garrison of Iniskilling have defeated Sarsfield. Major Baker (who is now in Derry, and not inferior to Walker) has sent over his lady to Chester, who has not a penny to buy bread ; the King lately gave two officers' wives who came from Derry £100 a piece, whose husbands have not deserved better than Baker.

Nottingham, Earl of, 26 Apr., about some newsletters from Ireland.

Osborne, Charles, 22 Dec., begging for help to pay debts.

——, to the Countess of Danby, 23 Feb., in relation to some offence given to the Earl, and about Lord Latimer's debts.

Parker, Abr., 25 July, sending some papers "of high consarne to the King, these kingdomes, and the Protestant religion."

Parrell, D., to Mr. Roberts at the Earl of Lindsey's ; has heard of two valets' places vacant, one at the Duke of "Norefoflk," the other at Adm. Harbort's. *French.*

Penington, Thomas, 30 Jan. 1689-90, urging that Jews should be no longer exempted from paying the alien duty.

Peyton, John, 21 May, asking for a major's place in a regiment going to Scotland.

Prickett, George, 19, 22 Feb. 1689-90; two letters about the election for York.

Purbecke, Visc., 21 March 1689-90, about elections in Radnorshire, and Mr. Duvall's exertions; and on behalf of his "poor grandson" who must be taken out of his mother's tuition.

Rastell, Thomas, Westby, 31 Jan., to Lord Latimer about elections in Lincolnshire, and asking for a place in the excise.

36   HISTORICAL MANUSCRIPTS COMMISSION.

MSS. OF THE　　Robinson, Will., High Sheriff of Yorkshire, 27 July; with complaints
DUKE OF LEEDS. against Col. Villiers' regiment for seizing the horses of Protestants.
1689.　　——— and Chr. Tanckred, 28 June, 24 July, about seizing Papists' arms, &c.

Rogers, Eliz., to Marchioness of Carmarthen, on behalf of her son Rhodes: "a good place will help a country farmer well"; Neitherthorpe, 29 Jan.

Rokeby, Thomas. Certificate in favour of Jasper Blythman, esq., a lawyer.

Russell, Jeremiah, 16 Aug., for a place as Secretary in one of the Leeward Islands.

Rutland, Earl of, Belvoir, 20 July, 3 Aug., declining the office of Lord Lieut. of Leicestershire unless he be also Custos rotulorum.

St. George, Sir Oliver, with proposal for supplying bread for the forces at a cheaper rate; Lond. 17 May.

Schomberg, Marshal, about embarkation of arms at Topsham; 27 March.

———, 25 May, in reference to Sir John Peyton.

———, 22 Apr., order for sending two soldiers from Hull to London.

Shales, John, six letters while employed on the commissariat service in Ireland; June-Dec.

———, to Marshal Schomberg, when in confinement at Belfast about his accounts; 28 Dec.

———. Petition to the King for release from confinement; 17 Feb. 1689-90.

Sheldon, Rich., to Charles Osborne, about the election at York; 17 Feb. 1689-90.

Shere, Sir Henry. Account of the arms required for 17 regiments of foot; Tower, 22 Apr.

Shrewsberry, Earl of. Summons to attend a meeting with the King.

Southwell, Sir Robert, 18 Dec., forwarding a paper respecting Irish accounts by one Mr. Waller.

Tanckred, Christ., 7 July, about the Yorkshire militia.

Tarbet, Lord, Edinb., 16 March. The fanatic party had so alarmed those who were not so, that there is a considerable party for King James, albeit the elections were in good hands; encloses a copy of King James' letter to the Parliament, with the vote passed thereon this day before it was read.

Tempest, Col. John, 7 May, about a customer's place the reversion of which was granted to his sons Rowland and John.

Thompson, Edward, York, 5 Aug. People are alarmed by scandalous news-letters from Scotland of the landing there of King James and the routing of Gen. Mackay. Knows not how to proceed against those who refuse the oaths, even priests getting quit for 40s. and being bound over to appear. Good service of Col. Villers in seizing Papists' horses. Encloses two letters brought by the postmaster; requests an order if any more are to be stopped. That from F. T. to Mad. Tempest is from one Wilson, a servant of Lord Fairfax, who lives in Northumberland to give an account of things: the other is for Mr. Midleton, though directed to one of his tenants. *Enclosures:—*

i. F. T. to Mrs. Tempest at Broughton near Skipton, Aug. 2; professedly about a trial soon coming off. Mackay is mortally wounded and taken prisoner by Dundee with the loss of 3,000 slain, at Uppermore, about 6 miles from St. Johnston's; we have it by a particular messenger from a person of quality in Scotland and a great friend to this house : " the posters gave out that Dundee was slaine, but he is certainly as well as ever."

ii. Thomas Gibson to Mr. Abr. Atkingson at Stockild ; 3 Aug. News of the fight in Scotland; " the Duke of Hamilton write to our Parliament man Mr. Forster that the losse was considerable on our side, but the rebells' losse was greater in regard Dundee was killed; and the same was write on the outside of the expresse ; but the silly Papists boldly affirme Dundee to be alive, and a glorious victory . . . . . . They brag too of great numbers of Irish landed."

Thornton, Alice, a "kinswoman," East Newton, 28 July, with thanks for a naval appointment for her son.

Waller, Robert, 9 Jan. 1688–9 ; 12 March, 1689–90. Two letters about elections at York.

Waterhouse, Tho., Braithwell, 29 June, requesting a place in the excise in Yorkshire.

Wheler, Will., 20 May. Is ordered to return to his command in Holland, but is ready to serve in America or elsewhere.

Wildman, John, Hull, 26 June, with an information against Col. Copley, the lieut. governor of Hull for imprisoning the postmaster and seizing letters.

Wykham, Oliver, Swakecliffe, [Oxon] 8 Dec., to Mr. Henry Rogers, at Grimsthorpe. Apparently an intercepted letter ; couched in enigmatical language, about a meeting before Christmas, which may establish a good trade : immediate letters to be written to Mr. Vall at the White Hart in Chipping Norton ; some letters have miscarried, through neighbours, as he fears, to doe him " diskindness."

York. The Mayor and Corporation, 17 Jan., recommending Thomas Jackson, who was a lieutenant in Monk's army at the Restoration, for a place in Chelsea College.

York. The High Sheriff and others ; 4 May. Alarms at meetings of Papists, particularly with Lord Fairfax of Gilling, and Lord Preston ; more troops wanted in the county. Copy of reply ; the King desires that the Roman Catholics may be carefully watched and further information sent.

York. The High Sheriff and others ; 5 July. About searching for arms.

York. The High Sheriff and others ; 21 July. Col. Villers has promised to make reparation to the country for injuries done by his soldiers, and that care shall be taken that nothing of like nature be done again.

Miscellaneous Papers, including—

i. Report of Rich. Gibson to S. Pepys, 28 Aug. 1689, on the victualling of the navy.

ii. Papers about the army in Ireland.

iii. Notes relative to preparations for the Coronation.

iv. "Case of the free shipwrights of England, with an abstract of their proceedings from 1605 to 1688."

v. Conditions granted by Hon. Will. Nugent on surrender of Sir Thos. Newcomen's house at Mosstown, Longford, 13 Jan. 1689.

vi. Proposals of Sir John Brodericke to raise a regiment amongst the Protestants in the county of Cork.

vii. Petitions.—1. Of Lord Peterborough to the Lords for release from the Tower. 2. Of the Earl of Sussex to Will. III. for arrears of a pension of £2,000 a year, granted to him on his marrying a natural daughter of Charles II. 3. Of Thomas Maynard to Will. III. for continuance in his place as consul at Lisbon, which he had held for 34 years. 4. Of Col. John Michelburne, one of the governors of London-

MSS. OF THE DUKE OF LEEDS.
1689.

derry, for payment of arrears, with a statement of his services in Ireland.

viii. Printed summons to the Earl of Danby, signed by the Prince of Orange, to attend the meeting of Parliament on 22 Jan. 1688–9.

ix. Summons to the same, signed by Will. III. and countersigned "Norfolke and Marshall," to attend, with the Countess, the Coronation on 11 Apr. 1689.

x. Processus ad Coronationem Gul. et Mar. R.R. Two copies. fol.

xi. A series of news-letters of proceedings in Parliament in 1689.

A large bundle of miscellaneous papers, for the most part without date, contains various proposals from projectors with reference to the revenue in the time of Charles II., petitions, and letters from many of the persons mentioned in the preceding lists, including the Countesses of Lauderdale and Yarmouth; but nearly all of no public interest. The following are exceptions:—

1. A complimentary letter to the Earl, in extremely good English, from "The Great Duke of Tuscany" (thus signed), expressing the hope "of seeing England againe," and the esteem and affection he has, for "all the nobility, who were so prodigal of their civilitys towards me."

2. Proposals by Sir Hugh Cholmeley for building the mole at Tangier.

3. Representation by "Mr. Hyde" of the charge requisite for his establishment, on his mission to attend a christening in the family of the King of Poland.

4. "A list of pensions paid annually by Sir Stephen Fox."

5. Account by J. Gilbert of the rogueries of Mr. Peter Stepkins, formerly clerk to the Coopers' Company, "whom Sir Edw. Seamor, &c., countenance to recover the Dissenters' mony."

6. Inscription on the tomb of the first Earl of Danby (died 28 Jan. 1643–4) in Dauntsey Church, Wilts.

7. A catalogue of the Admirals in England of the North and the West, and of the Lord High Admirals, from the time of Hen. III. to the administration of James Duke of York.

8. Proposal by Elias Palmer for the substitution of tin farthings for copper farthings.

9. Eight articles by Ed. Randolph against the government of Boston : "1. That the Bostoners have no right either to land or government in any part of New England, but are usurpers," &c.

10. Proposals by Lieut. William Serocold for the increase of the revenue by taxes in Newfoundland upon the fish called Poor Jack, on mud fish, on brewing, salt, hearths, and fur.

11. Estimates for the allowance by the King to Lord Plymouth, for damask, kitchen ware, &c.; with a "memorial" that if he ("Don Carlos") be sent to Cambridge, all his servants being Catholics may be removed, and at least the most pressing of his debts be paid.

12. Representation, in Italian, to the King, from "Jacob Aszik, Hebreo d'Praga" that the Jews in London are extremely rich and pay none of the taxes usually paid by them in other countries ; and offering that if he be authorized to collect these (of which he enumerates five) he will guarantee to the King in the first year 2,000 *lire*, and in the second 3,000.

13. Order from the Privy Council to Lord Latimer, Lord Lieut. of the Island of Purbeck, to search all the habitations of Papists for arms, in consequence of information of a dangerous conspiracy against the life of the King ; 30 Sept. 1678.   MSS. OF THE DUKE OF LEEDS.

14. Orders signed by the Earl of Bath for the better attendance of the Gentlemen and Grooms of the Bedchamber upon the King; 17 May 1684.

15. Petition of James Nailer for payment of £600 for black cloth supplied in 1666 for the funeral of the Queen Mother of Portugal.

16. Letter from the Earl of Lindsey with reference to Sir Christopher Wren's applying to Lord Danby for money for erecting scaffolding in Westminster Hall at the trial of a peer, 18 June, *n. y.*

17. Letter, in French from — Du Cros, an ambassador, about a proposed treaty of commerce between Holland and Sweden.

18. "A brief enquiry into leagues and alliances made betwixt Princes, and the nature of their obligation." 10 pp. fol.

19. Memorial in behalf of the right of the Earl Marshal to nominate to the King a person to be Garter King-of-Arms.

20. Proposal by the Dean of Ripon [Thos. Cartwright, afterwards Bishop of Chester ?] for an act for buying in impropriations for the better encouragement of preaching ministers, and for making some provision for the posterity of the married clergy.

21. "Plan du camp du Mont St. André" ; coloured plan of the army of Will. III. at a camp in Flanders.

22. "An antiphon à la mode de France ;" a political parody on Ps. I., *temp.* Chas. II.; "written by a French Jesuit, and translated out of the original for the use of his Majesties Cappell."

23. "A draught of Breste and the harbour, per J. Baxter."

24. Plan of the citadel of Hull.

25. "A specimen of a new Al-mon-ac for ever, or a rectified account of time by a luni-solar year ;" by Robert Wood. With a short printed paper to the same effect.

26. Copy of the Countess of Holderness' letter to her sons : a mother's advice.

In a parcel of very interesting printed papers of the second half of the 17th cent., comprising proclamations of James II., &c., parliamentary cases and miscellaneous tracts, I found a rare map of the voyage of Sir F. Drake in 1585–6: entitled " The famouse West Indian voyadge made by the Englishe fleete of 23 shippes and barkes, wherin weare gotten the Townes of St. Iago, St. Domingo, Cartagena, and St. Augustines, the same being begon from Plimmouth in the Moneth of September 1585, and ended at Portesmouth in Julie 1586. The whole course of the saide Viadge beinge plainlie described by the pricked line. Newlie come forth by Baptista B." At the foot of the map is a printed account of the voyage, month by month, but of this, unfortunately, the months of January and February have been torn away. Another interesting map is one of the Bermudas in 1622, engraved by Abr. Goos of Amsterdam (" to be sold by Tho. Bassett in Fleet Street and Ric. Chiswell in St. Paul's Churchyard "), marked out as apportioned amongst a company of Adventurers, a list of whose names is given at the foot with the number of their shares.

Twenty-five folio volumes; of docquets of Treasury warrants, &c., in 1672–9, with indexes of names; of minute books of Treasury proceedings; of books of accounts ; of caveats, 1674–9.

Fifteen folio volumes of quarterly accounts of the establishment in the office of Customs, in the years 1674–8 and in 1689; with two

MSS. OF THE DUKE OF LEEDS.

volumes of docquets of letters and orders and minutes of proceedings. "An abstract of the Inspector-General's accounts of imports and exports," Mich. 1697–Mich. 1698. 8vo.

Four folio account-books of the Exchequer receipts, 1674–1677.

Note-book of petitions to the Treasury, 1677–8. fol.

Two (beautifully bound) folio volumes of abstracts of Navy payments, 1671–4; "List of the Navy debt," on 4 Aug. 1670, incurred before 31 Dec. 1668; minute-book of the Commissioners of the Navy in 1672–3; docquet-book of a few orders in 1674; abstract of naval stores in the several dock-yards in 1674. A parcel of a few other naval papers, including "A discourse touching the past and present state of the Navie, by Sir Rob. Slingesby"; "A discourse concerning the regulation of the Navy"; "A briefe discourse of the Navy, by Mr. Holland" (69 pp. fol.); "Heads for instructions to the Commissioners for the office of L. H. Admirall"; "Reflections on our naval expedition into the Mediterranean, in answer to queries by the Marq. of Hallyfax; 1694"; &c.

MISCELLANEOUS MSS. AND PAPERS.

Fol., vellum. Commentary by Dean Colet on the *Hierarchia* of Dionysius Areop., prefaced by extracts, and a dedicatory letter to a friend in which the extracts are said to have been made yesterday and the day before. On the first page is the heading, written by an Italian hand, "Joannes Colett, sacre theologie professor, ex lectione Dionisii hec excerpsit et scripsit." Similar headings are given in other places, *e.g.* "traditus a Joanne Colet, decano Sancti Pauli London." The volume formerly belonged to a Knight of the Garter, whose arms are on the cover. This treatise was first published in 1869, by J. H. Lupton, M.A.

"A brefe summarie and demonstrācōn of the estat of England and Wales . . . mete for the vewe of her Majestie . . . . wrytten by an owld copie *verbatim*": a list of offices, officers, fees, &c. fol. ff. 47.

A similar list of state officers, &c. in 1617, beginning with "A catalogue of the nobilitie." fol.

A copy made in the 17th cent. of a book written in 1572, at the desire of Lord Burleigh, by Peter Osborne, esq., of the "Offices and officers of the Court of Exchequer." fol.

Readings in the Middle Temple by James Morrice on the Stat. of Westm. 1. cap. 49., with a dedication to Lord Burghley. fol. On the cover, "This is the book of Mr. — Grant: he lyes in the hous of his brother Grant, the minister of St. Dunstan's in the West, June, 1682."

Army List of the States General in 1607, entitled, "The substance and division of the souldiers and other charges of the warres of the high and mightie Lords the Staets Generall remaininge under them, anno 1607"; with the rates of pay. In English. Among English and Scottish names are those of "Cornell Horatio Veer" as commanding a regiment of 300 men with 600*l.* as pay, Colonels "Cicell" and Ogle, Adrian Robertson, Francis Baloch, Filistin Brooke, Morgan, Panton, Edw. Veer, Cooke, Horwell, Paggnam, John Burrowes, Fryer, Connaway, Ashley, Henry Wuddowes, Wynter, Carew, Linly,

HISTORICAL MANUSCRIPTS COMMISSION. 41

Courtney, Pears, Hollis, Ralph Dexter, Slingsby, John Veer, Edw. Harwood, Clark, Wrath, Schelton, Brinsley, Lovelace, Rookwood, Betham, Col. Brogge, Oliver Woodney, Caddell, Makugny, Aland Contis, Henry Balfour, Thomas Areskein, Lennog Stow, Archibald Austyn, Col. Bocclouch, Rob. Henderson, Fras. Henderson, Schot, William Douglas, Will. Balfoynt, Will. Hutton, George Botwell, Mungo Hamelton, David Balfoynt, Lambert Charles, Col. Broogh (Brooke?), Thos. Ewing, Colwell, Thos. Daniell, Rob. Masterson. The "minister over the Scottes" is Andrew Hunter; and among pensions is one to the widow of Capt. John Balfour. Among the officers provided by Nimeguen is a "Schoolmaster in the forme," Jacob Hallewin, with a salary of 100*l*.

MSS. OF THE DUKE OF LEEDS

"Concerning the jurisdiction of the President and Councell of the Marches of Wales in the four English counties." fol. pp. 12.

"Observations, rules and orders collected out of divers journalls of the House of Commons entred in the severall raignes of K. Edw. 6, Q. Mary, Q. Eliz. and K. James; with a declaration of the H. of Commons concerning theire priviledg." fol. Two copies.

"Nomina villarum in com. Ebor." fol. Two copies.

"A narration of the proceedings against Thomas Wentworth, earl of Strafford; by way of a letter to a friend." fol. pp. 91.

An account by Sir William Godolphin, of Sparger, in Cornwall, of the Duke d'Espernon's arrival and residence in England, 1638–1643, in French, entitled, "A breefe memorial of the arivall of the Duke of Valette into England, together with what hath therupon succeeded to him, since, the Duke of Espernon, written in French by him that best could tell the story though an English man." 4°. pp. 190.

"Epitome of the civill wars of England, by Thomas Hobbs of Malmesbury." fol.

Henry Elsyng's "*Modus tenendi parliamentum apud Anglos.*" fol.

Of the form of "Judicature in parliament." fol. Two copies.

Sir Rob. Cotton's Miscellaneous tracts, &c. fol. ff. 79.

"Observations on the case of customes cited in the booke called Cooke's 12th Report;" with reference to Sir Edw. Hales' case. 4°. pp. 44.

Letters patent of Oliver Cromwell, granting a fortnightly fair at Seaton, Yorkshire, to Sir Thomas Osborne, 8 Sept. 1656. The Protector's signature has been cut out.

Proceedings in the House of Commons on the impeachment of the Earl of Clarendon, Oct.–Dec. 1667. fol. pp. 237.

Report to the Lord Lieut. of Ireland by R. Bridges on the receipts and payments of the Vice-Treasurer of Ireland in 1660–1668; 16 Apr. 1670. fol.

Conference between the Lords and Commons, 19, 20 Apr. 1671, on the bill for impositions on merchandise, &c. fol. pp. 13.

Letter dated from Amsterdam, 30 Aug. 1672, on the taxation of the United Provinces; written to a friend in England who complained of the English taxes and of the burden of the monarchy. fol. pp. 18.

"A booke of articles of the custome of the mine, 1672;" being rules made at the "Great Court Bar-Moot" for the lead-mines at Wirksworth, Derbyshire, in 1665 and 1667. fol.

"Reflections upon the league with France, danger of Popery and arbitrary power, &c.; in a letter written by an ignoto to an ignoto, before the late peace concluded with Holland;" Lond., 7 Dec. 1673. fol. pp. 88.

MSS. OF THE
DUKE OF LEEDS.

Proceedings in the House of Commons—
20 Oct. 1673–24 Feb. 1673–4. fol. pp. 172.
3 Apr.–22 Nov., 1675. fol. pp. 183.
6 March–27 May, 1679. fol. pp. 704.

"A letter from a person of quality to his friend in the country" upon the Test Act; with Lord Shaftesbury's speech in the H. of Lords, 20 Oct. 1675. Endorsed, "For Sir Oliver St. George, Jan. 2, 1676–7." fol.

Proposal for the farming out of the King's casual revenues to citizens of London, to remedy the negligence and knavery of the collectors. fol. pp. 105.

Project of a treaty of commerce between England and France. fol.

Folio account-book of the "Weekly expence of the houshold [of the Earl of Danby] 23 June–21 Sept. 1677."

"Weights and measures, collected from the lawes and statutes of England, from the Book of rates allowed by the King's Majestie, and from other good authors; 1684." A curious folio vol., containing, in alphabetical order, notes upon things (precious stones, metals, provisions, &c.) mentioned in tables of rates, as well as the weights and measures, and miscellaneous notes on other subjects mentioned in statutes; e.g. "Gentlemen," "Head of the Church."

"The several debates in the House of Commons, pro et contra, relating to the establishment of the Militia"; 9–20 Nov. 1685. fol. pp. 68."

Arguments at the conference between the two Houses on the abdication of James II., 6 Feb. 1688–9. fol. pp. 261.

"Humanum est errare; or, False steps on both sides"; relative to the abdication of James II. fol. pp. 55.

Account of the defence of Londonderry in 1689, written in a dramatic form, in dialogues between the commanders and others, both of the garrison and of the army of K. James. 4°. pp. 136.

"A letter to a person of quality in Holland," dated 5 Jan. 1690–1, "The writer supposed to be Mr. Ferguson, with the assistance of Major Wildman." fol. pp. 82, of which, however, 59–74 are wanting.

"A discourse touching the decay of our navall discipline;" by Sir Hen. Sh[ere]s 1694." fol. pp. 46.

Return to the House of Commons of the grants made in England from Dec. 1696 to Nov. 1699. fol.

"Animadversions concerning the heralds;" a quarto tract (six leaves), by John Gybbon, Bluemantle, with a letter from him to the Duke of Leeds, presenting the tract, and complaining of one Russell, "the funerall-monger," who had conducted the burial of a daughter of Lord Carlisle, "with heralds of his own creation," and of the church of Westminster as claiming the heralds' perquisites before the Council; 9 Sept. 1695.

Two engraved views of Dunblane, from John Slezer's *Theatrum Scotiæ*, with a MS. description inscribed to the Marquis of Carmurthen.

Among distinctively family papers, of no public interest, are many letters in the time of Queen Anne from the Duke of Beaufort and Lord Godolphin. And in two parcels of such papers kept in box 15 of the Holderness papers, are extracts taken in 1678 from the Parish Register of Harthill relative to the family of the first Earl; a series of letters from Mr. L. Bérard, governor to the first Duke's grandsons while travelling abroad in 1706–11; letters from Lord Oxford to his son-in-law, afterwards the third Duke, in 1712–14; letters to the same from his father, while the latter was in exile abroad in 1722, written in a friendly-tone, and commencing " Deare Sonn," but which follow two others dated from Amsterdam in Dec. 1719 which commence respectively, " Thou most odious beast and brutall sonn," and " Unhewman sonn," upbraiding him in the most furious terms for not supplying him with money, and saying that he intends to come to England to give himself up for trial when of course he will be condemned to lose his head ; petition from the latter (the second Duke) to the King, for pardon for leaving the kingdom, " and for attempting those things I have in prejudice of your Majesty's service since my wandering," dated at Leghorn, Sept. 3, 1723, with a similar petition to the Lords Justices (who, he says, he is assured are " well acquainted with his follies and ridiculous proceedings against the interest and service of our royal Master "), upon his arrival at London; and a letter to Walpole which enclosed his petition to the King.

" Germanicus, a tragedy," by Thomas Cooke. A note is prefixed by the Duke of Leeds, dated Feb. 25, 1796, that he believes the dedication is to his father, and that it must have been written about 1731 ; of the author he knew nothing.[1] pp. 145. 4º.

Regulations of the Russian Navy, as approved by the Empress 9 Sept. 1788. In Russian and English. fol.

II.—HOLDERNESSE PAPERS. 1749-1776.

Folio MS. on vellum, pp. 48, " The Regester booke of the righte honorable Sir John Darcye, Knyghte, Lord Darcye of Chyche. . . . . . made and sett forthe by John Cooke, gentleman, the tenth daye of Maye in the xvii[th] yere of the reigne of our sovereigne lady Queen Elizabethe " (1575), containing the descent from Chaunceux, of Canewdon, Essex, with inquisitions p.m., the wills of Rob. Darcye, esq., 1448, Sir Rob. Darcye, Knt., 1469, and Thomas Darcye, esq., son of Sir Robert, 1483, patent of creation of lord Darcye, 1551, &c.; and coats of arms very elegantly painted.

Another folio volume of upwards of 250 pp. contains collections for the history of the D'Arcy family by the well-known Yorkshire antiquary, Dr. N. Johnston. It is noted on the cover that it was lent to Mr. Edmondson (Mowbray herald) by the Earl of Holdernesse in 1764. It bears the following title: " An essaye towards the illustrating of the antiquities of the right honourable familyes of the Lords D'Arcie, Conyers, and Mennill, and of the right worshipfull familye of the Meltons of Aston in com. Ebor. ; digested out of deedes, publique records and pedigrees, the Great booke of the collections of the right honourable Cogniers Lord D'Arcie of Hornbye, and the MSS. of Mr. Roger Dodsworth, Mr. Gascoigne, and Mr. Hopkinson, and the miscellany notes of Mr. Townley of Carr in Lancashire, and severall others, by Nathaniel Johnston, of Pontefract, in the county of Yorke, Dr. of physick, A.D. 1677."

Political Correspondence.

Fourteen portfolios of the correspondence, in 1749-51, of the Duke of Newcastle and the Earl of Holdernesse, while the latter was

---

[1] The title of the play is given in the 1812 edition of Reed's Baker's *Biogr. Dram.*, where it is said that a MS. was in the possession of Sir Joseph Mawbey. The author died in 1756, according to the account there given of him.

MSS. OF THE DUKE OF LEEDS. Ambassador at the Hague, largely with reference to the Barrier Treaty and a subsidy to the Elector of Cologne. Among the correspondents are Charles and Will. Bentinck, Duke of Bedford, Andrew Stone, Sir Charles Hanbury Williams, Walter Titley, Earl of Rochford, Henry Fox, Henry Pelham, Hugh Valence Jones, Prince of Orange, W. Fagel, M. Cressener at Liége, Dayrolles at Dunkirk, Comte de Finocchietti, and Baron Munchausen.

One portfolio of the correspondence of the Earl of Holdernesse with the Earl of Albemarle, ambassador at Paris, in 1749–51.

One portfolio of the correspondence and negotiations in Russia of the Earl of Hyndford, in 1749, and of the correspondence of the Duke of Newcastle with Col. M. Guy Dickens, in 1750–1.

One portfolio of the correspondence and negotiations of Mr. Onslow Burrish in Germany in 1749–51.

Two portfolios of the like correspondence of Mr. Robert Keith at Vienna in the same years, and (in box 11) a parcel in 1754–6.

In three iron boxes numbered 11, 12, 13, are many hundreds of letters to the Earl of Holdernesse, chiefly between 1750 and 1760, both of public and private nature. They are fastened up in separate parcels, packed closely together. I proceed to give an outline of the contents of the several series, arranging them, for the sake of ease in future reference, as they are now kept in the several boxes.

In box 11 there are 16 packets of letters from Gen. Joseph Yorke and 13 more in box 12, at the Hague in 1751–61, with copies of letters to him, on foreign affairs. In one of April 1, 1760, he says, "Your Lordship will recollect that some months ago I gave an account of the Pretender's eldest son's being at Bouillon." The informer now reports that "since he was there last, the young Pretender had considerably encreased his train, which was composed at present of an ecclesiastick, two gentlemen, a fine equipage, a great many hunters, eight footmen in livery, &c. The Intendant told this gentleman that he had the French King's orders to furnish him with everything he wanted, to shew him all the respect imaginable, and to make his abode at Bouillon as agreeable to him as he could."

Seventeen packets of papers, and four more in box 12, relative to East Indian affairs, and negotiations with France in 1753–5.

Four parcels of letters from and to Lord Albemarle at Paris in 1749–54. Among these is a curious series of papers relative to information by James Drummond, of Boheldie, of the clan of MacGregor, of a Jacobite plot in France, under the Earl Marischal, for the invasion of North Wales and Scotland simultaneously from Ireland by 14,000 Irish; with a licence under the King's signature dated 3 Nov. 1753 for Drummond's return to England, and minutes of his examination by Lord Holdernesse on Nov. 6. Drummond professes to give information of all the agents in Scotland and elsewhere, including two from England named Trent and Fleetwood, he being one of the most trusted ones himself; and advises that all letters directed to Patrick, George, or Edward Savage, merchants in Douglas, in the Isle of Man, or to Mr. Peter Pippard, merchant in Liverpool, should be intercepted and opened. In a letter of 16 Jan. 1754, Lord Albemarle sends a list of all the persons who had visited the Earl Marischal in Paris from 18 Dec. to 11 Jan. But it is satisfactory to read in the same letter that he advises Lord Holdernesse not to "give much credit to McGregor, for upon reading his long declaration I find in it many falsehoods, and very few material circumstances, and upon the whole I believe him a most notorious scoundrel." There is a letter from the Earl Marischal (signed "Keith") to Lord Holdernesse in 1759, dated at Madrid, Aug. 16, in which he returns his grateful thanks for the news communicated to him by Baron Knyphausen "that my pardon, which the King has of his goodness and clemency granted, has past the seals." MSS. OF THE DUKE OF LEEDS.

Four packets of the correspondence of the Duke of Newcastle in 1755. One packet of letters from Lord George Sackville, with the army in Germany, from Aug. 1758 to Aug. 1759, chiefly written from Munster, and six from the Marq. of Granby in 1759–60. Copies of letters from Sir Edw. Hawke, relative to his expedition to the Basque Roads in 1757, and to Lord Anson, from Quiberon Bay, in Oct. 1759. A few letters from Anson himself, in 1755 and 1759. From Lieut.-Governor Moore, of Jamaica, in 1758–60. One packet of letters from W. Pitt in 1755–9, chiefly on foreign affairs, and some of them only short notes. A few letters from H. Fox, 1754–9. Letters relating to election for the borough of Richmond, in Yorkshire, in 1759–60.

In a packet of miscellaneous letters of 1755 are two signed " Fidelis Brito," urging restrictions upon time bargains in the Stock Change, in which the writer speaks of " such ill practices as selling *bears* (as they call it) or stock for distant times"; and a letter from Capt. Denny, dated at Braemar Castle, Aug. 1, with a report on the woollen manufacture managed at Granada, in Spain, for a company, by — Kelly, an Irishman, who desires to break his engagement and leave, in order to settle at Norwich or in Spitalfields; with suggestions for a mode of escape. In this year also there are copies of two letters from Lord Drumlanrig, dated Nov. 8 and 19, with an account of the earthquake at Lisbon, where he was at the time. Narrative of hostilities committed by the French on the Ohio in 1754, with papers relative to the negotiations thereupon in 1755. Copies of letters between George II. and the King of Prussia in 1756–60. Letter from Capt. Peter D'Arcy, with an account of the capture of the French fort at Ticonderoga, dated 27 July 1759. Letter from Lord Mansfield on his accepting office as Lord Chancellor, 14 Sept. 1757. Letter from H. Walpole, choosing the title of Baron Walpole of Woolterton for his peerage, 20 May 1726.

Six packets relate to a report furnished by Mr. Charles Areskine, of Tinwald, Lord Justice Clerk for Scotland, to the Earl of Holdernesse, relative to complaints made to the Government in 1752 that various Episcopalians and non-jurors, and persons who had been engaged in the rebellion of 1745, had been appointed to various legal offices, such as Sheriff-depute, &c. The report, which disproves the charges in general, occupies 23 folio pages, and is accompanied by many documents and letters in proof. One charge was that persons arrested for wearing the Highland dress had been released from custody, which is chiefly met by the answer that " a new form of dress [had been] contrived by some of the Highlanders, which could not be said to be the Highland dress prohibited by law, or any part of it, and yet was not altogether the Low Country dress; and if a Sheriff substitute, in a case altogether new, doubted, and allowed his doubt to carry him so far as to admit them to bail until he was advised by his Principal, it does not seem to be unreasonable in itself, or detrimental to his Majesty's service, especially when effectual care was taken by the Principals to have even that new form of dress suppressed." In a letter from the Lord Justice Clerk, which was sent with the report, dated 17 Nov. 1752, the following mention occurs in a postscript of the James Drummond who, in the next year, attempted to gain pardon for a murder he had committed (of Colin Campbell, of Glenure,) by betraying an alleged

MSS. OF THE DUKE OF LEEDS. Jacobite plot, as noticed above. "Since writing this letter I have received an account from the General, for which I'm extremely sorry, that James Drummond, alias Macgrigor, who was in custody in the Castle of Edinburgh, and upon Munday next was to have received sentence of death, made his escape last night about a quarter after six. The particulars of the escape I have not as yet learn'd." With these papers is a small packet of documents upon which some of the charges were based, with extracts from letters of the Dukes of Cumberland and Newcastle in 1746, remarks in 1752 on the effect of the system of military stations and patrols in the Highlands, and some lists of names of attainted persons. Amongst others is the following list of "names of some of the attainted and excepted rebels who are, or have been lately, in Scotland, 1752. Lord Pitsligo, lives in Banffshire, and frequently at his house near Frazerburgh. Lord Lewis Gordon was in Scotland last year, but is said to be returned to France. Lord Ogilvie in Scotland, and lately escaped being taken by getting intelligence of General Churchill's having taken out a warrant to apprehend him; the General not being justice of the peace for all Scotland, as General Wade was, obliges him to apply for warrants to search houses, of which they get notice. Donald McDonald, of Clanranald, evades the attainder by a misnomer, his name being Ranald. Archibald McDonald, son of Col. McDonald, of Barrisdale, in Scotland. Sir William Gordon, of Park, lives in the same shire, and frequently at his house near Perth."

Another packet of Lord Justice Areskine's papers relates to suspected Jacobite movements in 1752, intelligence being sent that Kinloch-Moidart's two brothers, Æneas and Allan Macdonald, and Dr. Cameron, brother to the late Lochiel (who "remained at home during the rebellion, in the shape of an innocent man, and is now the chief director of them"), arrived in the Highlands in Oct., and remained some days at Fassifern's, in Sunart; Lieut.-Gen. Churchill is directed to be on the watch.

Other Scottish papers are: 1. A packet relating to an enquiry respecting Mr. Thomas Hay, nominated to be a Lord of Session, against whom it was alleged that he was a non-juror, and attended the meeting-house "kept by the person called Bishop Ke[i]th," that he had formerly had the pictures of the Pretender and his family hanging in his house, that his brother John Hay was attainted, &c.; with Thomas Hay's answer, dated 4 Nov. 1754, in which he says that since 1742 he had never attended non-juring meetings, that he never had "any painted pictures, mezzotintos, prints, portraits, figures, or representations whatsoever of the Pretender and his family," &c.; letters from Lord Justice Areskine, and the final confirmation of the appointment on 22 Nov. 2. Two letters from Ranald MacDonald to Lord Holdernesse, acknowledging gratitude for the King's clemency, procured by Lord Holdernesse, in permitting him to live in freedom in his native land, dated Edinburgh, 17 July 1754, and Benbecula, 1 Jan. 1755. 3. The Earl of Cathcart to the same, 3 June 1755, reporting his proceedings as Commissioner to the General Assembly. 4. Information that — Cameron, son to Dr. Cameron, and Capt. in Lord Ogilvie's regiment in France, came over into the Highlands in Nov. 1757. 5. Letter from Robert Dalyell (dated at Binns, near Edinb., 20 Oct. 1759), who was formerly in the Dutch service, desiring license to raise a troop of Light Cavalry, in anticipation of an invasion by the French. 6. Letter from Lord Justice Areskine, transmitting a copy of a printed "Plan" (34 folio pp.), drawn up at a public meeting, "for raising a militia in that part of Great

Britain called Scotland," in consequence of the expectation of a French attack by the squadron under Thurot, of which, however, nothing had been heard since its leaving Bergen on 7 Dec.; 15 Jan. 1760.   MSS. OF THE DUKE OF LEEDS.

There is one letter (in French) from the Grand Duchess Catharine of Russia (afterwards Empress) to George II. dated at St. Petersburg, 3 Aug. 1759, in which she asks that the bearer, Mr. Wroughton, may be continued in his post of Consul General.

In one of two small parcels of papers from Richard Wolters, a secret service agent at Rotterdam, there are copies of reports and memorials about the intercourse kept up through Jacobite agents in that town in 1747, with an application to the burgomasters to allow suspected letters to be intercepted at the Post Office and given to him, as had been done during the rebellion in 1745. The suspicious addresses are said to be those of Messrs. John Archdeacon, Peter Fox, Van Wyngaarter, and — Dillon, four merchants in Rotterdam. An officer named Coleman in the Scotch regiment of Ogilvie in the service of Holland is also named in 1748. Memorial to the Stadtholder in opposition to an application from Edinburgh in 1748 for the revival of the Scottish factory at Campvere.

Other parcels of foreign correspondence in this box are:—
Several (with four in box 12) from Mr. Andrew Mitchell, at Brussels, Berlin, Leipsic, &c., 1752–61; five packets (of which four are in box 12) from and to Sir B. Keene at Madrid, 1751–6; Mr. Robert Keith at Vienna and St. Petersburg, 1756–60; Sir Ch. Hanbury Williams in Germany and at St. Petersburg, 1754–7; Mr. Titley at Copenhagen, 1754–8; Lord Rochford at Turin, 1753; Sir James Gray; Sir Thomas Robinson, 1755; General Wall at Madrid, 1754–7; and Consul Smith at Venice.

Box 12 contains ten packets of the correspondence of the Duke of Newcastle in 1750–5, and one of letters from him and the Marq. of Hartington in 1755 relative to the Ministry and the affairs of Hanover. Four packets of foreign news-letters from Mr. Michael Hatton, chiefly from Paris in 1755–8. Two packets of letters from William, Duke of Cumberland, while in command of the forces in Germany in 1757, with two of replies, &c. Papers in 1760 relating to the place of the Duke of York in the House of Lords. Three letters to the Earl of Holdernesse, as governor to the young princes, from the Princess Amelia, aunt to King George III., one of which (Dec. 10, 1772) is an invitation for them to a dance-party, with a list of those who were invited.

An interesting series of forty letters (most of them very brief) from George III. to Lord Holdernesse, respecting the education of his sons, which display the greatest solicitude on his part for their moral and intellectual training; of these 16 are in 1771, and six in 1776 when Lord Holderness resigned his office on account of his difficulties in the management of the Princes and want of unanimity amongst the tutors. Of him the King speaks in the highest possible terms, as well as of Mr. Smelt, a tutor whom the King with difficulty prevails on in 1776 to remain two years longer, but who inflexibly declines beforehand to accept at the end of that period any appointment, honour, or pension, or even the gift of a house. In the choice of tutors counsel is taken with "so wise, able and honest a man as the Archbishop of York," (Markham) and the Bishop of Chester (Porteous). On 10 Sept. 1773 the King writes, "rules prescribed must be rigorously supported, and particularly with [the Prince of Wales], who too much inclines to evade application. I fear the word *duplicity* deserves a harsher epithet; I think so the more as you ever incline to the most lenient expressions;

MSS. OF THE DUKE OF LEEDS. the bad habit both my sons have of not speaking the truth gives me much more pain than any want of attention to their lessons. The first if not corrected may become a part of their characters; it is the worst of faults; it is not only unbecoming their rank but that of the meanest man. Truth is the constant attendant of an honest heart, and is more estimable than any of the advantages to be acquired by birth or education," &c. On 21 Dec. 1775 he writes, after a two hours' conversation with Mr. Smelt, that if a good understanding amongst the tutors "cannot be restored, it will be impossible to irradicate (sic) those failings in my sons that we have often deplored, and that, if they continue, will with age become vices that will choak every sentiment calculated to make useful and respectable members of society." And on 6 Apr. 1776, when sketching out a method of arrangement by which the Earl may be induced to continue in his post, he says, "The desire of fulfilling my duty as a parent alone actuates me on this occasion, and imposes on me first of all to see my children grounded in their religious duties, being well convinced that where the sentiments of love and fear for the Creator are wanting, all other tyes are but weak, and that passion, not principle, will then be the guide." On 22 May there is a letter which is apparently the reply to Lord Holdernesse's letter of resignation, " a step which though it gives me infinite pain, I am certain appears to you as the strongest proof you can give of your duty." Of letters from the Princes (chiefly during Lord Holdernesse's absence from illness) there are twenty from the Prince of Wales, in 1773–5, the same number from Prince Frederick (the Duke of York), two from Prince Edward and one from Prince William : in all which the professions of attachment to the Earl are profuse. In a letter of March 23, 1774, the Prince of Wales says, "I will take care to rectify the fault of inattention, for I shall take as a favour every fault your lordship marks for my improvement." On 18 Aug. : " an adventure happened to us at the fireworks [on Aug. 12] which had a very horrid appearance but in reality was nothing ; it came from a Mount Strombolo, which blew to pieces ; in the middle of its burning Secker opened the window at which the Queen was sitting, and called out as loud as he could, ' For God's sake save the Queen and all the royal family, for the house is on fire.' The King hit him a violent blow on the head, and pulled the window down. The Queen was obliged to take some drops, and to give some to the Duchess of Argyll."[1] Dec. 16 ; " I hope at your return you will have good accounts of us from Mr. Smelt and the other gentlemen, and that you will find no more the old trick of round shoulders. The King and Queen have put us quite upon the footing of men ; we not only go the Thursday and Sunday to them, but likewise we dine with them the Tuesday." Feb. 10, 1775 ; " The 7th of this month the House of Lords had a conference to propose an address of impowering his Majesty to take all the measures he thought fit about America. Lord Mansfield, as Papa told me, was scarce ever heard to speak better, when my Lord Shelburne caught at something Lord Mansfield said, and got up saying ' false, false, false,' upon which the whole house was in a hubbub, calling out ' to order, to order, to order.' After that Lord Littleton got up, spoke remarkably well, and gave my Lord a fine trimming for such an infamous thing." The Duke of York's letters are much longer than his brother's, and more natural. In one of them, dated 15 Sept., 1774, he dwells upon his appointment to the Bishopric of Osnaburgh, and in allusion to

---

[1] Of this false alarm, and the blow given by the King, Prince Frederick also gives an account in a French letter.

the motto upon medals then struck, "Spes publica," says it "made me think how much I had to do to render their hopes effectual . . . . When I have not used the time which has been given me to learn while I am a boy, I shall never have the possibility to regain it. And for that reason I shall be obliged to labour hard . . . . Though I cannot place myself as high as my brother, because his kingdom is much greater than my bishoprick, yet I must have as much care of it as my brother must have of his kingdom." On 17 March in the same year he writes, "I hope I shall gain both the love and esteem of the publick, which are my most ardent wishes." On 17 Feb. 1775 he writes thus about his uncle the Duke of Cumberland: "I was, my dear Lord, shockd to hear that the Duke of Cumberland was entered into opposition. I thought from the beginning it would be so, but I do not suppose you would think who was his adviser: Lord Mount Morris! Ev'n the opposition said, Block'd, what business has he to do here, when Papa told me the only thing he said was, He deserves that name."

MSS. OF THE DUKE OF LEEDS.

In parcels of miscellaneous letters in this box, of the years 1756–8, the following may specially be noticed. Long letter from Mr. James Nairne, as moderator of the presbytery of St. Andrew's, protesting earnestly against the appointment of one Mr. William Brown, formerly a minister of the Church of Scotland and now at Utrecht, as Professor of Divinity and Church History at St. Andrew's, he having some time before demitted his office, and fled the country for an immorality which would have been punished by deprivation; dated June 18, 1756.

From the Lord Advocate of Scotland, Robert Dundas, announcing the arrival at Edinburgh of "Mr. Macleod (commonly called Lord Macleod), eldest son of the late Earl of Cromartie, who stands attainted for his accession to the late rebellion," who has come from Sweden, in the service of which country he has been for some years: "I do not believe the young man has any bad intentions . . . . Your Lordship will no doubt remember that his Majesty was pleased to extend his royal clemency to both father and son"; dated July 11, 1758. Of a date two days later, there is a letter from Lord Macleod himself; he has come to avoid fighting in the Swedish army "against any of his Majesty's allies . . . . inconsistent with the duty and loyalty of a good and faithful subject to the King, penetrated with the deepest sense of gratitude for his Majesty's royal goodness and mercy to my father and to myself . . . . Penetrated as I am with the deepest grief and remorse for having been engag'd in the late unnatural (sic) rebellion, I should think myself happy cou'd I wash out with my blood the remembrance of that crime and of my past misconduct." There is a note also from Lady Cromartie, of July 17, begging for an interview with Lord Holdernesse.

Minutes by Lord Holdernesse, of examinations of Mr. Fosset in Feb. 1753, for his having said in conversation with the Dean of Durham and Lord Ravensworth, that Dr. Johnson, Bishop of Gloucester, nominated to a canonry *in commendam* at Durham, had been present at dinner at a Mr. Vernon's, when "disaffected" healths were drunk, viz., those of the Duke of Ormond, Lord Dunbar, and the Chevalier. There is also an examination of the Solicitor General (William Murray) he having also been said to be present.

Papers respecting a representation to the French ministers in September 1753, relative to works carried on at the harbour at Dunkirk, contrary to the stipulations of the treaty of Utrecht; with a report of a voyage made thither for inspection by Gen. Major Cornabé in December.

Box 13 contains several parcels of miscellaneous letters between 1751 and 1759, in which some in 1756 relate to riots in Warwickshire,

MSS. OF THE DUKE OF LEEDS. Nottinghamshire and Shropshire with regard to corn monopoly, with regard to which Lord Brooke writes that "the poor have just cause to complain." One from Orator John Henley to Lord Holdernesse, dated "The Oratory, Lincoln's Inn Fields, Apr. 18, 1752," assures his lordship "that if any officious sycophants, spies, informers, or personal and prejudiced enemies" represent Henley as being in the least disaffected or speaking a word against the ministry," they impose on them, as he proved six years ago when "an ignorant and spiteful justice was my enemy, and his own, for it broke his heart." In 1758 there are two letters from "Justice" Fielding at Bow Street, (in which the extraordinary scrawl of a signature, which is all that Fielding himself writes, would be impossible to be deciphered were it not for the endorsement,[1]) which relate to the prosecutions, 1, of a Mr. Page, against whom evidence was brought from Scotland; and 2, of one Rich. Will. Vaughan, for forging bank notes, not so much with a design to injure the Bank of England "as being an enemy to the Government." "Parkyns Macmahon writes a long letter on May 29, 1758, urging his being brought speedily to trial to clear himself from some suspicion under which he lies since his arrival in England, with allusions to his "literary correspondence" and to a proposed journey to Plymouth.[2] And John Newbery, the well-known bookseller of St. Paul's Churchyard, writes on Sept. 14, 1754 to intercede for one Solomon Jacob, a poor convict from Salisbury, sentenced to transportation for stealing something of the value of two shillings.

Letters to and from Ferdinand, Duke of Brunswick, 1758–1761. Four packets of letters to and from Lord Chancellor Hardwicke in 1751–9, chiefly relative to points of law and foreign negotiations. But among his letters of 1755 is a small packet of letters to him from an anonymous writer in France, offering to give information against the friends of Prince Charles Edward. The correspondence opens with a letter (in a large clear hand) dated 24 Dec. 1754, informing the Lord Chancellor that Mr. John Macleod, advocate, is pressing the sale of the estate of Sir James Campbell, of Auchinbreck, upon which he has a mortgage, before the Court of Session, in order that his son Alexander Macleod, who is attainted, may receive the money in France while his father lives, and not lose it by forfeiture to the Crown on his father's death. The writer then proceeds: "The person who gives this intelligence can, if properly rewarded, give more and of greater consequence; and will particularly discover the person intrusted at present, and for these eight years past, with the Pretender's affairs in Scotland. And as he is known to, and intimate with, many of that party, intrusted with their secrets for ten or eleven years past, and much connected with them, will probably have it in his power at any time, by giving proper intelligence, to prevent and disappoint any of their schemes taking place, or their disturbing the peace and quiet of the kingdom. A letter address À Monsieur Anderson, gentilhomme Anglois, à Sens en Bourgogne, will, tho' a borrowed name, find him. But as anything of this sort will be utterly ruin'd by the least discovery, he insists on corresponding directly with your Lordship, and not with any clerk or secretary.". With this letter is inclosed a copy of the

---

[1] A somewhat clearer signature is attached to a letter dated July 17, 1757, in application for some favour, which is found in a packet of miscellaneous letters of that year in Box 12.
[2] Amongst miscellaneous letters in Box 12 is another one from this writer, dated Oct. 5, 1758, praying for leave to go as a volunteer, or in any quality, to America or elsewhere, against the French.

reply, " London, Jan. 14, 1755. The person to whom a letter was sent by the post from Sens, dated December 22, 1754, acquaints the gentleman who writ it, that, if he will make good and perform the offers contain'd in the said letter, he shall receive all proper encouragement ;" with this note subjoined, " Jan. 13, 1755. Shew'd the letter from Sens above-mentioned to the King in his closet, who was pleased to give me his orders to write as above." The answer to this is dated Jan. 25, 1755, in which the writer begins ·by professing to state his reasons for wishing to serve the government. " He has been educated in the most rigid principles of Jacobitism, and taught to believe that the good of his country depended on the success of that family ; but his own observation, and comparing the present with former times, has convinced him, that, whatever are the professions of that family or party, it is almost impossible that the people can enjoy greater happiness than they do and have done under the present and late King, and that any change, how successful soever (beside the ruin and desolation that must ever attend the attempt to part of the people) is really no more than quitting certainty for hope." He therefore makes the following proposals, and if these are not agreeable, no further trouble need be taken on either side. A bill of exchange to be sent to him, with a blank indorsation ; the sum left to discretion, but if too small the bill will be immediately returned : that the amount may be proportionate to the person, he mentions that he has an income of 300*l. per an.* As he would wish to continue his services, and his employers would wish the same, he desires also to have an annual allowance for journeys or the living at Paris and elsewhere, so long as his services are thought to deserve it; but he insists on direct correspondence, and, as an indispensable condition, that he never appears as evidence in any court against any man. " His intelligence will generally be well-founded, for, beside his intimacy and familiarity with most of that party, he has an uncle, with whom he is in strict correspondence, who has been in the immediate service and trust of the Pretender these seven and twenty years." He will simply mention facts ; and if informed what pieces of intelligence are most desired, will " give immediate answers to such as he knows, and endeavour to inform himself of others he may not know." Endorsed, " Shew'd this to the Duke of Newcastle soon after it was rec'd, who tho't the terms c'd not be complied with, and that it did not deserve further notice." A letter of March 8 then follows, expressing surprise at the non-receipt of a reply, but saying that, trusting in the promise of " all proper encouragement," the writer now signifies " that the person employed as the Pretender's agent in Scotland these seven years past is Mr. Walkinshaw of Scotstown," and suggests that in arresting him care be taken to secure his papers. He desires that a proper reward shall at once be sent, upon which he will by return send such information as will easily lead to the discovery of the chief people employed in England ; and that some person of less note than the Chancellor may be named under whose cover letters may be sent, " the present address being rather too conspicuous. If an answer, as desired, is not received in course of post, there will be absolutely no further intelligence sent." No answer being returned, there comes finally a short letter dated 13 Apr. desiring to know whether the previous letters have been received, the writer concluding that they may have been intercepted. It appears, however, that though no return was made to the writer for his information, it was acted upon, and Mr. Walkinshaw [the father of Charles Edward's mistress] was arrested, for a letter from Lord Hardwicke to Lord Holderness of the date of April 12 runs thus, " As to your Lordship's

MSS. OF THE DUKE OF LEEDS.

D 2

MSS. OF THE DUKE OF LEEDS.
question relating to Mr. Walkinshaw of Scotstown, I apprehend it will not be proper to send him either to Newgate or the Tower before he has been examin'd, and that he should be confin'd in the custody of a messenger until his examination is over. I presume your Lordship will think it necessary that his papers should be perus'd before he is examin'd, because from thence the lights must arise whereupon he must be sifted."

Other letters relating to Scottish affairs, are, a series of papers in 1752 on the question whether Edinburgh Castle was a lawful prison; two letters, dated 22 Aug. 1752, to Lord Holdernesse and to the Lord Mayor of London, from P. Drummond, sending a pamphlet about the improvement of Edinburgh; a letter from Lord Hardwicke of 19 Sept. 1754 relative to a proposal of Gen. Bland that he be "authorized to dispense with the penalties incurred by the inhabitants of the Isle of Skye for wearing the highland dress and carrying arms, &c.;"[1] and a letter from Lord Holdernesse of 16 Apr. 1755, about the arrest of a person at Doncaster, going by the name of Salwyn, as a vagrant, who on being examined in the workhouse at Wakefield by Sir Rowland Winn, was suspected to have dealings with disaffected persons; he has therefore been brought up to London and has this morning confessed that he was in the rebellion of 1745, and has since been employed as an agent for the Pretender; his inability to find bail and his needy circumstances have induced him to promise that if he have protection and reward he will discover all he knows; he confesses that the name he goes by is a fictitious one, and that he is acquainted will all the principal agents the Pretender has in Great Britain, and can discover many important secrets; he is about 50 years of age, a sensible well-behaved man, and appears to have had a very good education.

Two or three letters of Hardwicke's, in July-Sept 1754, and a packet of depositions, refer to the verses, or "treasonable libels, drop't in the market-place at Oxford," a matter which created a considerable stir at the time. The Chancellor stigmatizes the paper as containing nothing, "but what is of the deepest dye, downright treason, and direct incitement to rebellion," and expresses great dissatisfaction with the conduct of the Vice-Chancellor and Mayor, who appear to have regarded it as a mere trick on the part of the pretended finder. The chief part of the remaining contents of this box is a series of books of summaries of accounts, with all the tradesmen's bills, for the Prince of Wales and his brothers Frederick and William, from 1771 to 1776, the Earl of Holdernesse having been governor to the princes during that period. Letters of summons to the Prince of Wales and Prince Frederick (as "Bishop of Osnabrugh") for their installation as Knights of the Garter on 25th July 1771, with letters of dispensation from taking the oaths; and to Prince Frederick for installation as Knight of the Bath on 15 June 1772.

In box 14 is a series of eleven portfolios containing foreign newsletters, or "Advices," written in a singularly large hand, from 1754 to the end of 1760, in French, and chiefly from France; interspersed throughout with a series of a quarto newspaper called *Le Courier*,

---

[1] In this letter the Chancellor complains of a letter from Cambridge in the *London Evening Post* of 10 Sept., which contains "a most direct audacious and seditious libel upon the Revolution and the settlement of the present government made in consequence of it," and proposing prosecution : "the licentiousness and insolence of that paper is intolerable."

printed at Avignon. There are also in this box and in box 15 the following MSS., in separate volumes :— *MSS. OF THE DUKE OF LEEDS.*

1. Minutes of the Privy Council Meetings with reference to foreign affairs, from 20 Sept. 1755 to 10 June 1756.
2. Index-book of Lord Holdernesse's letters in 1749.
3. "Plan général de la Marine de France," 1750-60. (Box 15.)
4. "The conduct of Admiral Knowles on the late expedition set in a true light ;" signed, Charles Knowles [1757].
5. "Reflections on the disputes subsisting between the companies of France and England trading to the East Indies ;" by Robert Orme, London, 24 Nov. 1753.
6. "General idea of the government and people of Indostan, by Robert Orme, Sept. 1, 1753."
7. Various papers, in French and German, 1746-50, on the succession of the House of Brandenburgh, with copies of two German works printed in 1718 and 1741; in a wrapper marked "Monsieur Seckendorff."
8. "Précis of the Dutch and Prussian correspondence of the years 1789, 1790."
9. Keys to cyphers; the Earl of Albemarle's in 1750, &c.

III.—CARMARTHEN PAPERS.—1784-1790.

In Box 15. Portfolio 1. contains 54 letters from Pitt to the Marquis of Carmarthen, in 1784-5, with copies of many letters from the latter. In one of Oct. 15, 1784, Pitt proposes to the Marq. his resignation of office, or change of office, in favour of the Duke of Grafton, as Lord Camden, whose inclusion in the ministry is greatly desired, cannot be brought to join unless united with the Duke. Lord Carmarthen's answer of consent follows, dated the same day. In a letter of 18 Aug. 1784, the latter suggests Mr. Eden as the Minister to be sent to America, as his abilities are "just of the nature fit for the business of that appointment, consisting chiefly of narrow and illiberal intrigues. I know nothing right or honourable about him any further than his being a Privy Councellor entitles him to claim." In answer to an application to send Sir John Henderson to Warsaw, Carmarthen writes, on 4 Sept., that that appointment is promised to Mr. Whitworth, but "I know some of Sir J. H.'s connections, and have heard him well spoken of; he seems a genteel man, and as to outward appearance very fit for the foreign line; probably Venice, or one of the smaller German Courts (when vacant), may be agreeable to him." In the same letter he objects very strongly to sending — Johnstone to Lisbon ; "whatever may be the consequences of his appointment, I beg I may only incur the censure of having submitted to, but by no means of having approved, the measure " Pitt's reply defers the settlement until they have an interview. With regard to a proposed prohibition by Austria, of the importation of English manufactured goods, specially affecting the woollen and silk trades, Pitt writes on Nov. 2 that "we have means of ample retaliation," the English imports from Austria having exceeded the exports by £50,000 in 1783, and it might therefore be stated " in a friendly way, that the clamor of our manufacturers might compel us, even if the measure seemed less justifiable, to prohibit all Austrian produce. Such a state of interdiction between two countries on terms of friendship, and especially when all restraints on commerce are growing out of fashion, would to be sure be singular."

MSS. OF THE DUKE OF LEEDS.

A letter of Dec. 16, 1785, relates to a memorial from the American Minister, Adams, of 30 Nov., of which Pitt says that "the demand seems itself fairly founded upon the treaty," but that the English also have claims which must go hand in hand, particularly satisfaction respecting the debts due from America to our merchants. The letters chiefly relate to suggestions respecting foreign despatches, and to proposed commercial treaties with Spain and France.

These are followed by a series of letters from the Duke of Dorset, ambassador at Paris, in 1784-5, and from the Secretary of Legation, Mr. Daniel Hailes, who is asked by Lord Carmarthen, on 22nd Oct. 1784, to write special private despatches, in the following words, "My dear Sir, for Heaven's sake have pity upon the Department, and either prevail upon our friend the Duke to write something worth our Master's perusal, or else suppose your principal absent, and let your own zeal and abilities have fair play. Consider but for a moment the importance of the present moment, and then reflect upon the situation in which we three are placed." The chief subject of negotiation in 1784 mentioned in these letters is with reference to French claims about the island of St. Eustatia. A few general extracts from the series may be noted.

"The new *Controlleur-Général* is a monstrous extravagant fellow; he pays all the debts of the royal family, and has just paid 28 millions French money for the Comte d'Artois"; 23 Jan. 1784. Other letters also speak of the extravagance of the French Court, as in the purchase of St. Cloud for six millions of livres, &c. Great frost in Feb. 1784: "the misery of the poor people is beyond all description, and it is impossible to say too much in the praises of the King and Queen upon this trying season." "I am convinced de Vergennes is an honest, well-meaning man"; 8 July 1784.[1] "I will endeavour to get you a print of Vergennes, and also a portrait of Prince Henry," of Prussia, "who, by the bye, is the most determined enemy to the English I ever met with, next to the King of Sweden": 14 Oct. 1784.[2] "Dr. Franklin sent me the two books addressed to his Majesty; it was the author's request to the Doctor that he would send them to me. Dr. Franklin and his grandson left Paris last Monday; he sails from Havre de Grace to Cowes, and from thence to Philadelphia:" 14 July, 1785. "There is a Baron de Kendall, a notorious spy, that I should guard you against. He is an active intelligent Irishman, and has been doing us all the mischief in his country that he possibly could, in the hope of advancing himself here. Pray venture to observe in general that every Frenchman of any condition that goes to England is more or less a spy, and brings back all the intelligence he can to ingratiate himself with the

---

[1] Mr. Hailes, on the other hand, says in a letter of 28th Oct., "M. de Vergennes is inordinately avaricious, and the love of place will in all probability sway him in his determinations."

[2] Of this prince Hailes says in a letter of 4th Nov., "His constant topic has been the abuse of this country, and he has frequently spoken of us in English company as a people without faith and without honor. Mrs. Buller, a very sensible woman, who has met him very frequently at the Duke de Nivernois, made one day so spirited an answer that I cannot omit mentioning it. The Prince, who had more than once attacked this lady on the subject of her country, its policy and conduct in wars, speaking at that time of the taking of Pondicherry in the war before last, went so far as to say that the English had not taken but bought that place. Mrs. Buller said, 'Monsieur le Comte, Je ne suis pas en état de disputer avec vous sur les affaires de guerre et de politique, mais permettez moi, de vous dire que les Anglais ne sont pas accoutumés à acheter la victoire, l'epée à la main.' She spoke, as I told her like an ambassadress."

Minister. The Duke de Liancourt spied as well as he could in England and got the *cordon bleu*. M. de Bombelles spied in Ireland, and has got an embassy. They are *sinons* all :" Mr. Hailes, 22 Sept. 1785. "I shall make an application to Mr. de Vergennes to-morrow for the permission for Mr. Howard to visit the Lazaret at Marseilles, and I dare say the request will be readily complied with ": Mr. Hailes, 17 Nov. 1785. "I find it will be attended with great difficulty, if obtained at all. The Emperor himself, they say, was obliged to see it in an irregular way:" 24 Nov. Mentioning Neckar's book upon finance published in Dec. 1784, Mr. Hailes says of him, " M. Neckar seems to be a disinterested enthusiast, who flatters himself that he can make an honest system applicable to a corrupt government. I rather think he will never recover his place." Some letters contain information as to French projects, including the improvement of Dunkirk, the French fleet, East Indian affairs, &c., furnished by one M. de St. Marc, who had been engaged as an informer, for three months, at a salary of 60 guineas a month ; but in August 1785, Hailes suggests that he is not to be trusted, and he ceases to be employed. On March 10, 1785 Mr. Hailes writes that he fears from the Duke of Dorset's coldness towards him,: hat his private correspondence with Lord Carmarthen is known to him, and desires therefore to give it up, and only to write at times with the Duke's knowledge. From this date therefore his letters are much briefer.

Portfolio 2.—Letters in 1784-5 relative to foreign affairs, from the Lord Chancellor [Thurlow], Lord Camden, Duke of Richmond, Lord Howe, Lord Sydney ; (difficulty with the Russian ambassador, Woronzow, respecting a treaty made by the Hanoverian Minister with Berlin and Dresden without communication with England, with regard to which the King considers his own personal honour engaged, and is not likely to retract one iota of his Electoral stipulations), Earl Cowper, C. J. Fox (one short note), Earl Chesterfield. Correspondence with Ministers abroad and others ; Earl Torrington, Sir Robert Walpole, John Trevor, Alex. Munro, Col. William Fullarton in India (strongly protesting against the forbearance shown to Tippoo Sahib, and the restoration of his forts, &c. when the English forces were ready to march to Seringapatam ; with a plan for order of battle of the army), Nath. Smith, Sir R. Keith, Mr. Alleyne Fitzherbert (the Empress of Russia particularly wishes for a telescope of great power, similar to that made specially by Henckel for Geo. III., but which Henckel will not make without the King's sanction), Mr. H. Elliot, Lord Dalrymple, Sir John Stepney, Mr. Jos. Ewart, Mr. Morton Eden (sends, as desired, a MS. copy of Graun's *Te Deum*). Letters of various foreign Ministers, &c. ; short notes from the first ambassador from the United States, John Adams, on his first arrival in London, 26, 27, 28 May 1785 ; Prince Adam Czartoryski ; Comte d'Adhemar, Sainte Foy, Chev. del Campo, Barthelemy, Woronzow, &c.

Three separate parcels of correspondence of, and with, various ambassadors abroad, and of letters and papers relating to foreign affairs, in the years 1787-1790. The larger part are the letters of and to Mr. A. Fitzherbert and Sir James Harris, at the Hague, with a few of Mr. Elliot, Sir R. Keith, Lord Dalrymple, Mr. Ewart, and two or three others. Three notes from Geo. III., one on 25 Jan. 1788 upon a conference held by Lord Carmarthen with the new French ambassador (M. de Calonne) which ends thus, " I cannot say the debut of the ambassador is to his advantage ; I hope it may mend." Letter from Calonne of 31 Jan. in that year to Lord Carmarthen ; has forwarded two copies of his book on the finance of France, in reply to Necker, one of which is for the King. A memorandum by the Duke of Leeds on

MSS. OF THE DUKE OF LEEDS.   16 Oct. 1739 records a conversation with M. de Calonne, in which the latter informed him that, being sent by the King of France to M. de Vergennes a few hours before his death, Vergennes entrusted him "with a secret which might some time or other be necessary for the King to be apprized of, which was the Queen's having obtained six millions of livres, which she had conveyed to the Emperor, in return for which he engaged himself to pay her an annuity, and have a respectable establishment for her, in case she should ever be under the necessity of flying from France . . . . . He had seen a great part of the correspondence between the Emperor and his sister, which was carried on by means of a Polish gentleman, and the Emperor had been very pressing for the money until it was actually remitted to him . . . . . . M. de Vergennes expired very soon after this interview with M. de Calonne. The latter before he left the house took down a note of what had passed, and sealed it up in the presence of Madame de Vergennes, and the paper remained sealed till opened in the King's presence some months afterwards." Short letter from the Duke of Luxembourg, at London, 27 Apr. 1790, enclosing French news of the 23, with the votes of the National Assembly on that day. Letter from the Earl of Massareene, 26 Nov. 1788, from prison in Paris, where he had been for 17½ years, for debt upon bills of exchange, representing his wrongs and sufferings in the most excited terms; "imprisoned abroad, robbed at home, misrepresented everywhere;" three times shut up in the *secret*, once for nine days in the "dungeon, the *cachot*, the cell, the grotto, where the lowest and most vicious of criminals are put," "the greatest part of the time without fire, candle, knife, fork, spoon, shoes, stockings, or shirt, perfectly *solus*, save the quantity of flees, bugs, lice, and some vermin," and a mouse which he had taught to come for food; sometimes in irons, once tied with cords.[1]

"Caractère du Prince de Galles par Mons. le Comte de B., 1789;" a scathing denunciation of the Prince for his vices, his profligacy, and follies, with a notice of his marriage to Mrs. Fitzherbert. He is represented as having worn out all the companions of his excesses but two, "un étourdi qui se nomme Hanger, et un Capitaine de vaisseau, Payne, écervélé sans fortune;" and is said on one occasion at Court to have said to one of the Ladies of Honour, pointing to his own mother, "Il n'y a rien que je deteste davantage qu'un visage riant et ouvert, avec un cœur faux et méchant."

Letters patent (in Latin), dated 13 July 1786, commissioning Francis Baron Osborne, Marq. of Carmarthen, as plenipotentiary for treating of boundaries, in pursuance of Art. 6 of the treaty with Spain of 3 Sept. 1783; with the Great Seal in a silver box.

Many boxes are filled with ancient deeds, chiefly relating to property in Yorkshire, from the thirteenth to the seventeenth centuries, including

---

[1] An account of Lord Massareene's imprisonment in the Grand Chatelet, for debts incurred through a speculation in salt, is given in the *Gentleman's Magazine*, Vol. LIX., p. 752, LXXV. 290. It is there said that his rigorous confinement in the dungeon was owing to his having attempted to escape; that the lengthened imprisonment (there wrongly stated to have continued for 23 years) was on account of his persistent refusal to pay the debts (which he considered were unjustly charged on him); and that he at length escaped in 1789 (the year following the date of the above letter) partly through the breaking out of the Revolution, but directly and chiefly through marrying the daughter of the governor of the prison, with whom he fled to England.

very early documents connected with the city of York. These I have not examined, as being outside my commission; but on a cursory inspection of two or three of the boxes I noticed two deeds of the first and second half, respectively, of the twelfth century, which I subjoin; and also a document relating to the city of Oxford, being the formal notification to Queen Mary II. by the mayor, bailiffs, and commonalty, dated 24 July 1694, of the election of Samuel Thurstan, gent., "a person of known loyalty and good affection to your Majesty and government," as Town-Clerk, in the room of Edw. Prince, deceased; with the city seal attached in a tin box.

The first of the following deeds is on a strip of vellum about thirteen inches long and seven and a quarter inches wide; the second is of the more usual shape and size.

"Sciant presentes et futuri quod ego Elyas filius Hugonis dedi Reginaldo de Waʒ [Warren] pro servitio suo et pro centum li. Esterlingorum quas dedit michi de pecunia sua: totam terram meam de Herthella cum omnibus ejusdem terre pertinentibus · in hominibus · in terris · in nemoribus · in campis · in pratis · in pasturis · in aquis · in molendinis · in viis · in semitis · et in omnibus eidem manerio prenominato pertinentibus · in feodo et hereditate · illi et heredibus suis ad tenendum per servitium quarte partis militis · de me et heredibus meis · ita bene · et honorifice · et libere · sicut ego et pater meus melius et liberius tenuimus de Comite Waʒ [Warren] domino nostro. Et de hoc: ipse Reginaldus et Willelmus filius ejus affidaverunt ad portandam fidem michi et heredibus meis · sicut domino de predicto feodo. Ego autem et filia mea Letiz que est heres meus affidavimus et sacramento assecuravimus ad warrantizandum hanc donationem Reginaldo et heredibus suis contra omnes homines. Et hoc fecimus coram Isabel Comitissa Waʒ domina nostra · et coram paribus nostris · et ita quod posuimus Comitissam in plegium versus Reginaldum et her[e]des suos de hac donatione warrantizanda · T. ipsa Isabel Comitissa · Rogero de Fraxnet' · Adam de Punig Rad' de Frevitt' · Symō de Petrapont' · Drogoñ de Frevitt. Witto de Bellomont' · Philippo de Jokintoñ · Bartholoñ de Chaisñ. Witto de Ely · Bernard de Blenvit · Ric. de Petrapont' · Mauricio de Cassett · Rad de Caisñ · Helya de Steinford · Patricio adhuc puero filio com. Patric' · Witto de Wennevatt · Rad· de Acra · Hugone Burdt · Roberto de Erleham · Richō. Witto Coco · Wigaro Camerario · Roḃto filio Sym' · Toma filio Hugonis · Jordan' de Furn' · Adam de Miclebric̄ · Witt· de Cuningburg' · Witto de Bailot · Roḃto Albo · Witto cler' de Dierñ · Adam clerico de 'Tefford'."

Small fragment of a dark seal attached by a silk ribbon.

"Sciant presentes et futuri quod ego Radulfus Selvan dedi · concessi et hac carta mea confirmavi Johanni Wacelin et heredibus suis unam carucatam terre in Richenildtorp · illam scilicet quam Osbertus pater meus dedit illi · cum omnibus pertinenciis et libertatibus suis que ad illam predictam carucatam pertinent · tenendam de me et de heredibus meis libere et quiete ab omni servicio excepto forensi pro servicio et humagio suo. Hujus donacionis et confirmacionis hii sunt testes · Robertus Wacelin · Racius de Bus · Rog' de Alneto · Witts filius Roḃt de Norton · Hug'iz de Riperes · Adam abas de Uuellebee [1] . John prior ejusdem loci · Hugo de Dranefeld Tomas et Michael filii ejus Witts persona de Torp Helias frater ejus · Witts persona do H[er]til · Rog' le Deune Roḃ filius ejus Ricard' Parent · Ricard' Wacelin et multi alii."

---

[1] Abbot in 1193.

MSS. OF THE DUKE OF LEEDS. Round green seal, attached by a cord of four strands; a rose; "Sigillum Radulfi Salvain."

A fine copy of the "*Roman de Rou*" of Jean Méon deserves notice. It is of the 15th century, written on 296 leaves of fine vellum, with 90 miniatures, painted in *camaieu gris*. It is bound in red velvet, and on the sides is stamped, in a cipher arrangement of the letters, the motto, " Amour, desir, regret, espoir et doubte." No trace of previous ownership is now found in the volume. The colophon is in the following couplet:—

" Cest fin du rommant de la rose,
Ou tout lart damous (*sic*) est enclose."

WILLIAM DUNN MACRAY.

MSS. OF LADY WATERFORD.

THE MANUSCRIPTS OF LOUISA, MARCHIONESS OF WATERFORD, AT FORD CASTLE CO. NORTHUMBERLAND.

By the kindness of Louisa, Marchioness of Waterford, I have enjoyed the privilege of examining a portion of the large collection of papers which are preserved in her Ladyship's residence in Ford Castle.

The Castle and the property in the midst of which it stands have descended to their present owner through a long line of illustrious ancestors.

King Henry the First granted to Robert de Muscamp the lordship of Wooler with its members, of which Ford was one (Hodgson, v. 210). It remained in this family until 34 Hen. III. (A.D. 1249–1250), when, on the death of Robert, it passed into the hands of Odenel de Forde, who had married Cecilia, one of the coheiresses of the deceased Robert (Dugdale's Baronage i. 557).

The family of Ford had settled at Ford at an earlier period, and one of them, a descendant from Odenel, having married a Heron, the property passed into the hands of that stirring border family (Dugd. i. 730). In them it remained until Elizabeth, daughter of William Heron (sheriff of Northumberland, 17 Hen. VIII.), married Thomas Cave, esq., of Etal. An heiress carried the property to Sir Francis Blake, whose daughter Mary became the wife of Edward Delaval, the ancestor of Sir John Hussey Delaval. Sir John was created Baron Delaval of Seaton Delaval 21 Aug. 1786, and died in 1808.

The documents which are preserved at Ford Castle fill twenty-three heavy chests, of which the larger proportion yet remains unexamined. Piled one upon the top of the other in a narrow closet, to move them was no easy task; and the time which I could afford for their examination enabled me to do no more than to exhaust the contents of seven boxes. The early Northumbrian charters are of especial interest. Among the documents which came to light, and which are here described, is a series of interesting charters relative to the Cistercian convent of Stixwold in Lincolnshire, about one hundred in number, and ranging from the reign of Henry the Second. Some Northumbrian documents are yet undescribed. But by far the larger number of the documents consists of the papers of Sir John Hussey Delaval, first baron Delaval, and the members of his family. A considerable proportion is of little value, but interspersed with them are many papers of no small interest. It is impossible to form a conjecture as to the contents of the boxes yet unexplored.

The documents described in the following pages speak for themselves. MSS. OF LADY WATERFORD
I gladly express my warmest thanks to the Marchioness of Waterford for the facilities which she had the kindness to afford me during the course of my investigations in Ford Castle.

King Henry the Second to Hugh [Cyvelioc] Earl of Chester.
" H. rex Anglie et dux Normanie et Aquitanie et comes Andigavie Hugoni comiti Cestrie* et Matildi comitisse, salutem. Precipio vobis quod sine dilatione et juste faciatis recognosci per barones vestros de Lincolne sirn si Arnulfus filius Petri terram de Hunintona in curia H. regis, avi mei, judicio amisit, et Lucia comitissa, et Ran. comes Cestric illam terram sanctimonialibus de Stikeswalda in elemosinam dederint. Quod si ita recognitum fuerit, faciatis eos bene et in pace et juste tenere. Et nisi feceritis Justicia mea faciat. Teste M. Bis. dapifero meo. Apud Gloce." With a fragment of a seal.

2. King Henry the Second to Hugh [Cyvelioc] Earl of Chester.
" H. rex Anglie et dux Normanie et Aquitanie et comes Andigavie, Hugoni comiti Cestrie et Matildi comitisse, salutem. Si sanctimoniales de Stikeswad [sic] poterunt monstrare quod Arnaldus filius Petri perdiderit judicio in curia regis H., avi mei, terram de Hundintona, tunc precipio quod ipse terram illam teneant bene et in pace, libere et juste, sicut carta comitisse Lucie† et comitis Ran. testantur. Et prohibeo ne super hoc inde injuste ponantur in placitis propter calumpniam predicti Arnulfi, vel heredum suorum. Et nisi feceritis vicecomes meus, vel Justitia faciat fieri. Teste, W. filio Johannis. Apud Clarend."

3. William earl of Romare to the Justices of Lincolnshire.
" Justiciar' vicecomitibus et omnibus ministris regis Licol'sire, Willelmus comes de Roumara,‡ salutem. Sciatis quod ego fui ibi ubi Arnulfus filius Petri in curia Henrici regis avi nostri regis, judicio amisit terram de Hundinton, quam calumpniatur super sanctimoniales de Stickeswald; et presto sum ad hoc demonstrandum sicut *comitatus Licol'. decreverit, et multi plures qui adhuc vivunt ibi fuerunt, et hoc viderunt et audierunt."

4. " Sciant omnes litteras hujus cyrographi videntes et audientes quod ego Hamo de Hundingtone, filius Toli, clamavi sanctimonialibus de Stickeswalde unam bovatam terræ in Hundingtone immunem de me et heredibus meis in perpetuum, quam pater meus emit de Lucia comitissa. Et præterea clamavi eis septem seliones post obitum meum immunes de me et heredibus [meis] in perpetuum, quas Lucia comitissa tenuit de patre meo in Warnabe pro quatuor denariis annuatim, quæ sunt . . . . villa apud aquilonem. Et prædictæ sanctimoniales reddent mihi annuatim duos solidos, scilicet ad festum Sancti Michaelis xij. denarios et ad pascham. xij. denarios, quamdiu vixero et illos recipere voluero. Et ego ero eis fidelis et legalis in omnibus, ut ego et sponsa mea, et pater meus et mater mea, et omnes parentes mei, simus participes omnium beneficiorum quæ fiunt, vel fient, in ecclesia sua. Et ipsæ suscipient corpus meum post obitum meum cum qualicunque catello ego potero eis dare ad illam horam." xij. cent.

5. Grant by Alexandra, daughter of Ralph Bernard, after the death of her husband, Robert de Hericrbi, to the convent of Stikeswald, all her

---

* See Dugd., Baron, 1-40.
† See Dugd., Baron, 1-36.
‡ See Dugd., Baron, 1-347.

MSS. OF LADY WATERFORD.
—·—

"maritagium" at Hundintun, viz. 12 bovates of land, the convent paying to her within the three Rogation days 3s. 8d. "in fraterna caritate" as long as she lives, with quit claim after her decease. If she should die in the secular habit the convent shall remove her body, and shall do for her the same full service as for one of their nuns. And if she should wish to change her life into holy religion she will give to the said church of her patrimony at Wilgebi, either in land or in rent, or in both, along with the said 3s. 8d., that willingly and with good will the convent would receive her honorably into their congregation. And she the said Alexandra has pledged her faith to Roger son of Roger de Stikeswald, and Alice, his mother, to observe the above, for the health of her soul and that of Robert, her husband, and William, her son, her father and mother, and all her relations, "in order that we " may be partakers in all the benefits which are done, or shall be done, " in their church for ever." With the names of many witnesses. With a seal. xiii. cent.

6. Grant by Hugh Scot to the convent of Sticheswald of 12 bovates of land in Undintune, which William son of Alexandra, and Alexandra herself, the mother of the said William, daughter of Ralph Bernard, gave to the said convent. The convent however shall remove his body and the body of his wife for burial, and shall do for them as much as they shall do for a canon and a nun. Witness Godfrey de Luci, Richard Bretone,* archdeacon of Coventry, &c. With a seal. xiii. cent.

7. Grant by Hugh Scot (for the soul of himself and his wife R.) to the nuns of Stikeswald of the church of S. Andrew of Wilchebi in pure alms. xiii. cent.

8. Grant by Michael Belet to the nuns of Stikeswald of a toft in Sichestan, formerly belonging to Gunchetel, in exchange for another toft at the gate of the cemetery of Sichestan, which is of the fee of the earldom of Chester and belongs to Hundinton. xiii. cent.

9. Quit claim by William son of Roger de Burle and Alice daughter of Hervey, and their heirs, to Margery Gubaud, prioress of Stikeswald, of their right in three carucates of land of the fee of Gilbert de Gaunt in Hundingtone. With a seal. xiii. cent.

10. Grant by John de Cormerie to the prioress and convent of Stykeswalde of his annual rent of 3s. which he ought to receive from them for the tenement which they hold of him in Hondyngtone. Witness Sir Robert de Barkewrd, knt. Sir Theobalde de Stykeswalde, knt. Sir Robert vicar of Stykeswalde, &c. With a seal. xiii. cent.

11. Grant by Symon de Crevequer to God and the convent of Stikeswald of all his lands, tenements, rents, men (free and villeins) with their homages and services there, &c. in perpetual alms. With seal. xiii. cent.

12. Grant by Gilbert Purmat of Great Hal to Symon son of John Schiken of Little Hall of a piece of land with the house built upon the same. With a seal. xiii. cent.

13. Quit claim by Hawisia, late wife of Alexander Bron of Hunsdington to William de Hounesby and Margery his wife, and to Richard son of William de Barkestone and Christiana his wife, of her right by dower after the death of the said Alexander, in the meadow which the

---

* Richard Brito was archdeacon of Coventry in 1184 and 1189. *See* Hardy's Le Neve, 1-568.

said Alexander sold to Nicholas the clerk of Hundington, in the meadow called Stondeyle. xiii. cent.   MSS. OF LADY WATERFORD.

14. Grant by Matthew son of Alan de Hundintone to the convent of Stikeswald of several portions of land in the territory of Hundintone, the respective boundaries of which are specified. With a seal. xiii. cent.

15. Grant by Matthew son of Alan de Hundintone to the convent of Stikeswald of several portions of land in Hundintone,* the respective boundaries of which are specified. With a seal. xiii. cent.

16. Grant by Nicolas son of Alan "ad ecclesiam de Hundingtone" to Margery Gubaud, prioress of the house of Stykeswaude, of various portions of land in Hundingtone,† the boundaries of which are specified. With a seal. xiii. cent.

17. Grant by Nicolas son of Alan "ad ecclesiam de Hundingtone" to Margery Goubude, prioress of Stikeswalde, of various pieces of land in Hundington, the boundaries of which are specified. With a seal. xiii. cent.

18. Grant by Nicolas son of Alan "ad ecclesiam" to Margery Gubaude, prioress of Stickeswalde, of various portions of land in Hundington,‡ the boundaries of which are specified. With a seal. xiii. cent.

19. Grant by Mathew son of Alan Wiles of Hundingtun to the convent of Stikeswaud of 2 seliones of arable land in the territory of Hundington, in exchange for the moiety of 2 seliones near "north-parte" of the grange and Riewang. With a seal. xiii. cent.

20. Grant of Margery daughter of Nicholas the clerk of Hunyngtone, widow, to Roger de Mamesfelde, clerk, of all her land &c. in Hunynygtone. With a seal. xiii. cent.

21. Grant by Roger de Mamesfelde, clerk, to Geoffrey de Lyle, son of Robert de Wodehouse and Marjoria his wife, of all the land which the said Marjoria daughter of Nicholas the clerk of Hunyngton, widow, had given him in the vill of Honington aforesaid. xiii. cent.

22. Grant by William son of Henry de Hundyngthone to his son Richard of one toft &c. in Hundyngthone, which he had by the gift of Ralph de Hondyngthone, clerk, son of Walter Abbot, by the annual payment to the master of Stykeswald and the convent of 2s. 9d. of silver. xiii. cent.

23. Grant by William son of Henry de Hundingtone to the convent of Stikeswolde of four seliones of arable land in Hundingtone, viz., in Spelhowe, Barkestone, Bramwonge and Heye. With a seal. xiii. cent.

24. Grant by Peter Mariot of Hundingtone to Robert his son of a toft and garden in Hundingtone, with eight seliones in the fields of the same. Witness, William vicar of Hundington &c. xiii. cent.

25. Memorandum that in A.D. 1247 brother Roger, master of the house of the nuns of Stikeswald (with the consent of the brethren of the said house), enfeoffed Peter called Mariot, his heirs and assigns, in the land which formerly belonged to Henry Lordecot in the vill of Honingtone, he paying annually to the convent of Stikeswalde 6s. of silver.

* Different from those in the previous grant.
† Different from all the previous benefactions.
‡ Different from those in the previous grant.

MSS. OF LADY WATERFORD. At the beginning of this arrangement the said Peter gave to the said master for the use of the convent 15s. of silver.

Affixed is a valuation of the property on the grange of Hunnington, viz., 2 cart horses, 20s.; 20 sheep, 40s.; 2 oxen, 20s.; 2 cows, 20s.; 10 qrs. of barley 100s.; 3 qrs. of "draget," 34s.; hay and forage, 10s.; 1 cart, 6s.; total 12l.

26. Quit claim by Avicia daughter of Ralph Redhod, of Hundintone, and Christiana, relict of the said Ralph, to Margery Gubond, prioress of Stikeswald, of her right in all lands and tenements formerly belonging to Henry Lurtkoc, her uncle, in the vill and territory of Hundinton. With a seal. xiii. cent.

27. Grant by Avicia daughter of the late Ralph Redhod, of Hundington, and Christiana, relict of the said Ralph, to Peter Mariot, of Hundington, and Robert his son, of all claim in the lands, &c. formerly belonging to Henry Lurtkok, uncle of the said Avicia, in Hundington. Easter [6 April] 1292.

28. Quit claim by Avicia daughter of Ralph Redhod, of Hundintonne, and Christiana, relict of the said Ralph, to Peter Mariot, of Hundington, of her right in the lands, &c. formerly belonging to Henry Lurtkoc, her uncle, in Hundington [A.D. 1292].

29. Grant by Eva, prioress of Stikeswald, "Roberto fabro de Hundigtun," and Emma his wife, of a toft and bovate of land which Henry Lurtecok formerly held in Hundigtun. With 2 seals. xiii. cent.

30. Grant by Matilda daughter of William son of Roger de Hundingtun, "domino Jolayno de Hecimere," his heirs and assigns, of a toft and bovate of land in Hundigtun, excepting two acres of land which Collegrim holds of the said Jolaynus. With seal. xiii. cent.

31. Grant by Robert son of Robert de Lincolnia in Hundingtone to the master, prioress, and convent of Stikeswald, of two seliones of arable land in the territory of Hundingtone. xiii cent.

32. A.D. 1223. Agreement between the Master of Stikeswald and the nuns there, on the one part, and William son of Peter Albus of Wymundham, on the other, as to the exchange of 2 acres and 3 roods of land in the territory of Wymundham.

33. Grant of John Ougel, of Freynish, to William de le Wirethes, for 4s. of silver, of 2 "saliones" of land in Lakefelde in le Stoniforlong and Shorteforlong. With a seal. xiii. cent.

34. Grant by William son of William Carpenter of Barkestone, to Richard Brun of Hundingdon and Giliane his wife, of 3 "selions" of arable land beyond "le beke" in the field of Barkestone. Dat. Hundingtone, St. John the Baptist's day, 25 Edw. [1]. [24 June 1297]. With a seal.

35. Grant by Roger Brun of Barkestone to Richard Brun of Hundingtone of one selion of arable land in Barkestone. xiv. cent.

36. Grant by William Boye, son of Thomas Boye, of Wymundham, to the nuns of Stikeswalde of two acres of meadow in the territory of Torpe and Wymundeham. xiv. cent.

37. Grant by John son of Robert Scragge of Sumerby to Henry Maulunel, son of Robert Maulunel, of a messuage and a half bovate of land, formerly belonging to Richard Turpin &c. near the wood of the abbot of Revesby. xiv. cent.

38. Grant by Robert son of Henry "Medic." of Hundingtone to William Lewyn of the same of one selion of arable land in Thorpedale in the field of Hundingtone, near Barkestone and Saltergate. Hundingtone, Ascension day [11 May] 1309.

MSS. OF LADY WATERFORD.

39. Grant by Mathew son of Peter Mariote of Huntingtone to Roger "ad Crucem" of the same, of a piece of garden land next the garden of the said Roger on the north. Hungindone, the Sunday before the feast of St. Clement [22 Nov.] 1310. With a fragment of a seal.

40. Grant by Matthew son of Peter Mariote of Hundingtone and Margery his wife to Hawisia, daughter of Robert de Lincoln, of Hundingtone, of the south gable of the house of the said Hawisia, with free entry and exit from the King's road to the well on the south of the said gable. For this grant Hawisia gives a certain plot of ground to the said Matthew and Margery. Hundingtone, Sunday after the feast of St. Martin, 5 Edw. II. [14 Nov. 1311].

41. Grant by Matthew son of Peter Mariothe of Hunyngtone and Margery his wife to Roger "ad Crucem" of Honingtone and Hawisia his wife of three plots of meadow &c. in the field of Honingtone near the land of the [prioress and convent of Stikeswald. Honingtone, Sunday before the Purification B.V.M. 10 Edw. II. [30 Jan. 1317.] With two seals.

42. Grant by Matthew son of Peter Mariothe of Hundingtone and Margery his wife to John le Pynder of the same of a piece of meadow in le Wotefoures in the field of Hundingtone. Hundington, the Purification B.V.M. 10 Edw. II. [2 Feb. 1317.]

43. Grant by Mathew son of Peter Mariote of Hundingtone and Margery his wife to William Lewyn of the same place, of one "selion" of arablel and in Holmewelledale in the field of Hundingtone, near the land of the prioress of Stikeswold. Honingtone, Sunday before the feast of St. George, 10 Edw. II. [17 April 1317.] With two seals.

44. Grant by Mathew son of Peter Mariote of Hundingtone and Margery his wife to William Le Loke of Hundington of two selions of arable land in the east field of Hundington. Hundington, St. John's Day "ante Portam Latinam," 10 Edw. II. [6 May1317.]

45. Grant by William Colgryme of Hundingtone to William Lewyn of the same of one selion of arable land in the Stayndale in the field of Hundingtone. Hundingtone, Thursday after the feast of St. James the Apostle, 11 Edw. II. [25 July 1317.]

46. Grant by Matthew son of Peter Mariothe of Hundingtone and Margeria his wife to Roger "ad Crucem" of two selions of arable land in the field of Hundington, near the land of the prioress and convent of Stikeswald. Hundingtone, Monday, the vigil of All Saints, 11 Edw. II. [31 Oct. 1317.] With two seals.

47. Grant by Mathew son of Peter Mariote of Hundingtone, and Margery his wife, to Roger "ad Crucem" of the same place, and Hawisia his wife, of two selions of arable land in the east field of Huntingtone. Hundington, Saturday after the Commemoration of Souls, 11 Edw. II. [5 Nov. 1317.]

48. Grant by Matthew son of Peter Mariothe of Hundingtone and Margery his wife to Robert Attehalleynte, of one selion of arable land in

MSS. OF LADY WATERFORD.

Hundingtone at Twene ye gate. Hundingtone, Monday the feast of St. Lucy, 16 Edw. II. [13 Dec. 1322.]

49. Grant by Robert de Carletone, dwelling in Honigtone, and Alicia his wife, to John son of William de Hunthifelde of Byrtone of three selions in Honingtone in le Dampdike, Northesteyndal and Nezergate. Honigtone, Monday in Cathedra S. Petri, 6 Edw. III. [22 Feb. 1332.] With two seals.

50. Grant by Margery, late wife of Mathew son of Peter de Houingtone, "Willelmo filio Henrici Medic' de Honingtone," of three scliones of arable land in Honingtone, viz. in le Midel furlonge, le Oldedikes, and le Longefurlonges "cum capite herboso." Honingtone, Tuesday after the feast of St. Ambrose, 6 Edw. III. [7 April 1332.] With a seal.

51. Quit claim by Richard de Hondyngtone, chaplain, to Isabella Broune of the same, of all his right in one toft and half a bovate of land in Hondyngtone, which he had acquired of Ralph "ultra aquam de Ancastre." Hondyngtone, Thursday before the feast of St. Barnabas [June 7] 1334.

52. Grant by Henry Engilie of Fraynyshe to Robert Troke, clerk, of all his land in Wythefeld and his croft in Fraynyshe. Fraynyshe, the Sunday after the feast of Benedict the abbot, 9 Edw. III. With a seal. [10 Dec. 1335.]

53. Quit claim by Mariota, late wife of Mathew son of Peter de Hondington, to Gilbert son of the late William Atte Kyrkeyat of Houtone, of one selion of arable land in the field of Hondington. Witnessed by Gilbert vicar of the church of Hondington &c. Dat. Hondington, Saturday, the feast of St. Vincent the Martyr [22 Jan.?] 1339, 13 Edw. III. With a seal.

54. Quit claim by Emma late wife of William Trewe of Hundingtone, to Robert "ad portam aulæ de Hundingtone" and Alice his wife, of his right in a house and land in Hundingtone. Hundingtone, Friday the Translation of St. Thomas the Martyr. 14 Edw. III. [7 July 1340]. With a seal.

55. Grant by William Loke of Hondyngtone to Gilbert de Houtone of Hondyngtone of certain pieces of land in Hondyngton, the position and bounds of each of which are described. Hondyngton, Sunday after the feast of St. Lucy. 19 Edw. III. [18 Dec. 1345]. With a seal.

56. Grant by William Loke of Honyngtone to Alice Lewyn of Honyngtone of a piece of land near the Cook's Well [juxta fontem coquinæ]. Honyngtone, Sunday after the feast of St. Barnabas the Apostle. 28 Edw. III. [13 June, 1354].

57. Grant by John son of Wylliam Cobard of Wynmadham to Robert son of John Asselyn of the same, of a cottage in the same, near the messuage of John de Reygate, knt. by the payment to the prioress of the abbey of Stykyswolde of 6d. per annum. Wynmadham, Thursday after the feast of S. Peter in Cathedra. 28 Edw. III. [7 Aug. 1354.] With a seal.

58. Grant by John son of William de Colby of Somerby to John son of Thomas of the same, of one selion of arable land in the field of Somerby lying upon Lynestanges, near the land of the abbot of Revesby, 37 Edw. III. (sic.) [25 Jan. 1363—24 Jan. 1364).

59. Grant by Walter son of Robert de Hunyngtone to William de Topclif, parson of Karltone in Kesteven, of certain his messuages and lands in the fields of Hunyngtone near Carletone aforesaid. Hunyngtone, 8 Aug. 40 Edw. III. [1366.] With a seal.

MSS. OF LADY WATERFORD.

60. John Lewyn of Honyngton appoints John Burbut of the same his attorney to deliver to John Appeller of Quappeode, chaplain, and others, seisin in a messuage &c. in Honyngtone. Stikeswolde, 2 April, 9 Ric. II. [1386.] With a fragment of a seal.

61. Grant by William Bernard and Alicia his wife to William Blyke of Haburley of a tenement and a meadow called Grenclond in Fraynessche, which they lately held by the gift of Edith Drede of Haberley. Fraynessche, on Friday, the feast of St. Andrew the Apostle. 10 Ric. II. [30 Nov. 1386.] With fragments of two seals.

62. Quit claim by Robert de Honigton (sic) son and heir of Alice daughter of Hawyse de Lincoln (?), to John Freman of Honigton, of all his right in . . . . . . Warston (?). Honingtone, Monday before the feast of St. John the Baptist. 12 Ric. II. [22 June 1388.] With a seal. Injured by damp.

63. Lease by John Wade of Systone, John Wilde of Ancaster, and Richard de Barugheby of Honyngtone, to Isabella Blauncharde, of a messuage with a garden &c. which they had of the gift of the said Isabella in Honyngton for the term of her life. Honyngton, Monday in the feast of St. Martin the Bishop. 22 Ric. II. [11 Nov. 1398.] With a seal.

64. Will of Richard Joy of Honyngtone and Johanna his wife, to the effect that after their decease their daughter Cecily shall have their infeoffment in a certain messuage with its appurtenances in Hunnington; and that their daughter Alice shall have the like rights in another messuage, &c. Honyngtone, Monday after the Circumcision. 14 Hen. IV. [2 Jan. 1413.] With a seal.

65. Quit claim by John Hamsterley of Bynbroke to Semann Grantham, citizen and merchant of Lincoln and others, of his right in a garden in the parish of St. Mary of Crakepole in Lincoln, now in the occupation of Margaret Ryby, together with his right in 8½ selions of meadow in the parish of St. Faith the Virgin, in the suburbs of Lincoln. Lincoln, Tuesday before the feast of St. Thomas the Apostle. 9 Hen. VI. [19 Dec. 1430.]

66. Grant by Alicia Colwelle, widow, to John Warde of Honyngtone, of a messuage in Honyngton near those of Richard Burbut and John Prat. Honyngtone, the feast of SS. Simon and Jude. 12 Hen. VI. [28 Oct. 1433.]

67. Grant by Alicia Colvylle, widow, to John, Robert, Richard, and William Warde of Honyngtone of a messuage near those of Richard Burbut and John Prat. Honyngton, 20 Dec. 13 Hen. VI. [1434.]

68. Letters by which Alice Colvylle appoints as her attorney John Colvylle to deliver to John Warde and others of Honyngtone her right in a messuage and certain lands in Honyngtone. Honyngtone, 20 Dec. 13 Hen. VI. [1434.]

69. Quit claim by John Colvylle of Newark to John Warde of Honyngton and others of his right in a messuage and land in Honyngton, which the said John Warde &c. held by the gift of Alice Colville of Newark. 25 Dec. 13 Hen. VI. [1434.]

MSS. OF LADY WATERFORD.

70. Quit claim by William Wrighte of Sugbroke and Margaret his wife to John, Robert, Richard and William Warde of Honyngtone in a messuage and 26 selions &c. of meadow in Honyngtone, which they hold conjointly by the gift of Alice and John Colville of Newark. 10 Jan. 13 Hen. VI. [1435.]

71. Quit claim by Richard Bykerstathe to Robert Cleydone and Margaret his wife of a tenement and garden in Kedermynstere, co. Worcester. Kedermynstere, Friday after the Annunciation B.V.M., 26 Hen. VI. [29 March, 1448.] With a seal.

72. Grant by Richard Burbutt of Honyngtone to John Wythere of Barstone and others of a messuage, orchard &c. in Honyngtone. Honyngtone, Sunday before the feast of St. Gregory the Pope, 37 Hen. VI. [11 March, 1459.] With a seal.

73. Grant by Edward Wythiforde of Kydermynstre to Thomas Hulle of Fraynche, of a croft &c. in payment of 30s. Assumption B.V.M., 37 Hen. VI. [15 Aug. 1459.] With a seal.

74. Grant by William Flecher and Dionisia his wife to John Bate and Agnes his wife, of all their messuages, lands &c. in Haburley in the manor of Kidderminster, on condition of providing them with certain lodging, provisions &c. during the life of both of them. Haburley, 6 March, 16 Hen. VII. [1501.]

75. Letters of Robert prior of Bever and the convent of the same, admitting master Robert Husy esquire into their fraternity. Dated in their Chapter House, 14 Dec. 1507. With a fragment of the common seal.

76. Quitclaim by Thomas Walker of Scotylthorpe and John Hurst of the same place to Thomas Nyxe of Lobthorpe and Katherine his wife, of their right in a cottage formerly belonging to John Freman of Honyngtone. Honyngtone, on the day of St. Lucy the Virgin, 1 Hen. VIII. [Dec. 13, 1509.] With two seals.

77. Letters of Thomas, chief Prior or Master of the Order of Sempringham, by which he admits Robert Husye esquire and Anne his consort to all the benefits of that Order, which are here enumerated. Dat. Watton, 17 April 1512.

Appended is a note, in another hand, to the effect that Anne Husye, the wife of . . . Husye, esquire, died on the fourth of the nones of September [2 September]. The year is not specified.

78. Letters by which friar William prior of the Greater Chartreuse admits master Robert Huse of the realm of England to participate in all the privileges of the Order, during life and after death. Dated in the General Chapter at Chartreuse, last of April 1532. With seal.

79. Inspeximus and confirmation of a grant by John Prior of the house or priory of St. Katherine near Lincoln, to Robert Hussey, esq., of an annual rent of 40s. from the rectory of Armestone,* co. Lincoln, for life. 7 Sept., 12 Hen. VIII. [1520], and confirmed 1 Aug., 32 Hen. VIII. [1540.] With a broken seal.

80. Grant by Edward Villars, gent. (for 13l. 6s. 8d.) to John Burbutt of Honyngtone, husbandman, of a messuage and lands in Honyngton. 14 Feb., 1 Queen Mary [1554]. With a seal.

---

* An early endorsement here reads "Harmthrop," included in the parish of Morton.

81. Grant by John Burbott of Huniugton, husbandman, to Edward Burbot his son, of a messuage &c in Hunington, which the said John had bought of Edward Villers of Loughborough. 26 May, 12 Eliz. [1570.] With a seal.   MSS. OF LADY WATERFORD.

82. Grant by William Burbott of Hunnington, yeoman (in consideration of 320*l.* received by him) to Charles Hussey of Hunnington, knt., of his messuage in Hunnington, with its appurtenances. 15 Oct. 2 James I. [1604.] With a seal.

83. Bond in the penal sum of 640*l.* by William Burbott of Hunnington, yeoman, to Sir Charles Hussey, of Hunnington, knt., to permit the said Sir Charles peaceably to hold his messuage and lands in Hunnington according to an indenture bearing the same date as the present bond. 15 Oct. 1604. With a seal.

84. Grant by Edward Burbott, of Fulbecke, yeoman (for 80*l*), to Sir Charles Hussey of Hunnington, knt., of his two messuages in Hunnington, with certain lands. 10 Nov. 1604. With a seal.

85. Presentation by Thomas Hussey. Baronet, of the rectory of Doddington Piggott to John Joynes, clerk, A.M., addressed to Robert [Sanderson] bishop of Lincoln. AD. 1661. Signed, with a seal.

Grant by Robert Templeman of Hortone to Gwyschard de Charrone and Isabella his wife, and their heirs and assigns, of all his land of Stobithorene, between the lands of Alan son of Adam Brac' and William Fayrechilde, and the march between Horton and Cupono [co. Northld.], "ad faciendum omnimodum proficuum suum inde pro eorum voluntate de capitali domino feodi illius." Test. Hugone de la Val, mil. &c. xiii. cent. 1.

Grant by Robert Templeman of Hortone to Guychard de Charrone and Isabelle his wife and their assigns of a silion of land called Aldehortone, near the land of William Fayrchylde. xiii. cent. With a seal 44.

Grant by Richard de Stykelawe, chaplain, to his lord Guychard de Charrone and Isabella his wife of all his land in the vill of Stykelawe. Test. Adam de Selcby, knt. Dat. 1270. 38.

Grant by Stephen de Charrun, son of sir Guychard de Charrun, to sir Guychard his brother, of all his right in the manor of Hortun near Bebseth, and in the vills of Herforde, Cramlingtone, and Stikkelaw [co. Nthld.]. Test. Hugh de la Wal and Hugh Gubione, knights, Walter de Selby &c. xiii. cent. 34.

Agreement made on the Friday before Pentecost, 27 Edw. I., between Guiscarde de Charrone, the Elder, on the one part, and Robert de Burendone on the other, by which the former grants to the latter a "selion" which he had from Hynynge the parker in the fields of Horton, in exchange for another "juxta fossas manerii prædicti." [5 June 1299.] 33.

Charter of William de Castre to Sir Gwychard de Charrone and Isabella his wife of all his right and claim in the manor of Hortone, formerly belonging to Thomas de Castre, the uncle of the said Wm. and the husband of the said Isabella, with remainder to Thomas her son, in the event of his having no issue by the said Gwychard. Test. Rob.

MSS. OF LADY WATERFORD. Bertram of Bothall and Hugh de la Val, knts., Adam de Seleby, &c. With a seal. xiii. cent. 48.

Grant by Thomas de Castre to Radulf son of Waleran de Hortone of all the land (being eight bovates) in the vill of Tyrringtoft, to be held in fee by the yearly rent of ten pence or a pound of pepper, whichever they please. Test. John de Rydale, Gilbert de Oggel, &c. xiv. cent. 41.

Quitclaim by Thomas son and heir of Richard de Stykelaw to Sir Gwychard de Charrone and his heirs and assigns, as to the lords of the fee, of his messuages and land in Stykelaw [co. Northum.]. Test. Ric. de Cramlyntone, John de Trewyke, "Tho. de Burthdune, manente in Hortone," &c. xiii. cent. 49.

Grant by William de Stikelawe to Simon de Newsum of seven acres of land in the vill of Stikelawe by the rent of 1d. at Pentecost. Test. Eustace De la Val, Henry de la Val, Gilbert de Oggil, &c., with a seal. xiii. cent. 37.

Grant by William de Steyclau to Simon de Neusum, for a certain sum of money by the granter received, of an acre of land in the vill of Stoyclaw near Wethermere and the land of Richard de Hortone, at the yearly rent of one penny. Test. Sir H. de la Wale, Ewstacius de la Walle, &c. xiii. cent. 45.

Grant by Henry son of Ralph de Stikelau to Richard son of Geoffrey de Neusum and his heirs of six acres of land in Stikelau, "de terra illa quam dominus meus Walranus habuit ad firmam de Johanne Mauduit," between Lidisdene and Horton [co. Northum.], at a yearly rent of 6d. Test. Thomas de Oggille and his brother Roger, &c. xiii. cent. 69.

Grant by William de Stickelau to Robert de Mitford of 12 acres of land in Stickelau [co. Nthld.], viz. in Floris, in Hefdis and in Welleside. Test. Adam de Gescum, then sheriff, knt., Adam de Seleby, &c., with a seal. xiii. cent. 70.

Grant by Nicholas, son of Osbert de Quelpingtona, to his sister Matilda, her heirs and assigns, of the lands in Horseley, which his father Osbert formerly held of Adam de Falderley. "Test. domino Waltero de Suethope, Waltero Scot, &c. xiii. cent. 9.

Grant by Symon de Neusome to Sir Guichard de Charrone and Isabella his wife of his right in eight acres of land in Styclawe [co. Nthld.] and all his other tenements there which he had of William de Styclawe, to them, their heirs and assigns "tanquam dominis feodi illius pertinentis ad Hortone Scyrref." Test. Adam de Seleby, &c. xiii. cent. 51.

Grant by Agnes de Vaus, relict of Sir Walrerau le Viscont, to Gwychard de Charron and Isabella his wife, of the whole land and tenement which she held in Hortone Shyrreve, Stikelawe and Herford [co. Northum.] in the name of dower, to hold by them from Michaelmas 1270 for ever, paying by name of dower 7l. 5s. to the said Agnes during her life, and after her death to be held by the said Gwychard and Isabella, their heirs and assigns, without any payment to any one. Test. Hugh de la Val, knt., Tho. de Dyvelestone, &c. xiii. cent. 43.

Grant by John de Belson, son of Adam de Trewike, to Sir Guychard de Charrone of 16 acres of land, &c. in Horton, which Alice de Bebesete, the mother of the grantor, late the wife of Adam de Trewike, gave to him in her widowhood. Test. Adam de Selcbi and Wm. de Framlington in Crambelington, knts., and Rob. de Burtdone, &c. xiii. cent. 54.   MSS. OF LADY WATERFORD.

Grant by Walranus de Hortone to Tho. de Castre of seven score and ten acres of land in the vill of Horton, "cum villenagiis, villanis, sequelis and catallis eorum," those namely which he had recovered from Sir John Waard in the king's court, "et postea per magnam assisam retinui, adeo integras sicut dictus Johannes easdem tenuit in maritagio cum Yssabella filia mea, habendas dictis Thomæ et Yssabellæ." Test. Sir William Heyrun, sheriff of Northumberland, &c. With an armorial seal. xiii. cent. 39.

Grant by Robert, son of Richard, son of Matilda de Horton, to Guyschard de Charron and Isabella his wife, of one acre and one rood of land in the territory of Horton, lying upon Sparwecester, by the payment of a red rose within the octaves of St. John the Baptist. Test. Adam de Selby, knt., &c. [xiii. cent.] 35.

Grant of Alexander son of Richard de Belhus, to Guichard de Charrone, of all the tenement which may be his by right in the vill of Daneby-upon-Yiore, of the inheritance of Sarra the daughter of Alan le Buiteiler, his late grandmother, along with the homage and service of Alan de Kilburn and his heirs. Test. Peter de Thoresby, rector of the church of Wathhouse, &c. xiii. cent. 15.

Charter of Alexander son of Richard de Belluse, next heir of Sarra daughter of Alan le Butiler, granting to Guichard de Charron all his land in Daneby-upon-Yore [co. York] of the inheritance of the said Sarra his late grandmother. He also grants to the same Guichard "Walterum filium Rogeri Clerici, villani mei, cum tota sequela sua, salvis mihi et heredibus meis omnibus aliis villanis meis, cum eorum sequelis." Test. Peter de Thoresby, rector of Wathous, Richard de Multon, bailiff of Richmond. xiii. cent. 31.

Grant by Thomas de Clyvedon to Gwyschard de Charrone and his heirs and assigns of "totum mesuagium meum et totam terram meam in Hortune et Styckeslawe," which he had by the gift of Robert son of Richard Templeman, knt., Michael the son of Robert, of William de Styckeslawe, Roger his son and Isabella daughter of William Maudut, at a rent of 6d. by the year. xiii. cent. 29.

Another copy of the above. xiii. cent. 30.

Agreement entered into on the day of SS. Fabian and Sebastian, 44 Hen. III., by which Alexander, son of Alexander de Belluse, grants to Sir Guichard de Charrone all the rents and services of his free tenants, villains, and cottars, in Daneby [co. York], for three years next following, under certain conditions here specified. Test. Richard de Multon, bailiff of Richmond, &c. [20 Jan. 1260]. 32.

Deed by which Thomas de Horsleye gives to Matilda, late the wife of Thomas Bottalle, his aunt, half an acre of land in the vill of South Horsleye, "in quandam cultura quæ vocatur le Hopesyde," in exchange for half an acre in the North Croftes in the said vill. xiv. cent. 17.

Release by Eudo de Paterby, clerk, to Gwelard (sic) de Charron, and his heirs of an annual rent of 20s. Horton, on the Sunday next before the feast of St. John the Baptist, 27 Edw. I. [21 June 1299]. 36.

Grant by Michael son and heir of the late Sir Thomas de Ryhil, knt., to his brother Guischard, of all his rights in the manor of Hortone

MSS. OF LADY WATERFORD. Schirrethe, Stikkelawe and Hereford, co. Northum., which his mother Isabella held, as also to his said brother of all his rights in a messuage in Heland and two acres "de petario in Merdeffen." Newcastle, "in loco Fratrum Minorum 1284, prid. non. Maii," [6 May]. 28.

Grant by Adam de Aula to Augnes (*sic*) his daughter, and her husband William, and their heirs and assigns, of all the lands and tenements which Sir Walleran gave to him in Hortone [co. Northum.], as they are described in the charter given to the donor by Walleran. Hortone, 6 ides of May [10 May] 1267. 55.

Grant by Eudo de Paterby, clerk, "domino Wissardo de Charrone, patri," and his assigns, of all his lands in the vill and field of Hortone formerly belonging to Adam de Aula. Test. Sir Rob. de la Vale, knt., &c. xiv. cent. 71.

Grant by John de Lomleye to William de Camera and Katherine his wi e of all his tenements in Southorsleye [co. Northum.], viz., one messuage and five acres formerly belonging to John de Whitchester and Eda his wife, and seven and a half acres of the grant of Robert de Unframville, earl of Angus. xiv. cent. With a seal. 68.

Quitclaim of Stephen de Charrone, son of Sir Guychard de Charrone the elder, to Sir Guychard de Charron, the brother of the grantor, of all his right in the manor of Hortone, Stickelaw and Herford [co. Northum.]. Test. Richard de Horssele, sheriff of Northumberland, &c. Newcastle, on the morrow of Trinity, 3 Edw. II. [6 July 1309.] With a seal. 57.

Grant by John de Plessys to Richard de Emeldone, of Newcastle, of a place of meadow in Holford [co. Northum.], called le Southandown, on the north of the meadow of the chapel of Shottone, and near the land called "les Twistes." Test. Gilbert de Bourghdone sheriff of Northumberland, knt. Holforde, 16 Sept., 18 Edw. II. [1324.] With a seal. 58.

Lease by Robert de la Vale, knt., to Ric. Scot, of Newcastle-upon-Tyne, and his heirs and assigns, "quod ipsi appruare se possint in perpetuum de carbonibus marinis" under both moieties of "le Chestres in Benwell," on the north and on the south, "et quod ipsi habeant in perpetuum cheminium sufficiens et competens (salvis bladis et pratis)," for carrying their coals to the Tyne. Test. John de Denton, the mayor of Newcastle, &c. Newcastle, 3 June 1334. 2.

Quitclaim by Richard, son and heir of John de Plessys, to Adam Graper and Agnes his wife, Richard de Actone and Matilda his wife, Sir Alan de Claveringe, knt., and Jacoba his wife, of all claim which he has in the meadow in Holforde in Shottone [co. Northum.], near "les Twistes." Newcastle, Tuesday in the vigil of the Invention of the Holy Cross, 14 Edw. III. [2 May, 1340.] With a seal. 60.

Indenture between Sir John Heron, knt., on the one part, and Rob. de Punchardon on the other, respecting the settlement of an annual rent of ten marks arising out of the manor of the said John of Crawlawe. Test. Will. Heron, knt., &c. Crawlawe, on the Friday next after the feast of St. Matthew, 27 Edw. III. [27 Sept. 1353.] With a seal. Injured by damp. 3.

Settlement as to the stipend to be paid to the chaplain of Erdesdone in the parish of Tynemouth, John de Whetley being perpetual vicar of the said parish. Durham, nones of December [5 Dec.], 1363. With the fragment of a seal.

MSS. OF LADY WATERFORD.

16.

Lease by Alan Whiteheved, chaplain, and John de Killyngworth, senior, to Sir William de la Vale, knt., of the manors of Sighalle, Benewelle and Bidelesden, with all their appurtenances in Hesilden, from next Michaelmas for ten years, by the yearly payment of one pound of cumin. Dated at Sighalle on the day after Michaelmas [30 Sept.], 1371. ·Test., Richard de Horsley, sheriff of Northumberland, Alan de Hetone, Robert de la Vale, knts. 2 seals. 4.

Grant by Cecily, late the wife of Robert de Punchardon, to John de Hexham and Eleanor his wife, of all the lands, &c. which the said Cecily holds for the term of her life in Bidelesdene, Buntyngfeld, Cotesfeld, and Fawelande, of which the reversion belongs to the said Eleanor. To be held during the life of the said Cicily at a rent of 40s. per an. Newcastle, on the Sunday within the octaves of the Holy Trinity, 3 Ric. II. [26 May 1380.] With a seal. 13.

Indenture made at Newsome on Wednesday, being the morrow of Michaelmas, 7 Ric. II. [30 Sept. 1383], by which Sir Robert de la Vale, knt., gives to his son John, and his wife Margaret, the daughter of John de Mitford, all his lands in Newsome, at an annual rent of 10l. during his life. Test. Henry de la Vale, William de la Vale, knights, &c. 2 seals. 6.

Grant of John Broun of Hawkewelle, to John Wodman, of all his lands and tenements in Haukwelle [co. Northum.], by the yearly rent of four marks sterling. Test. William de Karnaby, Samson Hareynge, &c. 16 Nov. 1395. With a seal. 53.

Grant by Osbert de Quelymtone to Matilda, his lawful daughter, of a messuage and ten acres of land in Horsseley. The names and position of the lands are specified. xv. cent. 5.

Quitclaim by Henry, son of Ralph, "Johanni filio Roberti Capellani," his heirs and assigns, of those twelve acres in the fields of Horton, with a toft, which Robert son of Walter gave him for six marks of silver, as they are described in the charter which the said John has from the said Robert. Test. Thomas de Hogil, &c. With seal. 14.

Deed of gift by John Wodman, mason, to Robert Wyse and John Baudwyn, of all his lands and tenements, &c. in Hexham and the liberties thereof. Dat. 20 Jan. 1402. With a seal. 64.

Letters of attorney by which John Remyngtone and Thomas Major appoint John Turpyn to give seisin to William de la Vale and Margaret his wife, daughter of John de Woddryngtone, knt., of ten husbandlands in Seghill [co. Northum.]. Seghill, 14 Oct., 13 Hen. IV. [1411]. With two seals. 56.

Grant by Adam Hagman to Robert Wyse of a messuage and croft in South Horsle, and 11 acres of land in the same, for the life of the said Robert, and after his death they shall remain to John son of John Wodman and his heirs for ever. South Horsle, in the feast of S. Matthew the Evangelist, 1 Hen. V. [21 Sept. 1413.] With a seal.
15*.

Grant by John Horsley, son and heir of John Wodmane, to Sir Walter Coke, chaplain, and Patom Wodmane, the brother of the grantor, of 2½ burgages and ten acres of land in Hexham, which he had

MSS. OF LADY WATERFORD. by right after the death of his father, John Wodeman. Last of October, 1 Hen. V. [1413.] 11.

A memorandum in a contemporary hand states that this John the son had it from John the father, who had it from John Bawdwyn of Hexham.

Grant by John Horslee, son and heir of John Wodman, to Adam Hagman, of a tenement in the Sotherawe of Sothe Horslee [co. Northum.], and 13½ acres of land, late in the tenure of Robert Wyse, and two acres late the property of John de Daltone, at the end of the Westwode of Horslee, at the yearly rent of 4s. Test. Robert Lylee, knt., sheriff of Northumberland, &c. Horslee, 18 Jan., 3 Hen. V. [1416.] With a seal. 40.

Grant by John de Horslee, son and heir of John Wodman, to Robert Elmet of an annual rent of 13s. 4d. from a tenement in Hawkewelle in the Hede Rawe in Westhidwyne. Westhidwene, 18 Feb., 3 Hen. V. [1416.] 10.

Release by William Gray, brother and heir of Robert Gray, deceased, to William de Orde, esq., of all claim on lands, &c. in Norham and Halielande, late the property of the said Robert, and which the same William has by the gift of this grantor. 20 Jan. 1420[-1.] 20.

Agreement as to the disposal of a certain great tenement upon the Sandhill in Newcastle, which had been sold by William Heroun, knt., and John Hall, chaplain, to Tho. de Pityngtone, vicar of Hartburne, and John de Fenwyke, chaplain. 4 Feb. 1422[-3]. 1 Hen. VI. 61.

Grant by Sir Thomas Gray of Horton, knt., to Laurence de Actone, John Raymes, and John Clerk of Nesbit, of all his manor of Horton and all his other lands in Northumberland, Elandshire, and Norhamshire, in the bishoprick of Durham. Horton, 10 Feb., 6 Hen. VI. A.D. 1427[-8]. With a seal. 50.

Duplicate of the above. With an armorial seal. 39*.

Grant of Sewallus Howghtone of Pylesgate, to Thomas Joy, son of Geoffrey Joy of Pylesgate, of certain land in the same. Pylgate, on the feast of the Invention of the Holy Cross, 9 Hen. VI. [3 May 1431.] With a seal. 18.

Grant by John Kendale of Newcastle, to John Horsley, of half an acre of land in Corbridge. Test. Adhomar Herynge. 8 Jan., 10 Hen. VI. [1432]. 26.

Quitclaim by William Holdene,* cousin and heir of Robert Hidwyne of Appirlee, to John Horseley of his [William's] right in the manors of West Hidwyne, Elfmelee, and Appirlee. He has caused the seal of the mayoralty of Newcastle to be affixed. Test. Laurence Actone, mayor of Newcastle, Adomare Heryng, &c. Newcastle, 16 Oct. 1433. 2 seals. 7.

Grant by John Burrelle of Holtelle, to William Burrelle, his son, of one husbandland in the vill of Holtelle [co. Northum.], which the donor had of the gift of John Rogerson of Branxtoune. Test. Ralph Gray, knt., John Herone, knt., Thomas Gray of Horton, Robert Maners of Etale, Tho. Strother, William Milne. Holtelle, 1 May, 32 Hen. VI. [1454]. 23.

---

* An endorsement states that he was "filius Agnetis, filiæ Johannis, filii prædicti Roberti."

James Delavale, cousin and heir of John Delavale, late of Newshame, appoints Edward Weddalle his attorney, to give seizin of his manor of Newshame [co. Northum.], and all his lands in Blithsnoke, to John Wodryngtone, esq. 6 April, 3 Edw. IV. [1463]. 27.

MSS. OF LADY WATERFORD.

Release by William Colvyle, of Swaledale, to John Herbotille, of Swareland, Thomas Herbotille, of Cramlyngtone, and Robert Sotherne, of Doram, chaplain, of all claim on the lands which he holds along with them by the gift of Bartram Herbotille, esq., now deceased, in Hamerden, Filsham, Morle, and Cortesle, co. Sussex; in the manor and vill of Suttone-super-Trent, co. Notts; in the manor and vill of Dalton-in-the-Gales, co. York, and also in all his possessions in the vills and manors of Beawmys, Caufeld, Hedle, and Pokerle, in the bishoprick of Durham. Test. Roger Aske, Robert Wycliffe, &c. 20 Jan., 5 Edw. IV. [1466.] 67.

Bond by William Ovyngtone to William Underwood in 8l. for the quiet possession of a tenement in Pilgrim Street, Newcastle, at present inhabited by Tho. Coke. 10 Oct., 6 Edw. IV. [1466]. 72.

Grant by Robert Southeron of Durham, chaplain, and John Herbotelle, of Tynmouth, to Ralph Herbotelle, esq., son and heir of Bertram Herbotelle, esq., of certain lands in the counties Sussex, York, and Durham. 1 June, 18 Edw. IV. [1478]. With 2 seals. 19.

Grant by Thomas Herbotelle, chaplain, John Herbotelle, and Rob. Herbotelle, esq., to James Delavall and Margery his wife, of all his lands, &c., in Blak Callertone and North Dissingtone [co. Northum.], which they had of late of the gift of the said James, as more fully appears in his charter to them granted. They also appoint Bartram Harbotille, son of the said Robert Harbotelle, as their attorney, to give seizin in the premises. 4 Oct., 18 Edw. IV. [1478.] 65.

Pardon by King Richard III., granted to James Delaval of Setone Delavale, esq., alias James Horsley, late of Seton Delavale, gentleman, for all offences by him committed before 1 Feb., I Ric. III. [1484.] Westm., 9 July, 2 Ric. III. [1484.] 62.

Grant by Ralph Herbotelle, knt., son and heir of Bartram Herbotelle, esq., lately deceased, son and heir of Robert Herbotille, knt., deceased, to Thomas Swynburne, Edmund de Herbotelle, Thomas Scott and John Richardsone, clerk, of his castles and manors of Prestone and Hortone, co. Northum., and of the manor of Kebelsworthe, in the bishoprick of Durham, which descended to him by the death of the said Bartram Herbotelle, his father; the manor and vill of "Dalton in the Gales," co. York; of the manor and vill of Suttone upon Trent, co. Notts; of the reversion of the manor and vill of Hamertone, Filsham, Morle, and Cortesley, co. Sussex, after the death of his mother Johanna, late belonging to his father Bartram. Test. Ralph lord Ogle, &c. 9 Nov. 8 Hen. VII. [1492.]

Dorso. Notice of livery and seizin given 19 May in the year aforesaid. 63.

Contract between Ralph Herbotell, knt., on the one part, and Henry Swynno, esq., on the other, respecting a marriage between John Herbotell, son and heir apparent of the said Henry, with Isabell, daughter of the said Sir Ralph, she to be endowed with lands and tenements in Swynno, Bedralle and Roke [co. Northum.]. 17 July, 7 Hen. VII. [1492.] 59.

Carta Johannis De le Waylle, ejusdem dominii De la Wayll in com. Northumbriæ, arm., "concedentis meo dilecto in Christo oratori

MSS. OF LADY WATERFORD

Johanni Reide, yeman, totum meum heremitagium sicut jacet in le Mekylden.... Quod quidem heremitagium est fundatum in honore B. Niniani, confessoris et episcopi, ... tenendum pro termino vitæ suæ." Dat. penultimo Octob., 13 Hen. VII. [30 Oct. 1497.] 52.

Deed of sale by William Ward of Bedlington, son and heir of William Ward late of Cowpen, to Sir Ralph Harbottell, knt., of his lands and tenements in Horton Schereff for a certain sum of money by him received (the amount not being named). Test. Anthony de la Valle, Robert de la Valle, his brother, Robert Blackden of West Harforthe. Horton, 4 Nov., 15 Hen. VII. [1499.] 42.

Indenture by which Thomas Harbotelle enters into certain arrangements with his brother Robert as to an annual rent of 10l. arising from the manor and vill of Horton [co. Northum.], which th.. said Robert had undertaken to pay to him. 20 Feb., 15 Hen. VII. [1500.] 75.

Grant by John Delavale, esq., to Rob. Wodryngtone, esq., of all his lands, &c., in Horsley, in the parish of Ovyngham [co. Northum.], together with his lands, &c., in Duxfelde. He appoints John Eryngtone of Levylls as his attorney for the same. 28 Apr., 15 Hen. VII. [1500.] 74.

Deed of entail by Thomas Hoptone, esq., to Richard Gray, esq., Roger Horseley, William Stanley, and Edward Store, clerk, of his manor, &c., of Morefelde, co. York, now in the tenure of John Walker and William Syckes, together with a messuage called "Gregory," in the parish of Eltone in the said county, to be held by them to the use of the said Thomas and Ann Delavale and the longer liver. Morefeld, 17 Nov., 23 Hen. VII. [1507.] Signed. With a seal. Seizin was given on the same day. 73.

Confirmation by Ralph Hopton, brother and heir of Thomas Hopton, esq., of a charter previously granted by him to Richard Gray, esq., now deceased, Roger Horslay, William Stanelay, and Edward Store, clerk, of the manor of Mirfelde, co. York, to the use of Thomas and Anne Delavale, during their life and that of the longer liver. 3 Nov., 1 Hen. VIII. [1509.] 22.

Grant by Guichard Harbotelle, esq., to his cousin Robert Delavale, of his windmill of Horton, for the life of the said Robert. He appoints Guy Delavale as his attorney to give seizin in the same. 2 Dec., 3 Hen. VIII. [1511.] Signed. With a seal. 47.

Indenture by which Sir Edward Storour, chaplain of the chantry of our Lady at Seton Delavale, with the consent of John Delavale, esq., now patron of the said chantry, lets to farm to Percevall Selby, of Byttilisdene, gent., all the lands called the Priest's lands in Byttilisdene [co. Northum.] belonging to the chantry for 15 years, at the annual rent of 5s. 4d. 15 May 1520. 21.

Deed by which John abbot of Newminster, Thomas abbot of Alnwick, John prior of Tynemouth, William prior of Brinkburn, Ewyn lord of Ogle, John of Wodringtone, sheriff of Northumberland, John Emley, master of Bamborough, John of Lilborne of Shawdene, William of Ogle of the same, Thomas Lile of Newton Hall, Robert Lile of Felton, John Horsley of Ulchester, John of Cransesture of the same, Thomas Foster of Eddirston, Thomas Carr of Lilborne, esquires, William Wodrington, under sheriff, Thomas of Bradford, John Herbotell of

Haroppe, Thomas of Fenwyke, Alexander Mitforde, John of Bewyk, crowners, John Carr of Chibborne, certify that James Delavale is next of blood to dame Elizabeth Burcesture. And as touching such land as the said dame Elizabeth had in Northumberland, that is to say, Callerton, Dissington, Seton, Hewsham,* Hartlaw, Halywelle, Betillisden, and fee farm of Branton, the said dame Elizabeth and her husband, Sir John Burcestre, sold the reversion of the said land to Robert of Mitford on this condition, that the said James and Margaret his wife, daughter of the said Robert Mitford, should have the said lands after the decease of the said dame Elizabeth and her husband, to them and to their heirs of their bodies lawfully begotten for evermore, and for default thereof to remain to the said Robert Mitford and to his heirs in fee simple. And thereupon the said dame Elizabeth and her husband reared a fine. Albeit, after this the said dame Elizabeth was variant, and through the labour and striving of ill disposed persons made a bargain with the marquis of Mountagu of the same lands; and after this it was so that the said James Delavalle was indicted of felony, the said marquis being sheriff of Northumberland and Sir William Bower, his under sheriff, "gart" attatch the said James, and the said James found "borowys" to appear at the next session, Alan Byrde of the Newcastle and John Harbotelle. Notwithstanding the said James was not quit of the said inditement. The said marquis had him to London, and there the said James released to the said marquis Mountague for fear of life we understand. The said James, incontinent after that the said dame Elizabeth Burcesture was deceased, as to his inheritance upon Callerton and Dissingtone, which is the chief of the said lands, took and occupied them, and took the former by the space of a year in the said marquis' days; and in likewise the said James at the same time went to Seton Delavale and asked delivery thereof, but it was kept from him [by] a stronger hand. In witness hereof we have set our seals. With 27 seals, nearly all imperfect.

MSS. OF LADY WATERFORD.

66.

Mortgage by John Burell the elder, burgess of Berwick, of the town and manor of Unthanke, in the county of Norham, to Anthony Murton, son to Lenert Murton of Berwick, until the payment of 26s. 8d., and with the further lease of the premises for 31 years after the payment of the debt, at the annual rent of 3s. 4d. Tweedmouth, 11 Sept., 28 Hen. VIII. [1536.]

12.

Lease (dated 8 Jan., 30 Hen. VIII., 1539) by Robert Blakney, prior of Tynemouth, to John Delaval, son and heir apparent to Sir John Delaval, of the tithe sheaves of corn in the town of Whitlayth [co. Northum.] for 40 years, at the annual rent of 50 sh. With the fragment of a seal.

24.

Limitation of the deed of infeoffment by which John Delaval of Seton [co. Northum.], knt., disposed of his lordship of Black Callerton [co. Northum.] in favour of John Delaval, son and heir apparent to the grantor. 26 Sept., 34 Hen. VIII. [1542.] 3 seals.

25.

NEWBORNE CHURCH.—"This indenture indented made the xxvii. day of March 1542, of the vestments, ornaments, plate, jewels, bells and lead belonging to the said church, signed and subscribed with the hands as well of Sir Thomas Hilton, Sir John Dalavaille, knight, and Cuthbert Horsley, gentleman, justices of the peace, there and thereto

---

* This one name is written in a different ink in a blank space left in the line.

MSS. OF LADY WATERFORD. authorised by the King's Majesty's commission, as of the curate and churchwardens of the said church."

In primis, iii. bells ; ii. chalices of silver ; ii. little bells ; i. faite of brasse ; viii. vestments; ii. albes; ii. capes ; i. pair of broken censers; iii. altar cloths ; i. hanging for the alter; ii. towels ; i. " corpix" ; one canopy. The church and ii. porches covered with lead.

   Thomas Hilton, knt.
   John Delavall, knt.
   Cuthbert Horsley.   46.

Address of the Lord Lieutenant, &c., of the county of Lincoln to the Prince of Orange, signed 13 Dec. 1688.

"Instructions to George Delaval, Esq., whom we have appointed our Envoy extraordinary to the Emperor of Fez and Morocco, &c." Kensington, 26 April 1707.

"Particulars of a present from Her Majesty to the Emperor of Morocco." Sir Cloudsley Shovell to His Excellency—thanks for delivering her Majesty's subjects that Vanitia had so wrongfully taken. The British fleet before Tolonne, 10 Aug. 1707. Copy.

"Instructions for George Delaval, Esq., our Envoy Extraordinary to the King of Portugal." 1710.

"News from Paris. An inhabitant of the parish of S. Martin des Champs has just arrived, and reports that he has seen the Young Chevalier at the Tuilleries ten or twelve times. He goes by the name of Prince Edward, is about 27 years old, between five and six feet tall, wears Le Cordon Bleu, the Garter and the Star of the order. He is generally attended by three or four Irish officers. His eyebrows and hair are red. His gait is ungracious, and his knees appear to be stiff. In other respects, he is a well made personage." French.

Bolton to his dearest son, "Kelly must give the gelding the best white oats he can get. I have dined at home by myself for five or six days together, and wished you with me, my dearest boy. To-morrow the Hampshire Club opens. The King has ordered a commission to prorogue the Parliament to-morrow to 8 Dec. The plague has got into the Isle of Man. Nov. 24, 1720.

Henry Fox to John Delaval. "The King has declared his intention to make me Secretary of State, and I must take the conduct of the House of Commons." Asks his attendance at the first day's debate. 30 Sept. 1755. Orig.

Dr. Arne to Sir John and Lady Delaval.

Has sent the harpsichord by two careful chairmen. She may pay the 22 guineas to Master Brown, who brings a receipt.

The same to the same.

Has sent the harpsichord away, and has paid the 22 guineas to the gentleman whose property it was. Assures her that it is worth 40 guineas. April 10.

Dr. Percy to Sir John and Lady Hussey Delaval with some trifling rhimes which accompany this billet. The Duchess and Lord Algernon have happily met in Germany, and are returned to the Hague, where the Duchess has had a slight touch of gout. Northumberland House, May 18, 1771.

The verses no longer accompany the letter.

Charles Nethercott to Sir John Delaval. Here I exist like a stray goose upon a wild and inhospitable common, knowing nobody, and everybody even with me. I was at my brother's seat in Essex [Thoby, near Ingatestone]. I lay at an inn the night before I saw him. Next morning I dressed and went to church, and directly into the pew where he was. For thirty years I had not seen him. The parson had begun divine service. At me my brother stared, and nature rose in his face. I looked at him. We were both silent. At last he spoke, seized me in his arms, cried out, "My brother, my dearest brother, brother," burst into tears, and the whole congregation melted. This brought crowds to see him while I stayed, and I lived in clover for a month till my evil genius dragged me here. Hull, 28 Oct. 1771.

MSS. OF LADY WATERFORD.

The same to the same. Wilkinson and his buffoons are gone hence yesterday for York, upon an average a very middling company. Wilkinson spoilt Townly in the Provoked Husband; and Mrs. Usher in lady Townly was deficient though pompous to the last degree and ungracious, two very capital faults. Wilkinson has humour in comedy, and especially in some of our pantomimes. He does Mungo well, and Midas, and [in] the Commissary he is inimitable. Powell totally destroyed Marc Anthony on Thursday evening last, and gave me great disgust, as that is a favourite character of mine. Cleopatra was ruined by Mrs. McGeorge, but Mrs. Usher made double amends in Octavia. When she appeared with the late Frodsham's two children by her side and presented the sweet, tender supplicants to Anthony, *that* scene tore my very heart-strings. In the Merchant of Venice Wilkinson is an excellent Shylock, and Mrs. McGeorge is very moving in Portia. They have lost Mrs. King, the best Mourning Bride in Europe, and the best Sir Harry Wildair I ever saw. She is gone to Dublin at eleven pounds per week, whereas Wilkinson could give but one guinea to her with a benefit, of which he always secures the best half to himself. So much for theatrical exhibitions. Hull, 9 January 1773.

Letter from Samuel Foote to [Sir John ?] Delaval.
Ten thousand thanks to you, my dear Sir, for your more than polite, your very kind and friendly letter. What cordial can so effectually soften the solitude or alleviate the anguish of a sickbed as the soothings of a sympathising friend ! why then would you wish to let the flames rob me of what is above all price ? Blessings on Lady Delaval's enterprising hand !
Will your Ladyship convey to Lady Northumberland my most grateful acknowledgement for two great goodnesses to me ? Can a lady whose extensive benevolence has showered blessings upon a whole people, descend to search out and pour balm into the wounds of a brokenhearted individual ? May that Providence, the amiable dispenser of whose benefits she has long continued to be, long, very long preserve to us her ministering hand; and when she is called to receive the reward of her humanity, charity and every Christian and moral excellence, may there never be wanting a lineal descendant to perpetuate her illustrious house and personal virtues to latest posterity.
I suppose you know that the Duke of York has been here these three days. You likewise know with what singular humanity and generosity he behaved at the time of my dreadful calamity. He warmly expressed a desire of securing me from the only additional distress that can now befall me ;—Poverty. I took the liberty to mention to his Royal Highness that a patent from the Crown for the house in the Haymarket during my life would protect me from want; that I had hitherto been permitted to exhibit there at only the time that no other playhouse would open

MSS. OF LADY WATERFORD. their doors; that I had been obliged to write all that was spoke there, I speak almost all that was wrote; that from the uncertainty of my tenure, the Chamberlain's staff so often shifting into different hands, I could not venture to engage proper assistants or decorate the theatre in a manner worthy the guests that I have very often the honour to see there; that my strength and helpless condition would prevent me from doing what I hitherto had done; that the grant would be an injury to none from the great increase of the capital, and that I had some reason to think the public would be rather pleased to see me possessed of this little provision. His Royal Highness had the goodness to approve of the plan, and to promise me all his assistance. I find the Duke has mentioned it to my Lord Chamberlain. His Grace most readily concurred in the propriety of the Duke of York's application, so that I am in great hopes my little scheme will succeed.

With regard to my health, about which I am sure your friendship will make you solicitous, I am better rather from what I am told than what I personally feel. I am week, in pain, and get no sleep but from opiates; but however the artery's bleeding is stopped, and they flatter me that in less than a fortnight I shall be upon crutches, and then with safety may be conducted to London. This I wish; not that change of place can make much difference to a man in my unfortunate way, but that I may have an opportunity of returning you and Lady Delaval my personal thanks for the goodness, humanity and friendship with which you have honoured your poor unfortunate, obliged and devoted servant,

SAMUEL FOOTE.

Cannon Park, March 19.

Mr. Townshend has wrote me a most friendly letter indeed, and so has Mr. Fitzherbert.

Samuel Foote to Sir Francis Delaval. Is afraid of the journey of 300 miles to Seaton. The fall of India stock has ruined both the Wades, Garsei escaped from the bailiffs by the coup militaire. "I took your friend Macklyn with me to Stafford... The Duke of Cumberland wanted me to take a trip to your brother's in Lincolnshire. I declined it, as supposing we should not have been very welcome guests." Congratulates him on the narrow escape of Lady Danvers and her daughter. North End, October 2.

The same to the same. Sorry to give Sir George Savil such an unfavourable opinion of his comedy. It is a most execrable composition. Is obliged to Lord and Lady Mexborough for their invitation. Tomorrow has the Garricks, male and female, Mrs. Hale and Chetwynd to dine with him. The King of Denmark has come; he does not understand a word of our language. Fulham, 11 August.

The same to the same. Congratulates him on his success at Andover. Is not astonished at Dr. Cameron's behaviour; persecution is the parent of obstinacy. His friend Mrs. Evan (?) has retired to a convent. The spirit of Mrs. Woym (?) is sowered against him. Encloses an answer to their friend Cleland. Lord Pulteny has arrived at Angers to digest his matrimonial disappointment. Anjou, June 7.

The same to the same. Lord and Lady Mexborough and Lady Stanhope are coming to visit him. Asks Sir Francis to come and to bring his brother Edward. Berham Wood, Monday.

The same to the same.

"I have fixed my abode at Blackheath. Has been to a ship launching at Woolwich, where we had the Royal family and Miss Roach.... Murphy promises greatly, both as author and actor. We have Hew

Daucus (?) Woffington, &c. &c., so that upon the whole I fancy Rich will make a powerful opposition next winter. . . Wade has renewed his flirtation with Woffington."

MSS. OF LADY WATERFORD.

The same to the same. Nothing new at Paris but a tragedy of Voltaire called Rome Preserved. The subject was chosen in direct opposition to Crebillion, but if crowded houses and universal applause are testimonies of merit, Voltaire must be allowed infinite . . . Taaf and Montagu are in the opinion of their judges perfectly justified. Wade is here, and we are generally together. Paris, Feb. 18. Chez Mr. Selwyn, Banquier.

The same to John Delaval, Esq. "The Dover Street cavalcade arrived here this morning." Is greatly distressed for want of a man cook. Compliments to the family in Downing Street. Watlington park, near Nettlebed.

The same to Lady Hussy Delaval. "The poor unfortunate Foote has designed himself the honour of thanking your Ladyship for your great goodness and humanity to him; but he was desirous of waiting till an hour's relaxation from pain might enable him to do some little justice to the obligations your Ladyship has laid him under, and his grateful sense of them. But not now knowing when that turn will come (an artery having burst yesterday and exhausted a large quantity of blood) he begs you will accept this mean but honest effusion of a heart warmed and truly sensible of your compassionate kindness to him.

God bless you! God bless you! and guard (as far as our nature is capable of) your door from every human ill. Thank my good, my constant, my worthy friend Sir John, for all his favours, and particularly for his tender benevolent feelings on the present melancholy occasion. What a trouble I have been to all your family! But don't let me add to it by the length of this scrawl, which I am afraid has tired your Ladyship and very near exhausted your most obliged, devoted and most grateful humble servant, Samuel Foote."

Charles Macklin to Sir Francis Blake Delaval, in Downing Street. Has received his of 30 January. The play has been introduced at Court by Lady Mannington, a woman of strict decorum, Sir Harry's guardian's daughter. Does not understand what he means by the condition of Plyades. "I get a great deal of money here, and a player's and an author's *summum bonum*, full houses and applause, but I have no Delaval. I live retired, quite sequestrated, and deep in the buskin. The subject is "The true born Irishman;" it comes out the first week in March. The public expectation is high, I am fairly on my country, to be tried by my Peers. Mirth and Satire send me a good deliverance! Sans puff, the stream is with us. "Love à la Mode" is the rage. 180*l*. every time it is played, which is equal to 270*l*. in Covent Garden. Barry plays Sir Callaghan well, and never appeared to such advantage. Missop has called in burlettas to his aid, which have wounded his pride and injured his consequence; for that part of the public who followed his tragedies have followed the burlettas for about twelve nights, but have neglected him, so that he cannot draw 40*l*., and now the burlettas begin to sink and will go quite down, it is thought. . . . . I can have a vast sum of money here for next winter; more than I have for this a great deal, for acting and producing two new farces. That is a retreat, however; if the London market is full the Dublin market is not. Well, I shall stop here till the play is over. P.S.—75*l*. was due in June, which I received in October; 75*l*. was due last December, that you are to pay directly."

MSS. OF LADY WATERFORD.

The same (in Dorset Street. Dublin), to the same in Downing Street. Reasons why he remains in Dublin, but anxious to return to London. Has agreed to act six nights with Barry at one or two nights a week Will not stir till he hears from him again. 13 Dec. 1766.

The same to Francis Blake Delaval, Esq., Andover. "Your hairbreadth escapes and the imminent political breach between you and the Governor of Andover, and your defeat of the turtle shielded, Highland-oaten-bonnetted-Haynau-American-here-and-thereian, mungrel hero, have made us laugh heartily. I have whole armies of wits, critics, scribblers, fools, men of sense and women to encounter, with an &c. &c. that would puzzle Shakspear himself to describe. In plain English, on Tuesday next the poetical fate of Macklin and the marry'd libertine is to be decided."

The same [to the same]. Advises prudence and patience in the present contest. "I could not afford to lose the winter, and my theatrical prospect in London was most precarious. Here I have a large sum of money, 600l. English, am to play but till the end of March but twice in each week and not at all in the Christmas holidays, and the managers will gain considerably by the agreement; for the Merchant of Venice hath brought in three nights above 450l. Love à la Mode was played for the first time against a burletta supported by subscription and powerful interest to 160, and the second time and within three days of the first to 170, and on Christmas Eve too, and the House is taken over and over again to it. In short, it is in much higher reputation here than ever it was in London. . . . Othello has brought three great houses. The other parts I played, which were the Miser, Wronghead and Don Choleric, had but common receipts to them, about 20l. each."

Half of the second leaf of this letter has been torn away, and the portion so mutilated is unintelligible.

David Garrick to [Sir John Hussey Delaval].

March 26, Hampton.

Dear Sir,

I have not had a single moment to myself since I came here; and upon consideration, any comments that I could write in the hurry I am in at present would only confound and mislead. It is a very difficult matter to describe with accuracy and precision the tones and actions which would be necessary to execute such and such passages. It is my opinion that every other method but rehearsals before the person you may think capable of instructing you, would rather be of disservice than otherwise to the speaker.

I shall therefore say in general that a *fix'd* attention to the business of the scene, which Lady Stanhope has to the greatest perfection, is the *sine qua non* of acting. In the speaking of soliloquies the great art is to give variety, and which only can be obtained by a strict regard to the pauses. The mixing of the different parts of a monologue together will necessarily give a monotony, and take away the spirit and sense of the author.

I shall always be happy to contribute everything in my power to your pleasure, and if you will favour me with a letter, and are of opinion that I can solve any questions in your present undertaking, I will send the best answer in my power and immediately. Therefore don't spare me; for I shall be proud to throw in my mite to an entertainment which will give so much pleasure to the spectators and do honour to the undertakers.

MSS. OF LADY WATERFORD.

I am,
Dear Sir,
Most truly your obedient and obliged humble servant,
D. GARRICK.

There was one passage in Lothario which I thought at the time his Royal Highness might have spoken with more levity, and a kind of profligate insensibility to the distress of Calista. It was this speech—
—"with uneasy fondness
She hung upon me," &c.*

I must beg you once again to employ me how you please and as often [as] you please, if you think I can be of the least service to you.

" A Catalogue of Books and Plays, French and English."
Among these occur " The Scotch Rogue," by General Græme.
" Long Meg of Westminster," by Miss Mary Rich.
" Tom Thumb the Great," in folio, by Sir Francis Blake Delaval.
" Male Coquet," by Lord March.
" Pattern for Husbands," by Sir John Hussey Delaval.
" Love in a Bottle," by Mr. Fielding.
" Restorer of Castles," by the Duke of Northumberland.
" The Poltroon," by Lord Orwell.

A note, of which the following is a copy :—
" Mr. Kemble asks Lady Delaval to patronise an evening's performance at the Theatre in North Shields for Thursday 10 inst. Appended is a Catalogue of Plays and Farces."

G. Inchbald to Lord Delaval, asks for the loan of two guineas. Theatre, Cardiff, April 15, 97.

JOS. STEVENSON.

THE MANUSCRIPTS OF LORD HOTHFIELD.

Lord Hothfield deposited in the Public Record Office for examination by the Commissioners a few packets of correspondence of the families of Clifford and Tufton,-Earls of Cumberland and of Thanet. The greater portion of these documents relates purely to domestic affairs, and their chief interest consists in the autographs appended to them. Among them are letters from George third Earl of Cumberland, when commanding at sea, to his wife ; others are from the Countess to her husband, and to her daughter the famous Anne Clifford, who became by marriage Countess of Dorset, Pembroke, and Montgomery. To the latter lady the greater number of the other letters are addressed, many of them being endorsed by remarks in her own handwriting. There are letters signed by Queen Elizabeth, and by James I. ; also a holograph letter of the Princess Elizabeth of Bohemia to Lady Pembroke dated

MSS. OF LORD HOTHFIELD.

---

* The passage here referred to occurs in Rowe's " Fair Penitent," Act 1, scene 1, p. 16 of Tonson's edition of 1766. A copy of this edition in old green binding, with the passages marked for omission, with stage directions and other notes, is in the collection of books at Ford Castle.

MSS. OF LORD HOTHFIELD.

from the Hague on the 1st of January, but no year is given, which is written in a very friendly style.

The following copies and abstracts of the papers include all matter of historical import that was noted when perusing them.

1578. Sept 27. Isleworth. Margaret Countess of Derby to her brother the Earl of Cumberland, touching the illness of the Earl's wife, and the preparations for her visit to Isleworth.

[1586] George Earl of Cumberland to the Countess.

My suite Mege,—I pray thy lett me here as soune as thou canst of the metynge betuixte your sunne Francis and you houe he dothe and hou poure vobci (?) got home. Sence your goinge I have allmost dispashad all my busines my shippes be upon the point of goinge, lyckelyer noue to sped well then ever for it is sertayne Sir Fra. Dracke hathe taken one of the chefest tounes in all the Indayes cauled Sante Domyngoe and in it thry hunderethe thousand duckettes and infinet other weltho, all the pepell of the cuntri folou him and he is very stronge. Ther is cum hether an embasator from the kynge of Denmarcke, he had open audience before the Quene in the presence chamber, the efecte of his message was to wyshe pece betuxte hus and Spayne which is thought will tacke noe effect noue this nues is cum from Sir Francis. All thynges in Flanderres gooe very well, sence your goinge doune ther hathe 5 or 6 hunderethe spanyardes bene slayne. Harry Cunstable is knyghted, my sute goethe well forward and I hope soune to be wythe my swite dery. Thus desierynge the to commend me to my brother and sister Wharton, to my ounc brother, a thousand to thye selfe with goddes blessynge and myne to all the litell ons I ende. Thyne ever

GEORGE CUMBRELAND.

1589-90, Jan. 5. Warwick House. George Earl of Cumberland to the Countess.

Announces his safe arrival with his ship and company, and though they have tasted some extremities, yet he himself was never better, and never lost fewer men. Would willingly have delivered the news himself, but with so many men lying upon his charge he can no way stir.

n.y. Oct. 23. From the Lion. Same to same.

Has taken a Dunkirk ship bound for Saint Lucas in Spain, has sent Lister to see her unladen in Portsmouth and to send all that is his to the Countess, which he would have her use according to her discretion. If there be anything fit to give the Lord Chamberlain he would have her do it; it will make him the readier to do for the writer if there be cause. The man he has taken tells him there are four ships now ready in Dunkirk going for Spain. Hopes within three days to meet them; if he does he will make a good voyage.

1589-90, Feb. 6. An affectionate letter of the Earl endorsed by Anne Countess of Pembroke as "writt to my Mother presently after my Berthe when hee then laye att Bedford howse att London."

n.y. Jan. 14. Newark. Same to same.

It is told for certainty my Lord of Huntingdon is made Lieutenant of the North parts, and is said in secret for truth that when he is to receive his commission he shall receive great sums of money, to what end is yet unknown.

n.y. March 13. Berwick. P. Willoughby to the Countess of Cumberland.

A long and high-flown letter of thanks and compliments from which the following extract will suffice. "I can not particular all the cause I have to give you thanks, my paper must be a worlde, the ink a sea and my hand a soule, but I may not forget these last, your elect history and your passionat Octavia [*Cleopatra* struck out]. To the last I say as Daniel to Nebucadnezur be this dreame far from the king and happen it on his enemies. If you have any she ones I wishe them worse than Antonies, for whan all is said that may be Antony was a good felow, Cleopatra a sunnshine day, and Octavia a ritch clasped boke wherein all the secrets of all good wifery is contayned. Good Maddam, let not my wife open it therefore least she become a proselite, forsake hur bible and mistake my name."

MSS. OF LORD HOTHFIELD.

1615, June 10. Anne, Countess of Dorset to the Countess of Cumberland. "Maddam, I have returned the kese of thos writings which your Ladyship sent mee agane to you, and for all the state of my bisneses Raffe can informe your Ladyship more perfectley then I can write, and houe my Lorde William Howord hathe shoed himsellfe verey constant to me in this bisnes, therfore if it wer not a thing to much contrarey to your minde I wolld humbley desire your Ladyship pase by all thoes unkindneses that heere to fore hathe bin ofred you, and to gooe to see his Ladey and to give him maney thankes for his favouer to mee, hee hathe parted with that rooge Bemond, which was onse your La. man, so as it seemes to mee hee is verey desirous of your love and frinship, and your Ladyship knos Soloman himsellfe sayes it is wisdome for a man to pase by an ofense, but I refer it holley to your plesner. I have sent you by Rafe my pictuer don in litell, which some sayes is verey like mee, and others sayes it dothe mee rather ronge then flatters mee, I knoe you will excepte the shodoe of her hous [whose] sobstance is com from yoursellfe. I hope you will requite mee with the same kindnes and lett me have yours when ether you come upe to London or when so ever aney that can draughe a pictuer comes in to thos parts wher nou you ar. For my muche desired jurney of coming to your Ladyship I can send you no good nues, for my Lorde will not by aney mens give his consent that I sholld gooe till the bisnes beetwene my Unckell of Comberland and him be ended. Thus nesesetey cares me from that whiche I most desire, I hope God will make ouer meeting joyfull, though it bee longe defered, for never was ther thinge more desired of one then that is by mee. My Ladey Margaret Sackvill hath sent your Ladyship 2 asses and on of her beggyles (beagles?) which is Jon's pupey, and I hope hee will bee a good water (*sic*). Thus humbley desiring your blessing to mee and mine I rest.

Your Ladyship's most loving and obedient daughter,

ANNE DORSET.

From Bellbrooke the 10 of June 1615.
To the Right Honorable my deere mother the Countes of Coumberland."

1615, Dec. 8. Mary Countess of Shrewsbury to the Countess of Cumberland.
Thanks for her sympathy with her hard fortuno in the heavy loss of the Lady Arabella. Hopes she died a Saint. Her weakness was not known to the writer till she was in all men's opinions that were about her to have died that night, which was about 2 days before her death, and the next morning I was made to believe she was much better. Is unfit to write of any other matter when her heart is possessed with this.

1616, April 1. "Memorandum that I Anne Countess of Dorset, sole daughter and heir to George late Earl of Cumberland, doth take witness

MSS. OF LORD HOTHFIELD.

of all these gentlemen present, that I both desire and offer myself to go up to London with my men and horses, but they having received a contrary commandment from my Lord my husband will (*sic*) by no means consent nor permit me to go with them, now my desire is that all the world may know that this stay of mine proceeds only from my husband's command, contrary to my consent or agreement, whereto I have gotten these names underwritten to testify the same."

Signed by Margaret Countess of Cumberland, Christopher Lowther, Mary Lowther, Christ. Pykeringe, Christopher Crakanthorppe, Ro. Doumvile, James Belassys, &c.

1652, May 12. The Earl of Northampton to the Countess of Pembroke, at Skipton Castle.

Concerning the unfortunate fate of his cousin Henry Compton, slain in a duel by Lord Shandoys. They did fight three to three, Lord Shandoys, Lord Arundel of Wardour, and Mr. Hatton Riche on one side, his cousins Henry and John Compton, and one Mr. Stuart Walker on the other; the survivors were all fled.

1660 or 1661. Draft of the reply to the Commissioners for taking subscriptions of Peers and Peeresses, upon the Act for a Free and Voluntary Present to His Majesty.

The Countess of Pembroke certifies that though her law suits and repair of her decayed houses in these parts have very much exhausted her, yet the zeal and duty she bears to his Majesty and his service are such as (though her ability be less) she would not be behindhand with any of her condition and quality in testifying the great joy she has for the King's happy restoration. She therefore takes the boldness to subscribe for the payment of £400 at the end of the following November, as soon as her jointure rents shall be received.

1661, October 22. Lincoln's Inn Fields. The Earl of Northampton to the Countess of Pembroke, at Appleby Castle.

Refers to the irreparable loss of his dear wife (daughter of Lady Pembroke), whose body is gone down to lie among his ancestors and family at Compton. All his brothers, except Henry who was commanded by his major to his troop there being suspicions of a disturbance, went quite through to Compton; his brother Thanet and his sister went 10 miles; the Countess of Devonshire and others had their coaches there; Dr. Hardy, Dean of Rochester, is to preach the funeral sermon.

1663, Sept. 11. Westminster. Commissioners for the Subsidy to the Countess of Pembroke.

Desire her to pay to John Clutterbook, gent., appointed Collector, the sum of four score pounds at which she has been assessed for the first two of the four subsidies granted to the King by Parliament.

The signatures of Lords Southampton, Clare, Roberts, and Newport, the Duke of Albemarle, Lord Craven, and Sir Chr. Hatton are appended.

1663–4, Feb. 22. Rose Castle. Richard, Bishop of Carlisle, to Anne Countess Dowager of Pembroke.

Understands by Sir Philip Musgrave that she is pleased to give way to the exchange of Brougham and Caldbeck, whereby two worthy men may be pleasured, and God and his Church in both places well served. Craves to be excused from making her castle his inn, his time being but short; purposes to have a confirmation at Penrith on Wednesday March 2, and at Appleby on Thursday March 3.

1664, May 10. Richard Clapham to George Sedgwick, at Appleby Castle.
Lord Thanet died on the previous Friday night. Particulars of his will, &c.

MSS. OF LORD HOTHFIELD.

1665, June 12. Compton House. The Earl of Northampton to the Countess of Pembroke.
Her ladyship will have heard of the great victory it has pleased God to bless us with over the Dutch, though with the loss of many worthy and eminent persons, as the Earl of Marlborough who commanded the great James, and in the Duke of York's own ship one shot killed the Earls of Portland and Falmouth, the Lord Muskerry (who married my aunt Clanricarde's sole daughter and heir), and Mr. Boyle, one of the Earl of Cork's sons.
Report (afterwards contradicted), that Lord Wharton was dead of the plague.

1665, June 27. Hothfield. The Earl of Thanet to the same.
The loss of Dick Boyle makes a sad house at Whitefriars, and little did my Lady of Burlington when she was so merry lately at Hothfield think of that fatal cannon shot that cut in two her son, and to aggravate the grief, the misfortune to have the rude sea-men fling the remaining part of his body which the cannon left into the sea.

1665, July 14. Epsom. Margaret Countess of Thanet to the Countess Dowager of Pembroke, at Brougham Castle.
Sir Kenelm Digby did not die in Somerset house, but at lodgings in Covent Garden.
The Queen mother went out of town on the 29th of last month, and the King and the Duke of York saw her on ship board, and she landed safe in France.
Where her daughter [Frances] Drax will lie in is uncertain, as the house they had bought is in St. Giles, where the plague is.

1665, August 7. (Winclandon?). Philip Lord Wharton to Anne Countess of Pembroke, at Brougham Castle.
Complains that some of her ladyship's tenants in Mallerstang very boldly and openly killed a sow, which very probably came out of Wharton Park, and suggests that she should proceed against and punish them. Refers to the obstruction of trade and commerce by reason of the sickness, and proposes that her rents due in the south should be paid to him at his house at Woburn in Bucks within 6 miles of Windsor, and from thence transferred to one of her ladyship's houses in Westmoreland or Craven.

1666, September 12. Stamford. The Countess of Thanet to the Countess Dowager of Pembroke, at Skipton Castle.
I thank God I came well last night to Stamford; and we are all very well; and I hear it confirmed that Thanet house is safe from the fire, and likewise Aldersgate Street, the nearest that it came my house was Surgeons' hall on the backside my garden, which is burnt down to the ground . . . the Goldsmiths have secured all their money in the Tower which is very happy. I hear that Dorset House is burnt down, but I hope it is not so. . . . Whether I have a bed left at Thanet house or no I do not know. . . . Lord Hatton doth confirm that all is burnt down from Pudding Lane that is near the Bear at the Bridge foot to Temple Bar. I have sent a man up to London to Fotherby, that if my beds be carried out of the house to get some of them in again, for it is

MSS. OF LORD HOTHFIELD. dangerous lodging for the plague and small pox, and scarce any lodging to be had.

1667, June 26 (endorsed August). Clarendon House. Lord Chancellor Clarendon to the Countess of Pembroke.

Some action of her ladyship in a suit before the Judges, having exposed her inferior officers to those inconveniences which the necessary course of law will bring upon them, he desires her for their sake to return a full answer to the Petitioner's Bill, and she may be assured not only of justice, but of all the respects which justly can be paid to her by the writer. The concluding portion only of the letter is in Lord Clarendon's handwriting.

1667–8, March 10. London. William Edge to the Countess Dowager of Pembroke, at Brougham Castle.

Lady Thanet will write to her ladyship concerning the election of Mr. Thomas Tufton, who is this day to be brought into the house by Sir Philip Musgrave and Mr. Dalston.

In addition to the above letters, three huge manuscript volumes of collections relating to the Clifford family and their connections were examined.

Part of the title page of the first Volume runs thus :—

"This is the First Booke of the Recordes concerning the two noble families of the Cliffords . . . . which Booke was compiled Anno 1649 By the care & industrie of the Lady Ann Clifford Countess of Dorsett, Pembrooke & Montgomerie, daughter & sole heire of Georg Clifford late Earle of Cumberland . . . . The cheife of which Records in this Booke was . . . . . gotten out of several Offices and Courts of this Kingdome" . . . . .

The heading of that portion of the third volume which contains the autobiography of Anne Clifford runs thus :—

"A Summary of the Records, and a true Memorial of the Life of me the Lady Anne Clifford who, by birth being sole daughter and heir to my illustrious father George Earl of Cumberland by his virtuous wife Margaret Russell my mother in right descent from him and his long continued noble ancestors the Veterriponts, Cliffords, and Vescies, was Baroness Clifford, Westmoreland, and Vescie, High Sheriffess of Westmoreland, and Lady of the Honor of Skipton in Craven, and was by my first marriage Countess Dowager of Dorset, and by my second marriage Countess Dowager of Pembroke and Montgomery."

Extracts from the manuscript containing this curious narrative, or from the copy of it among the Harleian manuscripts, have been printed before: but some of the selections which follow are new. The manuscript was evidently carefully revised by the Countess, as it bears occasional corrections and additions in her handwriting.

"I was through the providence of God begotten by my valiant father and conceived with child by my worthy mother the first day of May in one thousand five hundred and eight-nine in the Lord Wharton's house in Chanon Row in Westminster hard by the river of Thames, as *Psalm* 139. Yet I was not born till the thirtieth day of January following, when my mother brought me forth in one of my father's chief houses called Skipton Castle, in Craven. *Eccl.*, *chap.* 3. For she came down into the north from London with her two sons, being great with child with me, my father then being in great peril at sea in one of his voyages ; for both a little before he begot me and a little after it was ten thousand to one but that he had been cast away on the seas by tempests and contrary winds. Yet it pleased God to preserve him so as he lived to see my birth and a good while after, for I was fifteen years and nine months old when he died.

MSS. OF LORD HOTHFIELD.

And some seven weeks before my mother was delivered of me died her eldest son, the Lord Francis Clifford, in the said Castle of Skipton; and the two and twentieth day of February after my birth was I christened by the name of Anne in the parish church of Skipton, Philip Lord Wharton my aunt's husband being then my godfather, my father being then at London, as he was also when I was born. For he landed in England the twenty-ninth of December before I was born, by reason of his great business of giving accounts to the Queen of his sea voyages, and he lying then at Bedford house in the Strand, where Ambrose Earl of Warwick died the day before I was christened, who was husband to my mother's eldest sister the excellent Anne Russell Countess of Warwick.

About the last of March my father came down to Skipton Castle to us, which was the first time that ever he saw me (I being then near eight weeks old). And the second of April following, my father and my mother carrying my brother Robert and myself along with them, went quite away from thence towards London, and I never came into that after that time till the eighteenth of July in one thousand six hundred forty and nine, when my second Lord was then living, for he died not till the thirtieth of January following. And about six months before my then removing thither, the said Castle had then been demolished, and the principal buildings thereof quite pulled down by order of Parliament, having been made and kept as a garrison in the late civil wars. *Eccl.*, *chap.* 8, *ver.* 6.

I was but some ten weeks old when I came first up to London. Yet did not I nor my mother return again into the north till after the death of my father, remaining both of us in the southern parts as Northamptonshire, Hertfordshire, Kent, Berkshire, and Surrey, and in and about the court, and city of London all that time.

When I was about a year and four months old died my second brother Robert, then Lord Clifford, in Northhall in Hertfordshire the four and twentieth of May, in one thousand five hundred ninety-one; and ever after that time I continued to be the only child of my parents, nor had they any other daughter but myself.

I was very happy in my first constitution both in my mind and body, both for internal and external endowments, for never was there child more equally resembling both father and mother than myself. The colour of mine eyes was black like my father's and the form and aspect of them was quick and lively like my mother's. The hair of mine head was brown and very thick, and so long as that it reached to the calf of my legs when I stood upright; with a peak of hair on my forehead, and a dimple in my chin like my father, full cheeks and round faced like my mother, and an exquisite shape of body resembling my father; but now time and age hath long since ended all these beauties, which are to be compared to the grass of the field — as *Isaiah*, *chap.* 40, *verse* 6, 7, 8; 1 *Peter*, *chap.* 1, *verse* 24. For now when I caused these memorials of my life to be written, I have passed the sixty-third year of my age.

And though I say it the perfections of my mind were much above those of my body. I had a strong and copious memory, a sound judgment, and a discerning spirit, and so much of a strong imagination in me as that many times even my dreams and apprehensions beforehand

MSS. OF
LORD
HOTHFIELD.

proved to be true. So as old Master John Denham, a great astronomer, that sometimes lived in my father's house, would often say that I had much in me in nature to show that the sweet influences of the Pleiades and the bonds of Orion mentioned in that thirty-eight chapter of *Job*, *verse* 31, 32, 33, were powerful both at my conception and nativity. But happy births are many times attended on by cross fortunes in this world, which, nevertheless, I overcame by the divine mercy of Almighty God,—*Psalm* 121. And from my childhood by the bringing up of my said dear mother, I did as it were even suck the milk of goodness, which made my mind grow strong against the storms of fortune, which few avoid that are greatly born and matched, if they attain to any number of years, unless they betake themselves to a private retiredness, which I could never do till after the death of both my husbands. In my infancy and childhood by the means of my said aunt of Warwick, I was much beloved by that renowned Queen Elizabeth, who died when I was about thirteen years and two months old; and my mother outlived that excellent Queen the same time of thirteen years and two months over.

And the first of September in one thousand six hundred and five was the last time I ever saw my father in the open air, for then I took my leave of him on Greenwich heath in Kent, as he brought me so far on my way towards Sutton in Kent, where my mother then lay after I had been and stayed the space of a month in the old house at Grafton in Northamptonshire, where my father then lived by reason of some unhappy unkindness towards my mother, and where he entertained King James and Queen Anne with magnificence—which was a time of great sorrow to my saintlike mother till I returned back again to her from my father the said first day of September—*Psalm* 90, *v.* 15, 16, 17.

The thirtieth day of October (being Thursday) one thousand six hundred and five in the third year of the reign of King James died my noble and brave father, George Earl of Cumberland in the Dutchy House by the Savoy at London near the river of Thames, when he was almost three months past forty seven years old, my mother and I being present with him at his death, I being then just fifteen years and nine months old the same day; where a little before his death he expressed with much affection to my mother and me, and a great belief that he had that his brother's son would die without issue male, and thereby all his lands would come to be mine, which accordingly befell about thirty eight years after, for his brother's son Henry Earl of Cumberland died without heirs male in the city of York the eleventh of December one thousand six hundred forty and three.

. . . .

I must not forget to acknowledge that in my infancy and youth and a great part of my life I have escaped many dangers both by fire and water, by passage in coaches and falls from horses, by burning fevers and excessive extremity of bleeding, many times to the great hazard of my life, all which and many cunning devices of my enemies I have escaped and passed through miraculously, and much the better by the prayers of my devout mother, who incessantly begged of God for my safety and preservation.—*James, c.* 5, *v.* 6."

[After giving a lengthy account of the suits at law and other disputes between her uncle, the new Earl of Cumberland, and her mother the writer proceeds.]

"I must confess with inexpressible thankfulness that though through the goodness of Almighty God and the mercies of our Saviour Christ Jesus, Redeemer of the world, I was born a happy creature in mind, body, and fortune, and that those two Lords of mine to whom I was afterwards by the Divine providence married were in their several kinds worthy noble men as any there were in this kingdom, yet was it my misfortune to have contradiction and crosses with them both. With my first Lord about the desire he had to make me sell my right in the lands of my ancient inheritance for money, which I never did nor never would consent unto; insomuch as the matter was the cause of a long contention betwixt us, as also for his profuseness in consuming his estate and some other extravagances of his.

MSS. OF LORD HOTHFIELD.

And with my second Lord because my youngest daughter, the Lady Isabella Sackville, would not be brought to marry one of his younger sons, and that I would not relinquish the interest I had in five thousand pounds, being part of her portion out of my lands in Craven. Nor did there want divers malicious willers to blow and foment the coals of discontent betwixt us. So as in both their lifetimes the marble pillars of Knole in Kent and Wilton in Wiltshire were to me oftentimes but the gay harbours of anguish. Insomuch as a wise man that knew the inside of my fortunes would often say that I lived in both these my Lords' great families as the river of Rhone or Rhodanus runs through the Lake of Geneva without mingling any part of its streams with that Lake—for I gave myself wholly to retiredness, as much as I could in both those great families, and make good books and virtuous thoughts my companions, which can never deserve affliction nor be daunted when it unjustly happeneth, and by a happy genius I overcame all these troubles, the prayers of my blessed mother helping me therein.

The twenty-fifth day of February one thousand six hundred and nine as the year begins on New Year's day, I was married to my first husband, Lord Richard Sackville, then but Lord Buckhurst, in my mother's house, and her own chamber in Augustine Friars in London, which was part of a chapel there formerly, she being then present at my marriage.

And within two days after I was married died my said Lord's father, Robert Sackville, Earl of Dorset, in little Dorset House in Salisbury Court at London, by whose death my said Lord and I came to be Earl and Countess of Dorset.—*Job*, c. 7, v. 1.

And the twenty-fifth day of July one thousand six hundred and ten, a year and five months after my said first marriage was my cousin german Henry Lord Clifford, only son to my uncle of Cumberland, married at Kensington, near London, to the Lady Frances Cecil, daughter to Robert Earl of Salisbury, Lord High Treasurer of England, & then the greatest man of power in the kingdom, which marriage was purposely made that by that power and greatness of his the lands of mine inheritance might be wrested an I kept by strong hand from me. Which notwithstanding came not to pass by the providence of God, for the issue male which they had between them all died, and they left only one daughter behind them, who is now Countess of Cork."

[Then follow accounts of her children, three sons and two daughters— the sons died young, but the daughters became Countess of Thanet and Countess of Northampton respectively; of the great law suit in 1615 about her estates and its settlement; the death of her mother in 1616 at Brougham Castle in Westmoreland; the death of her husband in 1624, and the malice of his brother Edward. Her second marriage to Philip, Earl of Pembroke took place on 3 June 1630. In 1641 died her uncle

MSS. OF LORD HOTHFIELD. the Earl of Cumberland, and nearly three years afterwards his only son.]

"And when the Civil Wars between the King and the parliament began to grow hotter and hotter in England, my said Lord and I came together from Wilton (12 Oct. 1642) with my younger daughter, then the Lady Isabella Sackville, and the next day we came to London, where my said Lord went to lie at his lodgings in the Cockpit in Saint James's park over against Whitehall to be near the parliament. But I and my daughter went to live in Baynard's Castle, which was then a house full of riches and was the more secured by my lying there, where then I continued to lie in my own chamber, without removing, six years and nine months."

[In 1649 she visited Skipton and Appleby Castles, for the first time since her infancy, she having succeeded to the Clifford estates in Yorkshire and Westmoreland on the death of her cousin.

After the Countess's removal to the North, her narrative assumes more the form of a diary, but has little of historical value. It is mainly a record of her changes of residence from Skipton to Appleby, and from Appleby to Skipton, varied by occasional sojourns at Brougham Castle; the births and deaths of the members of her family, and their connections, and of the visits paid to her by them; the visits also of many of the judges when on circuit; her endless lawsuits with her Westmoreland tenants; and the rebuilding or repairing of the many castles, churches, chapels, &c. on her estates. The last event recorded is the death of her worthy cousin Sir John Lowther, when about 73 years old, on 30 November 1675. The Countess herself died at Brougham Castle on the 22nd March following, and was buried in Appleby church.]

W. O. HEWLETT.

THE MANUSCRIPTS OF FRANCIS DARWIN, ESQ., OF CRESKELD, CO. YORK.

DARWIN MSS.

THIS collection includes a very complete series of deeds relating to the manors of Gringley on the hill, and Eyleston or Elston, co. Notts. Among the earlier ones the following seem most noteworthy :—

n. d. Alice daughter of Eva de Grenley grants to Hugh son of Robert de Grenley lands in Grenley for one penny rent. Witnesses— John son of Robert de Grenley, Richard his brother, Adam son of Herbert de Grenley, &c.

n. d. Baldwin Wac confirms the grant made to the canons of St. Peter "de Brunna" by Baldwin son of Gilbert, Adelina his wife, and Hugh Wac his father, of the churches of Brunna, Morton, Helpingham, Westdeeping, Hicham, Scelingou, Bercham, Stowe, and Trapeston. Witnesses—Roger and Hugh Wac, Helias de Baiocis, Hugh and Walter de Boebi, Thomas and Peter de Anesi, Ralph de Briwecurt, Baldwin de Waspa, &c., &c.

1276. St. Wilfrid's day. Retford. Alexander son of Henry le Norays of Clawurth grants to Walter Prat of Retford, for a certain sum paid to him and an annual rent of one penny, five acres of land in Grenelay with a meadow lying in le Holmer. Witnesses—William de Grenelay, Thomas Daniel of the same, John Prat de Retford, Hugh Brun, Robert son of John the tanner, Adam Scotus, Adam Leveret, Elias de Retford, clerk, and others.

1278. Retford. Robert son of Henry of Tyreswelle and Alice Hirdman wife of Robert, grants to John son of Robert de Grenlay, for a certain sum of money paid to them, a rood and a half of land in Sulcroft in the territory of Grenlay, at one halfpenny rent in lieu of all services. Two seals attached.

DARWIN MSS.

1285. Hugh son of Hugh de Grenley grants lands to Ralph Prat of Grenley, for a certain sum of money paid to him, and an annual rent of two silver pennies.

1282. Vigil of St. James the Apostle. Derby. Hugh de Gurneye dwelling in Bolton by Derby, with the consent of his lords Robert de Saucheverel and Robert de Dethek, grants all his lands and tenements in Bolton and Alwaston to the abbot and convent of Parcho stanl'. Witnesses—Hugo de Stredleg, William de Shaddesden, John Fennel, knts., Ralph Saucheverel, William le Fraunceys de Osmund, and others. One seal.

n. d. Adam son of Ric. de Grenelay assigns to Thos. son of Ric. de Grenelay one acre of land in the territory of Grenelay, for one halfpenny rent and the sum of eight shillings paid down "in mea necessitate." Witnesses—Robert de Wuntona, Adam son of Ralph, William son of Leveneti, Geoffrey de Marcha, Thorald his brother, and others.

n. d. Magister Alanus de Bolleshouere brother and heir of Henry Norreus grants to Philip de Ulecotes his land "de Clay" in Stretton, in Fenton, in Leirton, in Greneley, in Retford, and in Weston, which the Lord J. king of England gave to Henry Norreus his brother when he (John) was Earl of Moreton, and afterwards confirmed when he was king, for the service "unius paris calcarium deaurator' domino regi ad Pentecost' reddendor'," &c. Witnesses—Reginald de Rupe, Richard de Wellebec', abbots, William, prior of Blida, Will and Elias de Buelwell, Robert de Wlrigton', Reginald de Bernevall, John de Harewrch, Robert de Clifford, and others. One seal.

1294. Retford. William son of Adam Leveneth of Retford grants to Roger son of William Leveneth of the same, for a certain sum paid to him, half an acre of land "in campo de Grenley." Witnesses—Robert son of John the tanner of Retford, Thomas Danyel of Grenley, &c. One seal.

All the deeds relating to Elston in this collection appear to have been copied into a large volume by Robert Darwin, who was born in 1682 and died in 1754; he began the work in Nov. 1743, according to a note made in the volume. The property to which the deeds have reference had passed into his hands from the Lascelles family in 1708. This volume also contains copies of seventeenth century deeds concerning lands in Kirton, Marton, and Lincoln.

Among the letters and papers of later date at Creskeld are the following:—

1643, Dec. 1. At our Court at Oxford. Charles I. to all Sheriffs, Colonels, &c. whom it may concern. Having formerly granted to Sir Robert Mansell and his assigns the sole making of all sorts of glass in the kingdom, for which a yearly rent was to be paid, which for sundry years past is in arrear, the said Sir Robert had assigned to Mr. Hercy (sic) Pate the making of all broad glass, 3s. upon every case of such glass being agreed to be paid to the King by Pate. Pate's workmen in Staffordshire, taking advantage of this time of trouble had combined with certain glasiers and others (rebels from London) to the damage of Pate. These workmen are straightly charged to perform their covenant

DARWIN MSS.

with Pate, and any glass sent to London or other place in rebellion is to be seized and disposed of.

1647, May 4. Inventory of the personal estate of Geo. Lascelles, Esq., late of Elston, exhibited in the Prerogative Court of Canterbury. 27 May 1647, amounting to 670*l*. 5*s*. 4*d*.

1654, Jan. 26. Inventory of the goods, &c. of Miles Chambers, of Grantham, woollen draper, deceased.

1659. A relation of his carriage when the Lord General Monck declared for the Parliament—by George Lascelles, Quarter-master to Colonel Hacker.

When left chief officer Lascelles received orders from Lambert to march the troop northward. Could not trust thirteen men in his troop, so left them at Oakham, and marched with the rest to join Monck. At Boroughbridge was unhappily surprized, and he with three others was carried prisoner to Newcastle. There Capt. Nicholas Lockyer exhibited some articles against him, and he was to have been tried for his life, when the news came to Lambert that Col. Wilkes and the rest had concluded a peace. Upon that he was dismissed and returned to Nottinghamshire, where he heard that Monck would not ratify the peace; so away he went to Coventry in the night, when he heard that place would be delivered up to the Parliament, which was so, Col. Sir John Norwich being instrumental in it. &c., &c.

Attached are "Articles (5) exhibited against Quartermaster George Lascelles."

Parchment endorsed " Capt. [George] Lascells certificate of his sufferings by his family and of his bravery, conduct and courage." His grandfather had given away to a son younger than his father an estate of 800*l*. a year. He was imprisoned at Northampton for a long time after the fatal fight at Naseby. After Worcester Henry Lascelles, his near relation, was instrumental in saving Charles from violence, &c., &c.

n. y., July 6. Coventry. Fra. Hawley to   . His Excellency Lord General Monck has given the writer a commission to command the regiment that was Col. Hacker's, now quartered at Warrington. Desires the person addressed to meet him there.

1660, Sept. 27. Cockpit. Ann Monck (Duchess of Albemarle) to Lieut. Lascelles. Her husband thinks that no more horses should be bought, he having two already, because of the speedy disbanding of the army. Sends her love to his mother.

1667, May to Nov. Book containing receipts and expenditure of the Duke of Albemarle, kept by Capt. George Lascelles (equerry ? to the Duke).

Some of the receipts were for rent of lands at Theobalds, Moor Park, Cheshunt, and Enfield, the Duke's pay as Colonel, 1*l*. a day, &c., &c.

Among the payments may be noted—for tobacco and pipes, 1*l*. 5*s*., three barrels of mum, 10*l*. 10*s*., three pairs of shoes for the Duke, 15*s*., hair powder, 9*s*., two shirts for the kitchin boy, by order of the Duchess, 5*s*., Mr. Hanmer for pictures and hangings, 10*l*. 15*s*., glazing Newhall House, 3*l*., Ottho Hoynck for four pictures, 6*l*., given a man that brought the Duke of York's picture by order of the Duchess, 2*l*., "for a shuite for Mounseir," 7*s*. 6*d*., 20 chaldrons of coals, 37*l*. 13*s*. 4*d*., bringing the same, 13*s*. 10*d*., various sums for the clothes and teaching of Lord Torrington, &c., &c.

1674, April 14. Commission of Arthur Earl of Essex to George Lascelles to be captain of foot.

1676, June 6. Mem. showing that Capt. Geo. Lascelles had sold his company of foot, then in Ireland, to Mr. Geo. Lyndon for 400*l*. DARWIN MSS.

1707–8, March 16. London. Edmund Lascelles to Mrs Ann Darwin at Elston Hall, near Newark. As ordered, he has furnished his cousin Natt. Thorold with 10*l*., who is not yet gone to sea, for the Government has taken 50 men out of his ship upon this critical juncture of affairs. The Queen's guards are now on their march towards the north.

1749, April (rec^d Apl. 26.) Chesterfield. Erasmus Darwin to his brother Mr Robt. Waring Darwin, Old Southampton Buildings, Holborn. Some verses and local gossip.

1749–50, March 17. London. R. Darwin to Robt. Darwin, esq., at Elston, near Newark. Endorsed, "from Bob, with the cause of earthquakes."

J. J. CARTWRIGHT.

CALENDAR OF LE STRANGE PAPERS SELECTED FROM THE MUNIMENT ROOM AT HUNSTANTON HALL, NORFOLK. EDITED BY HAMON LE STRANGE.—1887. LE STRANGE PAPERS.

The letters and other documents comprised in the following Calendar are mostly selected from a bound volume of miscellaneous papers, marked P. 20, in the Muniment Room at Hunstanton Hall, Norfolk. They are arranged chronologically, as far as it has been possible to ascertain the dates. A few letters which have been preserved unbound in the same collection are inserted in their proper places. Suggestions and explanations in the text for which the Editor is responsible are placed between square brackets [ ]. Where no name of a county follows the name of a place, the place may be assumed to be in Norfolk, the exceptions being well known localities such as London, Cambridge, &c.

1.—4 December — ? The King [Edward IV.] to Sir William Calthorp.

[Autograph initials.] R.E. [These initials were erroneously attributed to Henry VII. by the late Mr. Horwood in the third report of the Historical Manuscripts Commission, p. 272, and he gives the name of the recipient of the letter as Sir Willian *Hastings* instead of Sir William *Calthorp*.]

Forasmuch as it was agreed between Sir John Wyngfelde and Elizabeth [Wentworth] late wife to Calthorp's son and heir for the marriage of the latter's son and heir to one of Wyngfelde's daughters, and that the said Elizabeth deceased before the covenant was engrossed; and also that since that time Sir John Wyngfelde had agreed with "our cousine dame mergery the lady Roos Henry Wentworth and William Hopton having ful power and auctorite" to accomplish the covenant,

LE STRANGE PAPERS.

never the less it being reported that Calthorp was not "welwilled nor agreable therunto," but intended to withdraw and to aliene great part of the livelihood that by descent should appertain by right of inheritance to his grandson, the King wills and desires that he should cease and restrain his said purpose in doing "so great a wrong to the said childe orphelin and in the state of Innocencie," and that the said covenant of marriage "may take good conclusion and plain effecte, as ye desire to do us plesure and to deserve oure special thank. Yeven under oure signet at oure palays of Westmynster the iiij day of Decembre."

[A small fragment of the impression of the signet remains shewing the arms of France and England.]

2.—4 September . . The Duke of Suffolk to Sir William Calthorp.

Is credibly informed that he has condemned and grievously vexed the sureties of John Balhed late his under sheriff in Suffolk; "we think ye shewe to him gret rigo^r and no mano^r of favo^r;" desires Calthorp to assign to him a place and time in Suffolk "ther to acompte afore men lerned oen at yor denominacyon and an other at his" and to give him for payment of arrears "reasonable daies upon sufficiant suerte by obligation so that all his old obligatious may be broken and he relessed;" his costs to be paid to Sir William as the said auditors shall assign "and thanne ye to relesse alle the condempnations. And yif yeat our request and desire favo^r our seid servant we shall in tyme comyng do as moche for your pleasur and of your entente in the premisses we pray you to sende us writyng by the bringer herof. Wryten in our mano^r of Westhorp he iiij day of Septembr."

[Autograph signature.] Suffolk yor louyng cusyn.

3.—22 April [circa 1469.] The Duke of Norfolk to Sir William Calthorp, Steward of his household.

Gives him notice that it is his intention "to be on Monday at nyght next comyng at Norwiche for a direccion taking on the Tywesday next folowyng there in certaine matiers by the Kinges speciall comaundement concerning the weel of his persone and of these shires of Norff and Suff wherfore we hertily pray you at that day to giff us youre attendaunce and oure cousin youre sone Thomas with you And that it liste you to accompany us at our comyng in to the Citie as our speciall trust is in you And oure lord have you in his kepyng Written the xxij day of Aprill."

[Autograph signature.] Norff.

4.—xij day ? A—— C—— to her brother Sir William Calthorp.

Complaining that William Barle has wrongfully entered on Manor of Elsenham [Essex]. Encloses a letter to him which she asks Sir William Calthorp to sign so as to get her righted. [This letter has not been preserved.]

[Initialed] A. C.

5.—24 November . Dame Isabell Saquevyle to her nephew Sir William Calthorp.

She intends to carry out the wills of her late husband and of his father Sir Thomas Saquevyle. Her servant John Mathewe was to have an annuity of 40s. out of the Manor of Riddlesworth.

HISTORICAL MANUSCRIPTS COMMISSION. 95

6.—[No date or address.] J[ohn] Calthorp to [the Bishop of LE STRANGE PAPERS.
Norwich ?]

Commences "My Rygth reverent and worchipful Sir, onto your good fadyrod I me recomand." Requests him to send his men as before to help his mother-in-law Lady Roos in getting home her corn.

7.—4 June   . Robert Osborn to Master Calthorp. [Contemporary copy of a letter endorsed " to Bryan Stapilton, squier."]

Complains that his wife, Calthorp's sister, is not treated with love and favour by her own kin. Both he and she will agree to any reasonable course in order to mend matters.

8.—1 June [Between 1474 when Oxford was attainted, and 1476 when the Countess of Warwick died.] W. Dengayn, Staple Inn, to Sir W[illiam] Calthorp.

Recommends him to come to London next term for my lord of Suffolk's matter "butt Sir, in feith hadde noght this lending of him that is cleped the Erle of Oxenforth itt shall . . . . take effecte uppon ye Saterday or the Sonday next before this my writing " . . . . "my lord Howard went unto Caleys the weke byfore with whom mette iij shippes of Esterlingges and bikered to guyder and were slayn of his servants xvj persones, and he toke a botte and eskaped and his shippe driven upon the sandes. Sir also the king hath restored the countes of Warwick to all hir inheritaunce, and she have graunted itt unto my lord of Glowceter with whom she is, and of this foolkes merveyles greatley. I trust we shall have peas, but it is thought by lykelehod the contry. Sir horanges nor pongarnettes yet ther be come noon. Assone as any may come I shal sende w^t goddes grace who have you in his intier kepyng."

9—" The first Sunday of clene lenten."—Margery lady Roos to her brother Sir William Calthorp.

Complaining of the conduct of one Reynakyns, a tenant of Sir William's, who avers in excuse that he acted by Sir William's orders—"if it so be I mervayle moche."

10.—[Undated.] Frere Perys of St. Faiths to William Calthorp, Esquire.

As to certain matters in dispute between William Calthorp and Father Inglese with regard to lands in Dilham and Smalborough—requests that this letter may be burnt.

    Ends up " Be your owyn prest perpetuel "
          " ffrer^9 perys of Seynt feyths "
    Endorsed " To the worchopful ⎫
          " Sqwyyr William ⎬
          " Calthorp at Yerne
          " mowth dwellyng. ⎭

11.—4 October 1549. Duke of Somerset to Sir William Fermor.

William Bull has made complaint that he unjustly exacts sums of money; does not believe it; requests an explanation.

[Autograph Signature.—Dated at Hampton Court.]

12.—[Date torn off.]—Queen Elizabeth to . . . . .

"Whereas of late tyme our Treasorer of England the Marquis of Winchester did by o^r ordre cause a certain proportion of Grayne to be provided . . . . to have therwith gratified the King of Spayne's

LE STRANGE PAPERS.

subiect₹ in the Lowe countrey . . . . . being in the meane tyme infourmid that the prices of Grayne did ryse excessively and specially wheat, We did as it late appeered by our proclamation, resolve to forbeare the furdre proceeding therin at that tyme, so as we fynde the successe therof to have well insued, and the prices to have Reasonably abated; And now because we still perceave that the carryeng out of any wheat shulde be hurtfull, which we in no wise meane, and yet that the quantitie of Barley and Malte is so grete in that countrey as it may be better indured to sell som convenyent quantitie to strangeres, and therwith doo allso understande that suche ministers as our saide Treasorer did appointe, had shipped before knowledge of our proclamacion a quantitie of Barley and Malte by estimation neere fyve thousand quarters with intente to have also transported the same according to our first determacion, whicih somme being very small, and being allready shipped, is not well to be remedied with oute much loss of the grayne, We have resolved that the same shall passe to suche place as our Treasorer shall appoynte, and therfore we will and require you to permit the same so to doo according to his direction, And that therin such discretion be used by yoʳ order as no inconvenient reporte be made or notice given, to occasion any opinion of our Relenting contrary to the intention of oʳ Proclamation, which still contynueth to permit nether any wheat at all to passe out of the Realme nor any other grayne than this afore mentionid wherof any dearth shulde insue." A great quantity of other grain provided by the said Treasurer is to be sold by him and distributed to the "easing and abating of the excessive prices" . . . . and "to the relcef of our Citie of London."

[Sign Manual.—Dated at Greenwich, year and month gone.]

13.—1 June 1611. James I. to the Bishop of Norwich, Sir Edward Coke, and other Knights and Gentlemen of Norfolk.

Copy of a Commission under the Great Seal constituting them or any four of them Commissioners for enquiring into the misemployment of lands goods and money left to charitable uses within the county of Norfolk, "for the relief of aged impotent & poor people, maintenance of sick & maimed soldiers or marriners, schools of learning, free schooles, or schollers in universities, repayer of bridges, ports, havens, causeways, churches, sea banks, or high waies, Educacion or preferment of orphanes, relief, stock or maintenance for houses of Correction, mariage of poore maides, supportance or helpe of young Tradesmen, handecraftsmen, or persons decayed, relief or redemption of presoners or Captives, or aide or ease of anie poore ? . . . . . , fitting out of soldiers, or other Taxes, in anie parrishe, borow, or place with in our said County of Norff"; with power to make orders respecting them.

14.—24 June 1629. H. Colrane to Sir Hamon le Strange.

Offers to refer to arbitration some difference between his tenant Mr. Drury and Sir Hamon as to sheepwalks near Docking. He proposes Mr. Arminger as his umpire.

15.—25 July 1631. Charles I. to Sir Edward Bacon and the rest of the Commissioners for the County of Norfolk.

Appointment of Sir Hamon Le Strange as collector of fines on composition for Knighthood in the County of Norfolk.

[Sign Manual.—Dated at Bagshot. Signet gone. Countersigned by the Secretary of State, Windebank.]

16.—28 February 1631. The Board at Whitehall to His Majesty's Commissioners for Norfolk.

LE STRANGE PAPERS.

Empowering them to compound with any gentlemen in Norfolk for Knighthood, taking not less than 3½ times as much as the parties stand at in the subsidy, but more if they see cause. Further, giving them power to examine pleas put in by divers persons claiming discharge as not liable. They are directed to use all lawful means "by the assistance of the High Constables in every division as by your owne particular knowledg to enform yor selves of the true state and livelyhood of each person soe pleading" to take into composition those found "answerable to the vallewes for which others have compounded," and to threaten such as neglect with a legal trial in the Court of Exchequer.

Then follows a list of 65 persons, of whom 62 have pleaded that they were not seised of £40 per annum at His Majesty's Coronation and three years before, while the remaining three are marked as having pleaded other pleas that have been over-ruled by the Barons of the Exchequer as insufficient and dilatory.

17.—26 April 1632. Toby Pedder to Robert Banyard.

Banyard has been charged as disseizer of land from a poor orphan ; urges him to refer the matter.

18.—10 March 1633. Christ Church in Norwich. The Dean and Chapter of Norwich to their loving tenants.

" We suppose there is none among you but takes notice of the ruines fallen upon the spire of our Cathedrall Church by time and tempestuous weather, And we assure our selves that you and all the country doe concurr in your iudgmentes that very fitt it is it should be repaired according to it's former magnificence and state, as being a greate beauty to Godes house, a noble monument of reverend antiquitie, & none of the meanest ornaments of this Kingdome ;" for their own part they are resolved to do their best, but the rents are so small after deducting " the poore stipends " and other annual payments, that the remainder is " insufficient for soe expensive a work ; we are necessitated to pray in your severall aydes . . . ffor which wee shalbe ready to express our selves really gratefull . . . and in doeing every of you the greatest honor we caun by leaving a memorial to posterity of each man's bounty registered under his name in a fayre lidger booke which for that purpose shalbe forthwith provided."

Signed by John Hassall [Dean] and Foulke Robartes, John Spendlove, Nicholas Howlett, Edmund Porter, and Edward Younge [Prebendaries of Norwich].

19.—18 April 1634. Charles I. to the Earls of Portland, Lindsey, and others, and to all Justices.

Copy of Proclamation reciting that whereas he has at this time great need of Saltpetre, he empowers any three or more of them to enter break open and work for it " in the lands or possessions of us or any of our subjects in England & Wales and all priviledged places, & to make Saltpeter & thereof powder" to take carts, paying for them 6d. a mile, also to take for that purpose sea coals, outhouses, barns, &c. paying for the same at a reasonable price.

20.—2 July 1635. James Calthorpe to —— Armiger.

Encloses letters from Mr. Day and Mr. William Armiger. Is coming to Basham. Requests him to move Mr. Coke for the sight of evidence in his custody.

LE STRANGE PAPERS.

21.—19 June 1636. —— Myller to Sir Hamon Le Strange.
Sending extract from Lynn Charter as to their Admiralty rights. Thanks for kindness shewn to Thos. Lemon and other distressed neighbours put ashore 4 November last.

22.—9 May [16]37. John Whytyng to Lady Sydney.
As to the ownership of certain marshes. As to a debt due from one Simonds. Hanna Read has gone to New England; her sister Susan is with Lady Cooper, now Lady Alford, as her gentlewoman.

23.—13 November 1637. Thomas Coke to ?[Sir Hamon le Strange].
Sir Hamon is to have Heacham marshes. Legal arguments of the Lord Chief Baron shewing that ownership of Salt marshes is in the King. Argument respecting Ship money.

24.—21 April 1640. [No address or signature.]
[News from London in the form of a Diary from the 13th to the 21st April 1640.] Lord Loudon continues still in the Tower, close prisoner.
13th April. The King opened Parliament in State and in his speech declared that he had called it together for present supplies to reduce the Scots.
14th. Lord Loudon has been examined in the Tower touching his letter, which he says he wrote before the pacification of Berwick.
15th. The Commous presented Sergeant Glanvile for their Speaker to the King.
16th. "Sir Beniamyn Rudyard advised the house to procede with all humilitie to supplie the King with moneyes, and to take heede of the splints of a broken Parliament, for they sticke in the fleshe, but with all shewed a necessitie to reforme things amisse in church and commonwealth; then Sr Ffrancis Seymer in particular against shipp money and Innovacions."
17th. "Mr. Pymme made a speech allmost 2 howers long & particularizeing all the generall greivances of the Church and state without medling with any man's persone, Allsoe mencioned the Councell Table, and Starre Chamber together with the Pattents of Soape, Salt, Starch, Tobacco &c."
18th. Warrants sent to all the Courts to ask for the Judges' opinions as to ship money, also for the proceedings against Parliament men since the last Parliament.
19th. "My lord deputie [Strafford] came to Court, but sicke & weake, and my lord Keeper [Finch] is very sicke."
20th. The whole day spent in stating the question for the King touching grievances, & Dr. Mannering's being made a Bishop after he was disabled by Parliament. Mr. Jones of Lincoln's Inn chairman for Privileges, Mr. Grimstone for Grand Committee for grievances. Hopes that the King will give way to Parliament and allow those who have procured patents injurious to their fellow subjects to be questioned.
21st. The Lower house have joined the Upper in petitioning the King to name a day for a fast.
All ship money records brought into the House of Commons and viewed in part. Declaration made against such recoveries as have been acknowledged by infants to be voide. "Both howses attended the King this afternoone at Whitehall, who caused my lord Keeper to declare to them, that his armie was marcheing, and noe delay of supplies must be made, in a very gratious mild & meeke expression."

25.—15 July 1640. Norwich. Sir John Holland B*t*. Sir Hamon L'Estrange and others to L*t* Colonel James Calthorp.   LE STRANGE PAPERS.

Have received directions for the mustering of the trained fforces of the county, " for the safetie and defence of the Realme in this time of action "; requires him forthwith to call his company before him, to see that all the arms are repaired and made serviceable, that the company is augmented to the full number, and then to muster them completely armed and ordered, with all the inferior officers, at Hempton Green on Monday the 10th of August before 9 a.m. "Every Musquetteer furnished with a sufficient quantitie of powder and match, where an exact view is to be taken of their number persons and armes, and the true use of their armes." Further he is required to send in a Muster Roll of the whole Company, with the condition of their arms and the names of the inferior officers, the names of defaulters, returns of the quality and quantity of ammunition, and in what place kept and by whom. The Chief Constables are to collect the Muster Master's fee due from the hundred.

26.—7 October 1640, Norwich. Sir John Holland and others to Lieutenant-Colonel James Calthorp.

In pursuance of orders from the Lord General of His Majesty's Forces on this side Trent and the Lord Lieutenant, he is required to have the foot company under his command " compleatly armed and furnished on 24 houres warneing with all things necessary for march and service, ... amunition to be in a readynes and stored with the full quantitie of good and serviceable powder match and bulletts readie made, and that you cause to be in a readynes to every hundred trayned men ten pioners inroled & provided with spades shovells pickeaxes hatchets bills and the like for the making of workes of offence and defence ;" also two carts with men and ten horses for every hundred men to be kept ready, the owners of which shall be satisfied for any service they may perform : that beacons he watched and kept ready for fireing day and night. As to the payment of the trained men that in times of actual invasion every man is bound by law and custom " to serve in the publique and comon defence of the kingdome at his owne charge, ... without sticking or staying upon any tearmes or questions, and that the example of the subjects of the northern parts will invite them." " For the better encouragement of such men of qualitie as shall adventure their persons in this service that it is His Ma*ties* pleasure that such as shalbe slayne or dye . . . the whole benefit of the wardships of his heir under age shalbe granted to the mother, or to the next of kynne, and in case of full age the benefit of the livery to the heire himself freely without any composition to be paid." Full returns to be sent to Norwich by the 22nd October of the names of " the trayned men both piques and musquetteers, of officers, quantity of ammunition, names of pioncers, numbers of their tools, & of carts and carters."

27.—13 November 1640. H[enry] Mordaunt to James Calthorp.

Advice as to Calthorp's purchasing the Manor of Fakenham. £2,000 is too much, thinks it worth £1,500. [It was eventually purchased by him for that sum in 1647.] " Every day brings us rare news, my L. Leiftenant of Ireland accused for high treason by the lower house committed to Max[w]ell charge of the blacke rodd by the upper Sir George Ratcliff his favvorite sent for over out of Ireland as particeps criminis. My L. desiers that what he hath done by his ma*ties* command his

LE STRANGE PAPERS. highness would be pleased to justifie him in & what he hath donne by the advice of others that they may suffer the same punishment & what he hath donne of his owne head he desiers to stand & fall as the courte of parliament shall iudg of him. The first is totally denyed him. The king as he cann doe noe wrong soe cannot advise amiss but the actions of his instruments is their owne for which they must looke to it & if his Ma^{ty} direct amiss they must not put in execution that are his servants: some wagg or other hath sett over the parliament doore pray remember the judges as if they had been too long forgotten."

28.—10 April 1641, Lynn. Roger Bungay to Sir Hamon Le Strange.

Correspondence respecting some timber belonging to the Lords Adventurers for draining the Fens, cast up at Snettisham and detained by Robert Stileman.

29.—25 June 1644. Sir John Hobart to the High Sheriff & Deputy Lieutenants of Norfolk.

Enclosing copy of a letter from the Committee at Cambridge and one from Sir Samuel Luke; requests them to raise at once the best strength they can.

23 June 1644, Cambridge. Henry Myldmey and six others to [Sir John Hobart].

Requesting the Dep. Lieutenants to advance speedily all their forces to Thetford and Brandon, and to adjourn their committee to the place of the soldiers' rendezvous; the soldiers to bring a fortnight's pay with them.

22 June 1644, Newport Pagnell. Sir Samuel Luke to [the Committee at Cambridge].

Their horsemen have discovered the enemy in great strength at Buckingham. The Prince & Duke stay behind at Oxford. Encloses information of "one that this day cam from Oxford." Urges them to hasten on supplies to him with all speed.

One returned from Oxford this day, the 22nd June, reports that the King has this day marched with all his army to Buckingham; he has 9,000 foot & 3,000 horse. The Prince and Duke are in Oxford and intend to stay there until the King returns; he hears that they intend speedily to march upon Newport Pannell, and that they have 20 pieces of ordnance and much ammunition. There are 3,000 horse and foot left in Oxford.

25 June 1644. James Calthorpe to the Chief Constables of North Greenhoe.

To direct warrants to all who stand charged with foot arms requiring them to be ready to march at an hour's warning: "the feares of an approaching enemy invites them to itt." . . . . . "Every soldier be provided and furnished with a forthnight."

30.—5 July 1644. John Coke, High Sheriff of Norfolk, to James Calthorp and other Justices.

Sessions of the peace to be holden at Norwich on 23 July, at which all Justices, old and new, are to take the oath. Sessions at Fakenham on 1st August.

[On dorse.]

22 August 1644. Sir John Hobart and other Justices, to James Calthorp.

Requiring him to enforce punctual service of members of his trayned band which they hear is defective.

31.—[September 1644.] The Humble Petition of the Knights Esq[rs] Gentlemen and other inhabitants of the County of Norfolk to the Lords and Commons in Parliament.

LE STRANGE PAPERS.

"Whereas we have binn at Greate Charge to range and mayntayne the armye now under the command of the Earle of Manchester, which by Gods Blessing hath . . . . hetherto kept out the enimy from amungst us & may still secure us if not drawne fourth beyound the reach of our safetye; & whereas an expectation (from the reverend & lerned assembly of Divines) of some rules . . . . . for the settlement of the worship discipline & governement of the Church, ... which being published will preserve & establish quiet amungst us will bring us all unanimously to take the nationai covenant & . . . . . be an effectuall meanes for the obtayneing that blessed peace & truth which is so much wished, . . . we doe humbly desire that the sayd Army may be imployed nere the Confines of our association, that the Assembly of Divines may set fourth the resulte of there long & serious consultations, & that all (upon a payne) may be enioyned by a day prefixt to take the nationall covenant.

Subscribed by Sir John Hobart and six others.

[Beneath is a copy of a letter stated to have come with the above Petition.]

10 September 1644, Shipdam. Joshua Greene to Colonel Calthorpe & Mr. Russell.

At the desire of Sir John Hobart and the rest of the Committee encloses the Petition for their signature, and requests them to get it signed by all within their Hundred who are worth £100 in goods and lands, and at the same time to explain to the people that the "true intent is no more but to petition the parlament for a settlement in Church Government, that our owne Arrayes may be imployed for the safety of our owne countyes, and the national Covenant may be enioyned to be taken by al men."

On dorse is a list directed to James Calthorpe of eleven members (including himself), who are ordered to sit as the Committee during the last week of August under penalty of 10s. a day in default of appearance.

Order signed by Tho. Hoogan and 4 others.

32.—10 September 1644. Sir John Hobart and others to [? James Calthorp.]

Desiring him to be at Fakenham on the 17th to inspect the old soldiers and newly impressed men from the under-mentioned Hundreds, after which they are to go to Brandon "the generall Randevous, where "they shall receive their coates and conduct money."

		Men.
Hundreds	Smithdon	30
	Brothercross	10
	Gallow	30
	North Greenhow	28

Imprest men 98—besides old soldiers.

14 September 1644. William Haridance to the Constable of East Barsham.

"By Command from the Right worchippfull the deputie Livetenants & Comittee of Parliament" ordering him to impress one able and sufficient man within his town and "to take Idle serving men, & such other able persons as live dissolutely or Idly without Imployment," such men to be

LE STRANGE PAPERS.

delivered at Fakenham on the 17th inst. to such field officers as shall be appointed to receive them. Further, to give notice to all old soldiers fit for service then and there to appear upon pain of death, and a penalty of £20 upon the town and 40s. upon the harbourer.

[On dorse] "True coppyes of 2 letters received from the Committee the 19th Septemb. 1644.

Sir John Hobart and others to Sir Thomas Hoogan and others, "their affectionate frends and associates."

The letter of which copy is given below will shew how greatly they stand in need of their assistance—the trained bands are to be immediately called out and inspected, defects in arms &c. to be made good, and "that your selves and al other persons of quality will so furnish your selves with horse and furniture and have them in suer readinesse for defence of our country."

Trinity Colledge Septemb. 14th 1644. From Hen. Mildmay and seven others signing " Your Associated Frends & servants."

"'The extreame push of affaires that the associated Countyes are now put to by the emptying there fource into the west doe ernestly styr us up . . . . . . in your diligence the safety of your county resteth .
. . . . we see very playnely that matters will be brought very soone to such an adventure as to be prepared for the worst . . . . and this we do give you to take into your consideration as we have importuned other countyes to the like."

33.—6 October 1644. W. ? eeve to Sir Hamon L'Estrange.

Robert Stileman refuses to pay rates for his marsh land at Burnham Depedale and abused the constable. His proceedings concerning the Honour of Clare and Manor of Westronich.

34.—22 November 1645. Order of the House of Commons.

Sir Hamon L'Estrange and Robert Clench, or someone on their behalfe, directed to appear at Westminster on the 4th December when their Petition will be taken into consideration.

Signed by J. Potts.
John Wylde.
B. Whitelocke.

35.—2 January 1645–6. John Wylde, Chairman of Committee of House of Commons.

The Committee grant further time for the production of Sir Hamon L'Estrange's and Mr. Clench's witnesses, until the 15th January, when the case will be heard peremptorily.

36.— 2 January 1645–6. John Wylde, Chairman of Committee of House of Commons.

Order for the attendance of Sir Richard Hovell and nine others as witnesses at the hearing of Sir Hamon L'Estrange's and Mr. Clench's Petition on the 15th January inst.

37.—31 August 1646. Sir Hamon L'Estrange to ——.

Answer to a summons requiring him and nineteen others to shew cause why they should not pay damages to the town of Lynn for the destruction of the Almshouses during the siege. He declares that he has already paid more than the value of the property, and further pleads that under the terms of the Articles of Surrender to Sir Thomas Fairfax he was expressly freed from any such liability.

38.—9 October 1648. Sir Hamon L'Estrange to ——.   LE STRANGE
   Understands that Toby Pedder of Hunstanton (whom he made not   PAPERS.
chief constable to repay him with malice and ingratitude) has given
information concerning some clandestine favours shewn by him (Sir
Hamon) to some soldiers of the King's party lately landed at Heacham.
The facts are these:—About two months since there came to his house
one morning a keelman of Lynn who said that two gentlemen in the
outer Court desired to speak with him. He sent his servant; They told
him that many soldiers of the King's party had been sent as prisoners
from Lynn to Boston; they overmastered their convoy and wanted the
keelman to take them to Scarborough; he said he was not able but
would land them at Heacham, and that Sir Hamon L'Estrange who
lived near and had appeared for the King, would shew them favour;
they now desired to speak with Sir Hamon; he refused to see them so
they departed. Immediately after he sent for Pedder who asked his
advice. The Keelman confessed that he had used Sir Hamon's name to
get them to Heacham. Sir Hamon recommended Pedder to report the
affair and to use his own discretion as to hindering their escape. Afterwards some of the prisoners & their convoy came to his outer Court and
the weather being very hot asked for drink, which his butler gave them
without his direction ("tho' I might safely justifye that charity to a
Turk) and this is the sum of all that buysiness."

39.—19 March 1649, London.   William Beaumont to Sir Hamon
   L'Estrange.
   Since the receipt of Sir H.'s letter and the Conveyance inrolled has
been to London and finds that the Evidences of the Dean and Chapter
are come up "inclosed in a Greate Pipe vessell which is headed up, and
the Register is to take Care of them and to deliver them to the purchasers;
but he informeth me that untill all the lands of the Deanes & Chapters
through out England be sold, he shall have no leisure to break open the
vessell, and to deliver out any of the Evidences, which he saith will not
be yet these 3 monethes as he beleve. touchinge Mr. Fisher's Bills of
publique ffaith, I can not advise howe he may be payd the moneys; yt
is hoped the Parliament will take some Corse therein when their extraor-
dinarie Charges shall be over, yf they had bene doubled he might have
had 68 per cent, which is the most will yet be given that I can heare of."
Has given Mrs. Williams a gratification of 10s. to buy her a pair of
gloves as her husband refuses to take anything.

40.—1 February [circa 1650]. J. Whiting, Lincoln's Inn, to [James
   Calthorpe].
   Evidence as to the Pepper Rent due out of the Manor of Northwold
in Sculthorpe: an old inquisition book of 9 Edward II. speaking of the
hundred of Grymston says "Thomas Dackney tenet in Northwold dim.
feod de Comit. War. ut de manerio de Skulthorpe et idem comes de rege
per Servitm 2^{li} piper per ann. . . . I hear say that the Dutchman
hath petitioned the King to have all his marsh busines in Norff: to be
referred to the Counsell table or to some special lords of them. . . .
Upon Thursday last I attended upon the funerall of Sir Thomas
Richardson's lady who was buried at St. Buttolph in Aldergate St. in a
vault there by three of her children."

41.—10 September 1651.   Thomas Sotherton and others to Sir
   Thomas Guybon and the rest of the Commissioners.
   Enclosing an order from the Speaker to collect three months' assessment. Committee summoned to meet at Norwich. On the back is an
order to the Overseers and Churchwardens of the Hundred of Gallow to

LE STRANGE PAPERS.

make an assessment on real and personal estate for maintenance of the armies in England, Ireland, and Scotland.

42.—26 November 1651. The Commissioners for Compounding.

The cases of Sir Hamon L'Estrange and Thomas Dereham depending before the Commissioners for Compounding. They were concerned in the rebellion at Lynn and were Commissioners in the Treaty for its surrender; they plead the articles of surrender in their defence, but as it does not appear after search in the records of Parliament from 1643 to 1649 that those articles were ever confirmed, the Commissioners refer the whole matter to Parliament.

43.—[Undated, but in or after 1651]. Sir Hamon L'Estrange to the Commissioners for Compounding.

Draft petition [in his handwriting] praying that he may have the benefit of the late Act of Oblivion, and of the protection granted by the Earl of Manchester two days after the surrender of Lynn.

44.—25 February 1653–4. Matthew Manning to the Constables of North Greenhoe.

Precept from the Court of general Sessions directing them to collect and pay in £4 11s. 10d., being their proportion of the cost of repairing county bridges.

45.—9 March, 1679–80. John Fisher to [Sir Christopher Calthorpe].

As to new lease from the Bishop of Ely. It cannot be in Sir Nicholas's name as he is a minor. "The K. & D. and severall lords invited themselves last night to sup with my Ld Mayor, before they should leave the town, where they were most magnificently entertayn'd, and as much love & friendship as could be imagin'd, & they return'd late or rather early, his Majesty having first made Mr. Gulston a Knight, who is my Ld Mayor's partner. Tomorrow morning very early their Majesties and his R. H. go for Newmrket, their fore-runners being gon today, & their wagons yesterday, but the Dutches stays behind, in expectacion of her Mother's coming hither next weeke. This day his Majesty has taken leave of the Councell for 3 weakes at least (though they will sit in his abrence) & have put out 2 Proclacions, one for giving £10 to any man that shall bring in a highwayman or Robber, to be punctually paid by the Sheriff 15 days after conviccion, the other against Duells, & make any Actors or Abetters herein impardonable, where any person shalbe killed. Its now said the new Baron Norton (who comes o^r circuit) shalbe removed to the King's Bench, & Sir Job Charlton made Baron, & Sir George Jeffryes (the Recorder) made Cheife Justice."

46.—Copy, dated 8 January, 1683–4, of petition to H.M. Lord Petre to the King [Charles II.]

Hopes that H. M. will pardon the presumption of a dying but dutiful subject in giving a short account of himself. Having been now above five years in prison under a false calumny of a horrid plot against His Majesty's person and Government, and being now by God's Providence called into another world before he could prove his innocence by public trial, he protests solemnly that Titus Oates swore falsely that he saw him receive a Commission from Johannes Paulus de Oliva appointing him Lieut^t-General of an Army which was to come into England, and declares that he never saw or heard of any such commission to himself or anyone else. He renounces as contrary to the doctrine of the Roman Catholic Church, of which he dies a member, the aspersion that murdering Kings and taking up arms against one's Sovereign is an authorized principle of that religion. With his last breath will pray God to defend his Majesty and to forgive those who have endeavoured to make him appear to be one of the King's enemies.

LE STRANGE PAPERS.

47.—2 May 1684. Edward L'Estrange, clerk to the lieutenancy, to Sir Nicholas L'Estrange Bar^t and other deputy lieutenants.

Enclosing copy of an Order from the Duke of Norfolk directing that the Yellow Regiment of Trained Bands raised in the western parts of the county, shall, by reason of their great distance from the place of general muster at Norwich and the inconveniency of marching so far, hold themselves in readiness to meet near Lynn after Whitsuntide. To give notice to the Deputy Lieutenant and to the officers. Receipts from Sir Christopher Calthorp, Sir Thomas Guybon, Sir Edward Astley, and Francis Guybon.

48.—2 February 1684-5. The Duke of Norfolk to ?

Sending copy of a letter to himself as Lord Lieutenant of the county of Norfolk from the Earl of Middleton [Secretary of State] dated at Whitehall, 2nd February 1684, 4 o'clock; the King was seized by a fit at 8 o'clock this morning " but is thankes be to God much come out of it, and he continues so well that the Physicians have great hopes all danger is past." Recommends His Grace to send orders to his Deputy Lieutenants and Justices of the Peace to prevent all disorders that may happen upon any false report.

The Duke, writing at 10 p.m., says that since the above letter came into his hands he has been with the King in his bed-chamber who is very much better and thought out of all danger.

Signed, y^r affectionate Freind,
H. NORFOLK.

49.—7 February 1684-5. London. Fr[ancis] Negus, Secretary to the Duke of Norfolk, to [the Deputy Lieutenants for Norfulk].

Notwithstanding the physicians had declared that they believed King Charles the Second " in a condition of safety from the danger of his Fitt "; yet the fever returned the next day and yesterday between 11 and 12 H. M. departed this life. James II. was proclaimed at Whitehall, within Temple Bar, and at the Old Exchange, in the presence of great multitudes with great declamations of joy. A Proclamation was signed by the King, and published for the care of Government for the present. Deputy Lieutenants are desired to hold meetings in their respective Divisions and to give intimation to all justices and gentry, also to require the Militia to be in readiness.

Transmits copy of a letter from Lord Middleton to the Duke of Norfolk of the same date, officially notifying the death of Charles II. and accession of James II., and informs His Grace that he and all persons are continued in their respective offices of Government: requisite orders for preserving all things quiet should accordingly be issued by him.

Further transmits copies of three letters:

10 February 1684-5. London. Fr[ancis] Negus, Secretary to the Duke of Norfolk, to Mr. Edward L'Estrange, Clerk to the Lieutenancy.

As His Majesty has determined to call a Parliament in May, the Duke desires the Deputy Lieutenants to call meetings in their respective Divisions, and consult the Justices Militia officers and gentry, " in order

LE STRANGE PAPERS.

to the fixing on fit representatives, & more particularly for Knights of the county, which being communicated at a generall meeting, they may be resolved on two persons as may carry it without opposition. . . . . . It requires diligence & performance as well as a profession of Loyalty, which will appear by good Elections. When the gentry have met they will please to let my Lord Duke heare from them who they think fitt to pitch on for Knights." The Duke desires that Lord Townshend and Sir John Holland may be consulted.

12 February [16]84–5. The same to the same.

Th Duke had no leisure by reason of his attendance on the King to write to any of his Lieutenants by the last post. The Commission of the Peace will be renewed forthwith, "for those of the Lieutenancy not until a new broad Scale be made:" meantime they may safely act under H.M's Proclamation. The Duke met the Deputy Lieutenants and gentry of Surrey yesterday, "where his Grace desired them to agree amongst themselves to nominate persons that they thought fitt to stand for Knights, and when they had named 3 his Grace desired they would let their names be written in so many pieces of paper as there were Gentlemen who have voices, and that every one would mark 2 of this and then fold up the papers, & put them in a hatt, which being mingled together were open'd & counted, & by that means the two that had most voices were resolved on, and every one declared he would make his Interest unanimous for those two, they first haveing notice and declaring that they will stand, which in all probability may be a means to prevent any contest nor can any thing be more faire, because my Lord would by no means nominate who should stand, & his Grace is to meet those of Berkshire tomorrow, so that I hope the 3 counties in his Grace's charge will prevent the inconveniencies wch happen by delay."

12 February [16]84–5. London. The same to the Deputy Lieutenants of the county of Norfolk, or either of them.

The Duke has heard from Sir N. Lestrange & other Deputy Lieutenants that they will render a good account of the county to H.M. No immediate occasion for calling out the Militia. A Parliament is to be summoned. Recommends them to meet and settle on two candidates "to prevent unnecessary expences which contested Elections do occasion." The Duke is prevented from writing with his own hand by his attendance on His Majesty and giving orders for the funeral, which "tho' 'tis to be private so takes up his Grace's time."

50.—21 February 1684–5. London. Duke of Norfolk to [the Deputy Lieutenants].

Regrets that he is unable to attend the general meeting called to select Candidates for Parliament. Trusts that there will be no opposition; will readily concur in whomsoever they approve " which you cannot want choise enough off, since wee may say without braggery that no County affords so many loyall gentlemen to the Crown."

26 February 1684–5. Norwich Castle. Sir Nicholas L'Estrange & twelve others to [the Duke of Norfolk].

Acknowledging receipt of above. At a full meeting of gentry from all parts of the County, held to-day in the Grand Jury Chamber at Norwich Castle, Sir Thomas Hare and Sir Jacob Astley were unanimously selected as Candidates to represent the County. Their clerk, Mr. L'Estrange is forwarding for his Grace's approbation the form of an address which they have agreed upon to be presented to H.M. from

this County. They will endeavour in all things to make good the character which the Duke is pleased to give them. L'Estrange Papers.
[Copies certified by Edward L'Estrange, Clerk to the Lieutenancy.]

51.—17 February 1687-8. [Norwich]. E[dward] L'E[strange] to Sir Nicholas L'Estrange B^art, at Hunstanton.

Has lately heard from Mr. Negus that the Duke of Norfolk some days since received an order from the Earl of Sunderland to the effect that H.M. approved of the persons therein named to be Deputy Lieutenants of Norfolk; this much surprised the Duke who had not presented any of those persons to the King. As the order was not under the King's hand or Privy Signet his Grace could not legally comply with it, but had asked the King's leave to go beyond sea, and was going as soon as possible. At least five Roman Catholics were in the list. Some say the Earl of Yarmouth will be made Lord Lieutenant of Norfolk, but Edward L'Estrange thinks the Duke of Norfolk will continue to hold the office. The Bishop of Norwich has not yet been ordered to exhort his clergy to recommend the repeal of the test and penal laws. The Bishop exhorts gentlemen who are left out of the Commission of the Peace not to be discouraged, but to appear and serve on the Grand Jury at Thetford Assizes, if summoned. A list of the proposed new Commission of the Peace for Norfolk is enclosed. [From this are omitted the names of Sir Nicholas L'Estrange and other Justices who were opposed to the repeal of the Test Act.]

"Thus you see what care his Majestie has taken for to relieve the guard of this County, by calling of those Gent^mn who have so long bin upon Duty, least their longer continuance should make the burden & fatigue to great: How the Lieutenancy will be modelled, I cannot yet tell, neither whether there will be any further use for mee, God's will be done."

52.—31 May [16]88. W. Thursby to James Calthorpe.

Is much troubled because he cannot find certain writings touching the title of the Estate [Raynham] which were in the possession of the late Lord [Townshend]; they may have been in the care of some Agent and have now fallen into our adversary's hands. Has the house at Raynham been thoroughly searched? The young lord and Mr. Roger [his brother] have been above a week at Twittenham without leave from Calthorpe or himself. They would be better at school as Mr. Windham and others seek to obtain undue influence over the boys, to the prejudice of their guardians.

53.—5 June [16]88. W. Thursby to James Calthorpe, at Sir Christopher Calthorpe's house at Basham.

Begs him to search again for the missing writings. Has had young Lord Townshend to dine with him, and took him to see Lord Crew who told him how glad he was that his father had placed him in the hands of careful guardians. Thursby remarked that the young lord had evil counsellors among his relations who advised him to disobey his guardians. At this Lord Crew stormed. Lord Townshend promised not to listen to the advice he got at Twittenham. On getting home, Mr. & Mrs. Windham came in and offered their services to the young lord. "We had another little brush; Mr. Windham told me plainly hee would have Mr. Bech have (not Raynham but) Stowky liveing. I told him he might fayle of his resolves." Has written to Lady Ashe to hasten the children's return to school. Desires Calthorpe to tell Mr. Walpole about it and "that wee must all arme against Mr. Windham's designs."

LE STRANGE PAPERS.

54.—[? 1688]. W. T[hursby] to James Calthorpe.

Is in a peck of troubles and discontent about Lord Townshend's children : they have been 3 weeks at Twittenham and he proposed to go down and see them today, but Mr. Windham and his lady brought them up to town last night. Morell came to see him (Calthorp) late at night ; Calthorp told him he " was intrusted to govern " the young lord, "and ought not to suffer him to be carryed up and downe nor from school without his guardians or one of their leaves, nevertheless he had without any body's leave suffered him to goe a fortnight before the Holy-days frō school & now brought him or suffered him to bee brought to London in this sickly time." Morell replied that he could not prevent Mr. Windham from bringing him up. Calthorp waited on the young lord this morning and found him in bed with Mr. Windham's son ; the boy said he had come up to see his Aunt & go to a play—Calthorpe could not prevail on him to leave town. Had some words with Mr. Windham in the young lord's presence as to his inveighing him from his proper guardians. " My lord lay in bed and said nothing " ; told him " I hoped he would value those his father valued, & obey those his father had set over him ; that his father trusted you above all men." . . . . "they have got a great step into the government of the young man—how you will bring him off I know not."

55.—10 June 1688, Whitehall. The Earl of Sunderland, Lord President, and other Lords of the Privy Council to Henry Duke of Norfolk.

Announcing the birth at about 10 o'clock that morning of a Prince son of His Majesty and his Royal Consort ; desires that the intelligence may be communicated to his Deputy Lieutenants, the Justices of the Peace &c. to the end that at such time as H.M. may appoint they may all join in solemn thanksgiving and other expressions of public rejoicing.

Within the fold are endorsements shewing at what time it was received and sent on by each of the following : Edmund Wodehouse, Robert Walpole, Sir Nicholas L'Estrange, Sir Thomas Hare, Sir Henry Bedingfeld, Robert Longe junior, Bent Tasburgh, Edmund Blackborne, Gerard Cater, Valentine Pell, and Sir Christopher Calthorp.

56.—15 June, 1688 [Norwich]. Edward L'Estrange, Clerk to the Lieutenancy, to Sir Nicholas L'Estrange and other Deputy Lieutenants.

Transmitting (No. 55.) the announcement of the birth of the Prince of Wales, and requesting that it may be sent on from one to another with all speed, each setting down on the back of the order when it came into his hands, to whom he sent it on, and when.

57.—29 June [16]88. Lord Chancellor Jeffryes to Charles Viscount Townesend.

Robert Lewkenor Esqre having exhibited into the Court of Chancery his bill of complaint against his Lordship and desiring his appearance thereto " I do at his request according to the manner used to persons of your Quality desire your Lordshipp to give Order to those you imploy in such matters for your appearance to the said Bill.

[Autograph signature of Lord Jeffryes.]

58.—30 June [16]88. Christopher Dighton, London to Sir Nicholas Lestrange Baronett at Hunstanton in Norff. By Lynn Bagg.

Sending copy of the Lord Chancellor's order respecting the trial of the suit concerning Mr. Coke's Estate. " The tryall of Bishopps [cam]e on yesterday and held till about 6 o'clock [at n]ight and then the Court rise and left it with [the] Jury who sitt upp all night about it and this [mor]ning gave a Verdict not guilty there was never [befo]re soe many people in the Hall nor such Huzaing [as] there was after the Verdict was given."

LE STRANGE
PAPERS.

59.—2 October, 1689. Wm. Bullock, London, to [James Calthorpe].

Has sent him this week "2 rowles of chawing tobbacco from C. Calthorpe who sends it upon his word to be of the best . . . . I cannot but wonder how such falce reports should fly into the country, that the plague is here, and in the Fleete, for the first, thanks be to God, this city is in very good health. As for the Fleete, they have bin sickly, and not the Plague, and complaine their provisions were not putt up well. . . . . . . This day I heard from Mr. Moret that my Lord and his brother are in good health. On Wednesday the 9 instant Lyn coach shall not faile to be attended, for the box for my Lord which shall certainly be sent to Eaton next morning . . . . . . the King is now at Newmarkett. Noe certaine news from Ireland."

60.—14 October, 1689.

" The number of Sir Christopher Calthorp's Arms found in his house—
12 musquetts with 4 rests.
19 old useless head pieces.
12 old back & breasts with other old peice of armor.
18 Javelings & one Pike.
20 Holburts.
11 Old rusty swords.
One Snaphance.
One brass musquetoon.
One complete suite of Arms.
One case & 2 of broaken pistolls.
One suite of Indian Armor with a poll axe.
3 rusty daggers.
3 drummes whereof two belongs to the militia with 3 halberts & one pulleson with several old rotten twilled coats.

61.—2 November, [16]89. T. Saunders, London, to [Sir Nicholas L'Estrange, B^{art}] at Hunstanton.

As to suit respecting Mr. Coke's will. Lady Anne has put in a fresh appeal. This day the House of Commons in Committee of the whole house (Mr. Hambden in the Chair) has voted a sum of two millions to their Majesties for reducing Ireland, and joining with their Majesties allies abroad for a vigorous prosecution of the war with France both by sea and land. The Bill of Rights was read a second time. Little news from abroad, more than that Schomberg is advanced towards Dublin.

When 4 figures turned upside down
Make equal numbers and numbers years the same,
Down goe the Frenchmen and their crown
Together with their fame. 1691.
} An old prophecy found at Oxford.

62.—11 November, [16]89. The same to the same.

Lady Anne's appeal to be heard by the Lords in a week. Desires him to make interest with Lord Crewe and any other Lords whom he knows. This day the Commons " resolved into Committee to consider

LE STRANGE
PAPERS.

the state of the nation and to enquire into the miscarriages of the year past, after a long debate came to this vote. That want of convoys and guarding of the narrow seas was the occasion of those great losses which have happen'd to the merchants of this Kingdom. Wee shall enquire into severall miscarriages of the fleete for the year past, & who were the occasions thereof."

63.—23 November, [16]89. The same to the same.

"The Lords being on a debate upon the bill of rights put off o^r hearing till next Wensday. . . . I question not but you have had a dreadfull account of o^r Irish matter, but 'twas utterly false, and o^r army is gonne into their winter quarters, and in a much better condition then reported. Wee have lost a greate many men in the flux, and the enemy many more, but our sick men are in a fair way of recovery. Wee had an information in o^r house this day the severall of o^r men on board at Plymouth were poysen'd with bear, being prodigiously swell'd. Wee have order'd 4 or 5 to be sent for into custody who were concern'd in the horrid act. The Danes were very much dispers'd with bad weather, but 'tis believ'd it was the roguery of the pilots, & that they are now in irons, so soon as the Danes are refresh'd the King hath order'd their march."

64.—28 November, [16]89. The same to the same.

The appeal has been heard by their Lords, and the Chancery decree has been reversed but without prejudice. The land is to continue charged with our legacies, and the exceptions to be heard before the Lords Commissioners.

65.—3 December, [16]89. The same to the same.

The exceptions will be argued after Christmas The land remains charged. Mismanagement of affairs both in Army and Navy. "Wee have lost out of o^r army in Ireland at least 8,000 men by sicknesse, and many hundreds yet sick, besides that greate mortallity on board occasioned by bad meate and drink."

66.—14 January [16]89–90. The same to the same.

Arguments not yet heard. Mr Gwanas sick. "'Tis agreed on all hands that King Wiilliam intends for Scotland in March, & some will adde that thence for Ireland. I suppose when he hath received the crowne there, he will not go for Ireland to hazard the losse of it.

67.—15 February, [16]89–90. The same to the same.

Mr. Gwanas is dead. Names of his executors.

68.—10 May [16]90. The same to the same.

Has been dangerously ill. Dighton playing tricks. Case delayed. The King goes to Ireland about the 25th instant.

69.—3 June [16]90. The same to the same.

Case again delayed. Two of the Lords Commissioners changed. "The King goes towards Ireland tomorrow. The Irish have quitted & burn'd severall small garrisons (and 'tis said also that of Dundalk) on purpose to withdraw all their forces from the frontier townes, & are encamping their army in two severall places consisting of at least 60 thousand. I presume you have heard that yor friend Capt Calthrop who lately lived at Bassam was drowned about a fortnight since. Being on board Sr Cloudesly Shovell, he & a friend of his, & Sr Cloudesly's Leivtenant & about 12 seamen going off in the pinnace to see some curiosity fell into the sands & were drowned."

LE STRANGE PAPERS.

70.—8 July [16]90. The same to the same.

" As to o^r sea affairs (I think) the lesse I say the better. I presume you have an acc^t of the present state thereof ; which is that wee take what care wee can to keepe out of harm's way. I think it too true that 'twixt us & the dutch wee have lost nine ships, I meane sunk & burn'd to prevent falling into the enemy's hand. Wee are with all speede fitting out all the ships wee can ; & Mr. Wm Harbord is sent to Holland to get what assistance the Dutch can afford us, who ('tis say'd) have 17 ships ready besides 12 of the Swedes which are hourly expected, so that 'tis truly beleived wee may in one fortnight be able to confront that insolent mann . . . . . . you have here inclosed an account of proceedings in Ireland since which time (by an expresse this day) wee have a very satisfactory addition that King William safely [arrived] at Dublin last Friday. King James who fled [*end of letter torn off*]."

71.—24 July [1690]. The same to the same.

Cause part heard. Ordered to go back to a Master to have accounts adjusted. Endless delay. Report that the French have landed at Torbay.

72.—29 October [16]91. W. Thursby [London] to James Calthorpe at Sir Christopher Calthorpe's at East Bassam in Norfolk. By Swaffam Bagg.

Requesting him to come up to town to settle business of taking up security for £1,000. Our new Lord Westmoreland desires Mr. Roger may accompany his son, Lord Le Despenser to Morewood this Christmas : recommends that he be allowed to do so. J. Calthorpe has been called to the bench of the Middle Temple ; a chamber and a Treasurership when his turn comes will more than recompence him the £200 charges. Asks for news of my lord's health and progress at Cambridge.

73.—2 April 1692. James II. at St. Germains to the Privy Council.

Copy of Proclamation summoning, in accordance with usage of his Royal Predecessors, such of the Privy Councillors as can conveniently be had to be present at the labour of their Queen. In spite of having followed that example at the birth of James Prince of Wales, the precaution was not enough to hinder the aspersions of such as are resolved to deprive H. M. of royal right. Whereas his Consort is drawing near her time, he requires such of the Privy Council as can come, to attend at St. Germains as witnesses. The Most Christian King has given his most royal word for safe conduct going and returning.

74.—2 July 1693. Sir Roger L'Estrange to Sir Nicholas L'Estrange, Bart.

" My heart akes for feare of that addle-headed stubborne girle of mine that has the honour to be under the Protection and Charity at present of your roofe." If her behaviour to Sir Nicholas and Lady be what her Father trembles to think of, he will not suffer her longer to be an encumbrance to her best friends, in spite of the reduced condition of his own fortunes. Has been suffering much from gout, as a remedy for which he begs for a pot of conserve of Hipps out of the country. " I can tell you no newes now, but of the ravages of the ffrench in Flanders,

LE STRANGE PAPERS.

the Rhyn, Catalonia & all the open countreys wherever they come. The spoyleing of our trade by their Privatiers, the waneing (?) of some of the Allyes. The French letters write upon presumption that they have done execution upon Cadiz, and the Change here is in no small apprehension for the Smyrna fleet, though they say at Whitehall that Sr D^m Rook & his charge are all safe ; and one of the Dutch prints speaks of an expresse from the King to the States to the same purpose. But the most surprizing Rumour of all is the hot report now of 2 dayes standing, of a Peace in agitation betwixt France & the H. of Austria, & that the Spanish Junto hath declared upon the poynt of the succession, in case of the present King's dying wth out an heyre."

75.—7 Aprill 1694. 12 at noon. The same to the same.

His wife has just breathed her last. "Play and gaming company have been the ruine of her wretched self, her Husband, and her family : and she dyes with a broken heart. - . . . . but after all I have sayd never any creature lost a dearer wife. She made mention often of yours and yor Ladyes generous and charitable friendshippe to us both in yor goodnesse toward the poore girle."

76.—10 October [16]95. [Sir Roger L'Estrange] to Sir Nicholas L'Estrange at Hunstanton in Norfolk. Leave this at Lynne with Mr. Bromrig a Sadler to be sent as above.

As to money due from the Dolman family on his marriage settlement. News of Villeroy and the war in Flanders. The Turks have defeated Veterani and the Imperialists have withdrawn to the Iron Gates to secure that pass into Transylvania.

77.—29 February [16]95-96. Daniel Bedingfeld to Sir Nicholas L'Estrange at Hunstanton.

Has seen Sir Roger L'Estrange as to the Dolman settlement money. " I believe the reality of the designe of assasinating the King. Severall are taken & all under disguises & endeavoring to escape. You & I remember a plott they did not doe so in. Guynyes [guineas] will be brought to 26s. by what I hear of the proceedings of the Commons. I wish we doe not repent o^r not lowering them to 25s. 6d., which if they did, & would rayse the silver 1s. in six, it would make gold and silver of one price, wch might sett the trade right, keep silver in the nation, and bring more into it . . . . . The association in the House of Commons subscribed, they say, by 350 and odd, refus'd by 96."

78.—19 March 1696-97. Sir Roger L'Estrange, in Newgate, to Sir Nicholas L'Estrange at Hunstanton.

Has been committed to Newgate on suspicion ; has not been examined ; solemnly declares himself clear of contriving, fomenting, or being privy to any one point of the plot now in agitation. Has endeavoured to settle his accounts and make provision for his son Roger's education. His head is disordered ; has been almost three weeks a prisoner ; thanks Sir Nicholas and his Lady for all past favours especially towards his " poore deare childe." Takes leave of his family.

[This letter is initialed by Sir Roger, but is not in his handwriting. He was 80 years of age at the time.]

79. — 4 January 1696-97. Richard Sare to [? Sir Nicholas L'Estrange].

As to the Dolman settlement. Lady L'Estrange (wife of Sir Roger,) had raised money of Mr. Cope on her reversion ; affairs of Sir Thomas Dolman and his son. Sir Roger's health is good after his confinement.

80.—5 October 1700. Sir Roger L'Estrange to Sir Nicholas L'Estrange.   LE STRANGE PAPERS.

Is about to publish his "*History of Josephus*" by subscription. People have been mightily concerned a long time to know how he lived, some maintaining that he has an estate of his own, others that he is supported by his relations. He speaks with "a due reverence of acknowledgment" to Sir Nicholas for many charitable offices which he has received at his hand, but he has no settlements or annuities. He has "received very considerable presents from diverse persons not so much as known to mee by their names as a Reward for my good will to the Publique, but after all this, my pen has been my chiefe support." He was to have £300 for the translation of Josephus, of which he has received already £200. In addition he is to have 25 copies of the book in ordinary paper and 25 in Royal. The subscriptions are 10s. in hand for the common paper and 15s. more upon delivery, and 20s. in hand for the Royal paper and 25s. more upon delivery. He hopes that his friends who mean to have the book will take them of him, as it will be so much clear gain to him and not a farthing of loss to the contributor. After these 50 copies are disposed of he has an interest of a sixth part in the remaining copies.

81.—29 June 1702. The Bishop of Norwich to Sir Christopher Calthorpe.

He will not presume to judge "such as doe or shall runn into the Government, they must stand or fall to their own Master. If the Oath of Abjuration had not been entayled & left as a wofull legacy to the Nation, some what might have been said and offered to our ease and satisfaction, but it is such a cross stumbling block in my way, that I have no hopes to gett over it or any safe method to overcome it but Patience and Resignation to God's will. Our brethren here are agreed that we ought not to be so nice in our publick Devotions at this time so as to provoke and exasperate the Government, to that end they admitt some formes in the Publick Offices and make use of the word soverii where it is proper and inoffensive. This was practiced in the late Rebellion, & more particularly by Dr. Sanderson as appears from his own works. The Queen [Anne] is truly zealous for the Church of England, and tho' there may be some about her the are not so yett it's hoped there are many great ministers in her interest that may in due time assist her in giveing ease to those that suffer for conscience sake & for the true Interest of the Royal Family and the rights of hereditary monarchy.

82.—21 October 1702. Peter Le Neve to Sir Christopher Calthorpe.

Reporting on his old deeds which he has examined for him.

83.—1702. Sir Nicholas L'Estrange B^t.

Memorandum in his handwriting as to the double Land Tax charged on his and other Estates in accordance with the 4th Subsidy 1693. On the accession of Queen Anne and his taking the oath of allegiance, the Commissioners suspended the half expecting that Parliament would remit it. Mr. Walpole, a Whig, moved to do so, but it was thrown out by the Court Party, so next year (1703) the warrants order payment of the full 4s. Subsidy with arrears.

84.—29 February 1703–4. London. [No Signature or Address.]

Personal news as to divers friends in town. Boucher is condemned for high treason for coming from France and fighting in

Ireland. Great expectation of the Scottish Plot. "I believe you have in great measure hitt the secrett, that is the great ones endeavouring to ruin one the other. Ld Orkney has bought the fine seat of Hamsey, I think, butt I doe not know the name of the place, but you doe better.

85.—6 July 1704. Sir Christopher Calthorpe to [William Lloyd, the dispossessed] Bishop [of Norwich].

As to the Tithes of East and West Basham lately under sequestration. Vicarage House. Affairs both of Church and State are in a dangerous condition.

86. — 2 August 1704. H[amon] L'estrange to Sir Nicholas L'Estrange.

Has been to Basham. Excuses himself for not having come to Hunstanton—returned home for harvest—price of corn. News arrived of the battle of Blenheim.

87.—22 August 1704. Nicholas Parham, Swanton Morley, to [Sir Nicholas L'Estrange, Bart.].

Is willing to take £52 for the 18 acres 3 roods of land at Ringstead which he formerly offered him for £55.

88.—24 August 1704. John Taylor, Secretary's Office at Whitehall, to ——.

Enclosing the "Observator" wherein he will find a complaint of a Conventicle kept in his city by Nonjurors and Jacobites, and desiring him to shew it to the Magistrates that they may suppress it. The Council will shortly send down messengers to take the chief of them up. Unless the Magistrates take care of this affair themselves they will be regarded as disaffected persons, and particularly his chief. Sends down this notice as a friend.

[The "Observator," Vol. iii. No. 44, from Aug. 19th to 23rd, edited by John Tutchin, states that "at Norwich there is a Conventicle of some hundreds [of Nonjurors] where they constantly assemble, and of which I have given notice to the Ministry with the papers I received on that account, since which I have received other papers relating to the same, as also accounts of the same nature from other parts of the Kingdom; and is it any wonder that we have plots, when the enemies of the Government can assemble in a riotous manner without any notice taken of them.]

89.--10 March 1704-5. R[ichard] Sare to [Sir Nicholas L'Estrange, Bart.].

Concerning some books which he had furnished to him and others which he was sending according to his order. "The death of poor Mr. Roger was very surprising. The Capt gave me good reason to hope he would soon have made himself capable of Preferment and in order thereto I had gott the Queen's letter for him. The trouble about Sr Roger's concernes will now by this loss be quickly over, & all matters may safely be resigned to his daughter."

90.—13 December 1705. Thomas de Grey to Sir Christopher Calthorp.

Thanks for accounts. Glad to hear that his sister and nephew are well. " The house of Commons sate very late last thursday upon the

Union & resolved at last by a majority to bring in a bill to dissolve the privy Council of Scotland, to settle the Militia, and appoint justices of the peace with the same power as here in England, and the Sheriffs shall return the Parliament men as 'tis with us here. They goe this day agen upon the naval affaires, how the Admiralty will come off will not yet be decided, for 'tis thought they will not gett throw it yet of some time."
. . . . " The whiggs are mightily divided upon the present state of affaires, so as they do not know one another. There are the country w—-gs & the Court w-—gs."

LE STRANGE PAPERS.

91.—5 March 1705-6. Thomas de Grey to Sir Christopher Calthorp.

"Both houses joyned yesterday in an address to the Queen of, I thinke, a very extraordinary nature as to some parts of it particularly. They have desired her that she will not make peace with the King of France till he has acknowledged her title to these Kingdoms & the succession of them in the Protestant line as they are by us establish'd, and till he has banished the Prince of Wales out of his dominions and consented to have the fortifications & harbour of Dunkirk demolished and destroyed. 'Tis to be presented this evening so I can't tell you what answer the Queen gives to it. What was the occasion of the address or whether there be a secret in it or not I can't tell you. No body offer'd to speake a word against anything in it in our H. The Naturalization bill is engrossed & appointed to be read the last time on Monday next. Gentlemen are so fond of it that it was with much ado that there was a clause admitted to restrain it to such Protestants who upon their comeing over shall receive the Sacrament according to the Church of England.

92.—20 November 1707. James Calthorp to his brother, Sir Christopher Calthorp.

"There were great expectacions from the lords yesterday, which was appointed to consider of the state of the nation, Ld Wharton and Lord Havesham were the cheife speakers and pretty warm, as to miscarriages in the ministry; but ended for the present in appointing a Committee to examine the matter further, and Saturday I think is appointed for their Report. The Commons are this day considering the state of the Navy where no doubt but there will be some Heats. . . . . Partyes are divided amongst themselves, pray God send a good conclusion. The merchants of the City peticion against the Admiralty board for their great losses sustained for want of convoys and Cruisers; this is the best account I can give you of the publick at present."

93.—3 February 1707-8. The same to the same.

"This I believe has been a long and warm day in the H. of Commons where the affaires of Spain were to be looked into, and how the moneyes appropriated for the service have been employed, it appearing that the Army there was not half of what was provided for; the East India Company agree to advance Twelv hundred thousand pounds at 5 per cent. having their present tearm in the Government made up 21 years, how the remaining summ of about a million and half will be raised is not yet publickly known."

94.—28 February 1707-8. The same to the same.

No need for so great apprehension as there are "about 30 sail of ships ready to sail to Dunkirk, and more very speedily to follow . . . we are in great expectation what the secret Committee" [on the Union

LE STRANGE PAPERS.

with Scotland] "will produce, who have met severall hours every day for a fortnight, their Report to the House is expected next week . . . the small-pox is very mortall, and a dangerous feavour, but I think the bill decreased last week."

95.—15 April 1709.   Rev^d Mr. Lamb, Rector of Southwell in Nottinghamshire, to ——.

At Upton near Southwell a Roman urn was lately turned up by the plough. In it were some round balls which fell to dust, some coloured glass beads, a bit with chain and bosses curiously enameled, but so small that they seemed to have been made for some creature smaller than a horse. Lower still was found an entire egg covered with a hard mummy, blackish, pitchy somewhat like Spanish liquorice. Inside this were 20 silver coins " perhaps scarce to be equalled in England "; two were of Consular time, the rest of Augustus, Domitian, Vespasian, Nero, and other Emperors; they were nearly as broad as a sixpence but three times as thick; the faces very fine. Underneath were a number of human bones, so many that many men must have been buried there.

[Extract in the handwriting of Sir Nicholas L'Estrange.]

96.—16 April 1709.   James Calthorp to his brother Sir Christopher Calthorp.

"If the parliament breaks up next week I believe will be determined on monday next, the day appointed for the concluding consideracion about making Treason in Scotland upon the same foot with our English laws; the bill was sent down by the lords and sent back againe with amendments by the Commons, yesterday the lords return'd it againe with some alteracions, which after long and earnest debates in the Commons caused a division of the House, the question whether they should take the amendments sent down by the lords into consideracion on Monday next or that day three weeks, carryed for Monday by five votes 114 : 119: soe both partyes are trying their skill to encreas their numbers on that day : peace is yet much talked of, by the next mayles from Holland wee expect to know something of certaintye . . . price of corn falls dayly here, but still complaints amongst the poore."

97.—21 April 1709.—The same to the same.

On Monday the Treason bill was sent back to the lords withsome little amendment which the Lords agreed to on Tuesday. Yesterday the Queen sent a Bill of Indemnity, which passed in course both Houses, 'tis expected the Houses will be prorogued this day, but I have not been out soe I am not certain, the Duke of Marlborrow being hourly expected, some think may make some alteracion, by him 'tis believed wee shall know whether a treaty for peace or not."

Postscript :—" Near eight, the Duke is just come, the Parliament prorogued to ye 19th of May."

98.—3 May 1709.   The same to the same.

"My Lord [Townshend] took coach this morning about 4 of the clock in order to embark this evening at Margat with the Duke [of Marlborough] the, wind is contrary, and I fear the passage will be tedious, pray God it be safe ; till they arrive in Holland wee can only guess at what wee are to expect about a peace, which is variously discoursed off in the coffee houses in towne, as I hear oute of them.

99. — 27 August 1709. Eliza[beth] Lady Hare to Sir Nicholas L'Estrange. L'ESTRANGE PAPERS.

As to deeds relating to Mr. Harvey's mortgage. Mr. Hayes has paid £100 to Miss Eliza Hare. Asks Sir Nicholas to write to Mr. Harvey concerning payment of interest.

100.—26 September 1709. Sir Nicholas L'Estrange, Bart., to Lady Hare.

Enclosing letter for Mr. Harvey as to payment of interest. Was told on Friday last by Captain Host of an unfortunate shot her son George Hare had received on board the packet on his return from Portugal, while he and some other officers bravely defended their vessel against a French privateer. Hopes he may recover and asks for further news of him.

101.—27 October 1709. Lady Hare, London, to Sir Nicholas L'Estrange, Bart. at Hunstanton.

Has delivered Sir Nicholas's letter to Mr. Harvey, who has paid the interest due to her. Her son George only arrived in London last night, so she waited to see him before answering enquiries. His misfortune is not so bad as she expected ; he was shot through the face and tongue, but the scars are small and will not disfigure him. The worst is the loss of his teeth "being a pritty many makes him speak a little odly, but it's a very great mercy that he escap'd so well, and that his jawbone was not broke all to pieces, the bullet coming so near as his teeth, his cheek goes in with a little dent, where the bullet went in, so must all wayes ware a patch, but it will be noe great matter. He is in hopes of coming into Norfolk for recrutes, that is his business now of coming over. I wish he may ever escape as well."

102.—16 March 1709-10. Thomas L'Estrange, London, to his father, Sir Nicholas L'Estrange, Bart , at Hunstanton.

"The D^{rs} [Sacheverell's] speech has putt the rest of the proceedings out of everybody's head, & I think Sr Tho. Parker's reply, with one party at least as generally took place of it, especially since his sudden promotion, by which the Queen is supposed to have declar'd herself enough to turn the scale had it been equall before. We are yett in suspense to know the Lords determination. One side has shewn how absolutely resistance is forbid, upon any pretence whatsoever . . . . The managers by many instances shew that the means us'd to bring about the Revolution can have no other name but that of resistance." It was acknowledged by all that the Doctor's speech "was very artfully compos'd, since by what he spoke and his manner of speaking it, he so captivated the good will and benevolence even of some of his accusers, ... his very speech was prov'd an aggravation of his other crimes ; for besides the weakness of the cause was more manifest by his resort to art ; so after his 1st appeal to the mobb, in printing his answers, the business yett undecided, that of publishing his speech too must needs be to stir them up to further disorders, butt supposing it to have affected the Lords att the time of the delivery and to have been since misrepresented, as 'tis reported, he has given each of them one. I had the honour this morning to entertain Lady Ann, Lady Harpur and Sir John with some tea : the ladys I find who are acknowledg'd att this juncture to be very understanding in affairs of State, even to the degree of laying wagers, but all runs against the D^r, with some of them by a superiority of 10, some 15, butt within 5 allowing for accidents too they can be pretty positive. The hawkers

LE STRANGE PAPERS.

upon all occasions acknowledge themselves obliged to the D^r. The Press was nev[er so] fruitfull, nor did witt ever appear in more different shapes or m [*torn out*] to be taken notice of but most to the tune of

The Church is fallen, the Q^n is sad
The L^{ds} are puzled the Com^{ns} are —"

103.—21 May 1713. James Calthorpe to his brother Sir Christopher Calthorpe.

"I hear of more reioycinges for Peace [of Utrecht] out of towne then in towne, all I wish is that it may prove to the good of the Kingdome in generall and then it must bee to satisfaction, wee had yesterday a Proclamacion for a Thanksgiving upon the 16th of June, from which 'tis concluded that the Parliam^t will continue soe long."

104.—Easter Sunday [before 1719]. Lewkenor L'Estrange at Cambridge to Sir Nicholas L'Estrange Bart., at Hunstanton, to be left at the post house in Docking, Norfolk.

Enclosing copy found among the Bishop of Ely's papers of a letter from Sir Roger L'Estrange to Sir Christopher Calthorpe dated 16 Ffebruary 1702–3.

"The late departure of my daughter from the Church of England to the Church of Rome wounds the very heart of me, for I do solemnly protest in the presence of Almighty God that I knew nothing of it, and for your further satisfaction I take the freedom to assure you upon the faith of a man of honour & conscience that as I was born and brought up in the communion of the Church of England, so I have been true to it ever since with a firm resolution with God's assistance to continue in the same to my lives end. Now in case it should please God in his providence to suffer this scandal to be reviv'd upon my memory when I am dead and gone make use I beseech you of this paper in my justification which I deliver as a sacred truth."

"So help me God,
"ROGER L'ESTRANGE."

105.—28 October 1744. Roger L'Estrange at Falmouth to John Mendham, Saddler, at Dereham.

"After suffering so much as I have by sea I was in greate hopes in my return to England to have had the pleasure of haveing a letter from you. . . . . I went from on board His Magisty's shyp the *Royal Soverraiyn* on board the *Surprise* privitteare carreing twenty carrige guns and fourteen swivell wee have takeing four very riche prizes. Wee are now in Falmouth peare in order to stop our leake wich was so bad that wee wear oblidged to ceape two hands att the pumps night and day. Wee have had a greate loss in the Lowsinge the finest shyp in the navey of a hundred and twelve brass guns and a leven hundred men all lost iest of where wee took a prise, her masts was drove a shore in to ganszy and several chests of cloes."

THE MANUSCRIPTS OF THE LATE AUGUSTUS WILLIAM SAVILE, ESQ., OF RUFFORD ABBEY, NOTTS.

SAVILE MSS.

Among the historical characters who successively lived at Rufford Abbey after the dissolution may be named the Earls of Shrewsbury, for three generations, Sir George Savile, first Marquis of Halifax, and Sir George Savile, the popular member for Yorkshire in the time of George III. ; but the manuscripts still preserved there show few traces of these illustrious residents. The collection has, however, considerable value and interest. It includes :—

A Chartulary of the Abbey drawn up in 1471, a copy of which is among the Harleian MSS. in the British Museum. Thoroton, the historian of Notts, appears to have made careful use of this volume, and one or two brief notes in his handwriting are made therein.

Many deeds of gift, &c. to the abbey from the time of Henry II., and documents relating to the property of the Savile family in Nottinghamshire and the West Riding of Yorkshire ; the following seem noteworthy among them :—

Henry II. Grant "de teloneo, passagio, et pontagio" to the abbey and monks of Rufford. Witnesses : Thomas Canc', Richard Bishop of London, Reginald Earl of Cornwall. Dated at Westminster.

18 Hen. III. March 9. Oxford. Licence to Richard Folyot to enclose his mansion at Grymeston, co. Notts, with a moat and a crenellated wall of stone.

8 Edw. I., Aug. 18. York. Licence to the Abbot of Rufford " quod de propriis boscis suis qui sunt infra metas foreste nostre de Shirewode facere possit unam trencheiam latitudinis quadraginta pedum per pedem de foresta in circuitum boscorum illorum et commodum suum de bosco et subbosco trenchie illius facere prout sibi magis viderit expedire."
(Portion of seal remaining.)

13 Edw. I. A grant of free warren to the Abbey of Rufford in "Rufford, Cratele, Eykering, Almeton, Rolaghe, Parkelathe, Kirketon, Tokesford, Foxholes, and Morton" in co. Notts, in Rotherham and Carleton, co. York, &c.

35 Edw. III. 20 May. Carlisle. Renewal of grant of the manor of Barrowby, co. Lincoln, lately held by Stephen Peirson, a rebel, to John de Sandale.

2 Eliz. 20 May. Edw. Savile's marriage settlement with the Lady Mary Talbot, daughter of the Earl of Shrewsbury, of the manors of Tankersley and Haldisly, co. York. Signed by Edward Savile, George Lord Talbot, Francis Earl of Shrewsbury, Edward Earl of Derby, Henry Earl of Rutland, William Earl of Pembroke, Sir William Cecil, Sir William Cordell, Sir James Dyer, &c.

" The Inventory of all the goods ornaments playte ande bells belongyng or apperteynyng to the churche of Sandall magna mayde by the vicar and churchwardens withe other iij onest men of the parishe, maide at the commandment off the kinges maiesties commyssioners the xj day of marche in the thryd yere of Edwarde the sext.

In primis one Chalis withe a patene of Silver.

Item iiij^{or} bells hanggyng in the steple ij sakeryn bells ande ij handbells.

Item one payre of olde sensars and a crosse of laten.

Item ij kandyllstykks for the hey altar of laten and a crowett of pewther

SAVILE MSS. Item one suctt of vestments of redd saten of bryddgys lackyn ij albes andc a cope.
Item ij coopes the one of qwyte fustian bordred with ryde the other of dornyxe bordred withe changable velvett.
Item iij olde vestmentes havyng nothyng to theyme belongynge.
Item iij alter clothes ix towells beyng old.
Item a fruute for the altar of sondrye colours.
Item a whyte vestment of fustyan withe all thynges appertenyng.
Item ij hanggyngs for the alter for lent of lynnen clothe withe redd crossys.
Item a lenten clothe hanggyng in the quere withe fyve banerclothes of hurden payntyd.
Item one hullye water Fatt in the qwere
            per me Johannem Normavell vicar.   per me Hugh Savill."

About seventeen Subsidy Rolls for the West Riding of Yorkshire, chiefly 30–32 Eliz., George Savile, of Wakefield, principal collector, giving the names of contributors in the wapentakes of Agbrigg and Morley, Skyrack, Strafford, Osgodcross, and Staincross.

A small Collection of Letters (stitched together), of the sixteenth and early seventeenth centuries, chiefly addressed to the Earls of Shrewsbury, of which the following are abstracts:—

1545, April 21. Francis Earl of Shrewsbury to Sir Henry Seyvill, knight. (Much torn and decayed.) About musters and arms in the West Riding.

1546, August 1. Tankersley. Sir Henry Savile to the Earl of Shrewsbury. Has been killing stags at Tankersley and Wharncliff, in company with Lord Talbot. Other personal matters.

1547, April 6. Pontefract. Sir Henry Savile to ——. Encloses a paper of advice and instructions as to his conduct, &c.

1552–3, Feb. 19. Soothill. Sir Henry Savile to the Earl of Shrewsbury, lord president of the north parts. Asking repayment of loan.

1555–6, March 24. Soothill. Sir Henry Savile to the Earl of Shrewsbury, President of the North. Has continued in great sickness, yearly decaying from worse to worse. "By longe advyse I have de . . . . at the spryng to enter the new dyett " . . . . . " butt suerly I accountt myselff a dead man this yere or the next at the ferthyst."

1556, May 11. Soothill. Sir Hy. Savile, John Nevyll, and John Lacy to the Earl of Shrewsbury, President of the King aud Queen's most honourable Council in the north parts.

" Our duties remembred. Accordyng to the kynge and quene's commandement from your lordship to us directed, we have travelled in the mater for the murder of Doctor Haldisworth. First we have send unto you William Haworth which is taken of suspect for the said murder. Also we have appoynted certen other persons for dyverse causes to be examyned at such tyme as we most convenyently thynk it requisite for the same. Also for so much as we thynk that the wachemen in Halifax did not their duties that nyght, we have taken surties of theyme to appere before your lordship in the kyng and quene's counsell upon ten dayes warnyng to be giffen by Jamys Stanesfelde bayliff of Halifax or his laufull deputie in the church, or any other laufull warnyng that your lordship shall giff theyme."

1556, May 15 [Friday]. Soothill. Sir Henry Savile to the Earl of Shrewsbury, President of King and Queen's Council assembled in the North. On some business concerning William Haworth which the Council wished Mr. Nevile and himself to attend to. Edward Savile will wait upon his lordship that night with other prisoners; he went to Ferrybridge to know whether the Earl was at York or Sheffield. Mr. Nevile and Mr. Lacy will dine that day at Soothill, and he expects to hear of more prisoners.

SAVILE MSS.

1557, May 9. Sir William Cordell to the Earl of Shrewsbury, President of the North. " After my moste humble dewtye unto your good lordeshipp beynge glad to here that the same ys somwhat recoveryd of your disease. I thynke er this my letter shall come unto your L. hands you have receyved letters from my lordes of the Councell to send upp Bradford, the which made the traytorous proclamation thatt was sett forth by Stafford and likewyse the traytorous and hereticall book set forth agaynst the King's and the Queen's (majesties?). And I most humble requyre your L. to procede with the endytyng & arreignment of the rest that remayne with you of this Rebellyon with as (moche?) spede as convenyently yow maye accordyng to the tenor of ther LL. former letters. And that thendytements of Stafford, Bradford, Peter Sanders, Stowell & the Frenchman, the which be now in the Towre, maye be sent upp hether with all spede to procede agaynst them accordynge to justice. The king & the queen's majesties our lord be praysed are in good helthes, and wyshyng unto your L. the like good helth, &c. From London this ixth of Maye 1557."

1557, July 20. The Court at Richmond. Same to same. On behalf of his cousin Whalley of Notts, who has been directed by his lordship to put himself in order with his servants, tenants, &c. to be employed in such service as should be appointed them. Whalley's ability, owing to his long imprisonment and tedious suits, agreeth nothing with the forwardness of his heart to serve the king and the queen.

1558, Sept. 9. Court at St. James. Same to same. Complimentary. " Occurrents here be none but that yt ys reported that the kyng's majestie with his . . . ys gone towards . . . tterell. The quenes majestie our lord be praysed ys well recovered."

1560, April 25. From my house at the Rolls. Same to same. A long letter referring to his lordship's sickness, and to an interview with Lady Pope about the debts of Sir Thomas Pope.

1561-2, Feb. 24. From my house at the Rolls. Same to same. Referring to the marriage of Lord Shrewsbury's eldest son to the Earl of Pembroke's daughter.

33 Eliz. May 27. Articles of Agreement between Sir George Savile, of Heath, co. York, knt., and John Savile, of Howley, in the said county, Esq.

1573, Dec. 30. Accounts of Mr. Avercy Copley, receiver to Mr. Edward Savile, esquier, of all his rents and revenues due to him the said Edward for all his manors, &c. for one whole year, &c. (5 papers.)

1580, Sept. 3. From my poor house in Suffolk. Sir Wm. Cordell to the Earl of Shrewsbury, Earl Marshal of England. Acknowledging his efforts to compound the unnatural and unkind difference and questions between his cousin Francis Peake, and his brothers and sisters, although there had not hitherto grown such fruit thereof as the pains and travail deserved.

1589-90, March 11. Paper endorsed.—A note of Leases sealed at Sheffield to Sir George Savile's use out of Mr. Edward Savile's lands.

SAVILE MSS.

1564–5, March 7. Thornhill. Sir Henry Savile to the Earl of Shrewsbury. Being informed that his lordship is about to remove the keeper of Pontefract Castle, recommends Mr. Richard Bunny, "a gentillman of good habylytye & muche honestye," for the place.

1577–8, March 10. Bond of Elizabeth Countess of Shrewsbury. "Be yet knowen to all menne that I Elyzabethe Contys of Shrobery have resavyd of my lorde my hosbande towardes the pamente of my detes one thosante ponde, whyche thosante ponde I covente and bynde me my eares executoryes and asynes to repaye unto my sade lorde and hosbande yn maner and forme foloynge, that ys to say, two-honderythe ponde yn the yere of owre god one thosante fyre honderythe forescore, two hondryth ponde and . . (sic) that day twelve monte other two honderyth, and so yerly two honderythe ponde tyll the wolle some of one thosante ponde be payd yn wetenes therof I have potte to my hande and seal and wretyne thys with my owne hande.

E. SHROUESBURY.

Sealed and delevered the xth of Marche 1577 in presens of us here underwritten knowldginge the dett above mentioned.

WALTER GROSVENOR.
DAVID OWEN.
THO. BAYLY."

1591, Aug. 14. Court at Farnham. Lord Burghley to Earl of Shrewsbury (holograph).

"My very good Lord, I am right sorry that I am not hable as I am right willyng, to make your lo. a better satisfaction in this cases of your lieutenancyes. I shall hartely reteyne your letters patents for Darbyshyre being passed the Great Seal, but I will aventur (sic) to do it, untill I may farder consider therof, how and by what pretence I may staye it. I have attempted of late to have her Majesty apoynt you to be the lieutenant of Nottyngham as my L. your father was, but she is induced to alledg that whan the Erles of Rutland lyved, they war lieutenants ther. I answered that somctyme it was so, and sometymes not, and so I cold not obteyn it, and the rather as I se for that when Mr. Thos. Markham alledged some thyngs ageynst Sir Thomas Stanhop, hir Majesty hath sene his letters wherin he doth so flatly deny the complaynts to be trew, as hir Majesty semeth to creditt hym therin.

At this tyme I am also sorry that I cold not differ any longar the direction from hir Majesty, which now I do sygnefy by hir express commandment, for the sendyng upp of Mr. Savell, whose fortune is hard at (lx ?) yers of age to be examyned whyther he be a naturall foole or noe. As I perceave ther will be some errors fownd in the fynes and recoveryes passed ageynst Mr. Savell. And so I humbly tak my leave."

1590–91, February 15. From my house in Phillpott Lane. Sir Edward Osborne to the Earl of Shrewsbury. Reminds his lordship that he had become bound unto one Henry Lee for 105*l*. to be paid on Feb. 2 last past, for the which he had Lord Shrewsbury's hand and Sir G. Savile's to hold him harmless; and presses for payment of the amount.

1593, July 6. Lambeth Marsh. Richard Topclyffe to the Earl of Shrewsbury. Business matters.

1593, July 17. Gainsborough. Robert Somerscales to the Earl of Shrewsbury. Business matters.

1592, Dec. 16. Pomfret. Sir George Savile to the Earl of Shrewsbury at Sheffield Lodge.

1593, Sept. 22. Thornhill. Same to same. About his patent for the stewardship of the Isle of Axholme.   SAVILE MSS.

1598, May 12. Same to same.

1602, Aug. 14. Newington. Same to same. "Behold inclosed the manner of her Majesty's late entertainment at my Lord Keeper's house, whereunto I must add the doughty playing of 'Barly Breaks,' dancing of country dances by the boys of the Chapel, and excellent 'vawtinge of tumblers.' The feast so great, as six dishes upon head (*sic*) stood so furnished through the whole service which by report is greatly spoken of in London." The Queen likely to go forward from Oatlands to Lord Hertford's. The gifts many and great, the jewel presented by the Lord Keeper held richly worth 1,000*l.*, another jewel worth 600*l.*; and the gown of rainbows very rich embroidered.

1602, Sept. 14. Newington. George Savile to the Earl of Shrewsbury. Concerning Sir Henry Bromley, Mr. Curzon, and other personal matters. His father is come to Barrowby.

[1603]. Same to same. On like business.

1604, April 2. Cottesbrooke. George Savile to his aunt the Countess of Shrewsbury. Has come to this place to deliver the pill her ladyship had sent to Mr. Reade, whose senses and memory fail him. Concerning his affection for Mr. Reade's daughter, and her portion.

1604–5, March 4. Thornhill. George Savile to his uncle the Earl of Shrewsbury. Is informed Sir Carey Reynolds (having got a book of 50*l.* of the King in reversion for 41 years) hath put therein the three principal pastures his father (Sir G. S.) has in his lease of Wakefield mills, the taking whereof again his father will not meddle with, as he says the lease he has will serve his time, and therefore leaves the writer to take proceedings in the matter, who has no means of procuring money to take them again. Desires his lordship's advice therein. His father has begun to set up a saw mill in Emley park, and also smithies, if the water can be made to serve both.

1605, Sept. 21. Howley. Sir John Savile to the Earl of Shrewsbury at Worsopp. Describes his bad state of health. Regrets that his lordship has no intention to return to Sheffield before going to London, having a great desire to see him.

1606, Sept. 30. Thornhill. Sir Geo. Savile to the Earl of Shrewsbury at Sheffield Lodge. Thanks him for his good offices at court. His cousin Baron [Savile?] told him he thought his (the Baron's) disease was the gout; but he hears it was rather feared to be the palsy. Hears not of any "Poss" of Frison horses or mares to be gotten in these parts, but yet Lord Darcy bought one by chance at York of a captain. Has sent to York to enquire of captain, merchant, lawyer, gent., &c. if such can be found. Fray in Emley park between two bucks, one so sore wounded that the keeper easily took him.

1611, Oct. 1, and 1611–12, March 11. Welbeck. Chasrles Cavendish to Henry Butler. On business matters. Also an undated letter signed—
"Ca. Cavendysshe" to the same.

SAVILE MSS. Paper headed " The Account for the Journey to York 1666, July 3 —July 20."

		£	s.	d.
July 5	To the musick at Pontefract	0	10	0
	A messenger to Sir Wm Lowther's	0	1	0
Pontefract 6	The Bills of the Star at Pontefract	7	12	0
	To the servants of the house	0	8	6
York 7	To Lord Fleshevells (Frecheville's) trumpets	0	10	0
	a paire of spurs for the postilion	0	1	0
	The taking out the arms	0	10	0
	To Mr Gosling for a sword	1	0	0
	for Gilbert's sword	1	0	0
	for your Poskett	0	5	0
	To the barber	0	5	0
Selby July 14	To the 7 soldiers	1	12	6
	To one soldier more	0	7	6
Doncaster July 22	bottle of Renish & a rol	0	2	1

Sir George Savile, afterwards Marquis of Halifax, had a command in the Yorkshire Militia at this time.

A series of family letters ranging from about 1696 to 1733, the earliest being addressed to "Mr George Savile at Christ Church in Oxford." Early in 1700 is a letter addressed to the same "at Mr Wotton's at the Three Daggers near the Temple Gate Fleet Street," Savile at that time being a student in the Temple. In June 1704 is a letter to "Sir George Savile, Barron^t in Gerrard Street, near St. Anns Church, London," from his grandfather. The following are noteworthy among the remaining letters :—

1706, April 4. Council Chamber at Kensington. Copy of Order in Council about Papists, referring to the great boldness and presumption of the Romish priests and Papists in the kingdom, and requiring the Lord Lieutenant of Notts (John, Duke of Newcastle) to summon the Deputy lieutenants to take a distinct and particular account of all Papists or reputed Papists within the respective subdivisions of the county, with their qualities, estates, and places of abode.

This is inclosed in a letter from Haughton, dated May 22, of Robert Chappell to Sir G. Savile at Rufford, stating that the justices have had a meeting at the Crown inn in Mansfield, and will meet again at the house of Mr. Edward Jackson in East Retford.

1710, Sept. 4. Copy of a letter of Sir G. Savile to the Duke of Leeds, declining to interest himself on behalf of the Duke's candidates in Yorkshire and Notts.

1714, May 9. Edward Copley to Sir G. Savile. Thanks him for promoting his brother to Thornhill Church. Recommends a young lady to his prudent consideration, pretty young Madam Savile [of Methley] his worthy departed friend's only daughter; her mother may give her what fortune she pleases, she is very agreeable and pretty, of a fine mild temper and gentle behaviour, &c.   SAVILE MSS.

1715, Nov. 9. Southwell. Edward Becher to Sir G. Savile at Rufford.
Wishes to know the truth of a report that his outhouses and haystacks had been set on fire by some rogues in revenge for showing his good affection and zeal for the government, and offers help.

1727, June 15. London. B. Savile to her son Sir George Savile. On the death of George I.—Your sister and I saw him (Geo. II.) proclaimed at Charing Cross 'where there was vast hosays and we thought visible satisfactions.' Mrs. Devayn went close to the King and Queen's coach when they came from Richmond yesterday to observe them and saw the King look very heavy and thoughtful; and the Queen's eyes were so extremely swollen and red as she had not seen the like. This concern for a father at such a time I think adds to their good character.

1727, June 20. [London.] Gertrude Savile to her brother Sir George Savile.
"As to your enquiries about mourning upon this melancholy occasion I suppose you have the printed general orders in the country; but more particularly what we are informed by Mr. Lesure and several others is, that your dress must be cloth, with only three buttons, weepers, cambric turnover, black sword and buckles, "shamy" shoes and gloves, black worsted stockings, no powder for a few weeks. Mr. Lesure says your black for Lord Cadogan will not do . . . . We are told your children need not be put into mourning, Lady Pontefract (who is lady of the bed-chamber to the Queen) does not put hers in mourning. Lord Lichfield and Lady Hinchinbrook are two more precedents of the same. I believe you ought to have a night-gown of something of black and white, or grey, but will enquire further about that and let you know.
All things here are quiet (except the prodigious hurry about mourning) and peaceable, as if nothing of moment had happened. Joy is the universal fashion, without any mixture of concern; all parties seem pleased and full of hopes. The malcontent clergy who were so in the late reign (I know not why) now preach obedience, loyalty and unity. Those who have never been at court before, or not for thirteen years, go now there, never were such crowded drawing-rooms. . . The King and Queen's behaviour upon this occasion everybody agrees is very handsome, with a proper gravity and concern in their countenance, and condescension and goodness to all. There is a very just, I think, and fine character of the late King in last Saturday's Journal, whose memory deserves some gratitude from us, I think something more than I see paid to it."

1728, May 29. Note of a meeting at the King's Arms in Pall Mall of twenty-one gentlemen from the three Ridings of Yorkshire in support of Sir George Savile as member for the county in succession to Sir Thomas Wentworth.
Many other papers also relating to his candidature.
There is also a bundle of correspondence relating to Yorkshire elections dated between Sept. and Dec. 1733. Among the writers are Sir Wm. Strickland, Lord Carlisle, and Lord Malton.
Another bundle contains the following papers, among others of no importance :—

1715, Oct. 2. Owthorpe. Julius Hutchinson to Sir George Savile at Rufford.
Is apprehensive that by hauling so many people to gaol against whom there is nothing to object but that they are papists the executioners of those warrants and their friends too who have signed

SAVILE MSS. them may be rendered so odious in the sight of their country that they cannot be serviceable to his Majesty. They may seize indeed, but their persons will not be secure in the gaol unless they who are militia officers will be content to wait at the doors, as they have as yet no soldiers under them.

1715, Oct. 2. Letters of St. Andrew Thornhagh and J. White to Sir George Savile on the same subject.

1715, Oct. 18. Newcastle House. The Duke of Newcastle to Sir George Savile and the Deputy Lieutenants of Notts (Copy).

Thanks them for their services in preserving peace at this critical juncture, but asks pardon for differing in opinion about the construction of that part of the Order from the Council which relates to the seizing of Papists and Nonjurors. He thinks it extends to all papists' and nonjurors in general as they must be more or less disaffected to the government.

P.S. " We here make a slight business of the Rebellion in Northumberland, but you may judge better of it than we can, however the enemies of the Government appear every day so barefaced that all possible care ought to be taken to suppress them and to bring them to their deserved punishment, which can never be too great for men who at once endeavour to destroy the religion and liberty of a free people."

1715, Oct. 25. Newcastle House. Same to same (copy). Has received with the greatest pleasure the accounts of the seasonable loyalty of the towns of Nottingham and Worksop. Has spoken to the Duke of Marlborough about sending troops to Nottingham, and a regiment of dragoons is already marching there.

At Mr. Savile's estate office in Thornhill, Yorkshire, are many court rolls from the time of Henry VII. downwards, of the manors of Thornhill, Shelfe, Stainland, Eland, Skircote, Rawtenstall, Ovenden, Heptonstall, and Wadsworth. Dated 40 Eliz. 19 Jan. is an original indenture between Sir Geo. Savile, knt., John Lacy, of Brearley, Esq., and the freeholders of Wadsworth (Ambrose Greenwood, Thos. Naylor, Richard Wadisworth, Luke Stansfeild, and upwards of twenty others), whereby the right of common in Midgley is granted to the latter ; signatures and seals are attached.

J. J. CARTWRIGHT.

BRIDGEWATER MSS.

THE MANUSCRIPTS PRESERVED AT THE BRIDGEWATER TRUST OFFICE, WALKDEN, LANCASHIRE.

Some years ago nine boxes of miscellaneous historical and legal papers were removed from Bridgewater House, London, to the offices of the Trust. These were in the course of the year 1885, by direction of the trustees, sorted and scheduled by Mr. Strachan Holme, the Estate Clerk, and the order to which they were reduced by the care of that gentleman has greatly facilitated the examination of them for the purposes of the Historical MSS. Commission.

The papers consist, to a large extent, of the legal collections of Sir Thomas Egerton, the first Lord Ellesmere, who held the offices of Solicitor-General and Attorney-General from 1581 to 1594, of Master of the Rolls from 1594 to 1596, and of Lord Keeper and Lord Chancellor from 1596 to 1617. Of the rest, many are papers of the first two

Earls of Bridgewater in the 17th century, and some belong to the family of the Earls of Derby. The papers that fall within the purview of the Commission's inquiry are described in the following pages according to their present arrangement in parcels, for the object of facility in future reference. A collection of dockets of Letters Patent granted during the time of Sir John Puckering, Lord Keeper from 1592 to 1596, have not been noticed, because they are, as a matter of course, to be found on the Rolls. And of papers belonging to the last century the following have been passed over:—I. Papers about property in Marine *alias* Wellclose Square, London. II. A few business papers, including coal accounts, relating to the Bridgewater Canal. III. Papers in connexion with a trusteeship of the Waldegrave family, including many letters of the widow of George, the fifth Earl, who died in 1794.

BRIDGEWATER MSS.

Four charters relating to Buildwas Abbey, Shropshire, call for special notice, alike for their intrinsic interest and as being (with one other) the earliest documents in the collection, while with regard to one of them there is a curious question as to its date or authenticity. They will be found under *Shropshire*, in the alphabetical arrangement of counties.

None of the papers printed in Mr. J. Payne Collier's *Egerton Papers*, edited for the Camden Society in 1840, are to be found in this collection. They are still preserved at Bridgewater House, in London.

WILLIAM DUNN MACRAY.

The following table of the various parcels of papers described below will exhibit their diversfied character as well as the order in which they are arranged:—

   I.—*Select Documents.*
   II.—*Royal Papers.*
   III.—*General Autographs.*
   IV.—*Family Papers.*
   V.—*Cheshire.*
   VI.—*Lincolnshire.*
     a. *Charity Papers.*
   VII.—*London.*
   VIII.—*Northamptonshire.*
   IX.—*Shropshire.*
   X.—*Staffordshire.*
   XI.—*Warwickshire.*
   XII.—*Westmoreland.*
   XIII.—*Shire Papers.*
     a. *Bucks.*
     b. *Leicestershire.*
     c. *Lancashire.*
     d. *Nottinghamshire.*
     e. *Somerset.*

BRIDGEWATER MSS.

XIV.—*Wales : Denbighshire.*
    a. *Council of the Marches.*
    b. *Sheriffs.*
    c. *Abergavenny Papers.*
    d. *Carbery Papers.*
    e. *Herbert Papers.*
XV.—*Isle of Man.*
    a. *Priory of Whithern.*
XVI.—*Bolton Papers:* 1693–1700.
XVII.—*Brereton Papers.*
XVIII.—*Cheyne Papers.*
XIX.—*Derby Papers.*
XX.—*Howe Papers:* Manor of Kempley, Gloucestershire.
XXI.—*Ralph Rokeby Papers :* 1596.
XXII.—*Sutherland Papers.*
XXIII.—*Wrey Papers.*
XXIV.—*Official Papers.*
XXV.—*Ecclesiastical Papers.*
XXVI.—*Exchequer Papers.*
XXVII.—*Chancery Papers.*
XXVIII.—*Law Papers.*
XXIX.—*Star Chamber.*
    a. *Case of Lord Vaux, Sir T. Tresham, and others, for harbouring Edmund Campian:* 1581.
XXX.—*Bucks Militia:* 1696–1708.
XXXI.—*Trade and Plantations.*
XXXII.—*Privateers:* 1693.
XXXIII.—*Admiralty:* 1695–1703.
XXXIV.—*Peerage Patents:* 11 *Edw. III.*
XXXV.—*Bonds:* Sir Will. Courteen.
XXXVI.—*Miscellaneous.*

I. *Select Documents.*

In a parcel endorsed " Curious and historical Deeds," which contains a selection of some documents from the various other parcels which were judged to be specially noticeable, the following are to be found :—

Grant (*c.* 1180–1200) from Stephen de Nerbona to William son of Ralph de Filungele (Fillengley, Warwickshire), in consideration of his fighting a duel for him ("pro homagio et servicio suo, et propter duellum quod fecit pro me") of two virgates of land in Stivechala (in Warwickshire), with additional land near the high road leading from Allesle, with license to sell, or mortgage ("wagiare"), or assign to the house of the brothers of the Temple, or of the Hospitallers, or any other religious house : with a full warranty, " propter quod fecit pro me predictum duellum." Witnesses:—Bertram de Verdon, Rob. de Curli, Walter fil. Reginaldi, Rob. fil. Willelmi, Rob. Franceis, Rob. clerico de Alvaton',

Rob. Herlesheved, Ernaldo le Scirmersur, Walter de Filungeleia, Ric. fil. Turchil, Rob. de Overtona, Ric. clerico de Stivecheala, Jurdan de Filungeleia, Alex., Rob. Blanchebuche, Reg. de Childisbra. Seal lost.

BRIDGEWATER MSS.

Agreement between Sir John Basset and Sir Thomas Beek, for the marriage of John, son of the former, to Maud, daughter of the latter, Sir John Basset allowing them for the first six years 40s. annually, and afterwards 100s. annually during his life, and Sir John Beek allowing 26s. 8d. for the first six years and six marks afterwards. Dated at Chedulle, Monday after the feast of the Assumption 5 Hen. IV. (18 Aug. 1404). Seal of arms : " Sigillum Johannis Bassat " (sic). Articles of marriage between Ralph Basset and Ellen Egerton in 1474 are noted further on.

"Modus tenendi parliamenta" in Ireland ; exemplification by Sir John Talbot "de Halomshire," Lieut. of Ireland, at Trym, 12 Jan. an. Hen. [VI.] 6 (1428), of articles written on a parchment roll taken with Sir Christopher de Preston, at the time of his arrest at Clane ; together with articles written on a paper schedule and taken at the same time, as to the form of election of the King and doing homage ; fragment of Great Seal.

Act of the Irish Parliament suspending Poyning's Law ; [28 Hen. VIII. c. 4, 1537]. On vellum, with the Great Seal perfect.

"The Book of Garnsey (Guernsey,) and the Islands adjoining "—a folio volume, 1580-87, with table of contents prefixed. It contains the following articles :—

1. " Copie of Henry VI.'s graunt to those of Garnsie testified by the Bailives."

2. " Orders [of the Council] touching the Isle of Garnsey, xi of March, 1568."

3. " Articles by copie of chronicles, charters & privileges for Garnsey, of services done by those of the Isle against forreine enemies."

4. " Mr. D[octor] Hammon's report touchinge ye matters of Garnesie."

5. " Customes of the Isle of Garnesie differing from the customes of Normandie."

6. " The sum of the complaints exhibited by the inhabitants of Garnesie, with the bailifes and jurates awnswer thereto."

7. " An abstracte of such orders, grantes and privileges as the inhabitants of Guernsey do ground their complaints upon."

8. " Articles presented by the procurer for reformation of the Isle of Guernsie " (in French).

9. " The opinion of D[octor] Hammond and Mr. Norton upon certaine articles sent up by the procurer for reformation of the Isle of Guernsey, 6 Aug., 1580."

10. " Letter from D[octor] Hammond and Mr. Norton [to Sir Fr. Walsingham, London, 3 Aug., 1580,] touching the articles putte up by the procurer."

11. " An order sett downe by the Lords concerninge complaints of the Isle of G."

12. " Postilles to such articles as are thought meete to be presently answered."

13. " Orders for Garnesie sett downe by the Lords, September, 1580."

14. The Council " to Sir Thos. Leighton, sent with certaine orders concerninge the establishment of certaine things in Guernsie ; Sept. 1580."

U 24952.   I

BRIDGEWATER MSS.

15. "Points remained unredressed in the matters of Guernsey."
16. "The effect of the bill of complaint of the inhabitats of Alderney against John Chamberleyne and Edmond Sexton resident there"; May, 1585.
17. "Advertizement touchinge the state of Alderney, with a petition [to Sir F. Walsingham, from John Chamberleyne the Queen's farmer there,] for order by Commission for reformacion, &c."
18. "Articles to be observed by the Commissioners for the Isle of Alderney."
19. "Proportion of munition for the Isle."
20. "Orders from the Lords for the buildinge of an Conger house in Garnsey."
21. "Orders set down by the Lords in certain causes upon complaint of the inhabitants of Garnesey"; 9 Oct. 1580.
22. "Articles exhibited by the Queen's Commissioners to the bailyf and jurats of Garnesey"; with their answer.
23. Petition to the Queen by Lewes de Vyck, her attorney in Guernsey.
24. The Commissioners' report of their inquisition in Guernsey.
25. (*Loose.*) Petition to the Lord Chancellor Brackley from John Herault, bailly of Jersey.
26. (*Loose.*) Reasons offered to the King in council against an order of 23rd March 169¾ concerning a Register of Certificates in Guernsey.

Original draft of the Petition from Parliament to Q. Eliz. for the execution of Mary, Queen of Scots, with many alterations both by Burleigh and Egerton.

Copy of a grant of the office of Registrar of the Court of Chancery to Laurence Washington, 26 March, 35 Eliz. (1593); with a warrant for the apprehension of John Saunders, signed by the same L. Wasshington (*sic*). 28 July, 1595; and a letter without date from him ("La. Wasshingtō") and three others to the countess of Derby about the Brackley woods. It seems probable that this Washington was the great-great-grandfather of general Washington. The two last-mentioned papers are mounted in glass.

A folio volume, consisting of forty leaves, in parchment cover, containing descriptions, very neatly written, of various forms of horses' bits, with Indian-ink drawings of all of them, very well executed; by Arthur Senndye, 1594. The Queen's initials are placed at the head of the second leaf.

Heads of the indictment of Francis Lord Dacres, and deposition at his trial by John Whitfield, 15 Nov. 1593.

A folio book, containing, I., "A declaration of the decay of her Maj. revenue"; II., "Touching certayne particular persons": officers employed in the revenue.

Reasons submitted to the Privy Council by Bevis Bullmer, esq., for continuing the tax upon exported coals of 5*s.* per chaldron; 1599.

Return by Henry Fanshaw of the quantity of French and Rhenish wine imported 4-10 Ja. I.; 14 Apr. 1613.

Fortunia; a Latin comedy, in five acts, apparently one of the Cambridge plays. The epilogue is in the form of a dialogue between Cantebrigia and Trina. The chief personage is Susenbrotus, a pedant, whose school-boys in the 4th Act describe in English verse the Puritan's arms, the Jesuit's, the usurer's, and the pedant's. There is also an English love-letter from Susenbrotus. The play is dated 1615; it is in folio, and bound in parchment.

[Fr. Bacon's] "Consideracons touching a warre with Spaine"; a tract addressed to Prince Charles, in folio.   BRIDGEWATER MSS.

Report from the Navy Commissioners in 1618 on the state of the Royal Navy; together with Reports in 1699 and 1700.

" Estimate of the charge of his Maj. howse according to the late projecte of converting all the dyetts into boord wages"; in the time of Charles I.

A 12mo note-book of texts of sermons heard between 3 Aug. 1645 and 30 June, 1650, with the preachers' names; apparently in the handwriting of John, second earl of Bridgewater. The names are as follows:

Mr. Shaw.
Mr. Reeves.
Mr. Hooke.
Mr. Tutevill.
Mr. Ridley.
Mr. Adams.
Mr. Barwicke.
Mr. Lante.
Mr. Jones.
Mr. Hall.
Dr. Isaackson.
Mr. Humphreys.
Mr. Hudson.
Mr. Sparkes.
Mr. Baker.
Mr. Birkhead.
Mr. Anthropes.
Mr. Morris.
Mr. Popejoy.
Mr. Lee.
Mr. Newton.
Mr. Newcomen (10 May 1646).
Dr. Utie.
Mr. Morton.
Dr. Fowler.
Mr. Edwards.
Mr. Hunt.
Mr. Rowlandson.
Mr. Eaton.
Mr. Seddon.
Mr. Carter.
Mr. Haines.
Mr. Jeffereyes.
Mr. Wilson.
Mr. Moore.
Mr. Sanderson (29 Nov. 1646).
Mr. Haile.
Mr. Reackes.
Dr. Soames.
Mr. Thurman.
Mr. Mason.
Mr. Lloyd.
Mr. King.
Mr. Piggasse.
Mr. Holway.
Mr. Witcherley.

Dr. Bunbury.
Mr. Hatton.
Mr. Guin.
Mr. Squire.
Mr. Birch.
Mr. Smith.
Mr. Norton.
Mr. Flower.
Dr. Hewson (16 Jan. 1647, 26 March 1648 &c.).
Dr. Warmestray.
Mr. Knell.
Mr. Sadler.
Mr. Rockall.
Dr. Wild.
Mr. Chibald.
Mr. Cater.
Mr. Est.
Mr. Symmonds.
Mr. Feake.
Mr. Stephens.
Mr. Swan.
Dr. Pullen.
Mr. Bonniman.
Dr. Lesley, Bp. of Down (10 Dec. 1648).
Dr. Griffith.
Mr. Hardie.
Mr. Haftridge.
Mr. Williams.
Dr. Grant.
Mr. Sompner.
Mr. Moffet.
Mr. Heylin (13 May, 17 June, 1649).
Mr. Bispham.
Mr. Cooke.
Mr. Ashley.
Mr. Henchman.
Mr. Hone.
Dr. Hewit (7 Oct., 3 Feb., 1649).
Mr. Downes.
Mr. Thompson.
Mr. Davies.
Mr. Bridge.

BRIDGEWATER MSS.

Between 14 May 1648 and 4 Nov. 1649 there are also notes of many French sermons preached by Mr. d'Espagne. The sermon on 28 Jan. 1648 (two days before the execution of Charles I.) was by Mr. Williams on 1 Tim. i. 1, 2, " I exhort therefore that first of all," &c. On some Sundays noted as spent at Burghley, Ashridge, "in the withdrawing chamber," &c., the writer enters no sermons.

A fine impression in green wax of the rare Great Seal of the Commonwealth in 1651 "in the third yeare of freedom by God's blessing restored." In a box.

A collection of 65 coats of arms of peers, on folio pages, very cleverly pricked out with a pin.

A discourse on true happiness and the chief good; "for my lord of Bridgewater"; a folio treatise of 47 pp. End of 17th cent.

"An explanation of sundry tytles and antient obscure words which have bine conteyned in the Great Rolle of the Exchequer for diverse hundreds of yeares now last past." 4 pp., folio.

A neatly written pedigree, with arms, of the Fiennes family, to " Sir Rich. Fenis, knight, father to your suppliant," and son of Edw., lord Saye; written to accompany some Chancery petition.

A note from Edm. Malone to the Marq. of Stafford, asking for the loan of Greene's *Alphonsus*, 1599, the comedy of *Love and Fortune*, 1589, and Nash's *Terrours of the Night.* "Though Mr. Malone has perhaps the largest collection of old plays now extant, the above two playes are wanting in it." 30 March, *n.y.*

II. *Royal Papers.*

Two parcels so labelled, chiefly consisting of office-copies and drafts of various letters patent and other public documents, prepared while Egerton was Solicitor General.

Copy of an account book kept by Edmund Dudley of all the sums received by him for the use of K. Hen. VII. from 9 Sept. *an.* 20 (1504) to 28 May *an.* 23 (1508). Neatly written in a small 4° book by a hand of the time of James I., with fac-similes of the King's signature, and an index of names.

Exemplification by K. Philip and Q. Mary of the Act of Parliament for attainder of Henry, Duke of Suffolk, and his adherents; injured by damp. (No. 9.)

List of fines received for confirmations of charters to towns and corporate bodies, 1 Eliz. (11.)

Agreement between Q. Eliz. and Henry Lord Strauuge respecting his third part of the office of feodary of the Honour of Richmond; 31 Jan. 1567, signed by the Queen. (*Royal Autographs*, 1.)

Draft of letters patent granting to Sir W. Raleigh the control of wine licenses, and recalling a previous grant to him of 23 Apr. 1570; with many corrections and additions in the handwriting of Egerton as Solicitor General. (12.)

Court rolls of the royal manor of Rickmersworth and Watford, Middx. 15–18 Eliz. (1573–6), those for the latter years endorsed as being taken "by Mr. Goldwell of Greyes Inne, deputy to Mr. John. Hussey, nere kinnesman to the Lady Bridgett, late countesse of Bedd., stuard there under the then erle of Bedd." (18.)

Confirmation by Q. Eliz. to Thomas and Michael Heneage of the office of Keeper of the Rolls; 29 May, 1581. (19.)   BRIDGEWATER MSS.

Deed of sale by William Kircksham, jun. esq., and Thomas Thurleby, both of Finished, Northants, to Jasper Trice and Richard Campinet, both of Godmanchester, of the chantry of Rowds or Roodes and the guild of Corpus Christi, in Godmanchester; 30 May, 1592; injured by damp. (20.)

Three drafts of articles for the settlement of Munster, 28 Eliz. (1586) endorsed as being "penned by the L. Treasourer, and as the same are passed the great seale," with notes and alterations by Egerton as Solicitor General, and the following prefatory note, "Hyt may pleas my L. to consyder whether hyt shalbe better for her Maj. to passe these articles as they are here drawen, to be spoken by her hyghnes herselff in her owne person, or as the other boke drawen, as spoken by another off her Maj., which ys all the differens betwene these two draughts as hys l. may perceave." (27.)

Particulars of lands in various counties, extent and rentals, to be given by the Queen to the Earl of Huntingdon, in exchauge for the manors of Bradbury and Hilton in Durham, 1587; on parchment rolls, very much decayed by damp. (38.)

Draft of a charter for confirmation of Stourbridge Fair, with paper by Egerton giving an abstract of its provisions, and the reasons for them; signed at the end, under the words "This draught wee all allowe," by the Mayor (Nycholas Gaunt) and five others of the Corporation of Cambridge, and by the Chancellor (R. North), Vice-Chancellor (Thos. Nevile), and twelve others of the University, including Will. Whitaker. (42.)

Letters patent of Q. Elizabeth confirming a grant of the manors of Burfield, Amors Court, Arbor, Sulhampsted, Sheffeld and Uphton in Berks, and Horton in Oxon, by Henry Lord Norreis and Margery his wife to William Cecill, Lord Burghley and John Fortescue, esq.; 13 March, 1590. Great Seal perfect. (45.)

Roll of concealed lands in Devizes granted to Sir James Croft; 1586. (55.)

Draft of commission for survey of the forfeited lands of the earl of Desmond in Ireland. (62.)

Draft of a grant to Roger Lopez, M.D., one of the Queen's physicians, of the exclusive right for a term of years of importing aniseed and sumack. (64.)

Draft of the grant of lands to the Earl of Tyrone in 1587, with note of the articles of covenant on his part. (72.)

Letter from the Council (signed by Leycester, Burghley, Hatton and Walsingham) to Solicitor General Egerton thereupon; 25 Apr. 1587 (*Autogr.* 3).

Indenture of mortgage from the Queen to the City of London, for a loan of 60,000*l*. on condition that 63,000*l*. be paid in August next, prepared by Sir Edw. Coke; with the Queen's signature, and endorsed by the Council with an order that it pass "by imediatt warrant for expedition"; 3 Jan. *an.* 41 (1599).

Deed of sale, similarly prepared for the Queen's signature, of the rectory of Colston Bassett, Notts, to Rowland Dande and Anthony Nevyll; 28 Dec. 1599.

Warrant for expediting a case in the Star-Chamber; 7 June 1603.

BRIDGEWATER MSS.   Warrant from James I. for preparing a bill in Parliament to restore Thomas Lucas, gent., to his blood and gentry, who has been pardoned for the killing of Sir Will. Brooke, knt.; 18 March, *an*. 1 (1604).

Copy, on vellum of a grant from James I. to his Queen of "all the fishing in and upon all our streames seas and coasts of England, Scotland, and Ireland, and other adjacent islandes"; not dated. (80.)

Warrant for a special commission to examine the rights &c. of Sir Robert Dormer, knt., as Master of the Hawks; 20 June 1608. (Mounted under glass.)

Warrant for writs of adjournment of Michaelmas term; 26 Sept. *an*. 7 (1609).

Warrant for the staying the passing of a grant to Sir John Ramsey, knt. and Sir James Sandylandes, knt. of the goods and chattels of Sir George Rodney, knt., late *felo de se*, because Anthony, bishop of Chichester, claims them as the King's Almoner; not dated. (Mounted under glass.)

Holograph letter from James I. to Lord Ellesmere, desiring him to return two patents which had been ordered to be prepared of grants to Lord 'Rochester "of Winnike and Darcie's landes": "if thaye be all-readdie paste youre handes, you maye sende for thaime againe, as if ye waire in doubte of some words in thaime . . . . . . Close thaime up in a paper, & sende thaime sealed unto me . . . . & lette none alive knowe of this direction." Not dated. (Mounted under glass.)

Copy of an order concerning the King's deer in his forests in the Marches of Wales, and of letters in reply from the rangers of Feckenham Forest, Corselawne Chase, Kingswood Forest, Oakley Park, and Bringwood Forest; Nov. 1616. (88.)

Pardon to Francis Short, jun. of Datchett, Bucks, and others for the drowning of Robert Compton, 18 July, 1682. (89.)

Warrant (on parchment) from William III., in French, to the Sheriff of Surrey, for payments for the Royal Buckhounds; 10 July, 1690. (91.)

Note from William Lingard to the Duke (of Bridgewater) informing him of the King's removing the Prince and Princess of Wales from St. James's, and enclosing an order from the King that none who pay their court to them shall be admitted to his presence; 13 Sept. 1737. (90.)

III. *General Autographs.*

A series of documents in parcels thus endorsed, many having the signatures of Lord Burghley and others of the Council, and of Lord Ellesmere.

Grants of Crown lands, particulars and valuations of concealed lands in various counties, &c.

Cancelled commission from Charles Lord Howard of Effingham, to Sir Walter Raleigh to take cognizance of all matters relating to the Admiralty; 12 July, 1585. (Brackley 2, 13.)

Petition from Thomas Sekford, Master of the Requests, to Q. Eliz. for license to found an alms-house at Woodbridge, Suffolk, for 13 poor men; endorsed by Burghley, "I lyk of this booke as a charitable worke in this age, wherein manie such former charitable provisions hath bene subverted."

Petition from the Bailiffs of Colchester to Sir F. Walsingham for a re-grant from Q. Eliz. of two chantries formerly granted to the town by Hen. VIII. for the maintenance of a free school, &c.; not dated.

Seven letters from Sir F. Walsingham to Egerton and one to John Popham, about the preparation of various documents, in 1587-8; one for assignment of the rectories of Ayshbury, Berks, and Wytney, Oxon (which have been granted to the Queen by the Bishops of Bath and Wells and of Oxford) to the Queen's physician Dr. Baylye; and another about a petition from the inhabitants of Havering at Bower, Essex, for a renewing of their Charter.   BRIDGEWATER MSS.

A parcel of 58 letters from Egerton, sometimes with Popham and Coke, to Lord Burghley, in 1586-1593, about the preparation and issue of various legal papers. Two in March, 1593, are about the prosecution and sentence to death of two Portuguese, Stephen Ferera de Gama and Emanuel Louys Tynoco, and the arraignment of Dr. Lopez and John Anyas an Irishman.

Letter from Lord Chancellor Bromley to Egerton, on behalf of an application from Thomas Lawley to be clerk of the Crown in some Welsh counties; 24 Nov. 1582.

Letter from the Earl of Leicester to Egerton, about an office granted by the Queen to Ferd. Richardson, a groom of her Privy Chamber; 28 Feb. 1587.

Letter from Elizabeth, Countess of Lincoln, to Egerton, on behalf of the widow of an old servant, Geo. Yorke; Horsley, 24 March, 1587.

Two letters from Thomas Windebank to the same; 1589-1600. The second is about the rectory of Colston Bassett, granted to Rowl. Dande and A. Nevill, relating to which there is a letter from Sir Edward Coke to Windebank, of 14 July 1600.

From John Tyndall to the same, recommending his brother-in-law for his service; Much Maplested, 15 Aug. 1597.

From Sir Robert Cecyll to Sir Thomas Gerard about payments for provision of "furniture" required for the Isle of Man; at the Court at Nonsuche, 12 Sept. 1595.

Two letters from the same to the L. Keeper about "the extinguishing and effacing of the Records," and about a lease of Frodsham in Cheshire; June and May, 1603.

Copy, on a vellum roll, of a report from the Officers of Arms to James I. as to authorities for the precedency of the younger sons of Earls before Knights Councillors; with another and a smaller roll of authorities for the contrary order of precedency.

Interrogatories prepared by Sir Henry Hobart, Attorney-General, to be ministered to Francis Steuart, second son to the Earl of Murray, against Brian Gunter, and Anne Gunter, his daughter, of North Morton, Berks, the said Anne being accused of possession by the devil; with Steuart's answers, signed by him, and attested by L. C. Ellesmere; 29 July 1607. The answers show that the fits of frenzy were merely pretended ; the chief tricks consisted in the girl's untying her garters unperceived and conveying them away; and to the last interrogatory, which asked whether her breath in and about the time of her fits did not "smell allways very stronge and hott, as of brimstone or some such thinge," the deponent answers, "that he did allwayes observe in her fitts that her breath had a very strange smell, as yf she had taken some compounded drinckes." Other persons who visited her were Mr. George Hamden, M.A., of Christ Church, Oxford, and the Lady Effingham. On parchment rolls.

Three letters from the Earl of Lincoln to Lord Chancellor Egerton, respecting his prosecution in the Star Chamber by Sir Edward Dymock,

BRIDGEWATER MSS. complaining that the latter is upheld by Popish recusants, and of the great sums he had to pay a Scottish gentleman to procure the King's grant for his release from the Fleet prison, from which his second letter is written; May and Aug. 1610, March, 161$\frac{0}{1}$.

Two letters from the Earl of Buckingham to Viscount Brackley, about the proceedings for his creation as Earl of Bridgewater; March-Apr. 1617 (mounted under glass); and drafts of six letters from the latter on the same subject.

Order of the procession at the funeral of Queen Anne, 27 May, 1619. On a roll.

Two letters from the Council (signed by Archbp. Abbot, Bacon, &c.) to Alice, Countess Dowager of Derby, about payment of money due to the Crown; 8 Oct., 12 Dec. 1618.

Letter from the same Countess to her daughter, the Countess of Bridgewater; desires to know if Lady Killigrew be coming to see her, that, if so, she may send to London for provision, being not so well furnished in her own house as she could wish; "besides, I am sometimes from home at the house which I am building to set it forward; that if it should please God to call for me, I might have a place to lay my stuffe in, out of my Lord Castlehaven's fingering"; Haverfield, 14 June, 1630.

Letter from Katherine, Duchess of Buckingham, to Lord Bridgewater, desiring that Mr. Lewis Owen may be spared being made Sheriff of Merioneth; 28 Oct. 1632.

The Privy Council to the same, for return of names of persons to be Sheriffs in Wales; 12 Sept. 1636.

Sir John Brydgeman to the same, on the same subject; Prinknesh, 23 Sept. 1636.

Three letters from Sir Thomas Coventry to the same, on the same subject. Sept. 1636.—Aug. 1637.

Lord Keeper Littleton to the same, about the collection of subsidies; 7 Apr. 1641.

From Lord Bolingbroke to the Earl of Bridgewater, thanking him for a red deer; 18 Jan. 1663; with letter from the latter on behalf of Lady Eliz. Cranfield in a chancery suit; Ashridge, 24 Jan. 1663.

Letter from Rev. Jos. Rawson, Lecturer at Greenwich, to the Earl of Bridgewater, at his house in Red Lion Square, asking for a recommendation by him to Lord Lisle, for his favour for election to the vicarage of Clerkenwell, Dr. Sclater being a dying man; 12 Feb. 169$\frac{0}{1}$.

Orders in Council respecting the arrangements for the funeral of Prince George of Denmark; Nov. 1708.–March 1709.

Note from the Duchess of Gloucester to Mr. Gilbert. The King's Sedgemoor Inclosure Bill will come into the Upper House; 30 March, 1791.

IV. In several parcels endorsed as *Family Papers and Relics*, we meet with the following :—

Articles of marriage between Ralph son and heir of William Basset, esq., and Ellen daughter of Hugh Egerton, esq.; morrow after the feast of St. Hilary, 13 Edw. IV. (1474).

Articles of agreement between Sir John Bromley and Will. Harpur of Ruysshall, esq. for the marriage of John, son of the latter, to Margaret daughter of the said Sir John; July, 10 Edw. IV. (1471).

Dispensation from Peter Griphus, the pope's nuncio in England, to Ralph Eggerton and Margaret Rebyll for their marriage, they being related in the third and fourth degree of consanguinity; Lond., 11 June 1509.

BRIDGEWATER MSS.

Letter from Mary Egerton to her nephew Thomas, Solicitor-General, at Islington; Radley, 15 Oct. 1584.

Among documents relating to Lord Chancellor Ellesmere's public appointments and personal affairs is a large vellum sheet containing the descent of the family of Egerton traced back in full detail, with coats of arms, to David de Malpas, son of William Belward. Also, grants of annuities to Egerton of 2*l*. from the University of Cambridge, dated 20 May 1586, and from Thomas [Godwin] Bishop of Bath and Wells, 8 May 1587, as their counsel. Two letters to him from Sir John Puckering in 1593. License from the Archbishop of Canterbury to him, his son Thomas, their wives, and four other persons chosen by them, to eat flesh at forbidden times; he paying annually 13*s*. 4*d*., and his son 6*s*. 8*d*., to the poor's box of the parish in which they dwell.* Absolution granted by Richard [Bancroft] Bishop of London to him, his wife Elizabeth, widow of Sir John Wolley, and Ralph Hutchins, priest, M.A., from the sentence of excommunication which they have incurred by solemnization of marriage in a private house without banns or licence, 7 October 1597. Accounts of his plate, 1600-1616, with notes of plate given to and by him, and of plate sold. List of all the members of his household in 1603. Inventories of furniture, clothes, and other "stuff" kept in his chamber at the court, at Greenwich in May, 1596, and at other time. List of "rewardes" given by him to the officers of the King's household at New-year's tide 1611. A vellum roll, containing "A catalogue of my Ladies bookes at London, taken Oct. 27, 1627," containing 31 books in folio (amongst which, Spenser's *Faery Queen*), 59 in quarto ("Divers playes by Shakespeare, 1602"), and 111 in smaller sizes, of which some are in French. Further lists adds 42 vols. up to April 1632, among which are some "paper-bookes," apparently MSS., including *The Lamentations of Jeremy in verse*, by Dr. Donne, 8°, *The Gypsies masque*, 4° and Ravenscroft's book of Psalms. The last printed book added is Herbert's *Church Porch*.

Two letters from John Egerton (afterwards first Earl of Bridgwater) to his father the Lord Chancellor; Ashridge, 1613-4.

Wardrobe-inventories of the Earl of Bridgewater and his family in 1633-5. Letter from Lady Arbella St. John to her mother the Countess; Melshbourne, 13 September 1635. Many letters from the Earl's son-in-law Sir William Courteen about his debts and business affairs, 1643-8, with one from Lady Katherine Courteen, and several from Sir Robert Crayford. Inventory of goods at Ashridge, 21 Dec. 1663.

Letter from John, the second Earl, to John Halsey, esq.; Ashridge, 28 Nov. 1662.

Rules by the same for his household at Ashridge during his absence in London, headed "Memorialls for Bulmer to put in execution when I am gone to London," dated 17 Oct. 1673. None to be suffered to eat of his meat but his sons and his own servants; "this vigorously put in execution will suddenly stop that resort which hath hitherto beene so very

---

* A similar dispensation is granted to the Earl of Bridgewater in 1616, and afterwards in 1660.

BRIDGEWATER MSS. expensive to me." No strong beer, ale, or wine at all to be spent in his absence, except when his sons shall call for it. No frequenting of ale-houses, or drunkenness, on the part of any servants. Sundays, hitherto the days of greatest disorder, to be kept the most private; employed in the service of God, and not in debauchery abroad, much less at home.

V. *Cheshire.*—Parcels of deeds, numbering over 300, and extending from the time of Hen. III. (but more generally Edw. II.–III.) to that of the Commonwealth. They relate to Clutton, Malpas, Chester (the White Friars, &c.), Tarporley (where "Heremitorium," "le Ermitage" is mentioned in deeds of *t.* Hen. III. and 1343–6, numbered 66, 110, 304*) Cholmundeston, Cudington, Morton (as to which there is an account-roll of the bailiff of the manor in 1455–6), Knuttesford, and Prestbury (conveyance of manor and rectory in 1563 to Richard Massie; No. 49). Of the families of Caurthyn *or* Cawarthyn, Clutton, Hole, Bruyn, and Wettenhall, the documents are very numerous; and other families concerned are those of St. Pierre, Egerton, Cholmondeley, L'Estrange Bromley (Inq. p.m. Sir John Bromley, 1486, No. 19; &c.) Boydell, Harpur, Pesecod, Massey, Holford, Ridley, and Venables. Among the seals the following heraldic ones may be noticed:—

Vrian de St. Pierre, *temp.* Edw. II. (127) (father of Sir John de St. Pierre) a bend, with a label of five points.

Roger Bruyn of Stapelford, 1353 (92) on a shield a squirrel eating nuts: "S' Rogeri Bruyn Stapulford."

John L'Estrange, 1373. Two lions courant. "S' Johannis Lestrange."

Arthur Davenport, 1388 (104) a chevron (charged with a bezant?) between three crosses. "S' Artu de Donpor."

There are the wills of William Wettenhall, of Cholmundeston, gentleman, dated 28 Sept. 1570, and proved 16 Feb. following, and of Isabel his wife, dated 14 Oct. 1572 (31, 32). They both desire to be buried in the chancel of Acton church, he beside his father, and she beside her husband. Attached to No. 37 is a memorandum that Christian Kethine, late wife to Mr. Kethine, was buried in St. Katherine's chapel in the church of St. Mary on the Hill, Chester, 5 Aug. 1580.

Long statement (176) drawn out by William Whitgreve, suing *in forma pauperis* for the barony of Malpas, manor of Halton, and lands at Halifax, and tracing his descent through Alkok from the Egertons. Probably *temp.* Edw. IV.

Exchange of land (41) between Sir Will. Trussell and Elizabeth Rixton, prioress of the convent of St. Mary at Chester, giving *les Plekkes* at Chester for her lands in the demesne of Blakene. Seal of the priory, mutilated. The Virgin and Child, canopied; " S' cōe priorisse . . . ." 4 Aug. 20 Edw. IV. (1480).

Thomas, Bishop of Sodor (omitting the title of *Man*) executes a conveyance of the Cheshire property of Thomas Lord Stanley, 31 May, 15 Edw. IV, 1475. (51) This bishop was abbot of Vale Royal.

VI. *Lincolnshire.*—A collection of court-rolls and other documents relating to the manor of Earlshall in Frampton, which belonged

---

* The earliest of these (304) is a release by Rob. de Perers, rector of Torperley, of his action against John de Hulle, chaplain of the hermitage " de Roda," dedicated to St. Leonard, for tithes, in consequence of his inspection of certain authentic instruments. A. de Stanford, archdeacon of Chester [archd. in 1271], is a witness.

successively to the families of De La Pole, Brandon of Suffolk, and Stanley of Derby, and thence by marriage to the first Earl of Bridgewater, and was sold by the widow of the third earl. The court-rolls begin with a thick paper volume containing copies of those for 1561–1602, made by Thomas Doughtie, steward of the manor, who died shortly after the last court in the latter year, and of the first courts held by his son Anthony Doughtie, in the following year. In the cover of the volume is an indulgence granted by Pope Eugenius IV. to all persons visiting and contributing to the repair of the parish church of St. Margaret, Sybsay, Lincolnshire; dated at Florence in June, 1439. Of the original parchment rolls there are those for 1591–4 and 1635–63. There are rentals for 1573 and 1580. There are also a few rolls for Mumby, of which the earliest is 1531–2, and for Skirbech, near Boston, beginning at 1585 and 1599.

BRIDGEWATER MSS.

A folio volume, unbound, of 46 vellum leaves, containing a copy of a survey of the lands held of the Honour of Richmond in Yorkshire, Essex, Hertfordshire, Lincolnshire, Suffolk, Norfolk, and Cambridgeshire, made by the King's Escheator, in pursuance of a writ from K. Edw. I., dated 1 Dec. an. 10 (1281.)

A large vellum roll, consisting of 31 membranes, containing a report by five commissioners on the colleges, hospitals, alms-houses, and other charitable foundations, in the district of Lindsey, Lincolnshire, and the custody of their muniments; in pursuance of a commission from Q. Elizabeth, dated 13 Sept. 1593. Similar report, on six membranes, by three commissioners, for the district of Holland, unfortunately much injured by damp.

Copy of the will of Sir Hen. Cholmeley, 24 July, 1619.

Draft of a letter from the Earl of Bridgewater to Dr. Wivell, chancellor of Lincoln, about the repair of the chancel of Stainton church, for which he has been questioned, and which he now directs to be carried out in a fitting manner; 20 June, 1617.

The remainder of the documents in the parcel consist of legal papers and leases, &c., of no general interest, up to the time of Q. Anne.

In a parcel marked *Charity Papers* are the rolls of returns to the above-mentioned writ of enquiry respecting charitable foundations and bequests, for Berkshire, Cambridgeshire (mutilated), Cornwall, Dorsetshire, Monmouthshire, Staffordshire, and Surrey.

VII. *London.*—In a small parcel are the following. Grant by Sir Robert Southwell, knt. Master of the Rolls, to Robert Harrys and his brother Rowland Harrys conjointly, of the office of Clerk or Keeper of the Rolls in the Tower, on the death or surrender of Richard Eton, as fully as it was formerly held by John Gyles, Ralph Pexall, and others; 1 April, 3 Edw. VI., 1549. Composition between the said Robert and Rowl. Harrys and Edward Halys, that whereas Halys had been appointed to the same office by K. Edw. VI. by letters patent dated 8 May, 1549, in succession to Richard Eton, deceased, the said Halys shall enjoy the office for eight years, paying £4 yearly to Rob. and Rowl. Harrys, and shall at the expiry of the said eight years surrender the office to them. Appointment by Robert and Rowl. Harrys of Thomas Henneage and Michael Henneage, his brother, as their deputies; 8 Jan. 18 Eliz., 1576. Grant of the office by Sir William Cordell, Master of the Rolls, to the said Thomas and Mich. Henneage, as fully as it was held by Rob. and Rowl. Harrys or William Bowyer; 10 Apr. 18 Eliz., 1576. Petition to the Council in the time of Will. and Mary from surgeons

BRIDGEWATER MSS. dismissed from St. Thomas' Hospital because appointed by royal mandate, with special statement of the case of John Browne and his services. Rental of the estate of Wriothesley, Duke of Bedford, in the parishes of St. Paul, Covent Garden, and St. Martin-in-the-Fields, giving the names of all the tenants; not dated; [*t*. Anne or Geo. I.].

St. Paul's Cathedral. A parcel of fifteen papers relative to collections in Wales and the Marches in 1637 for the repair of the Cathedral, in pursuance of orders from the Privy Council, with letters from Sir John Brydgeman and Sir Marmaduke Lloyd. There are particular returns of contributions from the hundred of Dewisland, Pembrokeshire, the commott of Ardydwy, Merionethshire, the county of Monmouth, and the hundred of Oswestry, Salop, which are locally interesting as furnishing lists of names of persons in the several parishes.

Barbican House. In a parcel of leases, &c. relating to the Earl of Bridgewater's house in London, " called Bridgewater House, or Barbican House, formerly called by the name of Willoughby House, otherwise the Barbican, otherwise the Base Court," there is a deed of sale of the said house to Sir Christopher Wren and Roger Jackson, esq., for £4400, which has Wren's signature; 31 March, 1688. In a list of cottages adjoining to the house, given in a rental account of the time of Charles II., there is one, " on the east side of the mansion, called the Sicke Man's house and garden," no doubt intended as a place for removal of plague-infected persons.

VIII. *Northamptonshire.*—For the borough of Brackley, and for the manor (comprehending Halse, Brackley, Spratton, Woodford, Farthingho, Evenley, Crowfield, King's Sutton, &c.) there is a large collection of documents, in many parcels.[1] Court-rolls of the manor, from the time of Q. Eliz. to 1804; copied also in two vols. from 1695 to 1786. Records of the Port-mote, *tempp.* Edw. VI.—Mar. (very tattered), and of the Courts-Baron, *temp.* Eliz., &c.[2] Bailiffs' accounts of receipts, beginning in the reign of Hen VIII., comprehending also receipts from Holborn and Stratford-le-Bow, and from " Evensham " (Eynsham) and Shifford in Oxfordshire.

(*Parcel No.* 2.) Lease from Richard, abbot of St. Mary's in the Meadows, Leicester, to *dom.* Rich. Wood, vicar of Brackley, of the rectory of Brackley, lately in the tenure of Thomas Ingram, for 20 years, at an annual rent of £13 3*s.* 4*d.*, 16 March, 1519 ; and from abbot John to John Rudyng (in English) for 51 years, at the same rent, 12 Nov. 1535. Other leases of the rectory follow. Lease from the abbess (not named) and convent of Godesstowe, Oxon, to Will. Wylkyns, of the manor of Hals, for 10 years ; Monday before the feast of the Annunciation 28 Hen. VI. (1450). Letter from James Kent to the Earl of Bridgewater about the claim of some burgesses of Brackley to hold courts for Magdalen College, Oxford, independently of the Earl's, relying on an *Inspeximus* by Rich. I. of a charter " then formerly granted to the hospitall of St. John of Jerusalem there and their men, which is nowe belonging to the said college ;" 11 Dec. 1629.[3] Letter from Sir Will.

---

[1] The manor was inherited by the Bridgewater family from that of Derby; having been granted to Sir Geo. Stanley, Lord Strange, by Hen. VII., 8 March *an.* 4, (1489).

[2] In 3-4 Phil. & Mar. there is an " order that no maner of person nor servant to hunt no aylehouse or taverns on Sondays or alydays, in the service tyme, sub pena every tyme, iijs. iiijd."

[3] There is no *Inspeximus* either by Rich. I. or Rich. II. among the very numerous Brackley charters now preserved in the muniment-room of Magd. Coll. The hospital was founded by Robert Earl of Leicester, about 1160.

Noye to the Earl of Bridgewater on this claim, beginning, "He that BRIDGEWATER
sent this noate was deceived in his cronologye;" 29 Oct. 1629. MSS.

Petition from the burgesses of Brackley to Sir John Egerton to assist them in "the renewing, strengthening, and settling our corporation;" 4 June 1616, with the borough seal of the Derby device of the Eagle and Child, "Sigillum burgi de Brackley." Papers relating to the surrender of the Charter to James II. in 1688.

Letters relating to the fairs and markets at Brackley; cent. XVII.

Letter from Dr. Thomas Goodwin, President of Magdalen College, Oxf., to the Earl of Bridgewater (in reply to one from him) about the right of felling some trees ; 25 May, 1659.

Letter from John Elliot to the Earl's steward, Mr. Williams,1 May 1651. "The report of my good lord's enlargement, which came yesterday to my care, hath affected me with soe much joy that it caused a buzzing in my head all the last night, as if I had heard the bells ring from London to Brackly. Soe that I durst not drinke my morning's draught to-day till I had taken this opportunity to give a little vent to my affectionate rejoyceing, by congratulating with you this glad day (for I hope I doe not dreame)."

Letter from — Rye to — Hayton about rights of common at Maidford unjustly withheld from poor cottagers by two persons; Blakesley, 23 Sept. 1729.

Petition to the Duke of Bridgewater for the restoration of a town bull and boar, formerly kept by the impropriator of the great tithes of the parish of Brackley, "as is usual in other parishes."

(*Parcel "No. 3."*) Copies of various early inquisitions *post-mortem*, &c. relating to the manor; perambulations of the forest of Whittlewood; inquisition on the death of Lord Chancellor Ellesmere. Letters patent of Q. Mary granting to Edward, Earl of Derby, two fairs at Brackley; 4 May, 1554; seal lost. Copy of the charter granted to Brackley by James II.; 11 Nov. 1686.

Letter from Katherine Courten to "my dear and loving mother" the Countess of Bridgewater, about her health: "I intend to goe to London in a sidan ;" 21 Sept. *n. y.*

In a parcel marked "*M.P. papers*" are returns of the elections at Brackley for Parliament, and papers relating thereto, from 1695 to 1803.

Burgess-rolls of the borough, and other borough-papers.

Grant from Q. Anne to Scroope, Earl of Bridgewater, of four fairs yearly at Brackley; 22 Nov. 1708.

Copy of an agreement between the churchwardens and overseer of the parish of St. Peter Brackley with Matthew Oynon, to take the charge of the workhouse lately set up in the parish, and to maintain the poor sent there, for one year, for £100 ; 20 Jan. 1720.

Copy of a certificate from Philip Style that crown tenants of the Honour of Wallingford and Berkhamstead are free from service at assize or sessions, and from all tolls in fairs and markets, and that Rob. Wise of Middleton Cheney, Northants, is thus privileged ; 26 Dec. 1661.

Tattered letter from Geo. Smalman to the Earl of Bridgewater, dated 8 May 1656, with an account of the beating of the bounds of Brackley on 5 May.

A large mass of papers relate to the manor of Wollaston, which was acquired from the Crown and the Duchy of Lancaster by Lord Chancellor

BRIDGEWATER MSS.

Ellesmere. They consist chiefly of leases, and of a few court-rolls from the time of Q. Eliz. to that of Q. Anne, but amongst them is an agreement, signed and sealed on 13 Oct. 1631 by 25 freeholders and tenants, for the enclosure of certain lands by the Earl of Bridgewater and the assignment of other land in compensation, being a confirmation of a former agreement made to the same effect on 11 Oct. 1616. Of the 25 signatories only four affix their mark. In a series of letters from the earl's agents, one, John Lockman, in a letter which is not dated (written towards 1640) informs him of the death of Mr. Peele, vicar of Wollaston, and mentions that the annual value of the vicarage is between £50 and £60. There are lists of "quernkeepers" in 1630 and 1634, and from the latter of these we learn that this name designates "such as have and keepe maulte mylls or quernes." Those who had had them in use for many years in their families refuse to discontinue them, on the plea of prescriptive right; others promise to lay them down, and to make use of the lord's mill.

IX. *Shropshire.*—A parcel amongst miscellaneous *Shire Papers* contains deeds of the time of Edw. III. of Philip de Hanford and Constance widow of Philip de Presthope; and a grant (in French) by Roger Lestrange to Thomas Lestrange of the office of bailiff of the forest of Mailorsaysnek, formerly held by Richard Spygournel, witnessed by Sir Robert Corbet, Sir John Lestrange of Mudle, Sir . . . de Hopton, Griff. de Glyndowerduy, Richard de Wonere, steward, Morgan ap Jar: Moyl, Owayn Gogh of Havenem[un]d; dated at Knokyn Castle, 18 Jan. 9 Edw. III. (1336). Many papers relating to a law-suit with Sir Edward Kinaston, with a letter from him to Edw. Berker, esq., at Haughmond, dated at Dudleston, 7 Oct. 1592.

Separate from the other Shropshire documents, among the *Select Documents*, are the following deeds relating to the abbey of Buildwas, of great interest and very early date.

i. Commission from the abbey of Savigny to the abbey of Buildwas to assume the government of the abbey of St. Mary at Dublin.

" Venerando fratri et amico Rannulfo abbati de Bilduwas ejusdemque loci conventui frater Ricardus dictus abbas et conventus Savigneii salutem et dilectionem. In nomine Domini nostri Jesu Christi committimus atque concedimus vobis et domui vestre curam et dispositionem domus nostre Sancte Marie Duline in perpetuum habendam, ut vos et domus vester secundum tenorem ordinis Cisterciensis curam ejusdem domus, quasi filie vestre et sicut a vobis egresse in omnibus et per omnia habeatis, et ipsa vobis et domui vestre tanquam matri sue juxta eundem tenorem ordinis Cisterciensis semper et ubique respondeat et obediat. Facta est autem hec nostra commissio atque concessio in communi capitulo Savigneii anno ab incarnatione Domini M.° C.° L. VI.°, sexto kl. Decemb. Teste, Arraudo priore, et Gaufrido subpriore, et Unfrido cantore, et Roberto et Guillelmo et Gaufrido cellerariis, et Hugone sacrista, et Roberto magistro noviciorum, et Hugone infirmario, et Christiano hospitali, et Guillelmo portario, et universo capitulo." Oval brown seal: a hand holding a pastoral staff, " × Sigillum abbatis Savigneii."

This is printed from a certified copy made twenty years later, in a decision at Savigny confirming the subjection to Buildwas both of Basingwerk and St. Mary's abbey, at p. 51 of Joseph Hunter's *Ecclesiastical Documents*, Camden Society, 1840.

ii. Charter of King John, while Governor of Ireland, to the abbey of Buildwas.

"Johannes filius domini Regis Anglie, et dominus Hibernie: Omnibus ministris et baillivis suis de tota Hibernia Salutem. Sciatis me divini amoris intuitu et pro salute anime mee et omnium antecessorum et successorum meorum dedisse et concessisse et presenti carta mea confirmasse abbati et monachis de Bildewais in liberam et .puram et perpetuam elemosinam unum batellum ad piscandum in aqua juxta Duveliñ que vocatur Avenlif, ad sustentacionem infirmorum suorum. Volo autem et precipio quod ipsi et piscatores eorum de eodem batello talem libertatem piscandi habent in eadem aqua qualem piscatores de batellis meis propriis de Duveliñ habent. Et prohibeo ne quis eis molestiam aut gravamen faciat, nec eos inde aliquo modo disturbet. T. Bertram de Verdun, Will. Pipard, Alardo camerario, fratre Radulpho elemosinario, Will. de Flamar, Ricardo clerico. Apud Dyvelin." Seal lost.

BRIDGEWATER MSS.

iii. A charter which has been twice printed as a charter of Hen. II., but which presents considerable difficulties. We have here what professes to be the original, somewhat mutilated by damp, and wanting the seal. The witnesses' names would at once assign it to Hen. II., but the handwriting cannot be earlier than the middle of the thirteenth century, and is more probably thirty or forty years later. If therefore the grant itself be genuine, the inference must be that the document is a copy made because the original itself was perishing. It is printed in the *Monasticon*, and again in Mr. Gilbert's *Chartularies of St. Mary's Abbey* (Rolls' Series, 1884), vol. I., pp. 79-81; but as this document professes, at least, to be the original, and there are some few variations in the texts, it is worth reproducing in full.

"H. Dei gracia Rex Anglie, Dux Norm. et Aquitanie et comes Andeg., archiepiscopis, episcopis, abbatibus, comitibus, baronibus, justiciariis, vice-comitibus, ministris, et omnibus fidelibus suis Francis et Anglicis et Hibernicis, Salutem. Sciatis me concessisse et hac presenti carta mea confirmasse Rann. abbati de Buldewas et omnibus in posterum ejusdem abbacie futuris abbatibus, ad regendum, et secundum formam ordinis Cistercien. disponendum, monasterium sancte Marie juxta Duwelin. cum terris subscriptis: scilicet, Clunlif, Drissohe, Ratenham, Portmirnoch, Glassachet, Hurlegam [*Murlegan?*], Dovenachbirn, Karretbrennan, Karrechnecon, Balimachelin, Culmin, Kilmekeste, Dissertale, Balibawhel, Balilugan. Has terras cum omnibus pertinenciis suis in ecclesiis, in capellis, in bosco et plano, in sabulis et gliseriis, cum omni wrech quod in terra illorum venerit, in pratis et pasturis, in aquis et molendinis, in stagnis et vivariis, in viis et semitis, in piscariis et piscaturis, in portubus et villis, infra burgum et extra, et in omnibus aliis locis et omnibus aliis rebus concessi prefato abbati de Buldewas et successoribus ejus. Quare volo et firmiter precipio quod monachi predicti monasterii sancte Marie juxta Duwelin abbati de Buldewas subjecti sint, et prenominatas terras et omnes elemosinarum donaciones que eis facte sunt vel imposterum fient, tam in rebus ecclesiasticis quam in secularibus, ad ejus disposicionem tractent, habeant et teneant, adeo libere et quiete, plenarie et integre sicut aliqua abbacia vel domus religionis de terra mea melius et liberius tenuerit vel tenet, cum sach et soch et thol et them et infangenthef, et cum omnibus aliis libertatibus et liberis consuetudinibus et quietanciis, et sint liberi et soluti ipsi et homines eorum Anglici et Hibernici, et terre eorum, de schiris, de hundredis, de wapentach, de placitis,[1] de querelis, de murdro,

---

[1] The copy in the *Monasticon* ends here with "&c."

BRIDGEWATER MSS.

de furto, de scutagio, de hidagio, de assisis, de essartis, de wasto nemorum, de pastu forestariorum et sagittariorum, de geldis, de danegeldis, de horngeldis, de letgeldis (?), de blodwita, de fitwita, de leirwita, de herwita, de operacionibus castellorum et p[oncium] . . . . et de sumagio et meremio cariando, de armis portandis, de thesauro [portan]do et [con]ducendo, de wardis, ... scotali. .[regis?] [auxi]liis vel donis vicecomitum et ballivorum, et de prestura, et sint quieti de omni tolneto et passagio et pontagio et stallagio et lestagio, et de Scot et de Scat et de omni servicio et exaccione seculari et opere servili.   Hec omnia concessi predicto abbati de Buldewas et ejus successoribus et monachis prenominati monasterii sancte Marie in liberam et puram et perpetuam elemosinam pro amore Dei et gloriose virginis Marie cui servire creduntur, et pro salute anime mee et omnium antecessorum et heredum meorum. Hiis testibus, Ricardo de Luci, com. Ric. de Strigoil, Willelmo fil. Audele dap[ifero], Hug. de Laci, Hug. de Longo Campo, Will. de Stut[evile] Roberto de Stut[evile], Hug. de Creissi, Will. fil. Rad.   Apud Fekeham."

On the folded lower margin are written the following words, at varying distances from each other, in a hand of the end of the thirteenth cent., or beginning of the fourteenth :—

"de beatitudine Dublin benedictione loco benedicto de valle crucis."

iv. Consent by Henry de Lacy, Earl of Lincoln and Constable of Chester, to the exchange by the abbot and convent of Buldewas of their grange at Caldene in Staffordshire for lands at Edwyneye in Shropshire belonging to the abbot and convent of St. Mary at Crokesdene. Dated at Blankeford near Bourdeaux, 10 June, 1287. Seal lost. This is printed in the *Monasticon* from this original, which was in Dugdale's time in the possession of the Earl of Bridgewater.

X. *Staffordshire.*—A parcel of parchment deeds, numbering 134, almost entirely relating to property in the parish of Dilhorne (anciently *Dulverne*) and its township of Forsbrook (Fotesbroc), and chiefly of the reigns of Hen. III.—Edw. III., with a few of later date. In a grant from Letitia de Stantun to her son William, of the middle of the 13th cent. (No. 28), one English term is given, "unam acram jacentem in Morrfourlong, que vocatur Anglice *le poil acir.*" Nicholas, prior of St. Thomas without Stafford, is witness to a grant from Henry son of Roger de Kaverswalle and Mary his wife, *circa* 1300 (No. 37). In this grant there is the curious spelling of "aprowyamentis," "aprowy-andis," "aprowyare," for *appropriamentis, appropriandis, appropriare.* The wife calls herself on her seal, not Mary as in the deed itself, but Mariota de Pulv'he. Many of the seals in this parcel have been carefully sewn up in wool and paper, which, from writing on the latter, appears to have been done in the time of Q. Eliz., when the property came to the Egerton family. Ralph Basset of Sapcote has for his "sigillum secretum" a stag's head (22) ; to a very tattered early deed of William, lord of Caverswall, is attached a heraldic seal, fretty, thereon a bar, "[S'] domini Will. de Caresw." (21) ; and the same coat is borne by Richard, lord of Caverswall, in 1318 (112). Other armorial seals are those of Sir Ralph Basset of Cheadle in 1337 (64); Sir James de Stafford in 1354 (63) ; and a fine impression (but border broken) of that of Ralph, Earl of Stafford, in 1351 (62). There is one example of an inscription (that of "Roberti de Fotesb'c," 36) engraved in a reverse way, by a curious mistake on the part of the engraver which is occasionally met with. No. 139 contains "a table in forme of a pedegree directing the conveyances of the lands in Dulverne, Fossebrooke, Fulforde and Chedle unto Rauffe Egerton, esq., nowe owner thereof"; with references to the varicus deeds concerning them. No. 131 is a copy of the poll-book for the hundred of Seisdon, at an election [*t*. Geo. I.], when the candidates were "Wrottesley, Gower, Bagott and Crewe."

BRIDGEWATER MSS.

XI. *Warwickshire.*—A parcel of deeds relating to Astley, the impropriate rectory, and the site of the College, up to the time of James I.; commencing with two of the time of Henry II., as follows :—

i. Grant from Thomas de Estlein, with consent of his wife Ala and his heir Walter to Rich. de Cusinton of land in Soudleia. Witn., Hervie, clerk of Chelverdescote, Seer de Stokes, Will. Crusset, Robert the Cook, John de Flamville, &c. White seal; an eagle. (5.)

ii. Grant from the same to Robert the Cook of land which John de Hacking held on the day on which Philip de Estlege, the grantor's brother, died. Witnesses :—William de Hardredeshulle, Hugh de Bibbesworth, Seher de Stokes, Henry de Morton, Guy de Morton, Philip de Stokes, &c. Same seal. (7.)

In 26 Edw. III. a later Thomas de Asteleye uses a rose on his shield of arms : "Sigillum Thome domini de Astele." In 40 Edw. III. he, as Sir Thomas Asteleye, son of Giles de Asteley, makes a grant of rents to the Dean, Canons, and Vicars of the Chantry, of the Church of B. Mary of Asteleye in augmentation of the portions of the Vicars. To him on 9 Feb. 25 Edw. III. Margery, lately the wife of Thomas d'Asteleye of Hullemoreton, assigns (in a French deed) all her goods and chattels in the manor of Hullemoreton ; a fragment of her seal remains, bearing two shields, with two crosses of differing form. The official of the archdeacon of Coventry in 1407 issues a notification to Sir William de Asteley, lord of Asteley, and to the Dean of the collegiate church there, that he has sequestrated the profits belonging to the prebends of John Howbel and John Wynkepyry, on account of their neglect of duty with regard to the daily and nightly service in the church.

XII. *Westmoreland.*—A few papers of the last century about leadmines at Hilton and Morton, with a long letter about the working of the mines from John Gilbert to his brother, dated at Manchester, 14 June, 1758, and copies of letters from Edward Rawsthorn in 1737.

XIII. *Shire Papers.*—In a miscellaneous bundle relating to various estates, which is thus marked, and which consists chiefly of law papers of the time of Q. Elizabeth, are vellum rolls (decayed by damp) of returns of concealed lands in the counties of Berks, Bucks, Devon, Gloucester, Lincoln, Middlesex, Monmouth, Somerset, Sussex, Warwick, Wilts, York, and others. Inclosed with them is a notification to the Attorney and the Solicitor-General, signed by W. Burghley and Wa. Mildmay, and dated 4 March, 1585, that, the Queen having by a Great Seal dated 10 Aug. 1583 granted to Sir James Croft, knt., Controller of her house, power to search during two years for concealed lands, a book is to be prepared of the same, with reservation of yearly rents to the Crown ; and the value of such lands granted to Sir J. Croft in Bucks, Middlesex, and Sussex, is certified to be £12.5.11.

In this bundle there are also :—for *Bucks*, a deed by Robert Malet, of Quainton, in 1314, with his seal of arms ; rental of Pychelesthorne, 20 Rich. II. (1396), and several early rolls of persons entitled to loads of wood there ; some decayed rentals and court-rolls of Ivingho, &c. ;

U 21952.
K

BRIDGEWATER MSS. and the poll-book at the election for the county on 8–9 Jan. 1700. *Leicestershire* and *Staffordshire*. Examination before Will. Skeffington and Lord William Paget in Staffordshire of Mr. Walter Ferrers and others for supposed complicity as to the proceeds of a burglary committed at Leicester by Thomas Harrison of Elford, confession of Edw. Littleton, letters from Edward Bradshaw, Will. Skeffington and Peter Warburton, and warrants signed by Lord Stafford; March–Apr. 1605. *Lancashire*: lists of justices of the peace in 1590 and 1592, specifying those that have taken the oaths, with orders respecting the same. *Nottinghamshire*: deed of sale by Dame Margaret Stanhope, widow of Sir Thomas Stanhope, knt., of Shelford, to Sir John Holles of Houghton, of all the goods and chattels in the house at Shelford, saving the heir-looms, because her husband had not left enough to discharge his debts, defray the funeral charges, or keep his family together for two months as provided in his will; 31 Aug. 1596. Petition, &c., about the manor of Mansfield, 1602. *Somerset*: Manors of Curry-Revell and Bridgewater.

XIV. *Wales.*—i. A very imperfect series of account-rolls of receipts and expenses of the bailiffs of the lordship of Bromfield and Yale (including Ruabon and Wrexham) in the county of Denbigh.

The first roll is of the expenses of John Griffith, 21–22 Rich. II. (1397–8.) In the roll for 21–22 Edw. IV. (1481–2) there is a frequent entry, which is continued in the rolls of Hen. VIII., in the accounts of various officers, that the rents are lower than usual " pro eo quod adhuc quam plurima tenementa ibidem jacentia et domus eorum combusta fuerunt per invasionem et accessionem rebellium domini Regis de partibus Walliæ, et nondum reparata, propter absenciam quam plurimorum tenentium, et ob nimiam paupertatem eorundem tenentium." These rolls appear to end in 36 Hen. VIII.

ii. Court Rolls of the same lordship from the time of Hen. VIII. to that of James I. There are also single rolls of Wrexham of 39 Edw. III. and 14 Hen. IV., and one of Chaulton of 10 Hen. IV.

iii. Several parcels of leases and other legal documents, relating to the rectory of Gresford in Denbighshire (granted by the Dean and Chapter of Winchester to Q. Eliz. 1 Feb. 1581–2), and to Mold, Northop, Rhuddlan, Holywell, &c., in Flintshire, to lands (with a chapel) in Denbigh, Carnarvon, Flint Salop and Devon, formerly belonging to the preceptory of Knights Hospitallers at Halston, Salop, sold by Q. Eliz. to Geo. Lee, 15 March, 1560. These reach from the reign of Hen. VI. to the time of the Commonwealth. Inquisition *post mortem* of Henry Stanley, esq., 1589. Inventory of the goods and chattels of Sir Robert Salusburie, knt., deceased, in the counties of Denbigh and Merioneth, 5 June, 1601. Schedule of lands in Wales which descended to his son and heir. Anagram on the name of Lady Mary Herbert upon her marriage [*i.e.* " Sidney's sister," Mary Sidney, on her marriage to Henry Herbert, afterwards Earl of Pembroke]; signed W.R :—

"Ladie Marie Herbert,
  Ablie married, there.
          or
  Marie Herbert,
    Thear be merry.
Yow darlings of the Muses, man and wife,
No doubt but yow will live a merry life.
          So wisheth your servant,
                    W.R."

iv. A parcel containing letters and papers relating to the Lord President and Council of the Marches of Wales ; 1591-1642. Many letters of lawyers (Jo. Brydgeman, Sampson Eure, &c.) relating to a disputed case at law in 1636-7 as to the power of the Council respecting incontinency and matters of legacy ; and papers as to the jurisdiction over the four English counties, including Lord Bacon's arguments, in 1608. List of Royal Instructions preserved among the records at Ludlow. Entry-book of cases heard before the Council in Jan. 1631. Letter to Sir John Egerton from Thos. Stanley, dated Knokin, 18 Nov. 1616, about collection of rents. Letter to the Earl of Bridgewater from Magdalen Bagenall, dated at Conway, 8 Sept. 1637, about the purchase of some lands.

BRIDGEWATER MSS.

v. A parcel containing letters to the Earl of Bridgewater, the President of the Marches, from Capt. George Betts, one of the officers at Ludlow Castle, in 1631, and from Henry Eccleston, steward of the King's household there, from July 1640 to July 1642. These are endorsed by the Earl, and in many cases there are copies of his replies. Eccleston's letters frequently contain strong complaints of difficulties met with in the management of the household. The following extracts give all the notices that relate to public and political troubles.

1641, 25 Oct. "This present affords no other occasion whereof I might give your honour any advertisement, but that which is scarse worth notice : of Sir Ro. Harlow's vehement course in pullinge downe the cross at Wigmore the 27th September, and caused it to be beaten in peces, even to dust, with a sledge, and then laid it in the foote path to be trodden on in the church yeard ; and after, upon the 30th day, beinge Thursday, he puld downe the cross at Laynterden [Leintwardine], and broke the windowes in the church and chauncell, and beate the glass small with a hammer, and threw it into Teame, in imnitation of Kinge Asa, 2 Cron. 15, 16, who threw the images into the brook Kydron ; and because he could not come at Kydron, he threw it into Teame, as Mr. Yeates, one of h. chaplins, said. He was also at Enmstre [Aymstrey] to have done the lyke, but the parish and Mr. Lake the minister withstood him, and so he departed for that time."

1641, 22 Nov. "Here hath bene some sturr this last wicke by meanes of a letter sent by post on Wensday at night last the 17th of this instant, directed for his Majesties speciall service, to Mr. John Astone at Ludlow, and in his absence to Richard Griffyths, who hath taken his shope, and is after a sort his servant. Yt came from Sir Robert Harlow ; the effect was in these wordes ; ' looke well to your towne, for the Papists are discovered to have a blody designe, in generall, aswell agan this kingdome as elsewhere.' And the same newes it semes came to Bewdley, and caused them all in the towne to bo up in armes, with wnch all night in very great feare ; and here the towne hath kept wach ever since ; and at Brampton Bryan they were all in armes upon the tope of Sir Ro. castle, and tooke up provisions theyther with them, and in great feare ; all which puts the countrey in a great amase."

1642, 29 May. "Amongest many distractions and rumoures it is much reported that the Kinge, or the Prince, or both, are like to be here ere longe, which if it should so happen I humblie desire to know what your honour's pleasure is, wheather I shalbe anythinge forward in makeinge any provisions upon your charge, or wheather to offer the small store that is here remayninge to theyr officers, and leave the rest to them ; for loath I should be to doe more or less then what your honour's pleasure is, upon your charge." To this the Earl's reply, dated at Barbacan, 5 June, is, "All I can saye is, that I beleeve not the rumors and reportes

K 2

BRIDGEWATER **spreade amongst you. Yf either the King or Prince doe come to**
MSS. **Ludlowe, it is fitt they shoulde have their castle at their dispose; but I
knowe no reason why I shoulde finde them dyett ther. Their owne
officers can best tell howe to make provisions for them, for my purse is
not large enough to beare the charge thereoff. Therefore I thinke you
neede [not] to trouble yourselfe with that care or paines, unlesse your
helpe be desired by their officers without my charge."**

There are also two letters from Edw. Martyn at Ludlow castle, in 1637–41; and one from Sir John Brydgeman, dated 3 July 1636, endorsed by the Earl as relating to "custome of eating and drinking at Communion Table; case of Stretton in com. Salop, dismissed upon answere of the parson there," in which the following passage occurs :
"I have received your lordship's letters of the 25th of June last, and for the custome therein mentioned, it is true, as I heare, that it is claymed in many parishes both in Hereford and Shropshires, and hath bene usually performed in the churche, but I do not heare that there was ever any allowance geven thereof by this Councell; but it is true that some of the parishioners of Stretton in Shropshire of late exhibited a bill in this court against one Mr. Haukes, parson there, to compell him to performe that custome, whereunto he answered, shewing the unfittness to have eating and drinking in the churche, yett offering to do it in a convenient place; which matter was moved in the begining of this terme, being the first tyme I hard of it, whereupon we were so farre from relieving the plaintiffs that we dismissed the defendant with good costs."

vi. Three parcels of papers relating to the appointments of Sheriffs and Escheators in Wales, in 1631–1642, containing many letters as to the character and fortune of persons proposed for office; letters from gentry deprecating their appointment; list of sheriffs in all the Welsh counties, and the English border counties from 1624 to 1639 (No. 14); list of escheators in Wales, 1631–5 (No. 22);

Among the letters are :—one from Lord Carbery to his "brother" Lord Cottington, for the relief of his cousin Rowland Gwynn from being sheriff of Carmarthenshire, Golden Grove, 15 Oct. 1635; from Sir Peter Legh, "your lordship's olde unckle," to the Earl of Bridgewater, Haydock Lodge, 15 Oct. 1635; from Rowland Whyte, Richard Bulkeley, Sir Thos. Myddelton, Lady Audrey Dunsmore, "cosen" George Hope, "cosen" George Puleston, Walter Rumsey, Hugh Owen, Sir Nich. Overbury, Tym. Tourneure (one of the Welsh judges) &c. In a letter from Thomas Alured (who is addressed by the Earl as "Cousin") dated from Copthall, 21 Sept. 1636, the writer says, "My lord [qu. the Earl of Dorset?] I thanke God is well setled at Copthall, an house richly furnished within, and abundantly provided for without, as hay and wood and charcole; and within, the celler stored with beere, and the chambers so fitted that my lord removed nor brought either bed or stole, nor anything save plate and linnen. They have also taken Lowton, 3 miles of, where the Lady Wroth lived, for the Lady Savile, who is big with child, to lie in this winter. On Sunday last his lordship was at Otelandes, where the Spanish Embassadour had his audience, and layd that night at my lord Dunsmore's house in Surrey. The next Sunday the Lordes meete at Windsor, whither the King will please to come because he is not willing to have the Queen's Court endangered by the great resort which is usually on Sundays and Councell-dayes. And he is also desirous that the Lordes should be better accomodated, which at Windsor they may be rather than at Otelandes, where many are putt to thare shifts, which his Majesty very gratiously takes into consideration."

There are several parchment rolls pricked with the names chosen.   BRIDGEWATER MSS.

vii. A small parcel containing parchment and paper lists of the captains of trained-bands, their arms, ammunition &c. in 1637-42, very much decayed by damp.

viii. "Abergavenny papers." Paper roll showing the descent of Lady Mary Fane daughter of Hen. Neville Lord Abergavenny (who died 29 Eliz. 1587) from Drewe de Balun. "Certaine questions touchinge the dignity of Bergevenny, with the answers thereto." "The title of Edward Neville of Abergavenny to the dignitie of the baronie thereof." A few other papers concerning the descent of the barony.

ix. "Carbery papers." A small parcel of eleven deeds almost entirely relating to the settlements on the marriage of the Earl of Carbery to the Lady Alice Egerton, sister of the Earl of Bridgewater, in 1652, and to the settlement of Golden Grove in 1639.

x. "Herbert Papers." Papers in 1638-8 of the Earl of Bridgewater with relation to the Hon. Richard Herbert, son of Edward Lord Herbert of Cherbury, who married the earl's daughter Mary in 1627; the marriage settlements; and a series of rentals of the Herbert property in Anglesea and Carnarvonshire in 1598, 1609 (with comparison of value in a survey taken 1 Phil. and Mar. 1554), and 1637. There is also an account-roll of the bailiffs of Gilbert, Lord Talbot, for Tallibolyon and Turkelyn in Anglesey for 1414-15. To one of the deeds is attached a very fine impression of a double seal of the Earl of Bridgewater : on the obverse, the full coat of arms, with crest and supporters ; on the reverse, the crest of the lion rampant supporting a pheon.

The Welsh Shrievalty papers are supplemented by a few English ones, chiefly for the years 1632-7, amongst which is a letter from Sir Peter Legh to the Earl of Bridgewater, desiring exemption on the score of "ould age and untittnes," dated at Lyme, 26 Oct. 1632.

XV. *Isle of Man.*—In a parcel thus endorsed are the following documents :—

1. "Assedacio terrarum et tenementorum Thomæ comitis Derbiæ, domini Stanley, Manniæ et Insularum, de tribus lez shedynges ibidem, vz. de Rushen, Middell, et Garff, assessatis coram Johanne Irland, milite, locumtenente Manniæ . . . . mense Junii, A.D. 1512." A folio paper book of 21 leaves.

2. Account-books for seven years from 1599 to 1605 of receipts and expenditure at Rushen and Peel Castles ; in separate series, both signed "Gerard."

3. "The charge for the profits of customes for outgates and ingates in every severall port within the Isle of Mann, for five wholl yeres, beginning 24 June 1599, and endinge 24 June, 1604."

4. Copy of the grant of the Island to Sir John Stanley by Hen. IV., 6 Apr. 1406.

5. "The booke of fees and wages, 1575."

6. Letter to the Earl of Derby and the Lady Alice, Countess downger the younger, signed by Rand. Stanley, Humfr. Scarisbreck, and Will. Lucas, representing the desire of the inhabitants of the island "that the castels of Russhen and Peele, late dissolved, might be re-erected at Michaelmas next"; dated "from Castell Russhen, the last of August, 1594."

7. Copy of a letter from Q. Eliz. to the officers of the Island, appointing Sir Thomas Gerard to be captain on the death of Randolph Stanley, pending the settlement of a dispute as to the right of appointment between the Earl of Derby and the heirs general of his brother; 1 Aug. 1595.

8. Copy, attested by Humfr. Scarisbreck, of the oath administered to Sir Thos. Gerard, 15 Aug. 1595.

9. Copy of a letter from the Privy Council to Peter Leigh, esq., appointing him deputy-captain during the absence of Sir Thomas Gerard from the Island in the Queen's service; 3 July 1596.

10. Two tables of rates fixed for the prices of provisions supplied to the castles, &c.; the second dated 1601. A few other papers relating to revenue, garrison allowances, and the question of title.

Separated from this parcel, and included amongst a number of *Select Papers*, is a parchment roll of extracts made from the Register of the Priory of Whithern (" Candida Casa ") in Wigtonshire in 1504, which contains the following charters:—

i. Grant to the priory from Olaf, King of the Isles, of the hospital of Ballacgiuba and the churches of St. Ninian and St. Runan.

ii. Confirmation-grant by H[arold], King of Man and the Isles; headed, " Donacio terrarum de Kyrkmaroun et ejusdem ecclesie."

iii. Confirmation-grant by Regnald, King of the Isles.

iv. ——— by Alexander, son of Alexander the King of Scotland.

v. ——— by his father, Alexander [III.]

vi. Writ from K. Alexander to the Bailiff of Man to allow the Prior to receive the profits.

vii. Confirmation by Nicholas, Bishop of Sodor.

viii. ——— Simon, Bishop of Sodor.

ix. Grant to the priory by Alex. [III.] King of Scotland of the advowson of the church of the Holy Trinity at Ramsay. Witnesses, John Cumin de Buchan, Rich. Kynard, Patrick de Barklay, Andrew de Morzania, and David de Dorthorruld, knights. Dated at Glenlus, 20 May, *an*. 36 (1285). In the copies of the preceding charters the attestations are omitted.

x. Confirmation by Mark, Bishop of Sodor; at Kyrk-Andrew, [26] June, 1285.

xi. Confirmation by John, Bishop of Sodor, "sedis apostolice in tota Ybernia et Sodria nuncius et collector," of the title of the Priory to the churches of the Holy Trinity and St. Rune; headed, " super ecclesiis de Kyrkcrist et Kyrkmaroun." Dated at a general chapter in the church of St. Lupus in Man, 5 Feb. 1376.

xii. Bull of Pope Nicholas [iv] in confirmation of No. ix. 13 Apr. *an*. 3 [1291.]

Endorsed with this notarial certificate: " Hec est vera copia cartarum extractarum de autentico libro sive Regestro monasterii Candidecase per me Andream Meligan, canonicum dicti monasterii, ac apostolica auctoritate notarium, fideliter de verbo ad verbum copiata, signoque et nomine meis solitis et consuetis signata coram hiis testibus, Uthtredo Mak Dovell, domino de Garrhlayn, Patricio Dunbar apparente herede domini de Mochr[un], Cudberto Cunygham, Waltero Wauf, et Donaldo Mac Dowell, cum multis aliis, apud monasterium antedictum, penultimo die mensis Marcii, Anno Domini Millessimo quingentessimo quarto." With an

attestation of collation on the same day, before the same witnesses, by BRIDGEWATER Duncan Murray, "auctoritate imperiali notarium." In this certificate MSS. the first witness's name is written, " Wchtredo Mak Dowell, domino de Gercholaun."
These papers came to the Egerton family by intermarriage with the house of Derby.

XVI. *Bolton Papers.*—Amongst a mass of law papers relative to suits after the death of the first Duke of Bolton in 1699, are 14 letters from the Duke to his son-in-law, the third Earl of Bridgewater, from 1693 to 1698. In one, dated from Hackwood, 26 May, 1694, he says, " I send your lordship enclosed some news from Water Straford in Buckinghamshire, which is attested for a truth by an eminent minister here, one Mr. Acton. Sir Charles Wyndham was by . . . . . . and says they ought to be whipped and dispersed, but my opinion is they are fifth monarchy men. Mr. Barbon desires he may go to disperse them, they going naked, but my son William, Sir Charles Wyndham, and I, are of opinion your lordship will not give him that order."[1] There are also five letters from the second duke in 1699–1700, of which two in the former year are about the removal of his son, Lord Winchester, from Enfield School, Dr. Rob. Uvedale, writing to say that "he declines all businesse and refuses to be govern'd, absenting himself from schoole, and by no perswasions will bee prevayl'd upon to follow his studyes, but takes what liberty hee thinks fitt upon all occasions," and the Earl of Bridgewater writing, " in short, the matter is a danger of Lady Faukland's daughter, and no manner of complyance in the scoole, and the doctor declareing he could nott be answerable for him one hour."

XVII. Among a few *Brereton* papers relating to law-suits in Cheshire, and about the manor of Worsley, is an *Inspeximus* of an enrolment at Chester by Sir Ralph Brereton, on 1 Sept. 1525, of the will of his father Sir Rondulph or Ralph Brereton, dated 2 Aug. 1523, providing for the foundation of an almshouse at Malpas, with a bill of complaint and certain depositions relative to an alleged ejectment from the almshouse of one John Eyre.

XVIII. *Cheyne Papers.*—A large mass of papers relative to Charles Cheyne and his son William, Lords Cheyne and Viscounts Newhaven in Scotland. Account book of Francis Cheyne, esq., as Sheriff of Bucks, Mich. 1589–1590. Rent-rolls (from 1622), court-rolls, &c., of Drayton Beauchamp, Bucks. Minute daily account of provisions consumed at dinner and supper, from 3 Apr. to 17 May, 1630, a curious and interesting record, with a touching memorandum at the end (—which probably explains why this portion alone of the accounts of a good house-wife was preserved—) that the book was written by Anne Cheyne, wife of Francis Cheyne, of Chesham Boys, Bucks, that she was delivered of her fourth son on 18 May, 1630 (the day after the cessation of the entries) and died on 25 May. Account book of Lady Jane Cheyne (wife of Charles Cheyne) for household linen, &c., from 1656 to 1664; with inventory of her own clothes in 1635, of the plate in 1657, and of her jewels in 1656, with their prices, in which the first and largest entries are, " a neclase of

---

[1] This refers (in a very exaggerated way) to the "revival" movement at Water Stratford, under Mr. John Mason, the rector, whose preaching of the millennium, &c., was attended with the usual emotional extravagances. He died in the same year.

BRIDGEWATER MSS. pearls, wherein is 36 pearls, £725. A pare of lockets, wherein is 18 great diamands, and 16 littell ones, the prise £342." Two interesting entries in the household account show that Jeremy Taylor had baptized one of her sons (most probably in the house at Chelsea) shortly before his leaving London in 1658 for Ireland. " Oweing Mr. Cheyne more, what I had for Doctor Taler's chrisninge, £2 10s. oweing more, what I gave Doctor Taler, at his goeing into Irland, £5."[1] Folio account book of the personal expenses and receipts of her husband Charles Cheyne, from Dec. 1669 to June 1673. (Among the receipts are frequent entries of money won at chess; but occasionally money is also lost.[2] In London he frequently dines at a house called *The Quakers*, sometimes at *Sir John Oldcastle's*, and at *Lockey's*.) Accounts of the Pipe office in 1703 and 1712–27 (William Lord Cheyne being Clerk of the Pipe) with many notes and collections relative to the office,[3] including a list by Edw. Underwood in 1679, of all the Pipe Rolls from 5 Steph. [*rectius* 31 Hen. I.] to 18 Chas. II., then existing in the office at Westminster, or in the office of the Clerk in Gray's Inn, from which it appears that the Rolls of 1 Hen. III. and 7 Hen. IV., which are now wanting were then extant. Tax-book of the King's collectors at Acton in 1672. Entry-book of copies of letters patent relating to appointments to Exchequer offices, &c., 1671–9. Papers relating to the lands at Chelsea bought of the family for Chelsea Hospital, and manorial conveyances. Accounts of the trustees of the Duke of Kingston, with a series of letters from his tutors (Dr. N. Hickman and Mr. Peter Platel) at Plombiéres and Buisson, in France, 1726–7. Papers relating to an estate at Killeshin, Queen's county, Ireland, with letters from Sir Rich. Wolsely. Grant of a pension of £1,200 *per an.* to Charles Lord Cheyne, from James II., dated 24 March, 1687 (in a box, with a mem. that the pension was paid until Christmas, 1688, and that Lord Cheyne died 30 June, 1698). Among many letters there are some relating to the elections for the county of Bucks in 1713 and 1714 (in which William Lord Cheyne took an active part on the Tory side) from Lord and Lady Fermanagh, Lord Lichfield, J. Fletewood, Rich. Grenville and James Bertie, with printed papers, and accounts of the election expenses. Poll-books of the elections at Amersham in 1640 and 1680 ; with a petition to the H. of Commons in 1701, signed by a large number of the poorer inhabitants, against a vote which had passed for the restricting the right of voting, which had formerly been exercised by all householders, to such only as paid scot and lot. Abstract of the poll-book at the Bucks election in 1661, with marginal notes showing for which party many of the parochial clergy voted, marked *P.* for *Presbyterian* and *O.* for *Orthodox*: to most names *O.* is attached. Eleven interesting letters from Browne Willis, the eminent antiquary, of Whaddon Hall, extending from 1706 to 1714, (numbered 9 and between 57–72.) He mentions that he has traced the dedications of nearly all the churches in Buckinghamshire by means of wills, and sends copies of the wills of Agnes Cheyne, 20 Nov. 1494, and

---

[1] It must be remembered that the lady who makes these entries was the daughter of the Marquis (afterwards Duke) of Newcastle, who was then in exile for his loyalty.

[2] His fondness for chess-playing is evidenced also by an entry in his wife's account-book, that on New-Year's Day, 1658, she gave him a chess-board, with ivory men, which cost £2 10s.

[3] Amongst these notes is a copy of the epitaph in the south aisle of the quire of St. Botolph, Britain Street, on Will. Purde, Clerk of the Pipe, who died 15 Aug., 31 Hen. VIII., with notes of other burials there.

of a later Agnes Cheyne, which show the dedications of the churches of Cheynes and Chesham Bois. Asks for transcripts from the Augmentation office, &c., through Lord Cheyne's influence, and complains of delays and objections from Mr. Battely and Mr. Madox.[1] Desires a copy from the Augmentation office of the pensions assigned to the monks of Ashridge, and of the accounts of 16 chantries. Sends draughts of the monuments and arms in Drayton church: "I hear your lordship out of your great generosity designs to new beautify that church, which when you doe, if your lordship will be pleased to remove the painted glass out of the north window of the N. isle, and entirely compleat the chancell east window with it, in my poor opinion it will add very much to the magnificence of the church, and make the altar look very solemn. If that and the two east windows of the N. and S. isle were regularly glased, it would shew much more decent and ornamental then to let the glass be interspersed here and there, and the arms now in the east window might better be sett in the other chancell windows." Sends an account of Drayton church "copied from a MS. of my very worthy deceased friend, Dr. Hutton of Aynhoe," and an account of the lands from his own collections. Wishes Lord Cheyne might be created Earl of Amersham, "and real Lord Cheyne of your ancient seat of Cheynes, or some other eminent title in your neighbourhood, which you might derive from Cottslow, or Chilterne, and with good authority in relation to your ancestors might chalenge a title from the antient Honour and castle of Berkhampsted." Several letters about the county election in 1714, and about a book he is going to publish [the *Notitia Parliamentaria*] which he desires to dedicate to Lord Cheyne, who at first declines but is at length prevailed on to accept it. "My account of the 29 mitred Parliamentary Abbots . . when publish'd . . . . will doe me greater credit then my last appearing in print." A note in cipher from Lord Godolphin about exchequer business, dated 6 May, 1704 (686). Letter from Rev. John Ball, with profuse expressions of gratitude for presentation to two livings, Chesham, 27 Sept. 1711 (562). Draft by Charles Cheyne, esq., of an inscription to the memory of his wife Lady Jane who died 8 Oct. 1669, to be set up in Chelsea church, to which she gave the roof a few months before her death, which draft Mr. Cheyne sent to Dr. Adam Littleton to be put in Latin, and which is returned by Littleton with his version. (7) Also (559) directions for a burial vault for his family, by Mr. Cheyne, with inscriptions in Latin and English. A parchment-bound volume contains the Sessions proceedings in Bucks in 1702.

BRIDGEWATER MSS.

A small additional parcel is endorsed *Charles Cheyne Papers*. It contains thirteen letters from Edward Altham at Rome, about the carving of the above monument in Carrara marble at a cost of 700 crowns=£200, and the making of a telescope by sig. Divini, of 11½ palms long, with four glasses and a diaphragma, for 45 crowns, less 15 for an *objectivo* sent by Mr. Cheyne. There are also four letters from Altham's brother, Lewenthorpe Altham, and one from Edm. Chaloner, at Rome, dated 25 Oct., 1670. This parcel also contains an official account-book of receipts and payments at the Custom House in London in 1677-8.

XIX. *Derby Papers.*—Various legal papers relating to the estates of Henry, Edward, and Ferdinando, Earls of Derby, and to those

---

[1] In another letter he acknowledges obligations to Mr. Madox : "he is certainly most capable of answering my expectation of any one, being a thorough antiquary."

154   HISTORICAL MANUSCRIPTS COMMISSION.

BRIDGEWATER MSS. inherited through marriage by the Earl of Bridgewater; *tempp.* Eliz.—Charles I. Three thick volumes of rent-accounts. Valuations of the estates of Earl Ferdinando. Bailiff's accounts for lands at Burcester, Middleton, Streatley, Goring, &c. in Oxfordshire, 1–4 Eliz. Bailiff's rolls for the manor of Mayllorsays, 5, 8, Hen. VI., and 2 Rich. III. Nine letters from Mrs. Mary Fayrbairn to the Earl of Bridgewater in 1620–3, respecting a suit brought by her against him for a debt alleged to be due from the late Earl of Derby, with abstract of his reply to one of them. Representation on the part of the Countess of Derby to the Earl of Holland respecting a suit prosecuted by one Anne Willey, sister to his servant Mr. Anderson, who claims to be the widow of Sir Giles Bridges, and to have had a child by him, on whose behalf she claims estates in Wilts now held for the Countess's grandchild, Lord Chandos; about 1630.

XX. *Howe Papers.*—A small parcel relative to the manor of Kempley, Gloucestershire, mortgaged to the Earl of Bridgewater by Sir T. G. Howe in 1658.

XXI. *Rokeby Papers.*—Nine papers relating to the will and effects of Ralph Rokeby, Master of the Requests, who died 14 June 1596. 1. The charges of his funeral at the church of Lincoln's Inn, 18 June, 1596, amounting to £224 7s. 6d. 2. Account of moneys paid by Will. Lambard, for the funeral, debts and legacies.[1] To "Grigg, the marbler," for a monument, £6 10s.; legacies to the Universities, for poor prisoners, &c.; total, £1963 10s. 5d. 3. Account of the estate, of which Lord Keeper Egerton appears to have been executor and residuary legatee; total value £3,509 7s. 7d. 4. Inventory of books found in his study (125 volumes), with the probate valuation. Brook's *Abridgement of the Statutes,* two editions, bears the highest value, at £2: a "lardge church Byble," 13s. 4d.; two vols. of Holinshed's Chronicles, 10s. The miscellaneous books are chiefly theological, and against Romanism; among the smaller and fugitive pieces are, "The wofull crye at Pallace Garden," valued at a halfpenny, "A booke of erthquakes," 2d., " A lookinge glasse for England," ½d., " A new revenge for an olde grudge," ½d., "Jacke of both sydes," 2d. The whole valuation is £13 16s. 5d. 5. Inventory of plate and goods in the chambers at Lincoln's Inn, valued by John Bevington and John Stony at £200 18s. 9d.

XXII. *Sutherland Papers.*—A small parcel. Sketch of the history of the Sutherland family, to the year 1796, from Alan, thane of Sutherland, with whom Sir R. Gordon's *History* commences.[2] Dunrobin farm-journal, April, 1796—Dec. 1797; a daily record kept by John Bookless.

XXIII. *Wrey Papers.*—A parcel of papers relating to the estates of Sir Bourchier Wrey, who died in 1696, in Devonshire, Berkshire, and

---

[1] Another and final account of Lambard's payments, made up in 1600, which only exceeds this by £4, is printed pp. 308–312 of the Camden Society's *Egerton Papers,* 1840. A letter from Lambarde on the subject, *ib.* 228.

[2] In a little parcel endorsed "*Odds and Ends*" there are letters which seem to show that this MS. was at one time lent to Mr. Thomas Thomson, the well-known Scottish historical antiquary. In that parcel there is also a letter from Thomas Park to Archd. Todd, then chaplain and librarian to the Marq. of Stafford, asking permission to have a fac-simile made of the signature of Q. Eliz. to the warrant for the execution of the Earl of Essex, then in the possession of the Marquis. This fac-simile appears at p. 90, vol. II., of Park's edition of Walpole's *Royal and Noble Authors,* 1806.

Wales, and to the trust of the Earl of Bridgewater as guardian for his son. Inventory of goods and chattels, and list of books in his library. An interesting and somewhat touching series of letters from Lady Florence Wrey (written from Tavistock) to the earl, firstly about sending her son the young Sir Bourchier, to Eton, with Rev. Fermor Naylor, fellow of King's College, Cambr., and son of Canon Naylor, rector of Tavistock as his "tutture," as he "requiers one persone wholly to himself, who ought to be with him night and day"; and then, on his removal, in some disgrace, from Eton, (where, as the son himself writes, "I am forced by my discontent to absent myself so often from school that it makes me lead a very uncomfortable life") about the sending him to Ch. Ch., Oxford. Of Christ Church Major John Burrington writes in 1700, "The government of that house is much commended : they tell me that the Dean [Dr. Aldrich] has all the noblemen once a week at his own table"; and the earl also writes, "Christ-Church collidge has a great comendation." In that year he had no less a person for his tutor than Dr. Bull; "Geo. Bull" gives a receipt on Sept. 2 for money received for his pupil's use. There is also an entry of £3 4s. 6d. paid to Mr. Alsop for "making publick verses on the death of the Duke of Gloucester" ; this is a payment for Latin verses published in the Oxford collection on that occasion under the name of the young Sir Bourchier.[1] H. [Humphreys] Bishop of Bangor, writes two letters to the earl in 1697 and 1700; the former about the Welsh estates, the latter strongly recommending Owen Griffith (an agent employed by the earl) whom nevertheless the Bishop had dismissed from being his secretary for disobeying injunctions.

BRIDGEWATER MSS.

XXIV. *Official Papers.*—In a small parcel thus endorsed are some copies of appointments of officers in the Petty Bag office, Records, &c., and papers relating to fees, and (1620–21, &c.) to the patent for engrossing wills. Return of fees received for patents in 1594. Reply of the Clerk of the Privy Council to the Lord Keeper upon articles of enquiry respecting his fees. Petition of John Dessell (?), the Queen's clerk of the Market, to the Lord Keeper, with statements respecting his fees. Case of the Earl of Oxford as to his title to the office of Great Chamberlain.

XXV. *Ecclesiastical Papers.*—A folio volume, unbound, of the middle of the 16th century, (with an engraved number "9" on the back,) containing a common-place book of heads in controversial theology, alphabetically arranged, in which the opinions of heretics are first noted, and then quotations in reply follow, taken from the Bible, Fathers, and later writers, but especially from "Alfonsus." The heretics chiefly named are Wiclyff, Hus, the Waldenses, and Luther. At the end is [Walter Mapes'] poem beginning "Cur mundus militat sub vana gloria," and a table of "The authors' names alleged in the Treat[ise] of the Crosse."
Returns, or *significavits*, from the Bishops of Chichester, Ely, Gloucester, Hereford, Lichfield and Coventry, Norwich, and Salisbury, and from the Archbishop of Canterbury for Oxford and Peterborough, *sedibus vacantibus*, in Jan. and Feb. 1600, of the names of Recusants in the several dioceses.

---

[1] They occupy a page and a half in the folio *Exequiæ* printed in 1700. The "Mr. Alsop" was Anthony Alsop, M.A. (afterwards B.D.), of Ch. Ch., some of whose Latin poems were printed in the Oxford "*Musa Anglicana.*" The entry gives a revelation of the way by which so many young noblemen and gentlemen-commoners appear as practised verse-writers in the University collections of poems on state occasions.

BRIDGEWATER MSS.

Papers about Prohibitions.

Copy of a lease from Q. Eliz. to Edward Wingate for 30 years of the rectory and church of Dunstable Houghton, *alias* Houghton Regis, 10 Oct. 1588.

Draft of a deed of sale by Q. Eliz. to George Garth of the rectory and church of Sandall, Yorkshire; with corrections by Sir Thomas Egerton.

Draft of a lease from Q. Eliz. to Gilbert Gerrard, for 21 years, of the rectory and church of Eccles and the chapel of Deane, in Lancashire; with corrections by Sir T. Egerton.

Extracts from the Lincoln Registers of five presentations to the rectory of Long Ledenham, Linc., from the latter part of the reign of Hen. VIII. to 1603.

Fragmentary depositions in 16th cent. about the glebe of Great Ness in Shropshire.

Letter from James [Montagu] Bishop of Bath and Wells to Lord Chancellor Ellesmere, enclosing a question from the King about prohibitions; "from court at Royston," 20 Jan. 1609.

Articles against Mr. Carrier, vicar of Wirksworth and Carson, in the High Commission Court in 1633, for entire neglect of preaching in both parishes, for holding Romish opinions, for being busied in lawsuits, for employing one Mr. Botham as curate at Carson, who was a button-maker, a tailor, a soldier, and not in holy orders, and Edward Haslam as curate at Wirksworth who is charged with gross immorality.

Copy of the petition of Robert Lucy, Esq., to the House of Lords against [Thomas Watson,] Bishop of St. David's. [1698.]

Letter from four magistrates to the Earl of Bridgwater as Lord Lieut. of Bucks, certifying that they have searched all the houses of papists in the hundred of Desborough for arms, and have summoned them and the nonjurors to appear to take the oaths, being four papists and one non-juror, (Christopher Ingby, of Chipping Wycomb, foreign laceman); 17 Jan. 1715.

XXVI. *Exchequer Papers.*—Various papers by Chidiock Wardoure, Clerk of the Pells, respecting the tallies in the Exchequer, and their facility of falsification, with reference to complaints made by him against Robert Petre, writer of the tallies, in 1593, and to articles exhibited by him against Vincent Skynner, the next writer of the tallies, in 1599, with papers by Petre and Skynner in reply, and a letter to the Lord Keeper from the latter.

XXVII. *Chancery Papers*, chiefly of the time of Lord Keeper Egerton. Amongst Petitions are the following:—

i. Petition to the Queen from Arthur Hall, complaining of unjust dealing by the L. Keeper, and misrepresentation to her of the petitioner; with four letters from him to the Keeper, written from the Fleet, between 10 Nov. and 13 Dec. 1601, in which he upbraids the latter in strong terms, and two petitions, of which one is dated, 1 Jan. 1601, in regard to suits with Edward Sherland, serj. Hele and [Sir] Hugh Myddelton [Nos. 48-54]. The following extracts are worth noting. "Your lp. answers no letters of suyters by indorcements or in other manner by wryting, as I knowe I have bene tolde; wold yt please you otherwyse, yt were not much amys . . . as, before I was to desire your favor, by commendation from the highest, ... many tymes synce her majestyes raigne the greatest subjects in

England ever have, to whome more then often I have wrytten and they answered .... Your lp. said to my man this day .... that the Q's majestye wyl [not] wyl you to do what by justice you cannot. My good l., I know the Q. as well as you do: she wyl no doubt be unwylling therto: God graunte youre lp. wyll have as heedful, care therof as I am assured her highnes alwayes hath and wyll have; and long before you were called to the height you are at, I fealt her large favours to me, and I hope yet shall: tho hytherto you have muche hurte me, and not releived me, notwithstanding her majesty's graciouse mynd towards me hath spoken for me unto you .... Do not my l. disdayne or little regarde so meane a beggar as myselfe: make me bounde to you, if you will to end Hele and Sherland's causes. Else gyve me leave in my just question to have splene, as the sylly Pismyre hath, which oft too much abounds in wyse men of authorytye .... I must tell you I was so unhappie to be so yll advysed, as for the reverence I bare unto you, and oppynyon I had of your lp.'s conscience, to name you to be an actor for my releife . . . . I am not so simple, but I know what your lp. may do as but Mr. of the Rolls, nether what you have don in the lyke cases as myne are. If yt please not the Q. nor the lls. to heare the matter, I wyll lett yt notwithstanding be knowne to all men if I can, that I run not away with undoing and discredyt in the world. My l., cary a myld inclination to afflycted persons; the clamor is grevous (they say) of your sowernes to many, how trulye I knowe not: remorce is a qualytyo most commendable in all men of authorytye . . . . I have nowe to my great loss, being al the whyle in prison, performed your lp.'s strickt and inexorable order for a fewe dayes to be graunted for the last payment to Hue Myddleton. I beseech your Lp. to commaunde hym to fulfil what he shold, that so base and bad a man as he (which wel wold have appered yf yt had pleased youe to have loked into hys actyons to me) do not longer abuse me nor tryumphe over me. I am my L. dyverse ways quyte undon (which often som unmercyful men lyttle respect) by occasyon of matters before youe, and chiefly (tho bytterly besyde) in having her majesty's heavy displeasure, which howe I have deserved, and by what means yt ys procured, God wyl judge, and the worlde when yt shal hereafter have knoweledge of the same. I beseech your lp. I nowe may be delyvered of westward bred Myddleton." The petition to the Queen begins thus: "Most respectyve Quene Elizabeth, If I shold not be worthy of the grace to have yt graunted that the proceedings of my L. Keper in such causes as, of your majestye's most bountyfull favor in my behalfe, your highnes commended unto him, which he hath managed to my undoing, yet for your roiall clemencye and justice vouchsafe it: And that it may be tryed whether he have verry untruely informed your highnes against me or no . . . . I must with all humylitee remember your highnes what at Winchester nere 30 yeares past I requested and your majesty graunted me (that honorable gentleman Sir Jo. Stanhope being by in your highnes pryvye chamber), vid., that what sinister reportes shold come against me, your highnes would not beleeve. Most diva Quene Elizabeth aford me as much, and then shall your majestye fynde how unevenly my L. Keper hath caryed himself against me to your highnes." Papers numbered 96, 97, and 126, show that the matters in dispute were debts due from Hall, "a man of above £1,000 land of inheritance per annum, and his grounds stocked" (who "lives at his pleasure in the liberty of the prison"); and a judgment on 9 June 1601, orders him to pay £500 to Myddelton in several instalments. The Lord Keeper has underscored all passages reflecting upon himself.

BRIDGEWATER MSS.

BRIDGEWATER MSS.

ii. Three letters from Gifford Leeke, July—Sept. 1601 (Nos. 39–41) confessing in full detail his forging wine-licenses under the Great Seal, and acknowledging in the humblest terms the enormity of his offence.

iii. Statement of [Charles Yelverton] as to what passed between him and Sir William Cornwallis on Thursday, 15 Jan. [1599] in the presence chamber: "drawinge him privatlie toe the cubbord I used thies words followinge: 'Sir Will. Cornewaleis, I have your father in chasse for foule delings, and if I be nott able to make good proffe therof, he hathe remedie agenst me by lawe. In the mean space I wishe you forbeare toe give me evell reportts, holdinge it unresonable that your father should robbe me of my patrimonie and you of my good name.' This knight flinginge from me replied I was madd. This beinge spoken with a lowde voyce I followed him, intendinge toe have iterated my speeches in the hearinge of Sir Rob. Duddelie and Sir Rob. Crosse, therby to have cleared myself of that imputacon; but beinge interrupted by Sir. Wm. Cornewalies, whoe, shuffing me from him with his hand, used thies words, 'Awaye, thou art madd; thou art a beggare; thou arte unworthy to speak of my father; thou arte unworthy the Queen's service; I keep better men then thou arte; awaye, I will beate the'; my replie was, 'Sir knight, had I you out of this place I would pluke that periwigge of your pockie patte.' This was the forme of our speeches." Thereupon [Yelverton] writes to know when the knight would beat him, as he would not fail to keep any appointment he would make; but is ordered by the Lord Chamberlain to forbear the Court and to keep his lodging; "since which tyme I remayned prisoner ther." The name of the writer is learned from a judgment dated 11 June, 1599, in which a complaint of Charles Yelverton against Sir Thomas Cornwallis for breach of trust is altogether dismissed. (92–94.)

iv. Petition of 200 copyholders of the manor of Somersham, Hunts, that they may purchase the freehold of their tenements from the Crown, without extinguishment of their common in the wastes and fen-grounds. (34.)

v. Statements by Robert Naunton (afterwards Sir Robert) respecting a trust of property committed by him on going abroad in 1596 to Mr. Chester, about which there arose dispute on his return in 1599. He has a younger brother and three poor sisters depending upon him. "My case is ten times lesse, and lesse compatible with such a losse, then Mr. Chester's is, he being a man of £1000 by yeare, and I still forced to live a pore scholer in the University." (104.)

vi. Petition from Sir Richard Champernoun, on behalf of the parishioners of Modbury, Devon, against Mr. Serjeant Heale. Thomas Prydeaux, of Orcharton, esq., charged his lands with an annuity of £5 to be paid to the use of Modbury church, upon an exchange of land with the parishioners; but Heale, having purchased Prydeaux's lands, has for many years withheld the rent. "Moreover, besides this wronge, it pleaseth Mr. Serjeant Heale to beare out and uphould one Hen. Copleston, esq., whom the judges of our circuite for his lewde contempt against them bound to his good behaviour (but Mr. Serjeant Heale got him released) and John Copleston his sonne, in their dishonest and injurious and unlawfull courses, aswell against me as against other gent. and poore men." He forced a man to swear against himself; "nether makes he difference of men in his extreme, insolent and arrogant humour, for not long since he reviled the Maior of Exon, terming him foole and asse," because he would not punish a gentleman who had been wronged by one of Heale's name.

He has taken fees on both sides in a cause, and then spoken on neither. "I omitt many most shamfull and odious partes of his . . . . But otherwise, his userie, miserie, lawe, and pride of his purse, hath brought him to that height of insolencie, as he is growne insufferable in our countrey, and by some of theis doth he so subject the myndes of many to him as fewe or none dare to publishe their knowledg or conceit of him." (116.)

Other noteworthy papers are :—

i. Statement of the case of Thomas Rands, master of the Hospital of Spittle, against Sir William Wraie, knt., for pulling down the chapel of the hospital and the master's lodging and the dwelling for the poor, he having bought the hospital as concealed. (83.)

ii. Statement of the causes depending in the Star Chamber against Sir Sigismund Zinzan. First, he disturbed a licensed and authorized minister, ready to do service on the sabbath day, and appointed another neither licensed nor authorized, and wrote to Francis Drake, who had the gift of the place, to appoint his man ; and upon Drake's declining, because he had already appointed another, and because Zinzan's candidate was given to drink and notoriously unfit, wrote two scandalous and libellous letters, touching Drake in his place of justice of the peace. Secondly, because he beat Rob. Cley, the messenger who served process upon him, with the assistance of Henry Sturley, his brother-in-law, so that Cley was driven to run for his life into the Thames, where he continued for a quarter of an hour in the depth of winter. (115.)

iii. Case of Walter Aston, a ward of the Attorney-General, who was clandestinely married to Anne Barnes, (for which she was committed to the Fleet for nearly a twelvemonth) from which marriage he was freed by sentence of the High Commission Court, 12 March, 1600 ; and notice of a case of two men attached for beating Will. Heywood, curate of Corfe Castle, in 1601. (63.)

iv. Letter from Sir Thomas Areskyne to the L. Keeper, 7 June, 1603, interceding for the release from prison of John Arundell, on account of grievous sickness. "Much doth it move me to pittie that anie (thoughe never soe meane) without offence shoulde be soe distressed." (112.)

v. Long letter from Richard Barker, at Shrewsbury, 1 Apr. 1609, to the Earl of Ellesmere, about a warren. (46.)

vi. Letter from Henry Bowes, to John Halsey, esq., Lincoln's Inn, 12 Nov., 1655. Divers of the parishioners are petitioning my lord for Mr. Hanson ; others are desirous he would stay his hand " till some (as theire word is), sounde able man might be founde out for the place. . . . I have heard by two men endifferent well of Mr. Horne ; and now you know all I can say of that matter ; better him then a worse. Yesternight my lord's farme-house in Knockin, which Robert Stanley held, is burned downe to the grounde." (80.)

vii. Case of Col. M^cdonald ; in the time of Geo. I. Had served the late K. James in France, but was put on board a French ship to be exiled, on account of his killing a person in a duel ; the ship was taken by Capt. Peddar, and, as being a prisoner on board, he was not condemned to suffer as a pirate, but was ordered to be exchanged ; this cannot with safety be accepted, as he is liable to be tried for his life should he return to France ; now, after nearly eight years' imprisonment in Newgate, he prays for release. (18.)

BRIDGEWATER MSS.

In a separate bundle of petitions the following may be noted :—

From Jane, widow of Bartram Mitforth, endorsed, "This poore woman was first maried to one Sharpe, who was sister's sonne to the late Lord Keper" (Hatton, *or* Puckering ?).

To Lord Keeper Puckering from William Dowgle of Edmonton claimant of a moiety of the manor of Lydiard Millicent, Wilts, whose servant on going to take possession was seized by a pursuivant and others, who bound him, beat him, cut off his hair, "and notched him lyke a foole."

To the same from Irriell Offarell, chief of his name, son of Offarell Boye, respecting lands belonging to him in Ireland.

To the same from John Marcelline, M.A., clerk, for the living of Laiham, Suffolk, of the yearly value of £16 0s. 7½d., of which the houses are utterly ruinous, and the now incumbent is willing to exchange.

To Lord Keeper Egerton from Elizabeth Shawe against the Queen's purveyor, who on 10 Jan. 1598 and at other times took two dozen and eight mallards, 12 teals, 3 partridges, 2 capons, 3 dozen and nine plovers, 5 woodcocks, 22 blackbirds, and 44 dozen larks (larks being then worth 2s. per dozen) without payment.

XXVIII. *Law Papers.*—In a bundle of no general interest, there occurs in book-form the speech of counsel upon bringing a writ of error in the case of Fanshaw and Paschall about a lease of the manor of Denge in Essex from the Hospital of the Savoy, probably delivered about 1600, in which the speaker says, "there is an inscription upon the gate" of the hospital "ingraved in letters of stone in theis words followinge, *viz.:*

'Hospitium hoc inopi turbæ, Savoya vocatum,
Septimus Henricus struxit ab usque solo.'"

XXIX. *Star Chamber.*—A large parcel of papers relating to cases in this Court, beginning with some transcripts made *temp.* Eliz., of early orders.

23 Nov. 22 Hen. VII. [1506]. George Bardsay, a counsellor, forbidden ever to plead in the Court for advising a client to disobey an order.

17 June 10 Hen. VIII. [1518]. Commissioners appointed to hear poor men's causes.

11 July 22 Hen. VIII. [1530]. Injunction to Thomas, abbot of Haughmond, in a suit about property in which his predecessor Christopher had been concerned.

Temp. Eliz. Fragmentary notes on various cases.

28 Oct. 27 Eliz. [1585]. Sentence on John Meere, "a base man, of smalle or no reputation," in Dorset, for practising to entice and allure Ann Tilley, daughter and heir of George Tilley, esq., of the age of 13 years, to contract herself in marriage to him, and secretly conveying "himself into gardens and places adjoyninge to the windowes of the plaintiff's howse in the night tyme."

4 July 37 Eliz. [1595]. Judgment in the case of Edward Talbot, esq., against John Woodd for falsely accusing him of a purpose of poisoning his own brother the earl of Shrewsbury.

3 June 39 Eliz. [1597]. Rob. Long, Thomas Edwards, and others, for discharging listed soldiers for bribes.

5 Feb. 40 Eliz. [1598]. Examination of Will. Mille, clerk of the court, respecting his entering of an order.

12 June 42 Eliz. [1600]. Judgment in the case of Hen. Boughton, Leonard Gascoigne, Will. Eynes and Mary Fowler, for forging a treasonable letter to endanger the life of Rich. Fowler, husband of the said Mary.   BRIDGEWATER MSS.

3 Jas. I. Notes of the evidence in a case of Sir John Leveson *v.* George Shepherd and others for forgery and perjury.

4 Aug. 4 Jas. ⎱
3 Feb. 6 — ⎰ Cause lists, with notes.
24–5 Aug. 7 —

6, 7 Jas. I. [1609]. Notes about a case brought by John Hole, a clothier of Wells, employing about 500 poor people weekly, against Stephen Milward and a great many other persons (including the mayor of Wells) for libellous plays acted on Sundays in May and June 1607: including, minstrels, for playing at cards and drinking in time of divine service, "actors of the shewe, wherein the plaintiff and other tradesmen were deciphered, and acted by their persons and trades," one Will Gamage, author of a first libel, and who "acted the holing game with pictures, in the lewd manner described in the bill," painters of the pictures, &c.; William Williams, *alias* Morgan, who invented the second libel, with others who sent the first one to London to be printed; and various persons who in the Common Council voted money from the town-stock and church-stock to maintain the suit against the plaintiff. With a letter from the Earl of Hertford to Lord Ellesmere, dated at Littleton, 13 Nov. 1609, asking for favour to be shown to the Recorder of Wells, as being near to him, and to the mayor's son, as being his household servant. Notes of precedents for prosecutions for similar libels, viz., for a libel by one Colmer against Thos. Smalebrooke, a mercer in Bremingham, for his manner of buying and selling, usury, &c., which ended thus,

"Read now my frindes who this catchpoole should be,
The steward of the towne in plaine tearmes tys hee,
Smalebrooke by name, a Brooke that yeldes no fish,
But froggs and toads, and that's no deynty dishe";

for which Colmer in 5 Ja. I. was pilloried and fined; libel against three tradesmen of Gloucester and their wives; &c.

19 Apr. 8 Jas. I. [1610]. Cause list, with notes, chiefly on a prosecution against Sir John Mallory and many others in Yorkshire, for throwing down enclosures.

4 May —. Heavy sentences of fine, imprisonment, &c. on Sir Edw. Dymock, Roger Bayard, and others, for libel on the Earl of Lincoln, in " a very infamous and libellous stage plaie, acted on a sabboath daie, uppon a greene before Sir E. Dymock's house, in vew of 300 or 400 personnes purposely drawen thither, wherein they personated the said earle in apparell, speeche, gesture and name, with much disgrace and infamy, and so grossly that the standers by cryed 'Shame' uppon yt. And after the plaie ended, one of them appurrelled like a preacher with a booke went upp into a pulpitt fastened to the May-pole, and uttered prophane and scurilous matter in manner of a sermon, concluding with a most blasphemous and gracelesse praier, and thereuppon songe a *diridge* and fyxed a slaunderous ryme concerninge the earle on the mayepole, and the carles coate of armes over yt." With notes of other suits between Dymock and the Earl, beginning in 3 Ja. I., in one of which (8 Ja. I.) the latter was fined for depopulation in pulling down a house.

Many more cause lists to 1616, and from 1629 to 1634, with notes by Lord Ellesmere, and afterwards by the Earl of Bridgewater.

BRIDGEWATER MSS.

31 May 9 Ja. I. [1611]. Case of Sir Thomas Palmer for forging deeds.

9–10 ———. Case of Rich. Baker and his wife Jacomin Woodcock.

1 May 10 ——— [1612]. Case of Dr. Henry Manning, Chancellor of Exeter, for extortion.

Dec. 11 ——— [1613]. Robert Blundell, esq. v. Roger Hodgkinson and others for libelling by writing and pictures.

8 July 12 ——— [1614]. William Dale and five others prosecuted for pulling down crosses in Cheshire.

14 July ———. Sir John Yorke, dame Julian his wife, and 18 others, prosecuted for procuring and acting of a play, (at his house at Golthwayte) in profanation of religion. (Sir John Yorke and most of his men were recusants, and the play was probably one ridiculing Protestants.)

27 Nov. 14 ——— [1616]. John, Lord Darcy v. Gervase Markham, esq., for writing and dispersing of letters of challenge and other offences.

6 May 5 Car. 1. [1629]. Sentence of fine of 2,000l. and imprisonment on Rich. Chambers, a merchant, for saying at the Council Board in Sept. last that the merchants "are in noe parte of the world soe scrud and wrongd as in Eingland, and that in Turkie they have more encouragement."

2 June 6 ——— [1630]. Edward, Earl of Bath v. Sir Henry Bourchier, knt. for libellous letters and challenges to combat. The letters are enclosed :

i. Sir H. " Bourgchier " to Sir Alexander St. John, complaining of his withholding payment of an annuity given to the writer by William late Earl of Bath, " unles I woulde signe such an acquittance as you would tender, thinkinge thereby to constrayne me to acknowledge the right of him who hath none, but in the judgement of all æquall and indifferent men is a Bastard, and which I will mayntayne both by law, if I may be admitted to the tryall thereof, and by armes against any who shall dare to maynetayne the contrary ; . . . . . you have done most basely and vnworthilye, which I will likewise mainetayne as becomes a gentleman " ; London, 19 Sept. 1628.

ii. Copy of Sir A. St. John's reply, desiring to know " who is the bastard you intend, and what your meauinge is by maynetayninge of it by armes."

iii. Sir H. Bourgchier to Mr. William Skippon, desiring him to deliver to Sir. A St. John—

iv. His note of reply ; " . . . . . I would have you knowe that I meant him that usurpes the name and title of erle of Bath ; this I will mayntayne against you or any man that dares call me to accompt for itt " ; Lond. last of February 1268.

23 June ———. Full notes of the trial of John Trott, Richard Hull and John Clutterbuck for false and corrupt dyeing of silk, who are heavily fined.

1626–1630. A parcel of notes of depositions connected with the trial of Edward Vaughan and others of Montgomeryshire, for the alleged forgery of a deed of settlement after the death of Sir R. Vaughan, and for the substituting of a supposititious child for one born posthumously.

11 May 1632. Thomas Young v. Thomas Broughton and others for assaulting him in his pew in the Charnes chapel in Eccleshall church, Staffordshire, during sermon-time, with a counter-charge by Broughton, and a statement of the claims of both to the occupancy of the seat. Broughton is fined 100l., and each side 20l. " pro falso clamore."

6 June 1632. Cross-suits between Sir John Jackson, knt., and Thomas Viscount Savile for riot and assault, on a dispute about right of hunting. Lord Savile fined 1,000*l.* &c.   BRIDGEWATER MSS.

13 June ——. William Peterson, D.D. *v.* Samuel Travers, clerk, William Cotton, cl., Edw. Cotton, archdeacon of Totnes, &c., for slander. Full notes of evidence and opinions of the judges.

16 Nov. —— John Elwood *v.* Sir Edward Deering and others, in Kent. Hugh Trevanion *v.* Sir Francis Vivian, knt., (and others,) for oppressing the country as Captain of the castle of Mawes in Cornwall.

20 Nov. 1633. Philip Bushen *v.* Dominick Sarsfield, visc. Roscarbury, *alias* Killmallock, Sir Henry Bealing, and others, for accusing him of murdering his wife (for which he had been tried in Ireland). Long notes of evidence.

25 Nov. 1635. Thomas Temple, D.C.L., vicar of Bourton on the Water *v.* Bray Ayleworth, esq. and others, for accusing him of adultery; and a cross suit. Long notes of evidence.

Collections of notes of precedents, by Lord Ellesmere and others: corporations and noblemen fined, from the time of Edward I. to Eliz.; committals of juries and witnesses; killing deer; &c. In the parcel there is also the draft of replies to a bill in Chancery *temp.* Eliz. on behalf of the claim of Lord Roche to lands in the county of Cork entailed in the time of Richard II.

The following paper, containing the full report of the trial and sentence of Lord Vaux and others, on 15 Nov. 1581, for harbouring Edmund Campian, deserves printing in full, as the case does not seem hitherto to have had more than passing mention in the accounts of Campian's own trial.

"In Camera Stellata coram Con° ibidem, xv° die Novembris, anno 23 Elizabethe Regine.

Presentibus :

Thoma Bromley, milite, Domino Cancellario Angliæ.
Comite Sussex :
Comite Leicester :
Domino Cromwell :
Domino Hunsden :
Domino Buckhurst :
Domino Norris :

Walter Mildmay milite: s^b thess :
Wray, capitali Just. de Banco Regine.
Dyer, capitali Just. de communi Banco.
Manwood, capitali. Baron. Scaccarij Domine Regine.

Francisco Knolles milite : Thesaurario Hospicii Domine Regine:

This daie the Lord Vauxe, Sr Thomas Tresham, S^r Wiłłm Catesbye knights; Walter Powterell ; Jane Griffyn, the wife of Wiłłm Griffyn of Southladd in the county of Bucks, esq.: and Ambrose Griffyn, brother unto the same Wiłłm ; weare brought unto the barre as prisoners from severall places of imprisonment : To whom it was objected by her Mat^s Attorney gen'all,—That after divers & notable evill practises attempted, *by her Majs. knowne Enemy the Pope*,[1] seekinge and practisinge by whatsoever meanes hee might, either by hostilitie abroad, or by seacret practises within this Realme, as by his Bulls, Reconsiliaćons, Dispensaćons and such like doeings, to seduce and wyn the harts of her Mat^s lovinge subts, from their due obedyence for longe time borne towards her Mat^e, and soe to inclyne to his lewde treacheries & conspiracies, seekinge by such meanes to deprive her Mat^ie from her

---

[1] The italics represent passages underlined in the MS.

BRIDGEWATER MSS.

right, crowne and dignitie, and to subvert the state of this soe happie longe contynewed well-governed Realme & Common Wealth in peace & tranquillitie, to the great comoditie and benefitt of all her Highnes obedyent & lovinge subts; Hee hath now of late sent hither a rable of vagrant & seditious preists & ffryers of his confederacie, naminge themselves *Jesuits*, and *Seminary Priests*, for the same purpose; Amongst the which hee sent *one Edmund Campion* alreadie indicted of Highe Treason, takinge uppon him the name of one of the same Jesuits, most craftely seekinge howe to accomplishe his wicked and lewde devises, convayed himselfe into this Realme, beeinge misnamed, and disguised *in a very ruffianlike sorte*, and soe from place to place, by the space of one whole yeare, wandred in the same, where hee might fynde best oportunitie for his purpose, and thought himselfe to haue best securitie, throughe divers Sheires, ommittinge noe tyme nor occasion to put in ure and fynishe his lewde enterprise, whoe in the end being apprehended, taken & brought to examynačon, confessed, that in his wandringes abroad, where hee thought himselfe best welcome, hee was received, harboured and lodged divers and sundrie times in the severall howses of the said Lord Vauxe, Sr Thomas Tresham, Sir William Catesbye, Walter Powterell, and William Griffyn the husband of the said Jane Griffin, & brother to the said Ambrose Griffin, where divers secrett and lewde practises weare used as by divers circumstances in letters written by the same Campyon to his benefactors and brotherhood, beinge this day openly read in Courte, did more playnly appeare: Whereuppon the said Lord Vauxe, Sr Tho. Tresham, and Sr Willm Catesbye, beinge first examyned by severall parsonages by order from her Maties most ho: Privie Councell towchinge the premisses, utterly denyed, that hee the said Campyon had bin at any tyme in any of their howses. But the said Powterell in his examynačon taken by the right ho: the Earle of Shrewsbury, confessed that the same Campyon abowt three or fower daies after Christmas last past had byn at his howse, and had sayed Masse there, (a parte whereof hee heard) and likewise made a sermon there in his hearinge. Whereuppon the said Lord Vauxe was called and brought before the right hoble the Lord Threr of England, the Earles of Sussex and Leycester, beinge of her Highnes said Privie Councell, to be further examyned, where hee was made acquaynted with the confession of the said Campyon in that behalf, And thereuppon *It was required of the said Lord Vauxe on her Maties behalfe and by her Highnes expresse commandemt* That hee should *uppon his Oath* answeare whether to his knowledge the same Campion had bin in his howse or not, whoe refused soe to doe. Whereuppon he was required by their Honors to answeare thereunto, *uppon his Honor*, whoe likewise refused the same; And then hee was required to answeare the same *uppon his Allegiance*, which hee alsoe most contemptuously & obstynately refused. And it was likewise required of the said Sr Thomas Tresham by the said Lords That hee shoulde in like manner, *either upon his Oathe or Allegiance*, answeare to the same question, which hee very contemptuously and obstynately refused to doe. After which, the said Sr William Catesby beeinge called before the whole bodie of her Mats Privie Councell and required to aunsweare the same in forme as the said Sr Thomas Tresham was required, the said Sr William Catesby also verie contemptnously & obstynately refused so to doe, notwithstandinge many hoble pswasions used to them by the said Lords to the contrary. And the said Powterell beinge alsoe required to take his Oathe to aunsweare such articles as hee shoulde be examyned on concerninge temporall matters onely, and his due obedyence towards her Matie, the same Powterell very contemptuously & obstynateley refused soe to doe,

L. Vaux.

Sr Tho. Tresame.

SrW.Catesbye.

Powterell.

unless hee might first see and reade the same. It was alsoe informed by her Ma^(ties) said Attorney: That the said Jane Griffin and Ambrose Griffin beinge brought before him to be examined upon their Oathes, according to direction in that behalfe sent to him from her Highnes said Privie Councell, touchinge their knowledge of the receyvinge *of the same Campion, and one Parsons,* into the said William Griffins howse and of their meetinge there, they did likewise obstynately, maliciously and contemptuously without any sparke of obedyence refuse to aunsweare thereunto uppon their Oathes; ffor which contempts, and great malicious disobedyence, hee prayed on the behalfe of her Ma^(tie), That the said offend^(ors) might receive due correction and punishment by the order of this most ho: Court. Hereuppon the said Lord Vauxe, Sr Thomas Tresham, Sr William Catesby and the rest of the said offend^(ors) weare demanded what aunsweare they could make to the said accusaçõns; Whereunto the Lord Vauxe, Sr Thomas Tresham, Sr William Catesby, Walter Powterell, Jane Griffin, and Ambrose Griffin, confessinge their said contempts, craved the favour of this ho: Court *persisting notwithstanding in their former obstynacie,* which aggravated their offences soe much the more in the opynion of this ho: Courte. Nowe the whole Presence heer sittinge, gravely and advisedly waighinge the quallitie and depth of their offences, soe maliciously obstynately and disobediently comitted towards her Ma^(tie), by whom and under whose most gratious government this Realme and Comon wealth throughe the speciall grace of Almightie God, to her manifold daungers, and to the greate offence and dymynution of the power of her said capitall Enemy, hath received the Gospell freely preached and taught, and thereby innumerable comforts, benefitts & blessings, yea and by the good providence of God in her Highnes, by her gratious mercie and lenytie, soe long wealth peace and tranquillitie, notwithstandinge all the Abjuraçõns, Excommunicaçõns, Deprivaçõns, Bulles, Reconsiliaçõns, Dispensaçõns, Seditions, and all manner of lewde enterprises, attempted and most subtilly practised by the Pope and his confederats: All or the most part whereof have (throughe the goodness of God) bin intercepted and prevented by good order and pollicies; *amongst the which the examynac'ons of men upon their Oathes hath bin used, as one speciall Triall, and allowed both by the Lawes of God and the Lawes of this Realme, without the which many treasons misdemeanors and contempts, to the greate danger of her Highnes her Crowne and Dignitie, and this her peacable Realme and Comon Wealth, might heretofore and may hereafter escape unpunished, or not disclosed;* Have therefore thought the said offendo^(rs) well worthie to be most severely punished and deeply fyned for these their offences, *for examples sake;* And have ordered accordingly that they shall be comitted to the Fleete, there to remayne close prisoners *untill they shall conforme themselves in obedience and duty towards her Ma^(tie) in the premisses* and shall not bee delivered by the order of this Courte untill her Highnes pleasure be therein specially knowne. And further that they shall pay for their ffynes for the same offences to the use of her Ma^(tie) as followeth, vizt: the Lord Vauxe *a thousand pounds,* Sr Thomas Tresham *one thousand marks,* Sr William Catesby *one thowsand marks,* Walter Powterell, Jane Griffyn and Ambrose Griffin, every of them *five hundreth marks* a peece.   TH: MYNATT."

BRIDGEWATER MSS.

Griffin.

The charge of the offendo^(rs), and theyr awnswere in open Court.

Examynac'ons of offenders,&c.

Imprisonment untylle, &c.

Fines, &c.

XXX. *Bucks Militia.*—Commissions, lists, receipts; and papers relative to an order from the Council in Jan. 1704-5 for searching Papists' houses for horses and arms, and for enlisting soldiers, in pursuance of an Act of Parl. Letter from N. Hackett to the Earl of Bridgewater, Lord Lieut., excusing himself from acting as a' deputy

BRIDGEWATER MSS. lieut. as not having taken the oaths, &c.; North Crawley, 28 Jan., 1704. Letter from John Crosse; visited Mr. Dormer of Peterly, the only Papist in his neighbourhood, and found he had five ordinary cart-horses for farming and a small nag, one fowling piece and an old rusty carabine; "he is a very civil gent., and behaves himself as such;" 6 Feb., 1704. Another letter to the same effect in 1707. Letter from Edward Bate; searched the house of Mr. Minshall at Bourton, the only Papist and non-juror in the three hundreds of Buckingham and found no arms; in the stables "an old disabled race-horse (called Kibes) barbarously fired in his fore-feet. . . . . I know not (my lord) what prejudice he may have done his master, but I am sure he can now doe no hurt to the Government"; also a little pad for his daughter's use; Mayds Morton, 28 Jan., 1704. Letter from Robert Throckmorton: conceives the Act was chiefly intended against horses fit for military service, of which he has none; has some coach-horses for his wife, and a strong riding-horse for himself, but will keep none which may be offensive; Weston, 25 Feb. There are also papers about similar returns in 1696, and many in 1707–8.

XXXI. *Trade and Plantations.*—Chiefly notes by the third Earl of Bridgewater of business at the meetings of the Commissioners of Trade in 1694–7.

Draft (approved by the Queen) of a patent for Bevis Bulmer to put in practice a new device for cutting iron rods, &c., by a water engine; 9 May 1588.

Petition to Sir John Fortescue from Ralph Sparrow of Ipswich for licence to export some damaged corn to Bourdeaux. (159.)

"Abstract of some matters relating to the safety of the island of Jersey," against John Fitch; *c.* 1695.

Case of the Hudson's Bay Company against the Canada Company of France, 1696. (89.)

Printed "Factum for Gabriel de la Forest," a French prisoner. (41.)

Letter from Lord Bellomont, Gov. of New York, 9 June, 1697. (6.)

Address from the Bachelors of Virginia to Francis Nicholson, the Governor, thanking him for his intention of instituting annual games for the training young men "in the manly exercises and feats of activity," and desiring the publication of a sermon lately preached in his commendation. (148.)

Two representations to Parliament for bounties for Manchester linens and Blackburn cottons, about 1770. (160, 161.)

XXXII. *Privateers.*—Notes by the Earl of Bridgewater of business at meetings of the Lords of the Admiralty in 1693, with a memorial from the Portuguese ambassador, Visconde de Fontearcada, to the Lords of Appeal about a Portuguese ship.

XXXIII. *Admiralty.*—Copies of letters to the Lords from the Marq. of Carmarthen, commanding a squadron, with a convoy of merchantmen, on the west coast of England, 14 June–17 Aug. 1695. Navy lists, 1699–1700. A book of forms, instructions, signals, &c. copied by one Russell Revell. Household establishment of Prince George of Denmark in 1703.

XXXIV. *Peerage Patents.*—Copies of the patents in 11 Edw. III. (1337), creating the Earls of Suffolk, Huntingdon, Gloucester, Derby, and Northampton, with the grants of lands; and of the grant of the same date to the Earl of Salisbury, reciting his charter of creation. Certified copies made in 1606–7.

BRIDGEWATER MSS.

XXXV. *Bonds.*—There are many in which Sir Will. Courteen is concerned, for money borrowed from Lady Alice Hastings, with a copy of the commission of bankruptcy against Courteen, 26 Jan. 1661.

XXXVI. *Miscellaneous.*—A small parcel, in which are some curious printed papers :—

Some papers relating to coinage and the trial of the pyx, in the time of Q. Elizabeth (1599) and subsequently.

A printed memorial from the Earl of Egmont to Charles II. in 1673, about colonization in the island of St. John in the Gulf of St. Lawrence, and in the island of Dominique.

Papers relating to the case of Mr. Richier, governor of Bermuda, *temp.* Will. III.; with a folio pamphlet by Thomas Bulkley, printed at London in 1696 entitled " A pacquet of intelligence from New England . . . wherein the miserable state of the said province . . . . . under the tyranny of an indigent debauch'd idiot and most pernicious villain, named Cadwallader Jones, is briefly demonstrated."

WILLIAM DUNN MACRAY.

THE MANUSCRIPTS OF THE CORPORATION OF READING.

The muniments preserved in the Town Hall at Reading are both ancient and numerous. The earliest documents belong to the reign of Henry III.; the accounts begin imperfectly at the close of that of Edward I., and from the time of Edward III. are continued with some degree of regularity; while from the year 1431 there are but few breaks in the Register of the Acts of the Mayor and Burgesses, which thence dates its commencement. Many of the Account-rolls, as well as other documents, have unfortunately been at some time exposed to damp, which has greatly injured them, and left some in a state almost too tender for handling; but the whole collection is now well cared for. In 1866 a schedule was made, by the care of a then assistant Town Clerk, Mr. S. Preston, of the number and nature of the various parcels and volumes; and this (which was very well drawn up) affords a ready means for general reference. Some of the registers and miscellaneous papers were used by Rev. C. Coates when he was engaged upon his *History of Reading*, which was published in 1802; but any future writer on the antiquities of the place would find much of local interest, hitherto unused, in the earliest title-deeds, which it did not fall within my province to calendar, but which deserve full description. The series of letters and notices during the time that Reading was a centre of military movements during the Civil War will be found to repay examination.* A letter from a tenant of the Corporation, one George Varney,

MSS. OF READING CORPORATION.

---

* Of the history of Reading during that prominent period in its annals, I may mention that the Vicar of St. Laurence's parish, Mr. Guilding, has been for some time engaged in preparing a narrative.

to the Town Clerk in 1644, gives a graphic account of the losses suffered through the requisitions of the armies on both sides.

I have to acknowledge with pleasure the courtesy of Mr. Henry Day, the Town Clerk, who is greatly interested in the records under his care, and at whose suggestion, I believe, the Corporation invited the examination for the purposes of the Commission.

WILLIAM DUNN MACRAY.

June, 1886.

I. Fourteen Royal Charters granted to the borough of Reading from 18 Edw. III. to 6 Will. IV., with an exemplification of the Charter of Charles I., under the seal (of which unfortunately only one half remains) of the Keepers of the Liberties of England, dated 14 Dec. 1649. The Charter of Edw. III., dated 10 June (1344) at Westminster, is an *Inspeximus* of a Charter of Hen. III., with a qualifying clause excepting the privilege that the burgesses should be "quieti de omnibus placitis." It is printed by Coates in his *History of Reading*, Appendix, No. VII., who, however, omits the names of the witnesses in both cases. The witnesses to Edward's Charter are J[ohn Stratford], archbishop of Canterbury, R[alph Stratford], bishop of London, R[obert Stratford], bishop of Chichester, Will. de Bohun, earl of Northampton, Tho. de Beauchamp, earl of Warwick, Thomas Wake de Lydel, Ralph de Stafford, steward of the household. Unfortunately the entire Charter is greatly discoloured by the application of galls for the purpose of rendering it more legible, although in itself it is quite clear. The seal, in green wax, is perfect except for one half of the inscription.

Richard II., at Westm., 20 Feb. *an.* 2 (1379).—Confirmation of the Charter of Edw. III. Similarly discoloured. Seal in similar condition.

Henry IV., at Westm., 16 Feb. *an.* 2 (1401).—Confirmation. Discoloured. Seal almost perfect.

Henry VI., at Westm., 11 Aug. *an.* 5 (1427).—Confirmation. Discoloured. Seal almost perfect.

Henry VII., at Mayfield, 4 Aug. *an.* 2 (1487).—Confirmation ; but adds, i. the right to have two mace-serjeants; ii. exemption of mayor and burgesses from serving on juries; iii. supervision by the mayor of the clothworkers. Seal perfect.

Henry VIII., at Westm., 25 Apr. *an.* 34 (1542).—A new Charter. (*See* Coates, p. 63.) The initial letter contains a portrait of the King, enthroned, with three burgesses kneeling before him, whose names are written below. Only a fragment of the seal remains.

Edward VI., at Westm., 17 May *an.* 1 (1547).—Confirmation. An outline sketch of the King is given in the initial letter. Only a small fragment of the seal.

The subsequent Charters are of Q. Elizabeth (1560, Coates, p. 63), James I. (1604), Charles I. (1638, Coates, pp. 65–70), Charles II. (1667, *ib.*, p. 71), James II. (1686), Will. IV., 1830 (respecting Justices of the Peace), and 1835 (granting separate Quarter Sessions).

There is also a Confirmation by Hen. VIII. (dated at Westm., 17 Feb. *an.* 11, 1520) of articles, in English, for the regulation of the weavers' trade at Reading. The abbot of Reading is empowered to choose one person out of three who are to be yearly presented to him, to be the keeper of the seal for sealing the cloth. Of the Great Seal attached to this Charter there are three fragments. *MSS. OF READING CORPORATION.*

With these royal Charters there is also a box containing documents respecting the restoration of the rectories of St. Giles and St. Mary to the vicarages of those churches, dated 3 & 4 Phil. and Mary, and 16 Eliz.; with a letter from Lord Keeper Ellesmere, of 22 July 1614, directing their preservation in the custody of the Corporation.

A small box containing thirty deeds from the time of Edw. II. to II. Edw. VI. (omitting the reigns of Hen. IV., V.), together with a bond in the year 1665. These early deeds are almost entirely, throughout the whole collection, conveyances of property in Reading, and do not therefore come within the scope of this Report. It may be sufficient to mention as a specimen the earliest one in this box. It is a grant to John Vachel (afterwards Sir John Vachel, Knt.) from William and Edith, the son and daughter of the late Thomas le Vineter, of a messuage in High Street, bounded on one side by the water of Kenete; dated the Sat. before the f. of St. George, 19 Edw. fil. Edw. (19 Apr. 1326). The next, dated 24 Edw. III., relating to the same property, is witnessed by (amongst others) William Ruscel, mayor; and the third, 39 Edw. III., by Will. Warde, mayor. Nearly all the rest of the deeds in this box relate to the descent of the same property, (through Vachell, Cole, Appleman, David Atte Hatche, Hen. Lambyn vicar of St. Laurence, and Rich. Warde), which was finally sold by Rich. Way to the mayor and burgesses, 26 Nov. 1551. Will of John Hole, dated 3 Sept. 1461, proved 16 Jan. ensuing, bequeathing legacies to the churches of St. Laurence, Reading, and of Hurst, legacies for highways, &c. Will of Thomas Carpenter, dated 20 Aug. 1520.

Parcel endorsed, "24 ancient deeds from the time of Edward III. to III. Q. Elizabeth," but really commencing with two deeds of the time of Henry III.

38 Henry III., morrow of the Purification. Copy of an agreement in the King's Court at Westminster between the Burgesses and the Abbot of Reading, in a suit brought by the former about their privileges, in which the Abbot concedes the right of the burgesses to hold their corn-market in the accustomed place and to have their guildhall with the meadow called Portmannesbrok, paying yearly half a mark instead of one penny as before, the Abbot annually nominating a burgess to be "Custos Gildae," and having a fee of four shillings on the admission of each freeman's son to freedom, and half the sum paid by any stranger (*see* Coates, pp. 50-1, and App. No. V.). This is on a folio strip of vellum, cut out apparently from a roll of Statutes (written in the time of Edward I.,) since the line preceding the commencement ends with "*Expliciunt statuta*," and the rubric "*Assisa panis*" follows it at the end. On the back are prayers in French and Latin to the B. Virgin and St. John, and a French poem in 34 lines on the Passion, much rubbed and consequently partially illegible. The first four lines run thus:—

...	...	...	ke ew la croiz fu myse	
...	...	...	...	pur nus eit recoliz
...	parcele		...	pas kal munto Calvari fesis
...	...	..	...	... idonus e efferis.

MSS. OF READING CORPORATION.

The last four thus :—

"Eie merci de nus Jesu Crist e pite
Ke sul es sires e treis [?] e haute
Ou Deu la Pere e Seint Espirit enjoie en Deite
Amen car issint est sanz fin en verite."

IV. A small round wooden box, containing 13 vellum deeds, *tempp.* Hen. III.–Edw. III., and four of the year 1423; together with a copy on paper of the will of Richard Bedewynde, (mayor in 1385-9) proved 23 May, 1423.

V. Parcel endorsed "58 ancient deeds, bonds, &c. from the reign of Edw. I. (Hen. III.) to the reign of Charles I., &c."

Some of these are mutilated through damp. A deed dated 27 Edw. III. begins with the unusual form, "Salutem in Virgine gloriosa."

1500, July 28. Will of John Blunt of Swalowfyld; to be buried in the church of All Saints there; 6s. 8d. to buy a standard ("vexillum") of St. Margaret. Proved 9 October 1500.

One deed dated 1 Sept., 9 Hen. VI. has no connection with Reading, but is a grant by Robert Perneys of Abingdon, and Alice his wife, of a messuage in Abingdon.

VI. Parcel endorsed, "23 ancient bonds, releases, &c., from the reign of Edw. III. to Eliz."

VII. Parcel endorsed, "27 ancient deeds from the reign of Edw. III. to Edw. VI."

8 Hen. VI. (1429) Friday next after the f. of St. Mich. (Sept. 30) Indenture between the Mayor and Burgesses, whereby it is agreed that five marks shall be paid annually from the common chest for the maintenance of the Mayoralty, in exchange for the lands formerly assigned for that purpose.

VIII. Parcel endorsed, "14 ancient deeds, from the time of Rich. II. to Hen. VI."

IX. Small box endorsed, "Four ancient deeds in the reigns of Rich. II. Hen. IV., and Hen. VI."

X. Small parcel containing an award made 18 Nov. 17 Hen. VIII. (1525) by Thomas Englefeld, sergeant-at-law, and Walter Luke, gentleman, arbitrators between the Abbey and Convent of Reading and the Burgesses, respecting the flesh-shambles. This indenture has the town-seal, and is signed, "T. Englefild."

XI. 1311-12. 5 Edw. II. "Assisa armorum in villa Radinge." A vellum roll, very much injured by damp, containing, in three columns, a muster-roll. First come the names of eight persons, armed with " glad., arc., sag., et cultell."; viz., John la Acator, Rad. de Bello, Ad. le Politer, Will Eldesue (" obiit ") Ad. de Madenache ("obiit ") Joh. le Fogel[ere], Will. Cosin, Tho. Syward. Next follow 33, armed with bows and arrows and knives. Then follow over 235 (besides names lost at the foot through mutilation of the roll), armed with hatchets and knives ("hach' cult."). From this list an approximate calculation of the population of Reading may probably be made.

MSS. OF
READING
CORPORATION.

SERIES OF ROLLS of the ACCOUNTS of the MAYOR and the   XII.
TREASURERS of the COMMON CHEST.

1302. 30 Edw. [I]. "Item, cuidam menestrallo in abbatia, datum per communem assensum, vi^d. Item, quibusdam cokynis domini Regis venientibus in abbatia, ij^d. In stipendio Majoris, xx^s. In quadam commestione facta in la Gildhalle, xxiiij^s."

1356-7. 30 Edw. III. Very much mutilated. "Will Warde, pro expensis suis versus Parliamentum pro ix diebus."

1363-4. 37-8.—Very much mutilated.

1366-7. 40-1.— One pike, one tench, wine, &c., sent in this and the following year to Sir Adam, the Clerk of Windsor Castle. 40^d paid to Thomas le Clerk "pro transcripto novi statuti."

1367-8. 41-2.—(On the same roll.) "Edmundo de Chelreye et Joh. de Foxle, mil., 1 augwillam prec. ij^s"; "Waltero atte Grene et socio suo pro Parliamento 50^s"; 2^d. for the parchment for the account of the two years.

There is also one other roll of which the top lines with the date have been cut off, but which appears to belong to one of the later years of Edw. III. It contains references to the mayoralties of John Bythewode and Will. Calour, and apparently follows on one of John Farham (that of 1371 ?); and contains mention of the names of Henry Barbour, Walter Daunteseye, and others living at that time. It has copious details of the expenses of making certain bread-boxes or panniers ("panes.") for the carriage of food; but is chiefly occupied with the particulars of some levy of archers for service abroad, for whom the provisions were required. There are sums collected by the wardens of the several divisions of the town, *Veteris Vici, Novi Vici, Summi Vici, Castel Stret,* and *Vici London,* "pro hominibus existentibus apud Portesmuth"; and a separate collection "pro expensis apud Newebury." 12^d is given to a messenger from the Exchequer; one lucy, price 6^s viij^d, with wine, to Sir Warin de L'Isle and John Estbury at Reading; and wine to Nicholas Carrewe; expenses (particulars partly destroyed by damp) of the mayor, constables, bailiffs, and archers, going to Portsmouth; a great stock of fresh and salt fish bought at Abingdon "pro stauro"; expenses at "Maydenhuth, quo tempore dominus Rogerus Penbrugg et Ricardus Forester extiterunt ibidem pro eleccione sagittariorum," and at Reading when Thomas De La Mare and Richard Forester were there for the same purpose; expenses also at Newbury and at [South-]Hampton. There were two men-at-arms provided besides the archers. The arrows cost three halfpence each. "Item, missæ abbati pro la Lochehen, ij lagenæ vini, prec. xvj^d." This entry occurs also elsewhere.

1373-4. See *infra*, p. 33, XLV. *b*.

MSS. OF READING CORPORATION.

1378–80. 2, 3, Rich. II. On one roll, very much mutilated by damp. In the first of these years occur the following charges for the confirmation of the Charter.

"De fine facta pro confirmatione cartæ, lxvi^s viii^d. In denariis datis clerico scribenti cartam prædictam, ij^s. Et ad sigillandum dictam cartam, xxij^s iiii^d. Et pro una lace pro sigillo empta, xvj^d. Et cuidam clerico vocato Boulond ad prosequendum negocia cartæ, vi^s viij^d."

"In expensis Ricardi Budel, majoris, eundo et redeundo London. cum Ricardo Braunche per iiij^{or} dies cum equis, de commissione domini Regis si dominus abbas contribueret cum villa de decima domino Regi concessa, xiij^s vi^d. Item in uno jantaculo dato Laur. Drew et domino Johanni Colyngbourne ad certificandum de solutione domini abbatis prædicti, ij^s. In expensis Walteri Dauntesey existentis ad Parliamentum per iiij^{or} dies, iiij^s. Et Ricardi Selham vj dies, vj^s. Et in expensis Ricardi Budel, majoris, in eundo et redeundo London. et ibidem morando pro licencia habenda pro hominibus villæ de Parliamento [*deest*]."

1380–1. 4 Rich. II. "Ricardo Wycombe ac Ricardo Bromptone pro Parliament apud Norhamptone, xxxi^s iiij^d."

1381–2. 5.—

1382–3. 6.—"In denariis remuneratis ludentibus de Henle per assensum rldedignorum, v^s viij^d. Item ludentibus de Althermanstone, xviij^d"; and again in 1388–9.

1383–4. 7.—"In frenshebred, ii^d." Rich. Brompton twice attends Parliament, and John Balet three times.

1384–5. 8.—Henry Barbour and Walter atte Grove in Parliament.

1385–6. 9.—Thomas Drovere, "pro mora sua apud Westm. in Parliamento," 40^d, John Balet, "pro consimili," xv^d, Tho. Smyth, "pro consimili," x^s, John Doublet, "pro consimili," x^s. "Ludentibus de Wokyngham," ij^s.

1388–9. 12.—Nicholas Fachel and John Balet in Parliament ad Canterbury. "In denariis remuneratis armigero domini Joh. Denerose pro licencia petenda de Parliamento, xl^d. Pro uno *portyngaler* conducto per ij dies ad mundandum forum de fimo, viij^d. In l^a *saplacch* emptis ad emendandum le prive, ij^d."

1391–2. 15, 16.—A great eel and one pike given to the King's judges cost no less than 6s. 8d.

1393–1413 wanting.

1413–4. 1 Hen. V. (All the account rolls of this reign are much mutilated and often nearly obliterated through damp). "Roberto Moris pro vestura empta pro ij menestrallis, x^s vj^d."

1414–5. 2.—"Capellano Cantuariæ [*i.e.*, cantariæ] de Colle pro le clokhows per annum, xij^d." This occurs also in other years.

1415–6. 3.—

1416–7. 4.—

1417–8. 5.—In duplicate, but both copies mutilated. Payments from many persons (as also in other years), "ut moram trahere possint infra burgum extra gildam." Two "smytyngstokks" bought for the butchers' shambles.

1418-9. 6.—

1419-20. 7.—Work in fixing four "basys ad exaltandum iiij postes de Gildhalle." "In pane, serevicia et argento datis lusoribus de Yatele, iij˙ iiijᵈ, Et in vestura de mynsstrellis, vˢ."

1420-1. 8.—In duplicate. 9s. 8d. received "de diversis hominibus " pro porcis suis transeuntibus infra burgum contra ordinacionem inde " factam." Expenses "circa latrinam communem." "Pro proclamacionibus factis per omnes vicos burgi ad publicandum ordinacionem de porcis isto anno editam, famulo ballivi, iiijᵈ." "In donis Willielmo Vachelle et uxori suæ quando venit primo tempore nupciarum, in pane, vino et serevisia, xvᵈ." "In expensis factis circa Robertum Delamare quando solvit pecunias mutuatas domino Regi, iiijˢ." "In expensis factis apud Walyngford quando major et comburgenses sui fuerunt ibidem causa presti (?) domino Regi faciendi, viijˢ iiijᵈ."

1421-2. 9.—The receipts and payments connected with the impounding of pigs are numerous. "In expensis majoris laborantis ad Henle pro uno rotulo habendo, iiˢ viᵈ. Pro librata communis fistulatoris et servienciam suorum, xˢ." (This occurs also in other years.) Gifts to the players of Syrdelesham and of Sunnyngges. "Circa extracionem clocce, xvjdᵈ et in emendacione loci ubi per prius fixa erat, xijᵈ."

1422-3. 1 Hen. VI. "In expensis hominum veniencium de Wokyngham ad sagittandum cum hominibus burgi, xxᵈ."

1423-4. 2.—20ᵈ given to the players of Wokyngham, with bread, cheese, beer and sweet wine. In 1427-8, 15s. on two occasions to the same.

1424-5. 3.—"In i homine portante returnum pro Parliamento domini Regis de Redyng usque Oxon, ijᵈ (sic) et in cera rubra empta pro eodem returno, ob."

1425-6. 4.—22½ᵈ for bread, beer, wine, fish and spices "pro jentaculo justiciariorum domini Regis de pace quando Johannes Marham, jun., et Johannes Ede jurati fuerunt in officium constabulariorum." "vˢ pro capucio liberacionis majoris (the hood of the Mayor's livery) dato Johanni Boteler clerico de sessionibus." The name of a Welshman resident in Reading, "David Kedewelly," occurs frequently in the accounts about this time. The name of Lynaker also occurs. [See also under 1490-1.] "In expensis Johannis Gocelyn equitantis Oxon. pro returno Parliamenti, xiiᵈ."

1426-7. 5.—"In palustribus (read palæstribus) existentibus cum majore apud Perkyns pro rewardo, vjˢ viijᵈ. Et in serevicia eisdem data, ijᵈ. Et in fistulatoribus pro rewardo apud Perkyns, viijᵈ. Et in i corda empta pro communi campana, iiijᵈ." Parchment and wax for the return of Parliament, ijᵈ (and in other years). Three-halfpence for the parchment on which this account is written (which is two feet five inches long).

1427-8. 6.—Wine for the Recorder of Bristol, and ¾ᵈ to his two valets.

1428-9. 7. — "In rewardo dato palustribus apud Willielmum Perkyns, vjˢ viijᵈ. Et in expensis eorundem cum equis suis, iijˢ iijᵈ."

1429-30. 8.—12ᵈ received for the rent of the inn called le Belle in High Street, and 6ᵈ for a tenement near the High Cross in the same street; 8ᵈ for a stone-cart sold to St. Mary's church. (The receipts in this year are much greater than before.)

MSS. OF READING CORPORATION.

1430–1. 9.—"xx^d sol. a lez mynstrelles Ducis Gloucestriæ ad jentaculum majoris, iij^s iiij^d sol. palustribus apud Perkyns. vi^d quando mutacio fuit de pecunia domini Regis."

1431–2. 10.—" In expensis majoris Thomæ Lavyngtone et aliorum proborum hominum quando quesivere evidencias in communi cista pro concordia tenenda cum abbate de Redyng, in pane et vino, xii^d. Et alia vice quando venere de abbatia de consilio abbatis, in pane vino et servicia, xiij^d. Et in expensis majoris Thome Lavyngton et aliorum proborum cum eis apud Maydebythe, viij^s x^d ob."

1432–3. 11.—Rent for a great stable in " le Flexchepynge." " In i quaterno paupiri cooperati (sic) cum i nigro cooperturio, empto de Joh. Kyrkeby, xx^d." Repair of "la Pyndfold." "In expensis Roberti Morys, majoris, apud Maydenhede in presencia marescalli domini Regis ibi existentis, vj^s ix^d."

1433–4. 12.—" Roberto Morys et Simoni Peter ad equitandum London. pro certis causis majoris et communitatis, xl^s. Lusoribus in ecclesia sancti Laurencii, xviij^d."

1435–6. 14.—"In ix hewltes (?) emptis pro ix sagittariis transeuntibus ultra mare in Flandriam cum Duce Gloucestrie, xij^s. xij^d pro iij potellis vini datis archidiacono et officiali domini episcopi Sarum ad supervidendum evidencias Johannis capellani de Colle."

1436–7. 15.—" In scripcione rotuli de articulis inter abbatem et villam de Redyng, x^d."

1437–8. 16.—

1439–40. 18.—" In expensis i breve (sic) a retro missi vicecomiti quia nomina (sic) majoris non fuit infra, iiij^d. Et in cera empta pro communi sigillo, ob. Et in i box empto pro dicto breve, ob. Et in scripcione indenture de articulis inter dominum abbatem de Redynge et burgenses ejusdem ville, viij^d."

1441–2. 20.—" Le Pyllory" mentioned. (The "stokks" have been mentioned in earlier accounts.) " Pro indentura inter abbatem et villam, xiij^s iiij^d. Et in expensis circa consilium ad supervidendum evidencias inter abbatem et villam per diversas vices, viij^s vij^d."

1442–3. 21.—A large amount received from various persons "de donis ad reparacionem gildæ aulæ"; with corresponding details of the expenses of the repairs.

1444–5. 23.—"Sol. i peyntour in parte solucionis pro pictura ymaginis Regis Gild aulæ, xij^d."

1445–6. "In pergamino pro rotulo collect. denariorum datorum Regine, iiij^d. Et in pergamino pro rotulo collect. denariorum pro mut[u]acione denariorum domino Regi, ij^d. Et in expensis Johannis equitand. cum collect. xv^e domini Regis usque London, ij^s iiij^d."

1447–8. 26—.

1450–1. 29.—Several journeys to London and Canterbury "ad ostendendum evidencias gildæ aulæ" in connection with some law-suit; for which also consultations are held with " Lytiltone" (the famous judge) for his advice (for which his fee is xiij^s iiij^d), and with " Wynbusch," for whom journeys are made to Islip and Henley. And "ad prosequendum pro cart[a] gildæ aulæ," 4*l*. 15*s*. 10*d*. are lent by various persons. Fees to a trumpeter and to " le foteman" of the King."

1451–2. 30.—The law business is continued.

1452-3. 31.—
1453-4. 32.—
1454-5. 33.—" Ricardo Payne, goldsmyth, pro factura do le tokenes, iiij^d," and vj^d in 1457-8 and subsequently.
1455-6. 34.—Wine for Lord Lovell, and for John Norys.
1456-7. 35.—Expenses on the day of a muster. Wine to master Norys and master Rastold.
1457-8. 36.—
1458-9. 37.—
1459-60. 38.—" Ricardo Tawke, aurifabro, pro le tokenes, iiij^d."
1460-1. 39— and 1 Edw. IV. " Pro uno box ad ponendum literas 1^d."
1463-4. 3-4 Edw. IV. The first paper roll.
1469-70. 49 Hen. VI. "re-adeptionis reg. potest. 1." A tattered fragment of a parchment roll, almost reduced to tinder by damp.
1483-4. 1-2 Rich. III. Also on parchment with those that follow. The " Bere " [Bear] inn in Castle Street mentioned. " Pro pergameno ad faciendum lez indent. ad ij^{os} vicecomites pro parliamento, iiij^d." " Macellæ vocatæ le Copped halle."
1484-5. 2 Rich. III. and 1 Hen. VII. " Pro pictura ymaginis et lez panes" in the Guild Hall, viij^s. " Pro i hamo ad pendendum i de lez panes, i^d."
1485-6. 1-2 Hen. VII. "Pro i carecta focalium ad comburendum coram capella Omnium Sanctorum in vigilia Omnium Sanctorum, ex ordinacione Will. Baroun, et pro i cera ardente in eadem capella eadem nocte, viij^d."* Parchment, wax, paper, and a box, for the indenture of return to Parliament, xij^d.
1486-7. 2-3.—A tenement bequeathed by Will. Baroun, esq., to the town in the preceding year is said to be given in compensation for the customary payment called *Chepingavell* paid by the burgesses to the abbot, (" in exonia consuet. voc. le Chepingavell "). The fire and light on the vigil of All Saints, by his appointment, are repeated, and are said in the account roll for 1488-9 to be provided for out of the rent of the tenement bequeathed by him. Nothing was received of the issues of " le comune Beme " (the town's weights and scales) " quia Johannes Raynold eos expendit ob grave onus infirmitatis et paupertatis." " Solut. ballivis burgi de Reding pro le Chepingavell, xij^s, viz. pro quolibet burgensi, v^d."
1487-8. 3-4.—The rent of the tenement in Castle street given by W. Baroun is xiij^s iiij^d, and the amount of Chepingavell paid to the abbot for 22 burgesses at 5^d each was ix^s ij^d. Two new windows in the Guild Hall.
1488-9. 4-5.—
1489-90. 5-6.—
1490-1. 6-7.—The amount of Chepyngavell paid to the abbot this year is xij^s xj^d for 31 burgesses. " Pro script. quatuor supplic. et aliarum billarum domino Regi hoc anno, iij^s iiij^d. Pro transcripcione

---

* Baroun's death occurred in this year. He was at one time the owner or occupier of the inn called the " Bell."

MSS. OF READING CORPORATION.

sive transsumpto script. fundacionis cantarie de Colley, iij^s iv^d." Expenses of a journey by Roger Towcotts, John Kingesmylle and Morgan Kidwelly to the sheriff. Journey of Will. Lynacre to London. Indenture of return to Parliament.

1491-2. 7-8.—xiiij^s ij^d paid as Chepyngavell for 31 burgesses this year. The same in the next year.

1492-3. 8-9.—For the first time an entry occurs of expenses for a dinner at the election of mayor, x^s, "omnibus computatis"; and the same the week afterwards. Again in 1495, and subsequently.

1493-4. 9-10.—Nothing paid to Cristin Nicholas, the mayor, because neither he nor any one else charged anything on the office.

1495-6. 11-12.—Two candles are provided on the vigil of All Saints instead of one as before. "Pro tokyns de la comyne beme, iiij^d." No entry of Chepyngavell.

1496-7. 12-13.—The account is in English for the first time. "Paid for burgeis silver, x^s" [the Chepyngavell]. Indenture for return to Parliament, xij^d. Dinner at master Smith's to the burgesses of Parliament, iiij^s.

1497-8. 13-14.—(On the same roll.) Rent from Will. Mogge for his tenement in High Street "next to the crosse callid Gardener's Crosse." "For a brekefast at Shroftide for the Bredere[n] and Burgeis in bred and ale, ij^s j^d" (and a second time). "For befe, lambe, hennys, chekyns, suger, wyne, grese, floure, wode, orrengis and powther, vj^s. To men of the law and councell, xviij^s iiij^d." Bread, ale, and wine given to master John Williams, knight, at the Bell. Dinner kept at hall in Sept.; bread, ale, wine, salt fish, conger eels, pikerel and perch, a trout (viij^d), haddocks, oysters, pears, nuts, spices and sugar, mustard and vinegar.

1498-9. 14-15.—"Gevyne to my lady Chamberleyne in divers deutes at master Smethis, as apperith by a bille for the same made, ij^s. For a potell maletetyne dronk atte halle, and ale the same time for a congregacion had atte halle, x^d. For wine and deutes to master Sandes, vij^d. For a brekefast atte halle in bred, ale and biffe, iij^s. For fresshe samon presentid to my lord of Sarisbury, vij^s. For ij pikis and iij perchis send to my lord of Reding, v^s vj^d. For ij copulle capons gevyn to my lord of Reding, iij^s viij^d.

1499-1500. 15-16.—"Paid for fysshe sent to master Norreis, ij^s. For a pike bowt at London for the bisshoppe of Sarisbury, ij^s x^d. In expensis apon my lord of Sarisbury servauntis, viij^d. For a generall dynere made of fysshe and flesshe at Cristmas, liiij^s vj^d. For a galon Malmesey, xvj^d."

1501-2. 17-18 Hen. VII.—"To Thomas Hart for burges sylver, vij^s vj^d. To Thomas Smyth for the mayor and burgeis game of swannes, in chaungynge of the name, and for tyth of the same, ij^s. For fysshe that was sent to my lorde of Redyng to the Bere, iiij^s x^d. For a potelle of wyne to m. Noreys at Brylles, v^d."

1502-3. 18-19.—Burgess silver, viij^s ix^d. "For wyne gevyn by the maire to Sir John Williams, knight, x^d. For wyne gevyn by the said mayre to Sir William Noreys, xij^d. To Robert Brylle for burges money being behynd, unpayed in the tyme of Thomas Curpynter being coferer, viij^s ix^d. Delivered to maister Cleche for a dyner at Wyndesour to maister Bray and other, xxx^s iiij^d. For v capons sent to Wyndesour at the same tyme, iiij^s ix^d. To Thomas Myryman for rydying to Wynsour at the same tyme, xviij^d. For an hors to the same Thomas the same tyme, iiij^d."

MSS. OF READING CORPORATION.

1503–4. 19–20.—The two tapers at Allhallows Chapel become now 1lb. of wax. "For a quarte of Romney to Sir John Williams, iij^d. Delyvered to Richard Leche for the Kynges fotemen, ij^s." Indentures for Parliament, viij^d.

1504–5. 20–21.—"For bred and ale to the collectours when thei brought in the money for the burgeis of Parlament, iij^d ob. To the Kyng for the lyvelode of the seid gildehall, xviij^s j^d. For mendyng of the cuppys of the seid gildhall, v^s v^d. To the swanherd for his fee, x^d": (the first time of this entry).

1505–6. 21–22.—The Bell inn belongs now to master Richard Wrattesley, esq., in the "hold" of Thomas Dawson. Burgess money, vj^s iij^d. "Payed to a purcyvaunte for bryngyng of a prive seale to make enquyraunce of the content and payment of the benivolens to the Kynges grace, xvj^d."

1506–7. 22–23.—

1507–8. 23–24.—Burgess silver only iij^s iiij^d. For a quart of Malmsey to master Palmes, iiij^d.

Fragment, much injured by damp, of the account by Rich. Aman, cofferer, for one of the years of Hen. VIII. before the account next following, probably for 1510-11.

1512–13. 4–5 Hen. VIII. The tenement at "Gardener's crosse" is now called "at Jerard's crosse." "Payd for a dosene of bred when the Frenssh prisoners were here, xij^d. For a galone of red wyne gyvene to the Duke of Bokyngham, x^d. For wyne at another tyme gyvene to the seyd Duke, ij^s vi^d. For wyne gevyne to the commyssioners being at the muster, vj^d. For a brekefast for Mr. mayor and hys bretherne beyng at the halle, ij^s iiij^d. For bere and ale to my lord Chamberleyn's servaunts at the George, v^d. To Leonard Cokks for translatyng of an indenture out of French into Inglyssh, xii^d."

1513–4. 5–6.—Much mutilated by damp. "For wyne and suger gevyn to Mr. Westone when he went to Garnesey, ij^s iijd."

1514–5. 6–7.—Much mutilated.

1515–6. 7–8.—Much mutilated. "Jerard's crosse" is now called "Jarard's crosse." "Paid for the Kyngs sylver for the subsidy, v^s."

In the parcel with these rolls of Hen. VIII. is a fragment of a paper roll, with account, in English, of expenses on a journey to London on some business of the town, with the draft of part of a letter, strongly remonstrating with "my Lorde" (the person addressed, *qu.* the High Steward?) for favouring the commoners of the town, who are free from tribute, rather than the burgesses who pay tribute. Probably this paper belongs to one of the later years of Hen. VII.

From 1516 to 1584 the accounts are unhappily lost; then follows a short series from Mich. 1584 to Mich. 1600, but wanting several of these years. 1601–5 are also wanting, and the series is then resumed, but still with many deficiencies.

	£	s.	d.
1587–8. "To the earll of Leicester's players"	0	10	0
1588–9. "To my lord of Essex players"	0	10	0
16 Feb. For a salmon given to the Judges	0	15	0
To the Harold of Armes aboute our cullors and to know our armes	0	5	0

MSS. OF READING CORPORATION.

		£	s.	d.
2 Sept. "To the Queenes Maj. players" Frequent journeys to the Earl of Essex and the Court, and entertainment of the Earl.		1	0	0
1598–9. "To the Queenes players" Again in 1607. The King's, Queen's, and Prince's players in 1618–9, and frequently afterwards.*		1	0	0
1608. "The charge of breaking the ise in the great frost"		0	18	2

1609–1618 are wanting; but for the latter year see p. 32.
1622–1641 are also wanting, excepting 1630, 1631, 1635.

	£	s.	d.
1631–2.† "To Mr. Mayor that he gave to trompetars that came from the Ackte at Oxfforde"	0	5	0
1642–3. "For pulling up the bridge at Casom"	1	9	7
1643–5. "Paid to the Governor, Sir Jacob Ashley, 31 weekes' pay, at 9l. 6s. 8d. per weeke	289	6	8
For buryeinge of two souldiers	0	12	0
For a table cloth lent to the Lord Ruthen and lost at the abbey	0	3	4
Paid Joell Stevens for wares fetcht at his shoppe, and spent at the abbey by the Lord Ruthen's servants"	1	0	0
1648–51. (One account). "To Mr. Mayor to give the ringers att the 3 churches upon the newes of the good successe at Worcester	1	10	0
To Richard Paine for painting the States Armes in three frames for the use of the towne	4	0	0
. . . . more, in full"	1	0	0
1651–3. "For wyne and sugar presented to the Lord Generall Cromwell at the Beare"	1	12	0
1657–8. "For expences when the Lord Protector was proclaymed"	1	1	0

1659–1660. Expenses at the proclaiming K. Charles II., 3l. 12s. For the King's arms in the Hall, Council Chamber, and Compter, 9l. For wines when the King was proclaimed, 6l. 10s. For altering the mace, besides the materials of the old mace, 22l. 12s. To the bailiffs for serving the execution on the secluded members, 5l. 1s. To the under-sheriff for his fees for the same, 21l. 5s. To Mr. Simon Ford, late minister at St. Laurence, for half a year at Mich. 1659, 25l. To Mr. Rob. Howse, for preaching weekly on the Lord's Day at St. Laurence, for 6 months, 20l.

1662–3. For the King's use as a benevolence, 50l.

1663–4. To the Lady Hannah for sending a letter to Ireland about Mr. Carleton, 5s.

1664–5. To the Herald-at-Arms, 11 March, at the Bear, 2l. 10s.

1667–8. To Mr. Harris, towards renewing the Charter, 150l. For the curtain to hang before the effigies of the Bishop of Canterbury, 18s. 3d.

---

* These payments were in some cases made in lieu of permission to play in the town.
† The account of this year is sewn up in a letter from Edward Cery, Warfield, 24 Oct. 1637, to Mr. Curteys, draper in Reading, about the settling the son of Lady Harbert in some trade; she would think herself happy to settle him with Mr. Curteys.

1671-2. To Mr. Parr, for the King's arms in the oval glass, 10*l*.
1673-4. A present in wine to the Duke of Ormond, 19*s*.
1675-6. For bringing infected beef to the shambles, and burning the same, 7*s*. 6*d*.
1676-7. On 15 and 16 Aug. two fires broke out in hayricks in the town, and the fire-engines and buckets were employed; one engine was broken, and 32 buckets much damnified.
1684-6. For a bonfire on receiving the new Charter, 10*s*. For the ringers then, 1*l*. For beer for the ringers then, 1*l*. 2*s*. 8*d*.
1686-7. For a barrel of beer for the victory in the late rebellion in the West, 1*l*. 4*s*.
1688-9. 1688, July 6. "Paid Mr. Maior a bill for carricing the address and the entertainment of Princess An of Denmarke, 9*l*. 19*s*. 4*d*. July 30, Paid for wine at the Shipp at the day of rejoycing for the birth of the P. of Wales, 1*l*. 19*s*. Paid Mr. Morgan for wine on the same occasion, 1*l*. 16*s*. Paid Mr. Garraway for wine more, 1*l*. 10*s*. Aug. 21, Paid Mr. Grover for charges in prosecuting of Mr. Wilder for killing the boy, as by order from Mr. Maior. 1*l*. Sept. 10, For wood for a bonfier at the day of rejoyceing for the P. of Wales, 8*d*. Oct. 25, For a barrill of bear drink't at the rejoyceing for the P. of Wales, 18*s*."
1690-1. "Expended at summer assizes 1690 in prosecuting of one Awbrey, a Papist, for treasonable and seditious words against King William and his government, 15*s*."

From this date the accounts do not seem to present any entries specially worth notice, but only such as occur in ordinary course. They are far from being perfect during the last century.

MSS. OF READING CORPORATION

A thick folio volume, partly parchment, partly paper (bound in black calf, but back and clasps broken), containing a REGISTER or DIARY of the ACTS of the MAYOR and BURGESSES from 10 Hen. VI. (1431) to 44 Eliz.. (1602). [Compare entry in accounts for 1432-3, *supra*.]

XIII.

p. 11. xv. Hen. VI.—"Mem. quod remanent in communi cista vii cartæ sub sigillo domini Regis signatæ, et ii. aliæ literæ mangum (*sic*) sigill. dom. Regis." Similar entries are of frequent recurrence.

p. 17.—Juramentum gildæ aulæ Radingiæ. In English. Printed by Coates, p. 57, where he, however, omits to mention that over the word *heele* (to which he devotes a note) there is written a gloss in the same hand, "kepe close." All the earlier documents here, as well as many elsewhere, are discoloured by the application of some chemical, probably when consulted by Coates. The oath is entered again at p. 89.

p. 18.—Letters patent of Hen. VIII. confirming the Charters of Hen. VI., Rich. II., and Edw. III.

p. 22.—Record of the election of Richard Cleche and William Justice as members of Parliament, 1 Hen. VIII.

p. 35.—Charter of Hen. III., giving exemption from tolls, dated at Portsmouth 5 July, *an*. 37, with a note that it was read in the Hustings' Court at London the Monday after the feast of St. Martin, and entered in the Remembrancer's Black Book; and a further note that it was read and allowed in the same court on the Tuesday before the feast of the Annunciation, 11 Edw. II.

MSS. OF READING CORPORATION.—.

p. 48. 21 Hen. VI.—Ordered that no barber open his shop or shave any man after 10 o'cl. at night from Easter to Michaelmas, or 9 o'cl. from Mich. to Easter, except it be any stranger or any worthy man of the town that hath need; whoever doeth to the contrary to pay one thousand tiles to the Gild Hall.

p. 62. 27 Hen. VI.—Friday before the f. of Purif., Simon Kent and Simon Lodbroke elected burgesses of Parliament.

p. 63. 27 Hen. VI. 8 Aug.—"Ad istam diem Simon Kent et Simon Lodbroke, burgenses Parlementi, petunt habere pro expensis suis apud Parlementum tentum apud Wynton, decem marcas sterling."

p. 71. 29 Hen. VI.—Friday after the feast of K. Edward, John Orpyd and Thomas Beke elected for Parliament.

p. 81. 31 Hen. VI. 26 Feb.—William Rede and John Prut elected.

p. 84.—Petition to Hen. VIII. for that confirmation of the Charters, with additional articles, which is entered at p. 18.

p. 85.—Composition between the town and abbot, 38 Hen. III. *See* p. 2.

p. 94. 37 Hen. VI.—3s. 4d. paid "to Ricahrd Goldsmyth for makynge of a mace."

p. 95. 38 Hen. VI.—William Rede and William Lynacre elected burgesses of the parliament held at Coventry 20 Nov.

p. 96. 39 Hen. VI.—John Prowght and William Pernecote elected.

ib. 1 Edw. IV.—Thomas Beke and William Pernecote, for the Parliament at Westm. on 6 July.

p. 100. 2 Edw. IV.—William Rede and William Lynacre elected burgesses of Parliament.

p. 112. 9 Edw. IV.—Stephen Dunster and John Hunt for the Parliament at York on 22 Sept.

p. 113. 42 Hen. VI., 1 "readeptionis." William Lynacre and William Rede for the Parliament at Westminster on 26 Nov.

p. 115. 12 Edw. IV.—John Proude, esq., and William Lynacre for the Parliament at Westminster on 6 Oct.

p. 127. 19 Edw. IV.—Mem. of the delivery to the incoming Mayor of three silver cups, with covers, one gilt, of the gift of Elizabeth Clerke. This entry is repeated in most years to 32 Hen. VIII.

p. 127. 20 Edw. IV.—Mem. of an agreement that in future the sum of five pence paid annually to the abbot by every burgess of the borough by the name of *Chepyngavell* shall be paid out of the common chest.

p. 129. 1 Edw. V. 6 June.—Rich. More, esq., and Thomas Bestency elected burgesses for the Parliament on 25 June.

p. 130. 1 Rich. III.—Morrow of K. Edward Confessor, Henry Kelssale and William Erne, elected for Parliament on 6 Nov.

ib. ———. 19 Jan.—John Pers, of London, gent. (admitted burgess the same day), and William Hert elected for the Parliament to be held immediately.

p. 135. 4 Hen. IV.—SS. Simon and Jude, Rich. Cleche and Thomas Bye elected for the Parliament at Westminster on 10 Nov.

p. 136. 4 Hen. VII.—Morrow of St. Luke (*on preceding page*, St. Lucy), Richard Moore, esq., and John William elected for the Parliament on 18 Jan.

p. 139. 7 Hen. VII. The same.

p. 148. 12 Henry VII.—Friday after Epiphany. John Staunciall, esq., and Rich. Smyth, gent., elected for the Parl. on 16 Jan.

p. 162. 19 Hen. VII.—Friday after Epiphany. Richard Smyth and Christian Nicolas for the Parliament on 15 Jan.

p. 163. 19 Hen. VII. 5 July.—Writ from the King to the Mayor for payment to the above-mentioned members of Parl. of 14*l*. 8*s*. for their expenses for 72 days.

p. 165. 22 Hen. VII.—The swan-mark of the Corporation.

p. 166. Decree of arbitrament between the town and the abbey in 1507.

p. 173. 1 Hen. VIII.—f. of St. Stephen, Richard Clecke and William Justice elected for the Parliament on 21 Jan.*

p. 178. 2 Hen. VIII. 26 Oct.—Order of the King's Council respecting form of admission of burgesses.

p. 201. 14 Hen. VIII.— In the inventory are added a silver cup and cover, of the gift of John Crow, "a mase garneshed with sylver," a silver seal and chain, two "pesses of dornex called ij carpetts, to cover the exchequer," the common seal of brass, and other items.

p. 221. 28 Hen. VIII. 2 June.—Return to the Sheriff of the election of Thomas Vachell and John Raymond for Parliament (omitted under this date in Coates).

p. 224. 31 Hen. VIII. 9 Oct.—Thomas Vachell in the great hall of the abbey, as deputy of the High Steward, Thomas Crumwell, admitted the newly-elected mayor, instead of the deprived abbot.

p. 227. 33 Hen. VIII.—To the usual entry of the delivery of three silver cups is added the following,—" ac etiam unus alius ciphus, coopertus, argenteus et deauratus, ex dono Margaretæ Hide, viduæ, ac duas maces argenteas, parcell. deauratas."

p. 236. 36 Hen. VIII.—" In this yere, that is to witt the xiiith day of May, were prepared in arredynes to sett forth for the seid towne to serve the Kings Majestie in his warres in his graces voiage into France xiii men welle harnessed and horsed and xx fote men welle harnessed, at the charge of the said towne."

In this year the three old silver cups are not mentioned in the delivery of the plate, and there only remains Mrs. Hyde's cup, with the two silver maces, one of which is called in 19 Hen. VIII. " le new masse."

p. 245. 37 Hen. VIII.—The Mayor is summoned by a writ to the sheriff of Berks to appear and do homage to the King " pro le body et lez syde iles ecclesiæ domus dudum Fratrum Minorum, vulgariter nuncupatæ lez Grey Freres, ac una competente et sufficiente via ad eandem, quæ præfati major et burgenses nuper habuerunt ex dono domini Regis."

Charter of Henry VIII.

The delivery of the two maces is alone entered, without any cup; but even this ceases after this year.

pp. 250-2, &c. 1 Edw. VI.—*Ember* week is called (in reference to meetings then held) " the Imbryngweke."

p. 254.—List of the Mayors entered in this book from 10 Hen. VI.

---

* From this point the elections will only be noted when they differ from the list given by Coates.

MSS. OF READING CORPORATION.

p. 256.—"The articles of the Chartour belongyng to the maior and burgesses of the borough of Redyng."

p. 264. 4 Edw. VI. 4 Feb.—50 soldiers levied, armed with bills, swords, daggers, and bows and arrows, and every soldier 40d., at the town's charge, "appoynted for the Kyngis affares into Bolloyne."

p. 269. 5 Edw. VI. 3 July.—Proclamations entered that the teston is to be worth 9d. instead of 12d., and after the 17 Aug., 6d.; and all the lower coinage abased one half.

p. 270. ——.—The King's writ for election of a burgess notes that William Grey, the late member, died on 1 Feb.

p. 276. ——.—Articles of "the charge and dewtie of the Maior," and of all the officers.

p. 281. 6 Edw. VI. 13 Sept.—Account of the King's coming to Reading. (Printed in Coates, p. 17.)

pp. 284–5. 1 March, 21 July, 16 Aug.—Entries of the furnishing of soldiers for the Queen's service, the first being of ten men against the Duke of Northumberland (Coates, p. 18).

p. 287. 1 Mar.—John Sawnders, a burgess, expelled, who had been pilloried and had had his ears cut off for speaking seditious, slanderous and opprobrious words against the King's Council, to the great perturbance of his honest neighbours.

pp. 291–4. ——.—Copies of the letter sent by Q. Mary to the Privy Council on her brother's death, 9 July, and of the reply made by them on behalf of Lady Jane Grey, dated the same day.

p. 295. 2 Mar.—Note of the Queen's marriage, and account of her coming with Philip to Reading on 2 Aug. (Coates, p. 19.)

p. 312. 3 and 4 Mar. 9 July.—Forty men, in blue coats with red crosses, furnished for the Queen's service (ib.).

pp. 345–65.—Oaths of all the corporation-officers.

p. 351. 7 Eliz. 5 July.—Order of the Corporation of London that as soon as they are certified of the names of all the burgesses of Reading such burgesses shall be discharged of toll within the city, according to the ancient allowance of their liberties.

[For the first thirty years of Q. Eliz. the Register is simply a record of the elections of annual officers, not even including all the parliamentary elections.]

p. 582. 30 Eliz.—Robert Knowles, Esq., M.P., being likewise elected for the county, Thos. Egertonne, Esq., solicitor general, is elected in his stead (omitted by Coates, who puts the former election under 31 Eliz.).

p. 583. 31 Eliz. 21 Feb.—Order made for a taxation of the inhabitants to provide four ladders and two hooks, with iron chains, for the prevention of casualties of fire.

Thomas Charlton, M.A., elected Master of the Free School.

p. 591. 32 Eliz. 14 Dec.—Letter from the Privy Council deciding a dispute between the clothiers and dyers.

p. 598. 33 Eliz. 18 Dec.—Ordered that the house commonly called the Hospital shall be converted to a House of Correction, for setting poor people to work for their relief, and for punishing idle and vagrant persons.

p. 604. 34 Eliz. 7 Apr.—Orders for the reformation of the abuses of clothiers.

p. 616. 35 Eliz. 21 Jan.—Robert, Earl of Essex, elected High Steward.

p. 625. 36 Eliz. 24 May.—First entry of an election of a scholar from the School to St. John's College, Oxford, viz. Richard Lydoll, in the room of William Finnemore, B.C.L.

p. 628. ———. 20 Sept.—Order that no person put any kind of dyeing liquor or woad liquor into the street or the Hallowed Brook.

p. 639. 38 Eliz. 5 Mar.—Order that persons defrauding the city of London of toll under pretence that their goods belong to burgesses of Reading, shall be fined 10s.

The Register for the years 1603–1622 is wanting.

REGISTER, marked "CORPORATION DIARY, Oct. 1622–Oct. 1628, XIV. No. 1." In folio, as also those that follow.

24 March 1622.—Goods that were drowned by the oversetting of a boat in the Thames, when nine persons lost their lives, having been claimed as deodand, "Resolved that a petition to the Almnor shall be made and exhibited by the boatmen and inhabitants, owners of the goods, and a certificat from this Corporacion that oftentymes the like losse hath happened, but noe demaund of any deodand before this tyme."

11 Aug. 1623.—"At this daye question was made for the charges of the mayor, constables and officers, in their journey to Salisburye, beinge sent for by warrante, concerning the tumult at the passage of the Spanish ambassadour throughe the towne. Referd untill further consideracion."

22 March 1623.—Orders in a dispute among the town musicians.

2 June 1624.—"Ordered that Mr. Richard Winch and Mr. Anthony Brackston shall have forty shillings allowed them towards their chardges in travelling into the west countryes to viewe the manner of making their white cloth."

25 Oct. 1624.—"Mem. that the armes confirmed the last yere by the herraulds be called for, to be in hall kept."

17 Nov. 1624.—A warrant read "for the impressing xiiij strong and able men fitt for the warres, to serve under Count Mansfeild."

7 Feb. 1624.—"A funerall sermon was made at St. Mary church by Mr. Doctor Denison, for and concerninge Mr. John Kendricke, late of London, deceased," (a benefactor to Reading.)

21 April 1625.—Sir Francis Knollys and John Saunders, elected burgesses in Parliament, give engagements that they will attend Parliament at their own proper costs and charges, and hold the Mayor and Burgesses acquitted from payment of any wages or fees. (Repeated in 1627).

7 May 1625.—Warrant for impressing xviii men fit for service.

1 July 1625.—The plague supposed to be in Reading, a child being dead "full of blue spots."

July–Sept. 1625.—Orders for precaution against the plague.

23 Jan. 1625.—20s. given for relief of Henry Bell, esq., captain of a foot company, on his journey to Cork (?) from Plymouth, where he hath been long sick.

MSS. OF READING CORPORATION.

31 July 1626.—" A second meetinge of the most able men was had in the Towne hall concerning the raisinge of moneys to supply the Kinge's wantes, according to letters to the justices, viz. of fre guift, by the second letters explayning the former. And it was then and there, generally, with one consent and with one voyce, resolved and aunswered, that every man was willinge his Majesties want of money should be supplyed, but not in manner as it is required; and desire there maye be a Parlyament, for then all men should be bounde to paye a part by subsidyes and fifteenths."

12 Dec. 1626.—" The right hon. Erle of Banberye and the Lord Carleton, and divers Knights of this countye, commissioners for the K. Majestie about the loane, satt all day in the counsell chamber, and all the subsidy men of the towne, beinge warned, did attend in the hall, but about 4 of the clocke in the afternoone they were dismissed untill a new warninge ; and nothing at that time done, to my knowledge."

May 1627.—Twenty-one men pressed for service, and in Oct. ten more.

11 Dec. 1627.—Letters from the King and the earl of Baubury read about raising money for effecting the saltpetre work in the town, but answer returned that the clothiers and dyers make daily use of most part of the urine, and cannot spare it from their trade.

XV. DIARY, No. 2, Nov. 1628–May 1637.

4 Aug. 1629.—Resolved that on the King's coming to Reading in his progress, a gilt cup, of £20 value at least, shall be given to the Prince, and another to the Queen. (There is no subsequent mention of any actual visit at this time.)

30 March 1630.—Complaint signed " Tho. B "[unbury, D.D.], vicar of St. Mary's, against Kath. Hobson that she said his doctrine, if his people followed it, would bring them to hell, charged him with believing lies, and said that he was not temperate, and was fitter to go to sleep than to talk, &c.

9 June 1630.—Dr. Bird, the schoolmaster, complained that divers strangers, viz., Mr. Rich. Grenehill and Mr. Peters, teach grammar and other Latin books, but Mr. Grenehill showed his license from the Bishop of Salisbury to teach *quocunque loco* within his diocese; but an inhibition was obtained, and both forbidden on 16 June. However, Grenehill petitions the King and obtains an order to the Bishop, which is considered at his visitation on May 4, 5, 1631.

8 Sept. 1630.—A warrant read from the King's commissioners for compositions, for the not receiving the order of knighthood.

23 Oct. 1630.—The King's proclamation and Book of Orders read.

15 Feb. 1630.—The clothiers petition the Council (as before in 1626) for liberty of trade.

10 April 1631.—Letters from the Earl of Holland read, accepting the High Stewardship.

2 May 1631.—A strict account of the town charities required by the Privy Council.

7 June 1631.—Will. Creed elected scholar of St. John's Coll., Oxford.

18 July 1631.—Ellys Guest and Rich. Errington and their company of players showed their license from the Master of the Revels, and desired leave to play, but did not.

MSS. OF READING CORPORATION.

13 Aug. 1631.—Another company of players, Joseph Moore's, come under the name of the Princess Elizabeth's players, and desire the use of the Town hall; but 20s. are given to them to forbear their play at this time.

14 Nov. 1631.—Return of the charities ready for the King's Commissioners.

28 Nov. 1631.—Mr. Grenehill forbidden to teach grammar in the borough.

12 June 1632.—Certificate to be made to the Privy Council of the apothecaries and grocers as the fittest persons to sell tobacco. (Further proceedings, 30 Oct. 1633.)

3, 15 Oct., &c. 1632.—Enlargement of the Charter desired in specified points.

22 March 1632.—Warrant read for a collection for preventing the great ruin of St. Paul's Cathedral.

26 June 1633.—Order on the King's proclamation for preventing frauds in drapery.

11 Sept. 1633.—"Lodowick Bowyer, servant to the Duke of Lenox saith, upon his examination before Mr. Mayor, that on Thursday night last Sir Thoby Mathew dyed at Gravesend, and upon his deathbed delivered certen letters written to the Pope to the Deane of Rochester, and the Deane brought the letters together with 6 bishoppes to the Kinges Majestie. And that yesterday morninge he came from Whitehall about five of the clocke, and came to Fulham, and at Fulham Thomas Newton, William Airesbury, and George Price, three of the guard, told him, the said Lodowick, that Dr. Laud, nowe Archbishoppe of Canterbury, was confined by his Majesties direction to the bishoppe's house at Fulham for some matters that were discovered in the said letters written to the Pope.

By me, Lodowick Bowyer.

Commended to the keeping of constable Symes untill Mr. Mayor should further advise of the busynes."

13 Sept.—Bowyer is further examined by direction from Sir Francis Windebank, and the depositions forwarded.

21 Dec.—Lodowick Bowyer brought down from the Fleet prison, and set in the pillory, with his ears nailed thereto, in accordance with an order from the Court of Star-Chamber (of 17 Dec., of which a copy is given), in presence of the Mayor, burgesses, " and abundance of other people," and then delivered again to the custody of the servants of the Warden of the Fleet.

2 June 1634.—William Wallis and his wife Edith, accused of bewitching Edward Bonavant, so that he has constant fits of shaking. Wallis is searched, and found to be a man as other men, "not having teat bigg or small about his bodye, but a blewe spott or two," which, when pricked, bled. He is bound over to appear at the assizes, and his wife is committed to gaol. "Vide lez files."

16 July 1634.—Ordered that on the coming of Sir Nathaniel Brent to hold a visitation for the Archbishop on 26 July, he be presented with two or three pottles of wine and a sugar-loaf, and be invited to dinner on Sunday at the Mayor's.

MSS. OF READING CORPORATION.

16 Dec. 1634.—John Ricaelt, a limner, born in the Low Countries, living at Odiham with his uncle John Ricaelt, a distiller of metals and waters, for the Lord Arundell, examined as to his reason for coming to Reading; it was only by his uncle's directions, to sell a piece of silver of two ounces, "not spoone silver nor trencher silver, but onely of a powder." Committed to ward till further examination.

31 Aug. 1635.—260*l.* to be levied for ship-money.

9 Sept. 1635.—Ten shillings allowed a poor women for carrying her child for cure of the evil.

29 Oct. 1636.—260*l.* again to be levied for ship-money; "advised to petition the higher powers to have abatement of some parte thereof." 9 Nov.—The steward to be sent to the Secretary of State.

29 Nov. 1636.—Dr. Bird, the schoolmaster, died.

12 Dec. 1636.—Those who deny payment of the ship-money to be proceeded against as the counsel of the Corporation shall direct.

20 Dec. 1636.—William Page, M.A., admitted schoolmaster.

27 Dec. 1636.—Two good sugar-loaves to be given to Secretary Windebank, he being at his house at Hayne's Hill.

XVI.   DIARY, No. 3, June 1637–Sept. 1647.

6 Sept. 1637.—Two books formerly belonging to the School brought in and delivered to Mr. William Page to be chained and locked in the School as before, one being Cooper's Dictionary, given by Mr. Gabriel Barbour, late master of the lottery holden in Reading.

14 Nov. 1637.—Lionel Jackson, a teacher of dancing, convented to show cause why he stayed in Reading; promised to go within a fortnight.

1638–41.—Tax levied for relief of the people "visited" (with the plague).

13 Feb. 1638.—The new Charter read.

31 July 1639.—Writ for ship-money read, and assessment made.

15 Jan. 1639.—Another writ read, and assessment ordered.

12 March 1639.—The Archbishop of Canterbury recommends Edward Herbert, the Solicitor-General, to be one of the burgesses in Parliament, and the Earl of Holland recommends Sir John Berkley for the other. Six voted against both of these as being strangers to the Corporation; twenty for Herbert, and sixteen for Berkley.

30 April 1640.—Sir Francis Knollis, sen., and Sir Francis Knollis, junior, unanimously elected for Parliament, against Sir Robert Heath, for whom not a single vote was given.

15 June 1640.—The Mayor asks advice as to his best course for having the ship-money paid.

19 Oct. 1640.—The same members re-elected for Parliament, "in open hall, without any contradiction, but with general alacrity," no votes being given for three other candidates, Tanfield Vachell, esq., Sir Humphrey Forster, bart., and Edward Clarke, esq.

23 Nov. 1640.—Letter from the Archbishop of Canterbury sending £100, half-year's rent of land given by him for binding out apprentices.

17 Feb. 1640.—Ordered that in case the Mayor or aldermen be called in question for doing the King's service at any time, their costs and charges shall be borne by the hall.

MSS. OF READING CORPORATION.

29 Sept. 1641.—" Agreed that those persones within the towne which were distreyned for shipmonyes shalbe agreed with, and have their monyes repaid unto them by the hall."

1 Nov. 1641.—A letter read from the Archbishop of Canterbury, desiring that a safe and speedy messenger may be sent unto him for the money given by him; agreed that Mr. Mayor shall attend my Lord's Grace. A similar letter read on 25 Oct. 1642.

28 March 1641.—The High Sheriff of the county, Tanfield Vachell "openly read the booke of propositions for Ireland, and a letter sent to him from the Lord Keeper and Mr. Speaker, touching the promotinge and speedinge of that service, and did then also move " the Corporation "to subscribe what they would doe therein. But Mr. Sheriffe expectinge other bookes of directions from the Parliament touchinge that busynes, they referred their answer untill another meetinge."

15 Aug. 1642.—Agreed that every one will be ready to assist by counsel and purse about the setting up the posts and chains, and other such like charges, in these times, for the defence of the town.

2 Sept. 1642.—" Consideration being had of the greate dainger that this towne and the inhabitants thereof are in (by reason of the Cavaleers abroad, *interlined with fainter ink*), it is therefore ordered and agreed for the better safety of the same (preparation of their suddayne comminge and for their defeate, *interlined*) that forthwith a monethes taxe shall be made (and levyed, *interlined*) . . . . . to raise monyes to beare the charges of men and horse in·this towne, to ride out (dailie, *interlined*) us a scout to informe the towne of such dainger as they may learne and understand."

8 Sept. 1642.—Two men brought before the mayor whom one Richard Deane had taken near Marlow, by virtue of a warrant to him from the Parliament, supposing them to be Popish priests or seminaries ; the oaths of supremacy and allegiance being tendered, one refused them, and was by the said Richard Deane on his own authority committed to gaol ; the other freely took both, and was discharged.

9 Nov. 1642.—" Consultations were had aboute the execution of·the King's warrants and dispatch of other his majesties busynes."

17 Nov. 1642.—A tax levied " to pay those greate charges which are now layed upon the borough concerning cloth, apparrell, victualls, and other things for his Majesties armye."

30 Nov. 1642.—500*l.* a week required by the King for a month, by way of loan.

14 Dec. 1642.—Eight men. to attend the several sentinels for the quiet passage of such townsmen and countrymen as pass and come to the market, according to the governor's command.

14, 16 Dec. 1642.—1,000*l.* borrowed of Mr. John Struggell for the King's army, on the security of the market tolls, towards the 2,000*l.* lent to the King.

16 Dec. 1642.—List of those in the corporation who have taken the oath tendered by Sir A. Aston, the governor.

2 Jan. 1642.—" Agreed that the towne shall joyne with the countie in a petition as well to the King as to both Howses of Parliament for an accommodation."

MSS. OF READING CORPORATION.

6 Jan. 1642.—A further loan of 2,000*l.* required by Sir A. Aston, whereupon it is agreed that a petition be forthwith presented to his Majesty praying to be herein excused, " for that they are altogether unable by reason of their great payments, burthens and losses, which they have already and do daily undergoe, since the first advancement of his Majesties armie to the towne. Which petition with his Majesties answer thereupon endorsed is upon the fyle of this yeares busynes."*

18 Jan. 1642.—By order from the King through Sir A. Aston Henry Bradley is dismissed from being an attorney of the court, and Francis Seakes admitted.

6 Feb. 1642.—A meeting of the clothiers summoned by Sir A. Aston, at which he declared the King's good intentions to the town to be that they should have free liberty to trade to London, and desired them to procure like liberty from the Parliament. The Governor also read the Parliament's petition to the King and propositions for accommodation, and the King's answer, with his propositions. Some persons are double taxed towards the payment of the second 2,000*l.* "loaned" to the King.

10 March 1642.—100*l.* lent to the town by Sir A. Aston.

15 March 1642.—Petition to the King for security for the 2,000*l.* "loaned" to him. His answer " appeares upon the fyle, under the foot of the petition."

20 March 1642.—Petition that the goods and cloth now in the town of the western men may be stayed until free trade be procured for Reading.

5 and 7 Aug. 1643.—Money raised in pursuance of a letter from Col. Thomas Blagge for the fortifying of Wallingford.

Aug., Sept., Oct., 1643.—Several aldermen resign, or refuse election. One, Edw. Hamlin, refusing both to serve and to pay the fine, is committed to the Compter, but is released a fortnight afterwards on payment.

6 Oct. 1643.—Agreed that Sir Jacob Asteley, the governor, shall have 7*l.* a week for his allowance.

18 Oct. 1643.—Agreed that the King be petitioned to release the town from the monthly contribution.

16 Feb. 1643.—A petition to be sent to . . . . [*blank*] at Oxford for free trade in cloth for the town.

27 March 1644.—Robert Westmerland presenting a bill amounting to 40*l.* for materials and work had and done about the garrison, " was promised to be paid when the King payeth the towne."

6 April 1644.—Letter read from the King requiring the town to supply men for duty during the absence of that part of the garrison which is gone to the Lord Hopton.

16 April 1644.—Sir Jacob Asteley and divers officers were present when divers instructions sent from Oxford were read, and a new oath taken.

8 May 1644.—Petition to the King that no one of the Corporation may be sued by any shopkeeper, tradesman, &c. for anything had for the King's use, until he repay the 4,000*l.*, or the county pay 1,500*l.* according to his former directions.

---

* The "files" here referred to, and in several other places, are not now in existence.

15 May 1644.—The Mayor to undertake for 40l. worth of bread required for the army. "Agreed as touching the some of money demanded by the Lord Generall from the towne, that answere shalbe given to the said Lord, that the Kings Majestie hath graciously freed the towne from the payment thereof, and that the towne is so much impoverished that they are utterly unhable to pay any money."

20 May 1644.—"In obedience to his excellencies the Earle of Essex warrant," the carpenters are called, and agreement made with them for the making up of Cawsham bridge.

19 June 1644.—Letter from St. John's College, Oxford, announcing the death of Will. Brackston, fellow ; and on 21 June, John Blackman, aged near 17, "a modest, ingenious and hopefull young scholler, very fitt to learne logique," was elected in his place.

25 June, 27 June, 1644.—Letters from lieut. col. Lower, the lieut. gov. of Wallingford, with an order from the King for 150l. for three weeks' contribution for the maintenance of the garrison at Wallingford. "Submissive" answers sent, alleging utter inability, notwithstanding willingness.

18 July 1644.—Warrant from major-gen. Browne and others for the making up of a sufficient drawbridge in Caversham bridge.

14 Aug. 1644.—Mr. Thomas Pocock permitted, in the absence of Mr. Page, to teach scholars in the Free School. 12 June 1645. 5l. paid him for his pains in supplying the School.

22 Aug. 1644. The Parliamentary committee for Berks desire the removal of three aldermen and two assistants as being "notoriously disaffected to the State" ; the Company desire further time to consider of it.

2 Dec. 1644.—"Agreed that a petition shalbe forthwith preferred to the Parliament for the relief of the towne against the insolencies and violences of the souldyers."

27 March 1644.—Warrant from the Parliamentary committee for a weekly tax of 37l. 11.; petition thereupon for mitigation, acknowledging former favours.

8 April 1645.—The said tax assessed.

4 June 1645.—25l. paid to Dr. John Pordage, out of the late Archbishop's gift, for his pains in officiating the cure in St. Lawrence's church the last half-year. Also 9 Nov. 1646, to him as Vicar of St. Lawrence.

9 July 1645.—A tax (of 220l. 6s. 6d. for twelve months) ordered for relief of the British army in Ireland.

28 Aug. 1645.—A petition made for respiting of the said tax, but rejected.

13 Oct. 1645.—Tanfield Vachell elected burgess in Parliament in the room of Sir F. Knollys, jun., deceased. Will. Ball, esq., desired a poll, but it was refused, the voices being two to one.

1 Dec. 1645.—A fresh election held upon a new warrant, and a poll taken ; Vachell, 560, Ball, 309. But the Mayor delays to sign and seal the indenture for Vachell, and on 3 Dec. a petition (of which a copy is given) is agreed on to the House of Commons against him.

17 June 1646.—"Ordered that the wholle company shall forthwith in some convenient time attend his excellencie Sir Thomas Fairfax concerninge the aspersion laid upon the towne."

MSS. OF READING CORPORATION.

8 July 1646.—"Mr. Mayor desired to know when the company would attend the Generall, Sir Thomas Fairfax, about the aspersion laid upon the towne. Resolved within few daies to attend his excellencie about that and the freeing of the towne from the military part." Thomas Skinner, one of the three serjeants, sharply reprehended for his ill manner of presenting the Lord Fairfax's gift from the Company.

Aug. 1646.—Tax for relief of the people " visited " (with the plague), and also on 26 Aug. 1647.

31 Aug. 1646.—Mr. Pocock to be examined by the ministers touching his sufficiency as schoolmaster.

1 Oct. 1646.—"Agreed that a letter be sent to Mr. Vachell to free the towne from free quarter of soldiers, in regard of the infection and their great chardg in building posthouses." In Aug. 1647 a "great number of poor people " infected.

9 Oct. 1646.—Tax levied for quartering capt. Morris' company, consisting of 3 sergeants, 2 drummers, 3 corporals, one gentleman of pikes, one gentleman of arms, and 60 common soldiers. "Many questions about a newe schoolemaster, but nothing resolved upon."

21 Oct. 1646.—40s. allowed to John Blackman of St. John's College "to supply his present necessities."

4 Nov. 1646.—Mr. Pocock's sufficiency as schoolmaster to be forthwith proved by Mr. Fowler and Mr. Wylde. 9 Nov. 10l. paid to him. 18 Dec. further order for his examination. 6 Jan. 1646, 14 July 1647, 4 Aug. 1647, further proceedings thereon.

30 Aug. 1647.—"Agreed that a petition shalbe forthwith presented to the hon. Sir Thomas Fairfax for the vindication of the Company and towne from the aspersions laid upon them by capt. Goddard and others," and that the Company or the greater part of them, shall go to Sir T. Fairfax.

XVII. DIARY, No. 4, Oct. 1647—April 1655.

19 June 1648.—Daniel Blagrave, esq., elected burgess in Parliament in the place of Sir Fr. Knollys, deceased, over George Starkey, esq.

(The dating by the year of the King is continued up to the day before his beheading, 29 Jan. 1648, " annoque xxxiiii^{to} r. r. Caroli, Angliæ, &c.")

4 July 1649.—"The daunceers of the rope were this daie forbidden to stay any longer in towne."

20 Aug. 1649.—Mr. Thomas Pocock's proposals for payments to be made to him at his leaving the School at Michaelmas next. Mr. Will. Wise recommended as his successor by Mr. Dan. Blagrave, but takes time to consider it. Further proceedings, 17 Oct.; 21, 26 June 1650. Pocock continues to keep a private school of his own, "for he knew noe lawe to contradict itt."

25 Aug. 1651.—No toll henceforth to be taken for bread brought to be sold in Reading market.

14 Jan. 1651.—The mace to be new-gilt, the head to be made 3 inches larger, the cross at the top and the King's arms to be left out, and the State's arms to be set in the place, according to the pattern prescribed in the Act of Parliament.

24 Jan. 1651.—The cost of making a new mace (weighing 80 oz.) being estimated at 26*l*. or 27*l*. besides the price of the old one (weighing 52¼ oz.), it is ordered that the old mace be sold in London, and a new mace made on the best terms.

19 March 1651.—The new mace, silver gilt, weighing 91¼ oz. cost 44*l*. 12*s*.; the old mace was sold for 14*l*. 7*s*.

7 Oct. 1652.—Mr. Will Page, formerly schoolmaster, claimed arrears due for 9 months; but it appeared that he had received all that was due at Mich. 1642, and in Nov. following the School was made a magazine for the King's army, and Mr. Page thenceforward never officiated; further, he was sequestered about 1644 by the Committee for Berkshire, and Mr. Pocock appointed; there was, therefore, nothing due.

22 Nov. 1652.—"Agreed that the cucking-stoole be sett in the markett-place, and chayned to the pillory."

19 Sept. 1653.—"William Sample, clarke of St. Giles, was sworne parish register here."

19 April 1654.—John Gripp and Edward Woodward elected for St. John's College.

18 Dec. 1654.—The Right Hon. Bulstrode Lord Whitlocke chosen High Steward, in the place of Col. Robert Hammond, deceased.

DIARY, No. 5, April 1665—May 1656.   XVIII.

23 July 1655.—Mr. Reeve leaves the School because no house is provided.

30 July 1655.—Mr. Robert Jennings, M.A., appointed schoolmaster.

17 Dec. 1655.—Mr. Will. Brackston discharged of his offices of alderman and justice of the peace in pursuance of the Lord Protector's Declaration for settling the peace of the commonwealth.

2 Jan. 1655.—"Upon the motion of Mr. Fowler in the behalf of himself and Mr. Ford for removing of the scandall raysed upon them whereby they are charged to have the swaye of the towne in point of government, Mr. Mayor and the rest of the aldermen now present that have been mayors do affirme that the said Mr. Fowler and Mr. Ford and either of them neuer exercised any such authority."* [Mr. Simon Ford was the well-known Puritan minister and writer, who after the Restoration conformed, and died in 1699. Christopher Fowler was ejected from St. Mary's in 1662, and died in 1679.]

"Mr. Thomas Gerrard produced (which was openly read) an order from his Highness the Lord Protector constituting the said Mr. Gerrard schoolmaster of the Free Schoole in this Corporacion during the life of Mr. Page from whome the same was sequestred. Whereupon (the said Schoole being under sequestracion), it is ordered that Mr. Jennings the present schoolmaster be imediately removed, and that possession of the said Schoole be delivered to the said Mr. Gerrard accordingly." Mr. Gerrard produced a certificate of his godly life and conversation from Edw. Paris, Vice-Pres. [of St. John's Coll.], Will. Padden and Tho. Wyatt.

40*s*. granted to the son of John Tripp at St. John's College.

---

* In a certified copy of this vote printed at p. 13 of Part II. of Fowler's *Dæmonium Meridianum*, the words "to have the sway of the town" are altered to "to have intermedled with the affaires of the town," and the last words are altered to "have not intermedled with the authority."

MSS. OF READING CORPORATION.

1 Feb. 1655.—" Resolved upon the question that the answere of the Company to the pamphlet (subscribed *Rams most Rich*, &c.) be as it is nowe read and written in the paper nowe produced. And that Mr. Fowler be desired to insert the same into his booke of his answere to the said pamphlet." [Printed pp. 54–6 of the second part of Fowler's *Dæmonium Meridianum*, a reply to *The case of Reading rightly stated*, in behalf of J. Pordage, 4°, Lond. 1656.]

6 Feb. 1655.—" Agreed that the answer to the scandalous pamphlett be sent to Mr. Fowler to London with the additions thereunto nowe read, to be inserted in Mr. Fowler's booke," &c.

18 Feb. 1655.—The schoolhouse was used at the assizes as the court of Nisi Prius.

17 March 1655.—Daniel Blagrave discharged from the office of steward of the borough for insufficiency and neglect, and also from that of one of the assistants. He was again " removed and discharged," 10 Aug. 1657.

7 April 1656.—Agreed that a petition be made to the Lord Protector for confirmation of the Charter. 3 June, agreed that " such additional privileges " be desired " as shalbe thought fitt."

19 April 1656.—Richard Bulstrode elected steward, on the recommendation of the Lords Whitlocke and Fleetwood. Elected again (the former election having, apparently, been annulled for informality) 3 Oct. 1657.

XIX. DIARY, No. 6, 17 May 1656—21 Oct. 1657.

23 June 1656.—Ten shillings allowed to the bellman for warning the inhabitants to hang out lanthorns and candles in the dark nights the two last winters.

7 July 1656.—Lord Whitlocke advises that the Charter be renewed as speedily as possible. Sir John Barkstead and Sir Thos. Pride to be arbitrators in a difference between Mrs. Harrison and the Corporation.

14 July 1656.—Sir John Barkstead thanked for his pains therein.

21 July 1656.—" At this tyme the Company with the ministers and divers other people assembled in the Townehall to seeke God for a blessing in the choice of a burges for this borough to serve in Parliament. And Mr. Jemmatt and Mr. Ford performed the duties of exhortacion and prayer for that purpose." Sir John Barkstead, lieut. of the Tower of London, elected.

22 July 1656.—Sir John Barkstead admitted a freeman.

15 Oct. 1656.—" Mr. Garrett, schoolmaster of the Free Schoole, made complaint against John Jemmatt for comming into the schoole and beating and misusing the schollers."

22 Oct. 1656.—" Agreed that the Company will joyne with the rest of the freeholders of Southstoke to defend them against the inclosure of the commons there."

25 Oct. 1656.—Debate concerning additional points to be considered in the renewing of the Charter; i. whether the Company or those that pay to the poor elect the burgess for Parliament; ii. whether the assizes for the county shall be held only at Reading.

15 March 1656.—Mr. Garrard, the schoolmaster, cited by an order of the commissioners for ejecting scandalous ministers and schoolmasters

to appear at Speenhamland on 8 Apr., upon a reference from the Lord Protector upon the petition of Mr. Robert Jennings.

MSS. OF READING CORPORATION.

11 July 1657.—" This daye in the open markett in Reading the proclamacion of his Highness the Lord Protector and the Parliament, and the Petition and advise of the knights, citizens, and burgesses in Parliament to his Highness, were read and published, according to the tenor of the said proclamacion."

27 Aug. 1657.—A perambulation of the outbounds and limits of the borough made, in accordance with the Charter. About twenty boys of the Free-School accompanied the mayor and others.

DIARY, No. 7, 23 Oct. 1657—17 Dec. 1658.   XX.

6 Sept. 1658.—The Lord Protector Richard solemnly proclaimed in the market place between the hours of 10 and 11; the warrant of the sheriff, and form of proclamation, with a copy of the order of the Council, "remaine in the press cupbord in the councell chamber."

17 Dec. 1658.—Mr. Joel Stephens voted out of the office of mayor, for that he "hath knowingly and willingly, by forreine and private advice and practice, attempted to acte and acted severall things against the judgement and consent of the major parte of the said Corporacion, and to the disinherison of the said Corporacion of their rights and priviledges."

DIARY, No. 8, 30 Dec. 1658—30 Sept. 1659.   XXI.

30 Dec. 1658.—Henry Nevill, esq., and Daniel Blagrave, esq., unanimously elected burgesses in Parliament by near 1,000 persons.

9 Feb. 1658.—Peter Burningham and William Brackston restored as aldermen, upon writs.

12 Feb. 1658.—Richard Bulstrode removed from his place of steward, and Daniel Blagrave chosen.

Account of a disturbance at the meeting on 17 Dec. last, when, in consequence of a dispute about a suit at law upon the former "false" return of Sir John Barkstead as burgess in Parliament, the mayor was voted out of office, the cupboard and great iron-bound chest broken open and the books, mace, and common seal removed. In consequence, all those aldermen and assistants who took part in "these great insolent and notorious misdemeanours and offences" are this day removed.

2 March 1658.—The expelled aldermen come and take their seats, and refuse to withdraw, whereupon the meeting is adjourned. Lawsuits follow thereupon.

17 June 1659.—Rich. King elected from the School to be a fellow of St. John's College. Again elected as a scholar, 29 June, 1661.

19 Aug. 1659.—Forty shillings allowed to John Gripp, a young scholar chosen from the School; and again on 27 Aug. 1660. Similar payments afterwards to other scholars.

10 Sept. 1659. The expelled aldermen and assistants desire to treat for re-admission.

19 Sept. 1659. Mr. Thomas Gerrard summoned to show by what title he holds the School.

MSS. OF READING CORPORATION.
—

23 Sept. 1659. Mr. Gerrard appears, and desires he may not be interrogated, no man being bound to accuse himself, but refuses to own the Company to be patrons of the School.

XXII. DIARY, No. 9, 3 Oct. 1659—31 Oct. 1660.

3 Oct. 1659.—Mr. Gerrard disowned as schoolmaster. The mayor closed the School-door last Friday (30 Sept.) to prevent his entrance.

Letter sent to Mr. Jennings to tell him that possession of the School is kept for him.

12 Oct. 1659.—Resolved that the order of Oliver late Lord Protector appointing Mr. Gerrard, schoolmaster, and all proceedings thereon, are groundless, illegal and null. Gerrard removed and Jennings restored.

31 Oct. 1659.—Mr. Fowler is desired to perform divine service in St. Mary's church every morning, six days in the week, according to Mr. John Kendrick's will, and to continue the weekly Friday lecture.

Mr. Edwards being nominated as schoolmaster, he is desired to come and exercise the scholars.

5 Nov. 1659.—Mr. Edwards is desired to enter on the School next Monday (7 Nov.), and a letter to be written to Mr. Jennings to resign his interest.

29 Nov. 1659.—Mr. Gerrard is told that if he keep possession of the School he shall have no further pay.

2 Jan. 1659.—Mr. Edwards to be sent for to teach the School. Again on 13 Apr.

13 Feb. 1659. Mr. Gerrard is ordered to be paid up to Mich. last, but refuses to give up possession of the School. Orders that he is to be paid, deducting law-costs, 22 Oct. 1660, 1 Apr. 1661.

10 Apr. 1660.—Thomas Rich, esq., and John Blagrave, esq., unanimously elected by more than 1,100 persons burgesses in Parliament.

10 May 1660.—King Charles II. "with greate solempnity and rejoycing proclaymed upon a stage sett upp for that purpose in the open markett-place."

23 May 1660.—"Agreed that the mace of the Corporacion be forthwith altered, and the King's armes put upon it.

Edw. Dalby, esq., chosen steward.

28, 30 May, 1660.—Resignations of the secluded members of the Corporation, upon composition.

12 June 1660.—Consultation about the 1,600*l*. lent to the King for the garrison in the time of the wars.

24 Sept. 1660. Mr. Gerrard being evicted by law, Mr. Edwards is desired to come to the School.

29 Oct. 1660.—Thomas Singleton, M.A., appointed schoolmaster His appointment sealed, 7 Oct. 1661.

XXIII. DIARY, No. 10, 20 Nov. 1660—21 July 1662.

3 Dec. 1660.—Dr. Will. Page brings a writ of restitution to the schoolmastership.

6 March 1660.—Dr. Page resigns his right to the School.

22 April 1661.—20s. to be given to each parish to provide "bonefires" and beer on the day of the King's coronation, 23 Apr.

MSS. OF READING CORPORATION.

23 Sept. 1661.—A cripple-carrier appointed, with the ancient allowance, on condition that in case of necessity he provide some out-room and straw for the lodging of poor diseased people.

30 Sept. 1661.—£50 voted as a voluntary gift to the King.

7 Oct. 1661.—Agreed that a sugar-loaf and a gallon of sack be presented to the Bishop of Sarum in the afternoon at his coming to Reading. Again on 10 Sept. 1666.

16 Oct. 1661.—Agreed that "six instruments for the quenching of fire" be provided.

17 Feb. 1661.—Appointment of searchers for flesh in the butchers' shops in Lent.

27 May 1662.—Signatures of 17 members of the Corporation, before Commissioners under the Corporation Act, to the renunciation of the Covenant. Order of the Commissioners removing S. Jemmatt, the mayor, and 13 others, for non-subscription, &c. Other subscriptions on 20 Aug.

DIARY, No. 11, 23 June [*rectius* 7 Aug.] 1662—27 March 1665. XXIV.

This book is noted as having been produced in a suit in which Christ's Hospital, London, was plaintiff, in 1847.

14 Oct. 1662.—Thomas Thackham, M.A., appointed schoolmaster.

21 Nov. 1662.—Agreed that some course be taken for recalling the patent given formerly to Mr. Whitelocke for the High Stewardship.

4 Feb. 1662.—License to a man for one year to have a lottery of small prizes of plush-ware, silver-ware, glasses, &c., with ten blanks to every prize.

14 Apr. 1663.—Scapula's *Lexicon*, Cooper's and Rider's *Dictionaries*, and Erasmus' *Adagia*, to be bought for the Free School.

24 Aug. 1663.—" Agreed that at the King and Queene's comming to this towne on Thursday next (27 Aug.) fifty 20s. pieces in gold, in two purses, amounting to the value of £56 6s. 4d., now provided for that purpose, be presented to their Majesties by the Company."

26 Aug. 1663.—" Agreed that £30 in gold be presented to the Queenes Majesty at her comming to this towne, besides the £50 to the King."

27 Aug. 1663.—" This day upon the comming of the King and Queenes Majesties through this towne, the Company (on foote) attended their comming in the Orte lane, and upon their approach met their Majesties, and after a congratulatory speech made by Mr. Steward, presented to the King's Majesty 50 pieces in gold, which cost 22s. 6d. a piece, and to the Queenes Majestie 30 pieces of the like gold, in 2 severall purses curiously wrought, which cost 18s." The fees paid to the King's servants amounted to 37l. 6s.

28 Oct. 1663.—The Duke of Albemarle elected High Steward.

23 Nov. 1663.—" Jeremiah Rich, a professor in the art of short writing, produced his authoritie to teach."

MSS. OF READING CORPORATION.

23 Dec. 1664.—A collection to be made "for the providing of instruments to convey water upon howses in case of any danger that shall happen by fire."

XXV. DIARY, No. 12, 10 Apr. 1665—18 March 1667.

5 July 1665.—Agreement to be drawn up with John Shawe, a founder at the Dial in Lothbury, for the making the engines for quenching fire. (Order for payment on 4 Sept.) "At this time (Sir William Armorer and Mr. Aldworth being present) it was ordered . . . . that the hackney coaches belonging to this Corporacion be restrained from bringing any passengers or goods from London to this Corporacion during the time of the visitacion with the Plague in London, and that the coachmen be prohibited from bringing any such persons or goods." Further order on 14 July.

15 Sept. 1665.—Tax ordered for payment of searchers and buriers of those who have died of the plague, and of the warders employed to keep suspicious persons and goods from entering the town.

22 Feb. 1665.—The King's Declaration for war against the French King proclaimed.

10 Sept. 1666.—Ordered that the fire-engines be exercised and kept ready for use.

22 Oct. 1666.—Ordered that the effigies of archbp. Laud and of "that worthy benefactor" Rich. Aldworth, be brought into the Council Chamber, to remain as memorials of them.

17 Dec. 1666 and 7 Jan.—Mr. Blake authorised to receive the interest for the 500*l*. lent to the King upon the Act for the royal aid. The 500*l*. repaid 10 Feb. 1667.

18 Oct. 1667.—The charge of the new Charter is 229*l*. 17*s*. 9*d*.

25 Jan. 1667 (wrongly dated 1663).—The Right Worshipful Dr. Peter Mewe brought in and presented as his gift the "effigies and portraiture of that worthy benefactor," archbp. Laud.

XXVI. DIARY, No. 13, 30 March 1668—26 July 1672.

17 July 1668.—A chief fireman appointed, who is to be freed from all taxes, and to have a leathern coat, an iron cap, and other necessaries.

31 Aug. 1668.—Mr. Thackham resigns the School.

7 Sept. 1668.—Mr. Thomas Ireland, of Wallingford, elected schoolmaster.

14 Dec. 1668.—A committee appointed to survey the writings in the Hall and make an entry of the same.

21 Dec. 1668.—A catalogue of the writings remaining in the Hall, bonds, leases, &c., committed to the custody of the town-clerk.

25 Feb. 1669.—A letter sent to the two burgesses in Parliament (Sir Thos. Dolman and Richard Aldworth) expressing the thankfulness of the Company for the happy union between his Majesty and the two Houses of Parliament.

30 July 1670.—Samuel Howse expelled from his place as alderman for endeavouring to force Mr. Thackham to take Mr. Singleton, a nonconformist, as his assistant in the Free School, and for attempting to hinder the suppression of conventicles. A law-suit follows, but on Good

Friday, 17 Apr. 1674, at the request of Dr. William Lloyd, Dean of Bangor, who was present, the matter was ended by the restoration of Mr. Howse.

7 Oct. 1671.—Out of the six poor maid-servants elected to partake of the annual gift of archbp. Laud, one, Anne Bigg, is described as being "kinn to the Bishop." She was daughter of Richard Bigg, of Reading, cordwainer. Another daughter, Mabel, was elected 8 Oct. 1677.

2 Apr. 1672.—A letter to be sent to Sir Bulstrode Whitelocke desiring him to resign the office of High Steward.

21 June 1672.—Compton Read elected to a scholarship at St. John's College in the place of Mr. Page, deceased. Constantine Phipps first elected, but requested his election might be postponed. (An earlier entry of one Blackman has been accidentally omitted in this abstract.)

DIARY, No. 14, 26 Aug. 1672—25 Sept. 1682.   XXVII.

13 Jan. 1672.—Mr. Thomas Ireland, the schoolmaster, removed as being lunatic, and Mr. William Gostwicke appointed, on the recommendation of the Bishop of Bath and Wells.

5 Feb. 1674.—Henry Earl of Clarendon elected High Steward.

29 May 1676.—Number of oaks and elms on the several lands belonging to the Corporation at Bray.

13 March 1676.—"A letter to the maior of Bridgwater, with the impression of *sigillum officii* for this Corporacion."

15 June 1677.—Francis Barnard and Thomas Poke elected to the scholarships at St. John's College, vacant by the resignations of Mr. Thos. Tuer and "Sir" Read (*i.e.*, B.A.); the former on the strong recommendation of the Bishop of Bath and Wells, who also advised that none should be chosen whose parents were dissenters. The latter was rejected by the College as incapable, because he had been some time employed in a trade, and David Webb was elected in his place on 23 June.

13 July 1677.—"Agreed that the Maior and aldermen doe attend the Queenes Majesty upon her retourne from the Bath hither on Tuesday next [17 July], and that in the meane time a banquett of sweet meates be provided ready at her lodgings, to be then and there presented to her Majesty."

8 Oct. 1677.—Four maid-servants elected to partake of Archbishop Laud's charity, who are all bracketed as of kin to him; Mary Mayott, Jane Smith, Mabel Bigge and Eliz. Bowland.

18 Oct. 1678.—A petition to be presented to the Duke of Monmouth for easing the Corporation by removing two out of the five companies quartered in the town; the Earl of Clarendon to be requested to assist. Again on 5 March.

11 Nov. 1678.—The soldiers at the guard to be supplied with one bushel of sea-coals every night, at 8*d.* per bushel.

5 Feb. 1678.—Poll for two members of Parliament: John Blagrave, 927; Nathan Knight, 766; Thomas Vachell, 426; Sir Will. Kenrick, 384. Blagrave and Knight re-elected without opposition, 12 Aug, 1679. Re-elected again, 9 Feb. 1680, Thomas Coates, an alderman, retiring from a contest.

MSS. OF READING CORPORATION.

18 June 1679.—Will. Wotton elected to a scholarship at St. John's College, vacant by the death of David Webb.

7 Oct. 1680.—Sarah Mayott, maid-servant, elected to Laud's charity as being of kin.

23 May 1681.—Ordered that an humble address be presented to his Majesty, to give "their most humble and hearty thanks for his princely favour in publishing [his] Declaracion, and to beseech him to accept their loyal resolutions to oppose their lives and fortunes to the greatest extremity in defence of his Majesty's person, royall prerogative, his lawfull heires and successors, and for the preservacion of the Protestant religion as by lawe established against all Popish and factious endeavours whatsoever." [The Declaration was on the dissolution of Parliament.]

7 Nov. 1681. A collection made in each parish on account of a fire caused by fireworks in the market-place on 5 Nov., one of which set fire to the thatch of a stable.

24 Dec. 1681.—Letter from the King to the Mayor, requiring him to restrain all riots.

26 Dec. 1681.—Warrant from the King for a brace of fat does from the park at Windsor.

27 March 1682.—Agreed that an address to his Majesty be drawn up signifying abhorrency and detestation against all unlawful associations.

8 April 1682.—The said address signed by all the members present except two; Thomas Blake, an assistant, saying he would have nothing to do with it, and Francis Terrell, jun., another assistant, desiring time to consider of it.

17 April 1682.—The address sealed, and a deputation appointed to present it to the King.

5 May 1682.—The address having been altered was again read, approved, and ordered to be sealed and presented.

1 Aug. 1682.—The Lord High Chancellor being appointed to come this day to Reading, it is agreed that the Mayor and aldermen attend him at his lodgings in their gowns, and that a present be made him.

XXVIII. DIARY, No. 15, 2 Oct. 1682--18 Jan. 1685.

17 May 1683.—The Duke [of York] being to pass through this Corporation to-morrow, it is unanimously agreed that the Mayor and aldermen shall meet him in their formalities, and congratulate his welcome.

13 July 1683.—Address to the King on the discovery of the Rye-House plot, congratulating his "happy deliverance from the dreadful effect of the most horrid and traiterous conspiracy that hath beene hatched in any age, contrived, and fomented by persons of phanatike and antimonarchicall principles."

7 Sept. 1683.—Sunday being appointed as a thanksgiving day for the discovery of the plot, it is agreed that the Corporation attend church in the afternoon, and after sermon go to hall; "and it is agreed that the bells shall ring, and that a bonefire be made in the markett-place, and a barrell of beere, fower bottells of sack, and twelve of clarett be carryed thither."

26 March 1684.—"Agreed that the Maior and Company will assert their rights in keeping their fower faires throughout the Forbery, as it

is graunted by their Charter, and that Sir Thomas Clarges be spoken with to remove all incroachments there, and that if hee refuse soe to doe that then an action at law be brought against him at the suite of the Maior, &c. as they shall be advised." MSS. OF READING CORPORATION

9 Feb. 1684.—A letter received from the Earl of Clarendon, High Steward, announceing the death of Charles II. " of blessed memory," and the proclamation of K. James at Whitehall on the 6th inst. K. James consequently proclaimed this day in the market-place by the town-clerk at 12 o'cl. "in the presence and hearing of the said Maior, aldermen, and assistants, being in their formalities, and accompanied with the clergy and abundance of gentry and the inhabitants with greate acclamations, the bells ringing, drummes beating, and trumpetts sounding. God blesse King James the Second. Amen."

20 Feb. 1684.—Address sent to the King on his accession.

12 March, 1684.—Sir Henry Fane and Sir Will. Rich, bart. (candidates for the representation of the borough in Parliament) desired to be admitted freemen of the borough ; the question was put to the vote and carried in the negative.

13 March 1684.—Election for Parliament ; Sir H. Fane, Sir W. Rich, John Breedon, esq., and Thos. Coates, gent., candidates. The two former demanded a poll ; but the question being put to the vote, it was carried in the negative, for that they were not freemen of this borough ; and Breedon and Coates were declared elected.

15 June 1685.—The King's proclamation of the 13th inst., declaring the Duke of Monmouth and his adherents traitors, published by the town-clerk in the market-place.

26 June 1685.—The late election for Parliament made void for want of a poll, and a precept received for a new election.

27 June 1685.—The election held, George Blagrave, esq., standing in the place of Sir H. Fane. Votes : Sir W. Rich, 473 ; G. Blagrave, 483 ; J. Breedon, 507 ; T. Coates, 530 ; the two latter consequently returned.

28 Sept. 1685.—The question being put whether the Charter shall be surrendered to the King, it is unanimously agreed (with 16 votes) in the affirmative.

6 Nov. 1685.—The surrender to be sealed ; those who go with it to London empowered to advise touching the preserving the fairs to be kept in the Forbury and upon anything else.

11 Nov. 1685.—The Charter surrendered.

16 Nov. 1685.—Precept received for election of a burgess in Parliament on the death of John Breedon, esq.

17 Nov. 1685.—William Aldworth, of London, esq., admitted a freeman on the recommendation of the High Steward as a fit person to be a representative in Parliament. The precept having been read in the Guildhall, "the said Will. Aldworth, and George Blagrave, of Bulmarsh Court, esq., were cryed upp by the commonalty there, some for the one and some for the other ; the said George Blagrave (being then and there present) did publiquely deny and refuse to stand in election, and did forbid them to vote for him. Soe none other being cryed upp, the said William Aldworth was elected, and soe then and there declared by Mr. Major to bee duely elected, there being noe poll demanded for any other."

15 Feb. 1685.—A letter of thanks to be writ and delivered by Mr. Coates and Mr. Aldworth to the Lord Treasurer.

MSS. OF READING CORPORATION.

DIARY, No. 16, 8 March 1685-6—19 Oct. 1688.

XXIX. 29 July 1686.—John Dalby, esq., elected Recorder in the place of Sir Thomas Holt, deceased.

2 Aug. 1686.—Notice to be sent to the High Steward of this election, and of the death of Mr. Coates.

23 Aug. 1686.—The Corporation meet the King (according to a resolution passed on the 21st,) at his passing through the town from Windsor westward, at Ort Lane end, and after a congratulatory speech by the Recorder, present him with fifty guineas in a purse, and attend him through the town to their utmost bounds. £36 6s. allowed as fees to the King's servants.

8 Sept. 1686.—Upon the Queen Dowager Catherine's passing through the town, the Corporation meet at the Bear at 1 o'clock in their gowns to attend her coming, and to present her with some wine, fruit and sweetmeats.

15 Nov. 1686.—" Mr. Gyles Hinton (nominated an alderman in His Majesty's gracious letters patents lately graunted to this borough), being summoned to take his oath to execute the said office did this day appeare, and hee being acquainted therewith, and the oath tendred, hee refused the same for severall reasons, and now signed and sealed his resignacōn of that place and office, which was accepted and recorded, and his said place and office declared to be void."

17 Jan. 1686.—Mr. William Gostwyke gave notice of his intention to resign the Free School at Lady Day.

26 March 1687.—Mr. Thomas May, fellow of St. John's College, elected as Mr. Gostwyke's successor.

9 May 1687.—Account of the perambulation of the bounds of the borough.

10 Aug. 1687.—Ordered that the Corporation meet the Queen on foot in their formalities, on Tuesday next, at her coming through this Corporation, and that the Mayor present her with thirty guineas in a purse.

29 Sept. (Thursday) 1687.—" Mr. Maior and the aldermen having certaine intelligence that the Queenes Majesty in her retourne from the Bath intends to lodge at the Beare here, on Wensday night next, it is agreed that a banquet of sweetmeates shalbe by Mr. Maior and the aldermen in their gownes presented to the Queene that night in her chamber. Mr. Head is desired to send to London for the same, and to laye out about 50s."

21 Oct. 1687.—" Mr. Henry Bulstrode, gentlemen usher to Queene Mary, having beene very kinde and civill to the Company at their attendance on her Majesty upon her retourne from the Bath, [they] have thought fitt to present him with two ginneyes for such his civillity. This was done as a voluntary gift and not otherwise, there being noe fees due to the Queenes servants in her progresse."

29 Dec. 1687.—" Upon reading His Majesty's gracious letter . . . . dated 17 Dec. inst., and his late gracious letters patents of Charter to the said borough, and upon debate of the wholle matter, the question being then and there putt whether they should immediately proceed to elect Mr. Hugh Champion to be Maior of and for the said borough, it was carried in the affirmative." Mr. Champion is then elected assistant, alderman, and Mayor in succession; on that day and on 13 Jan., nine

new aldermen are admitted, eight assistants, Recorder (Thos. Pettitt), and Town Clerk, and two more aldermen on 27 Jan.

MSS. OF READING CORPORATION.

14 Feb. 1687.—Order for three of the aldermen to survey the writings in the Hall at their leisure and inventory them.

20 Feb. 1687.—An address of thanks to the King.

16 March 1687.—Letter read from the King (date not given), ordering that three of the lately elected aldermen be turned out (Sam. Howse, Tho. Stephens, and Edw. Braxton) and six of the burgesses, and nominating others in their places. The mandate is obeyed.

15 May 1688.—"This day it was debated whether the Major and Company should waite upon the Princess of Denmark ["Orange" *first written, and struck out*] att her passing throug this towne to the Bath to wellcome her Highness into this borough, and it was carryed, nemine contradicente, in the affirmative, but withall that there should be no present made. Soe it is hereby ordered that the Major and aldermen doe waite upon the Princess att her lodgings in a complement, and that no present be made."

17 May 1688.—"Ordered that the Princess of Denmarke be presented with a dish of sweetmeates, and that there be eighteene yards of woolen cloath bought and provided for the said Princess to walke upon."

1 June 1688.—Mandate from the King read, removing Mr. Sebastian Lyford from being alderman and chamberlain. "The election of Mr. Clare who was nominated in his place is respited until a farther time, *there being no such man.*"

6 Aug. 1688.—"Ordered that every alderman and assistant of this borough shall cloath himself with a neate and hansome gowne made of purple cloath by the first Monday in September now next ensuing."[1]

25 Aug. 1688.—£5 allowed to John Foster for translating the Charter granted by James II. into English.

27 Aug. 1688.—"This day John Bigg, esq., the late elected Mayor delivered the King's letters mandatory to the mayor, aldermen and burgesses of the borough, bearing date 25 Aug., whereby they were commanded to remove the said John Bigg from the office of one of the aldermen of the said borough, and to proceede to elect Mr. Joseph May (one of the assistants of the same borough) to be alderman in his roome and place.

---

[1] Orders respecting the wearing of gowns (as authorised by the Charter of Charles I.), and inflicting fines on those who neglected it, are frequently met with. After the passing of the Municipal Act, it was ordered on 29 January 1836, "that the wearing of gowns be altogether abolished"; but on 20 Dec. 1838 it was resolved that "as such custom is conducive to the honour and respectability of the corporate body, the custom of wearing gowns on public and solemn occasions be now revived." It was also subsequently resolved that the shape of the gowns should be the same as those worn by the Corporation of London. The material is black cloth, trimmed with Russian sable, with a roll collar extending down the front, for those who have passed the chair, and trimmed with black-silk velvet for those who have not passed the chair. The town-clerk has a black silk gown with black silk-velvet collar, tippet, and facings. The three mace-sergeants and two wardens also wear on state occasions black beaver cocked hats trimmed with gold lace, and brown cloaks with scarlet collars, similarly trimmed. On their cloaks they have silver badges with the arms of the town, dated 1744, and in one case (as noted below) 1688. The senior sergeant carries the mace, and the two wardens have long staves tipped with silver balls. (Collections respecting the mace, official dresses, &c., made by Mr. Henry Day, town-clerk, and kindly communicated by him to me.)

MSS. OF READING CORPORATION.

And in obedience thereunto Mr. Joseph May was (nemine contradicente) elected to be one of the aldermen of the same borough." Mr. Charles Calverley was elected Mayor in Bigg's place.

16 Oct. 1688.—Two or three new lights, "such as are used within the city of London," ordered to be set up in the most convenient places within the town; and as they are approved of, more shall be added for the whole town.

24 Oct. 1688.—"This day the members present did send to Mr. Calverley, the late mayor, for the mace, keys, and other things belonging to the Hall, which being sent they possessed themselves of it, and also of the Hall, and of the presse, chests, and trunck of writings."[1]

XXX. DIARY, No. 17, 24 Oct. 1688—6 Dec. 1694.

30 Oct. 1688.—An Order of Council brought in by the Steward dated 17 Oct., ordering the late mayor, aldermen, assistants, recorder, town-clerk, &c. to be removed, displaced and discharged.[2] Also the surrender of the Charter, &c., cancelled by the Attorney-General, with his letter thereon.

21 Dec. 1688.—"The oath being tendred to Mr. Francis Terrell, jun., lately elected an alderman, [he] did refuse to take the same."

9, 10 Jan. 1688.—Sir Henry Fane, knt., and Sir Will. Rich, bart. elected members of Parliament (in pursuance of a circular letter from the Prince of Orange), over Edward, Lord Cornbury.

9 Aug. 1689.—Francis Terrell, jun., takes the new oaths of supremacy and allegiance.

21 Aug. 1689.—"Mr. Mayor saith he hath the booke called *The Phanaticall Plott.*"

11 Sept. 1689.—Two sugar-loaves, six bottles of canary, and six of claret, presented to the Bishop of Sarum, now in the town. Again 19 Sept. 1695.

20 Feb. 1689.—Sir Will. Rich and Sir Hen. Fane re-elected for Parliament over John Wyldman and Nathan Knight, esqs.

Various entries in this year relate to a law-suit with Christ's Hospital relative to Mr. John Kenrick's gift.

8 Sept. 1690.—"Mr. Maior and the aldermen and assistants having notice that His Majesty is landed in England (out of Ireland), and supposing hee will passe through this borough this day or to-morrow towards London, mett togeather to consult how to receive him. After severall consultacions it was agreed that they should attend in their formalities beyond the Forelorne Hope, and that after a speech made to him by Mr. Steward, and the mace delivered to him by Mr. Mayor, hee should be presented with forty broad pieces of gold in a purse."

---

[1] I learn from Mr. Day's collections, referred to in the preceding note, that although Calverley was only mayor for two months, he has perpetuated his memory in the borough by a silver badge on the left arm of the cloak worn by that one of the two town-wardens or beadles who acts as crier or bellman. This badge has on one side the town arms with the date 1688, and on the other the inscription "Charles Calverley, maior."

[2] The preceding entry shows that although the official document was only now brought in, the order it contained had been previously received and acted on.

9 Sept. 1690.—"His Majesty came through this borough, and went to Windsor that night. Mr. Mayor and the Company attended, and presented him as abovesaid, which present and purse cost £47 5s."

MSS. OF READING CORPORATION.

28 Sept. 1691.—John Smith, cripple-carrier, is allowed 20s. more than his salary for his extraordinary trouble in carrying the cripples. Again, 20 Dec. 1693.

25 Nov. 1691.—Agreed that the mayor, aldermen, and assistants appear at the Town-hall to-morrow at 4, being a thanksgiving-day appointed by proclamation, in their formalities, and that three barrels of beer, and 10s. in money to buy wood for a bonfire, be allowed in order to rejoice; the beer not to exceed 20s. per barrel.

25 March 1692.—"Ordered that the Towne-hall shall not be let to any dancers or others, to shew any sports or pastimes, &c."

26 Sept. 1692.—£80 voted for the Mayor's salary instead of £60 as before.

6 Dec. 1694.—"Agreed that the booke of the Life of Archbishop Laud writt by his owne hand, and bound neately, in royall paper, be forthwith provided by Mr. John Blake upon the charge of the Hall revenues, for the use of the maior, aldermen and assistants for the time being."

DIARY, No. 18, bound in parchment, 12 Dec. 1694–9 March 1712. XXXI.

12 Dec. 1694.—"Sunday next being appointed a day of thanksgiving for His Majesty's safe retourne out of Flanders to Whitehall, it is agreed that the aldermen and assistants shall meete in their gownes at Mr. Maior's house after dinner on that Sunday, and goe with him to St. Lawrence church, and after sermon to goe with him to the Towne-hall to rejoice, and drinke their Majesties' health in a glasse of wyne, and to that purpose Mr. Chamberlen Watlington is ordered to provide wyne in the like manner and quantity as was provided the last yeare, and to provide tenn shillings' worth of wood for a bonfire, and two barrells of beere."

4 Feb. 1694.—An address to the King approved, to be presented by the Recorder.

13 March 1694.—Agreement for water-works to supply water to the town. Also, 19 Aug. 1696.

1 July 1695.—Representation to be made to the King's Council that one cornet Smith, quartered here, did give the Mayor "many opprobrious and villifying languages, and also threatned to knocke Mr. Maior on the pate," and the cornet to be prosecuted.

19 Sept. 1695.—Sunday next being a thanksgiving-day for the taking of Namur, similar proceedings ordered as on 12 Dec. above; the wine to be two dozen bottles of claret, and half a dozen bottles of sack.

The Life of Archbishop Laud to be chained with a small brass chain on a desk fixed to the wainscot in the council chamber.

23 Dec. 1695.—Order to provide for the justices at the sessions, one cake at 12s. price, one gallon of claret burnt, and two bottles of sack.

11 March 1695.—Deputation appointed to go up to the King with an address and association.

19 Aug. 1696.—The Mayor's salary fixed for the future at £40. £50 granted in the next year, and the amount varies afterwards, although fixed at £30 in 1700, the Mayor's public feast being then given up.

MSS. OF
READING
CORPORATION.

8 March 1696.—Mr. Will. Grover is fined £10 for refusing to take the oath as assistant.

22 Oct. 1697.—Peace with France to be proclaimed to-morrow. Four barrels of strong beer, three dozen of claret, and one dozen of canary to be provided.

24 Nov. 1697.—An address of congratulation to the King on the peace. On the thanksgiving-day, 2 Dec., 10s. to be spent on a bonfire, and three barrels of beer, one dozen and a half of canary, three and a half of claret, and one dozen of white wine to be provided.

27 Feb. 1698.—A petition to the House of Commons to encourage the woollen manufacture sealed.

31 May 1700.—Samuel Weller and — Payne elected scholars of St. John's College.

7 Oct. 1700.—The Queen to be met on horseback next Friday, when she passes through the borough for the first time, and to be presented with forty broad pieces of gold.

20 Oct. 1701.—An humble address to the King, in the name of the mayor, aldermen and burgesses, "that they will defend His Majesty's person, right, and title to the ymperiall crowne of these realmes against all princes, pretenders, and opposers whatsoever."

11 March 1701.—Three barrels of beer to be set in the market-place to drink the Queen's health " at the time of proclaimeing her Queen of England."

24 March 1701.—An address to the Queen on her accession.

22 April 1702.—Order for wine and beer for the next day, being the day of the coronation.

7 Oct. 1702.—The Queen to be met on horseback next Friday when she passes through the borough.

22 Oct. 1705.—"It is the opinion of the Board that for the time to come, the mayor, aldermen and burgesses in their common counsell, in case of members to serve in Parliament for this burrough, doe first determine and resolve amongst themselves whoe shall be deemed fitt representatives for that purpose." (From 1689 the elections cease to be entered in the Diary ; only the notice of the days.)

4 June 1708.—The return of Owen Buckingham and Anth. Blagrave, esqs., as members of Parliament, sealed.

18 Nov. 1709.—Wine, beer, and a bonfire, to be provided on the thanksgiving-day.

(There is no Diary for the period from 9 March 1712-3 to 8 Jan. 1714-5.)

XXXII. DIARY, No. 19, in rough calf, with clasp, 8 Jan. 1714-25 Aug 1726.

5 March 1715.—Ordered that the judges have their usual present, six bottles of claret, six of sack, and two sugar-loaves. (This had been a customary present for a long period, reaching back to the time of Charles I., or earlier. In 1656 it was one gallon and a half of sack, two barrels of beer, one sugar-loaf, and a quarter of oats for the horses.)

26 Apr. 1721.—Petition to the House of Commons to redress the present [South-Sea] grievances the nation labour under.   MSS. of READING CORPORATION.

8 Oct. 1722.—Order that all elections in the Corporation be in future by ballot.

7 Nov. 1722.—Order that about £3 be paid for painting the King's arms set up in the mayor's seat in St. Lawrence's Church.

DIARY, No. 20, in marble paper cover, kept "by Mr. John Watts, alderman, [Mayor, 1722-3] for his own private satisfaction;" 26 Apr. 1721—7 Oct. 1730. (Produced in Chancery in the suit with Christ's Hospital, 27 Jan. 1847.)   XXXIII.

20 Oct. 1721.—John Merrick elected to St. John's College in the place of — Beadel, resigned.

13 March 1722.—Application from the officers of Colonel Clayton's regiment of foot quartered in the borough for an allowance of coals and candles; it is refused, there being no fund for such expenses, and the War Office providing allowance for them. It is made a standing resolution that coals and candles shall never hereafter be allowed for soldiers quartered in the town.

30 Sept. 1724.—A general order that no strolling stage-players or puppet-showers shall have the use of the Town-hall.

27 Apr. 1726.—Six bottles of sack, six of claret, and two sugar loaves to be presented to Benjamin [Hoadly] Bishop of Salisbury, on his first visitation, as hath been usual.

7 May 1726.—The Bishop waited on by the Corporation at the Golden Bear, where in a large parlour, after a speech by the Recorder, the present was offered, and the Bishop and his Chancellor were sworn justices of the peace, according to the Charter.

21 Dec. 1726.—The order against the lending the Town-hall for stage plays and puppet shows discussed and confirmed, both because such practices tend to the corrupting the youth of the borough, and also to prevent damage being done to the hall, which has been lately beautified by the contributions of neighbouring gentlemen and ladies.

30 March 1727.—Address to the King on the discovery of the secret attempt upon Gibraltar, and upon the delivery by a foreign minister [Palm, the Emperor's Resident,] of an infamous libel into his hands, and publication of the same. Sealed 3 Apr., and presented on the 5th.

1 July 1727.—Address to Geo. II. on his accession,

15 Apr. 1728. — Princess Amelia waited on, at Col. Fellow's house in St. Mary's churchyard, on her way to the Bath, and an address presented.

28 Oct., 18 Jan. 1728.—Application made by the President of St. John's College for £4 to defray coach hire from Oxford for the visitation. Refused, there being no warrant or precedent. But at length, the Visitors being strange to the method adopted, and not having travelled with their own horses, £3 are allowed on this occasion, but not for the future.

DIARY, No. 21, in broken parchment cover, 20 Sept. 1737—16 Sept. 1758.   XXXIV.

1737, 7 Oct. Ordered that no person in future be taken to be kin to Archbishop Laud unless he or she produce a satisfactory pedigree. Ordered that £2 2s. be given to the "Prince of Marinites" [the Maronites].

MSS. OF READING CORPORATION.

1742, 15 May. The portraits of Mr. Kendrick, Archbishop Laud, sir Thos. White, Mr. Aldworth, and Sir Thos. Rich, ordered to be cleaned by Mr. Vanderhaghen.

23 Aug.—Hymns and Psalms to be printed for the Blue School boys, "for the encouragement of Mr. Allcock to teach them to sing."

1743, 7, 9, March.—An address to the King ordered and approved.

1745, 7 Oct.—" Ordered that the Mayor do offer 200 guineas towards the Association."

1746, 29 May.—An address to the King approved.

1749, 12 June.—Mountague Rush, son of Sir John Rush, knt., elected scholar of St. John's College, in the room of Rev. James Poynter, resigned.

1750, 13 Apr.—Rev. John Spicer elected master of the Free School.

1751, 11 Apr.—Petition to the House of Commons against a bill for the naturalization of foreign Protestants.

1753, 29 Sept.—An address from the Corporation to each of the parliamentary candidates for the borough, complaining of the many grievances of the nation, but specially deploring the recent unexpected step, which has so alarmed the whole nation, in the late Act for the naturalization of the Jews, urging them to use their utmost endeavours to get it repealed. " To enumerate all the massacres and persecutions of the Jews upon the score of religion, the many extortions and crueltyes arising from their usury, and the treasons and conspiracyes from their covetousness, would be an endless task, and in great measure a repetition of what has been already published."

1753, 18 Oct.—Answers of the several candidates to the preceding letter. Mr. John Dodd avows his principles to be " truly revolutional," but knows that the Corporation are deeply engaged with his opponents; the abettors of the late horrid rebellion are in part accountable for the taxes we now labour under, "under the most mild and gentle government that this nation was ever blest with "; will use his utmost endeavours to get the Act for the Jews repealed, and will oppose any subsequent bill in their favour. Mr. Will. Strode has always believed the bill to be prejudicial to Christianity but more particularly to Protestantism, and temporal interest ought not to be an excuse for countenancing the avowed enemies of our sacred religion, and consequently of our present happy constitution. Lord Fane hopes for the speedy repeal of the Act.

1756, 25 May.—Loyal address to the King, in warm approval of the war with France.

1757, 24 Jan.—Petition to the House of Commons on the dearness of corn, necessities of the poor, &c. A subscription to be entered into to distribute bread to the poor at a price much below the present price.

XXXV. DIARY, No. 22, in rough calf, 3 Oct. 1751—20 Sept. 1786. (Exhibited in Chancery, in the Christ's Hospital suit, 27 Jan. 1847.)

1760, 30 Oct.—Proclamation of Geo. III. " Two hams, some chickens, and what wine shall be necessary," to be provided, for an entertainment in the evening.

14, 15, Nov.—An address to the King on his accession.

1761, 4 March.—Declaration that the Corporation never intended to deprive the inhabitants paying scot and lot of their votes at parliamentary elections.

25, 29 Sept.—An address to the King on his marriage.   MSS. OF
1763, 2 April —Peace with France and Spain proclaimed.   READING
                                                         CORPORATION.
3 June.—Address to the King thereon.
1769, 14 June.—Joseph Gill elected scholar of St. John's College in the room of Rev. Mountague Rush, resigned.
1769, 10 Nov.—A new mace procured, about the weight of 160 oz., the old mace being much decayed and broken. In the accounts for the year the payment for the mace (in addition, apparently, to the value of the old one) is entered as £57 6s. 8d.
1770, 7 Feb.—Mr. Wise of St. John's College elected to succeed Mr. Spicer as Master of the Free School on his resignation at Midsummer twelvemonths.
1773, 21 May.—Ordered that every candidate for a scholarship at St. John's College shall in future undergo examination. [From this date I omit the elections, because they must be all registered in the School and College.]
1774, 21 Dec.—Resolution to prosecute all persons inoculating any strangers or outdwellers, &c. 1,000 handbills to be printed.
1781, 18 Sept.—Rev. Mr. Valpy, of Pembroke College, Oxf., elected master of the Free School, to succeed Mr. Wise at Michaelmas.
1782, 18 May.—A letter from Lord Shelburne as Secretary of State, inclosing a plan for raising corps in the principal towns in Great Britain was read, upon which the following motion was made, "That an answer be returned to Lord Shelburne's letter in the most respectful manner acquainting him that the Mayor having convened the Corporation on the subject of his letter, the plan contained in it was not approved by the Corporation. Only ten strueck (?), and they were for the motion. The Mayor accordingly wrote the answer by the next post."

DIARY, No. 23, Oct. 1786—Sept. 1809.   XXXVI.

1789, 4 March.—An illumination ordered at the Hall on 19 March, and a tea and ball to the town and neighbourhood, on the King's recovery from his late indisposition.
Complaint by Mr. Valpy that the noises in the Hall prevent his teaching the children in the room under it, and by the parents that the boys are sent home neglected, because they cannot be taught in the schoolroom ; a committee appointed to confer with Mr. Valpy.

1792, 1 Oct.—Permission to Mr. Coates to examine the ancient deeds and writings with a view to his *History of Reading*.

1795, 12 July.—£30 ordered to be distributed amongst the resident poor, towards reducing the present high price of bread.

1796, 3 Oct.—£52 10s. ordered to be paid immediately in part of one hundred guineas subscribed to the internal defence.

1798, 11 Feb.—£500 subcribed "towards the present exigence of public affairs."

1 Oct.—£10 10s. presented to Mr. Mann, who is requested to send a plan of the borough published by him.

8, 25, Oct.—Right Hon. Henry Addington elected High Steward, and the freedom of the borough presented in a gold box.

MSS. OF
READING
CORPORATION.

1803, 12 Aug.—One hundred guineas advanced to the general subscription for those "members of the Association" (volunteers) who cannot afford the expense.

1807, 5 Jan.—Address to Francis Annesley, LL.D., Master of Downing Coll., Cambr., on his resigning his seat for the borough in Parliament.

23 Jan.—Mr. Annesley's answer, dated 7 Jan.

1808, 8 Dec.—Twenty guineas subscribed towards a public monument to be erected to the memory of Lieut.-Col. Taylor, a native of this town, who died in the service of his country at the battle of Vimiera.

1809, 22 Sept.—Committee appointed to prepare a plan for celebrating the King's jubilee, "as an affectionate remembrance of his mild administration and government."

26 Sept.—Long details of the plan adopted.

29 Sept.—The Mayor reports that a general meeting of the inhabitants was proposed by Messrs Valpy, Marsh, and Monck to consider the celebration, but that he declined compliance, as a plan was already adopted ; the Mayor is thanked for his manly and decided conduct herein.

30 Oct.—Address to the King.

1813, 12 Feb.—Petition to the House of Commons in support of the Court of Record held at Reading every Wednesday in pursuance of the Charter.

1813, 14 Sept.—Address to the Prince Regent at Basildon Park, with an account of the presentation.

1815, 24 March.—£50 reward offered for discovery of persons writing inflammatory and seditious words on the walls and public places of the town.

Subsequent entries do not appear to require notice.

XXXVII. Small parcel endorsed "Miscellaneous old counterpart leases, &c., 26 Hen. VIII., 1534 to 1612." Amongst these are the following :—

a. 29 Sept. 1534, 26 Hen. VIII.—Lease from the Mayor and burgesses to Thomas Turner, burgess, of their tenement new builded called "the weyng howse for yerne," with two chambers over the same, in the street called " Chese Rewe," for twenty-one years, at an annual rent of 23s. iiij^d. There is a subsequent lease of this weighing-house in 4 Edw. VI.

b. 6 Sept. 1545, 37 Hen. VIII.—Lease from Rich. Turner of Reading, and John Maynesforth, vicar of St. Laurence in Reading, wardens of the Mass of Jesu founded in the said church, to John Richards of Burghfield, of ground and water-course at Shynnyngfield for thirty years at an annual rent of 3s. 4^d and for a fine of 10s.

c. 22 Dec. 1550, 4 Edw., VI.—Lease from the Mayor and burgesses to Thomas Benwell, of the beam, scales and weights called "the comyn beame," for the weighing of wools and yarn, for twenty years at an annual rent of 13s. 4^d.

d. 1564, 17 July.—Lease from Robert Boyer, of Reading, yeoman, to John Royse, of Henley, mercer, for 14 years, of the tithes of St. Mary's, Reading, which he holds under Richard Tomyowe, of London, gentleman ; paying an annual rent of 12l. 16s. 8d.

Parcel endorsed "Miscellaneous Papers in the reigns of Eliz., James I., Charles I., Charles II., and James II."   MSS. OF READING CORPORATION.

A mutilated parchment roll of 25 Edw. (1) containing a "Taxatio uonae partis bonorum in villa de Radinge."   XXXVIII.

Assessment roll used for the fifteenths levied from 1595 to 1611.   b.

Printed Proclamations :—

Charles I.—A proclamation against frauds and deceits used in draperie :   c. 16 April 1633. Five leaves.

Charles II.—Proclamation touching the King's majesties audit now shortly to be kept and holden at [Maidenhead, *Ms.*] for the year ending at the feast of St. Michael 166[5, *Ms*].

James II.—Proclamation for restoring Corporations to their ancient charters, 17 Oct. 1688.

Plea on behalf of the Corporation in answer to a *quo warranto*   d. information exhibited by Gilbert Gerrard, Attorney General, 4 Eliz., respecting their privileges.

A bundle of warrants for musters of the trained bands, muster-rolls,   XXXIX. orders for levy of taxes, &c. 1604–42, but chiefly of the time of Charles I. In the muster-roll for June 1642 the name of "Mr. Milton" *i.e.*, Christopher Milton the poet's brother, occurs among the inhabitants of St. Laurence's parish under the head of "suplies"; of those, that is, who were not bound to personal service but to supply arms.

The bundle contains also two fragments of a taxation-roll for a ninth, apparently in the time of Edward II., which had been used as wrappers for the parcel.

Parcel endorsed "Accounts of monies raised for the relief of the   XL poor, &c."

Accounts of fifteenths levied in 1598–1606, including taxes for   a. furnishing soldiers for service in Ireland, and for furnishing 140 men "for the defence of thys realme against the entended invacion by the Spannyard, taxed the 9th of August 99."

Taxation in the parish of St. Laurence "towards the relief of those   b. people who are visited with the plague, or suspected to be visited and kept in," 27 Feb. 1606.

Levies for soldiers of Col. Ramsey's regiment billetted in Reading in   c. 1628.

The names of those who refuse to pay the billetting and conduct   d. money.

"The names of those that have bequeathed [and given] gwifts unto   e. the parish of St. Gyles," 1635.

Poll-book of the voters [850] for Nath. Knight at an election 9 Feb.   f. 1680.

Account of the overseers for the relief of the poor in various years   g. from the time of Charles I. to that of James II.

Parcel endorsed "Miscellaneous Papers, comprising some accounts of   XLI. fifteenths & sundry other old parchments."

10 Eliz., 21 Aug. Indenture between Martin Dare, John Elliot, and   a. Roger Carew for the joint working of mines, &c., in the Scilly islands (apparently preserved here as having been used as a wrapper for other documents).

U 24952.   O

Taxations in the time of James I.
- b. 1726, 20 Dec.—Order of the Town Council that the Town Hall shall
- c. not be let for strolling stage-players or puppet shows. Formerly nailed, as it seems, on some wooden tablet, probably outside the Town Hall.
- d. 1751, 25 George II., 30 Nov.—Agreement between the bargemasters and mealmen of Reading respecting the rates of water-carriage to London.
- e. 1756, 17 May.—Printed broadside of the Declaration of war against the French King. Printed by Thomas Baskett, the King's Printer.

XLII. Parcel endorsed, "Miscellaneous Papers, relating principally to the period from the reign of Q. Elizabeth to that of Charles II., but none apparently of importance or of any particular interest."
- a. Copy of letters patent granted by Q. Eliz. 25 June, 1569, granting to Sir Thos. Benger a moiety of estates held of the Crown which had been forfeited by alienation without license, &c.
- b. Tax roll for a fifteenth, 9 May 1581, and 1597.
- c. Copy of a conveyance from William Earl of Banbury and his wife to Sir Francis Knollys, the elder, of Reading, of Whitley Park; 12 Feb. 1630.
- d. Muster-roll of the trained band, 1637.
- e. Miscellaneous receipts, memoranda, &c. reaching to 1770.

XLIII. A parcel containing 66 receipts for quit-rents paid to the Crown in the time of Eliz., Jas. I., and Chas. I.

XLIV. Parcel endorsed as having papers relating to the pontage, tolls, &c., a Quo Warranto in 1618, assessments for the poor, "and various old papers," some in a state of great decay.
- a. Copy on parchment i.. the 15th cent., of the agreement made in 38 Hen. III., at Westminster, between Daniel Wolveseye, "seneschallus gilde de Radynge," and Richard, abbot of Reading, as to the services due from the town to the abbey and the privileges of the town.
- b. 1644, 23 June. Letter from Thos. Maynwaringe to the Mayor while detained at Wallingford. Has seen Secretary Nicholas, but finds no hope of easing the town from the contribution (see above, pp. 16, 17). This letter is a mere shred, from damp.
- c. Answer of the Corporation to a bill of complaint of Francis lord Hollis and others about the parsonage of Shinfield.
- d. In a bill of charges in 1518 connected with the Quo Warranto are these entries:—

	£	s.	d.
"Given to the King's players the 3 of Nov.	0	11	0
Given to the Queene's players the 11 of Nov.	1	2	0
Given the Prince's players the 30 Nov. that they should forbeare playing in the town	1	2	0"

XLV. Parcel containing the Proceedings at the Court Leet, from the time of Q. Eliz. to 1810, and in the year 1830.
In this parcel there are also the following documents:—
- a. A parchment roll of the 15th century, containing copies of ten deeds relating to property of the family of Coppemor in Reading, from the time of Edw. I. to Hen. V.
- b. Account of receipts (£4 20d.) and expenses (£6 10s. 8d.) of William Catour, Mayor, Mich. 47—Mich. 48 Edw. III. (1373-4).
- c. Mutilated fragment of a longer account-roll, in which the sum of expenses is 10l. 19s. 6d., exceeding receipts by 2l. 1s. 0¾d. There are gifts

to the Abbot of Reading, the Chamberlain and Sub-Chamberlain, and MSS. OF READING
the Prior; and to Thomas, "nuncio Principis." "In expensis meis CORPORATION.
apud Lond. pro Parliamento, per iij etas in quindena sancti Hillarii,
xx^d."

One folio volume containing entries of cases heard in the borough XLVI.
court 26–30 Eliz.; and three volumes of the like register from the reign
of James II. to that of George II. There are also later volumes.

A thick folio volume, bound, containing the Register of the admis- XLVII.
sions of freemen from 1603 to 1700.

A folio volume containing a Register of elections of members of the XLVIII.
Corporation and officers, with notes in the latter part of leases sealed,
&c., from 1603 to 1665. Among the occasional entries in it are the
following :—

1614[-5], March 3.—" The letters from the Lordes of the Counsell, a.
concerninge the Lottery for the helpe of the Englishe in Virginia were
openly read, and referred to further consideration."

1625, October 11.—Copy of proclamation for the further adjournment b.
of Michaelmas Term. Note of the buildings at Reading occupied by
the courts-of-law and the chief members of the legal profession (See
Coates, p. 22).

1658. Proceedings concerninge the attempted ejection of Joel c.
Stephens from the office of Mayor.

1660, May 23.—"Agreed that the mace of the Corporation be d.
forthwith altered and the King's armes put upon it."

1661, April 22.—" Agreed that twenty shillings apiece to each parish e.
be given for the providing of wood to make bondfires and for beere to be
then spent in way of rejoyceing," on account of the Coronation.

1661, May 21.—Orders against beggars. f.

1662, May 27.—Proceedings before the Commissioners for the g.
government of corporations.

1663, Aug. 27.—Short account of a royal visit to Reading. (Printed h.
in Coates, p. 46.)

Parcel endorsed "Miscellaneous Papers from about 1620 to about XLIX.
1775." Chiefly concerned with the Reading charities and municipal
elections.

Privy-seal warrant from Q. Mary I. to John Owen, esq., of Wotton, a.
Surrey, for the loan of £40, 17 Sept., an. 4 & 5. [1557.]

Letter from Thomas Taylor, the well known Puritan minister, a b.
lecturer at one of the churches, to the Mayor and Corporation, dated
Sept. 2, 1625, complaining of accusations brought against him for
allusion in a sermon to Mr. Alder's intended gift for a lectureship, and
desiring "leave in this same place and hearinge" to clear himself.

Several letters from lawyers employed by the Corporation; viz., c.
three from Walter Knight, of Staple Inn, 1636–1659, one from Edward
Clerke and John Saunders in 1632, and three from Edw. Dalby in

o 2

MSS. OF READING CORPORATION.

1663–6. In the last of Knight's letters, dated 3 Nov. 1659, he writes, "My Lord Lambert is gone this daye with an armye towards Scotland, but (it) is hoped that General Monke and hee will not fight. Ther are mediators gone before. My Lord Cheife Justice that was, although hee doth practice, yet hee will not practice at the upper bench wher hee was a judge . . . . . Mr. Rolles is cryed upp in Middlesex for a rare man."

d. Copy, without signature, date, or address, of a letter about a conventicle :—

"My Lord,
"Yesterday (being Sunday), towards the evening I went with my constable to the house of Mr. Fowler in Castle Streete in this towne, to prohibit the great meeting of people there upon pretence of religious worship, and finding a greate number of people there I charged Mr. Fowler in the King's name not to suffer any such meeting for the future. Whereupon he answered that he had beene with your Lordshipp, and acquainted your Honour of those meetings, and that your Honour seemed not to be displeased thereat, as hee thought, but rather satisfied therewith ; which I thought in my duty to signifie unto your Honour."

e. Memorandum of the distribution (in the reign of Q. Elizabeth or James I.) of 1,182 mulberry plants.

L. Parcel endorsed "Miscellaneous Papers in the reign of Charles I."
a. Various taxatious and orders relative to the billetting of soldiers, &c.
b. Two peremptory letters to the Corporation from W. [Knollys, Earl of] Banbury, the High Steward, respecting the admission of a freeman, and the payment of an accustomed fee of £6 to Sir Edward Clerke, the steward of the town; the last dated 23 Nov. 1626.
c. Counsel's opinion, signed "Nich. Ducke, Wm. Noye," about the above-mentioned case of admission to freedom.

LI. A large parcel endorsed "Various papers of special interest of the period of the 17th century."

1. Abstract in English, written in the 15th cent., of the composition made between the Abbot Richard and the burgesses in the 38th year of Henry III. ; slightly mutilated (*see above*, p. 2). An English version from another MS. is printed in Appendix V. to Coates' *History*.

2. "This is the answere of Richard Cleche to the bille of complaynt of (John Thorne) the Abbot of Redyng:" between 1490 and 1508. (A draft.) He bears no malice or grudge against the abbey, as the abbot alleges ; but by default of the abbot no "maister of the gilde otherwise called the Mayre," had been appointed by the space of three or four years, for the which cause the burgesses elected Cleche, and for as much as before the time of Christmas last past "mysruled people dayly encresed and contynued, as carders, disers, hasarders, vacabonds and mony oder unlawfull gamys were used as wele by nyght as by day," and the abbot had taken upon him to admit simple and perjured persons to the office of constable, who in nothing regarded the good rule of the town, therefore Cleche desired certain burgesses to help to see such misruled people punished during the said time of Christmas, and further, until matters were settled with the abbot.

HISTORICAL MANUSCRIPTS COMMISSION.   213

3. Various warrants for musters in 1616, 1618, and 1642, and for providing conduct-money for troops coming from Devonshire in 1627.

MSS. OF READING CORPORATION.

4. Receipts from two fellows of St. John's College, Oxford, Thomas Walker and Thomas * * * * in 1619-1620, for the exhibitions of £2 per ann. allowed them by the Company of burgesses.

5. Copy of a letter dated Sept. 22, 1622, from the Lord Keeper, Bishop J. Williams of Lincoln, to Sir Richard Lovelace, *custos rotul.*, and the justices of Berkshire, calling for the strict and immediate execution of the laws against beggars, for that "his Majestie is justly offended at you, who, being entrusted with the care and execution of theis statutes, do suffer your countrie notwithstanding to swarme with whole troupes of rogues, beggars, Agiptians and idle persons," "sumptomes of Popery and blinde superstition." Also, because the last years have yielded abundance of grass and hay and corn, and cattle have been very cheap in markets, but notwithstanding, all have "everywhere borne such excessive and intollerable prices, that people could take no knowledge of the blessing of God, nor lifte up their hands to praise him for the same," therefore such reasonable rates are to be fixed for hay, oats, flesh and bread, as shall in equity be found fitting, "especially in those townes and villages within your countie where his Majestie's servaunts and retinue are enforced by their attendance upon the court to lodge and sojorne." Followed by an order made at the Quarter Sessions at Newbury on 1 Oct. in accordance with these injunctions. The mayors and bailiffs are to fix the price of bread and flesh in their several jurisdictions; at inns, oats, being now 15d. per bushel, are to be sold at 20d., beans, being 2s. 6d. the bushel, are to be sold at 3s.; and hay being 20d. by the hundred, the traveller may have the half-penny bottle to weigh two lbs.

6. Petition from John Strip of St. John's College, Oxford, for an allowance of £2.

7. 1624, 24 Aug.—"From my schoele within Temple-bar." Letter from William Grippe to the Corporation thanking them for help "in mine extreamity."

8. Letter from Edward Clercke to "Mr. Barnard" sending £3 from the Corporation to enable "one Grippe of Magdalen Hall borne of poor parents in Reading" (whose necessities they have often before commiserated), to discharge "such dues as the Batchelor's degree requyres, and alsoe to put him into apparell decent and becomminge, that sitting to receive his grace he meete not with disgrace and discorage·ment too."

9 1625, 14 Aug.—Copy of a letter from the Privy Council at Woodstock, to the High Sheriff of Berkshire, desiring two clothiers to attend the board at Southampton on 23 inst., to give advice to what towns the staple of cloth shall be removed while the plague continues in London. Endorsed with draft of a report on the state of Reading; four houses are infected, and two suspected.

10. 24 Aug.—Copy of a letter to Sir James Whitlocke, judge, with further report on the state of Reading ; a pest house has been provided, but the infection has not spread ; in spite of the King's orders, however, some people persist in receiving wares from London, "more respecting their private gayne and profitt then the public calamity."

11. 8 Aug.—Copies of the orders referred to in the preceding letter, and of an order for collection of a tax levied for relief of persons infected with the plague.

MSS. OF
READING
CORPORATION.

12. Letter from W. (Earl of) Wallingford to the Corporation, dated "Grayes, the 30 of Oct.," without year, complaining that they have not complied with his application for the restoration of John Ne[wman] to his ancient place, which he cannot but judge proceeds from "a peevish humour"; desires they will make no further delay in granting so menu a request.

13. Representation (without date) to the Corporation, complaining of the number of disordered persons in the town, " whoe are very dissolute in their lyves, very obstinate, stubborne, and disobedient to their parents and governors, and suche as are not onelye gadders and spinners of streete webbs in the daye time, but very unruly in the evenings, ordinary nightwalkers," and "that the keeper of the House of Correction (Ballard by name) intertayneth poore men's children, other men's servaunts, both by daye and by nighte." The names of eight women being " some of theis disordered persons" are subjoined.

14. 1629, 24 Feb.—Letter from James Heron, at Abingdon, to the Mayor, about taking recognizances for the observation of Lent.

15. 1630, 13 June.—Copy of an order from the Privy Council for restraint of malting and brewing, on account of the scarcity of corn.

16. 1631, 11 April.—Certificate of the election of Henry, Earl of Holland, as High Steward of Reading.

17. 1631, 4 April, 12 Sept.—Orders for summoning persons possessed of £40 a year in land to appear before the King's commissioners to compound for not receiving knighthood.

18. 1631-2, 13 Jan.—Warrant signed and sealed by Sir James Whitelocke for the apprehension of the engrossers and forestallers who frequent Reading market.

19. 1632, 30 Apr.—Copy of a letter from the Privy Council to the justices of Berkshire for a return of places and persons fit for the sale of tobacco, and list of persons licensed in Reading, 1 Nov. 1633.

20. 1635, 31 March.—Copy of a letter from the same for a return of the names of all maltsters, with a view to the regulation of the trade, and limitation of their numbers.

21. 1636, 31 Jan.—Articles to be propounded by the King's Commissioners for regulating the trade of maltsters.

22. 1635, 14 Jan.—Copy of a license from the Earl of Holland, as High Steward, for a butcher to sell meat in Lent.

23. 1636, 18 June.—Certificate signed by John Squier, vicar, Roger Ley, curate, and the churchwardens of St. Leonard Shoreditch, that Will. Mosely hath had his house clear and free from the plague this year hitherto.

24. Copy of a petition from the Corporation to the King's Commissioners for grievances, setting forth the number of persons unemployed through decay of the clothing trade, arising partly from small sale, partly from competition of the northern clothiers, who have altered their lengths from 12 yards to the length of Reading cloth, and sell their cloth in the name of Reading cloth, and partly from high rates of shipping.

25. An opinion signed by "Dn. Jenkins" (afterwards the famous judge), as to the power of the Corporation to appoint attorneys of the borough court, make bye-laws, etc.

26. Copy of the King's declaration at the head of his army 19 Sept. 1642, and of the reciprocal declaration to be made by loyal subjects, 6 Oct.

MSS. OF READING CORPORATION.

27. Copy of a warrant from the King for impressing all the tailors in Reading and within 6 miles, for making clothes for the soldiers, Reading, 8 Nov. 1642; with order to the constables thereon, dated the same day.

28. " A particular noate of all such charges as hath been disbursed since the Kinge's majestie came first to Reading," for provisions, clothes for the soldiers, and the King's own use, amounting to £6697.

29. Order for supply of 1000 suits of clothes, Abingdon having supplied 1644, 9 Nov., no year.

30. Note of the payment in various sums of £2000 lent to the King by the town.

31. Receipt signed by Sir Arthur Aston for £2000 lent to the King in December, 3 Jan. 1642.

32. An amusing paper of trivial counter-recriminations made by two attorneys, Francis Seakes and Henry Bradley, against each other, as being friends to the Parliament, with depositions of witnesses; the real reason apparently being, that Bradley had obtained the office of attorney of the borough-court which Seakes claimed. Bradley's wife had been heard to say that she wished Prince Robert had been hanged 7 years ago. Dated 9 Jan. 1642

33. Copy of a petition to the King from the Corporation praying that they may have security given for repayment of £4000 which they have lent him, and for which they have engaged themselves and the hall-lands, rents, and revenues; with an order dated at Oxford, 18 March, 1642-3, for the procuring security.

34. Copy of a letter from the King to Sir Jacob Astoley, governor of Reading, ordering him to provision Reading for three months, to provision Greenland, and to send out scouting parties to watch the enemy and to prevent carriage of supplies to London; with the following postscript: "You shall have a weeke's pay by to-morrowe at night, or Jacke Ashburnham shall bee canvast." Oxford, 3 March, 1643.

35. Petition from the clothiers of Reading to the King, praying for liberty to trade with London notwithstanding his proclamation for restraint of the same.

36. Petition from the same to the same, praying that the clothes seized by Sir A. Aston may be kept in safe custody until they can obtain from the Parliament freedom of trade again with London.

37. Letter from Sir Thomas Maynwaring to Mr. Willmer; the King has, in answer to the petition, ordered the Governor to deliver the cloth; Oxford, 22 March, 1642.

38. Copies of four petitions to the King from the Corporation, for protection from plundering, for imposing a contribution jointly upon the county with the town, and for release from certain weekly and monthly assessments.

39. Draft of a petition to the Parliament for licence to trade with London.

40. Letter from col. Thomas Blagge, to Thomas Thackham, the mayor of Reading, forwarding accompanying copies of warrants, dated

MSS. OF READING CORPORATION.

26 June, from the King and Prince Rupert, directing him to receive the contributions assessed on Reading and the neighbouring hundreds, for the fortifying of Wallingford town and castle; Wallingford, 30 June 1643.

41. Letter from John Clarke, Sheriff, to the same, in obedience to an order from the King, for a return of the contributions paid for the horse since the King's residence at Oxford; and enjoining the proclaiming next market-day of some proclamations sent the last week. 5 July 1643.

42. Letter from Thomas Thackham, the mayor, without address, stating the inability of the town, through great sickness and utter decay of trade, to repay borrowed money, or to pay any further taxes. 1 Sept., 1643.

43. Copy of an oath of allegiance to be taken by the soldiers in the regiment raised by the town of Reading.

44. Copies of a petition from the Corporation to the King, praying for release from £700, being arrears claimed by Prince Rupert; and of an order dated at Oxford, 15 March, 1643, granting release from arrears, and from future contributions while the town remains garrisoned.

45. Copy of an order from the King for the levy of men in Reading for the garrison, in consequence of the withdrawal of a part of the garrison to re-inforce Lord Hopton's army. Oxford, 5 April, 1644.

46. Copy of a petition from the Corporation to the King for license for the merchants of London to come to Reading to make purchases; sent with a letter to Sir Thomas Maynwaring, 20 April, 1644.

47. Copy of a letter from the King's commissioners of excise at Oxford to Mr. Henry Gardener, ordering him to go to Reading to publish the proclamation of excise, and to collect the dues at the next market, 1 May, 1644.

48. Letter from capt. Edward Clerke to the Mayor, with major-general Browne's order that the drawbridge at Caversham be forthwith made up, 16 July, 1644; with a letter from the Mayor, &c., to Browne, on the same day, saying that they "have made up Caversham bridge fitt for any carriages to pass over," and desiring that if it be his pleasure to have a drawbridge made, he will send his warrant to the two town-carpenters to take timber and impress other carpenters.

49. Order from the Parliamentary Committee of Deputy Lieutenants for Berkshire (signed by Francis Pile, E. Dunch, Tanfield Vachell, and col. Henry Martin) for the immediate muster, at 3 o'clock in the afternoon, of the trained bands, 26 July, 1644.

50. Order from Col. "Jere. Horton" to the Mayor and aldermen, for the levy of money for provision for prisoners, 26 July, 1644.

51. Draft of a petition from the town to Parliament showing "that since the tyme the two armyes came into this towne your petitioners have had their sufferings so multiplied upon them, the souldiers growing to that height of insolency that they break down our houses and burne them, take away our goods and sell them, rob our markets and spoile them, threaten our majestrates and beate them, so that without a speedy redresse we shalbe constrained, though to our utter undoing yet for the preservation of our lives, to forsake our goods and habitation, and leave the towne to the will of the souldiers, who cry out they have no pay,

they have no beds, they have no fyer, and they must and will have it by force, or they will burne downe all the howses in the towne, whatever become of them."

52. [1644.] Letter from George Varney to William Wilmott [Wilmer] the town-clerk, not dated, but written from prison, where he was brought by the soldiers ; stating his inability to pay his rent for the farm held of the town, which is three yard-lands, and on which the taxes last year were 10s. a week. " We cannot injoy our land we rent of you because the armies of both sides lie so nere us, consumeing the profits of our grounds. Besides taxes are so hard, we are not able to pay them ; ther is but threscore and 8 yards lands within the parish, which comes to, at 10l. a yard land, six hundred and fower score pounds a yeare, and the taxes that are layed apon us by both armies is above 12 hundred pounds a yeare, besides quartering with us. Yet notwithstanding I will plow it so long as I can, and soe soone as I can I will send you money. I had eleven horses taken away by the King's soldiers, and fower of those eleven were well worth 40 pound ; I rode after the eleven horses, and bought nine of them againe, and brought them home ; then, rideing after the other two, whiles I was abroad the King's souldiers tooke the other nine away againe, and I could never have them more. Since againe this last winter, goeing to market with a load of corn, the earle of Manchester's souldiers mett with my men, and tooke away my whole teame of horses, letting my cart stand in the feild, 4 milles from home ; never had them more. You know by ordinance of Parliament landlords should pay there taxes for their tenaunts. Besides all this, when the King's souldiers comes to us, the[y] call mee roundheaded rouge, and say I pay rent to the Parliament garison, and they will take it away from mee. And likewise when the Parl. souldiers, they vaper with me, and tell me that I pay rent to Worcester and to Winchester ; therefore the Parliam. souldiers say they will have the rent."

53. Six letters from the Parliamentary Committee, ordering assessments for the Parliamentary forces and for the relief of the British forces in Ireland, 25 March, 1645–21 Feb. 1647.

54. Draft of a petition from the Corporation to the Committee of both kingdoms, against the assessment for Ireland ordered by warrant of 26 June, 1645.

55. Printed summons " in his Majestie's name," from Philip Daroll, auditor of crown revenues, to attend for payment of rents at Reading on 23 Oct., dated 10 June, 1647, with a written copy of a proclamation relating thereto, of the same date, on the part of the said auditor, as authorized by both Houses of Parliament; subscribed at the foot " God save the Kinge and Parlyament."

56. Petition to the Mayor and aldermen from John Blackman, elected fellow [of St. John's College] Oxford, after being three years at Oriel College, praying for money to enable him to take his degree ; noted as having been referred on 7 July, 1647, to a fuller company for consideration.

57. Copy of an order from Sir Thomas Fairfax to Col. Vincent Goddard, dated 14 Aug. 1647, to take account of the arms in the custody of the Mayor of Reading ; with a note subjoined that on 18 Aug. Mr. Curtis " went into the armor-house under the Hall, but there was noe armes there."

58. Letter, signed by Sir Thomas Fairfax, to the Mayor, recommending Mr. Wells, who had served many years in Fairfax's own troop, for

MSS. OF READING CORPORATION.

admittance to the freedom of the town in his absence, Westm., 22 Jan. 1648, with Fairfax's seal, broken.

59. Copy of a letter from the Corporation to the Recorder, Daniel Blagrave, of 8 Oct. 1650, inclosing a petition to the Council of State from some of the inhabitants of Reading, complaining of the Mayor and aldermen as disaffected to "the present power by their malevolent practise in opposing the cordiall friends of the Parliament."

60. Reply from Daniel Blagrave, advising the Mayor to slight all the "weak threats and ridiculous practises" of the "godly-pretending party," "for they may bark but not bite. . . . . . As for my parte, I contemne their poor projects, and pitty their folly, for I am (blessed be God) out of the reach of this malitious rable." Westm., 2 Nov. 1650.

61. Three letters about the Dutch prisoners at Reading, May–July 1653.

62. Copy of the certificate of the election of [Col.] Robert Hammond as High Steward, 26 June, 1654.

63. Draft of the certificate of the election of Bulstrode, Lord Whitlocke as High Steward, 18 Dec. 1654.

64. Letter from Thomas Bulstrode to the Mayor, informing him that he had, as desired, acquainted Lord Commissioner Whitelocke with his election. "Parliament was dissolved on Munday last, without any thing acted." Hare's Court, Inner Temple, 25 Jan. 1654.

65. Three letters from Richard Bulstrode to the Mayor, respecting a law-suit between Bulstrode and Daniel Blagrave as to the stewardship of the borough, of which the latter had been deprived, the judges at last giving decision in favour of the writer; 9 Feb. 1656, 28 Jan. 1657; 8 May, 1658.

66. Copy of the certificate of re-election of Daniel Blagrave as steward, 13 Apr. 1660.

67. [1662.] Petition from the cobblers in Reading to the Corporation against the shoemakers for mending and repairing old ware, in violation of the ancient orders of the borough; with a note that the defendants appeared and received warning not to offend against the orders at their peril. (See Man's *History of Reading*, p. 364.)

68. Letter from R. Aldworth, sending licences from the Privy Council for butchers to kill meat in Lent; Lambeth, 27 Feb. 1662.

69. Particulars of the fees paid to the King's servants on his visit to Reading, 27 August, 1663.

70. Letter to the justices of peace from the Earl of Southampton and Lord Ashley, about the collection of hearth-money, 7 Oct. 1663.

71. Copy of a letter from the Corporation to the Master of University College, Oxford, asking him to assist one Richard Pawley, who has been admitted into that College, a poor fatherless youth, brought up at the free-school in Reading.

72. 1672, 20 April. Copy of a letter from the Mayor, John Blake, to Sir Bulstrode Whitelocke, requesting him, in the name of the Corporation, to resign the office of High Steward, conceiving, "as your circumstances are, it may not be so proper for yourselfe to appear for us," should they soon have occasion, for the preservation of their rights and immunities.

73. Copies, with signatures of the Corporation, of two loyal addresses to Charles II; the one thanking him for his declaration, 27 May, *an.*

HISTORICAL MANUSCRIPTS COMMISSION.   219

33 (1681); and the other vehemently inveighing against the Earl of   MSS. OF
Shaftesbury's Association, 5 May, *an.* 34 (1682). [*See* p. 23, *supra.*]   READING
                                                                              CORPORATION.

74. Copy of a letter from the Mayor to Sir Leoline Jenkins, giving
(as directed in a letter from him of 15 Dec.) an account of proceedings
against some rioters, and of the endeavours made to suppress conventicles.
" As to the conventicles, myself and the rest of the justices here have
oftentimes resorted to their meeting-places, and disturbed them, and
dissipated their meetings, and have dilligently endeavoured the taking
their preachers, but cannot as yet, for that as often as they meete they
sett spies everyway to give them notice of our comming, and then the
preachers escape, and the persons mett are silent, or gone by that time
we can gett to them " ; 15 May, 1682.

75. Resolutions of the Corporation, 6 Nov. 1685, about the surrender
of the Charter to James II. with a note that the surrender was delivered
to the King on 11 Nov.

76. Answer of the Corporation to " the scandalous pamphlett intituled,
The case of the towne of Reading stated." [1656. *See* p. 19.]

Parcel endorsed " Miscellaneous papers relating to the period of the LII.
reign of Charles I. and the commonwealth, but none of any apparent
importance or of any particular interest." The contents are :—

Taxations for the King's garrison in 1643–5 ; rough memoranda of
the preceedings of the Corporation at their meetings ; letters to them
from Edw. Dalby, T. Vachell, Will. Verney (Bedford, 1646), Walter
Knight, and others, on Corporation business ; rightly described as being
of no particular interest.

Small parcel endorsed " Papers of Special Interest," &c.   LIII.

1633, 27 Aug. Woodstock.—Order from Charles I. to the Mayor and *a.*
burgesses for the removal from Broad Street of the fixed flesh-shambles,
whereby " the beautie and pleasure of that streete [are] utterly lost."

1643, 24 July.—T. . . . [Maynwaring? *signature lost*] to Mr. Edw. *b.*
Willmer, town clerk. Has delivered the several petitions to the King
for discharge from contributions to Wallingford, but cannot obtain it.

1644, 3 June, Oxf.—Copy of an order from the King to Col. Blagge *c.*
and Lieut.-Col. Lower for the levying weekly contributions for the
garrison at Wallingford.

Letter from William Brackston, mayor of Reading, to the aldermen, *d.*
sending the preceding. He was carried away to Wallingford by a party
of horse last night, and will be detained there as a prisoner until the
contributions which are due since 3 June of 50*l.* a week are paid.

22 June.—Copy of the answer of the aldermen, desiring to know the *e.*
exact amount required.

1644 [23 ? June].—Letter to the aldermen from Lieut.-Col. Lower, *f.*
lieut.-gov. of Wallingford, urging, in a friendly tone, the payment of
what is due, and promising to abate future contributions as far as
possible. If two aldermen will go to Wallingford the Mayor shall be
dismissed.

1644, 25 June.—Draft of a letter from the aldermen to Lieut.-Col. *g.*
Lower, declaring their utter inability to levy any contribution now.

h. 1644, 26 June, Wallingford.—Reply of Lieut.-Col. Lower. Their letter gives him little satisfaction, since they do not so much as promise their endeavours to raise what is required. If they will send 100*l.* he will forbear the rest, and abate the weekly sum of 50*l.*; till then the Mayor will be detained. "If we shall heare you contribute anythinge under hand to the Rebells, we shall require it double; but I have a better opinion of your loyaltie and affection to the King's service."

i. Draft of a petition to the Council of war at Oxford from the aldermen for relief.

j. 1644, 1 July.—Copy of a warrant from the Council at Oxford to the Commissioners for contributions in Berks, directing that Reading shall pay only a proportionable rate of the 1,000*l.* levied weekly upon the county.

LIV. A bound folio volume, lettered, "Autographs."

1. Order from Charles I. to the Mayor and aldermen. "Whereas I (*sic*) have received information that the bridge over the river of Thames at Causeham was lately broaken downe, our will and expresse commaund is that you imediately uppon sight heereof cause the said bridge imediately to bee rebuilt and made stronge and fitt for the passage of our army and artillery by tomorrow eight of the clocke in the morneinge as the bearer shall direct. Of this you may not fayle at your utmost perill. Given at our Court at Benson, this 3d of November 1642."

2. Order from the same to the Mayor that he do not permit any wheat, barley, or other corn or provisions to be conveyed away out of the house of John Dee without the King's leave. Reading, 8 Nov. 1642.

3. Order from the same to the Mayor and aldermen to take up such carts and boats within the county of Berks as shall be necessary for the speedy conveyance of suits of apparel for the soldiers and of provisions, which are supplied by the town of Reading; "and heerein I (*sic*) require you to use your utmost care and diligence." Colebrooke, 12 Nov. 1642.

4. The same to the same, approving of their election of Francis Seakes to be one of the four attorneys of the town, on the recommendation of Sir Arthur Aston. Oxford, 23 Jan. 1642.

5. The same to the some, licensing the clothiers (at their desire) to follow their trade, and promising that henceforward no clothes shall be taken from them without payment, provided they do not send clothes to London. Oxford, 4 Nov. 1643. Countersigned, "Edw. Walker."

6. Prince Rupert to the same. According to the King's agreement with the county for £1,000 per week, Reading is assessed at £65 weekly, but no part thereof hath been paid, nor attempted to be collected, from Michaelmas last; "by which neglect of yours and disservice to his Majestie and your country, the soldier is unpaid;" immediate collection, therefore, and regular weekly payment are ordered; payment to be made to Edmund Turnor, gent., who is appointed to pay the horse quartered in the county. *No place, and day omitted,* Jan. 1643.

7. Letter from Sir T. Fairfax to Col. Harrison, "or the cheif officer with his regiment at Gilford." "I have received information this morn-

ing from some of the well affected in Reading that there hath beene of late severall meetings of cavileirs and other disaffected persons in an hostile manner in that towne, and that they have threatned to make the same a garrison for the King. I desire yow would upon receipt hereof send two troopes of your regiment unto Reading, and to quarter there untill the Major and well affected may put themselves into a posture of defence to preserve that towne for the service of the Parliament." This order to be communicated to the Major, who is to be assisted in apprehending such persons as may disturb the peace. Windsor Castle, 8 May, 1648.

8. Warrant from "Oliver P." to the Mayor to send up some suspicious persons who are in his custody, together with the examinations taken concerning them. Whitehall, 30 Apr. 1655.

9. "W. [Earl of] Wallingford," High Steward, to the Mayor and burgesses, complaining sharply of the meanness of some contribution collected in the town for the King, in which they have not given according to their several abilities, but by an equal scale. It is "for the K. Majestie's dawghter," and "divers towns farr enferior to the towne of Readyng have gyven more." Mr. Kenrick gives but 15s., whereas he might well give £5. He is ashamed to see this penury in so weighty a cause, and desires they will double the sum at the least: the head burgesses should give 40s. a piece, and the second 20s., and so the rest; none to give under 5s. "I praye you to let the world know that I have some power with you." Grayes, 10 Dec., *without year. Holograph.*

10. The same to the same; *signed.* Desires the restoration of John Newman, a second burgess, to his ancient place as a head burgess. *Not dated.*

11. The same to the same; *holograph.* Upon the same subject. Hears they have not fulfilled their promise, made at his last being with them, of Mr. Numan's restoration; desires he may be speedily replaced "without eny further daliance." *Not dated.*

A third letter is noticed at p. 35.

12. The same to the same; *signed.* Understanding that they have kept back part of the £6 which formerly (at his request) they gave towards bettering the stipend of their schoolmaster (who is fundamentally in their Charter, and for whose maintenance, amongst other things, their lands, which have been much improved, were first given), he requests that they will restore what has been detained, and in future pay the £6 quarterly. Caversham, 18 Sept. 1623.

13. The same to the same (*signed*) recommending Sir Francis Knollis the younger, for election as one of their burgesses in the new Parliament, and leaving to them the nomination of the other, "presuming you will make choise of Mr. Sanders, whoe served for your borrowe the last Parliament." Grayes, 8 Apr. 1625.

The Mayor notes at the foot: "This I did so performe the 21 of Aprill, 1625, with almoste the hole company, wantinge but to only."

14. The same, as Earl of Banbury, to the same; *signed.* Now that age and infirmities have made him unable to serve them as he was wont, the love which he has ever received from them makes him desire to provide them with such a patron as may best protect them in the free enjoying of all their just privileges and lawful immunities. "To this purpose, as I made choise to succeed me in my liftenancy of Berkshire of my deare and noble nephew the Earle of Holland,

MSS. OF READING CORPORATION.

see there is no man I can so worthily recommend to your election for your Steward as he, who for the emminence of his person and noblenes of his disposition is so well knowne to you." 8 July 1630.

A copy of the reply of the Corporation (who subscribe as, "your humble servants and beedsmen most devoted") is inserted, in which they profess the utmost respect and gratitude, and beg the earl to retain his office (which he has held nearly 30 years) for the whole of his life ; for the resignation, also, of which they have no precedent. Dated 24 July, 1630.

15. The Earl to the same; *signed*. Consents to retain the stewardship for life, as they desire, taking no small comfort in this demonstration of their love, but hopes they will not forget his request to them for the earl of Holland when he is dead. "From Bowton neere Northhampton," 12 Aug. 1630.

16. Letter from the King's Commissioners for defective titles "to the pretended owners and occupiers of the hospitall called Leeche Almeshouse in Reddinge," calling on them to appear on or before 20 Oct. next before Rob. Tipper, esq., in Fetter Lane, London, to prove their title or make composition. Signed, Middlesex, Rich. Weston, Jul. Cæsar, Thomas Coventrye, and Rich. Fortescue. Whitehall, 6 Aug. 1623.

17. Judgement in the Earl Marshall's Court (signed E. Worcester, Pembroke, T. Arundell), in a dispute about precedency in the borough between Roger Knight and Christopher Turner. Whitehall, 24 Apr. 1619. (Printed in Coates, appendix, No. XV.)

18. Notice to the Mayor from Sir William Killigrew, by direction of the King, that if the inhabitants do not, in obedience to the proclamation, bring in all arms and armour to the town hall by one o'clock, any house in which any such arms are found will be given over to the soldiers to plunder. 7 Nov. 1642.

19. Letter from the Privy Council to the Mayor and burgesses. Considering how the poor may be relieved in the present scarcity of corn, they find that a great quantity of barley (which in time of scarcity is the bread corn of the poor), is unnecessarily consumed by the excessive quantity of strong beer consumed in alehouses. They require, therefore, that all such alehouses be suppressed as shall not be needful for the ease and convenience of the people, the same being now growne to so great a number, and for the most part places of disorder, and entertainment for lewd and ill-governed persons. And also that care be taken that the beer and ale which are brewed be so moderated and reformed that there be no vain consumption of the grain of the kingdom. Whitehall, 31 Dec. 1622. [See order in 1630, at p. 35.]

20. License from the Earl of Holland to a butcher to kill meat in Lent. 6 Jan. 1631. [A license in 1635, at p. 35.]

21. Letter from Will. Juxon, President of St. John's College, Oxford, (signed also by ten Fellows), to the Mayor and burgesses, informing them that there is a place vacant in the college by the preferment of Mr. Thomas Walker, which belongs to the School. 24 May, 1631.

22. Order from John Clarke, High Sheriff of Berks, to the Mayor, to cause 25 able men to be brought to Abingdon on 28 June, as the Reading quota of 500 men ordered to be raised from the county by the King, (whose order of 22 June is given at full). 23 June, 1643.

23. Orders made at a Council of War at Oxford, 14 Apr. 1644, present the King and twelve others, concerning the defence of Reading. A regiment of auxiliaries to be raised of well affected persons in the town and neighbourhood, to be commanded by Col. Richard Neville, High Sheriff, which regiment shall not upon any occasion be drawn out, but only employed in the defence of the town ; a tax to be levied for the support of those who cannot bear their own charges ; an oath to be taken by those who are enlisted ; the governor, Sir Jacob Astely, speedily to return thither, with arms and ammunition ; muskets to be provided at Reading, at 12s. each. [For the oath see p. 36.]

MSS. OF READING CORPORATION

Lying loose in the same volume are the following letters to the Mayor and burgesses relative to the appointment of a master of the Grammar School on the death of Dr. Bird in 1636.

1. From Archbishop Laud. It will not be an easy thing in all respects to equal Dr. Bird, who hath taken a great deal of pains and done a great deal of service. Proposes to thank the King next Sunday, in their name, for the care he has taken for the furnishing of the School. Two great hindrances to the getting an able schoolmaster are the poorness of the stipend (£10) and the want of a house, the old house not having been renewed when the time was. Advises their asking the President and Fellows of St. John's College to name some sufficient man. Croidon, 1 Dec. 1636.

2. The same to the same. Wrote to St. John's College ; approves of the letter which they also wrote, and thanks them for their respect therein to them ; is glad to hear that they propose to better the master's allowance ; recommends the bearer, Mr. Page, M.A., a Fellow of St. John's College, as sufficient in learning, honesty, and soberness in conversation. Croydon, 15 Dec.

3. The President (Rich. Baylie) and five Fellows of St. John's College to the same, recommending Mr. William Page. 5 Dec.

Parcel endorsed " Writs for the restitution of members of the Corporation in the time of Richard Cromwell and Charles the II."

LV.

Order by the Parliamentary Committee for the removal of three aldermen (Anth. Brackston, Thos. Harrison, and Will. Turner), and two assistants (Sir Thos. Mainwaring, knt., and Will. Gandye), as delinquents ; Reading Abbey, 21 August, 1644.

a.

Order by the Corporation for the removal of the above with several others ; *not dated*.

b.

Two letters from Thomas Harrison claiming repayment of money lent by him to the Corporation.

c.

Draft of a petition from the Mayor and burgesses to the House of Commons, praying for relief against Harrison who is suing them for £600 advanced by him to the enemy during the war.

d.

Petition from inhabitants of Reading to the House of Commons against the return of Daniel Blagrave as member for the borough.

e.

Sixteen writs for the restoration of 16 aldermen and assistants who had been deprived ; two dated 5 Feb. and the rest 20 April, 1659.

f.

Writ for the restoration of Will. Page, " in medicinis doctor," to his place of head master of the School ; 21 Nov. 1660.

g.

Writ for the restoration of Daniel Webb to his place as one of the burgesses ; 30 May, 1674.

h.

MSS. OF READING CORPORATION.

LVI. Small parcel endorsed "5 ancient books of regulations and ordinances," &c.

i. Small quarto book of 12 parchment leaves, written in the time (as it seems) of Mary I., with the duties of the mayor, steward, and sergeants, articles of the Charter, and various orders made between 1 Henry VII. and 1–2 Philip and Mary.

ii. A paper book, containing eleven written leaves, endorsed "The booke of the names and ordinaunces of the Cutlers' and Bellfounders' Company," but containing also the names of the tradesmen of 17 other trades who were admitted into that Company; and "Perticuler orders" and "Generall orders" of the Mayor and burgesses for the regulation of the smiths, barbers, carpenters, joiners, and sawyers. Under the head of "Barbours" it is ordered that no toothdrawer being a foreigner shall draw any tooth in any other place than in the barbers' shops, under a penalty of xij$d$., and that no barber shave, trim, dress, or knot any person on the Sabbath day, the fair-days only excepted, under a like penalty. At the end is a table of the fines from the several trades for admission to the Company.

iii. A similar book of the Tanners' and Leathersellers' Company, including also the shoemakers, curriers, glovers, sadlers, jerkin-makers, bottlemakers, collarmakers, and coblers, with particular and general orders, and the table of fines. Nine written leaves.

iv. A similar book of the Mercers' and Drapers' Company, including also the "poticharys," haberdashers, chapmen, hosiers, tailors (35 names), and clothdrawers, with the particular and general orders and fines. Nine written leaves.

v. A similar book for the Clothiers' and Clothworkers' Company, including the dyers, weavers (30 names), shearmen (29 names), shuttlemakers, and ashburners, with the like orders and fines. Ten written leaves.

LVII. Vellum roll (of two membranes) containing "Divers actes and decrees by Edmund Plowden, Thomas Stafford, John Okeham, Richard Warde the younger, esquieres, and William Wollaston and Thomas Berington, gent.," commissioners appointed by Q. Elizabeth, by commission dated at Windsor, 22 Oct. an. 12 (1570) touching the rivers of Kennet and Loddon and all other rivers and brooks falling into the same. The orders (which are dated 7 March 1575) provide minutely for the deepening of a portion of the Hallowed Brook (parcel of the river Kennet) by the occupiers of the Abbey Mill, and for the careful cleansing of the brook and its protection from pollution, since the inhabitants of Reading "have chifely theiere water to brewe, bake, and dresse theire meate out of the broke." The precautions taken show sufficiently how the brook had been treated as a receptacle for all manner of refuse and filth. The mayor for the time being and such other inhabitants as have been mayor are appointed conservators of the river within the borough. There are also regulations for the floodgates of the mills, and a provision that during the months of April, May and June all the floodgates of the three mills shall be opened every Sunday morning before 4 a.m., and remain open until 6 a.m. on Monday, and be also open during the whole of Monday and Tuesday in Easter and Whitsun weeks. The roll is a certified copy of one of two originals, deposited with the clerk of the peace for the county; the other being deposited in the Court of Exchequer.

Parcel endorsed "Various ancient papers relating to the House of LVIII. Correction or Bridewell."
Orders for the government of the house; 18 James I. Payments, 1641–1651. "In the year 1642 the King's army tooke uppe their winter quarters in this towne of Reading, which was made a garrison for them, and likewise a garrison here in the year 1643, in which yeares the said House of Correction was made a court of guard by the soldiers, who did ruinate and pull downe a great parte of the said house."

A folio volume containing an account of "the practice of the borough LIX. court of Reading in personal actions." Written apparently about 1800.

Two framed tablets containing the arms of Reading, as attested by L. Heralds at their visitations; i. by Will. Hervye, Clareneieux, 6 Oct. 1566; ii. by Hen. Chitting, Chester, and John Philipot, Rougedragon, in 1623. (*See* Coates, pp. 453, 454.)

Small parcel endorsed "Grammar School."

1630, 13, 28 June.—Copies of two letters from the Mayor and bur- LXI. gesses to the bishop of Sarum, complaining of one Mr. Greenhill, who, 1. under the cover of the bishop's licence, teaches grammar in Reading to the prejudice of the Free School.

1631, June.—Draft of a letter to St. John's College announcing the 2. election of Will. Creed to the scholarship vacant by the preferment of Mr. Thomas Walker.

1636, 2 May, Westm.—Letter from Sir Francis Windebank, convey- 3. ing the King's pleasure that whensoever the School shall become vacant by avoidance of Andrew Byrd, M.D. (by whose pains and diligence it has become very considerable), it be not filled up without the consent and approbation of the Archbishop of Canterbury and the bishop of the diocese.

1636, 30 Nov.—Copy of a letter from the Mayor and burgesses to 4. archbp. Laud, informing him that Dr. Byrd died on Monday night last, and asking, in accordance with Secretary Windebank's letter, his direction.

Copy of a letter to St. John's College, Oxford, asking them to 5. recommend a master. [*See* p. 41.]

1640, 23 Nov.—Receipt from William Page, master, for his salary. 6.

1644, 4 Sept.—Copy of an order from the Committee for Berks for 7. the admission of Thomas Pococke, M.A., as master, with a copy of a certificate from the Mayor and others on his behalf.

1648, 7 Oct.—Account of the visitation of the School, and of orders 8. then made, signed by Ed. Reynolds, Vice-Chancellor of Oxford, Fr. Cheynell, President of St. John's Coll., and John Palmer, Warden of All Souls.

1649, 5 Oct.—Letter to the Mayor from Dr. Ed. Reynolds, Vice- 9. Chancellor of Oxford, and Fr. Cheynell, President of St. John's College, desiring that a sum of 20*l*. be given to Mr. Pocock on his removal from the School.

1649, 19 Oct., Oxf.—Letter from Francis Cheynell, President of St. 10 John's College, to the Mayor, recommending Mr. Waddon for the School, as civil, godly and learned, and wanting nothing but experience.

MSS. OF READING CORPORATION.

11. 1655, 5 July.—Copy of a letter to St. John's College, requesting recommendation of a master, on avoidance of Mr. Reeve.

12. 1651 (*sic*, mistake for 1655), July, Temple.—Letter from Bulstrode Whitelocke to the Mayor and aldermen, recommending Mr. Jennings for schoolmaster, on the testimony of Mr. Dighton, a bencher of the Temple, and Mr. Libbe, a neighbour to the Corporation.

13. Copy of a certificate from St. John's College in behalf of Robert Jennings, M.A.

14. 1655, 30 July.—Copy of a letter to St. John's College from the Corporation, acknowledging a letter of the 24th, recommending Mr. Jerrard; but having *this day* received a letter from the High Steward, the Lord Whitlock, and having also seen a certificate from the College giving a fair character of Mr. Jennings " our country man," they have elected the latter.

15. 1659, 4 Jan.—Appointment by the Mayor and Corporation of Rob. Edwards, M.A., as master. On parchment.

16. 1659.—" Bill of charges layd out by mee Rob. Jennings in defending the title of the Schoole of Reading from an order of sequestracion," amounting to £9 4s. 6d. Ordered that £5 of this be paid, 13 Feb. 1659.

17. 1660, 20 Feb.—Resignation by Will. Page, M.D., of his place as master. On parchment.

18. 1661, 10 May.—Release by Thos. Jerard, M.A., late schoolmaster, of all actions against the Corporation.

19. 1665, 6 Oct., Oxford.—Letter from Rich. Baylie, Pres. of St. John's Coll., to the Mayor. Wrote last Tuesday about the inability of the Vice-Chanc. to hold the visitation this year; they desire that no maid partake of Archbishop Laud's charity who has not showed herself careful in conformity to the doctrine and discipline of the Church of England, and has not lately received the Sacrament of the Lord's Supper; they recommend Sarah Hulebert, a maid-servant to the Lady Armorer.

20. 1686, 31 May } Receipts from Will. Gostwyke for his salary as
     1 Nov. } master.

21. 1680, 20 Nov.—Receipt from Thos. May, master; with one from S. Hughes, as vicar of St. Laurence.

22. 1770, 17 Feb. 2 April, 21 Miles Lane, London.—Two letters from Mr. W. Wise, to the Mayor, on information of his election to succeed Mr. Spicer in 1772.

23. 1770, 26 Feb., St. John's College, Oxford.—Letter to the same from Tho. Fry, on Wise's election.

The present Town Clerk has brought to light a volume of some interest in reference to the School. It is the record of the annual dinner of old members on the Visitation Day, 18 Oct., from the commencement in 1768 to 1817. The volume begins with the entry of a resolution that the undersigned persons agree to dine annually on 18 Oct., or pay 3s. 6d., "for the ordinary to the landlord of the inn where the meeting is appointed." The names throughout are arranged under the dates of entrance into the School.

The list of Mayors given in Coates' *History of Reading* (1810), begins at 1 Hen. IV. (1400). It may therefore be worth while to subjoin a list of earlier Mayors whose names I noted in the course of inspection, but which possibly might be further enlarged by still closer examination. MSS. OF READING CORPORATION.

18 Edw. II.	(1324–5).	John le Goldsmyth.
9 Edw. III., March	(1335).	The same.
9–10 ——	(1335–6).	Henry Foliot.
16 ——	(1342).	Walter de Staunton.
24 ——	(1350).	William Ruscel.
29 ——	(1355).	William Warde.
30–32——	(1356–8).	John Chaunterel.
34 ——	(1360).	William Warde.
37 ——	(1363).	John le Akatour.
39 ——	(1365).	William Warde.
40–42——	(1366–8).	John Farham.
44 ——	(1370).	William Catour.
45· ——	(1371).	John Farham.
49 ——	(1375).	The same.
51 ——	(1377).	Thomas Smyth.
2 Rich. II.	(1378).	William Catour.
,, ——	(1378–9).	Thomas Smyth.
3 ——	(1379–80).	Richard Budel.
4 ——	(1380–1).	William Catour.
5 ——	(1381–2).	Henry Ropere.
6 ——	(1382–3).	David atte Hache.
7 ——	(1383–4).	William Catour.
8 ——	(1384–5).	Thomas Berefeld *or* Thomas Smith.
9–11 ——	(1385–8).	Richard Bedewynde.
12 ——	(1388–9).	William Catour.
13 ——	(1389–90).	The same.
15 ——	(1391–2).	John Kent.
20 ——	(1396–7).	John Harald.
21 ——	(1397–8).	William Skoryare.
6 Hen. VI.	(1427–8).	William Huntyndon, omitted in Coates' list.
13 Hen. VII.	(1497–8).	Cristin Nicholas is described as " Magister gildæ burgi."

To the deed witnessed by Mayor Warde in 39 Edw. III. (noticed above p. 2), the town seal is attached, because the seal of the grantor was unknown; it has the same bearing as that which is now in use, five heads, with the inscription, partly broken, " [S'] communi[ta]tis Rad. . . . ."

WILLIAM DUNN MACRAY.

REPORT ON MSS. IN THE LIBRARY OF THE INNER TEMPLE.

The greater part of the rich stores of historical materials contained in this Library came to the Society of the Inner Temple by the bequest of William Petyt, Keeper of the Records in the Tower, the well-known writer on constitutional law, and controversial opponent of the historian Brady, who died 3 Oct. 1707. His own vast collections and transcripts from Records have been occasionally used and referred to by Daines Barrington and others; and the invaluable volumes of ecclesiastical MSS. OF THE INNER TEMPLE.

MSS. OF THE INNER TEMPLE.

papers, relating chiefly to the time of Queen Elizabeth, have been largely made use of by Strype. But no calendar of the contents of Petyt's books has hitherto been compiled, and their character is little known.; while of the materials for the history of the Roman recusants in the latter part of the 16th century, which are alike abundant and interesting, largely dealing with the conflict between the secular clergy and the Jesuits, no public use appears ever to have been made. Of two of the ecclesiastical volumes a portion of the contents was calendared, as a specimen of the collection, by Mr. H. T. Riley in the Second Report of this Commission; and additional notes, with some corrections, on this portion are here included. Whence it was that these volumes of ecclesiastical documents came into Petyt's hand does not appear. It may be conjectured, however, that he acquired the official papers of some one of the law-officers of the Court of Arches, possibly those of Dr. Richard Cosin. Some of the papers are stained with damp and injured, in the way in which such accumulations of a lawyer's chambers might be expected to suffer.

Besides the MSS. bequeathed by Petyt, the Library contains:—i. A large number of MSS., chiefly Law Reports, sent by the executors of Bishop Barrington, of Durham (which had doubtless been previously in the library of Daines Barrington) in 1823; ii. Some which were sent by the executor of Baron Maseres in 1825; iii. Reports purchased at Sir Charles Wetherell's sale; and, iv. Reports and common-place books, given by the Duke of Northumberland, through Mr. Martin, the late librarian to the Temple, who was also librarian to the Duke. Of the library of printed books of Sir Martin Wrighte, which were given to the Society, there is a MS. Catalogue. The whole series of MSS. —throughout are now sumptuously bound, chiefly in red morocco.

The following catalogue contains all the MSS. which possess historical or biographical interest. The purely legal MSS. are omitted, with a few theological and general MSS., which, with the exception of a beautiful copy of the *Somnium Scipionis* of Macrobius, of the early part of the twelfth century, are of trifling character. The catalogue was commenced some years ago by the present Deputy Keeper of the Public Records, but then laid aside; it has now been made *de novo*, but with the incorporation of a large portion of the notes then made for some of the volumes; for the free use of which the writer's best acknowledgments are due.

---

502. The Journals of the House of Commons from March 19, 1603–4 to Feb. 21, 1707–8; in 83 vols., folio.

Of the five vols. from Nov. 7, 1693 to Feb. 13, 1695–6, the late Mr. Saxe Bannister has made a note that they "are not to be found at the House of Commons."

503. fol.—Processus ad coronationem Geo. I. Given by G. Wrighte, clerk of the crown, in 1716.

504. Vellum. fol. ff. 242. Cent. XIV. 1. Natura brevium, p. 5. 2. Magnum Hengham, p. 21. 3. Parvum Hengham, p. 42.

4. Registrum brevium. This Register occupies 206 leaves; and is preceded by a table of contents. Among miscellaneous notes on some leaves at the end is an account in doggrel Latin of the "Curia de Domino Rege dicta sine lege," held before dawn at the manor of Kingshill in Rochford, Essex, written by a hand of the 15th cent. And on the last leaf is a list of successive owners, which affords a very rare instance of a record of ownership nearly from the time of the writing of the

volume to the present day. The name of "Welles" is written in large characters, and below is this note:—"Liber Ricardi Welles olim, nunc Willielmi Savage; ac postea datus per eundem Williclmum Savage Roberto Gayer nunc possessori vero; et, 1532, ad presens, Ricardi Fytt ex dono Petri Marker; et postremo Willielmi Barnesley." And by the last-named the volume was given to the Inner Temple. [MSS. OF THE INNER TEMPLE.]

505. Vellum. fol. ff. 260. Cent. XV.—The Statutes of England from 1 Edw. III. to 29 Hen. VI. An alphabetical index of matters is prefixed which occupies 38 leaves.

At the end of the 15th cent. it was "liber Ricardi Bukheved, ex dono Willielmi Massy, Interioris Templi generosi." Given to the library by Daines Barrington.

506. Vellum. fol. ff. 315. Cent. XV.—Another copy of the same Statutes, with the index; but wanting the first leaf in year 1 of Edw. III., and ending imperfectly in 23 Hen. VI. Also given by D. Barrington. Both these MSS. are well written, and in fine condition.

507. Sm. 4º. ff. 517. Proceedings in Parliament from 6 Feb. to 12 May, 1626.

508. Vellum. 8vo. ff. 220. Latter part of cent. XIV. One of Daines Barrington's MSS. The Statutes of England from Magna Charta to the stat. "de Scaccario," 14 Edw. II.; followed by "expositio vocabulorum," "assisa panis et cerevisiæ," "compositio monetæ," &c. At the end are added rules for calculating the golden number, leap-years, &c., based on Latin mnemonic verses; written apparently in the year 1400. They are headed, "Hic incipit le compound manuel."

509. Judgments in cases in the King's Bench, from 14 to 27 Geo. II. inclusive. 14 vols. fol.

510. fol. Year-book for the years 10–17 Edw. III. This is now in course of publication in the series of Year-books published by the Master of the Rolls, and the vol. is described at pp. x.–xii. of Mr. L. O. Pike's preface to the books for years 11 and 12, issued in 1883.

511. 1. Vellum. fol., in double cols. ff. 343. Cent. XIV.—The *Speculum Historiale* of Vincent of Beauvais, with many marginal corrections. On the first leaf is this note of ownership, in a hand of the 15th cent.: "Johannes Armorer, vicarius de Sutton Valince Hedecronkforde (?), modo rector de Penshurst."

511. 2. Vellum. fol., in double cols. ff. 132. Beginning of 13th cent.—"Historia Anglorum, sive Saxonum, post venerabilem Bedam, edita a magistro Roberto de Hovedan (sic)"; to the year 1181. At the end (f. 126b): "Explicit pars prima hystorie Anglorum post venerabilem Bedam illius gentis hystoriographum."

This beautiful and precious MS. was formerly "Liber Sancte Mariæ de Ryevallis"; afterwards of Rob. Constable, of Will. Bowyer, and of Rob. Bowyer of the Middle Temple in 1595. It was unknown to the Bishop of Oxford (Dr. Stubbs) when he edited this portion of the history in 1868–9; and has never been collated. That it would well repay collation may be conjectured not only from its age, but from a single passage which I have happened to note under the year 1176. Where in the printed text (II. 89) the Constitutions of Clarendon are inserted, the following note is given instead, which does not seem to occur in any other copy: "Si quis tamen eas videre aut legere desideret, in libro qui dicitur *Curialis* querat, et ibi plenarie eas inveniet." The text

MSS. OF TH INNER TEMPLE. of the history (in which Glanville's book *de legibus Angliæ* is omitted) ends on f. 125, with the words "titulo pignoris obligare. Vale" (Bp. Stubbs' edit. II. 257); and then follow these documents, in most instances agreeing with the Arundel MS. 150 (described *ibid.* 215 *note*). 1. "Quedam sentencia Willelmi Bastard." 2. Articles xxxii., xxxiii., xxxv. of Glanville's book. 3. "Descripcio genealogie ducum Normannorum." 4. "Decreta Alexandri pape tercii sicut superius promisi." 5. "Decreta Ricardi Cant. archiep. in conc. suo apud Lundonias postquam reversus est a predicto generali concilio." 6. "Ex decretali epistola Alex. papæ tercii ad Rogerum Wigorn. episc. de presbiteris fornicarias habentibus." 7. Extracts from decrees of various early councils and popes. On the last leaf is entered a copy of the acknowledgment by the Scottish lords of the sovereignty of Edw. I. in 1291, as sent by the King to the Abbey of Rievaulx; and a note of the decision given at the General Chapter of the Cistercian order in 1301, in a dispute between the abbot of [Savigny] and the abbot of Buildwas respecting the patronage of St. Mary's Abbey, Dublin. [See *Chartularies of St. Mary's Abbey*, edited by Mr. J. T. Gilbert, vol. I. 1884, p. 381.]

511. 3. Vellum. fol. Cents. XIII., XIV.—A curious collection of forms in ecclesiastical cases, with directions for the drawing up of pleas, interspersed throughout with original writs and documents of various kinds between the years 1278 and 1323. What appears to be a table of contents is prefixed on several mutilated leaves. It is probable that the volume may have formerly belonged to the Court of Arches.

511. 4. Vellum. fol. Cent. XIV.—"Registrum brevium;" imperfect at the beginning and end.

511. 5. Vellum. fol. ff. 267. Beginning of cent. XV.—The *Polychronicon* of Ralph Higden, in seven books, ending at 1377. The first leaf of the chronicle is wanting. In 1559 the book belonged to Francis Babington (who says in a note written in Greek characters that "Richarde Babincton is a knave as he saithe himself who best doth knowe") and afterwards to Edmund Parkinson.

511. 6. Vellum. 4°. ff. 446. End of cent. XV.
i. "Modus tenendi parliamentum."
ii. The Statutes, from 1 Edw. III. to 3 Hen. VII., inclusive.

511. 7. Vellum. fol. ff. 195. Cent. XIV.
1. "Historia Britannie conscripta per Robertum [Manning, de Brunne] in materna lingua." At the end (f. 95*b*): "Explicit historia Britannie transposita in linguam maternam per Robertum." The prologue, and the account of Stonehenge, are printed in the Appendix to Hearne's pref. to Langtoft, pp. xcvi–ci., clxxxviii–cxcvi. An edition of this earlier part of Manning's work has just been edited for the Master of the Rolls by Dr. Furnivall.

2. "Gesta Anglorum secundum Petrum de Langtoft, transposita per eundem R. Mannyng." Printed from this MS. by Hearne, in 1725, who gives the prologue at pp. cv–cvii of the Appendix to his preface. On a fly-leaf is "Iste liber pertinet Edmundo Pymond, vic. de Laghton"; and on others at the end are these notes, "This buke be delyverd at the syngn of the Bell in Doncastre for to be send to John Wyre dwelling at the parsonage of Laghton, a° 1522, x° die Marcii"; "Sell this book for v^s if you can."

511. 8. Vellum. fol. ff. 247. Cent. XV.—The Statutes, from 1 Edw. III. to 29 Hen. VI. inclusive, with the alphabetical index. Formerly "liber Johannis Croxton," and of John Leueson.

511. 9. Vellum. fol. ff. 136. Cent. XIV.—" Liber Johannis Byrche." MSS. OF THE INNER TEMPLE.

i. Statutes: Magna Carta, de Foresta, Merton, Marleberge, and Westm. I. and II.; with some later ones, ending with "Articuli statutorum Exoniæ."
ii. f. 65.—" Summa, Cadit assisa."
iii. f. 70*b*.—Parva Hyngham.
iv. f. 77*b*.—Tractatus bastardiæ.
v. f. 78*b*.—Excepciones contra brevia.
vi. fol. 85*b*.—Summa pro brevibus cessandis.
vii. f. 89. Registrum de Cancellaria. Forms of Chancery writs, with legal notes, amongst which occur the two following: (f. 119*b*.) " Sequitur nunc de brevibus de avo et avia que tempore domini H. Regis patris Regis E. per discretum virum dominum Walterum de Mertone, tunc secratarium (*sic*) et prenotarium clericum cancellarie domini Regis primo fuerunt inventa"; (f. 126) "Notandum quod istud breve consignatum fuit apud Cestre in excercitu (*sic*) Regis existente apud Rothel ad expugnandum Lewelinum et David inimicos domini Regis." Imperfect at the end.

511. 11. Partly vellum, chiefly paper. fol. ff. 247.

i. John Lydgate's Life of St. Alban in English verse (beg. "To calle Clio my dulnesse to redresse," end. " O prothomartir of Brutis Albioun,") with the colophon as in the MS., No. 44, described on page 23, vol. I., of Sir T. D. Hardy's *Catalogue of Materials*. ff. 1–65.

ii. ff. 66-169. The Brute Chronicle of England to the beginning of the reign of Henry VI. Begins :—" Here men mowe knowe how Engelonde firste was callid Albion and thorowe whom it hadde the name of Albion; In the noble londe of Surrye." Ends (after the account of the murder of King James of Scotland): —" peple that ar evell disposid he puttith hem under fote."

iii. ff. 172–208.—" The protestation of Walter Brute, sinner, layman, husbandman and a Christian, exhibited to the Byshop of Hereford for his defence." (Printed in Foxe's *Acts and Monuments*.") A transcript made about the beginning of the 17th century.

iv. ff. 221-247.—A sixteenth-century transcript of the work of Ailred, Abbot of Rievaulx, on the early kings of the English. Begins:— " Illustrissimo duce Normannorum ;" ends, " de te ad posteros transmittamus." (Printed in Twysden's *Scriptores Decem*.) The following notes, written in the same hand as the transcript itself are prefixed, the second being evidently copied from the MS. from which the history was transcribed. " Illustrissimus hujus nominis, Rogerus Hovenden historiographus splendidissiman hanc de Regibus Angliæ historiam contulit." "Liber magistri Willelmi Reed Episcopi Cicestrensis, quem emit a venerabili patre, domino Thoma Trilleck Episcopo Roffensi, Oretis igitur pro utroque, continens historiam de quibusdam Regibus Angliæ, inventam ac repertam in celeberrima bibliotheca monasterii de Merton."

511. 12. fol. Reports of cases *tempp*. Edw. VI., Mary, and Eliz. with a few of earlier date.

511. 13. fol.—A thick volume of miscellaneous legal collections in the time of Q. Eliz., including reports by judge Dyer, cases in the Star Chamber, Treatises of the Understanding the laws of England and of the Masters in Chancery, (printed by Hargrave in his *Tracts*), " Customes del citie de Londres."

511. 14. fol. Year books 38–42 Edw. III., and 3 Hen. VI.

511. 16. 4°.—Collections relating to ecclesiastical jurisdiction, and the dispute with the Archbp. of Canterbury respecting prohibitions and *modus decimandi* in the time of James I.

MSS. OF THE INNER TEMPLE.

511. 17. 4º.—Collections, chiefly from the Records in the Tower, relating to Scotland, from the time of Edw. I., including, "Commissions taken out of an auncient wrytten booke of the time of Edw. 4, found in the study of Mr. Rigby, Master of the Requests, and lent to mee by Mr. Serjent Harris, and by mee to my L. Buckhurst;" and "A journall of Scottish accidents" from 1581 to 1594, at ff. 35-51.

511. 18. Vellum. 4º. ff. 124.—Imperfect at the beginning, the first page being numbered, by an old pagination, 15. Cents. XIV., XV. A chartulary of the cathedral church of Sarum. (Privately printed by Sir Thomas Phillipps at Middlehill.)

511. 19. Vellum. 8vo. ff. 148. Cent. XIV.

i. "Litera a Sarazenis quibusdam in litera prescriptis domino Clementi pape nuper transmissa," "dat. anno Machametis viiº xli. die xviii. mensis Kalden;" (in a hand of 15th. cent.) f. 1.

ii. A short chronicle of England in rhyming Latin hexameters, with a genealogical table from Will. Conq. to Edw. III. Begins:—
"Dux Normannorum Willelmus vi validorum
Rex est Anglorum bello conquestor eorum."
Ends:—
"Princeps Edwarde, non sit tua lancea tardo
In Scotis mota, per te sit Cambria nota."

iii. A few French riddles, with English translations and answers. Cent. XV. f. 7. E.g.—"Plus haut que larbre, Hegher þan þe tree; þᵗ is þᵉ firmament. Plus profound que la mere, Depper þan þᵉ see, hell."

iv. f. 7 b.—Introductory note in French of the size of the rest of the volume, and its cost:—"En cest volume sount contenuz 19 quaiers et chescun quaier de perchemin jd. Et pur les alumpner vd. Et pur lescrive de chescun quaier iijd. La somme en tut " (erasure).

v. f. 8.—A Brute chronicle in French; how Albion was named England; headed " Ci comence lestoire des geantz." Begins :—" Ci poet homo saver qaunt et de quele gent les grauntz grantz vindrent Re Engleterre." Ends (f. 12b):—" Keen escripture les mettreit. Amen."

vi. f. 12 b.—Two notes in Latin about the contents of the chronicle.

vii. f. 13.—"Ci comence la Romaunce de Bruyt" (rubric). Begins:— "En la noble citee de graunt Troie." Ends (f. 146 b):—"pristrent totes les bestes et biens qe illoqes furent et ent firent lour volente," referring to the battle of Haddington. (See an account of similar manuscripts in the "Catalogue of the Arundel Manuscripts in the College of Arms," 1829, pp. 57-59, and the Second Report of this Commission, p. 7.)

viii. f. 146b.—Latin hexameters, etc. on the characters of "Sanguineus," "Colericus," "Malencolicus," and "Flemmaticus." (Cent. XV.)

ix. f. 147.—Translation into French of a letter from Pope Boniface to the English barons at Lincoln. (Cent. XV.)

511. 23. Sm. fol. ff. 137.—Arguments in various law cases, by, and in the handwriting of, W. Prynne. Amongst them are the following :—

i. f. 1.—" The case of the burrough of Tewksbery about Mr. Edward Stephens' election."

ii. f. 8b.—Case of Barking parish and the sequestrators of the vicarage, March, 1642.

iii. ff. 14-25.—Case of the printers of London before the committee for printing, with regard to the patents, 17 Chas. I., with notes on the origin of printing, and a list of early printed Bibles, especially English.

iv. f. 26.—St. Giles Cripplegate, concerning their vestrymen and vestry.
    v. (*MS. reversed*). — Case of Thomas Worsley, of Manchester, a recusant.
    vi. Case of John Reynolds, M.A., curate of St. Ivo's, against Will Court for libel, 18 Car. i.
    vii. Case of Cornelius Maguire, baron of Eneschallan in Ireland, Mich. 20 Car. I.
    viii. Mercantile and Admiralty cases.

512.—Collections by W. Petyt, in 26 vols. folio (distinguished by the letters of the alphabet up to BB.) respecting the government of England from the time of the Britons, the authority of Parliament, (including Petyt's printed tracts in his controversy with Dr. Brady) Scotland, Ireland, regal writs, &c. The volumes are frequently referred to by Daines Barrington in the third edit. of his *Observations on the Statutes*, and are cited by Strype and others. They contain many transcripts of documents from records in the Tower, as well as from printed books. Vol. F. consists of " A supplement to Dr. Brady's introduction to the old English history, by the author of *Jani Anglorum facies nova* " [Will. Atwood]. Vol. U: " Speculum Scotiæ, or a short view of the antient and modern government of Scotland, together with a brief account of that of England, by way of paralell," with an appendix of documents. Vol. W. " Historica collectanea de regno Scotiæ ex chartis antiquissimis, codicibus MSStis, chronicis typis exartisa, rotulis, schedisque pervetustis, in archivis Turris Lond. aliisque monumentis membranaceis alibi conservatis ; quæ appendice in qua varia instrumenta conjiciuntur, notis illustrata." AA. Royal charters, writs relating to ecclesiastical matters, election of bishops, &c. in the time of the Norman Kings, especially Will. I., II. BB. Collections relating to the reigns of John and Hen. III. Of the contents of all these volumes (with the exception of W. and partially of BB.) there are full lists in an old MS. catalogue of Petyt's collection preserved with his books.

515. 1. fol.—Placita de juratis et assisis temp. Edw. I.; at Worcester, Shrewsbury, and Newcastle-upon-Tyne.

515. 2.-5.—Placita coram Rege : tempp. Edw. I.–III.

515. 6.————tempp. Joh.-Hen.V.; with a glossary of obsolete words. These six vols. only contain short abstracts, made in the 17th century.

515.-7. fol.—An account for one year, from Oct. 1621 to Sept. 30, 1622, of petitions and orders thereon, of payments, warrants and letters, referring to and issuing from the office of the Lord Chamberlain.

There are warrants for payments to John Hemmings and his fellows as the King's players, to Ellisworth and his fellows, late servants to Queen Anne and now the company of the Revels, and to the Prince's servants, for the following plays : *The woman's plot* (5 Nov.) ; *The woman is too hard for him* (26 Nov.) ; *The Island Princes* (Dec. 26), *The Pilgrim* (1 Jan.), *The Wildgoose Chase* (24 Jan.), *The Coxcomb* (5 March) ; *Gramarcie wit* (30 Dec.) ; *The man in the moon drinks claret* (27 Dec.), and *The witch of Edmonton*, (29 Dec). There is also a privy-seal warrant (signed 25 July) for licensing Rob. Lee and others, late comedians to Q. Anne, " to bring up children in the quallitie and exercise of playing commedyes, histories, enterludes, morralls, pastoralls, stage playes, and such other like, as well for the solace and pleasure of his Majestie as for the honest recreation of such as shall desier to see them, to be called by the name of The Children of the Revells."

MSS. OF THE INNER TEMPLE.

MSS. OF THE INNER TEMPLE.

515. 8. fol.—Account of annuities, fees and allowances paid by the Exchequer in 1599.

515. 9. fol.—[Sir T.] Fanshaw's *Short compendium of what every officer of his Maj. Exchequer ought to do.*

516. fol.—Law reports, in the reigns of Eliz., Jas. I., and Chas. I., in six vols.

517. fol.—"Instructions for the Maister of our Wardes and Liveryes."

518. fol.—Arguments on the ecclesiastical question of Prohibitions, *temp.* Jas. I.

519. Large fol.—The arms of the nobility of England, in number 547, ending with the creations on 4 May, 1605; emblazoned in their proper colours. Given to the Society by John Hales, a Bencher.

524. Vellum fol.—Walter Hilton's *Scala Perfeccionis*: to which are prefixed "viii chapitres . . . . . founden in maister Lowis de Fontibus booke at Cantebrigge, and turned into Englissh by maister Waultier Hiltone de Turbaton." Well written and in fine condition. One leaf, or more, appears to be wanting at the beginning. It belonged to Bishop Gardiner, the inscription "Stephani Winton et amicorum" being on a fly-leaf at the end. One fly-leaf is part of Lydgate's prologue to his *Siege of Troy.*

526. f. 1. ff. 1–32.—Transcript of Sir F. Vere's narratives of the expedition to Cadiz in 1596, the " Island Voyage " in 1597, and the battles at Turnhoult and Newport; as printed in his *Commentaries* published in 1657.

2. f. 33.—Transcript of Bacon's dedication of his *Maxims of law* to Q. Eliz.

3. f. 42.—" Sir Walter Rawleigh's Apollogie " (*Works*, 1829, vol. VIII., p. 479).

527. fol. 1.—Transcript of the whole of Sir F. Vere's *Commentaries.*

ii. f. 39—Copies of letters from John Van Oulden Barnevelt to his wife and children, 12 and 13 May, 1619.

528. 4º.—Articles of the Treaty of Munster, 30 Jan. 1648, translated into English.

529. 4º.—Rich. Hakluyt's translation of Grotius' *Mare Liberum.*

529. A. 4º.—" The Life and Death of Henery our late famous Prince, together with his Funeralls " (by Sir Charles Cornwallis. Printed in 1641, and in Somers' *Tracts*, vol. II., p. 226, but with a different preface).

530. A. 4º. ff. 194.—A brief History of Scotland from 1436 to 1561, written by John Leslie, Bishop of Ross, in 1573, and dedicated to Q. Mary. (Printed for the Bannatyne Club in 1830.) On the fly-leaf there is the following note :—" This copie is not perfyte, and therfore is to be reformed in dyvers places conforme to the principall, quhilk is in the Quenis Majesties hands." This note, as well as the title of the book, is written in a Scottish hand different from that of the scribe of the volume, which is very neatly written.

530. B. 4º.—Three sermons preached by Alexander Strange, B.D., minister of Buntingford, Essex ; 1. at St. Mary's, Cambr., dedicated to Ralph Sadleir, esq., 1 Jan. 1610 ; 2. at the assizes at Hertford, 4 March, 1607 ; 3. at Woodhall Hatfield, at the anniversary commemoration of Sir Henry Butler, knt.

530. C. 12º.—Sermon for Christmas, by the same; presented to Mrs. Anne Sadleir of Standon.

530. D. 4°.—Two sermons by Th. Newcomen, dedicated to Mrs. Sadleir of Standon, dated at Clothall, 9 July, 1660.

530. E. 4°.—Meditation upon I. Cor. II. 24, by Ph. de Mornay, sieur du Plessis, "translated into English by R. C., Paris, 1609, September 22."

531. A. 4°.—Form of coronation of Kings and Queens of —England; "transcr. ex veteri chronico quod dicitur Brute." f. 1*b*. f. 4. Creation and succession of dukes, marquises, and earls, from the Conq., "gathered by D. P." In alphabetical order, from *Albemarle* to *Shrewsbury*. In 1590 the vol. belonged to "Fraunces Morre."

531. B. 4°.—Four sermons, in a somewhat singular hand, of the 16th cent.; to which is added by the same hand the often-printed "Relation of the desperate estate of Frances Spira in 1548."

531. C. 12°—"Israel and England parallel'd"; a sermon by Andrew Marvell, dedicated to Mrs. Anne Sadleir, 28 Apr. 1627.

531. E. 4°.—"A sermon preached at the funeralls of Sir Thomas Sadleir, knight, at Standon in Hertfordshire upon Shrove-Tuesday, being the xviith of February, 1606, by Robart Tounson," with a "narration of the life and death of Sir Thomas Sadleir" prefixed. On a fly-leaf, "Anne Sadleir."

531. F. 12°—Four sermons; amongst which, "A sermon preacht att Corby on the feast-day, 1654."

531. G. 12°—"A sermon at St. Sepulchre's the 29 of Januarie, 1623, at the funerall of that worthie citizen-vintner Mr. Anthony Cookson, by that famous divine Mr. Shoote, resident at —-—— in Lumbard Streete, London."

533.—"Records": Extracts from the Rolls, Proceedings in Parliament, Placita, and other records, from the reign of K. John to that of Edw. IV., both inclusive, in 38 vols., folio. The extracts are of the most general kind, relative to all the subjects within the scope of the documents from which they are taken. Full lists of the contents are given in Petyt's MS. catalogue before referred [to. Four volumes relate to the rights of the Commons in Parliament by prescription, in the reigns of Hen. III. and Edw. I., II., III.; from the second of which the returns printed at p. 35, vol. I. of Sir F. Palgrave's *Parliamentary Writs* were taken. Vol. 37 is "De electione et coronatione Gul. I. Hen. I. Steph. Hen. II. et Rich. I."; and vol. 38 contains "Monumenta parliamentaria tempp. Rich. I. et Joh."

534.—Rolls of Parliament from 5 Edw. II. to 6 Hen. VIII., with two volumes of Summons to Parliament; 33 vols., folio.

535. 1-2.—Charters of London, &c. collected by W. Petyt, when employed by the city to peruse their records for defence against the Quo Warranto brought by Chas. II.; 2 vols., folio.

535. 3. fol.—Extracts from the *Liber de Antiquis Legibus*; extracts about coronations, the reign of K. John, &c.

535. 4. fol. i.—Various private Acts of Parl., *tempp.* Edw. VI.-Eliz.

 ii. ff. 200–316.—Arguments of the judges, and other papers, concerning Mary Q. of Scots; with copies of papers of Sir R. Sadleir relating to his negotiations in Scotland.

 iii. f. 370.—Anglo-Saxon coronation oath.

 iv. f. 374.—Foundation charter of Ramsey Abbey.

 v.—Various ecclesiastical charters of Anglo-Saxon Kings, from books then or since printed.

 vi.—Writs and pleas relating to baronies and reliefs.

236   HISTORICAL MANUSCRIPTS COMMISSION.

MSS. OF THE
INNER TEMPLE.

535. 5. fol.—Statutes, Rich. II.-Rich. III.

535. 6. fol.—Various Acts of Parliament, Rich. III.-Hen. VIII., selected with the object of showing the wide extent of the "authority of Parliament." (See f. 115.) Transcript from Cotton Cleop. E. III. of the bull of Alex. VI. (f. 59) respecting the marriage of Hen. VII. John Leland's *New Year's gift* (f. 30). Ends with, "The unpresidented case of Sir Ralph Sadler, 37 Hen. VIII., and therein of the authority of the most high court of Parliament." (f. 335.)

536.—A series in 14 folio volumes of collections from the Rolls, Records of Parliament, and other sources, on various subjects; the volumes being entitled as follows:—

1. De pardonationibus.
2. De moneta. (At f. 172, "Sir Richard Sackvill's discourse (in his owne handwriteing) about decryeing of money."
3. Literæ procuratoriæ cleri in Parliamento. (At f. 42, "A most memorable record never before found out by anybody but myselfe that I ever heard of concerning a marriage to be had betweene Prince Edward and Alianor sister to the King of Castile, anno 38 H. 3, which marriage was assented to by the common counsell of the whole kingdome.")

4–8.—Theatrum criminalium. State Trials from 4 Edw. I. to 1631. In the first volume of this collection an example occurs of the probable value which may attach to many of the transcripts through the subsequent loss of the originals, in the following entry, at ff. 36–46. "Annales acephali ab anno 1195 a Ric. I. ad 35 E. 1., nempe 1307, ac etiam res sb 10 E. II. gestæ, luculentissime narratæ, in bibl. Cotton. sub effigie Othonis B. 3, f. 157*b*." This Cotton MS. was burnt in the fire of 1731.

9, 10.—Two volumes, "De provisionibus papalibus in Anglia;" including copies of bulls and letters.

11, 12.—Two volumes, "De creatione nobilium in parliamento et extra." "From these Rich. West, Lord Chanc. of Ireland, compiled a book entitled *Enquiry into the manner of creating peers*, 8vo, 1719." (MS. note in printed Catalogue.)

13, 14.—Two volumes "De cartis concessis civitatibus et burgis," from the time of K. John to Hen. VI.

537.—Journals of Parliament, Henry VIII.-Chas. II. 46 vols. folio.

538.—A series in 56 vols. folio, with the general heading of "Proceedings in Parliament, and Miscellanies": as follows—

538. 1-5.—Proceedings in Parliament, proclamations, manner of proceedings, rights of the House of Lords, chiefly in the time of James I., with a few papers in the first vol. of the time of Queen Eliz. Amongst the latter is, "a discourse of the providence necessary to be had for the setting up the Catholick faith when God should call Q. Eliz. out of this life;" from a MS. in Petyt's own custody.

538. 6.—Copies of commissions issued during the reign of Q. Eliz., with a few warrants for execution, &c.

538. 7-9.—Journals and Proceedings in Parliament, 1604, 1627-8, &c. including (in vol. 7) original rough Journals of the House of Lords in Jan.-March, 1620-1, and March-Apr. 1628; with earlier collections for the 14th and 15th centuries.

538. 10. i.—A curious series of transcripts of letters and petitions written by persons about the Court of Q. Eliz. between, as it seems, 1578 and 1588, but unfortunately without the signatures or addresses, except in a few instances. Some are from one F. A.; several refer to an application from a layman (an ecclesiastical lawyer and M.P.), for the prebend of Combe Nona in the Church of Wells, which he obtains and afterwards resigns,* with other applications from the same for church preferment, including Dr. Renniger's prebend at Lincoln; others, in Latin and English, are about a proposed history of Q. Elizabeth, apparently by the same person, which he begs may be recommended to the Queen; a vindication of himself from being supposed to favour the Q. of Scots by a speech made in Parliament, with a notice of his services in France. Several letters from Sir C. Hatton. The Earl of Arundel's letter to the Queen when he purposed to leave the realm. "A praier made by her Maj^{tie} vpon the setting furth of the army to Cales" (f. 6). Her speech touching the treasons of the Q. of Scots (f. 6b). ff. 4–81.

MSS. OF THE INNER TEMPLE.

On ff. 1–3 are prefixed these copies of verses :—
1. Epitaph on Will. Herbert, Earl of Pembroke, signed L. Ll., 88 lines.+ "Yeld, Phebus, teares, come, Muses mourne, come grone, you Graces three."
2. Twelve lines dedicatory of some translation to the Q. of Scots: "O Quene whose scepter prudentlie doth Scotland nowe defend."
3. Eleven lines struck out, beginning "Ah! silly pugge."
4. Fourteen lines, beginning, "The begger which from dore to dore doth wander with his mate."
5. "In praise of a contented minde. My minde to me a kingdome is, such perfect ioye therin I finde"; 8 triplet-stanzas. [By Sir Edw. Dyer?]
6. "*Per Reginam.* The doubt of future foes exiles my present joye." 16 lines.
7. Twelve lines: "The lowest trees have toppes, the ant her gaule."
Former possessors of this portion of the volume were "Thomas Aldwell," and John Maynard in 1639.
  ii. ff. 86–121.—"That Knight-service and other tenures were before the Conquest"; a long and closely written treatise.
  iii. ff. 122–125.—Answer of Jas. I. to the petition of the House of Commons, 11 Dec. 1621; with their protestation on 18 Dec.
  iv. ff. 129–140.—"An humble supplication to her Majestie, 11 Dec. 1595," on behalf of her Roman Catholic subjects.
  v. ff. 145–176, 190–202.—Journal, transcribed by Robert Bowyer, Clerk of the Parliament, of the Proceedings of the House of Lords, 19 March–7 July, 1601, 7 Feb. 1604–5, 5 Nov. 1605, 22 Jan.–6 May, 1606.

538. 11.—Miscellaneous notes and collections about Proceedings in Parliament.

538. 12.—Collections about summons to Parliament.

538. 13.—Miscellaneous Parliamentary collections; amongst which, 1. "A letter written to the Lower House touchinge divers inconvenyencies and grievances of State" (f. 12). 2. "Balaam's Asse, or a free discourse touching the murmurs and fearefull discontents of the tyme, directed to his then Majesty K. J." (f. 20). 3. The argument of W. Hakewill against impositions (f. 160).

538. 14. i.—Selden on Judicature in Parliament.

---

* The succession of prebendaries at this time is not given in Le Neve's *Fasti.*

MSS. OF THE INNER TEMPLE.

ii. f. 88.—"A discourse off the Highe Courte of Parliament and of the aucthoritye of the same."

iii. f. 127.—Titles of "Acts of Parl. remayning in the chappell of the Rolles," 1 Rich. III.–7 Jac. I.

iv. f. 199.—Copy of a letter from recusants to Sir Francis Hastings, remonstrating against the proposed aggravation of the penal laws.

538. 15.—Collections about the forms of Proceedings in Parliament.

538. 16.—Miscellaneous collections about the authority of Parliament, &c.; among which, i. W. Prynne's first reading on 17 Feb. 1661⁄2 on the Petition of Right (f. 2). ii. Sir Rob. Cotton's "Extracts out of the records . . . by what meanes the Kings of England have and may raise moneys" (f. 297).

538. 17.—Miscellaneous Parliamentary collections. The contents are as follows, omitting a few fragmentary notes of no importance.

f. 1. "Mr. Peter Wentworth his speech in the Parliament House, anno 1576, for which he was put into the Tower."

f. 8.—A speech in the House of Lords against the right of the King to be present at their debates.

f. 12.—Speech of the Duke of Buckingham, with his answers to the Speaker's questions, Jan. 14, 1673.

f. 16.—Table of the contents of a book of law collections, including the franchises of London and the liberties of St. Martin's-le-Grand, written on parchment by Mr. Fleetwood in 1576.

f. 16b.—List of the different Courts of Law in the realm (extracted from Fleetwood's book).

f. 17b.—Lord Bacon's advice to Sir Lionel Cranfield and all great officers of the Crown, "to remember a Parliament would come."

ff. 19, 126–184.—Notes from the Journals of Parliament; tempp. Edw. VI., Mary, Eliz., Jas., and Chas. I.

f. 31.—Notes from the Acts of the Privy Council 1547–1552, relating to Parliament; with a letter to Hen. Elsynge from Ra. Starkey (who collected the notes) dated at London, 3 Aug. 1624.

f. 33.—Speech of Queen Elizabeth in the Council Chamber to the House of Commons, Nov. 30, 1601.

f. 37.—Extract from the Lords' Journals, 7, 9, June, 1610.

f. 38 and 56.—Copies of a writ for the borough of Tewkesbury, March 30, 8 James I.

f. 40.—Copy of a letter giving an account of the state of affairs in England in the time of Charles II.

f. 44.—Argument in Council of Edmund, Archbishop of Canterbury, against Peter, Bishop of Winchester, and others, 1234.

f. 45. b.—Articles of Humphrey, Duke of Gloucester, against Cardinal Beaufort.

ff. 50, 58.—Notes from Rushworth's *Collections*, and the Lords' Journals, temp. Jas. I.

f. 62.—Answer to a letter concerning the jurisdiction of the House of Lords in cases of appeal.

f. 70.—"Cases of Priviledges of the King's servants during the time of Parliament."

ff. 80, 108.—Extracts from Foxe's *Acts and Monuments* about authority of Parliament.

f. 86.—"Sir Robert Holborne's replie to Mr. Sollicitor's argument in the case of the ship-money."

f. 90.—Extract from the Supplication of Souls by Sir Thomas More.

f. 94.—A letter from G. Evelyn to Roger James, dated Nutfield, Aug. 7, 1676. Mr. Hampton says that his good friend and intimate acquaintance Sir Henry Spelman often complained to him that the Licenser had dashed out a great part of the Epistle Dedicatory prefixed to his Collection of Councils reflecting a little on Bishop Laud's designs of hierarchy, but that he never complained of any injury done to him with respect to his Glossaries.

MSS. OF THE INNER TEMPL.

    f. 92.—Queries about the Parliament of Scotland.
    f. 93.—Queries relating to the English Constitution.
    f. 100.—Observations on Magna Charta.
    f. 105.—Observations on the Parliament of Scotland.
    f. 107.—Notes from various chronicles.
    f. 120.—Observations on miscarriages which have occasioned the poverty and low condition of Tangier.
    f. 124.—Letter from John Mainwaring to Mr. Petty (Petyt) concerning the county palatine of Chester.
    f. 185.—Precedents to show that the Kings of England have been acknowledged to have the sovereignty of the Sea; in a letter.
    f. 217.—" A draught of an intended act against Popery"; 1674.
    f. 225.—Draft of " A bill for a general Test to distinguish between Papists and Protestants, etc."
    f. 231.—The Act prohibiting appeals to Rome.
    f. 237.—Protest "before the Lord Jesus Christ" against "Lord Henry Darby" (Henry IV.) after his accession to the throne, in ten articles.
    f. 245.—Proclamation against the Lord Protector Somerset.
    f. 251.—Peter Wentworth's report of the proceedings against him in the Court of Star Chamber.
    f. 257.—Notes about writs of *habeas corpus* and mainprise, being apparently heads of a speech upon a bill in Parliament.
    f. 262.—Mr. William Daniell's speech to the Irish submitters, delivered before the Council in Ireland, April 27, 1609.
    f. 264.—A letter from Ralph Cudworth to William Petyt, dated March 2, 1677, thanking him for his gift of Poole's *Synopsis* and Castell's *Lexicon* to Christ's College, Cambridge.
    f. 266.—Notes about the office of " Philizer " (Filazer) in the Courts of King's Bench and Common Pleas.
    f. 268.—Letter from the Earl of Salisbury and Sir Julius Cæsar to Rob. Bowyer and Henry Elsyng, the keepers of the records, authorizing Will. Tipper to make searches without paying fees; 16 May, 1609.
    f. 270.—Sir Edw. Coke to Bowyer, for copies of Acts of Parl. *temp.* Hen. VI.; 16 Dec., 1609.
    ff. 271, 281.—Two letters from Archbishop Bancroft to the same for loan of books, &c.; 9 Mar. 1608, 4 Nov. 1608.
    f. 273.—Sir Henry Hobarte (Attorney-Gen.) to the same, for copies of records relating to the forest of Mendip; 8 Dec. 1609.
    f. 274.—Proofs desired by the Earl of Northampton, Lord Warden of the Cinque Ports, as to his authority in certain cases; 4 Nov. 1609.
    f. 275.—The Earl of Salisbury to Bowyer, authorizing his servant Will. Hill to make searches without fees; Basing, 8 Aug. 1609.
    f. 288.—The same for John Watkis, 3 July, 1608.
    f. 277.—Particulars by Mr. Baron (George) Snigge of lands belonging to the monastery of Bath ; 27 June, 1609.
    f. 278.—Lord Ellesmere to Mr. Robson, clerk in the Records, for a copy of a record ; 4 Feb. 1608.
    f. 279. Sir Francis Bacon to Bowyer for the loan of copies of records about the King's prerogative collected by Mr. Heneage; 27 Feb. 1608.

MSS. OF THE INNER TEMPLE.

f. 283.—E[dward, Lord] Bruce to Bowyer and Elsyng, for information; Rolles, 29 Oct. 1608.

ff. 285, 314.—Two letters from John Parkinson to Elsyng, for copies of some records *de natis transmarinis*, for the Attorney General, 10 and 27 Apr. 1608.

f. 287.—Order from Henry Hobarte (Attorney-Gen.) for verification of copies for Mr. Marrett, the King's advocate in Jersey; 14 May, 1608.

f. 289.—Letter from Gerard Langbaine to John Selden; about the readings in Oxford MSS. of the first Epistle of St. John of the text of the Three Witnesses; about Selden's forthcoming edition of the *Decem Scriptores*, and the works of Ailred of Rievaulx; Queen's Coll., 17 Nov. 1651.

f. 291.—Letter from Cudworth to Petyt, thanking him for the gift to the College of his book on the *Commons' Right*; Chr. Coll. 16 Oct. 1679.

ff. 293, 298.—Two letters to the same from his cousin, Thomas Barlow, Bishop of Lincoln; will do what he can for the young man he recommends; (*in both*) desires him to thank "that excellent and worthy person" lord Essex for kindness shown by him; acknowledges gift of the book on the *Commons' Right*, which he will carefully read; Buckden, 6 Oct., 11 Dec. 1679.

f. 294.—Case of Capt. Waters and a serjeant of his company, in K. B., 25 Car. II.

f. 296.—The Earl of Essex to Petyt, about a debt due from the executors of the Duke of Richmond to the Earl of Chesterfield; 2 May, 1680.

f. 298. Latin letter from Joseph Idzikowski, a Pole, formerly of the Order of Preachers, to the same; has returned from Holland to this "Angelicam, Anglicam loquor, patriam"; begs help for the printing of a book which is to be dedicated to the Prince of Orange.

f. 302.—J. Tyrrell to the same; finding that Petyt is writing on the same subject as himself, against Sir R. Filmer, begs him freely to use the papers he has sent; Oxford, 12 January.

f. 305.—Edward Pococke to Selden, about a MS. of Albumasar which was in Mr. Greaves' hands, but probably pulled in pieces when his study at Gresham College was ransacked; Oxon. 11 Feb. 165¾.

f. 307.—The Earl of Rutland to Sir Francis Windebancke, about a petition respecting his rights in one of the royal parks; Belvoir, 21 June, 1640.

f. 309.—The Earl of Bedford to Sir Archibald Primrose, Lord Register of Scotland, desiring him to expedite the hearing of a cause; Bedford House, 6 Dec. 1661.

f. 315.—Rich. Connock to Bowyer, for searches by Mr. Paddon on behalf of some business of the Prince's; 15 Dec. 1607.

ff. 317, 320.—Hen. Hobarte to the same; two letters for searches by J. Parkinson, &c.; 5, 11, March, 1607.

f. 318.—Letter from Bowyer to Connock, in answer to the letter above; 17 Dec. 1607.

f. 321.—E[dward Lord] Bruce to Bowyer and Elsing for searches by Will. Hackwell under special order from the Queen; Rolls, 23 March, 1606.

f. 324.—Sir Lawrence Tanfild, for searches by Edm. Duffild concerning the manors of Tew and Spelsbury in Oxon.

f. 326.—Draft of a petition from inhabitants of Middlesex to Parliament about Sheriffs' bills of Middlesex; *imperf.*

f. 332.—Warrant from the Earl of Salisbury to Bowyer for searches by Rob. Treswell; 22 Sept. 1610.

MSS. OF THE INNER TEMPLE.

f. 334.—Submissive acknowledgments of the Filacer and Exigenter of London in the Court of C.P. of the mistakes and offences of their clerks in the making of process of Exigent against Isabella, Lady De La Warre.

f. 336.—Warrant from the Earl of Salisbury for searches by Henry Mason concerning the possessions of the Duke of York; 14 March, 1609.

f. 338.—Warrant from Ranulph Crewe, Speaker of the House of Commons, for a new writ for the borough of Chippenham, 11 April, 1614.

f. 340.—" A particular of such Records as are in the Round Tower in Yorke, and were under the custody of Mr. Beesley, 6 Nov. 1610." An interesting list of 137 chests and boxes and 7 bags, with notes of their contents.

f. 341.—Letter from Will. Atwood to Petyt, on Petyt's book and Atwood's own collections.

f. 343.—Warrant from Lord Burghley to Thobic Houghton the King's Woodward general in the counties of Northampton and Rutland, respecting the manor-house of Collyweston; 10 Feb. 1589.

ff. 345, 350.—Two letters from Obadiah Walker to Petyt, concerning the preparation for publication of various Chronicles, Plot's *Oxfordshire*, and the *Life of Ælfred*, and concerning the oath of the Saxon Kings; University College, Oxford, 9, 30 Nov. 1676.

f. 347.—Letter from Kingsmill Lucy to his cousin Petyt, inviting him to Lord Berkeley's house, Durdens, near Epsom; 11 July, 1674.

f. 348.—Michael Tisdall to the same, about the records preserved at Dublin, of which the oldest is a small Pipe Roll of K. John; many were destroyed during the rebellion; Dublin, 4 July, 1674.

ff. 352, 354.—Two lists of the books and writings of Sir Edward Coke delivered to Sir John Bankes, the Attorney General, by Sir Francis Windebank, 9 July, 1636, and returned by him to Windebank, 20 March 1639.

f. 356.—Letter (in English, without address) from Don Alonzo de Cardenas the Spanish Ambassador, signed by him and dated June 9, 1640, stating that he has appointed Mr. Anthony Morgan to levy and transport the residue of the two thousand soldiers graciously afforded to him by the King of Great Britain, Captain Edwards who was lately charged with that duty having been ordered to return speedily into Flanders.

f. 358.—Letter from Sir John Marsham to Petyt, on the name *Parliament*; sends him a collection of the parliaments of Will. I., II.; Halling, 12 June, 1677.

f. 359.—Copy of the funeral certificate of Sir Thomas Windebank, deceased 23 Oct. 1607, with a trick of his coat of arms.

ff. 361–368.—" Of Thomas Lord Coventry, late Lord Keeper of the Great Scale of England. Some notable observations in the course of his life and ultimum vale to the worlds." Begins:—"To trace him in the beginning." Ends:—" his posteritie surviving remaines in his honor and fortunes."

f. 372.—Copy of an inscription for a monument of Edward, Earl of Clarendon, made by Payne Fisher,

f. 373.—Letter from the Earl of Shaftesbury to the Countess Dowager of Arundel and Surrey, desiring her to appear in Chancery to answer a bill preferred against her by Will. Williams; Exeter House, Jan 29, 1672.

f. 375.—Historical notes about the Temple and Clifford's Inn in London, from Records in the Tower.

MSS. OF THE INNER TEMPLE.

f. 382.—Copy of a proclamation made by the Lord Lieutenant and the Council of Ireland, Jan. 24, 1672, in support of the Act of Settlement.

f. 384.—Letter from Edw. Peck to "Mr. Petty;" is unable to act as counsel in some cause; 27 March, 1669.

ff. 386–412.—Historical notes about the Temple and the Templars, with "Finch's argument" in a suit between the Temple and the City of London; Order in Council of 7 Apr. 1669; and a history of the two Inns. Some extracts from these notes are given in Addison's *History of the Knights Templars*, 1842.

f. 415.—Notes on the office of Clerk of the Council to the Prince.

ff. 417, 419.—Valuation of the lands to be assigned to the Prince of Wales in different counties, and list of the advowsons belonging in the 17th cent. to the Duchy of Cornwall.

f. 421.—Description of the ruinous condition of Carnarvon Castle, and notes on the constable's fees, subsequent to the death of Sir John Harington, constable.

f. 423.—Fees agreed on by the Council of the Duchy of Cornwall, 18 May, 1618, for the passing of leases to the tenants in the county and bishopric of Durham; with 9 signatures, including that of Sir Oliver Cromwell. f. 432.--Another table of fees, with 10 signatures; 16 May, 1623.

f. 425.—Table of the revenues and debts of Henry Prince of Wales drawn up after his death by Richard Connock, 22 Dec. 1613. It mentions " certen meddalls of gould and strainge coyne which cost his Highness £2,200."

f. 427.—Letter from the Lords Commissioners of the Admiralty to the Council of the Prince of Wales, rebuking them for summoning the Vice-Admiral of the North of Cornwall to appear before them in Fleet Street; signed by the Bishop of London, Earl of Lindsey, Sir Francis Cottington, and others; 11 Nov. 1637.

ff. 430–439.—Schedules of the property of the Duchy of Cornwall, etc.

f. 440.—Letter from Sir Edward Hyde to Will. Loving, auditor to the Prince at St. Ive's, desiring him to call on the following morning as soon as possible, bringing with him all the money he could get. Pendennis, 1 March 1645. In Edgeman's handwriting, signed by Hyde.

f. 442.—Lord Cornbury to the same; will be with him in Westminster to-morrow morning; not dated.

f. 444.—Holograph letter from Sir Edward Hyde to the same, addressed, "Monsieur Loving, chez Monsieur Carew, marchand a Dunkerke," thanking him for congratulations on his "unseasonable promotion" to be Lord Chancellor, and for sending him some books; desires also to have the Statutes made this last Parliament "by this noble Protector;" Bruges, 24 Jan. [1658].

f. 448.—Copy of the Latin hymn *Dies iræ*, subscribed as written "by Shaftesbury, 1710."

f. 450.—Rental of the manor of Spalding, 1604.

f. 452.—Fines levied of the manor of Spalding in the reign of Henry VIII.

f. 461.—Privy Seal warrant for the restoration of Ulick, Earl of St. Alban's and Clanrickard, to his estates in Ireland, signed by Charles II., but not dated. See below, f. 469.

f. 464.—Letter of William (Juxon) Bishop of London, notifying the appointment of one Mr. Sydney to the office of Clerk of the Commission of Recusants' Compositions; 20 Oct. 1640.

f. 466.—Letter from Sir Francis Cottington. The Bishop of Lincoln has offered to give the adowson of Wheathamstead which is worth at least £300 a year, and where there is a very old incumbent. The King has signified his pleasure for the passing of the Great Seal in Lord Bedford's affair. "We might have had £6000 reddie money for the revertion of Mr. Brounlo's place," if the King had not, as he understands, given it to the Marquis Hambleton, if that must be, "put his Majestie in mind how much he wants the office of *Contador de mercede*, concerning which I have spoken so often to him. Money of necessitie we must have from the farmors, and how it wyll be gotten with the course we hold for my part I know not." Desires to know whether the Committee for the Treasury meets on the following morning. "I pray tell the King that the pale in the new parke is now finished all but the gate." Salisbury House, 19 May 1635.

MSS. OF THE INNER TEMPLE.

f. 467.—A letter from Christopher Wren to his "very worthy friend Dr. Stokes, at his lodging in Eaton College," dated 23 Oct. 1639, "horâ somni." It his impossible for him "in such a scantlinge of time" to draw up the state of the dennery lease, but he will draw a breviate of the particulars of most moment, and give or send it to Mr. Secretary. There are two great persons that greedily seek it and make very great proffers to some that are Wren's agents in the cause, but he has very great reasons to decline these solicitations, and has resolved to throw it into the arms of so honourable a friend unclogged and free from such conditions as may deter him from meddling with it. (Seal of arms.)

f. 469.—Privy Seal warrant for the restoration to the Earl of St. Alban's and Clanrickard of castles, manors, etc., within the King's intended plantation in certain counties in Ireland, signed by Charles II., but not dated.

f. 471.—Copy of a commission from the Committee of the Revenue appointing Sir William Brereton, Bart., to the office of Keeper of the Castle of Eccleshall, co. Stafford, during pleasure, 24 June, 1646, and of an order of the same for delivering possession to him, 14 Sept. 1646.

f. 472.—Copy of an order of the same Committee that Sir William Brereton should have the manor and park of Brewood, co. Stafford, for one year, at a rent of £66 3s. 24 June, 1646.

f. 473.—Letter from Lord Wentworth (afterwards Earl of Strafford) to Francis Windebank at Holyhead. Sends the bearer with a boat of Howth to await Windebank's return and to bring over his packet if the wind will not suffer the post-bark to come over, and then Windebank himself is to follow in the post-bark. If, however, the post-bark be ready and the wind stands right, Windebank is not to deliver the packet to the bearer, but to bring it over himself and deliver it into the writer's hand with all convenient speed. Dublin Castle, 9 May 1634.

f. 475.—A letter in Latin from Thomas Reade to his uncle [Sir Fr. Windebank], commending his fortitude, and deploring his possible imprisonment and execution. New Coll. [Oxford], 23 Nov. 1640.

f. 476.—Letter from Sir Robert Heath to Mr. Read. Begs him to move Mr. Secretary to move the King to sign a warrant for a writ of error in parliament to reverse a judgment given against Mrs. Hyde, a poor widow, in an ejectment from her dwelling house in Fleet Street. 5 Nov. 1640.

f. 477.—An order from Lords Manchester, Bridgewater, Anglesey, and others, for the production of certain records concerning capital cases *tempp.* Edw. II.-Hen. VI., to the House of Peers to-morrow; 27 Nov. 1667; with a rough list following.

Q 2

MSS. OF THE INNER TEMPLE.

f. 479.—Note on the privilege of the servants of the nobility; 27 Jan. 1628.

f. 481.—Letter from J. M. [John Mill ?] to Will Petyt, thanking him for reading some difficult and "rude characters" in a MS. for him. Queen's College, Oxford ; 8 June 1676.

f. 482.—Copy of a letter from Petyt to Sir John Cotton, concerning the antiquity of the House of Commons. Inner Temple, St. Jude's day, 1676.

f. 483.—Copy of a letter from Petyt to [John Mill ?] at Queen's College, Oxford. Has ascertained from Mr. [Obadiah] Walker that the edition of Sir Henry Spelman's "Glossary," printed in 1664, is not really genuine, incorrect additions having been made, of which he mentions an instance under the word *parliamentum*. Mr. Walker is willing to print a third edition with 1,000 additional words, if sufficiently subscribed for. Questions about the original MS. at Oxford. 19 March 1675.

f. 483b.—Copy of the answer to the above. Mr. Walker says that the University does not possess the original of the additions to the Glossary. It was made from loose papers and printed by Spelman's grandchild with thousands of errors, which will be in some measure corrected when a third edition is published ; both Mr. Hide, the library keeper, and Anthony Wood, assure him that the University does not possess the original MS., but they bought the printing of all Sir Henry's works of Henry, brother of George, son of John, son of Sir Henry, as Mr. Walker, who was a great promoter of the purchase, informs the writer. "I suppose you have heard that the Countesse of Pembroke is dead. It was so customarie to report her to be so about the great Rent-dayes, that I could not beleive itt, till the other night that I received a letter by post, which acquainted mee punctually with the day and houre of her departure, scilicet one Wensday before Easter about 6 a clock at night." 7 Apr. 1676.

f. 485.—Copy of a letter from Petyt to Mr. Bowyer, concerning the supposed falsification of Sir Henry Spelman's Glossary, and Sir Henry's complaints in his lifetime (as alleged by one Mr. Hampton, a learned divine near Blechingley, in Surrey), of alterations made in his books by the licensers. 20 June 1676.

f. 487.—"Apology of the Commons touching their priviledges." 1 Jac. I.

ff. 511–13.—Extracts from the Journals of Parliament about Rushe's case of privilege 1 Jac. I., and Ensign Bower's case in 1628.

f. 513b.—Report of the case of Capt. Waters in B.R. 25 Car. II.

ff. 517–533.—Extracts from the Lords' and Common's Journals, about cases of privilege ; *temp.* Car. I.

ff. 534–8.—Extracts from Foxe's *Acts and Monuments*.

ff. 540–548.—Extracts from the Lords' and Commons' Journals about debates on the defence of the nation in 1625, and Sir John Bennet's case in 1621.

f. 550.—Legal questions about the impeachment of Lord Strafford.

f. 554.—Extracts from the Lords' Journals about proceedings against the judges, 1640-1.

538. 18. — Contemporaneous reports of speeches, petitions, the "Remonstrance," etc., and Journals of Proceedings in Parliament in the years 1623, 1625, 1626, 1627, 1628, some of which differ a little from those printed in Cobbett's *Parliamentary History* and in the Lords' Journals ; ff. 1–442. Among other papers bound together in this volume are :—

f. 29.—"The danger wherein the kingdome nowe standeth," by Sir Robert Cotton (printed in his *Posthuma*, p. 311). Another copy occurs at f. 400. MSS. OF THE INNER TEMPLE.

f. 120.—A paraphrase of the first and second Psalms, said to have been "written in high Dutch by a blasphemous Jesuite." It begins, "Blessed is the man that doth not walke in the councell of the Kinge of Denmark, nor standes nor treades in the way of the States, nor sittes in the seate of Mansfeild, but his delight is in the lawe of the Emperor." "Mounser Tilly" is mentioned several times.

f. 143.—Copy of a letter from a minister of the King of Poland to the King of England, asking for aid against the Turks.

f. 160.—Proceedings against Roger Manwayring, D.D.

f. 183.—An abstract of a writing presented to the Emperor by tho Electors and Princes of the Diet at Ratisbon, 21 Feb. 1623, and of the last resolution of the Emperor two days later.

f. 187.—Arraignment of Frances Carr, Countess of Somerset; 24 July 1616.

ff. 200b–254.—Copy of a letter from the Lords of the Council to the King, on behalf of Lord Chief Justice Coke, 26 June 1616, followed by copies of letters from Queen Elizabeth to Sir A. Paulett, Sir Walter Raleigh (21 March 1617, with account of his voyage to the W. Indies, and to his wife, &c.), the Earl of Essex, Sir Thomas Egerton to Essex, and many other well-known papers of the time, taken from an old commonplace book.

f. 265.—"Mr. Burgess his catachisme, vicear of Whitney, Oxon.," against the Puritans, with the articles exhibited against him in Parl.

ff. 275–296.—Notes as to the liability of peers to arrest.

f. 301.—"A collection out of the antient statutes [&c.] as of the nature and order of a parliament; liber secundus."

ff. 311–330.—Notes as to procedure in Parliament.

ff. 339–350.—Copies of a few letters and speeches by Sir Henry Sydney in Ireland in 1566, Lord Lucas in 1671, &c.

f. 356.—"Repertorium sive Elenchus Parliamentorum" Edw. III.-Edw. IV. An alphabetical table compiled in 1644.

f. 383.—The verses by the Earl of Essex, entitled "The discontented Courtier." Beg. :—
"It was time when sillie bees could speake." Ends :—
"T'was not tobacco had stupified my braine."

f. 385.—Apology of the Earl of Essex, addressed to Mr. Anthony Bacon, 1599. (Printed in 1603.)

f. 404b.—"Copy of a letter which was found amonge Jesuits that were lately taken att London and addressed to the father rector at Bruxells" concerning the state of the kingdom.

f. 420.—"Note of such monyes as I have received since I first came to London from Mr. James Ravenscroft."

ff. 443b–4.—An index of proper names in some book.

f. 445 —Notes about the legislative power in Ireland.

538. 19. fol.—Miscellaneous collections.

f. 1.—Examination of the Earl of Southampton and others, 1621.

f. 5.—Proceedings in Parliament, 21 Edw. III.

f. 12b.—Proceedings in Parliament, 5 Edw. II.

f. 14.—"A recitall of the celestiall apparitions of this present trigon now in being"; by Sir Christopher Heydon, commencing at 1603, with interpretations of the conjunction and eclipse in 1603-5, and the comets in 1607 and 1618, and prognostications to the year 1623.

—f. 37.—George Cavendish's notes of the life of Cardinal Wolsey.

MSS. OF THE
INNER TEMPLE.

f. 61.—Causes of "the want of moneys in this land: a representation to Parliament from the merchants of London in 1622.

f. 69.—"A cronologicall deduction concerning the . . . . treaties between the crown of England and the House of Burgundy," with reference to the exportation of English cloth.

f. 75.—Arguments in the Exchequer, Mich. 4 Jac. I. (1606) respecting impositions, in the case of the monopoly of currants.

f. 91.—The protestation of the House of Commons for their privileges, 1 Jac. I.

f. 107.—"A collection of the severall recordes in the fower treasuries at Westminster, in the office of recordes in the Tower, and in the King's remembrauncer's office"; with a list of all the Fine rolls, and of the treaties between England and other States preserved at Westminster, from 1 Hen. I. (1100–1) to 1593; written after 1615.

f. 150.—How "the Kings of England have supported and repaired their estates": [by Sir Robert Cotton.] Printed in Cotton's *Posthuma*.

f. 185.— Considerations upon the treaty for the Spanish match. Beg. "The essentiall pointes thereof seeme to be."

f. 190.— "The fishing project," for encreasing English shipping and fisheries; submitted to James I. (Lubeck has 700 great ships, Hamburgh about 600, Embden "late a fisher towne, and within the memory of man knowne not to have above 60 shipps at the most, hath nowe fully 1,400, which are allmost as much as belongs to all England," Holland "20,000 sayle of shipps and hoyes, which is more then are in all England, Fraunce, Spaine, Portugall, Italy, Scotland, Denmarke, Poland, Sweden, and Russia, all put together.")

f. 200.—A list of all the public bills passed and under consideration in Parliament in 1621–2.

f. 206.—"A treatis touching the auctoriti and practis of the Starred Chamber." Beg. "As in the governement of all commonweales."

f. 226. — "A discourse concerning the antiquitie of the Starre Chamber, occasionyed by certaine articles made by the atturnyes againste the Courte and Clarke of the same;" 1590.

f. 271. — The case touching the monopoly of playing cards, granted to Edward Darcy, Esq., argued in Mich. term. 44 Eliz. (1601).

f 284b.—A commission touching ordinances to be observed by the Warden of the Fleet, and his fees, 3 June, 3 Eliz. (1561).

f. 290. — Speeches in the Star-Chamber, 14 Nov. 1619, at the judgment on the Earl of Suffolk and his wife, and Sir John Bingley, or corruption in the office of the Treasurership of England.

538. 20. fol.

i. p. 1.—Copy of a Journal of the House of Commons, 35 Eliz.; 19 Feb.—9 Apr., 1593, "very laboriouslie collected, though in divers places somewhat defective." Collected by a member. Notes of speeches by Sir W. Raleigh frequently occur.

ii. p. 199.—"Diurnall occurrences, or the heads of proceedings in both Houses of Parliament," 3 Nov. 1640—18 April 1641, in May, July, Aug., Nov. 1641, and April and May, 1642, confusedly bound.

iii. p. 617.—The judges' arguments in the case of ship-money, 1638.

iv. p. 680. "Orders betweene the Heralds at Armes and Serjants at Armes touching their places, made 3 Sept. 1417." With an explanation of the service and fees of the Serjeant-at-arms.

v. Copy of a petition from Richard Terrell, esq., Warden of the Prison of the Fleet, and all the prisoners in the said prison to Sir Nicholas Bacon, knt., Lord Keeper.

vi. p. 684. "Constitucions and Orders to be renued, graunted, and established touching the government of the Fleet and prisoners there by the Warden thereof," 1561. (Twelve of the thirteen articles here given are printed in a volume entitled "*The Œconomy of the Fleete*," published by the Camden Society, pp. 157–159. The twelfth article in this MS. runs :—" Item that the said Warden shall take of every man or woman that shall sitt at the parlor commons twoe shillings foure pence weekly for his bedd and chamber, and of every man or woman that shall sitt at the hall commons weekly 14*d*. for his bedd and chamber, lyeing like prisoners 2 in a bedd together." The thirteenth article in this MS. corresponds with the twelfth in the printed version.) — MSS. OF THE INNER TEMPLE.

vii. p. 685.—Copy of the answer of the Warden of the Fleet and the prisoners there to Sir William Petre, Sir Robert Catlin, and the other members of the Royal Commission, concerning the prices which they thought meet that every prisoner might reasonably pay for his weekly commons. —" Wee the prissoners here undernamed haveing deliberatly consulted thereopon doe now condiscend and agree with the assent of the Warden there that every persone of the degrees hereunder written for there weekly commons and wine, over and besides the rate for their bedd and chamber by your honors in the booke of Constitucons already assigned, shall weekly pay according to the rates hereafter declared : That is to say, a knight and a lady the wife of a knight, a doctor of divinitie and other of like calling haveing 200 markes a yenre liveing, xviij*s*. & vj*d*. An esquire, a gentlemen or gentlewoman, that shalbe at the parlor commons or any person or persons under the degree that shalbe at the same ordinary commons of the parlor, shall pay weekly for their weekly commons and wyne x*s*. A yeoman that shalbe at the hall commons or other man or woman shall pay weekly for their commons there v*s*.

Richard Blaston.	Xrofer Laicles.	Tho. Large.
Cuthbert Scott.	George Felton.	Edw. Thurland.
Henry Cole.	Tho. Dymoche.	William Wharton."
Nich. Herpefeild.	William Crouch.	
Jo. Mordant.	Robert Colton.	
Arthur Poole.	H. P.	

(The second of these prisoners was the deprived Bishop of Chester, the third the deprived Dean of St. Paul's and Provost of Eton, and the fourth the well-known historian.)

viii. p. 686. " Orders and directions for the better explanieng and establishing of the Warden of the Fleet and his officers their severall fees." It begins :—" At the Court at Whitehall, 30 Aprilis 1598." (The MS. differs somewhat from the version printed in *The Œconomy of the Fleete*, pp. 118–119.)

ix. p. 686. " The orders for his Majestie's Chappell, Anno Dñi 16—." Begins:—" Imprimis for our Chappell and Closett wee ordaine and command that in our goeing and comeing thence all men keepe their rancks."

x. p. 691. " Orders for the Queens wayters chamber concerning such persons as are allowed to eate there." As issued by Edw. Earl of Dorset, Chamberlain and George Lord Goring, vice-chamberlain [about A.D. 1642] after approval by the King and Queen.

xi. p. 692. " Orders made by the Lord Wentworth, Lord Deputie of Ireland, to be observed by his secretaries and gentlemen ushers." [A.D. 1633–1639.]

xii. p. 694.—" The passages in Parliament against Francis Visc. St. Albans," etc. 1620.

MSS. OF THE
INNER TEMPLE.

xiii. pp. 717, 729.—Speeches of John Glanvile and Sir Henry Martin in a committee of both Houses, 23 May 1628.
xiv. p. 733.—" Touching the Lord High Admirall's place, vested in the Council of State."

538. 21. fol.—Abstract, under the heads of orders, committees, petitions, and reports, of Proceedings in Parliament, Edw. VI.-Car. I.

538. 22. fol. Henry Elsing's *Modus tenendi Parliamentum*.

538. 23. fol.—Selden's treatise *Touching judicature in Parliament*.

538. 24. fol.
i. f. 1.—"The severall opinions of sundry antiquaries touching the antiquitie, power, [&c.] of Parliament."
ii. ff. 65, 84, 111.—The Commons' declaration and impeachment against the Duke of Buckingham, 10 May 1626, with the Duke's answer and the Commons' Remonstrance to the King.

528. 25. fol.—" Explanatio brevis de nominibus et naturis omnium rotulorum in archivis Turris London repositorum."

528. 26. fol.—" A kalendar of all the Acts which are in the Clerk of the Parliament his office," from 16 Jan., 12 Hen. VII. (1497) to 10 Jan. 32 Car. II. (1681).

528. 27. fol.
i. f. 1.—"Considerations for the repressinge of the increase of preists, Jesuits, and recusants, without draweinge of blood, written by Sir Robert Cotton, knight and barronett." (Printed in his *Posthuma*, ed. 1672.)
ii. f. 38.—Remonstrance of the House of Commons to Charles I. on the cases of the Duke of Buckingham and the proceedings against Sir John Eliot and Sir Dudley Digges.
iii. f. 46.—Declaration of the Scots against the Earl of Strafford.
iv. f. 54.—Argument of the Lord Chief Justice Finch concerning ship-money, 9 June 1638.
v. f. 96.—Speech of Sir Francis Bacon at the arraignment of Robert, Earl of Somerset.
vi. f. 112.—Copy of the petition of the grand jury at the assizes, co. Berks, July 11, 1640, to the King for redress of grievances.
vii. f. 114.—Copy of the petition of the gentry in the county of York, July 28, 1640.
viii. f. 116.—" A note of the townes which are to contribute towards the settinge out and mainteyninge ot 20^{tie} snips and 4590 men," from March 1, 1634.
ix. f. 118.—Copy of the humble representations of several aldermen and others of the city of London to Oliver Cromwell, Captain-General of all the forces of the Commonwealth, and to the Council of the army, 20 May 1653, against their being deprived of the right of electing representatives, with order of the Council of State thereupon.
x. f. 120.—Copy of a grant by James I. to Sir Thomas Shirley, the elder, of Wiston, co. Sussex, concerning the newly erected office of alienations and pardons. 17 Sept. 5 Jac. 1 (1607).
xi. f. 135.—" The case of the Tynners stated " by — Worsley.
xii. f. 137.—Translation of an *inspeximus* of several letters patent confirming the original grant of privileges by Edw. I. to the Stannaries of Cornwall; 1 Nov. 2 Eliz. [1560].
xiii. f. 141.—" The King's case [for ship-money] with the judges' resolutions thereupon [7 Feb.] and my Lord Keeper's speech in the Starr-chamber, 14 February 1636."

xiv. f. 149.—"A displaye of bastardy, for mayntaynenge the lawfull clayme and challenge of the heire apparent of the Right Honourable Sir Thomas Cusacke, knight, sometyms Lord Chancelor of Ireland, deceased, to his inheritance. Composed and sett forth by the plaintife [John Cusacke], and dedicated to the Lords of the Court of Exchequier Chamber of Ingland," with a table of pedigree.

MSS. OF THE INNER TEMPLE.

xv. f. 162. — A case on a writ of *Quare impedit*, Woodley v. Manwaring, Hil. 18 Jac. I. (1620).

xvi. f. 170.—A treatise of the High Court of Chancery.

xvii. f. 229.—A reading on the Statute of Limitations, given at Gray's Inn by John Bauckes (afterwards Attorney-Gen.) in 1630.

538. 28. fol.

i. f. 1. — Copy of the bull of Pope Lucius III. to the Order of the Templars in 1183; from the records in the Treasury of the Exchequer, with representations of signatures and *bulla*, by Tho. Fauconberge, 22 May, 1638.

ii. f. 5b. — Extracts from the Register of the muniments of the Hospital of St. John of Jerusalem in England which begins in 1442, and copies of several records relative to the Temple in London.

At the other end of the volume are some notes of family and personal accounts in June—Aug. 1664, including receipts of 7s. 10d. from Mr. James for christenings, and of 2s. 6d. from Sir Tho. Woodcock for his child's christening and registering.

538. 29. fol.—Various notes from records, arranged under these heads: Pardons, Offices, Quinque Portus, Equisium Regis, Officium Pincernæ Regis, Foresta, Moneta et Monetarii, Cambium Regis, Scaccarium, Hibernia, Purveiancia, London, Admiralty, and Cartæ Libertatum. At the end are copies of several Inquisitions *ad quod dampnum* and other records relative to the manor of Stoke Goldington, co. Bucks, Edw. II.-Hen. VI.

538. 30. fol.—"The sovereignty of the seas of England, and a summary relation concerning the inestimable riches and commodities of the Brittish seas, by Sir John Burgh." Printed in 1651.

538. 31. fol.—"An answeare made by commaund of Prince Henrie to certayne propositions of warre and peace delivered to his Highnes by some of his militarie servaunts; written by Sir Robert Cotton." Printed in 1657 and 1675.

538. 32. fol.—i. Instructions to the Master of the Wards and Liveries; discourse on tenures and wardships; &c.

ii. (*Vol. reversed.*)—The Reading of W. Prynne at Gray's Inn, 17 Feb. 1661, on the Petition of Right in 1627; with observations on the right of bishops to sit in Parliament, on the laws with reference to royal castles, &c. Described as being in Prynne's own handwriting.

538. 33. fol.—Collections from records by W. Petyt relative to the army, and navy, fortifications, war, victualling, pay, truces, and various other subjects relating to military affairs; including a collection of orders in the time of Edw. II., III., for prayers for success. A table of the various heads is prefixed. ff. 518.

538. 34. fol.—" A brefe summarie and demonstracion of the estat of England and Wales, as well generall as particuler, mete for the vewe of her Majestie and of her heyghnes most honorable previe Counsellers, and to be kept from all others excepting souche as be very dyscrete and dutifull subjectes." 45 ff.

It gives the names of the High Commissioners and Privy Councillors, the number of churches in the different counties, the values of the

MSS. OF THE INNER TEMPLE. different bishopricks and deaneries, the names of the *custodes rotulorum* of the different counties, the names of persons certified into the Exchequer as fugitives over the sea, the names of the noblemen, tables of precedence, abstracts of musters taken in 1574 and 1575, the names of the Queen's ships with the number of men and furniture requisite for them, the names of the captains in charge of the different forts and castles, the number of men appointed to be trained in the different counties, list of the charges at Berwick, an estimate of the value of the ordnance in the Tower of London and elsewhere, a list of the different sorts of ordnance and munitions of war.

These are followed by tables of the salaries and fees of the officers of the Custom House, of the Exchequer, of the Court of Wards and Liveries, of the Court of First Fruits, of the Counties Palatine, of the Queen's Court, of the Admiralty, of the Ordnance, of the Armoury, of the Mint, of the Works, and of the Wardrobe, and by tables of the fees for tents, for hunting, for musicians, for surgeons, for bargemen, for artificers, for officers and servants of the household. The date of this compilation is 1579, inasmuch as it mentions Sir Roger Manwood as Chief Baron of the Exchequer and William Whittingham as Dean of Durham. Some of the tables given in it are printed in Peck's *Desiderata Curiosa*, 1789, pp. 51-78, but with many variations. The list of the different sorts of munitions of war is curious.

At f. 49 is an account of Exchequer payments received at Norwich 10 Apr.-2 May 1594, and at f. 53 of payments received at Huntingdon on 15 Apr.

538. 35. fol.—i. f. 1.—" Altera secretissima instructio Gallo-Britanno-Batava, Friderico V. data, ex Belgica in Latinam linguam versa et optimo publico evulgata. Hagæ-Comitis, permissu Senatus. 1626."

ii. f. 18.—Translation into Latin of the Lord Keeper's speech at the opening of a Parliament, *temp.* Jac. I. Begins:—" Si me delectasset oratio proclivior, exempium tamen Regis."

iii. f. 23.—An abstract of the valuation of all the lands belonging to the Religious Houses in England taken out of the Court of First-Fruits and Tenths, according to counties, showing a total of seven hundred and fifty-four religious houses.

iv. f. 37.—A copy of the proceedings at the justice-seat held for the Forest of Dean at Gloucester Castle, 10 July 1634, before Henry, Earl of Holland, Lord Chief Justice in Eyre, and others.

v. f. 49 *b*.—" A treatise of Ireland " by John Dymmoke. It begins : " The Realme of Ireland conteinethe in length from the south forelaude to the northe pointe named Thorach about 300 miles." Treats of the conquest and division of Ireland, and, very briefly, of its present state and government. In a short dedicatory letter to a friend, the author speaks of " these rude leaves " as having been " abortivelie brought forthe in an other shape."

vi. f. 94.—" A treatise concerning the Nobilitye according to the Lawe of Englande," by Sir John Doddridge, Judge of the King's Bench. (Printed in *The Magazine of Honour*, 1642.)

538. 36. fol.

i. f. 2.—Notes of arguments in the matter of the divorce of the Earl of Essex. 1613.

ii. f. 9.—" A Discourse against the peace with Spaine, directed to the King's Majestie at his first enterance into this Kingdome."

iii. f. 20.—" Advertisements of a loyall subject to his gratious Soveraigne, drawne from observations of the people's speeches." Begins:—

"It is sayd your Majestie will not continue the protection of the Low Countries."   MSS. OF THE INNER TEMPLE.

iv. f. 24.—"An Advertisement written to a Secretary of my Lord Treasurer's of England by an English Intelligencer, as he passed through the Mayne towards Italie, concerning another booke newly written in Latine and published in divers languages and cuntries against her Majesties late Proclamation for search and apprehension of seminary priests and their receavers; also of a Letter written by my Lord Treasurer in defence of his gentrie and nobilitie, intercepted, published and answered by the Papists. Anno Domini 1592."

v. f. 56.—"The coppy of an humble Supplication to her Majestie in answere to the late Proclamation," [by Robert Southwell. Printed in 1593.]

vi. ff. 78-89, 95.—Copies of petitions from John Lilly to Q. Elizabeth, and of letters from Sir Walter Raleigh to James I., to his wife, to Sir Robert Carr, and to the Queen, from Lord Rochester to the Earl of Northampton, from Sir Fulk Grevill to his kinsman Grevill Varney, from the Earl of Arundel to the Queen, from Lord Mountjoy to the Earl of Essex, from the Secretary of Scotland to the Secretary of England, January 4, 1566, and from the Queen to the Earl of Essex.

vii. ff. 99-110.—Copies of letters from the Council to the Archbishop of York, to the Lord Mayor of London and to the Earl of Hertford; Mr. R. C. to the Earl of Leicester, 29 Nov. 1586; the Lord Keeper Egerton to the Earl of Essex; from Lady Rich to the Queen in behalf of her brother Essex; and of a few anonymous letters of the time of Elizabeth, with a letter from James I. to the city of London.

viii. f. 111.—"The Earle of Essex his device one the Queenes day, presented before he rann at tilt" [17 Nov. 1595] being speeches written by Fr. Bacon. (Nichols's *Progresses of Q. Eliz.* III., 372.)

ix. f. 115.—"An Apologeticall Epistle written by Count Arundell, and directed to the Lord Treasurer of England, as concerning his Title of *Comes Imperii*."

x. f. 140.—"Vita Prothoplasti nostri Adæ et Evæ uxoris suæ." Inc. "Factum est cum expulsi essent."

xi. f. 149.—George Cavendish's *Life of Wolsey*.

xii. f. 199.—"A collection of certaine matters touching the death of our late Queen Elizabeth, and the Proclayming, Coronation, etc., of the most renowned Prince James the Sixt, King of Scotland, her lawfull successor."

xiii. f. 207.—Speech delivered to the King at his approach to London in the name of the Sheriffs of London and Middlesex, by Richard Martin, of the Middle Temple. (Printed in 1603.)

xiv. f. 211.—An apology for, or vindication of, Robert Cecil, Earl of Salisbury [by Sir Walter Cope], addressed to James I. (Printed in Vol. I. of Gutch's *Collectanea Curiosa*.)

xv. f. 219.—"The Life and Death of our late noble Prince Henry"; in a letter, [by Sir Charles Cornwallis]. (Twice printed.)

xvi. f. 243.—"A briefe relation of the arraignement of Philip Howard, Earl of Arundell, at Westminster, on the fourth day of Aprill, Anno Domini 1589." (Printed in Howell's "*State Trials*" under the date of April 18.)

xvii. f. 249.—"The manner of proceeding against the Scotish Queen," at Fotheringay on the 12th of October and following days. (This narrative differs from that given in Camden's *Annals* and in the "*State Trials*").

MSS. OF THE INNER TEMPLE.

xviii. f. 273.—"A Relation of Sir Walter Rawleigh's arraignement."
xix. f. 284.—"The Araignment of Sir Walter Rawleigh." (Printed in the "*State Trials*.")
xx. f. 315.—Copy of the Act of Association, made in the time of Elizabeth.
xxi. f. 319.—"Certaine motions wherupon a Conference is humblie to be desired before the Lords of the higher House and a Committee of the lower House," for the maintenance of her Majesty's prerogative, etc., against the abuses of the Bishops and the Commissioners Ecclesiastical.
xxii. f. 324.—"Meanes of Unitie," a memorial from Puritans for relaxation of uniformity in ritual, and for encreased care in ordination ; *temp.* Eliz.
xxiii. f. 327.—Address from the House of Commons to Queen Elizabeth on ecclesiastical affairs, praying for toleration and suspension of the penal laws.
xxiv. f. 331.—"The Flowers of Grace; or the Speech of our Soveraigne Lord King James, 5° Aprilis 1614, at the session of Parliament then begunne." (Printed in the *Parliamentary History*, vol. i.).
xxv. f. 335.—Remonstrance from the H. of Commons to James I. on the grievances of the kingdom ; taxes on ale-houses, coals, merchandize ; the Marches of Wales, patent for wines, proclamations, &c. (1610).

538. 37. f. i.—"Observations concerning the royall navy," by Sir Walter Raleigh (printed in Ralegh's Works 1829, Vol. viii., p. 335).
ii. f. 18.—"A breife discourse by way of question and answer of estates of inheritance," etc.
iii. f. 54.—"A very pathetically or heart affecting and selfe-convincing speech for the supply of the King's debts" (James I.), by the Lord Treasurer Cecil.
iv. f. 70*.—"Concerning a Parliament," by Sir Francis Bacon.
v. f. 71.—Answers to certain petitions against the Court of Chivalry.
vi. f. 106.—On the election, confirmation, and consecration of Archbishops and Bishops; in two chapters.
vii. f. 114.—"A proposition of divers Roman Catholiques in this kingdome, being a moderate expedient to remove jealousies of danger by their increases, with reasons to inforce the same and answers to objections. Anno 1647."
viii. f. 124.—Instructions given by Robert Earl of Warwick, Lord High Admiral of England, to be observed in the fleet. Beg. :—"First and above all things you must provide that God bee duly served publiquely twice every day in the shipp under your command."
ix. f. 136.—The Antiquity, etc. of Parliament, by Sir John Doddridge. (Printed in 1658.)
x. f. 153.—Justice Hutton's argument against the ship-money, 28 April, 1638.
xi. f. 163.—Charge of Sir John Finch to the judges of England, 13 Feb. 1639, before their circuit.
xii. f. 171.—"An excellent treatise against Jesuits and Recusants written by the Earle of Salisbury, or rather the Lord Treasurer Burleigh, to Queen Elizabeth." Begins :—"Most gracious Soveraigne and most worthy to bee a soveraigne."
xiii. f. 183.—Judge Hutton's argument upon the ship-money, 1638. A different report from that given above.
xiv. f. 193.—Judge Jones's argument on the ship-money. 28 Apr. 1638.

538. 38. f. i. On the case of a sovereign prince who flies to another prince for protection, is kept in safe custody, and practises against the life and kingdom of that prince ; whether such a practiser may be justly put to death.

ii. f. 5.—Suggestions for " a collection of the heades and branches of all controversies betwixt us and the Papists," to be submitted to learned men for arguments thereon, then submitted to the Bishops, and finally drawn out into a short catechism ; with a list of such principal heads (4) and their branches. Endorsed on the last leaf, " Certaine advertisments geven by Mr. Secretarie to Dr. Fulk."

iii. f. 11.—A Latin treatise (endorsed as being by " a learned father ") on the question of the rightful authority for carrying out ecclesiastical reformation ; that it is to be done by civil magistrates if others fail in their duty.

iv. f. 18.— " *Camarina*, a discourse against the profane Lollardes commonly called Puritanes; Auctored by John Lloyd, Doctor of Divinitie in Oxford ;" only the first two pages of the preface (as it seems), with dedication to Charles Earl of Nottingham, Lord High Admiral of England.

v. f. 22.—List of dioceses in England and Wales, with their estimated firstfruits.

vi. f. 23.—A treatise in Latin on the Lord's Supper, endorsed " The Archbishop of Canterbury de Cœna Domini." Beg. : " Quid est cena dominica ? est sacramentum ab ipso Christo institutum." Apparently autograph.

vii. f. 25.—Letter in Latin from Matthew Hutton, dean of York to [the Archbishop of Canterbury ?] criticising the " Formula " of John Sturmius " *de Cœna Domini.*"

viii. f. 27.—Copy of the draft of a letter from the King to the Universities in 1604, concerning the imposing of the oath of Supremacy, &c.

ix. f. 29.—" Certeyne reasones to be offred to the Quene's majesties consideracion why it is not convenient that the Communion shulde be mynystred at an Altare."

x. f. 33.—Extracts from St. Augustine on the lawfulness of punishment of heretics, with a marginal note " Etsi Episcopus Winton se contra (sine causa) opposuit."

xi. f. 34.—Autograph treatise in Latin by " Mr. [John] Castoll," [minister of the French church in London] on the thesis, " Homini peregrino apud eam gentem in cujus ditione non commorandi sed habitandi domicilium ecclesiamque regendam habeat, nativi Regis, et contrariam religionis profitentis, legato mandatario et procuratori esse, nec licet nec expedit."

xii. f. 40.—" Articles for Institution," being questions for examination of some suspected person, beginning :—" Were you borne in lawfull matrimony ?" Among the questions are the following :—" Have you not offered to fight hande to hande with any other, or being offered by him have you not accepted of the challenge ? " " Have you not unsealed and opened letters directed to others ? " " Were you not suspended from execution of your ministery by your ordinary the B[ishop] of Excester the firste day of Aprill being Thursday, and the sixte of Aprill after, being Tuesday, in the yeare of our Lorde God 1595 ? " " Are you not the authore of a certaine libell against the B. of Excester, the B. of London, and others lately cast abrode in Excester Diocess ? " In the handwriting of Dr. Rich. Cosin ; *cf.* f. 201.

MSS. OF THE INNER TEMPLE.

xiii. f. 41.—" Notes to be considered of in the Convocation Howse;" about the article in the Creed of the descent into hell, about prohibitions, and about obstinate excommunicate persons.

xiv. f. 43.—Notes on the power of Christian princes as against that of the Pope.

xv. f. 45.—Notes on tithes, by Mr. Hampton.

xvi. f. 48.—Notes on the excommunication of Princes, by Dr. Crompton.

xvii. ff. 49–50, 85–6.—Part of a long letter from John Duport to his "neighbours and brethren," being twenty-five of his parishioners who have, apparently, desired him to resign his living on account of non-residence, with marginal notes; dated " Boresworth, 14 Nov. 1588."

xviii. f. 52.—Answers by Nicholas Shepperd (Master of St. John's College, Cambridge), to twenty articles of inquiry as to his orthodoxy and conformity.

xix. f. 54.—Extract from the Register of Matthew Parker, Archbishop of Canterbury, by the Registrar, of the excommunication of Rich. Cheney, Bishop of Gloucester, 20 Apr. 1571. Printed from this MS. in Strype's *Life of Parker*, III , 182. App. No. lxi.

xx. f. 55.—Copies (sent to the Archbp. of Canterbury) of letters from Sir W. Cecil, Chanc. of Cambridge, to the Vice-Chanc. of Cambr., 10 Dec. 1565, and of a letter from Bishop Cox of Ely to the Master and Fellows of Peter House, 15 Dec., concerning the use of the surplice.

The former is printed from this copy in Strype's *Life*, III., 128–131, and the latter in abstract in Strype's *Annals*, I., ii., 159.

xxi. f. 58.—Notes on predestination; *Lat.*

xxii. f. 59.—An address to the bishops on behalf of those who denied predestination of evil, by Thomas Talbot, parson of St. Mary Magdalen, Milk Street.

Printed from this original in Strype's *Annals*, I., i., 495.

xxiii. f. 60.—Letter from John Whitgift to the Archbp. of Cant., about the depriving Cartwright of his fellowship ; 21 Sept. 1572.

Partly printed, as from the original, then " penes me," in Strype's *Life of Whitgift*, I., 95–6. The last words there, printed in brackets, are not in the MS., but the paper has in that place been cut in two and afterwards neatly rejoined.

xxiv. f. 62.—Certified copy of a public confession by John Travers of his unreverend speeches against the Bishop of Exeter and Sir Will. Courtenay, knt., his contumelious abuse, &c. Probably the person referred to in Art. 12.

xxv. ff. 63, 68.—Letter from Whitgift to the Archbp. of Cant., 21 Oct. 1572; has sent him a copy of the second part of his book, which has been perused by the Bp. of Lincoln. Mentioned in Strype's *Whitgift*, I. i., 86.

xxvi. f. 65.—Copies of a letter from Tho. Norton to Whitgift, 20 Oct. 1572, dissuading him from answering the *Admonition*, and of Whitgift's reply, 25 Oct. Printed from these copies, *ibid.*, pp. 58–65.

xxvii. f. 68.—" Mr. [Edward] Dearings false prophesie " at " Mr. Lonison's," 11 Dec. 1572, that Matthew Parker would be the last Archbishop of Canterbury, at which Cartwright said " Accipio omen," and Blage said " Ye will first rue it." Dering also said that Parker's bill might be taken on the Exchange, as he was the richest prelate in England. *See* Strype's *Life of Parker*, II., 241.

xxviii. f. 69.—Draft of an ordinance for restriction of excommunications, ecclesiastical censures having come into contempt by over-frequent use.

xxix. f. 71.—" Notes for some reformacion of the mynistrye and mynisters in this corrupt tyme," signed by Thomas Lever, Archd. of

Coventry, and by him sent to the Bishop of Coventry and Lichfield, Thomas Bentham.

xxx. f. 75.—" Whether all ministers of the Church should be preachers." *Affirm.*

xxxi. f. 79.—Arch. Whitgift's answer to the petition of 16 articles from the House of Commons about the ministry. A.D. 1584. Strype's *Whitgift,* I., 254–360.

xxxii. f. 83.—Extract from the Register of Archbishop Warham of a bull of Pope Julius II. about appointment to the see of Rochester in 1504, and of the oaths taken by the bishop elect.

xxxiii. f. 87.—" Papa non posse principes deponere; " a short treatise in Latin.

xxxiv. f. 89.—Memorial to the Archbishop and Bishops on the liberties of the Church, and grievances of the clergy, praying that some remedy may, by her Majesty's special grace and favour, be found.

xxxv. f. 92.—" Inconveniences in the petition moved for a graunte of the parishe clerkshippes or for surveying them." Printed in Strype's *Annals,* IV., 63.

xxxvi. f. 93.—" A breefe of some differences in statutes and customes of Emmanuel College in Cambridge from all other foundations there."

xxxvii. f. 95.—" Inconveniences ensuing upon the passing of landes as concealed belonging to churches."

xxxviii. f. 97.—" Inconveniences arising by farming forth the first frutes and tenths of spirituall livinges."

xxxix. f. 99.—" Brevis et vera narratio eorum quæ Genevæ sunt ab Hugone Broughtono, Anglo, patrata." Signed, " Theodorus Beza dictavi." 1595.

xl. f. 100.—" Reasons whic beneficed men lyvyng and doeng their duties in their benefices should not be counted non-resident, though they dwell not in their parsonage or vicarage howse."

xli. f. 101.—Letter from Archbishop Whitgift to Lord Burghley against the commission *ad melius inquirendum.* 1584. Copy in his own hand. Printed in Strype's *Whitgift,* I., 405–408.

xlii. f. 102.—His " Notes *de melius inquirendo.*" Printed *ibid.,* 403–4.

xliii. f. 103.—Fragment of other notes against the same.

xliv. f. 105.—" The liberties of the Isle of Ely ; " by Bishop Cox ; half in his own handwriting.

xlv. f. 108.—Short notes in Latin " de Contemptu."

xlvi. f. 109.—" Directorium expediendorum in negotio confirmationis electionis domini episcopi A "[saphensis].

xlvii. f. 110.—Latin notes " de Episcopis " and " de Presbyteris."

xlviii. f. 113.—Examples collected out of English history of the grievances suffered by the nation when the Bishop of Rome had his full sway in this realm.

xlix. f. 122.—Three schedules relating to the bishops, deans, and chapters, and several clergy, in the dioceses of Canterbury, Ely, and Oxford, each signed " Fra. Walsyngham." The several papers are in this form :

" Cantuar. The Archebushoppe, iiii. The Deane, ii. The Chapter, iiii. John Bungey, parson of Chartham, ii.," &c.

l. f. 125.—" The great, absurd, and blasphemouse praises given to the Pope ;" examples from various Latin writers.

li. f. 127.—Latin notes "de natura institutionis, collationis, etc."

lii. f. 129.—" Formula Johannis Sturmii de Cœna Domini." See f. 25.

liii. f. 131.—The oath of supremacy taken by a Bishop.

liv. f. 132.—The oath of a member of the Court of Star Chamber.

MSS. OF THE INNER TEMPLE.

lv. f. 134.—Reasons against the payment of 38s. demanded of the Archbishop of Canterbury by the Commissioners of Sewers for fifty-seven acres of land at Lambeth.

lvi f. 135.—" A note of the Lords of Scotland which comes to London with his Majestie." [A.D. 1603.] The list (twenty in all) ends with " The Abbott of Blantire."

lvii. ff. 136, 139, 140.—Copy of four legal opinions on the Act 18 Eliz. for reserving rent in corn for the Universities, and " Answers to the doubts upon the statute."

lviii. f. 137.—Proposals for the bestowal of benefices in the Queen's gift on preachers being graduates.

lix. f. 142.—Paper by Dr. Will. Drury, entitled " Particulars by every bishop within his dioces to be collected and certified unto your Grace ;" being advice to Archbishop Whitgift with a view to stop the commission *ad melius inquirendum.* 1584. Printed by Strype, *Annals*, III., i. 333–5, and ii., 317–9.

lx. f. 144.—The oath of a councillor.

lxi. f. 146.—" The reasons of the schollers of both the Universities against the Provisoe propownded by the townesmen of Cambridge and Oxforde."

lxii. f. 147. Some Latin verses and epigrams, copied, apparently, from the fly-leaves of mediæval MSS.

lxiii. f. 148.—" The proceeding of two sutes in the Star-chamber against certeine of the townsmen of Cambridge for two ryottes." Feb. 1602. (Cf. Cooper's *Annals of Cambridge*, vol. ii., p. 612.)

lxiv. f. 149.—" The reply of the Universitie of Cambridge to the exceptions of Mr Thomas Wendie, concerning the Sheriffes oath for the mayntenance of the University priviledges." Noted on f. 145b as being " Dr Bing's " reply, *i.e.* Dr. Thos. Byng, reg. prof. of Civil Law.

lxv. f. 151.—A copy of a letter from Stephen, King of Poland, to Queen Elizabeth ; 4 March, 1585.

lxvi. f. 152.—" Disorders in the University of Cambridge anno Domini 1601."

lxvii. f. 154.—" A briefe collection of some of the causes of the decay of the Universitie of Oxford."

lxviii. f. 155.—" Reasons alledged by the late Archbishop of Cant[erbury] for Dr. Bancroft's preferment to the B[ishopric] of London." Printed from this MS. in Strype's *Life of Whitgift*, II. 386–388.

lxix. f. 157.—A memorial to the Archbishop of Canterbury, showing " howe those places that have not sufficiente maintenance for able men to execute the function of preachinge, may in some parte bee made more sufficiente, with some commoditie to the revenue of the Crowne of this realme, and yet no man wronged."

lxx. f. 161.—The Lambeth Latin articles on predestination, approved 20 Nov., 1595. Strype's *Whitgift*, II. 280.

lxxi. f. 162.—Part of the answer of Thomas Cooper, Bishop of Winchester, to the Petition of 16 Articles in 1584. Strype's *Whitgift*, I. 369–376.

lxxii. f. 165.—Archbishop Grindall's " forme of doinge publike pennance," prepared in 1580. Endorsed, " A forme of pennance devised by my L[ord] himselfe." Strype's *Life of Grindal*, pp. 387–9.

lxxiii. f. 168.—" An othe of Allegeance [to Queen Elizabeth] thowght upon by some Catholikes."

lxxiv. ff. 167b, 170.—A declaration of the royal supremacy, etc. " sent by Mr. Attorney to be generally subscribed."

lxxv. f. 172.—Notes about the papal supremacy, addressed to Dr. Cox, Bishop of Ely.

lxxvi. f. 174.—" Dr. Barlowes aunswer touching the Sabboth, 1603." MSS. OF THE INNER TEMPLE.
lxxvii. f. 176.—" The names of the Lordes Spirituall and Temporall the upper howse of Parlament, as they take place in the saide howse " ; June 1604.
lxxviii. f. 178.—" The chief heades of the Articles to be conferred of with the Lordes concerninge the matters of Religion," *temp. Jac. I.*
lxxix. f. 179.—Notes " concerning the exemptions of the clergie in Purveyances."
lxxx. f. 182.—" Inconveniences of grawnting the penaltie of Statutes," and of " grawnting the goodes of men before they be attaynted."
lxxxi. f. 183.—Notes on the manner of appointing bishops.
lxxxii. f. 184.—Notes out of various Roman Catholic books of the sending children to Seminaries abroad.
lxxxiii. f. 186.—" A project of Articles to examine Papists upon ; " marked " my drawght, 1604."
lxxxiv. f. 188.—" Articles delivered to the Lords from the Lower Howse off Parlament, concernynge, 1 makynge off Mynisters, 2 Faculties, 3 Commutations off penance. 4 Excommunications for contumacie, etc. 1580."
lxxxv. f. 192.—Fragment of the printed Greek and Latin text of Barlaam *de papæ principatu,* printed at Oxford in 1592.
lxxxvi. f. 196.—Proposition " concerning the reformation of excommunication."
lxxxvii. f. 127. — Notes of " Mr. Wincott" on the valuation of benefices in the twenty-first year of Henry VIII.
lxxxviii. f. 199.—Notes on reformation of ecclesiastical censures and on excommunication : " being an answere to the 4 pointes referred to owr consideration."
lxxxix. f. 201. — Draft of an Act for the furnishing of benefices with sufficient and able ministers; marked as being in " Dr. [Rich.] Cosins' hand."
xc. f. 202.—" Certayne abuses touching " appeals, delays, *significavit,* simony, unlearned ministers, &c. " worthy redresse," with suggested remedies.
xci. f. 204.—Letters from John Clark, parson of Laceby, co. Lincoln, to the Archbishop of Canterbury, requesting him to procure some good laws in Parliament for the maintenance of tillage. Four years ago he complained to the Archbishop that, in consequence of an agreement between the freeholders and lords of Laceby for enclosures, whereas there were 27 ploughs there are now only poor 3. Now the state of Laceby and many more towns in Lincolnshire is lamentable by means of the utter decay of tillage ; whereas in Dr. Dallison's time and during the incumbency of the Archbishop the tithe corn of Laceby was yearly about nine score quarters, it is not now eighteen quarters," whereby it is apparent that the common wealth is impoverished by the decay of tillage in Laceby, above one thousand and eight hundred quarters of corne."
xcii. f. 206. — " Remembrances concerning tillage and decaie of townes " through enclosures.
xciii. f. 208.—" Additions to the arguments against the Bill for suppressing of three weekes courtes."
xciv. f. 210.—" Certaine remedies for the strengtheninge of the borders, with reformation of divers decayes in Northumberland," *temp.* Eliz.
xcv. f. 212.—An oath of allegiance for Roman Catholics. A.D. 1605.
xcvi. f. 213.—Arguments " that Deanes and Masters of Colleges may be restrayned from marriage." Among the " Inconveniences found by experience " the writer urges :—" Young students have theire myndes

MSS. OF THE INNER TEMPLE. withdrawne from theire studies and are moved to unchast thoughtes by the lodginge of woemen in Colleges. And this for the mo t parte are the sennes of noble men and greate men most subjecte unto, who doe comonly lye in the Master's lodginges. Fewe men can be preferred to fellowshipps or schollershipps, and fewe leases passed, without a bribe to the Heades wife . . . . . . Weston of Lovaine taxeth many of the Heades of houses by name for keepinge their wyves in Colleges." "In Christchurch in Oxford above 50 woemen have been lodged att one tyme."

xcvii. f. 215.—Articles agreed upon by the Convocation of Canterbury "towchynge thadmission of apt and fitt persons to the ministery and thestablishing of good orders in the Church." A.D. 1575.

Printed from this copy in Strype's *Life of Grindal*, p. 537.

xcviii. f. 219.—"An Act to reforme the abuse of excommunication in diverse cases"; to carry out a constitution made in Convocation restraining excommunications.

xcix. f. 223.—"Resolutions concernynge the Injunctions"; drawn up by (as Strype supposes) Bp. Cox and revised by Archbp. Parker. 1560. Printed from this copy in Strype's *Annals*, I.; 318–22.

c. f. 227.—Latin Articles, put out in 1560. *Ibid*, 323–5.

ci. f. 228.—"Injunctions to be confessed and subscrybed by them that shalbe admitted Readers": 1562. The last order, for deacons, is apparently added by Archbp. Parker's hand. *Ibid*, 514–5.

cii. f. 229.—"Project of the bill for clergy leases," for lives.

ciii. f. 231.—" Orders in ecclesiasticall jurisdiction," (*endorsement*); being a contemporary translation of part of the *Reformatio Legum*, from chap. 2 of tit. *De crimine falsi* to chap. 19 of tit. *De dilationibus;* pp. 240–278 of Cardwell's edition in 1850.

civ. f. 247.—" Theses touching the contention between D. R [eynolds] and B." respecting the chronology of Scripture, by Hugh Broughton; in his own hand, and signed by him. See Strype's *Whitgift*, II. 117.

cv. f. 253.—Hugh Broughton's "Reasones against Doctor Renoldes," on the same subject. Written by another hand.

cvi. ff. 356–298, 315.—Copies of twenty-eight Injunctions or Ordinances of Q. Eliz., concerning proceedings in Ecclesiastical courts, relative to excommunication, tithes, prohibitions, &c.

The first is headed: "The aunciente writt *de excommunicato capiendo* not to be impeached by any device or construction."

The last; "The liberties of the Churche and cleargie, not to be impeeched by any acte of Parliament but in expresse termes."

cvii. f. 300.—"Orders fitt to be observed by his Majesties commissioners for causes ecclesiasticall touching the sessing and rating of fines," &c. 1 May, 1609.

cviii. f. 316.—"Notes for redresse of divers abuses about payingof tithe."

cix. f. 317.—"The motion of the late Earl of Lecester for judges delegates." In Dr. R. Cosin's hand.

cx. f. 319.—Letter from R. [Cecil] Earl of Salisbury, to the Archbishop of Canterbury [Bancroft], declaring (in his office of Lord Treasurer) the exemption of "those of the clergie that are only incumbents," from the necessity of contributing to the aid in respect of their glebe; no man seeking to charge them in respect of their tithe; Whitehall, 12 Oct. [1609].

cxi. f. 321. — " Certaine reasons why the Register of the Arches should continewe the office of a procter in the corts of Audience and Prerogative."

cxii. f. 325.—Copy of a letter from Matthew (Hutton) Bishop of Durham to the Archbishop of Canterbury reporting a long conversation between himself and the Lord Treasurer and Mr. Secretary Walsingham, on three subjects; i. The judicial laws of Moses: ii. The authority of a prince in causes ecclesiastical: iii. The antiquity and lawfulness of a bishop. 10 Oct. 1589. Printed from this copy in Strype's *Life of Whitgift*, III. 224-8.

MSS. OF THE INNER TEMPLE.

cxiii. f. 327.—A draft of the same in Latin, evidently in Hutton's own hand.

cxiv. f. 331.—Copy of a long letter from M. J. [*i.e.*, J. Mush] a secular priest "to Mr. Wis:" [Mr. Wiseman, afterwards Sir William Wiseman, of Broadoaks, Essex,] vindicating the secular priests, in reply to his depreciation of them, and his great commendation of the Jesuits in preference. " Of late certain lines taken out of a booke made as they say by you of 3 fairewelles (if I mistake the author, *nihil ad te scriptum putes*) were showed to me and others." . . . . " Since the Jesuits entred, indeed the numbers of God's people zealous and resolute have increased dayly everywhere, the prisons have bin and are filled with Catholiques, many have bin spoyled of their goods and livings, many have constantly sustayned greivous torments, many have joyfully suffred death alredy, and many stand resolutely prepared to endure the uttermost cruelty of the persecutors. But, Sir, yourself and others must know that the good industrie of the secular (God's holy grace cooperating) hath principally wrought these effects: for that to the most of all these saints of God onely the secular preists have bin continually since the beginninge, and are still, their pastors and guides, without these relations and guidings of yours." Very closely written, in a small hand.

cxv. f. 333.—" Capita quædam accusationum quibus doctor Giffordus et dominus Pagettus, Angli, aliique eorum sequaces, societatem Jesu immerito apud Summum Pontificem . . . . . traduxerunt, quas justum est ut vel probent, vel ut societati fama, tam iniquis et manifestis calumniis impetita, restituatur," 1596.

cxvi. f. 387.—Another copy of the preceding, marked in the margin, "Articuli patris Personii contra D. Giffordum, decanum Insulensem."

With some additional papers in the same hand probably intercepted in England: Articles in Latin [for the regulation of the College at Rome] headed "A monsieur le provoste de nře Dame de Cambraye" [Dr. Hugh Griffin], dated at Rome 15 May. 1597, "agreed upon by fa. Persons, &c. and confirmed by Card. Burghesius"; and a letter from Parsons to father Will. Holt dated at Genua, 15 March 1597, signed 215, marked in the margin "Deciphered by Mr. Worthington," and at the end, " Per famulum magistri Bluet, xvii Decemb. 1601." (An Italian version of this very interesting letter is given from a copy in Parsons' own hand in Dodd's *Church History* ed. Tierney, vol. iii., pp. lvii–lix. This manuscript contains the passage in which Parsons expresses his opinion that the most suitable candidate for the English throne would be "the Infanta with the Prince Cardinal").

cxvii. f. 341.—Copy of the examination of John Jerrard (Gerard) a Jesuit, respecting Southwell's doctrine of equivocation, which Jerrard also maintained, 13 May 1597.

cxviii. f. 342.—" An abstracte of the memoriall sent by certaine English owte of the lowe Cuntreys to the Pope's holines Clement the Eight, against the Jesuites laboring in the Englishe vineyarde, September 1597. The inscription of the memoriall ; A breife declaration of the miserable state of Catholiques in England."

cxix. ff. 344-5. Two copies of the same, in Latin.

cxx. f. 347. Another copy of the "Capita accusationum" given at f. 333, with English notes at the end about one Fisher, an agent

R 2

MSS. OF THE INNER TEMPLE. at Rome against the Jesuits. "All this ensueth vpon the cominge over of Fisher from England."

cxxi. ff. 349, 353. Two copies (the first by Bluet?) of forty-nine articles, *Lat.*, extracted from Rob. Parsons' *Memoriale pro reformatione Angliæ*, 1596. The first copy is in the same handwriting as art. 115.

cxxii. f. 355. An English copy of the "Capita accusationum," with the same notes about Fisher as in art. 120.

cxxiii. ff. 358, 359. Two copies of Parsons' letter, the first apparently in Parsons' own hand, to Holt, as in art. 116. The first is endorsed. "For Mr Dr Bushope, &c."

cxxiv. f. 360. Copy of a circular letter (in Lat.) from Henry Garnet, "reverendis dominis presbyteris universis per Angliam constitutis," in reply to the Memorial of Sept. 1597 against the Jesuits; dated 1 March 1598.

cxxv. f. 361. Copy of a Latin letter to the Archpriest Blackwell, from English priests, repudiating agreement with the Memorial of Sept. 1597. Beg.: "Rumores sparguntur, P. R^{de}, sacerdotes Angliæ."

cxxvi. f. 364. Letter (in a hand greatly resembling Mush's), signed "Parker", to Dr. Bag[shawe]: sends 12*l*. 2*s*. 6*d*. "I am hartely sorrie to hear of a certayne memoriall that hath bin exhibited unto the hygher powers," &c. 10 May. Noted at the foot: "This Parker is now Assistant," and endorsed "Oliver Almand."

cxxvii. f. 365. Copy of a letter from Parsons to Holt, then in the Low Countries, informing him that the troubles at the College at Rome are happily settled; Rome, 5 May 1597. "Within 4 or 5 monethes after 2 new breeches hapnd, as Parsons confesseth in a letter to Walley or Blackwell." The letter is printed in Tierney's edition of Dodd, III., lxxviii–lxxx.

cxxviii. f. 367.—Another copy of the same.

cxxix. f. 368.—Copy of a letter from Cardinal Allen to the Roman Catholic sufferers in England, 12 Dec. 1587. His sympathy with them in the persecutions they endure. He would have such of them as be priests use great compassion and mercifulness towards such of the laity as from mere fear or for the saving of their families from ruin "are so far only fallen as to goe sometymes to theire churches or to be present at the tyme of theire service. For though it be not lawfull to doe so muche, nor yet in itself any way excusable, yet suche necessity in that kinde of men maketh the offence lesse, and more compassionable, yea and more easelye by you to be absolved. And therefore be not hard nor rough nor rigorous nor morose in receyving agayne and absolving them when they confesse their infirmityes and be sorry for the same, and yelde some reasonable hope that they will hereafter stand more strongly or have hope to have meanes to escape and not to be led into the like temptation." The priests must use this mercy though they fall more than once, and though they have some "probable fear" that they will of like infirmity fall again; for God may give them more strength; so that more must not be required of the penitent than in any other sins that be subject to the sacrament of penance. On the other side the priests must be careful not to teach or defend "that it is lawfull to communicate with the Protestants in theire praiers or service, or conventicles where they meete to minister theire untrue sacraments." This is not a positive law of the Church which can be dispensed with upon occasion, but God's own eternal law. Lest however any of the brethren should not be satisfied with the writer's judgment or with such proofs as have been made in this matter, he has demanded the sentence of the Pope who now is, "who expressely tolde me that to participate with Protestantes either by prayinge

with them or goinge to theire churches or service or suche like was *MSS. OF THE INNER TEMPLE.*
by no meanes lawfull or dispensable ; but added withall that suche as
of feare and weakenes or other temporall force and necessity do it,
ought to be gently dealt withall and to be easely absolved, as before
said."

cxxx. f. 370.—Copy of a letter (in Latin) from Octavius, "Episc.
Tricaricensis" (in Naples) Nuncio Apostolic to the Catholic priests
resident in England. The Pope has revoked certain faculties granted
to three English priests, Edward Tempest, Thomas Hill, and Robert
Benson who, seduced by their lusts, have renounced the study of the
more perfect life. The bulls that they have, however authentic, must
therefore be treated as void, and not as permitting any exercise of the
said faculties. Brussels, 29 Dec. 1597.

cxxxi. f. 371.—A report (in Latin) of the answer of Pope Clement
VIII. to the speech (made by Edw. Bennett in the name of the rest)
of certain English priests who were about to start for England, Sept.
3, 1597, in the presence of Cardinal Cajetan and Father Robert Parsons. The Pontiff addressed them sharply, upbraiding them with the
quarrels that had broken out in the College through the spirit of pride,
and warning them that they would do no good in England unless they
left the spirit of strife behind. When Father Hill, one of the chief
ringleaders in the disturbances, came up to kiss his feet, the Pontiff
again urged agreement with the Fathers of the Society (of Jesus) in
England, and added to a bystander that he recognised Father Hill by
his face and his long beard, and that he knew him to be very seditious.

cxxxii. f. 372. Letter from R. C. [Charnock ?] to Mr. B., endorsed as
being to Bagshaw. Reasons why the writer has been through the winter
unable to meet him ; sends a copy of a letter to be delivered to the Pope,
to which it is fit that many should set their hands. Not dated.

cxxxiii. f. 373. D. U. to Mr. D. Account of the writer's incessant
engagements in travelling, specially at the times of the greater feasts. Will
copy out the proposed Rules of Association, about which a message came
from Dr. Barret, from Douay. " Here came a message twoe severall tymes
frome you concerning Mr. Till. Yt maybe yow there do trust Fisher,
but so do not we, nether make him acquaynted with any suche messages.
As I here, he spake of yt not onelie here to my ostice, but also talked
of yt at the next towne. We are not willing that owre youthe or laye
people should here of moe defects in priests then they needs must ; *quia
fragiles sunt.*" When therefore there is occasion to send any such
message, let it be written, and not sent by word of mouth, not only by
Protestants but also by Catholics, " for even they some tyme will shewe
weaknes in theire speuches, and be sone scandalized." Said mass yesterday for the soul of " Mr. D. Nor :" [Norden ?] desires to know particulars of his death, " for stopping of fowle mowthes and selanderous persons." The latter sent two knives to the writer to be given to the person
whose name began with B. who had one before : will give them to his
brother, if Mr. D. knows whether they were intended for him. Has
been earnestly requested to come " to your house, to visit yow all ; "
desires to know whether it be convenient, and can be done safely ; " yf
I thought your keper wold be at Sturbrige fayre I wold come then."
[*It appears from this that the letter was written to one of the prisoners
in Wisbeach Castle.*] " I pray put her name into the Societie that this
bearer shall deliver yow, but ye nede saye nothing to him of yt, for yt
is none of his howse, and therfore I have sealed yt up, because I wold
not have her name knowen ;" 23 July. " Burne my lřc, burne my
lře."

MSS. OF THE INNER TEMPLE.

cxxxiv. f. 374. Letter from [Robert] Fisher, to Dr. Bag[shaw], bitterly inveighing against the Jesuits or "Ignatians." There was never a more fit time for the passage from England. Laxity of the searchers; a student of Douay and a priest came over without any search. A number of Dutch ships are now at London, and within twenty miles, and only waiting for the wind. On the previous Friday the writer saw a good many soldiers start for Flanders, to enlist there because they could not get their living in England, and the searcher passed them at once, saying he wished all who had not wherewithal to live would do the like. Reports a long conversation with Mr. Barras, who refused to help the writer with money to leave England, while professing to be a great friend, and rebuked him strongly for what he had spoken and written against the Jesuits. "And I did smell a rat, for it is hard to halt before a creple. I had his meaning presently, and therefore I did plie him with a carde often," and said all he had done was to tell the truth about the College at Rome. Mr. Barras then said that he would hinder this confraternity as much as he could, and would write his mind about it to those at Wisbeach. "After that I ranne uppon him with a fresh *vi*," and spoke of the ungodly dealing of the Jesuits and the unmerciful dealing of Rome. Barras then spoke most falsely of the great difficulty of getting out of England: "when I hard him speake thus, I was about to breake this jest uppon him, *Fie, goe far, for you smell of tar;* he hath beene so long under Mr. Gerard that he cannot but cog and lie; *lie* I must not say but *equivocate.*" News brought from Rome by Mr. Bartley, and of "some little jarring betwixt the President of Doway, sc. Mr. Dr. Barret and father Conyers, one whom I know to be a prating companion." Desires to know, if Mr. Bluat "be not a quene Marie's priest," where and when he was made so, and what orders he had in Q. Mary's days; also what bishop it was that died here, and how long he was prisoner, and how long Bagshaw and Father Edmonds have been prisoners in Wisbeach. Not dated.

cxxxv. f. 376. The same to the same. Has been unable to deliver the letters Bagshaw sent him; cannot find Mr. Collington; Mr. Long has left England, and Mr. Heb[urne] refused to receive the letter. Has vainly endeavoured to procure money from Mr. Barras for his passage; Bagshaw's brother only gave him 5s.; ever since he came to England has not been in any Catholic's house one week together, and has had to pay for his meat, his bed and his journeys. If he had had 30s. or 40s. he might have passed (the sea) finely. A man lately came to his lodging and asked for him under the name of Brathait, which not any of London knew, and said that whatsoever his name was, he was sure he lodged there. This made his host suspicious and put him to his shift, for he durst not stay there. The few people who knew his lodging deny having sent the man to him. It is plainly given out by the Jesuits that the writer is a crafty spy, and that he only pretends to be a Catholic. He has been told that there is a plot against him. He now fears the Jesuits more than the heretics. If a navy had gone he would have gone with it anywhere, so that he might have landed out of England. In waiting so long for it he has not left anything unsold. He even begged when three miles from London, until told that if he did he must not stay in that town. But let the Jesuits, the world, and devil spit and spite him as much as they will, he is content to bear it. Desires Bagshaw to tell him what to do. Dated May 16. In a postscript he adds that "Mr. D. Norice" is sore sick in Warwickshire, and that he hears that one of his schoolfellows, chamberfellows and bedfellows, named Robinson, was lately martyred at Carlisle.

cxxxvi. f. 377. The same to the same, about a Dominican friar, called Father William, who came into England a little before Easter, and was apprehended, but, by means of his brother and others, was bailed; having supported the cause of the English students (including the writer), who were expelled from the College at Rome, he is now reported by the Jesuits to be a spy; Dr. Norice, Mr. Fletcher, a priest, Mr. Mauger, a priest, and divers others of the same coat, affirmed it to the writer. The latter therefore found the friar in a tavern, and conversed with him, and found him very zealous for the Church of Rome; and has vindicated him to Mr. Barras and others, who accused the writer of conferring with a spy. When the friar was apprehended, there was also taken a young man who served Dr. Elie of Mussipont, and had been sent by his master to Mr. Major upon his fall, a fall which Dr. Elie had bitterly lamented to the writer; and then Elie was said to have sent over a spy. "I se that many wold have men spies who are more honest than themselves. If an honest man come from Rome or Flanders, and not follow their vaine, he is no lesse at first than a spie; and if he come from Spaine or from hel, if he serve them he is no lesse the first day than a seint. Mr. Atkinson came from Spaine in September last, who gave information against his owne fellow being a preist, and hath done much hurt in the North. Mr. Warwicke came from Spaine in Februarie last, and is the cause of all this persecution there. Mr. Nelson came from Spaine of late, and is knowne to be a spie. Theis are honest men, allwayes had in account, never talked of nor taken for knaves." Not dated.

MSS. OF THE INNER TEMPLE.

cxxxvii. f. 378. Letter from G. G. to Dr. B[agshaw]. Received his letters by R. F. and J. H. The tyranny which he sustains; they have far worse to bear than that which they endure of heretics. The only remedy is to send two or three of the gravest of the body to Rome to declare the true state of affairs, and seek redress. Their adversaries have declared that all is quiet and in concord with the fathers, and solicit for a head either a Jesuit or one at their devotion. There are false brethren. Send word of some safe means in London for sending news without fear of interception. Let Dol[man], Mich[ell], Blu[et], Nor[ris], or Butt[on] come; else all is lost. 20 Sept. 1597.

cxxxviii. f. 379. A memorandum endorsed :—" 19 October 1598. Bagshaw of Fisher's coming from Rome, of CardinalToledo his inclination, of the association; the names of the [nine] assistants of the [Archpriest]: " the cause of Fisher's coming to England; the proposal for an Association of priests, and the reasons (including the opposition of lay Catholics) why the device " was utterly disliked and lefte of."

cxxxix. f. 380. Letter from [John Musshe], signed " M. J. Rat." to Dr. Bagshaw and Mr. Bluet. Sends for their consideration and amending ("for I am out of use in writing Latine") a letter which he has written at Mr. Anth. Heb[urn's] request, to be sent to Rome. 28 May, 1598.

cxl. f. 381. Heads of instructions for Fisher on his being sent to Rome to oppose the Jesuits, and to deal with Cardinal Toledo to prosecute his purpose for removing them out of the English college at Rome and out of England; with the objects of the Association of priests. Subscribed " From D. B. to Mr. Wade, in presence of the B. of L. [Bishop of London] and Mr. Lieft." (?) [Lieutenant of the Tower ?]

cxli. f. 382. Another letter from J. Musshe, signed M. J., to Dr. Bagshaw. Sympathises with him about the divisions in their company at Wisbeach. Mr. Gwyn tells him that Fisher is " ungone " as yet from London. He marvels why the man stays all this while, unless it be to carry news of the foul dealing of the Jesuits who band themselves thus mightily against the Association. Had been often warned by Bagshaw and others

MSS. OF THE INNER TEMPLE. against them, but he was ever too incredulous. They accuse him of being the author of the tumults at Rome, of which he knew nothing, and of being the head of a faction to expel them the realm; and, fearing that the credit of the confraternity might countervail theirs, will never endure any union of priests; but the Association should have gone forward, to the confusion of their slanderous tongues, had not Bagshaw's godson, Michell, and others been faint-hearted. Unless the secular clergy seek for redress at his hands that can command them, they will have small credit with the people, or concord among themselves. Hears that "Til" has come out. 8th . . . .

cxlii. f. 383. The same to the same, and to "Mr. Blew [ett]," signed "M. J. Rat." Hears that the Jesuits have succeeded in getting an Archpriest, with twelve coadjutors of their own appointing; if this be so, all their intendments will surcease. Sends by Mr. Thewles 50s. for the common purse; Mr. Barlow will pay 50s. more; and 5l. will be sent through Mr. Coope. 13 July 1598.

cxliii. f. 384. Short anonymous letter, but signed with a monogram " | Ro | " stating that Father Parsons had been trying to obtain superiority
  Px
for the Jesuits in England, and that he was supported by all the Jesuits in and near Rome, but that the Pope would not give them any superiority over the secular clergy, but that the secular church was to be above all the Orders.

cxliv. f. 385. Copy of the commission from Cardinal Cajetan to George Blackwell, S. T. B., 7 March 1597. (Printed in Dodd's *Church History*, ed. Tierney, vol. iii., p. cxix.)

cxlv. f. 387. Original copy of the same, signed and sealed by Card. Cajetan. Signed, "Uti frater, Hen. Car^{lis} Car^{lis} Caetanus, Protector." The word "clarissimam" occurs here (as also in the preceding copy) near the beginning of the document, as originally printed by Dodd, not "durissimam," as altered (with a special note) by Tierney.

cxlvi. f. 389. Copy of Cardinal Cajetan's "Instructiones pro officio Archipresbyteri in Anglia melius exequendo;" 7 March 1598.

cxlvii. f. 391. Statement by Dr. Bagshaw (in his handwriting) of the case of the English clergy against the Jesuits, whose proceedings during the 23 years they have employed themselves in English affairs they have great cause to mislike, and to fear their ruin by them, which Card. Allen foresaw and foretold. They now endeavour (in spite of all remonstrances from grave and learned persons, to whom they have returned replies farced with indignity, contumely, lightness and unlearnedness) to set up a superiority in the form of an Archipresbytery. "From which authority " (" derived from on Cardinall Caietane whom the[y] name the Protector of England"), "as prejudiciall to the dignity of the See Apostolique, and promise and piety of his Holinesse, and obtained only by intervention, shufflinge, glosinge, and false intimation, reputed by our Prince and countrye as trayterous and disloyall, prejudiciall and nowayes profitable to our religion and calling, for many just causes at large to be declared, we have appealed and doe appeale to the Pope's holinesse himself," which appeal they will prosecute.

cxlviii. f. 392. Copy (apparently by Bluet) of a letter (in Latin) from George Blackwell, the Arch-Presbyter, to Bagshaw and Bluett, vehemently censuring them for their opposition to him. 22 Aug. See art. 150 *infra*.

cxlix. f. 395. A long original letter (6 pages) from Father "Rob. Persons" to Mr. Constable. Acknowledges the receipt of his correspondent's letter of July 20, and refers to previous letters from the same.

Alludes to the recent sending of an Ambassador to England who was "a Catholique in profession but none in re." He wrote authorizing the dealing with secretary Cecil, but no word has been sent him of what was done. It is said that the Queen will send new ambassadors to treat of entering into the peace already made between France and Spain. If it so fall out, it will be a good time to deal effectually by means of the King of France that liberty of conscience may be given to the Catholics. He has received many lamentable and earnest letters from England, where the persecution is more rigorous than before. Mentions Robert Pett and his brother, whom he caused to be made priest. Mentions "the turbulent company" and "disordinate proceedings" at [the English College at] Rome. Congratulates his correspondent on having procured some means of maintenance for the English in Paris. The more help there be for their nation the better, if it be well employed. Some persons have written that it may prove a matter of schism and division if the persons be not well chosen. They do not suspect his correspondent's intentions so much as the event itself by reason of the variety of humours that reign, through the art and iniquity of some sticklers among Catholics themselves. His correspondent must be very wary what manner of men he gathers together. The condition would be fittest for good priests who have laboured in England and have been driven back upon particular and personal persecution. As for priests of the seminaries who come to perfect their studies, it would divert their purpose and rebate their fervour of going towards England "wherein all the good of the seminaries consisteth." As for the Masters of Arts that Constable names from the Universities, if they have no inclination to live in seminaries of more strict discipline, Douay would be most proper for them where they may have more liberty, and yet such instruction for the end of helping our country as is needful to frame in them an ecclesiastical spirit. With regard to the succession to the crown people may do and think as they judge best either in respect of conscience or commodity. For himself he could heartily wish that he might attend only to matters of the kingdom of heaven without thinking about the affairs of any earthly kingdom. The misery however of their countrymen in spiritual matters forces them to reflect upon the latter, for otherwise they could have no hope of the restitution of religion. He has no other eye in the world about this affair, but only that the person to be preferred be a tried Catholic, be he of what nation soever. He has no personal aversion from any pretender be he of what religion soever; but so far as he is no true Catholic, "so far am I and shall ever be agaynst him." As to Constable's request for his assistance for obtaining a cross of the Order of Malta, he cannot tell what hope of success he may give, for divers other English gentlemen as Mr. Capt. Crips in Spain, before he was married and since, Mr. Robert Warram, Mr. W. White that serves the King in Sicily, have earnest and long suits, with the recommendation of the King and of "our" Cardinal [Allen] while he was alive, and yet have not sped; and at present Mr. Arthur Poole has all the favour and friends of Cardinal Farnese, and three principal Irish gentlemen came lately, greatly recommended by the King of Spain and by the Ambassador, and with the Pope's letters, and yet are put back hitherto. Sir Andrew Wise, Prior of England, told the writer lately at Naples that the Order had determined not to create any more of these nations, that they enjoy no wealth, until these kingdoms be reduced; for that they cannot send knights thither to make the lawful proofs of lineage according to their statutes, as also that such men admitted are not able to bear out their state without burden of the Order. Indeed he thinks that one principal cause hath

MSS. OF THE INNER TEMPLE.

been that Sir Andrew himself hath wrung (?) from them this dignity of Grand Prior (a principal dignity amongst them for making the Grand Master) against their wills, and also hath constrained them to give him a *commendam* in Italy for his maintenance. But Sir Andrew saith that the true cause is that the French faction, which is most potent in Malta, hold that the English and Irish Catholics are partial to Spain. Denies that any men are ever sent by him as spies to watch what others are doing. Hears it said there is talk of making suit in England to the Queen and Council for peace for Catholics by means of the King of France; others say, that it may be done on condition of the expulsion of the Jesuits. Naples, 31 Aug. 1598.

cl. f. 399. Information from the Keeper of Wisbeach Castle.

"Mem. I do afferme that Calverly, one of the prysts under my charge in the castell of Wysbyche, tould me that Edmunds the Jezuet and his Jezueticall faction did usually resorte together, and had ther pryvat counsayles howe the State should be determyned of after it should pleas God to call hyr Majestie, and that nowe it was fully determyned of by them that then the Cardinall should be our Kynge and the Infanta of Spayne our Queene, and that we should have no other Kynge or Queene but them. Calverlye, in manner pyttyenge them in ther follye, sayde unto me, I praye God helpe them and send them more wyte, for they ware busye-hedded fellowes.

Blewet, presently after Doctor Bagsho was sent for upo by my LL. of the Counsayle, with teares in his eyes, tould me, that himselfe with the secular prysts ware in moste mysserabell takynge, and that he fered ther should letters cume frome a Cardinall that was governer of the Ingleshe Colledge at Rome to Edmunds and his Jezueticall faction to swere all the prysts to the obedience of the Infant of Spayne, as Parsones had caused the prysts that ware in Spayne to be sworene; but Blewet sayd, before he would take suche an othe he would starve in prysson, as himselfe and his fellowes ware lyke to do that would not be factious with them, for the Jezuets had wrought so here in Ingland that they should have no mayntenance from any of ther frynds but suche as should be distributed by the Jezuets. And thus moche of my owne knowledge I cane saye that synce Edmunds was sent for from the Castell ther haue not one penye for ther releife beyne sent thether, the Jezeticall (*sic*) prysts beinge alredy well furnyshed, and the secular prysts havinge scarse monye to releve them.

Ther is under my charge a ffryar they call Sir Wotter, and one Wyges a Jezueticall pryste, who when I stayed my 3 prysonors that would have broken out at ther wyndowes, gave me, ther sayd keper, Richard Blunte, beinge the hygh cunstabell, and Tho. Edwards, one of the right ho. the Lord Noorthes mene, that came to my assystance, verye wylde and leuved speches, in so muche that by multeplyinge of woords they justyfyed Walpoole his actiones that was in Spayne, callynge us knaves and traytores, and that all thoes who so evar ware knaves and traytores that would saye that Walpoole was a traytor.

Wotter reviled me, and sayed that myselfe was the cause that they ment to escape; his reason was, for that he had sent him woord from a secretarye (as he sayde) who was appertaynynge unto a great Counsaylor, that Bagsho was a spye, and myselfe was the caues that Edmunds, Archer, Southwoorth, and Pound, ware sent for from the Castell, tellinge me that if Edmunds had byne here styll he would nevar have attempted to have goone awaye."

cli. f. 400. Draft, in the handwriting of Dr. Bagshaw, of a Latin letter without address, but written to Blackwell, vindicating himself [and Bluet] against the charges brought against them in Blackwell's letter of 22 Aug.; 2 Sept.   MSS. OF THE INNER TEMPLE.

The charges considered are these four : " 1. Illustrissimi domini Protectoris institutiones exagitatas. 2. Permissos ad nos excursus hominum indisciplinatorum. 3. Discerptum exemplar litterarum nuncii Apostolici. 4. Pœnas ex mandato supremæ auctoritatis inflictas (verbis tuis utendum quo sensu tu videris) accusatas." He passes over the employment by Blackwell of such terms as "inconsiderationem, conspectius crimen, obsoletum senium, in moribus splendorem, multa peccata et inhærentia, bonorum offensionem, linguæ petulantiam, parum modestiæ, contemptum, fæcem dissentientium humorum, aculeos verborum, et alia."

clii. f. 401. Draft of a letter from Ro. Bluet to the same, in answer to the same letter of 22 Aug. Did not expect when spending a 22nd year in imprisonment to receive letters with no brotherly love "sed animositatis, contumeliarum, ac detractationum satis plenas." With regard to the tearing of the Cardinal's letter, "agnosco peccatum esse gravissimum, Diabolo instigante commissum, idque excommunicatione dignum, sed alienum, non nostrum." They are compelled to appeal to the Pope, whose sentence they wait for, "cujus sermones sani et recti sunt, firmantes et dantes intellectum." In the same handwriting as ff. 337, 349, and 392 *supra*.

cliii. f. 402. Letter signed C. R. (no doubt Rob. Charnock) to Mr. John Smith; dated "Dominica in albis." They want to see Mr. Blackwell's first letter, and his decree against Paris; "we would gladly see yours, which he sayth be ike to owrs. .... We have sent Mr. Blackwell an answeare to his suspension and interdicte, which I pray yow see sent unto him. In any case, good Sir, fayle not to certifye us uppon what grounde he excepteth againste Mr. Button, Mr. Potter* and Mr. Cope." Great need of money for relief of their wants. "It would grieve you, and it maketh me lawghe and disdayne, to see how some of his seditiouse laymen, ether of feare or simplycyty, looke at us, as if yt were true what John a Greene wrote, that we were to be avoyded as men haveinge the plague soare." "So deale with Mr. Bluett as he may be assisted and counsayled by you and the rest."

cliv. f. 403. Draft by Bagshaw of a letter to the appellants at Rome of the points to be submitted to the Pope, and "cum firmitate petendos."

The first is, " Archipresbyteratus domini Bla., utpote nec expetitus nec utilis futurus, revocandus est." The letter ends thus : " Albanus Dolmannus, sacerdos, publica ludibria in veste sacerdotali Londoni insigni constantia perpessus, ob incarcerationem non semel fortiter toleratam et quadraginta annos in excolenda vinea Domini Anglicana egregie impensos nobilis fidei confessor, idem sentit."

clv. f. 404. Copy, in Bagshawe's hand, of a letter, or part of a letter, to the Pope, representing the case of the appellants against Blackwell. Noted as having been sent "by Mr. Bisse."

clvi. f. 406. "The condicions of yeldinge;" offers "made by the priests about London, as Mr. Collington and the rest," of submitting to Blackwell's authority, "yf any authenticall instrument of his Holiness shalbe shewed unto us wittnesshinge the same to be instituted by him," and with seven other conditions. "Blackwell tooke this in great scorne, and writ accordingly to them."

clvii. f. 407. Long letter from Jo. Sicklemore to Dr. Bagshaw, " prisoner in the castle of Wisbighe;" 3 Aug. 1598.

---

* *i.e.* Dr. George Trensham. Tierney's edit. of Dodd, iii cxlv.

MSS. OF THE INNER TEMPLE.

With reference to the proceedings at the college at Rome, strongly urges Bagshaw to submit to the judgement of others, especially "of the right reverend ff. Per[sons] whose shooues I wish myself worthie to kisse . . . . . whose learning, wisdome, labours, goodwill to our common cause, England hath tried, France *ex ore infantium et lactentium* testifiethe (to confound *inimicum et ultorem*), Spaine with erected colledges largelie witnesseth, and Italie, in Rome in self (*sic*), with established peace most highlie commendeth; finallie, credite, yea familiaritie with the holiest, most potent, most glorious, most godlie, maketh most famous." "The greatest griefe in this matter is the publishing of defames:" what was done herein in the College was by commandment of the Protector; what was done in England was through Bagshaw and others who extorted it, against the will of the superiors. Only some few priests at present know hereof, and no one is named; "it is an easie matter as yet to drowne all before it be imparted eyther to catholyke or heretyke. For Gods sake let us follow ff Gar[net] his counsaile in this, which is wholie to conceale the enormous and beastlie offences: he is wholie bent to yt, that is the mynd of our assigned superior Mr. Blackwell, of his coadjutor, and our dearest friends." Otherwise, the persons will be known and publicly punished, and thereupon must "fall a publike infame both of our cause, churche, and clergie."

clviii. f. 409. Copy of a long letter, in Latin, from John Mushe to [Thomas] More, [great-grandson of Sir T. More] at Rome, representing the wishes of the secular clergy; 27 May 1598.

They desire 1. The appointment of a bishop; 2. The restoration of the English college at Rome out of the hands of the Jesuits, of whose mismanagement there is a long account, with a counter-representation of its condition under Cardinal Alan: 3. The prohibition of the introduction into England of books treating of the affairs and government of England, by which persecution of their religion on its own account is provoked and the priests have to bear the consequences, while those who write them, and particularly father Parsons, live in safety abroad; 4. License to the clergy to meet together for the purpose of laying down rules for their common guidance.

clix. f. 414. Examination of Christ. Southworth, a priest, taken 28 Jan. 1598. Confesses that divers priests have come to them at Wisbeach from beyond seas, and that one Bolt came last summer; that they have often had prayers for hours ("howars") which they call *quarent*, but not since last Lent, and that these prayers were for the conversion of the realm, the good of the country, and for God's glory, "as he supposeth," Signed, "Christopher Sothworth;" examined by John Peyton and another justice.

clx. f. 415. "A true cope" of a letter from Francis Tailour to Blackwell; not dated. Is credibly informed by sundry persons of good reckoning that his wife is here in London, and kept from him by Blackwell: not that he would for the world charge him or any other of his coat and "prospision" with the least unhonest act committed with her or any other woman, nor has he that opinion of her. But she has been withheld from him for almost two years for no cause save that he has showed his poor affection towards the secular priests, to whom he wholly leans, and has spoken on their behalf against the Jesuits and their bad dealings. He cannot impute it to any one so much as to Blackwell alone, shift it off as he can. He came to London, and desired Mr. Watson to entertain him, being persecuted by the Jesuits, who gave out that he was excommunicate and a lewd fellow, and his wife was

drawn away by these persuasions and made to believe that she must MSS. OF THE
not come into his company. He has not been able to hear from her, INNER TEMPLE.
much less to meet her, ever since Father Fleeminge and others of them
got her into Lancashire. But Mr. Watson, hearing that he was a
married man, declared absolutely that he could not entertain him without his wife's consent, and would not believe his explanation until it
was confirmed by others. Had it not been for Watson, who made his
innocency known, the writer had died in the Marshalsea, where that
faction had sought to bring him to the gallows. Because he has
vindicated the secular priests from unjust slanders, they hinder his
living in service, have taken away his good name, and caused him
to 'lose seven hundred marks which they have gotten amongst themselves. He desires to have his clothes returned by his wife. "Aske
father Walley [i.e. Garnet] your great case man . . . . . with
what face he can carye a gentlewoman up and downe the cuntrye
with him . . . . Laste of all, as for my wyfe
herselfe, keepe her and use her as you list and can agree among yourselves, for she shall not, if she and you bothe woulde, seeke to come
any more at me ; let me have a good rounde reckoninge made by you
for her in money after tenne in the hundred, and that is all I looke
for ; you shall never be called unto any counte aboute her by me."
clxi. f. 416. Copy of a long letter (12 pages) from Father Parsons to
Blackwell, dated at Naples, July 12, 1598.
The writer dwells on the causes of the unruliness of the English
students at Rome, and enters into many curious details about the recent
disputes in the College ; in reply to statements in a letter from a priest
in England to Blackwell. The last great broil fell out on the death of
Cardinal Allen, and was due to a secret negotiation of some English
for the advancement into his place for the faculties of "the former
principall man ; " in which all the scholars and the rector of the
college joined ; but the Pope flatly refused. Hereupon they all banded
together by oath against the Protector and the fathers. Such
obstinancy on the part of youths was never before heard of at
Rome. Many wise men begin to suspect that the sufferings of the
martyrs and confessors in England were not so much due to virtue
and love of God's cause as to "a certayne choller and obstinate will
to contradict the magistrate there." "Your friend Robert" [Parsons]
therefore took a long journey from Spain to Rome, where he found
the College divided into two hostile camps, the Father General and
his assistants determined to leave, and the Protector thoroughly
wearied, and the rest of that order extremely scandalized, and
namely, Baronius, who often said that the youths bragged much of
martyrdom, but had no part of martyrs' spirit, which was in humility
and obedience. His holiness often told [Parsons] that he was
never so vexed with any nation in the world, and then related the
different measures that had been taken in the matter. When " your
friend " left Rome eight years before to set up a College for English
youths in Spain, the College in Rome was in good condition. He is
often asked whether the College in Spain will not prove equally unruly in course of time. After much trouble and discussion [which is
related at some length] he made the scholars perceive the evil of their
course ; and peace was at last made on Ascension Day, 1597. But
on the 27th of September next, some scholars were taken at a tavern
on a Sunday morning, and were accused by the taverners of repairing
thither frequently, and others of some worse behaviour. The Pope
therefore ordered a visitation, and some members were dismissed. Some
accordingly declared that the former peace was dissembled, but " your

MSS. OF THE INNER TEMPLE.

friend" assures his correspondent that this is false. Six or seven were quietly dismissed by mission in September, and had their faculties, vinticum, and Pope's benediction, but with a sharp reprehension (*see* art. 131). "Your friend" does not understand why some men in England call his action in the matter "tyrannicall, Turkish, and Machiavillian." Particulars of the withdrawal of faculties from three priests when on their way to England.

In a postscript he adds that his health is somewhat better, and that he hopes the baths will do him good. His companion is sick of an ague. Mr. Martin Aray only is with him. They have been much occupied about the delivery of thirty-four Englishmen whom they found in the galleys at the oars in extreme misery. One was a young gentleman of very good parts, who has been sent to Rome to study at the seminary.

538. 39.—i. [Sir Francis Bacon's] "Certaine observations upon a Libell" (probably by Parsons) "published this present yeere of 1592, intituled, A Declaration of the true causes of the great troubles presupposed to be intended against the Realme of England."

ii. f. 58.—"A Briefe out of the booke of the rites of the Coronacion called *Liber regalis*, for the crowning of the King and Queene together." June 4, 1603. (The coronation of James I. took place on July 25.)

iii. f. 61.—A list of the Peers who were at Winchester for the trial of Lord Cobham and Lord Grey. Nov. 26, 1603.

iv. f. 62.—"The plea betwene the Advocate and the Antadvocate concerning the Bathe and Batchler Knightes, wherein are shewed manye antiquities touchinge Knighthoode, by Frauncis Thynne, esquier, Lancaster Harrold," dedicated to James I., April 2, 1605; dated at the end, "from my house on Clerkenwell greene, this xiii[th] of Maye, 1605." This treatise is not mentioned in the lists of Francis Thynne's printed works.

v. f. 134.—"A booke of all thoffices belonginge to the Quenes Majestie our Sovereigne Ladie Elizabeth . . . . with the names of the officers executing the same, together with theire severall fees and other allowances."

This compilation differs considerably from that which occurs in 538, vol. 34. The date of it appears to lie between A.D. 1569 and 1572.

vi. f. 164.—List of the original Governors of the Charter House, and of the Governors in April 1650, with extracts from the Statutes of the house.

vii. f. 184.—"A catalogue of severall officers in severall Courts whose offices are grantable by the Kinge by Patent," drawn up during the reign of James I.

viii. f. 198.—Ordinances of Edward IV. for the guiding of his eldest son under the care of the Earl Rivers; and rules of the household of the Princess Cicely, mother of Edward IV.; in English.

ix. f. 205.—"A discourse or relation both of the auncyent and moderne estate of the Principality of Wales, Dutchie of Cornewall, and Earledome of Chester," by Sir John Doddridge; not quite perfect at the end. Printed in 1630.

x. f. 269.—Copy of letters patent appointing Sir Edward Denny clerk of the recognizances. 5 May, 31 Eliz.

xi. f. 270.—Translation of a writ for letters patent concerning the settlements of suits with the Church of Norwich concerning grants of concealed lands 31 May, 30 Eliz.; with a rental of the lands of the Church.

xii. f. 276.—Copy of an ordinance of Queen Elizabeth concerning the office of cursitor of the Court of Chancery. MSS. OF THE INNER TEMPLE.

xiii. f. 280*b*.—Account of the receipts and expenses of the See of Norwich after the death of John Parkhurst, Bishop [A.D. 1574].

xiv. ff. 301-311.—Fragment of an entry-book of cases heard in the Archbishop's court in Lambeth Church, from 8 Oct. 1505 to 26 June 1506.

xv. f. 312.—The argument of Mr. Edward Bagshawe against the late Canons in the House of Commons, 9 Dec., 1640.

xvi. f. 356.—The information of Sir Robert Heath, Attorney-General, for citation before the Star Chamber of Sir R. Cotton, John Selden, Gilb. Barrell, and the Earls of Clare, Somerset and Bedford.

xvii. f. 366.—Proceedings against Francis, Earl of Bedford and others aforesaid by Sir R. Heath, Attorney-General; 6 Car. I.

xviii. f. 372.—" Notes touchinge monarchicall governement."

538. 40.—A catalogue of the Cottonian MSS. made in 1674, arranged under subjects.

At the end (f. 178) is a catalogue of books "in the custody of the first secondary in the King's Remembrancer's office, at present Mr. Hall," which were "in the outer roome where the Clerks write at Westminster in Curia Scaccarii," 30 March, 1675; and also (f. 180) " A further catalogue of such books as are in the Augmentation Chest, where the records of late time doe lye."

538. 41.—Another catalogue of the Cottonian MSS., under the heads of the Cæsars' names; with an index of some of the subjects.

538. 42.—" The forme of proceeding upon an appeale of Treason &c. before the Conestable and Marshall in the Court Military where the Combate was to be awarded, represented by Thomas, Duke of Gloucestre, to King Richard the Second, in French, and now translated into Englishe, with annotations out of Recordes, Stories, Manuscriptes, Statutes, and Common Lawe bookes, by Sir John Burgh, knight." The original treatise is not noticed in Walpole's " Royal and Noble Authors." A Latin version of it is printed in Spelman's *Glossarium Archaiologicum* under the title of "Campus" (ed. 1687, pp. 99-103). The annotator, Sir John Burgh or Burroughs, was Garter King at Arms.

538. 43. f. 1. — "Instructions for Francis Walsingham, esquire, sente by the Queen's Majestie to the French King," Aug. 1570; with copies of other instructions and correspondence to 22 April 1571. (Printed in Digges's *Compleat Ambassador*.)

f. 60.—" Of Robert Devereux, Earle of Essex, and George Villiers, Duke of Buckingham, Some observations by way of parallel in the time of theire estates and fortunes." See Art. 9 *infra*.

f. 84.—" A discourse touching a marriage betweene Prince Henry of England and a daughter of Savoy;" by Sir W. Raleigh. (Printed in Raleigh's Works.)

f. 106. — " Certaine Remembrances to Prince Charles, written by Sir Charles Cornewallis, duringe his committment in the Tower, with a copy of a letter written by him when he was Embassador in Spaine, expostulatinge to the Kinge of Spaine the oppressions and injuries done to the Kinge of Englandes subjects, and delaies in givinge justice and remedies to them. July 1609."

f. 133.—" Interrogatories ministred unto the Lord of Bristoll at his returne from Spaine." With his answers.

f. 155.—" The case for a legall reformacon of one of the greatest home trades in the Commonwealth of England, vizt—Sea-cole."

MSS. OF THE
INNER TEMPLE.

f. 163. — "The opinions of the Judges of assizes upon diverse questions concerninge Parishes [the apprenticing of poor children], &c. And Justice Jones his opinion touchinge the commissions by which the Comissioners sitt at Newgate, 1633."

f. 177. — "The Bill in Star Chamber against the Nobilitie and Gentrie, for living and abydinge in the Citties of London and Westminster, contrary to his Majesties Proclamacon," by William Noy, Attorney General. 17 Feb., 8 Charles I.

f. 188.—"An Answer to the Paralell, or the difference and disparitie betweene the estates and condicions of Robert Devereux, Earle of Essex, and George Villiers, Duke of Buckingham."

f. 209.—"Tell truth and Shame the Spaniards, or The certaine manner of Mr. Vice Chamberlaine's [Sir John Digby's] reception and entertainement in the court of Spaine at his last being there, then his Majestie's extraordinary Ambassador," by Francis Phillipps.

f. 224.—"A second Present to the King's most excellent Majestie that now is, touching the furtherance and reformation of Trade," by William Sanderson, gent. 1640.

f. 262. — Proposals by the Cursitors of the Court of Chancery for restraint of the Courts of King's Bench, Exchequer, &c. from encroaching on the Chancery; addressed to the Earl of Clarendon, Lord Chancellor.

f. 268. — Copies of the letter of the Council for the levying of Ship-money, with the assessment of ships, &c. 1635.

Copies in a small neat hand, of various poetical pieces, etc., as follows:—

i. f. 284.—Versions of Psalms 51, 104, and 137, by Mary Sidney, Countess of Pembroke, and "The Triumph of Death," a poem translated by the same out of Italian.

ii. f. 289 b.—Epigrams "out of a pamphlet called Misacmos-merriements," by Sir John Harington.

iii. f. 291.—Two poems addressed to the Earl of Essex.

iv. f. 292 b.—Latin verses addressed to King James, by Alexander Seton, Earl of Dumfermline, Lord Chancellor of Scotland.

v. f. 293.—Analysis of the play called "Vertumnus" by Dr. Gwynne, acted before the King and Queen at Oxford. [1607.]

vi. f. 293 b.—"A foolish song upon Tobacco," [against it] by J. F. It begins:—

"Will you drink a pipe of Tobacco? bis.
'Tis good for the head, and nought for the braine.
'Twill make a man sick, and sober againe."

vii. f. 294.—"The speache of a Prince requiring the opinion of som of his Counsellors, touching the scope of his government;" with three replies.

viii. f. 295 b.—A long and obscene poem entitled "The choosing of Valentines," by Thomas Nash. The first 17 lines are printed at p. lx. of the pref. to vol. i. of Mr. Grosart's edition of Nash's Works as if they formed the whole piece.

ix. f. 299.—"A dialogue betweene Constancie and Inconstancie, spoken before the Queene's Majestie at Woodstock," by Dr. Edes.

x. f. 300 b.—"The Melancholie Knight's complaint in the wood," by Dr. Edes.

xi. f. 301.—A loose Oxford libel, by Thomas Bastard of New College, with the names in the margin of the persons satirized. It begins:—

"Fy, bretheren schollers, fy for shame
Such yonkers tricks amongst you still?

This is one of the lampoons mentioned by Anthony Wood (*Athenæ Oxon.*, vol. ii. p. 228), of which his last editor was unable to find a copy.   MSS. OF THE INNER TEMPLE.

xii. f. 303 *b*.—Presentation letter to Lucy, Countess of Bedford, from Sir John Harington, sending the Countess of Pembroke's Psalms and his own Epigrams. 29 Dec., 1600.

f. 304.— "An Antidote against Jesuitisme, written by the Lord Treasurer Burleigh, to Queene Elizabeth, concerning a pretended peace with Spaine."

f. 315.—Argument of Judge Croke in the Exchequer Chamber, in Hampden's case, 14 April, 1638.

f. 331.—"A Narrative or true Relacion of the death of John Holland, gent. and the prosecution and tryall of Henry Howard, esquire, for the same." 1654.

f. 335.—Arguments of Mr. St. John, Sir Edw. Littleton and Sir John Banks, in the Exchequer Chamber, concerning Ship-money in 1637, with the argument of judge Croke in 1638.

538. 44. f. 1.—Copies of documents concerning the precedence of the Earl of Nottingham, and the Viscount Rochester ; 1619.

f. 13.—"A Treati[s]e of dignities and degrees of all estates, noble and ignoble." Begins :—"All sortes of people created from the beginning are divided into two, noble and ignoble."

f. 25.— Copy of letters patent of William Dethick, Garter King at Arms, concerning the precedence of noble women. Dated Dec. 31, 1591. In Latin, with an English translation.

f. 29.—" The order of all estates of nobles and gentry of England, sett forth this 8th of October in the yeare of our Lord God, 1399," and other tables of precedence in the years 1431, 1479, 1519, and other years, transcribed from manuscripts in the possession of Sir Henry St. George.

f. 39.—" Touching the placeing of the Earle of Arundell in the Parliament howse."

f. 41.—" Questions touching a controversie of precedencie hapned of late betweene two gentlemen."

f. 43.—" An ordinan[c]e or decree made by the Commissioners of the Office of Earle Marshall of England for the precedency of all Estates according to their birth and callinge, dated on Tewsday the 16th of January, anno 1594."

f. 45. — "An acte concerninge placeinge of the Lords in the Parliament Chamber and other Assemblyes and Conferences of Councells. 31 Henry 8."

f. 47.—" Evidences and records prooving the antiquitie and precedency of the Lord Thomas Fitz morris, Lord and Baron of Kirrie."

f. 55.—" Objections and answers betweene the Lord Slaney and the Lord of Kirrie for place and precedencie."

f. 59.—" The question betweene the younger sonnes of Earles and the Knights of the Privie Councell for place and precedencie, which was deliberately heard by his majestie the second of May 1620."

f. 76.—Copies of various documents concerning the precedence of the Lord Mayor, Knights, and Aldermen of London, with the opinion thereon of Ralph Brooke, York Herald, 1607. (See Gutch's *Collectanea Curiosa*, vol. i. p. 95).

f. 90. The opinion of Richard St. George, Norroy King at Arms on " the questions betweene Knights commoners as they call them and Aldermen of London, concerning place and precedency."

f. 102. — The opinion of Richard St George, Norroy King at Arms, and Ralph Brooke, York Herald, on the claim of the wife of

MSS. OF THE INNER TEMPLE. the Mayor of St. Alban's to rank above the wives of Esquires within that town and borough, " that Mistris Mayresse ought not to take place above Esquires wives."

f. 104. — " Orders according to auncient statutes made by John Tiptofte, Earle of Worcester and Constable of England, in the sixth yeare of Edward the fourth, for the placeing of all Nobilitie."

f. 108.—" The placeing of the greate officers according to the Act of Parliament, anno Henrici 8, 31."

f. 110.—" The order of placeing Lords and Ladies according to their degrees."

f. 114. — Copies of writs concerning the precedency of George Talbot, brother of the Earl of Shrewsbury, 1627–30; Sir Francis Seymour, grandson of Edward, Earl of Hertford, 1619; and John Craven, brother of William, Lord Craven, 1637.

f. 122. — Copy of the petition of the House of Lords concerning the precedence of the Scotch and Irish nobility. A.D. 1628.

f. 130.—Copy of a writ of Charles I. for the precedence of the grandchildren of Roger, Lord North, 29 Sept. 1627.

f. 132.—" The decree and establishment of the Kings Majestie concerning the controversie of precedency betweene the younger sonnes of Viscounts and Barons and Baronetts."

f. 136. — " The agreement of the challendge made by John, Earle Marshall, to have his place in parliament above Richard, Earl of Warwick, with the answere of the said Earle of Warwick."

f. 142. — " Orders to be taken for the placeing of Lords and Ladies according to their degrees."

ff. 154, 172, 174, 182, 188, 198, 200, 206, 210.—Copies of various papers relating to the creation of the order of Baronets, and their precedency. Among them (f. 198) is a paper entitled, " Motives to induce the Knights, cittizens and Burgesses of the House of Commons of Parliament, to petition his Majestie for the revoking and abolishing of the degrees of Baronett lately created by his highnes' letters patent." The last paper (f. 210) is a list of the first baronets in order of precedency.

ff. 214, 228. — " The charges belonginge to them that be made Knights of the Bathe, with the charges of the officers of the Kynges howse."

ff. 215, 229.—" Rewardes and payments which was payde by Sir John Legh of Stokwell in the countie of Surrey, whan he was made Knight of the Bathe att the mariage of the most noble Prince Arthure, son and heire to the moost victoriouse Kynge our Soveraigne Lord Henry the 7th, the 27th day of November, the 17th yeare of his most royall raigne."

ff. 216, 230. — List of the Knights of the Bath made at the marriage of Prince Arthur, and Knights of the Carpet. (See Nicolas's *Orders of Knighthood*, vol. iii. Appendix, p. xi.)

ff. 217, 232 —" The maner of makynge of Knyghts . . . . of the Bathe." (*Ibid.*, vol. iii., p. 19.)

ff. 222b, 237.—" The charges of the Knyghts of the Bathe."

ff. 223b, 239.—Lists of Knights of the Bath created in 1475 and in 1477. (Nicolas, vol. iii., App., pp. viii, ix.)

f. 240.—List of Knights dubbed by Henry VI. and his successors down to Elizabeth, arranged in reigns, and in alphabetical order.

f. 252.—List of Knights and bannerets created by Henry VII. at his landing at Milford Haven, at the battle of Redmore, at his coronation, at the battle of Stoke, at the Queen's coronation, at the creation of Prince Arthur, at the creations of Prince Arthur, the

Duke of York, and Prince Henry, and at other times in the course of his reign.   MSS. OF THE INNER TEMPLE

f. 256.—Copies of a writ concerning the fees for Knighthood, 13 Dec. 1606, and of an order in the Court of Requests.

f. 260.—The degradation of Sir Francis Michell from the degree and dignity of a knight. A.D. 1621.

f. 264.—" Sir Robert Knollis, his project concerning esquiers."

f. 274.—Order of precedency drawn up for a procession by Robert Cooke, Clarencieux King at Arms.

f. 278.—Lists of fees paid to the Heralds at Christmas 23 Henry VII., and at the funeral of Queen Elizabeth, A.D. 1604.

ff. 280, 284.—The order of procession to Parliament, March 17, 1627, and April 5, 1614.

f. 286.—Roll of peers. 1614.

f. 292. — Copy of the petition and case of Sir Henry Beaumont for restoration as Lord Beaumont.

f. 296.—Copy of the opinion of the Lord Treasurer and others on the claim of Margaret, sister and sole heir of Gregory, late Lord Dacre, to that dignity.

f. 298. — Copy of an Act for the restoration in blood of the brothers and sisters of the Earl of Kildare. 11 Eliz. c. 13.

538. 45. ff. 1–78. — A large and curious collection of French proverbs with their equivalents in English, arranged in alphabetical order.

f. 81.—" The ancient manner and order of the officers at Armes, to be truely by them observed in tymes both of peace and warr, made and confirmed A.D. 1568 ;" a transcript in the 17th cent.

f. 97b. "The first foundacon of the office of Armes."

f. 113. " A Breviat or direction for the Kinges learned Counsell, collected by the Lord Chancellor Ellesmere, mense Septembris anno 13° Jacobi Regis."

ff. 130, 131. Copies of the grant by Randulph, Earl of Chester, to St. Werburgh's of "Escham at Bruneburgum," in satisfaction of the evils done by him to that church, and of the confirmation by Hen. I.

f. 132.—" Extracts out of the Records wherein may be collected by what meanes the Kings of England have and may rayse moneyes," by Sir Robert Cotton. (Printed in his *Posthuma*.)

f. 153. — " Of the lately erected service called the office of the compositions for alyenacons ;" by Sir F. Bacon.

f. 177. — The Life of Sir Thomas More [by his great-grandson Cresacre More]. This transcript has at the end some English lines beginning :—

" Who with as curious care should veawe,"

which are not given in the edition by Hunter.

f. 275.—" The History of the Earle of Leicester," or, Leicester's commonwealth, [by Father Parsons]. This transcript contains an Epistle to the Reader, and Epistle dedicatory to Mr. G. M. in Gratious Street, London.

f. 334. — " A treatise of the Court of Starre Chamber," in two parts, written by different hands. Beg.:—" I cannot but with admiration reverence."

f. 477.—" Of the suing forth of originall supœnaes."

538. 46.—Original State Papers, *temp*. Hen. VIII.–Jas. I.

A calendar of the contents of this volume by Mr. H. T. Riley is given in the Appendix to the Second Report of the Hist. MSS. Com-

MSS. OF THE INNER TEMPLE.

mission, pp. 151–2; to which the following corrections and additions may be made.

f. 2.—The letter is from the magistrates of Dantzic, and has no reference at all to Cadiz, as stated.

f. 4.—The Princess Mary is to give credit to what her chaplain Dr. Hopton is instructed to utter.

f. 5.—Original.

f. 9.—About news of K. Edward's late illness, and thanking him for a "token" sent to the Princess Mary, the writer.

f. 10.—In French.

f. 12.—For "Decembris" read "Novembris."

f. 279.—A translation of an oration delivered before the senate of Poland.

f. 369.—*Add*, Treaty between England and France in 1498.

f. 379.—The number of houses in the various sea-port towns of Kent is given amongst the other particulars. The date of the return is 18 March 1565, and it does not belong to the time of Hen. VIII.

f. 438.—For "prenthing" read "preaching;" and for "xxiiii June" read "xxiii June."

f. 467*b*.—The letter is in reply to a letter from the Duke of Somerset, in which he urged the coming to his help, and declining to do so since the matter is only a private quarrel between him and the nobility, and the King's person is not in danger; written in the plural number, and subscribed, " From Andover, the viijth of October, 1549, your Grace's loving friends."

f. 469.—Dated from the "Castell of Wyndsor."

f. 470.—Dated "from Wilton."

f. 481.—The Life of Archbishop Edm. Riche is unfinished. It begins, "Beatus Eadmundus Cantuar. Archiep. ex piis parentibus Abendonie genitus," and ends, " post epulas autem et somnum."

538. 47.—This volume of State Papers during the same period is also partially calendared by Mr. Riley with the preceding volume, pp. 152-5.

f. 2.—The word omitted after "addere etiam" is "oportet."

f. 3.—The first part of Bonner's letter is with reference to property of the see of London lost "in the tyme of the wicked [duke] of Somersette," afterwards called "that naughty duke." The latter part, about the heretics, begins thus : "concernyng thees obstinate heretikes that doe remayne in my house, pestering the same, and doyng moche hurte many wayes, some order may be taken with theym, and in my opinion, as I shewed your grace and my lord chanceler, it shuld doo well to have theyme brunt in Hammersmythe," &c. as printed by Mr. Riley.

f. 5.—In the same handwriting as art. 1.

f. 9.—The letter contains ten charges against Wyat, for misdealings in his embassy to the Emperor, while commending him as "wittie and pleasant amongs companye."

f. 25.—A copy, not original.

f. 27.—*Add*, letter from Archbishop Grindal to Archbishop Whitgift; 9 Dec. 1573.

f. 29.—Dated from Leicester.

f. 30.—Endorsed, "Epistola D^{ris} Cox : de nomine Jehova."

f. 32.—Dated "From my Lord Keper's house at Gorhamburie besides St. Albons."

f. 38.—For "15th of June " read " 17th of June."

f. 39.—A copy.

f. 41.—A copy of John Knox's letter to Q. Elizabeth of 28 July, MSS. OF THE INNER TEMPLE. 1559, not of any letter of Chr. Goodman.
f. 43.—Printed in Strype's *Annals*, I. i. 184.
f. 45.—Letter from Jean De Ferrieres, vidamus de Chartres. Dated at London, 3 March.
f. 50.—For " 1 Aug." read " 20 Aug."
f. 51.—A copy, headed, " A letter sent of a precher to the bishope of Norwiche."
f. 58.—Signed by 26 fellows of Magdalen College Oxford, about their being subject only to their visitor the Bishop of Winchester: 5 cal. Mart.
f. 65.—The date is 15 Jan. 1564.
f. 66.—Dated 31 May, 1552.
f. 69.—Refers to a proposed discussion between Wallaye, Lister, and other Jesuits on one side, and some of the secular priests on the other, as to whether the latter are guilty of schism.
f. 73.—*Add*, letter from George Blackwell to Mr. John Collington, Mr. Anth. Wyburne (? Heyburne), Mr. Thomas Moore, Mr. Robert Drurie, " and the rest of their adherents " ; in vindication of himself and the Jesuits.
f. 75.—The heading of the letter is :—" The cause of this letter proceeded of Blakwell's wordes that the Jesuits had many exceptions against him," *i.e.* against the writer of the letter.
f. 76.—Not a " defence of Blackwell," but a long letter to a " very Reverend sir," in defence of the English seculars against Blackwell and the Jesuits.
ff. 84, 85.—The first paper is endorsed, " Mr. Bagshaw of the dealings of the Jesuits " ; the second, " Mr. Bagshaw, that he hath been slaundered at Rome by the Jesuits, to receive an annuall pension of her Matie &c.", being a letter to " Good Mr. John."
ff. 86–90.—Arguments against the opponents of Blackwell as being schismatics.
ff. 91–2.—For " gubernation " read " subordination."
ff. 94–7.—The title is, " A breife colleccion of the causes moving me never to yeeld to the Jesuites thoughe all other sholde, onely in regard of their Machiavelian practises, as heere in parte doe ensue." The list of persons named under art. 22 comprehends about 80 English priests, with several of the English nobility. By W. Watson ; the paper being in the same hand as the preceding and with the letter following of Watson.
ff. 97–105.—The first copy is the original by Watson himself. He gives the history of his own life; the controversy about Doleman's [Parsons's] book on the succession to the Crown, and prays for release from prison. He was sent to Oxford at 10 years of age, to the Inns of Court at 14, at 16 went to Rheims, and at 26 returned home, when he was arrested and committed to prison, and afterwards by Mr. Topcliffe's cruelty to Bridewell, where " all the plagues and torments of that place " were inflicted upon him. The date endorsed upon the second copy is not " 1577 " but 1599.
ff. 106–112.—No " series of small tracts," but 45 heads of articles for enquiry, probably by the Attorney-General or some law-officer, respecting the movements of the Jesuits in England, and the opposition to them of the secular clergy; after 1598. The supposed " titles " given in Mr. Riley's list do not at all refer to this paper.
f. 113.—Answer in Bagshaw's handwriting to the preceding 45 questions.
f. 116.—Signed " Henricus " (Henry Garnet) not " Herring ;" the name of the person addressed is possibly " Payn."

MSS. OF THE INNER TEMPLE. [*The following papers, up to f. 317, are not entered in Mr. Riley's list.*]

f. 117.—Letter, noted as being from "Mr. Heburne," about a letter which Blackwell calls an infamous libel, and of which he supposes Heburne to be the writer.

f. 118.—A letter from John Maister, chiefly about Mr. Mush; 9 Dec. 1598.

ff. 119–22.—Two copies of a letter sent to the Pope, and approved by the Jesuits in England, thanking him for the appointment of Cardinal Cajetan as Protector.

f. 123.—" Out of Mr. Doctor Had[dock's] letters, Nov. 19," about the arrival and proceedings of Bishop and Charnock at Rome.

f. 125.—Letter from W. B[ishop], with an account of the proceedings of himself and Charnock ; Rome, 20 Feb. 1599.

f. 127.—Report by the Earl of Bath to the Council (under his signature) of his examination of Thomas Bridges, 15 Apr. 1599.

f. 131.—Letter from " Ed. T." to Dr. Bagshaw. Complains of Blackwell and " that route," whose " persecution is more greavous and hurtful then the hereticks." From the Clink, 13 June. " Read and burne."

f. 132.—Letter signed R. (or P.) B.; Corpus Christi day, 1599. " Holcorne hath ben at Ofchurche, to establish that syllie man in his conceited opynion of their cause."

f. 133.—A third letter from M[artin] A[rray], [one of Blackwell's agents], about Bishop's and Charnock's proceedings at Rome.

f. 135.—Letter from Blackwell's proctor [Haddock] at Rome giving account of the pleadings before the Pope in reply to Bishop and Charnock ; 20 Feb. 1599.

f. 137.—Cajetan's grant of faculties to priests in England submitting to Blackwell ; 2 Feb. 1599.

f. 138.—" Objecta de seditione, ser. D. oblata contra duo (*sic*) presbyteros Bish. et Ch. per Rich Haddo[ck] et Mart. Ar[ray] in causa Archipresbyteri procuratores, 10 Jan. 1599."

f. 140.—" Exemplar literarum d. Joh. Wrighte, decani Cortracensis ad Card. Cajetanum." 3 id. Nov. 1599.

f. 141.—Extract from a letter of Blackwell's.

f. 142.—Answer (*Lat.*) to the libel of Haddock and Array against Bishop and Charnock, presented to Cardinals Cajetan and Borghese in the English College, 17 Feb. 1599.

f. 146.—Latin letter from Rome [from the Nuncio Apostolic to Blackwell] ; prid. id. Jan. 1599.

f. 146.*—Copy of the brief of Clement VIII. confirming the appointment of Blackwell; 6 Apr. 1599. (Printed in Tierney's Dodd, III. cxxviii.).

ff. 147–154.—Four original letters of Robert Parsons ; of which two are to Mush and Collington, and one to Dr. Cecill; 1 Aug. 1598, 9 Apr., 17 July, 4 May, 1599.

f. 155.—Anon. letter to Dr. Bagshaw against Parsons, who is said to have intercepted letters of Dr. Gifford's to Bagshaw in which he said that Parsons had prepared knives to cut the King of Scots' throat, &c. ; 4 June.

f. 156.—Copy of a long letter from Parsons to Bishop; Rome, 9 Oct. 1599.

ff. 165, 166.—Original and copy of an angry letter from Blackwell to Mr. Francis [Francis Clerke], threatening him with suspension ; 27 Feb.

f. 167.—Letter signed Fra. Cle[rke].
f. 168.—Reasons against submission to Blackwell; *Lat.*
f. 171. Anon. letter to Bagshaw, which accompanied copies of a letter from the writer to Blackwell and of the latter's reply; 9 March.
f. 172.—Long narrative, addressed (as appears from marginal notes) by Collington to Walley [*i.e.*, Garnet], in vindication of himself.
f. 186.—Long letter, in the same handwriting, to a lady, signed . Duckett; but noted in the margin, "Holtcby, the Jesuit, against the secular priests, answered by Mr. Collington."
f. 198.—Letter to Blackwell, signed T. M. Ratcliffe, but endorsed as being from Mush, in answer to two letters from Blackwell; 2 March.
f. 199.—Unsigned letter to Giulio Piccioli at Venice, with particulars of the expenditure of money, dated at London, 21 July 1599, and endorsed, "This is from Garnet, the Jesuyte, alias Walley, of his owne hand."
f. 200.—Anon. letter to Collington, mentioning a report that twelve articles were presented to the Council for removing the Jesuits out of England; 3 March.
f. 200*.—Short letter from F. Gray to Bagshaw.
f. 201.—Prohibition by Blackwell of the publication of books offensive to the State, or injurious to the unity of the Church; 17 Jan. 1599.
f. 202.—Copy of the decree of Cardinals Cajetan and Borghese of 21 Apr. 1599. [Tierney's Dodd, III. cxxvii.]
f. 203.—Letter from John Blacsaw, a Jesuit abroad, to John Floyd, a Jesuit "en Balverde," about news from Garnet, &c.; 7 Sept. 1599.
f. 204.—Letter from John Mush to Bagshawe; he, Collington, and Heburne are deprived of their faculties: warns Bagshaw to be on his guard.
ff. 205, 6.—Copies of two anonymous letters of submission to Blackwell; 7, 16 Jan. 1600.
f. 207.—Letter from R. B. to Bagshaw, complaining that he is worse off, as regards his maintenance, since he submitted to Blackwell than before.
f. 208.—Letter from Blackwell to Mr. Thomas Barlow, urging him to continue his hospitality to Mr. Nicholas; 16 Feb. 1600.
ff. 209, 210.—Copies of an order from Blackwell for the examination in the Clink of Will. [*al.* Francis] Clerke, priest, a prisoner there, as to his having written a seditious letter dated 17 Nov. 1600, and of a sentence of suspension against him on 10 March 1600.
f. 211.—Statement, in Latin, by Blackwell of the controversy between him and those who repudiate his authority; 14 March, 1600.
ff. 212-213.—Copy of a letter from Blackwell to Collington, demanding the names of the persons who framed a supplication to him; 16 March, 1600; with a reply from Collington.
f. 215.—Very long letter from W. Bishop in answer to a letter to him of 9 Oct.; 10 Apr. 1600.
f. 223.—Copies of some letters that passed between one of the seculars and Blackwell in May and June 1600.
f. 224.—Letter from Arthur Pittes, dean of Liverdun, to Blackwell, commending Charnock, who had been staying for some time with him; 11 Apr. 1600. (A copy?)
f. 225.—Extracts from various letters.
f. 227.—Letter from Bagshaw to Thomas Bluett, with the following curious endorsement by the latter: "Mr. Parsons about 3 yeares since was tempering and hatching a plott to set up Essex against her Matie.

MSS. OF THE INNER TEMPLE. Hereof he brake with a priest, and acquaynting him with the hopes that he should have out of Spayne and the Lowe Contries, moved the said priest to be his messinger of this matter unto the Earle. But the priest refused to be a dealer in any such cause, and yet gave hym good words lest otherwise he might have procured hym to have been sent to the galleys. The said priest told me thus much : and I having written of it to Dr. Bagshaw, he desyred here to be better instructed."

f. 228. Announcement by Blackwell of the granting of a jubilee by the Pope to English Catholics.

f. 229.—Copy of the opinion of the Theological faculty at Paris about the authority of the Arch-presbyter; 3 May, 1600. (Tierney's Dodd, III. cxxx.)

f. 230.—Circular letter of Blackwell's containing his decree against the preceding opinion; 29 May. [The decree is printed *ib.* cxxxi.]

f. 231.—Letter [from Parsons] to Mr. Collington, deprecating the revival of strife ; 3 June, 1600.

f. 233.—Letter from John Darell upon Blackwell's censure of the Paris opinion ; Agen, 14 Aug.

f. 235.—Copy of a letter from Parsons to Mr. John Bennet, on the same subject as the letter to Collington above ; 24 Sept. 1600.

f. 238.—Copy of a decree from Blackwell, dated 18 Oct. 1600. *Lat.*

f. 240.—Letter from Francis Clerke [to Bagshaw ?] expressing his abhorrence of all traitorous attempts ; with particulars of a proposal made by Mr. Oldcorns (about the time of the appointment of the Archpresbyter) to a gentleman to form one of a band who should seize the Tower of London, and hold it until help should come from Spain ; and Mr. Jones' boasting that he had 60 or 100 tall fellows ready in Wales, "when tyme should serve . . . . . either by invasions, civill mutinies, or deathe of her Majestie."

ff. 241-243.—Draft of orders drawn up by Will. Brewster, Keeper of Framlingham Castle, and submitted to the Privy Council, for the better government of the priests and recusants imprisoned there ; with a list of the prisoners, divided into three classes : i. "thoes which do reforme themselves and obeye their orders, all poore, and shortly will have no monye," in number 8: ii. "thoes which be moste obstynate and deserve hangynge," in number 20 : ii. "the more temperat," in number 12.

ff. 247, 249.—Copies of a letter from Cardinal Borghese to Charnock, dated 15 Sept. 1600, and of Charnock's reply, dated at London, 4 Nov. 1600. *Lat.*

f. 254.—Report by Sir Thomas Challoner that the English at Rome are regarded as traitors to their country.

f. 255.—List of all the members of the English college at Douay ; with an account of the Jesuits' seminaries ; endorsed as being " Swift's declaration."

f. 256.—Latin version of the appeal of 33 priests against Blackwell of 17 Nov. 1600, of which an English version is printed in Tierney's Dodd, III. cxxxiii.

f. 261.—Unsigned letter from Mr. Drury (*endorsement*) to Blackwell ; 16 Dec. 1600 ; with copy of another letter, and of a sentence of suspension by Blackwell on 17 Dec.

f. 265.—Copy of a Latin letter from Blackwell upon the appeal against him, 20 Dec. 1600.

f. 266.—Statement by Thomas Bluett respecting the proceedings of Bishop and Charnock at Rome.   MSS. OF THE INNER TEMPLE.

f. 267.—Copy of a letter (noted as being by " Mr. Clarke") giving a narrative of the proceedings in the controversy with the Jesuits, to the time of the Paris sentence ; 20 Dec.   Injured by damp.

f. 270.—Letter, mutilated by damp, to " Good Mr. Jhon," representing the sufferings of the writer.

ff. 272-6.—Copies of six Latin memorials to the Pope, one of them in behalf of John Fisher.

f. 277.—Memorial to the Cardinals, 6 Sept., on behalf of the priests deprived of their faculties by Blackwell. *Lat.*

f. 279.—Long letter from Franc. Clerke, arguing on the charge of schism ; 27 March.

f. 282.—Reply from E. Hall to the preceding letter, described as " your long and passionate letters stuff with manic bad words and uncivill termes." See f. 288 *infra*.

f. 283.—Rejoinder from Clerke, very temperately worded.

f. 284.—" Certayne considerations" in defence of those who withhold obedience to Blackwell, by F. Clerke.

ff. 286-296.—Copies of various letters from Clerke to Blackwell, and from the latter to Clerke. In some of them Clerke signs as " Francis, *alias* Will. Clerke," and Blackwell addresses him simply as " Francis." See f. 165 *supra*.

f. 288.—Letter to Clerke from E. Hutton, in the same hand as the letter signed E. Hall, above. 8 March.

ff. 292, 3.—Two copies of a letter to [Clerke] in vindication of the Society of Jesuits, dated 11 Nov. 1598, and signed " Henery," *i.e.*, H. Garnet.

ff. 298, 301, 302.—Three letters from Charnock to Bagshaw, one dated 9 Aug. 1598.

f. 303.—Sixteenth century transcript of the Latin version of Sir Th. de la More's Life of Edw. II.

[*At this point Mr. Riley's list recommences for a few pages, and the following are only additional notes as far as f. 371.*]

f. 318.—The proposed sumptuary laws of Edw. V. are printed in J. G. Nichols' *Literary Remains of Edw. VI.*, vol. II., pp. 496-8.

f. 321.—Letter from Dr. Laur. Humfrey to Bishop Jewell, who had objected to Humfrey's having preferment in his diocese on account of his nonconformity, promising conformity when there. Strype's *Parker*, I. 370.

f. 323.—Letter from Dr. Thomas Sampson to Archbishop Parker. Lond. 3 June 1565. Parker's *Corresp.* 213.

ff. 325, 7.—Letters from Parker, printed in his *Corresp.*

f. 336.—The letter is to Archbishop Grindal, and is printed in Strype's *Life of Parker*, III. 319.

f. 342.—For " Mr. E." read " G. H.," and for " cared not a curse " read " cared not a rushe." The inquiries are about the hearing mass, the having popish books, including one called *A knacke to knowe a knave*, knowledge of papal bulls, &c. The other persons examined are T. P., the under-treasurer, J. S., E. P., and Matth. Shastowe.

f. 344.—For " Liner " read " Lever."

ff. 347, 372, &c.—Letters from W. Cecill, Lord Burghley, to Archbishop Parker, all printed in the *Parker Correspondence* published by the Parker Society.

MSS. OF THE INNER TEMPLE.

f. 364.—Copy of the bull of Pope Pius absolving the subjects of Q. Elizabeth from their allegiance, 1569.

f. 371.—A copy of Bishop Scory's letter to Edw. VI., reminding him of things petitioned for in one of his sermons. Printed in Strype's *Memorials*, II. ii. 431.

f. 379.—Copy of a letter written by Dr. John Bate to Mr. Ashley, touching the troubles and controversies between the Protestants and Puritans in 1556.

f. 381.—Copy of the archbishop's mandate for publication and observance of the Queen's Injunctions for reformation of the Calendar, and setting up the tables of the Commandments; 15 Feb. 1560.

f. 384.—Copy of a letter signed H. (most probably from Garnet) on the publication of the Pope's brief of 5 Oct. 1602, urging obedience on the part of the Jesuits and the restraint of intemperate speeches, &c.; 16 Nov. 1602.

f. 385.—Letter in French to Dr. Cecill; signature mutilated, but probably from the French ambassador at Rome; has written to the King, M. Villeroy, and M. de Beaumont, the ambassador in England, on his behalf; Rome, 4 Nov. 1602.

f. 386.—Letter from W. Stannee to "P. Nang.," recommending one who wishes to enter the Society of Jesuits; 10 Apr. 1602.

f. 387.— Letter from Blackwell to T. Darcie, recommending the same person, who desires to show his penitence for having been influenced by Watson's *Quodlibets against the Jesuits*; 11 Apr.

f. 388.—Letter from J. Percee to H. Fitz., in behalf of the same, who had been the cause of the apprehension of two Jesuits.

f. 394.—Copy of the commission of Edw. VI. for the deprivation of Bishop Gardiner.

f. 397.—Draft of a letter from a Cardinal legate to the Pope.

f. 398.—Contemporary copy of the will of Hen. VIII. Endorsed, "Received of Mr. Grafton."

f. 407.—Copy of a mandate of the Archbishop of Canterbury for execution of an order of the Council for the removal of images; 24 Feb. 1547.

f. 409.—Letter from [the Queen of Hen. VI.] to the Prior of Christ Church, Canterbury. "By the Queen. Right trusty and welbeloved in God, We grete you welc. And for the grete zele, love and affeccion that ye have towards my lords helth and welefare as tacerteine us of suche holy water and relik as ye have, We thanke you with al our hert. And to that entent that my lord may have sume of that blessed water We sende therefore unto you at this time his aunner, Maistre Henrye Seyver* for to bringe it hider, after your mocion and benevolence in this partie. And our Lord haue you in his koping. Yeven under our signet at Wyndesore, the xxx day of Avrill."

f. 410.—"De ecclesia confessio magistri Johannis Wickleff;" a 16th cent. transcript.

f. 415.— Commencement of Archbishop Chicheley's foundation-charter of All Souls' Coll., Oxford.

On the back of f. 415 is a "note of [a] monster," seen, apparently, by a labouring man in June at Mitcham, Surrey.

f. 416.—Draft of clauses " to bee conteyned in my last will as parcell thereof," *sc.* the will of Edw. VI.; in the same hand (that of Secretary Petre) as the agreement of the Council about the succession at f. 316,

---

* D.D., Chancellor of London, died 1471.

described in Mr. Riley's list.   Printed in J. G. Nichols' *Literary Remains of Edw. VI.*, Vol. II. pp. 574-6.

f. 418.—Letter from Edw. VI. and the Council to Bishop Gardiner; 8 July, 1550.   Printed in Strype's *Memorials*, II. i. 373.

ff. 419, 435.—" General notes of matters to be moved by the clergie in the nexte Parliament and Synod." 1562. Two copies; one the rough draft. Printed in Strype's *Annals*, I. i. 473-184.

ff. 426, 462-6.—Extracts out of the *Admonition to the Parliament*.

f. 448.—The judgment of W. Alley, Bishop of Exeter, about doctrine and discipline.   1562.   Printed *ibid.*, 518-522.

f. 450.—" Certen articles in substance, desired to be granted by the Q. Majestie."   *Ibid.*, 522-5.

f. 451-5.—Copies of letters from Lord Burghley to the University of Cambridge, and of the reply.   Feb.-March, 1572.

f. 456.—Forms of protestations of allegiance for Papists and Puritans. Printed in Strype's *Life of Parker*, II. 64, under date of 1571.

f. 457.—Copy of the order for the apprehension of Thomas Cartwright; 11 Dec. 1573.   Strype's *Annals*, II. i. 418.

f. 458.—" Argumenta quædam quibus probatur non debere ministros verbi obtemperare principi cerimonias et formam amictus prescribenti." Endorsed, " From the Superintendent."

f. 459.—Answer to a sermon preached by Thomas Cooper, Bishop of Lincoln at Paul's Cross, 27 June, 1572. In a very small, close hand. Strype's *Annals*, II. i. 286-304.

f. 461. Letter from Thomas Norton to Archbishop Parker; 16 Jan. 1572.   Strype's *Parker*, II. 143, with omission of a few words.

ff. 467-8.—Copies of articles ministered to Edw. Dering in the Star-Chamber, of a letter accompanying them from Sir T. Smith, 7 June 1573, and of Dering's answer.   See Strype's *Annals*, II. i. 415-7.

ff. 470, 479-81.—Notes of the preparation of some papers before the examination of Dering and Wiborne, and of the proceedings in the Star-Chamber; articles proposed to them; Dering's assertions, &c.; in the same hand as some of the extracts from the *Admonition*. The Articles and Assertions are printed in Strype's *Parker*, II. 239, 240.

f. 471.—Copy of three articles affirmed by John Browning, of Trin. Coll. Cambridge, in explanation of a sermon preached 25 Jan. 1572.

f. 472.—" Certeine articles holden by divers in Elie diocess, soe declared by the Lord Northe."

f. 473.—" To our Catharytes or brethrene of the puritie, as they call it, which franticly have reported the Communion of our booke to bere the face of a popishe Masse."

f. 474. Short answer, with regard to the controversy about apparel, " to all that can be objected against the refusers of those idolatrous garments."

ff. 476, 478.—" Certaine things sediciously uttered [by -- Crick] at Paules Crosse, 19 July, 1573," as reported by Will. Gravett; with Crick's answer.

f. 477.—Notes out of " The Cobler's book " against the Church, entitled, " This is the healthe both of Elizabeth our Quene," &c. See Strype's *Whitgift*, I. 565-6.

f. 482.—Long letter, in Latin, from Andrew Kingsmill, to Archbishop Parker, against the surplice; Oxon, 13 Cal. Febr. [1564]. See Strype's *Parker*, I. 313.

f. 491.—Letter from Andr. Perne, John Whitgift, Tho. Byng, and John Still, to Archbishop Parker in favour of Dr. Styward; Cambridge, 17 March, 1574.

MSS. OF THE INNER TEMPLE.

f. 492.—Declaration of Rob. Sharp, and others, suspected to be of the Family of Love, before Dr. Perne at Cambridge, 13 Dec. 1574. Strype's *Parker*, II. 382–5.

f. 494.—Letter from Dr. Perne to Archbishop Parker, recommending Dr. Styward; 17 March 1574. *Ibid.*, II. 398.

f. 495.—Propositions for restraint of the Puritans. *Ibid.*, 354–5.

f. 496.—Translation from the French of the will of Raoul le Chevalier, or Cavalerius, 8 Oct. 1572; attested by Paul Typoots, notary at London. Cf. *ibid.*, 146–7.

f. 499.—Letter from Whitgift to Archbishop Parker, sending the first part of his answer to Cartwright; 2 Oct. 1572. *Ibid.*, III. 207.

f. 500.—"Ministrorum petitio" to the Archbishop of Canterbury and the Bishops for limiting the sense of subscription to the Prayer Book, relaxing its obligation.

f. 501.—Copy of the Queen's mandate for the consecration of Rich. Rogers as suffragan Bishop of Dover; 12 May, *an.* 11.

f. 502.—Letter from Lord Burghley to Archbishop Grindal, in behalf of Mr. Ramsden, parson of Spofford; 25 Nov. 1575. Part in Strype's *Grindal*, 201.

f. 503.—Reasons [by Archbishop Parker] why bishops may be called lords. Strype's *Parker*, II. 285–7.

ff. 504–5.—Three articles of subscription to the Prayer Book and 39 Articles, signed by Thomas Sartore (?), John Walker, Will. Fulke, Rob. Tower, James Yong, Tho. Edmund, and Rich. Pickering. Again, with qualification, by James Yong, at f. 512.

f. 506.—Draft of letter from Archbishop Parker to Sir W. Cecill; 6 Feb. 1570. Parker's *Corresp.*, 378.

f. 507.—Letter from the High Commission to the Duchess of Suffolk for the sending up of her chaplain Browne; 13 Jan.

f. 508.—Copy of a letter from Archbishop Parker to Bishop Sandys; 24 Nov. 1573. Parker's *Corresp.*, 451.

f. 509.—Letter from Bishop Cox of Ely to Archbishop Parker; 5 Dec. 1573.

f. 510.—Printed folio leaf of "The Charge geven to the Inquest at Chelmsford, 15 Dec. 1573."

f. 511.—"The Protestacōn of the Puritanes." Strype's *Parker*, II. 283–5.

f. 513.—Letter from Whitgift to Archbishop Parker; 4 June 1573. *Ibid.*, 253–4.

f. 514.—Copy of the preface to the Advertisements of 1564, as in the MS. cited by Strype, *ibid.*, I. 314.

ff. 515.–21.—The original copy of the Advertisements; signed by the bishops whose names are attached in the printed book. Printed by Strype, from a copy which he describes as "penes me," in the *Life of Parker*, III. 84–93, where, however, at p. 37 for "receve sometymes" read "receve foure tymes."

f. 518.—Letter from Archbishop Parker and Bishop Sandys to another Bishop; 6 July, 1573. Parker's *Corresp.*, 434.

f. 519.—The three Articles given at ff. 504–5 *supra*, with the subscriptions of John Lane, John Scarlet, Rob. Buckberd, John Stybbynge, and Tho. Knell, vicar of Hackney.

f. 522.—Latin letter from Dr. Andr. Perne to Archbishop Parker; 25 Oct. 1564. Abstract in Strype's *Parker*, I. 349.

f. 524.—Sir W. Cecill, just recovering from sickness, to the Duke of Northumberland, about the preparation of his own robes, &c. as a knight of the Garter; 14 May [1572].

f. 525.—Letter from Grindal, Bishop of London, to Archbishop Parker; 2 Jan. 1563. Parker's *Corresp.*, 201–2.

f. 526.—Letter from Richard Kechin to Mr. Pearson, Archbishop Parker's almoner; 3 July 1564. Strype's *Parker*, I. 304–6. MSS. OF THE INNER TEMPLE.

ff. 528, 536.—Two copies of a letter from Bishop Pilkington of Durham to the Earl of Leicester; 25 Oct. 1564. Strype's *Parker*, III. 69–73.

f. 531.—Suggestions for orders to be made about private baptism, omission of the sign of the cross, &c. and for orders to be made " in this present synode " to be observed by the bishops, &c.

f. 532.—Copy of a letter from Whittingham, Dean of Durham, to the Earl of Leicester; 1564. Strype's *Parker*, III. 76–84.

ff. 538, 539.—" Imagines in templis Christianorum non esse tolerandas." Two papers on the subject.

ff. 542, 545.—Draft of the letter from Archbishop Parker and Bishops Grindal and Cox to Q. Eliz. urging her to marry. Strype's *Parker*, III. 44–6.

f. 543.—Letter from Ed. Campion to the Privy Council, written on his coming to England, to be in readiness in case of his apprehension. Printed in Strype's *Annals*, III. ii. 182-6 as from " Foxii MSS."

f. 646.—" Resolutions concerninge the Injunctions;" endorsed, " A declaration to have been made of the Injunctions, by Dr. Cox," 1560. Strype's *Annals*, I. i., 318–322.

f. 553.—Draft of the Preface originally prepared for the second book of the Homilies, 1562. Strype's *Annals*, I. i. 516–8.

ff. 555–557.—Draft of Bishop Cox's letter to the Queen on refusing to minister in her chapel on account of the lights and cross remaining there; with his *Considerations* thereon. Strype's *Annals*, I. ii. 500–503.

f. 561.—Nineteen articles in Latin subscribed by licensed preachers " in Bp. Cox his tyme ; " with the signatures of Rob. Beaumont, Edw. Harnys, A. (?) Bedford, John Lakin, John Andrew, Andr. Plandon, and Rich. Harryson.

f. 562.—Notes in Latin against the use of images.

f. 564.—Notes on the increase of ministers' livings, on rites and ceremonies, marriage, &c., with reference to some book of injunctions or articles.

f. 569.—" For reformation concerning desolation of churches, by reason of exilitie of stipends."

ff. 572-3.—Two letters from Sir W. Cecill to Archbishop Parker for licenses to eat flesh in Lent; 23, 27 Feb. 1562. Parker's *Corresp.*, 172.

ff. 574, 588.—" Acta in inferiori domo Convocationis die sabbati xiii. die Feb. 1562." *Engl.* Strype's *Annals* I. i. 502, 504-5.

f. 576.—Copy of the request of 33 members of Convocation, for alterations in ceremonies, &c. *Ibid.*, 500-1.

f. 577.—Propositions in Latin, sent to " Mr. Elmer " [Aylmer], prolocutor of the Lower House of Convocation, by Tho. Thornton, proctor for Ch. Ch. Oxford, for additions to the 37 Articles.

f. 579.—Letter from Dr. Laur. Humfrey to Archbishop Parker, in defence of his non-conformity; 11 Feb. [1564 ?].

f. 581.—" The requestes and petitions of the Clergie in the Lower House of Convocation," 1562. Strype's *Annals*, I. i. 508–12.

f. 585.—Draft of an Act for providing better stipends for the clergy. *Ibid.*, 514.

f. 586.—Articles of enquiry with a view to the aforesaid Act. *Ibid.*, 513.

f. 589.—" An order for the serving of curys nowe destitute."

MSS. OF THE INNER TEMPLE.

f. 592.—Copy of the commencement of the Queen's instructions to Dr. Rob. Horne and Dr. Tho. Huyck, visitors of the dioceses of London, Norwich and Ely (1559).

538. 48. f. 1.—Copy of the instructions sent by Queen Elizabeth to Sir Henry Nevill, John Herbert, Robert Beale, and Thomas Edmunds, appointed to treat with the Commissioners for the King of Spain and the Arch-Duke of Burgundy, for the conclusion of a peace. 1600.

f. 40.— "The negotiations of Sir George Carey (Carew), knight, during his residence in France." (Printed in 1749 in Birch's *Historical View of the Negotiations between the Courts of England, France, and Brussels.*)

f. 90.—" Sir Richard Weston, his negotiation with the Arch-Duchesse at Bruxells." 1622.

538. 49. f. 1. — " The death of Queene Elizabeth, with her declaration of her successor." (Printed in Nichols' *Progresses of Elizabeth*, vol. iii., pp. 607–609.)

f. 3.—"The manner of the sickness and death of Prince Henry, sonne to King James. Anno 1612." (Printed in Nichols' *Progresses of James I.*, vol. ii., pp. 478–485.)

f. 14b.—" A discourse of the Queenes marriage with the Duke of Anjoue, drawne out, as is thought, by the Lord Keeper, Sir Nicholas Bacon, anno 1570."

f. 22b.—Notes of proceedings in the Court of Star Chamber against the Earl of Hertford, and against John Hales.

f. 23.—" Certaine articles of Comes Imperii taken out of an epistle of Count Arundell."

f. 23b.—" An answere to the King's letter for staie of justice, made by all the justices the 25 day of Aprill, anno 1616."

f. 25.—"The copie of a letter written by the Lord Chancellor Ellesmere to the King, desiring to be discharged of his office." 1612.

f. 26b.—" The Pollitica of the United Provinces."

f. 35.—Copies of a letter from the Archduke Ernest to Queen Elizabeth, October 14, 1595, and her answer, October 30, 1595.

f. 36b.—" The Ladie Elizabeth, her grace's answer made at Hatfield the 26 of April 1558, to Sir Thomas Pope, knight, being sent from the Queenes Majestie to the same, to understand how her grace liked of the motion of the marriage made by the King elect of Swethlandes (Sweden's) messenger." (Printed in Nichols' *Progresses of Elizabeth*, vol. i., pp. 23–25.

f. 38.—Copy of a letter from Henry Cuffe, secretary to the Earl of Essex, to Secretary Cecil, concerning the title of the King of Scots to the crown of England.

f. 41b.—Protestation of Sir Thomas Smith, one of the Sheriffs of London, concerning the words which he used to the Earl of Essex, when the latter fled into the City [A.D. 1601], with notes of some remarkable occurrences connected with his execution, such as the fall of his portraits in the houses of Lord Willoughby and Lord Mountjoy.

f. 42b.—Copy of a letter from W. Liddington, [*i.e.* Will. Maitland, laird of Lethington] Secretary of Scotland, to Sir William Cecil, concerning the title of the Queen of Scots to the crown of England. January 14, 1566.

f. 49.—" Directions of Queen Marie to her Councell, touching the reformation of the Church to the Roman religion, out of her own originall."

f. 50b.—Copy of a letter from Queen Elizabeth to the King of Scots, concerning Valentine Thomas, and other persons and matters. May 11, 1601. MSS. OF THE INNER TEMPLE.

f. 54.—Copy of a letter from the same to the same, against the reception of an ambassador from Spain.

f. 55b.—Life of Sir Thomas Bodley, written by himself. (Printed in 1647.)

f. 59.—Copy of a letter from the Lords of the Council to James I. concerning means for the increase of the revenue.

f. 64b.—" The examination of Sir Anthonie Browne touching the Lady Marie's submission to King Henrie the Eighth, her father."

f. 67.—Copy of enquiries made by the Commissioners at Boulogne, June 20, 1600, concerning treaties, etc., and of the reply of the Lords of the Council, dated June 30, 1600.

f. 71b.—Copy of a letter from the Lords of the Council to the Commissioners at Boulogne. July 25, 1600.

f. 76.—Copy of a letter from Sir Robert Cecil to the same, July 25, 1600.

f. 77.—" Questions propounded by Queene Mary, and answered by her Councell touching the continuance of a treaty made by Henry VIII. with the Emperor and [the] King of France."

f. 80.—" Abatementes now in being or to be verie shortlie upon the marriage of the Ladie Elizabeth to the Count Pallatyne of the Reigne (Rhine) anno 1613, and otherwise for the Kinges benifitt, by the Comisioners of the Treasury."

f. 82.—A table of the ordinary revenue and expenditure of Great Britain, temp. Jac. I.

f. 84.—Propositions made by the French ambassador to the Assembly of the States General of the United Provinces, December 12, 1618.

f. 87.—Copy of a letter from Viscount Cranborne to Sir Thomas Parry, Ambassador to the King of France, April 14, 1604.

f. 89.—The opinion of "auntient doctors" concerning the right of reprisals and embargo in international law.

f. 92b.—Account of the charges paid by Walter, Earl of Essex, for his installation as a Knight of the Garter, June 18, 1572.

f. 94.—Copy of a letter written by Lord Norris to the King after he had slain one of Lord Willoughby's servants. 1615.

f. 95.—Epitaph on Rich. Burbage, the player.

ib. Commencement of Fr. Tate's treatise on cities and boroughs.

538. 50. f. 1.—Bishop Lesley's Discourse of the affairs of Mary Q. of Scots, 1571-2.

f. 39b. — Arraignment of matters objected to Mr. Davison, late Secretary, in the Star Chamber, with his answer, &c., 28 March 1587.

f. 51.—Discourse sent by Davison from the Tower, of what had passed between him and the Queen in the cause of the Scottish Queen.

f. 102.—The death of Q. Eliz., with her declaration of her successor.

f. 104.—The sickness and death of P. Henry.

f. 114.—A discourse of the Queen's marriage with the Duke of Anjou, by Sir N. Bacon, "as is thought." And other small items as in the preceding vol.

f. 125.—Fragmenta regalia ; [by Sir R. Naunton].

538. 51.—Copies of various State Papers of the time of James I. and Charles I.

f. 1.—" The arraignement of the Earls of Essex and Southampton," A.D. 1600.

MSS. OF THE INNER TEMPLE.

f. 18.—" The particulars wherein the Master of the Temple findes himself agreeved." A schedule of twelve complaints by Dr. Micklethwaite against the Societies of the Inner and the Middle Temple, with the answers thereto of the Middle Temple. (See Addison's *History of the Knights Templars*, p. 392.)

f. 21.—" A Letter from the King of Morocco to the King of England."

ff. 23, 27.—Speeches of Mr. John Finch, before the King at Canterbury, May 30, 1625, and before the Queen at the same place, June 13, 1625.

ff. 30, 32b.—" The Lord Keeper's speech to Sir John Finch, when he was called to be made Lord Chief Justice of the Common Pleas," Michaelmas 1634, and his answer thereto.

f. 36.—" A Commission for makeing lawes and orders for governement of English colonies planted in foraigne parts, 1634."

f. 39.—" The Lord Chancellor Elsmere, his Letter to King James, desiring to be dischardged of his office of Chancelorshipp."

f. 40.—" A Letter written afterwards by the said Lord Chancellor, when Sir Edward Cooke entended to question him upon a Premunire."

f. 41.—" A generall Band voluntarie made by the good subjects of the Kingdome of Scotland to the King's Majestie for the preservatione of his hienes persone in the persuit of his undoubted right to the croune of England and Ireland, in anno 1599."

f. 43.—" A collection of former King's revenues and what it is at this time."

f. 44.—" The copie of a letter written by Sir Walter Rawlegh to the Earles of Southampton, Suffolk, and Devonshire, and to the Lord Cecill." August 14, 1603.

f. 47.—" A letter from Sir Walter Rawlegh to the King, delivered by the Parson of Stapeley." August 1, 1603.

f. 49.—" A letter written from the Earl of Desmond to the Earle of Ormond, upon his false report of rebellion." June 5, 1583.

f. 49b.—" A letter from Sir Henry Wallopp, Treasurer of Ireland, to Queene Elizabeth, by way of appologie to purge himselfe of some false rumours." Dundalk, August 11, 1583.

f. 51.—" A letter from the Lord Norris unto King James, upon a quarrel betwixt him and the Lord Willoughby. A.D. 1615."

f. 52.—" A letter from Mr. [Edm.] Anderson to Sir Francis Bacon, to move his Majestie for a pardon."

f. 53.—" A letter from King James to the Parliament House, concerning the point of remanding. This letter was sent 1° Junii 1607. Not to be entred."

f. 55.—Letter from James I. to Sir George Calvert, one of his Secretaries of State. Dec. 16, 1621.

f. 55b.—Letter from James I. to the Serjeant-at-arms of the Lower House of Parliament. May 17, 1621.

f. 56.—Letter from Sir John Popham to the Lower House of Parliament. Read in the House, March 4, 1606.

f. 57.—Letter from James I. on behalf of Sir George Marshall, one of the gentlemen of the Privy Chamber; 12 Nov. an. 18.

f. 58.—Letter from James I. to the Lords of the Council, about a dispute between two of the Heralds, Brooke and Treswell. December 8, 1621.

f. 58b.—Letter from James I. about the accident of Archbishop Abbot in killing a keeper.

fol. 61.—Letter from Sir Charles Cornwallis in the Tower to the King.

f. 67.—" A letter directed to certaine commissioners appointed by order from his Majestie for compounding for the wardshipp of the children in the lifetime of their parents." MSS. OF THE INNER TEMPLE.

f. 69. — " A letter from King Charles to the Privie Councell of Scotland for composition of renovacions of their defective titles of lands."

f. 70.—Translation of a letter from Pope Gregory XV. to Charles, Prince of Wales. Dated April 20, 1623.

f. 74.—Letter from Lord Carleton to the Queen, "touchyng the tragycall end of my Lord Duke of Buckingham," 23 Aug. 1628.

f. 76.—" Notes out of a Protestation of the House of Commons." 1 James I.

f. 80.—An original treatise entitled :—" A Comparison between Phisique and Lawe," setting forth the superiority of Divinity to either, " written against John Ferne, the author of the Blasonist of gentrie." " Per me X^rA.L. (?), 10 die Dec. 1637."

f. 94. — " A letter written from Philipp, Earle of Arundell unto Queene Elizabeth, as an appologie for his departing out of the kingdome. A.D. 1590."

f. 100.—" A coppie of a letter sent by the Right Reverend Father in God, Edmund Grindall, Archbishop of Canterbury, to the Queene Elizabeth, concerning settling of religion, A.D. 1598 " [*rectius*, 1576]. Strype's *Life of Grindal*, 558.

f. 110.—" A coppie of a letter written by Sir Phillipp Sydney unto Queene Elizabeth, touching her marriage with Monsier."

f. 119.—" A coppie of a letter written by Mr. Thomas Alured unto the Marques of Buckingham, concerning the Prince his then entended match with Spaine." (Printed in Gutch's *Collectanea Curiosa*, vol. 1, p. 170, from a different version.)

f. 125.—Apology of the Lord Pres. of Ireland about proceedings against Phelim Phleak, with copies of letters and orders concerning the pay and uniform of the soldiers in Ireland. A.D. 1595-1597.

f. 134.—Notes of a speech made by Sir Edward Coke at the installation of eleven Serjeants-at-Law in the Temple Hall, 1614 ; explaining the symbolical meanings of their coifs, their hoods, their robes, and their caps.

f. 137.—" The speech uttered by the Lord Chancellor in the Kinges Bench att the tyme of the admission of Sir Henry Mountague to bee Lord Cheife Justice of the same Court, viz.: November, A.D. 1616," with Sir Henry Mountague's reply. This speech is wrongly attributed to Lord Bacon at the head of the page, the Lord Chancellor in 1616 being Lord Ellesmere.

f. 142.—Original letter from the Privy Council, signed by the Archbishop of Canterbury, Thomas Egerton, the Earl of Essex, the Earl of Nottingham and six others, concerning a controversy between Thomas Beauvoir of the Isle of Guernsey and Peter Beauvoir his uncle, and Peter Beauvoir the younger, son and heir of Henry Beauvoir deceased. Greenwich, June 6, 1598.

f. 143.—Complaint of the Irish to James I, with a copy of the King's reply for redress of grievances.

f. 147.—" A speech made by the Lord Primate of Ireland before the Lord Deputie and the great assemblie at his Majesties Castle of Dublin in Ireland, the last of Aprill, 1627."

f. 152.—" The speech of the Lord Wentworth, Lord Deputie of Ireland, to the Parliament there. 15 July, 1634."

MSS. OF THE INNER TEMPLE.

f. 158.—Notes of the Acts of Parliament that were made in Ireland in 1634, with a table of the chief towns, etc. There is the following note :—"His Majesties certain revenues in Ireland besides casualties is worth per annum—52420*li*. 3*s*. 6*d*¼.

The Lord Deputies entertanement in Ireland is 10*l*. 10*s*. 10*d*. per diem, which is per annum 3864*l*. 8*s*. 11*d*. Besides he hath the lands of Kilmaynhaune, rent, corne, impost, wyne and the guift of diverse offices worth per annum 2000*l*. In toto at least per annum 5804*l*. 8*s*. 11*d*."

f. 162.—"The Speech and execution of the Earle of Essex."

f. 164.—Petition of George Fowch, one of the messengers of the King's Chamber in ordinary, to the Earl of Dorset, Lord Chamberlain. See *post*, f. 174.

f. 165.—Petition of the churchwardens and other officers of the parish of Christ Church, London, to Sir Henry Martine, knight. In order "to prevent the oppression of an exacting parson, and the fall and ruine of their decayed church," they have lately procured a grant of their parsonage, and thereupon undertaken to repair the church at a cost of 800*l*. "As their said parishe is the greatest, soe it is the poorest within the walls of London, having above 800 poore people in it which receive relief." Most of the parishioners are therefore unable to contribute towards the repair of their church. They cannot raise more than 400*l*. and they pray Sir Henry Martine to assist them with money, according to his accustomed goodness.

f. 166.—Petition of John Parker, citizen and goldsmith of London, senior Churchwarden of Christ Church, to the Lord Mayor, praying for the remission or respite of the order that he should move from his present house into Cheapside, inasmuch as he is of a mean estate, and "unable to undergoe the great fyne and yearly rent" of a house in Cheapside.

f. 166*b*.—Petition to the Master, Wardens and Assistants of the Company of Leathersellers from Alice Wright of London, widow, "the sorrowfull mother of her distressed sonne Thomas Wright, late of London chirurgion, but now a poore prisoner in Argeere." Her son being bound for Genoa in the ship called the Adventure of London was taken by Turkish pirates and thrown into prison. 80*l*. is demanded for his ransom, and as she and her friends cannot disburse half of that sum, she requests the Master, Wardens, and Assistants "to remember the afflictions of Joseph," and to contribute towards the release of her son.

f. 167.—Petition of James Crux of Hastingleigh co. Kent, yeoman, to the Master and Governors of St. Thomas Hospital in Southwark, against the exactions of John Taylor, B.D. the parson.

f. 168.—Petition of William, Lord Monson, Peter De la Motte, and four other inhabitants of Covent Garden, to the Lords of the Privy Council, against the proposal of one Brett a chandler to build twelve tenements between Covent Garden and Drury Lane. They contend that these tenements being in a blind and obscure place will be fit only for poor and mean people who will cause them much inconvenience. They protest against "such pestering of multitudes of families and poore people together in such by-places to suffocate each other," urging that "it wilbe an evill example for all such other (more affected to their own private lucre then the publique good) to build and erect like tenements in every piece of ground or garden plott nere the said Convent garden."

f. 169.—Petition of James Guthree, a poor prisoner in the Fleet, to Sir Humphrey Davenport, Lord Chief Baron of the Exchequer, praying for release or admission to bail.

f. 170.—Petition of Hugh Morrell and Charles Snellinge, to the King. The petitioners were formerly merchants at Rouen. On the late breach between England and France all their estates, goods, and debts to the value of 7,000*l*. were confiscated by the French for reprisal of the goods taken by the English ships at Conquett. In June 1627 they petitioned for recompence out of the profits of the French prizes, or by abatement of customs, and Sir Henry Martin and Mr. Burlimachi, to whom the question was referred, reported favourably. They have, however, had no relief. They suggest that they may be recompensed out of an additional impost on coals carried from Newcastle and other places in England by Hollanders and French, who make great profits thereby. They say that in the reign of James I. coals were sold at Rouen and elsewhere "for 12*l*. and 13*l*. the 100 barrels, a measure proportionable to three Newcastle chaldrons, but now for some few years past and at this present the coles are growen soe usefull and nessessary abroad and soc greatly is that trade augmented that the same measure is sould for 20*l*., 22*l*., and 26*l*., and the price they pay for them at Newcastle and other places continuing the same." They propose an addition of 3*s*. 4*d*. per chaldron to the existing import of 6*s*. 8*d*., which is farmed to Sir Thomas Lake and others for 6,000*l*. a year.

MSS. OF THE INNER TEMPLE.

The matter was referred to certain Lords on the 20th of October 1630, and they, two months later, required the Attorney General to call the farmers of the coals before them.

f. 172. — Original writ of Henry Hopkins, Warden of the Fleet Prison, appointing James Crux, and two others to guard Thomas Taylor, officer of the Court of Exchequer, until the return of a writ of habeas corpus. June 4, 1633. Impressed seal of arms.

f. 173 and 178.—Two copies of a petition of Edward Crowe, gent., to Sir Thomas Trevor, Baron of the Exchequer. The petitioner being newly come of age in January, 22 James I., borrowed of one John Osborne, woollen draper, the sum of 174*l*. on five notes of receipt, and for security mortgaged to him by bill of sale " a fayer cabinett very curiously made, richly sett forth with Pearles, Rubies, Saphers, Emeraldes, and gold worth 600*l*., and 2 very fayer precious stones worth more 100*l*., upon condition for the repayment of the said principale and use amounting together to 179*l*. 4*s*. 4*d*. the 10th of May then next following." Osborne dissuaded five different merchants from taking the notes, and caused the petitioner to be arrested. The latter prays that he may not be obliged to pay any costs or damages beyond those awarded by a jury in the Court of King's Bench.

f. 174.—Petition of George Fowche, one of the messengers of the King's Chamber, and collector of chantry rents in the county of Cornwall, to the King. The petitioner states that he was employed about seven years since to collect divers rents of the King in the counties of Somerset, Dorset, Devon, Cornwall, and Gloucester, and that as he was returning to London his horse fell and so cruelly bruised him that he was obliged to lie in the mire all night. He has consequently been under physicians and surgeons for five years at a cost of at least 300*l*., " to his utter undoeing." His landlord Mr. Mullins and other creditors proceeded against him and they daily endeavour to cast him into gaol. " there to endure the loathsome plagues of Egipt, without cleane foode or sweet ayere (worse than beastes), most miserably to suffer a lingering death by loathsome imprisonment." He prays that they may be ordered to take an extent of 200*l*. against the lands of Sir Nicholas Halse, knt., in Cornwall, for the satisfaction of his debts to them.

T 2

MSS. OF THE INNER TEMPLE.

f. 175.—Another petition of the same George Fouche *or* Fowthe. A.D. 1683.

f. 176.—Report to the King upon the same case.

f. 177.—Petition of the Kings, Heralds, and Pursuivants, of Arms, to the House of Commons, in vindication of their ancient rights. The first name is that of William Seagar, Garter King at Arms, and the last that of Augustin Vincent, Rouge Croix. The date is probably, therefore, about or shortly after 1621.

f. 179.—Petition of John Walton, a poor distressed prisoner in the King's Bench, to John, Bishop of Lincoln, Lord Keeper of the Great Seal.

f. 180.—Petition of Richard Marten of Cranbrook, co. Kent, husbandman, to Thomas, Lord Coventry, Keeper of the Great Seal, praying that an attachment against him may be stayed.

f. 181.—Part of a petition of the two clerks of parcels of the Court of Exchequer, to William, Bishop of London, Lord High Treasurer, and Francis, Lord Cottington, Under-Treasurer.

f. 181b.—Petition of Margaret Thurston, a poor distressed widow, to William, Bishop of London, Lord High Treasurer of England. She prays that she may receive 250*l*. out of the 750*l*. which was lately paid for the place of waiter at the Custom house. Her late husband died before completing the arrangements for surrendering the place, and his successor, formerly one of the King's coachmen, will not satisfy her claims out of the 500*l*. which he has received.

Petition of the same for the nomination of her son John, to a place at Sutton's Hospital.

f. 183.—Petition of poor John Chafy, of the parish of Stoke under Hambdon, co. Somerset, labourer, about eighty years of age, to the King, praying for the grant of a cottage and rod of land, built on the King's waste, at an annual rent of 4*d*. He will during his life pray that the King " may live Nestor's yeares to raigne over this royall kingdome."

f. 184.—Petition of the Company of Leathersellers of London to the King, that they may be heard with regard to the demand of the Glovers to be a separate corporation. A.D. 1635.

f. 184.—Petition of Elizabeth Kerrill, widow, to the Master, Wardens and Assistants of the Company of Merchant-Tailors, on behalf of her son John Kerrill.

f. 185.—Petition of Wooding Waller, a poor oppressed and very distressed maid, to William, Archbishop of Canterbury.

Petition of Thomas White, an under-keeper of otter hounds, to the King.

f. 186.—Petition of Edward Holmewood, gent., one of the esquires extraordinary of the King's body, to Sir Laurence Tanfeld, Lord Chief Baron of the Exchequer. A.D. 1622.

f. 187.—A letter of Edward Hornby about a law suit.

f. 188.—A treatise on merchandise, by Sir F. Bacon.

f. 194.—" A letter wherein directions are given to a traveller for his observations of such things as are fitteing to be observed in his travells in forraigne parts," from F. R. London, Dec. 17, 1630.

f. 196.—Letter from the Earl of Essex [to ——] beginning : " My verie good Lord, though there is not that man this day living."

f. 198.—Two letters from James VI. King of Scotland, to M. Du Plessis, principal Secretary to the King of France. A.D. 1590.

f. 199.—Letter from the King of Navarre to Queen Elizabeth.

f. 200.—Letter from Queen Elizabeth to the King of Scotland. April 21, 1595.

MSS. OF THE INNER TEMPLE.

f. 200b.—Letter from Queen Elizabeth to Sir William Bowes, ambassador in Scotland. July 25, 1596.

f. 202.—Letter from Queen Elizabeth to the King of Scotland. Dec. 7, 1597 [or 1598].

f. 203.—Letter from Queen Elizabeth to Sir Robert Carew, son of Lord Hunsdon, Warden of the East Marches against Scotland. July 22, 1596.

Letter from Queen Elizabeth to the Lord Deputy of the North.

f. 203b.—Letter from Queen Elizabeth to Sir Robert Carew, Warden of the East Marches. A.D. 1596.

f. 204.—" A coppie of a letter from King James, shortly after he was proclaimed King of England, to the Councell of England, for the delivery of the Earle of Southampton out of the Tower." April 1, 1603.

f. 205.—Speech delivered by Mr. Witherington, Recorder of Berwick, before the King, when he went to be crowned in Scotland. A.D. 1633.

f. 206.—Speech delivered by the same, Sir Thomas Witherington, before the King, at York. March 30, 1639.

f. 207.—Speech delivered by the same, before the King, at Berwick. May 27, 1639.

f. 209.—" The coppie of a letter from the Helvetians to the Archbishop of Canterbury concerning the Scotts' business, with his answer." A.D. 1639. The Archbishop's answer is printed, in Latin, in Laud's *Works*, vol. VI., p. 563.

f. 213.—Abstract of the speech of Lord Mountnorris in the Castle Chamber. May 25, 1636.

f. 215.—" The antiquitie, use, and priviledge of citties, borroughs, and townes, written by Mr. Francis Tate, of the Middle Temple, esq."

f. 220.—" A letter written by the Lords of the Councell to the King . . . . touching means to advance the Kings revenues by unusuall means." A.D. 1608.

f. 223.—" A collection of such things as Robert late earle of Salisburie thought fitt to offer to his Majestie upon the necessitie of calling of a parliament." 1609.

f. 234.—" A copie of a letter from G. D. to his freend A. W. at Middlebrough, advertising him of the occurrents in the Parliament, and withall sending him a coppie of the late Lord Treasurer Cecill's speech as followeth." London, July 27, 1610.

f. 236.—" A copie of the Lord Burlie, thesaurer, his Lordshipp's last speech delivered unto his Majestie in the presence of both the housses of Parliament assembled at Whitehall on Thursday the 29 of July 1610, wherein is declared the true cause of his majesties laying the late imposition uppon merchandize."

f. 241.—" My Lord Treasurer Cecill his treatees to his Majestie, shewing as well by argumentes as presidentes that his Majesties state cannot be supported in any proportione without levies from the people."

f. 249.—" Considerations uppon his Majesties estate. 23° Januarii 1610."

f. 252.—" Propositiones made by his Majestie to the Lordes of his Counsell after he had receaved a declaratione of his estate by the Erle of Salisburie, Treasurer of England," Jan. 12, 1609, with the answer of the Council.

294   HISTORICAL MANUSCRIPTS COMMISSION.

MSS. OF THE INNER TEMPLE.

f. 262.—"The effect of the Lord Chancelor Egerton his speech to the judges in the Starchamber, the last sitting day there in termino Sti. Hil. anno Regni 1° Jacobi."

f. 265.—Proclamation issued by Lady Jane Grey on her succession to the crown. July 10, 1553. Printed in Somers' *Tracts*, Vol. I., p. 53; &c.

538. 52.—A transcript (41 leaves) of a register of important letters and documents, mostly written to or by Archbishop Whitgift; 1579-1585. Most of the contents are printed or noticed in Strype's *Life of Whitgift* (ed. 1822). Vol. I., pp. 228, 238, 249, 250, 290, 327, 328, 331, 340, 343, 380, 390, 391, 426, 429, 430, 534, 563, and Vol. III., pp. 104-124. The following, however, do not appear to be given in that work:

f. 1.—"A letter from the Counsell to certaine chosen commissioners in everie shire for the execution of the Proclamation for uniformitie in religion and common prayer by way of Oyer and Terminer, in Mr. Secretary Smithe's manns hande, penned bylike by his master."

f. 2.—"A letter to the Bishop for the execution of her Majesties Proclamation for the uniformitie sett forth in the Booke and other injunctions, penned by Sir Thomas Smith."

f. 3.—A letter from the Council to the Archbishop of Canterbury. Jany. 17, 1579. Printed in Strype's *Life of Grindal* p. 363.

f. 4.—"A letter from the Councell to the Bishop of London, to cause common prayers, sermones, and thanksgivings for a victorie gotten against the Turke, penned by Mr. Frem, with the Lord Treasurer's correction." 1571. Printed in Strype's *Annals*, Vol. II. i. 156, without the name of the author.

f. 5.—"A letter to the Lord Mayor to the same effect." (*Ibid.*, p. 157.)

f. 11.—Letter from Lord Burghley to the Archbishop. 17 Sept. 1584.

f. 11*b*.—Reply by the Archbishop. 18 Sept.

f. 17.—A letter from Lord Burghley to Archbishop Whitgift, dated at Richmond, July 17, 1584. Noticed in Strype's *Whitgift*, pp. 316-7, where, however, the notice is so brief that the following abstract may be given:—He has received the Archbishop's letter; knows he has many faults, but hopes he has not given such cause of offence as that letter expresses. The Archbishop promised to deal with such only as violated order, but now by examination seeks to make them accuse themselves, a proceeding which the writer considers "scant charitable." Has no leisure to write more, and writing will but "increase offence," and he does not mean to offend. The Archbishop and the Bishop of London may use Browne as they think fit; if it is meant to sift him with twenty-four articles, he has cause to pity the poor man.

f. 21.—A letter from Archbishop Whitgift to Queen Elizabeth about the objectors to the Book of Common Prayer.

f. 25.—Answer of the Archbishop to the Petition of the Commons, presented to the Queen's Majesty.

f. 31.—A faculty to Robert Merrick to hold the vicarage of Staines together with that of Horton. August 5, 1587.

f. 32*b*.—"The summe of the Lord Treasorers speach in Parliament against pluralities." With other notes on the same subject.

538. 53.—A sixteenth-century transcript of the "Liber Niger Domus Regis Edwardi IV."

538. 54.—Papers relative to the ecclesiastical laws and to the recusants in the reign of Q. Elizabeth.

f. 1.—Animadversions upon 18 articles of complaint about the laws against recusants, about the licensing of books, about preachers, about the translation of the Bible, and other ecclesiastical matters, concluding that the true remedy for disorders will be by a royal visitation, as in the first year of the Queen's reign. MSS. OF THE INNER TEMPLE.

f. 7.—" Touching the superiority claymed by the Officiall of Canterbury of the Court of Arches above the Vicar Generall;" an answer by Dr. Tho. Yale, to a " reasonlesse Challenge," 1576. See Strype's *Grindal*, 309.

f. 10.—Petition to the Archbishop of Canterbury for the reform of certain disorders in the Prerogative Court of Canterbury.

f. 13.—An answer, in Latin, by the Official of Canterbury to the claims of the Auditor, signed " Bartholo Clerke."

f. 16.—" The reasonable answere of the Officiall of the Arches, who never made challenge to superioritie but (beinge challenged by him that pretendeth him sealfe Vicar generall nameth him sealfe Officiall princepall and weeneth him selfe Chauncelor of Canterbury) is driven to defende the aunscient dignetie of the Courte of the Arches and Officiall thereof, not withe triple titles and gaye termes, but by reason, lawe, custome and statute." By Dr. Barth. Clerk. See Strype's *Grindal*, 309.

f. 19. — " Articles of agreement concluded upon betwixt Thomas Bing and Richard Cosin, Doctors of the lawe, and whiele they doe covenaunte and graunte eche unto other respectyvely to observe, touching offices to them granted, and claymed by them." July 17, 1595. Signed by Byng.

f. 21.—" That there was a Chancellor or Vycar Generall to the Archbishop from the first institution of the Archbishoprick."

f. 23.—" Touching the course that hath been used by the proctors of the Arches in their use of seales annexed to proxies and certificates."

f. 25.—Draft of the condition of a recognizance relating to the appointmen t of John Parker, esq., as surrogate of the Judge of the Prerogative Court of Canterbury, during the archiepiscopate of Parker.

f. 27.—" A remembrance in the matter of variance betwixt the Archbishop of Canterbury and his suffrigayns for the approbation of testaments."

f. 29.—" Reformacions of the Prerogative Courte wished to be had for the Cittie and Diocese of London."—February 1592.

f. 30.—" An order for avoyding the greivance in probate of wills and committing administrations."

f. 34.—Copy of a letter from the Archbishop of Canterbury to his suffragans on the state of the Ecclesiastical Courts. Nov. 19, 1594.

f. 35.—" The names of severall Courts for determining all controversies and offences, according to their jurisdiction."

f. 36.—Copy of a petition of George Kirkham and Nicholas Byrd, old servants of the Queen, that they may be appointed sole appraisers of the goods of persons dying within the city and suburbs of London. August 2, 1594.

f. 38.—Copy of the answer sent to the Lord Treasurer concerning the foregoing petition.

ff. 40, 41. — Some reasons "why the appraisemente of dead mens goodes and the making of inventaries " cannot be granted to any man.

f. 42.—A letter from Dr. W. Lewyn to the Archbishop of Canterbury, on the same subject. August 16, 1594.

f. 47.—Draft of a letter from the Archbishop of Canterbury to the Queen, praying her not to grant any application made to her relating to his courts without enquiry. October 26, 1594.

f. 48.—" Touching granting of licences for marriage without banes."

MSS. OF THE INNER TEMPLE.

f. 49.—"Considerations why Bishops' temporalties shuld not be taken away," by Bishop Cox.

f. 51.—"Touching Bishopps, their revenues and priviledges." In Cox's hand.

f. 54.—Draft of a letter from Bishop Cox to the Queen, requesting her to order her officers not to proceed any further in the exchange of bishops' lands.

f. 55.—"The names of her majesties ships, with their nomber of men and furniture requisite for the setting forthe of them." Printed in Peck's *Desiderata Curiosa*, vol. 1. p. 72.

f. 56.—"Touchinge the bill late exhibited against excessive fees exacted by ecclesiasticall officers."

f. 26.—"A declaracion of abuses in the officers of the Prerogative Court of Canterbury, usurping uppon the jurisdiccion of the Lord Bushopp of London and the rest of the Bushopps of the province of Canterbury, for and concerninge causes of probates of testaments and comittinge of administrations, which causeth greate discencion betwene the officers of the said Courtes, and is a greate trouble to the comon wealthe and stirreth upp many exclamacions in the poore subjects against all ecclesiasticall government," presented to the Archbishop, to be read in Convocation.

f. 64.—A civil law argument in Latin, as to the authority of the official of Canterbury in the case of Doyle v. Waynman for a contract of marriage. 1576.

f. 68.—A paper about the rules of the Prerogative Court.

f. 69.—"Articles concerning the execution of the Commission for redresse of extraordinary fees in Courtes. 19° Novembris 1594."

f. 71.—Considerations, in French, as to the desirability of effecting a peace in the Netherlands.

f. 72.—French verses entitled :—

"Postilion du Compte de Buquoy pour chercher le Palatin Roy de Boheme." They begin :—

"Je suis le grand postilion
Qui en bottes et esperons
est despeché de Buquoy
pour chercher le nouveau Roy
qui vaincu sen est enfuy
de Boheme sans faire bruit.
Dittes n'aves vous pas veu
Le Palatin qui est perdeu."

f. 75.—"Dictata Reverendi Patris Politiani," on the 2nd part of book II. of the *Summa* of Aquinas, *de fide*.

f. 97.—A narrative in Latin (written by an Italian hand) of the proceedings of John Cecil, Thomas Bluet, John Mush, and Anthony Champney, the four English priests sent to Rome on behalf of their secular brethren. It begins on the 14th of February, and extends to the 16th of October 1602. This very curious and valuable record was unknown to Mr. Tierney, the learned editor of Dodd's *Church History*. It is entitled, "Brevis veraque admodum relatio, ... ab uno ex ipsis sacerdotibus fideliter recollecta." It is followed by some remarks in Italian on Father Parsons' "Conference on the Succession to the Crown of England," and by transcripts (in the same hand) of many interesting documents in Latin relating to the quarrel between the secular priests in England and the Jesuits. Among them are, (fol. 116 and 150) observations to show that all armed attempts to reduce England to the Roman obedience had been more injurious than profitable to the English Catholics ; (fol. 117*b*) reasons why the Jesuits should be forbidden to meddle in politics, and be recalled from the courts and camps of Princes ; (fol. 122*b*) remarks (in Italian) on a proposal for the granting of liberty of conscience by Q. Elizabeth to the Catholics of her realm; (fol. 126) extracts from books, etc. written by the Jesuits to discredit the secular priests; (fol. 128*b*) speeches (in Spanish) delivered before the King of Spain in the English Colledge at Valladolid ; (fol. 134*b*) notes on the authorship and contents of Parsons' Life of the Earl of Leicester; (ff. 143*b*, 151) paper (in Ital.) for father Holt, apparently from Parsons, as to the reasons of the writer's coming to Rome from Spain ; (fol. 146*b*) account of the condition of the Catholics in England from 1587 to 1602 ; (fol. 163*b*) refutation of Parson's Reply to the proposals made by the English priests to the Pope.

f. 149.—A Latin paper to show that the Spanish King is not animated by religious zeal, apparently headed " S. J. Holt ad R. G."

f. 153.—A narrative of the journey of the appellant priests to Rome ; in English.

f. 155.—An original letter, in Latin, from the Archpriest George Blackwell to Mr. Hebborne, Mr. Clerck, and Mr. Collington, dated February 3, 1602. He rejoices to hear that they intend to behave in a manner worthy of Catholic priests with regard to the Pope's brief.

f. 156.—Copies of a letter from "the discontented about the œconomie " to Blackwell, 13 December 1602, and of his reply, 22 Dec.

f. 189.—Letter from Thomas Bluet " to the ryght reverent father in Godd, my good Honorable Lord my Lord Bushope of London." He promises to give forthwith an account of his negotiations at Rome and elsewhere, " a poynt not unfitt to be knowen unto her majestie." He means to come as secretly as may be, in order " to avoyd the speaches of the clamarouse puritans that take upon them to direct her majestie in matters of government." The Ambassador [at Paris] has treated him most honourably, and the writer intends to come over under the conduct of one of the ambassador's gentlemen. *Dated,* f. of St. Nicolas.

f. 190.—A diary in English of the proceedings of John Cecil, Thomas Bluet, John Mush and Anthony Champney, at Rome, from the 14th of Feb. to the 19th of Oct. 1602. Endorsed as being by Mr. Mush.

f. 200.—Letter from Sir Robert Cecil to the Bishop of London. He is growing very tender because he sees how the priests would encroach and so give cause to carry anew harder hands of them. By God, the priest[s] swarm. He never loved persecution but, by heaven, he is loth to be considered Popish. He must neither go too low nor too high. Barrow is a dissembling lying fool. He has sent a warrant for Wright ; who, he believes, will keep open house in the Clink, " which, if he do, or suffer resort, he shall back againe."

f. 202.—A passport for the four English priests, John Cecil, Thomas Bluet, John Mush, and Antony Champney, signed by Cardinal Aldobrandini at Rome. October 22, 1602.

f. 204.—A similar document signed by Cardinal Borghese. Oct. 23, 1602.

f. 206.—A printed copy of a brief of Clement VIII. to the Archpriest, George Blackwell, beginning " Venerunt nuper ad nos nonnulli sacerdotes Angli." October 5, 1602. (Printed in Dodd's *Church History,* Tierney's edit., vol. iii., p. clxxxi.)

f. 207.—Another narrative in English, of the journey and negotiations of the four appellant priests, Cecil, Bluet, Mush and Champney ; 1601-

MSS. OF THE INNER TEMPLE. 1602; with an introductory account of their being released from prison by the Privy Council for the purpose, as being sent into banishment.

f. 207.—A long letter from Dr. Humfrey Ely dated at Pont a Mousson in Lorraine, August 30, 1602. On behalf of the secular priests and Catholic gentlemen he declares to the "Right Honourable" to whom he writes (Cecil?) that they are "most ready and willing, both at home and abroade to suffer imprisonment, racks, and death itselfe, for the defence of our naturall and lawfull Prince, of her life and estate, against all whosoever shall attempt any thing against her royall person or crowne, be he Spaniard, Frenche, Scott or whosoever els." This they have often testified in words and by printed books to the whole world. Their case is very miserable both at home and abroad, "at home afflicted for our consciences, abrode persecuted for our fidelitie to our Prince." If the Queen knew this, she would surely of her clemency make a distinction between them, her natural children and subjects, and "those unnaturall Bastardes who do attend to nought else but conquester and invasions," by giving them leave to serve God freely and securely, and easing the yoke of the severe laws enacted against them. They desire freely "without feare of pursuyvants" to offer up their sacrifices for her prosperous health and happy reign, as indeed they do yet daily, notwithstanding the execution of her severe laws. His correspondent, he says, is envied, maligned, and hated by many. "The partizantes and favorers of the late seditious Puritane Erle doo beare your honor in special cancred hartes, poysoned entrailes, and unspeakable hatred, swelling with desired vengeaunce." He would therefore be greatly strengthened by the support of the Catholic party. The writer prays his correspondent to give him an audience, upon the least intimation of which, made through her Majesty's agent at Paris, he will be soon with him.

f. 215.—A very long letter from William Watson, dated the last day of August, 1602, denouncing the "calumnies, slanders, lies, forgeries and such like trash" of the Jesuits.

f. 221.—Letter from Christopher Bagshaw to the Bishop of London, dated at Paris, Sept. 27, 1602. Mr. Bluet is on his way to Paris. He has received no letter from Rome by the last three or four posts. From Flanders they hear that all is going well with the Jesuits; at Paris the King's ministers are informed that all is going well with the priests. There are many matters that require particular discussion. Ingress and egress is necessary for their despatches. He has written to Mr. Secretary about his own affair. For Fisher he has written more fully to Mr. Watson, so as not to trouble the Bishop whose "wonted prudence and respect of innocency" will direct him to manage the examination for the best. He would like to have some time in England. *Mutilated.*

f. 222.—Draft of a Latin memorial to the Pope from the Appellants.

f. 223.—Draft of a Latin petition of John Cecil and Antony Champney to the Pope, for vestments, chalice, paten and cross for use in England.

f. 224.—A long statement of the points at issue between the secular priests and the Jesuits; in Mush's handwriting.

f. 228.—A narrative by Humphrey Ely of the things that befel Mr. Arthur Pits, "a worshipfull priest," after his banishment out of the Tower of London in 1585 (originally sent with the letter at f. 207). *Mutilated.*

f. 229.—Draft of proposals for an agreement between the secular priests and the Jesuits, after the return of the four appellants from Rome : *Latin.*

f. 231.—Draft of a Latin petition to the Pope from an English priest for a grant of his faculties.   MSS. OF THE INNER TEMPLE.

f. 232.—A passport for the four English appellant priests, Cecil, Bluet, Mush and Champney, signed and sealed by M. Philippe de Bethune, the French Ambassador at Rome. Oct. 31, 1602.

f. 233.—Copy of a form of submission in which certain English priests, liable by law to death, profess their loyal allegiance to Queen Elizabeth, on the assurance of mercy on this condition.

f. 236.—Letter from William Byshop to Mr. Watson "at my Lord of London's," about his books.

f. 237.—Letter from Dr. John Cecil at Rome to James Hyll, esq. at Paris. Oct. 7, 1602. He describes the state of the negotiations. He and his colleagues were summoned to be at the Palace " at 20 of the clock " on the previous Thursday. When they had waited half an hour, Parsons appeared with his proctors, and salutations were exchanged without any further communication. The writer and his friends feared that the Pope would order them to join hands with Parsons, and they prayed to God and our Lady to divert this "malheure" from them. Cardinal Farnese came in, but only for a while, and after waiting two hours Parsons went away. They also went away, and repaired to the French Ambassador. He the next day persuaded the Pope to abandon his intention of making the priests embrace Parsons in his presence. They cannot decide about their return from Rome until they see the Bull.

f. 240.—Letter from A. H[ebbourne] to the Archpriest Blackwell, dated November 11, 1602. When the writer happened to visit Fremingham Castle in the month of June, the appellant priests there imprisoned told him that for several months past they had not received more than 2s. 4d. a week between them all. They now write to say that for the last three months they have not received so much as 18d. a week between them, and that they expect to receive yet less. The Archpriest knows that they are Catholic priests, suffering for the name of their Lord Jesus, and that they have no means of livelihood, but depend "for meate, drincke, clothes, fireing, housrome, and other requisites to lyfe, upon the providence of God, to be mainteyned by the oblations of his people, as others of their qualitie are." The alms are not evenly distributed. The number of priests in Fremingham Castle who are in want is six; they differ only from the others there in that they are appellants to the court of Rome. A letter from the Archpriest would soon redress their grievance.

f. 241. — Letter from the Archpriest George Blackwell dated Nov. 17, in reply to the above. He bids his correspondent not to be so vehement. By being content to live in a mean condition he has been able to send above six score pounds to the prisoners at Fremingham. The disposition of the alms is not committed wholly to him. He blames none so much for defect of alms as Mr. Collington and his adherents, from whom, since the begining of his troublesome office, he has not received one mite. If his correspondent knew how much he gave "towardes the reliefe of poor priests at their coming in, towards the succouring of prisoners in the Cittye, and towards afflicted Catholikes at libertie, and priests" in great need, he would be ashamed to forge accusations against him. Within the last week he has given away 10l. and 40s., and 4l. to different persons. He has now to provide 20l. for Fremingham Castle.

f. 242. — Letter from William Gifforde to his sister, dated at Lille, Dec. 17, 1601. He is glad to hear of her welfare. In his long

MSS. OF THE INNER TEMPLE.

exile it has been an extreme grief to him that for thirty years he has not been able to have ordinary intercourse with his family. This he imputes to those who "by stratagemes and crafty devises" have wrongfully made him hateful to his prince. By God's special assistance he will ever continue a Catholic, but he has ever detested those violent spirits who "unnaturally practise against their prince and country," and seek to expose it to invasion. He would be very sorry that his good sisters or any of his Catholic friends should through simplicity be intangled with such persons. They must be very careful. He denounces the foolish books that have been written about the right to the crown and about the lives of particular men.

f. 243.—Letter from C[hristopher] B[agshaw] at Paris to Mr. William Watson, dated February 7. He has read his correspondent's *Quodlibets* and has asked the judgment of others on them. The style is disliked, as being too bitter.

ff. 245, 246.—Epistle to those united with the Archpriest, and preface general to Catholicks prefixed to some book by F. B.

f. 247.—Thirteen articles offered to Parliament, 1580, with an answer by the Bishops; endorsed by Archbishop Whitgift. Strype's *Whitgift*, III. 47–63.

f. 263.—Representation by Dr. Lewin, judge of the Prerogative Court, to the Archbishop, about irregularities in the Ecclesiastical Courts; 31 Oct. 1597.

f. 265.—"Remembrances touching reformation of certen disorders in the corts of the Arches, Audience and Prerogative;" " D. H[arvey]." 28 Apr. 1576. Strype's *Grindal*, 305.

f. 267.—Representation by Rob. Forthe to the Archbishop about dissensions between the Judges and the remedies.

f. 268.—Representation to the same, in accordance with his desire, by W. Aubrey about the Arches Court; Kew, 30 Apr. 1576. Strype's *Grindal*, 307.

ff. 274–8.—Three anonymous papers relating to the Ecclesiastical Courts.

f. 280.—" A note of divers incestuous and unlawfull marriages made by licences by vagrant ministers in lawlesse peculiars."

f. 282.—Paper addressed to the Archbishop by about the Court of Audience, by Tho. Yate, auditor of the court. Strype's *Grindal*, 307.

f. 284.—Letter to Archbishop Grindal from Dr. Henry Jones on the courts; 25 Apr. 1576. *Ibid.*, 303–5.

f. 286.—"A breyffe treatyse of othes exacted by ordinaryes and ecclesiasticall judges," 1590. (Another copy is in Cotton MS. Cleop. F. 1.) See Strype's *Whitgift* II., 31.

f. 318.—A few Latin notes *de matrimonio*.

f. 320.—Copy of an order about the fee of the Registrar of the Court of Canterbury. 12 March 1391.

f. 322.—A paper by Robert Bluet about Blackwell.

f. 324.—Copy of a long letter to a lady from A. Duckett, 30 June; endorsed, " Holtebye against the secular priests."

f. 334.—Copy of a letter from a priest [to Blackwell?] desiring to be informed of the charges brought against him; 5 Nov. 1598. Endorsed, " My first letter."

f. 335.—Copy of a letter from Cardinal Pole to the Emperor. *Lat.*

f. 337.—Latin oration made by Dr. L. Humfrey to Q. Elizabeth at Woodstock, 1572.

f. 342.—Copy of a letter from Ulrich [Duke of Holstein] to [James 1.] thanking him for his book [*Apologia pro juramento*] he has sent. If " Guillaume" exceeds the time assigned him, desires he may be excused, as he attends after the writer, and the latter after his brother the King of Denmark. Bubzow, 8 Sept. *Fr.*

f. 344.—Copy of a letter from Christian II. Duke of Saxony to James I., also thanking him for his book, which he has not yet had time to read. Schwartzenberg, 14 Aug. 1609. *Lat.*

ff. 346-364.—Copies of similar letters from Henry Julius, Duke of Brunswick, Erichsburg, 30 July 1609, *Lat.*; John Sigismund. Elector of Brandenburg, Stendahl, 23 Aug., *Lat.*; Frederick, Elector Palatine, Heidelb., 2 July, *Lat.*; Louis Frederick, Prince of Wirtemberg, Stutgardt, $\frac{8}{18}$ July, *Fr.*; John George, Prince of Anhalt, Dessau, 6 Aug., *Lat.*; Maurice, Landgrave of Hesse, Smalcald, 19 July, *Lat.*; John Adolphus, Duke of Schleswig Holstein, Gottorp, 16 Sept., *Lat.*

f. 356.—Copy of a complimentary letter to the same from John George, Marg. of Brandenburg, after meeting with Sir Rob. Ayton, the King's envoy to the writer's brother, the Elector; Cologne, 3 Sept. *Fr.*

ff. 358-368.—Copies of letters on public business and the affairs of the Palatinate, to the same, from the Duke of Wirtemberg, 8 July, and Louis Prince of Anhalt (?), 2 Aug., after interviews with Sir Rob. Ayton, both in French; and from the Elector of Brandenburg, accrediting Christian á Bellin, 24 Aug. and Charles, Duke of Mecklenburg, 4 Sept., both in Latin.

ff. 370-374.—Three letters about the proceedings at Rome and the Pope's brief. i. The first without address, somewhat mutilated; the writer uses the opportunity offered by Mons. Acaria to answer letters of 24 Feb., 10 March, &c.; signed " Will. Persens." ii. The second to Mr. Bluett at Paris ; " yours off 23 off November wear most gratfull to my lord ;" Parsons " dar not visit my lord, but with the card. he was bold to utter his fears, forsoth he hath off your negotiations, the cair he saith (?) off the publique good and off his nation. O vox serpentina !" It includes also a letter to Dr. Bagshawe. Signed, " Will Persens," and dated Rome, 25 Dec. iii. The third is to Mr. Midleton, an English gentleman at Paris. " Hear Persons and his ar strok dead with his newes " [of the Pope's brief and of the restoration of faculties to the English priests]. The proclamation of King James as King of England " was geven to his holines in Latyn by my L. Embassador upon the 19 off this instant." Signed " Persens," and dated at Rome, 21 Apr. The handwriting strangely resembles the dashing straggling hand of Rob. Parsons. The letters were originally endorsed as being from Dr. Cecill, but this name was afterwards crossed out.

f. 375.—Account in Latin, in the same handwriting as Champney's papers following, of the scholars admitted into the English College [at Rome] from 1597 to 1602.

f. 376.—Letter from Dr. Will. Byshop to the Bishop of London, on the progress of the appeal, and requesting leave for some of their company to come to him safely, for the settling of better correspondence ; Paris, 27 Oct.

f. 378.—Unsigned letter from a priest to the Bishop of London, asking for the Queen's clemency, and ease from the rigour of the laws, on the ground of his steadfast loyalty, proved by his opposition to Parsons and the Jesuits when in the College at Rome; by the danger he incurred of imprisonment or murder in the Spanish dominions when coming to England ; and by the persecution he has suffered since. 14 Nov. 1602. (*Qu.*, from Watson ?)

MSS. OF THE INNER TEMPLE.

f. 380.—Constitutions of the English College at Rome. *Latin.* In the same handwriting as the next.

f. 384.—Long but imperfect (as it seems) paper against the allowing the Jesuits to have the control of the English seminaries. Endorsed as being "in Mr. Champney's hand," but resembling Mush's.

ff. 390, 391.—Copies of two letters from J. Cecyll to Mr. Mush and Mr. Watson in February 1603.

f. 392.—" A forme of submission exhibited to her Majestie of England by the pryestes and Catholiques of the same nation."

ff. 393, 394.—Legal questions as to the force of the brief about Blackwell; with the replies thereupon of " Monsieur Seraphin." *Lat.*

f. 396.—Copy of a declaration of loyalty, under three heads, to the Queen, and of submission to the Pope as supreme spiritual pastor, signed by 15 priests.

f. 398. — Petition to the Privy Council from the prisoners in Fram[l]ingham Castle, praying for better treatment; with 23 original signatures.

f. 399.—Letter from A. H[ebborne] to Blackwell with reasons for not obeying his order to publish the papal brief in the Clink; 14 Dec. 1602.

f. 400.—News from Rome respecting Parsons' book and the plots of the Spanish faction.

f. 401.—Copy, in Mush's or Champney's hand, of a very long letter (ten closely written leaves), of expostulation to Blackwell, and account of proceedings at Rome; subscribed, "Yours as yow are in will to deserve of us the so unjustly defamed priests." With the attestation, " Concordat cum originali, Will. Clerke."

538. 55. f. 1.—Collections about Prohibitions.

f. 39. A treatise on the Court of Star Chamber.

f. 85.—Fifteenth-century copies of letters from and to Pope Martin V. the Archbishop of Canterbury, Hen. VI., &c.; with a letter from the University of Oxford of 25 July 1427.

f. 100.—" The etimologie, antiquity, and authority of Sheriffs and their deputyes."

The rest of the volume contains readings on Statutes, and various collections relative to the Charters of London, the Chancery, and the office of Compositions for alienations.

Barrington MS. 22.—A very thick folio volume of law collections.

ff. 1–64, 129–576.—Briefs, bills in Chancery, and other law papers, of the 17th century.

f. 65. Transcript of " Some notes and observations upon the Statute of Magna Charten ca. 29, and other Statutes concerning the proceedings in the Chancery in courses of equity and conscience, collected by the Lord Elesmere for the Kinges learned Counsels direction, the month of September 1615."

f. 80.—Copy of a letter from the Lords of the Council to the King on behalf of Sir Edward Coke, June 26, 1616; with account of his appearance before the board and submission on June 30.

f. 85*b.*—Notes on the Court of Chancery, etc.

f. 577.—Copy of the Will of Henry VIII.

f. 588.—Copy of an encyclical letter of Pope Alexander VII., 20 Sept. 1655.

f. 591.—Notes on the laws about religion made 1–23 Eliz., dated " August, 1581."

f. 609.—The original brief of Thomas Egerton (afterwards Lord Ellesmere) in the proceedings against Mary, Queen of Scots, in the Star Chamber. MSS. OF THE INNER TEMPLE.

It is endorsed "Mr. Sollicitor his Breviate in the Queene of Scottes cawse, 20 Octob. 1586." It begins "The Commission recitethe" and ends "her Majesties pryvy counsell." It is incorporated in the report of the Trial at Fotheringay printed in Hardwicke's "State Papers" vol. 1, pp. 225-249, of which the credibility has been called in question by M. Chantelauze in his work on "Marie Stuart, son Procès et son Exécution."

f. 621b.—An original undated letter from Sir Anthony Ashley to a person whom he addresses as "Right Honorable." He encloses a document which "was compiled longe since in the yeare of our Lord 1571, not longe after the death of the Duke of Norfolk, by very learned clarkes on that side the sea." He suggests that his correspondent should add what has happened since. "Tyme suffers not to annexe the tragicall historie towchinge the conjuracons made against her husbande and the adultery comitted. All which (no doubt) wold make for your better satisfaccon in manie pointes."

The paper enclosed is headed "A briefe collection of the conspiraces made by the Queene of Scottes against the person and state of the Queene of Englande." It begins, "It is well knowen that the Queene of Scottes hath all waies." It ends (on f. 624b.) with "A discourse uppon the detencon and custodie of the Queene of Scottes, and whether she ought to be drawen into justice by the Queene of England, or not," in the form of an imaginary dialogue between "The Hystoriographer" and "Pollitick."

f. 635.—An epitome of the foregoing dialogue; in the same hand.

f. 641.—"The Reasones abridgede tendinge to the delivere of the partie from the peyne of deathe," with answers thereto.

f. 646.—Copy of Letters Patent (25 June, 3 Eliz.) to Robert Purseglove sometime prior of Gisburne, licensing him to found a hospital and free school at Guisborough, co. York, with the statutes of the school, a list of the books given to the School by the founder, for the use of the Masters, noting the very few which remained in the year 1630, and a rental of the lands, &c., which formed the endowment.

f. 657.—Copy of the will of John Cosin, Bishop of Durham, 13 Dec. 1671.

f. 667.—A collection of original treatises, in English and Latin, on the Courts of Record, on the Courts Spiritual (dedicated to Drs. Rich. Cosin and Thos. Bing), and on legal procedure, by Richard Robinson, "dwelling in Cowe Lane, London," A.D. 1588-1597.

Barrington MS., 67, 4°.—1. "Mr. Litleton, of the Inner Temple, his argument, and others, in defence of Mr. Stephens his plea concerninge knyghthood"; with the arguments and resolutions of the Barons of the Exchequer.

2. Serj. Whitfield's Lectures at Gray's Inn, 1633, and Staple's Inn, 1628.

3. Mr. Fuller's Argument against oaths *ex-officio* in eccl. courts.

Barrington, 82. fol. ff. 62.—MS. on vellum, of the middle of the 15th cent., containing part of Littleton's treatise on Tenures, beginning, "Tenaunt en fee simple est celluy," and ending at chap. 7, book III. An old MS. note at the beginning suggests that as the book came from the study of Mr. William Colles, of Leigh, Worcestershire, to his son and grandson, Michael and Humfrey Colles, while the family of Colles

MSS. OF THE INNER TEMPLE. "were well acquainted with Mr. Littleton," the book may have been had direct from the author himself.

Barrington MS., 83 fol. ff. 56.—MS. on vellum, of the first half of the 14th cent., containing *Placita de Quo Waranto* and *Placita Coronæ* at Bedford, and *Placita communia et coronæ libertatem et burg. tangentia* at Dunstaple, before the Judges itinerant, Rob. de Arderne " et sociis suis," John de Cauntebrigge, Thos. de Louthe, and Thos. Rudeclyve, 4 Edw. III., and beginning of year 5 (1330–1). Among the contents are, " Placita de libertate Prioris de Dunstaple ; " " Allocaciones amerciamentorum hominum nostrorum nobis factæ in Scaccario; " a copy (on paper) of a composition between Richard, prior of Dunstaple, and the burgesses ; and a case extracted from " Placita aulæ dom. Regis apud S. Albanum die sabb. prox. post fest. S. Valentini," 15 Edw. III. The volume appears to be one of much interest in connection with the history of Dunstaple and the neighbourhood. On a fly-leaf is this note : " Nota, cest liver cite par Sur Coke, 2 Inst. 298 ; infra, p. 23."

Maseres MS. 1. fol.—Entries of leases which passed under the Great Seal, 20 Eliz.—6 Jas. I.

Maseres MS. 2. fol.—Copy of a report on the State of Quebec, its fortifications, government, revenues, church government, Indian nations, soil, population, trade, and character of the people, by James Murray, the Governor, A.D. 1762 ; with extracts about Customs' duties, etc., in Canada, A.D. 1664–1754, and " Liste des navires venus en Canada en 1754."

Maseres MS. 3. fol.—" Instructions for Georgia. 1758."

7226. A volume of miscellaneous foreign papers, mostly relating to Spanish Flanders (many in Dutch), presented to the Library of the Inner Temple by Mr. Francis Turner in 1860. Among the contents are the following pieces :—

4. An invitation to a councillor to attend a solemn Te Deum in the church of St. Gudule (at Brussels) in thanksgiving for the peace. Dec. 29, 1678.

16. Copy of regulations for the government of the archers belonging to the body-guard of Philip II. King of Spain.

17. Copy of a letter, partly in French, partly in Latin, from Peter Van Heele to Monsr. Castol, Minister of the Word at Blackfriars (" Blachyers ") in London. The writer had a good journey from Hamburgh. After visiting the Duchy of Lunenburg and the University of Helmstadt, he went to Magdeburg, and thence, by advice of his friends, to call on the Princes of Anhalt at Dessau, who gave him the best cheer in the world, and almost adored him, because he was able to give them a true report on the state of foreign affairs. They seemed to think that God had sent him on purpose to remove them from their state of ignorance. They consulted him on divers weighty matters. The expenses of his stay were paid for him, and at his departure the Princes gave him a gold medal and a number of thalers for his journey, with the promise of a larger stipend if he would write to them. He would to God that their power was greater. They consider that the Queen (of England) will do great harm to the common cause if she make peace with the enemy, who if at peace with England and Holland would be able to trouble all the world, and especially Germany. Other Princes are careless of this, knowing no more about the affairs of Christendom than those of Africa. The Princes of Anhalt say that one might search all Germany for Princes worthy of the name. There is a great quarrel between the

Prince of Brunswick and the Landgrave on account of the disorders of the army of Germany. The Elector Palatine has tried in vain to reconcile them. He himself has been at issue with the Landgrave for some time past, on account of a report which Monsr. Bongars had made of one to the other. This however seems now at an end, and they both lay the blame on Bongars. Germany is so constituted that if the Spaniard were to attack her he would make himself master of her. The emulations and dissensions among the Princes and the factions of the theologians, Calvinist and Lutheran, ruin the Princes, who for the most part are simpletons and brought up to hunt and drink, and for the rest believe whatever the Church believes. Every minister wishes to appear to know something more than his brethren, and to raise a standard of his own, striving for victory rather than for truth. The Princes being badly trained by these ministers mismanage their affairs. From Anhalt the writer went to Wittemberg which abounds in theologians who believe in Luther only, and give over all others to the Devil. Thence after two days he went to Berlin, where he arrived on the 22nd of November. On the following day he presented his letters to the Chancellor of the Elector, and to the Marshal. He did not however present his royal letters as the Elector was absent for three weeks for hunting. In the evening there came a messenger from the Prince of Anhalt with letters requesting him to return in order to discuss certain important matters which had been overlooked. He accordingly started on the 24th, and reached Dessau on the following evening, where he was honourably received at the Castle. He returned to Berlin on the last day of the month, but he has not yet seen the Elector. He sends messages to his relations. If his correspondent wishes to write to him he should address the letter in Latin, "Nobili viro Petro van Heyle," for such is the way in which the King and the Senate of the Kingdom write to him. It is wrong to err in such matters in Germany. He sends messages to [Fr.] Bacon, and to the good Earl of Essex, whom he has been extolling to the sky in Denmark and in Germany alike, so that he alone of the English nobles is known there to be a good citizen of that common Republic of which the good Princes of Germany are citizens. Would that the Earl might know how zealous the writer has been in describing his incomparable virtues. Dated at Berlin, Dec. 3, 1599.

31. A collection of eight, extracted from fourteen, Protestant songs written in French in the sixteenth century, with notes of the tunes to which they are to be sung. The first one (of 12 stanzas, each beginning with the same words) commences:

"O presbytre, presbytre, oyez votre chanchon,
En voz matinez chantez ceste lichon."

The tunes mentioned are "La voix, O hermite, sainct hermite,". &c. " le chant dy more par ta foy," "le cant, mon poure est prison," &c., " le chant, Jay le cœur souvent bien Mary," "le chant, dame Dorleanes ne pleurez plus."

40.—Monita privata Societatis Jesus.

50.—"Nouveau Reglement pour le gouvernement du Pays Bas Espagnol."

90.—Account (on seven leaves, written by a French hand) of the household of Mary, Queen of Scots, entitled :—" Estat de la Reyne Marie d'Escosse, d'Angleterre, et de France, par elle dressé a Cheofold (Sheffield) le dernier jour du mois de Juillet, mil cinq cens soixante treize, pour le reglement de sa maison." This very interesting docu-

MSS. OF THE INNER TEMPLE.

ment gives the names and the wages of about one hundred and fifty persons who were then in attendance on the royal prisoner, including the Archbishop of Glasgow as "embassadeur." It is not mentioned in Mignet's Life of Queen Mary, in the later work of Mr. Hosack, or in Mr. Leader's *Mary Queen of Scots in Captivity*.

Miscellaneous MSS., not numbered.

Fol.—A collection of letters to the Benchers and Treasurer of the Inner Temple, from—
1. The Earl of Leicester; four letters, 1570–84.
2. Roger Manwood; six letters, 1577–1590.
3. Judge Will. Peryam.
4. John Aylmer, Bishop of London, recommending Mr. "Travis" [Travers] for Reader; 29 June 1581.
5. The Privy Council: 31 March 1583.
6. Robert Rolt to Mr. Pagrave, Reader.
7. Sir Christ. Hatton; six, 1583–1592.
8. The Privy Council desiring the allowance of a pension to Travers, whom they highly praise; 19 Feb. 1585.
9. Sir F. Walsingham; two letters, 1586–9.
10. The Privy Council; 22 Jan., 1586.
11. Francis and Adrian Stoughton; 28 Nov. 1589.
12. Tho. Norrys; 8 July 1590.
13. Lord Wray; 13 Nov. 1591.
14. E. Walter and Rich. Daveys; 12 Jan. 1591.
15. Will. Hyldyard; five letters, 1591–5.
16. Will. Watson; two letters, 27 Jan. 1591.
17. Sir Thos. West and Thomas Tasburgh, desiring leave to make a door from the White Friars into the Temple garden; 5 Feb. 1591.
18. Thos. Lucas; Colchester, 3 June 1592.
19. Will. Hughse, the Treasurer to — Pyrton, 29 Jan. 1592; to the Benchers, from Higham Ferrers, 9 Nov. 1593.
20. Sir John Puckering; four letters, 1593–5.
21. Ralph Rokeby; two letters, 1593.
22. Thomas Wrothe.
23. Rob. Sackeville; Sackvill House, 24 Feb. 1602.
24. Sir John Popham, L.C.J.; two letters, 1605–6, with orders made by the judges, and a letter thereon signed by 14; 7 June 1605.
25. Lewis Tresame.
26. John Mershe; 1 Dec. 1606.
27. J. Pagrave; Northwoodbarningham, 9 May 1606.
28. Will. Howpill, Treasurer of Lyon's Inn; 10 May 1614.
29. Order under sign manual of Charles I. for the strict observance of the proclamation for keeping Lent, during the time of the reading in the House; 18 March, *an* 8.
30. Sir Rob. Heath; two letters, 1634–41.
31. Tho. Nash; 1634.
32. Sir John Laurence; Chelsea, 14 June 1635.
33. Francis Hemsworth; 14 Feb. 1637.
34. W. Lord Wentworth (afterwards Earl of Strafford), giving up his chamber in the Temple which his father bought; York, 23 Feb. 1637.
35. Rich. Tailboys; 9 June 1638.

36. John Lane; 9 June 1638.   MSS. OF THE INNER TEMPLE.
37. Francis Jackson; 13 June 1638.
38. Petition from Nich. Rolf and Will Style.
39. Remonstrance of the Society to the Privy Council; 5 Jan. 1630.
40. Order of the House of Commons for the tendering the oaths to the Irish students and other suspected persons; 9 Nov. 1641.
41. Sam. Lodington; 25 Nov. 1647.
42. Order from the King for admitting Roger Fielding into the place of prothonotary of the Court of Common Pleas; 3 Aug. an 14.
43. Order from the House of Lords for a list of all students that are Irish or Papists; 29 March 1679.
44. Sir N. Bacon, C.S.
45. Petition from James Heath.

Where not otherwise specified the letters are almost entirely respecting applications on behalf of students, admission to chambers, fines, and the like.

3059. fol. pp. 154.—A copy-book of letters to the Earl of Essex, Lord Lieut. of Ireland, from 9 Jan. 1676 to 29 Aug. 1677; from Sir H. Coventry, H. Thynne, Earl of Danby, Duke of Ormonde, Lord Ranelagh, — Wyche, &c.; with a large number from Hen. Capell, the Earl's brother.

Miscellaneous MSS., not numbered.

fol.—"Certaine observations upon the Eyre of Pickeringe, by Will. Fletwoode, serjeant of the lawe and Recorder of London, written by him 6 Apr. 1592." At the end are messages from James I. to the House of Commons, with addresses from them in 1621. Formerly, as it appears from the binding and the handwriting of a list of contents, in the libraries of Lord Somers and Sir Joseph Jekyll, although not included in the sale catalogue of 1739; and given to the Inner Temple in 1867 by E. R. G. Robertson.

fol.—A catalogue of the Nobility of England, with the Courts of record, King's household, public officers, &c., in 1616.

fol.—An 18th century transcript of Sir Robert Cotton's Treatise of the Court of Chancery.

fol.—An English treatise, in two books (pp. 114), "De synedriis Britannicis," to the time of Edw. Conf. Formerly in B. Bright's library, 253, who supposed that it was written by W. Petyt, under whose name it subsequently appeared in a catalogue of T. Thorpe's. This, however, seems very questionable. The commencing words would, of themselves, render it doubtful: "Haveing allready given an acc^t of the Jewish, Gretian, and Roman assemblies and councells, tis time now to say something of those of our own country." The MS. (apparently in a transcriber's hand) is of the latter part of the 17th cent.

Small 8vo.—A metrical version of Psalms I.-LXXX. Apparently the first draft in Archbishop Parker's own hand of his version of these Psalms. See *Notes and Queries*, 3rd Series, VII. 357.

8vo.—A MS. Note-book on the forms of practice in the Court of Chancery, by H. Finch, Earl of Nottingham, Lord Chancellor. Given to the Library in 1842 by John Wyatt.

MSS. OF THE INNER TEMPLE.

fol.—Note-book of miscellaneous matters written in the latter part of the 17th cent. 1. Notes on gunnery. 2. On dialling, with mention of a dial made by Sir C. Wren for the King at Newmarket, and description of a "weather clock" made by him. 3. On organs, with a list of stops in the Temple Organ. 4. Notes about Major "Knaspole's" house at Eastwell. 5. Charge to Freemasons, by Hen. Heale, 1675, including a sketch of the history of freemasonry. 6. Architectural drawings of details of roofs, including the Duke of Norfolk's at Weybridge, and of a "very antient" roof of Irish oak at East Coker, taken 23 Jan. 167$\frac{7}{8}$. From Mr. J. O. Halliwell's library, who bought it at M. Libri's sale, March 28, 1859, lot 65.

fol.—Copies of correspondence on the subject of precedency claimed by the Queen's Advocate; being letters from the Attorney and Solicitor-Gen. (Cockburn and Bethell) and the Advocate (Harding) in 1855 to the Lord Chancellor Cranworth, with his reply. Given to the Library in 1857 by Sir J. D. Harding.

fol.—Vellum MS. of the middle of the 14th cent., in double columns. Bracton's Treatise *De legibus Angliæ.* The last leaf, with chap. 33 of book V., *De Exceptionibus,* is wanting. A fine MS., in good condition, bought of Mr. R. Howarth in 1886, who bought it in Lancashire about 1870. On a fly-leaf is the name of an earlier owner : " Ex libris Adriani Stokes, Medicinæ Doctoris, de vico Yate, in com. Gloc." Amongst some fragments of early MSS. which formerly formed part of the old binding are four pages of a MS. of Ovid's *Metamorphoses* of about the beginning of the 13th cent., or end of the 12th, containing rather more than a hundred lines from book I., including vv. 600–700.

WILLIAM DUNN MACRAY.

INDEX.

A.

"A.," intelligence concerning ; 24.
"A. A.," letter signed by ; 25.
Abbot :
    Archbishop ; 136.
    —— accident caused by ; 288.
    Walter, son of ; 61.
Abbott, Thomas, letter of ; 31.
Abergavenny:
    family of, papers relating to ; 49.
    peerage of ; 149.
    Henry Neville, Lord ; 149.
Abingdon ; 170, 171, 222.
    Earl of, counterfeit name of ; 30.
    —— letter of ; 31.
    —— his mission to the Prince of Orange ; 23.
Acaria, Monsieur ; 301.
Acra, Radulphus de, witness ; 57.
Acton :
    church of ; 138.
    tax book for ; 152.
    Rev. Mr. ; 151.
Actone :
    Laurence de, grant to ; 72.
    Richard de, and Matilda, his wife ; 70.
    —— quitclaim to ; *ib.*
"Adam, Anna," intelligence from ; 25.
Adam :
    Sir, the clerk of Windsor Castle 171.
    son of Ralph, witness ; 91.
Adams :
    John, American minister ; 54, 55.
    Mr. ; 131.
"Adams," *alias* Mr. Russell ; 30.
Addington, Henry, steward of Reading ; 207.
Admiral, Lord High, office of ; 40, 248.
Admiralty :
    the ; 134.
    Board, charges against the ; 115.
    Court of, fees and salaries in the ; 250.
    Lords Commissioners of, letter of ; 242.
"Adventure," the, ship ; 3, 290.
Agbrigg, subsidy roll for ; 120.

Ailesbury :
    Earl of, letter of ; 22.
    —— petition signed by ; 21.
Airesbury, William ; 185.
Akatour, John le, mayor of Reading ; 227.
Albemarle :
    Duke of ; 3, 4, 5, 84.
    —— household accounts of ; 92.
    —— letters of ; 7, 20.
    —— orders to and by ; 4, 5, 7.
    —— petition signed by ; 21.
    —— steward of Reading ; 195.
    Anne, Duchess of, letter of ; 92.
    Duchess of, character of ; 22.
    Earl of, cipher of ; 53.
    —— correspondence of ; 44.
Albus :
    Peter, of Wymundham ; 62.
    —— William, son of, exchange by ; 62.
    Robertus, witness ; 57.
Alder, Mr., benefaction by ; 211.
Alderney :
    bill of complaint of ; 130.
    papers relating to ; *ib.*
Aldobrandini, Cardinal, passport signed by ; 297.
Aldwell, Thomas ; 237.
Aldworth :
    Mr. ; 196.
    —— portrait of ; 206.
    R. ; 218.
    Rich., effigy of ; 196.
    William, election of ; 199.
Alexander :
    witness ; 129.
    III., Pope ; 230.
    VI., Pope ; Bull of ; 236.
    VII., Pope, encyclical of ; 302.
Alford, Lady ; 98.
Alkok, —, descent from ; 138.
Allcock, Mr. ; 206.
Allen :
    Captain Thomas ; 3.
    Cardinal ; 264, 265, 268, 289.
    —— letter of ; 260.
    Jos., letter of ; 11.
Allesle, lands near ; 128.
Almand, Oliver ; 260.
Almeton, grant of free chace in ; 119.
Alneto, Rogerus de, witness ; 57.
Alnwick, Thomas, abbot of ; 74.
Alsop, Mr., verses by ; 155.
Altham :
    Edward, letters of ; 153.
    Leventhorpe, letters of ; 153.

Althermanstone, players of; 172.
Althrop; 21.
Alured:
    Col., imprisonment of; 32.
    Thomas, letters of; 148, 289.
Alvaton, Rob., clericus de; 128.
Alwaston, lands in; 91.
Aman, Rich.; 177.
Amelia:
    Princess, at Bath; 205.
    —— letter of; 47.
America; 37.
    commercial negotiations with; 54.
    peace negotiations with; 53.
    state of; 48.
Amersham, election at; 152.
Amors Court, manor of; 133.
Amsterdam, letters dated at; 10, 41, 43.
Ancastre:
    water of; 64.
    Ralph of; ib.
Anderson:
    Mr.; 154.
    Monsieur, a Jacobite agent; 50, 51.
    Edm., letter of; 288.
Andover; 78.
    letter dated at; 276.
Andrew, John, licensed preacher; 285.
Andrewes:
    Will., petition by; 30.
    —— loan by his wife to the Crown; ib.
Anesi:
    Peter de, witness; 90.
    Thomas de, witness; ib.
Angell, Will., scrivener, petition of; 5.
Angers; 78.
Anglesea, rentals in; 149.
Anglesey:
    Earl of; 8.
    —— conventicle held by a former chaplain of; 15.
    —— his sister reported to attend a conventicle; ib.
    Lord, order of; 243.
Angus, Earl of; 70.
Anhalt:
    John George, Prince of, letter of; 301.
    Louis, Prince of, letter of; ib.
    Princess of; 304.
Anjou, Duke of, project of his marriage; 286, 287.
"Anne," the yacht; 4.
Anne:
    Princess; 179.
    —— at Nottingham; 27.
    —— determined to go towards Oxford; ib.
    of Denmark, Queen; 240.
    —— grant to; 134.
    —— funeral of; 136.
    Queen, grant by; 141.
    —— her attitude in Sacheverell's case; 117, 118.
    —— players of; 233.
    —— proclamation of; 204.
    —— at Reading; ib.
    —— her zeal for the church; 113.
    —— her regiment of guards; 93.

Annesley, Dr. Francis, address to; 208.
Anslow:
    Mr., reported to hold a conventicle; 16.
    Peter, reported to hold a conventicle; ib.
Anson, Lord, letters of; 45.
Anthropes, Mr.; 131.
Antrim, Randolph, Marquis of, liberated on bail; 2.
Antrobus, Benjamin, reported to attend a conventicle; 16.
Anyas, John, trial of; 135.
Appeller, John, of Quapprode, chaplain 65.
Appirlee, manor of; 72.
Appleby:
    Confirmation at; 84.
    lease of the manor of; 12.
    Castle; 84, 85, 90.
Arbor, manor of; 133.
Archdeacon, John, suspected Jacobite agent; 47.
Archer; 266.
Arch-Presbyter, the; 264.
Arches, Court of:
    register of the; 258.
    precedence in; 295.
    irregularities in; 300.
Ardydwy, commott of; 140.
Areskine:
    Charles, report of; 45, 46.
    Col. Thomas; 41.
    Sir Thomas, letter of; 159.
Argeere (? Algier); 290.
Argyll:
    Marquis of, prisoner in the Tower; 2.
    Duchess of; 48.
    —— family of, safe with both sides; 24.
Arlington:
    Earl of, warrants by; 7, 8.
    —— marriage of his daughter; 9.
    —— letter of; 10.
    —— information against a priest of; 17.
Armestone, parish of; 66.
Armiger, William; 97.
Armerer, Nich.; 4.
Armorer:
    Johannes; 229.
    Lady; 226.
    Sir William; 196.
Arms, description of; 132, 145, 234.
Armytage, Thomas, letter of; 31.
Arne, Dr., letter of; 76.
Arnulfus, filius Petri, case of; 59.
Arran, Lady; 117.
Arras, camp before, letter dated at; 9.
Array:
    Martin; 270.
Array, Commissions of; 278.
Arthur Prince, marriage of; 274.
Arundel:
    Earl of; 273.
    —— exile of; 237.
    —— letter of; 251.

Arundel—*cont.*
  Philip Howard, Earl of, arraignment of; *ib.*
  —— letter of; 289.
  Lord; 186.
  —— petition signed by; 21.
  of Wardour, Lord, duel with; 84.
  and Surrey, Countess Dowager of, bill preferred against; 241.
  John, case of; 159.
  Lieut. John; 3.
  R. of Trerise, letter of; 10.
  T.; 222.
Ashburnham, Jack; 215.
Ashe, Lady; 107.
Ashley :
  Lord, letter of; 218.
  Colonel; 40.
  Mr.; 131, 282.
  Sir Anthony, letter of; 303.
  Sir Jacob, governor of Reading; 178.
Ashridge; 132.
  monastery of; 153.
  letters dated at; 136, 137.
Ashton, Mr.; 25.
Aske, Roger, witness; 73.
Asselyn :
  John, of Wymundham; 64.
  —— Robert, son of, grant to; *ib.*
Assheton, Ralph, letter of; 28.
Association :
  the (1745); 206.
  of Priests; 263, 264.
  of the Eastern counties; 101, 102.
Asteleye :
  Giles de; 145.
  Sir Thomas de; *ib.*
  Thomas de, of Hullmoreton and Margery, his wife; *ib.*
Astley :
  Sir Edward; 105.
  Sir Jacob, selected as candidate for Norfolk; 106.
  —— Governor of Reading; 188, 215, 223.
  rectory and college of; 145.
  —— Dean and Canons of; *ib.*
Aston :
  Sir A., Governor of Reading; 187, 188.
  —— Governor of Reading; 215, 220.
  Walter, case of; 159.
Astone, John; 147.
Aszik, Jacob, proposal of; 38.
Atholl :
  Marq. of, intelligence from; 31.
  —— position of; *ib.*
Atkins, J., letter of; 10.
Atkinson :
  Abra., letter to; 37.
  Mr.; 263.
  John, "the Stockener" committed to the Tower; 7.
  Rob., committed to the Tower; *ib.*
Atkyns, Edward, letter of; 31.
[Atte Crosse,] Roger and Hawisia, his wife, grants to; 63.
Atwood, Will., letter of; 241.

Aubrey, W., representation by; 300.
Auchinbreck, fraudulent sale of; 50.
Audience, Court of; 300.
Aula :
  Adam de, grant by; 70.
  Agnes, his daughter; *ib.*
  William, son-in-law of; *ib.*
Austria :
  commerce with; 53.
  rumoured peace with France in; 112.
  threatened by the Turks; *ib.*
Austyn, Col. Archibald; 41.
Avignon; 53.
A. W., letter to; 293.
Awbrey, a papist, prosecution of; 179.
Axholme, Isle of, Stewardship of the; 123.
Aylisson bank, on the march to Edinburgh; 25.
Aylmer, Mr.; 285.
Aymstrey, sacrilege at; 147.
Ayshbury, rectory of; 135.
Ayton, Sir Rob.; 301.

B.

"B."; 258.
B., ——, Baptista, plan by; 39.
Babington :
  Francis; 230.
  Richard; *ib.*
Backwell, Edw., letters of; 9, 10.
Bacon :
  Anthony; 245.
  Francis; 251.
  —— considerations by; 131.
  Sir Francis; 136, 147, 252, 270.
  —— dedication by; 234.
  —— letters of and to; 239, 288.
  —— speech of; 248.
  —— treatise by; 275, 292.
  Lord Chancellor; 238.
  Sir Nicholas, Lord Keeper; 246, 286.
  —— letter of; 307.
Bagenall, Magdalen, letter of; 147.
Bagley, Thomas, of Lothbury, reported to attend a conventicle; 16.
Bagott, ——; 145.
Bagshaw :
  Mr., letters of and to; 261, 277, 278, 279, 280, 281.
  Christopher, letter of; 298, 300.
  Dr.; 266, 267, 268.
  —— letters to; 262, 263, 301.
  —— statement by; 264.
  —— brother of; 262.
  Edward, suit of; 271.
  —— committed to the Tower; 7.
Bagshot, commission dated at; 96.
Baliol, Willelmus de, witness; 57.
Baiocis, Helias de, witness; 90.

Baker:
 Lady, reported to frequent a conventicle; 15.
 Major, his position in Derry; 35.
 —— his wife destitute; ib.
 Mr.; 131.
 Rich., and his wife, case of; 162.
Baldock, Edw., order for, 25. :
Baldwin :
 son of Gilbert, grant by; 90.
 —— Adelina, wife of; ib.
 Mr., merchant, reported to frequent a conventicle; 15.
Balet, John; 172.
Balfour :
 Col. Henry; 41.
 Capt. John, pension to his widow; ib.
Balfoynt :
 Col. David; ib.
 —— Will.; ib.
Balhed, John, under sheriff, case of; 94.
Ball :
 Rev. John; 153.
 William; 189.
Ballacginba, hospital of; 150.
Balletti, Abbot, information against; 17.
Ballymartin, letters dated at; 8.
Baloch, Colonel Francis; 40.
Bamborough, Master of; 74.
Bamfield, Joseph, discharged from the Tower; 2.
Banbury :
 Earl of; 184.
 —— letter of; 221.
 W., Earl of, letters of; 212.
 —— conveyance by; 210.
 Countess of; ib.
Bancroft :
 Dr., preferment of; 256.
 Archbishop; 239.
Bandwyn, John, grant to and by; 71, 72.
Banfshire; 46.
Bangor :
 Bishop of; 155.
 Dean of; 197.
Banks : ·
 Sir John; 249, 273.
 Attorney-General; 241.
Banstead Downs, Royal visit to; 12.
Banyard, Rob., letter to; 97.
Baptism, orders concerning; 285.
Barbadoes, letter dated at; 10.
Barbon, Mr.; 151.
Barbour :
 Gabriel, benefaction by; 186.
 Henry; 171, 172.
Bardsay, George, disbarred; 160.
Barebone, Praisegod, committed to the Tower; 3.
Barker, Richard, letter of; 159.
Barkestone; 63.
 lands in; 61.
 Richard, son of William de and Christina his wife; 60.
Barkewerd, Sir Robert de, witness; ib.

Barking :
 conventicle held in; 16.
 case of the parish of; 232.
Barklay, Sir Patrick de, witness; 150.
Barkstead :
 John, conveyed to the Tower; 4.
 Sir John ;¯192.
 —— case of; 193.
Barle, William; 94.
Barlow :
 Mr.; 264.
 Dr.;·257.
 Thomas, letter of; 279.
Barnard, Francis, elected to a scholarship; 197.
Barnes, Anne, clandestine marriage of; 159.
Barnesley, Willelmus; 229.
Barnevelt, John van Oulden, letters of; 234.
Baroun, Will.; 175.
Barow, ——; 297.
Barras, Mr.; 262, 263.
Barrell Gilb, proceedings against; 271.
Barret :
 —— reported to hold a conventicle; 16.
 Dr.; 262.
 —— at Douay; 261.
 · Geo., letter of; 33.
Barrington, Abraham, letters of; 31, 73.
Barrow, Dr., of Cambridge University; 9.
Barrowby; 123.
 manor of; 119.
Barry, ——, actor; 79, 80.
Barthelmy, ——, letters of; 55.
Barugheby, Richard de, of Hundington, lease by; 65.
Barwicke, Mr.; 131.
Basham; 97, 107, 110, 114.
Basildon Park, the Prince Regent at; 208.
Basing, letter dated at; 31.
Basingwerk, abbey of; 142.
Baskett, Thos., King's printer; 210.
Basque Roads, expedition to the; 45.
Basset :
 Sir John, deed by; 129.
 —— John, son of, marriage contract of; 129.
 Sir Ralph, of Cheadle; 144.
 Ralph, marriage contract of; 129, 136.
 Thomas, bookseller; 39.
 William, son of; 136.
Bastard, Thomas, lampoon written by; 272.
Bate :
 Edw., report by; 166.
 Dr. John, letter of; 282.
 John, and Agnes his wife, grant to; 66.
Bates, Charles, letter of; 9.
Bath; 205.
 · Katharine of Braganza at; 197.
 Mary of Modena at; 200.
 monastery lands in; 239.
 peerage of; 162.
 Princess Anne at; 201.

Bath—*cont.*
Earl of, letters of; 12, 22.
—— orders by; 39.
—— report of; 278.
—— *v.* Bourchier, case of; 162.
—— petition signed by; 21.
knights of the, creation of; 274.
and Wells, Bishop of; 197.
—— bishopric of; 135.
—— James Montague, Bishop of; 156.
—— Thos., Bishop of; 137.
Battely, Mr.; 153.
Batto, Jasper, reported to hold a Quaker's meeting; 15.
Baxter:
Mr., reported to hold a conventicle; *ib.*
J., plan by; 39.
Bayard, Roger; 161.
Baylie, Rich., President of St. John's College, Oxford; 226.
Bayly:
Charles, committed to the Tower; 7.
Tho., witness; 122.
Dr., Queen Elizabeth's physician; 135.
Baynes, Jeremy, petition of; 5.
Beadel, —, resignation of scholarship by; 205.
Beale, Robert; 286.
Bears, on the Stock Exchange; 45.
Beaufort:
Cardinal, case of; 238.
Duke of, letter of; 31, 42.
Beaumont:
M. de, ambassador; 282.
Sir Henry, petition of; 275.
Col. John, letter of; 31.
Rob., licensed preacher; 285.
William, letter of; 103.
Beauvais, Vincent of; 229.
Beauvoir:
Henry; 289.
Peter; *ib.*
—— the younger; *ib.*
Thomas; *ib.*
Beawmys, manor and vill of; 73.
Bebesete, Alice de; 68.
Bebseth; 67.
Becher, Edw., letter of; 125.
Becket, Thomas, chancellor, witness; 119.
Bedewynde, Richard, mayor of Reading; 227.
Bedford:
letter dated at; 219.
A., licensed preacher; 285.
Bridget, Countess of; 132.
Lucy, Countess of, letter to; 273.
Countess of, reported to frequent a conventicle; 15.
Duke of, letter of; 44.
Wriothesley, Duke of; 140.
Earl of; 132.
—— letter of; 240.
Lord; 243.
Francis, Earl of, proceedings against; 271.

Bedingfield:
Dan., letter of; 112.
Sir Henry; 108.
—— letter of; 13.
Bedralle, lands in; 73.
Bedwynde, Richard, will of; 170.
Beek:
Sir Thomas, deed by; 129.
—— Maud, daughter of, marriage contract of; *ib.*
Beesley, Mr.; 241.
Beke, Thomas, election of; 180.
Belasyse:
Lord, letter of; 11.
—— information of mass said by his steward; 17.
James, witness; 84.
W., intelligence from; 29.
Belcarras:
Lord, his influence in Edinburgh; 24.
—— behaviour of; 25.
Belet, Michael, grant by; 60.
Belfast; 36.
troops landed at; 34.
Belhus:
Richard de; 69.
—— Alexander, son of, grant by; *ib.*
—— Alexander, grandson of; *ib.*
Bell, Capt. Henry, sickness of; 183.
Bellbrooke, letter dated at; 83.
Bellin, Christian á; 301.
Bello, Rad. de; 171.
Bellomont:
Lord, letter of; 166.
Willelmus de, witness; 57.
Belson, John de, grant by; 68.
Belvoir, letter dated at; 240.
Belward, William, descent from; 137.
Bemohd, —; 83.
Benbecula, letter dated at; 46.
Benefices:
bestowal of; 256.
valuation of; 257.
Benewelle, manor of; 71.
Benger, Sir Thos., grant to; 210.
Bennet:
Sir H., warrants by; 5, 6.
John, letters of and to; 280.
Sir John, case of; 244.
Squire; 30.
Bennett, Edw., speech of; 261.
Benson:
letter dated at; 220.
Robert; 261.
Bentinck:
Mr., counterfeit name of; 30.
Charles, letters of; 44.
W., minister of the States-General, letters of; 19, 20.
Will., letters of; 44.
Benwell, Thomas, lease to; 208.
Bérard, Mr. L., letters of; 42.
Bercham, church of; 90.
Bergen; 47.
Berington, Thomas, commissioner; 224.
Berker, Edw., at Haughmond; 142.

Berkeley:
Lord, petition signed by; 21.
John, Lord, letters of; 10, 11.
—— his salary as ambassador in arrear; 11.
Sir John; 186.
Will., letter of; 10.
Sir Will., governor of Virginia; 14.
Berkhampstead:
honour of; 153.
liberties of; 141.
Berkshire:
charitable uses in; 139.
the civil wars in; 187-190, 215-220.
direction for parliamentary elections in; 106.
grand jury of; 248.
grants of lands in; 133.
justices of; 213.
High Sheriff of; ib.
high prices of provisions in; ib.
concealed lands in; 145.
Lord Lieutenant of; 221.
sheriff of; 181.
Parliamentary Committee for; 189, 216.
Royalist contributions in; 220.
Berlin:
correspondence from; 47.
letter dated at; 305.
negotiations with Hanover at; 55.
Bermuda, governor of, case of; 167.
map of (1622); 39.
Bernard:
Ralph, Alexandra daughter of, grant by; 59, 60.
—— —— husband and son of; 60.
William, grant by; 65.
—— Alicia, wife of; ib.
Bernevall, Reginald de, witness; 91.
Berry:
Col. James, transported; 4.
John, Commissioner of Virginia; 19.
Bertie:
Chas., letters of and to; 8, 9, 10, 19, 22, 26, 32.
Henry, letter of; 22.
James; 152.
Peregrine, letters of and to; 7, 8, 9, 10, 13, 25.
—— engagement by; 20.
—— his proposal for manning the Navy; 31.
Philip, intelligence from; 28.
Robert, letters to; 10.
—— petition for a place by; 13.
Bertram, Robert, of Bothall, witness; 67, 68.
Berwick:
charges at; 250.
Charles I. at; 293.
Recorder of; ib.
letters dated at; 12, 28, 82
mayor of; 13.
corporation of, address by; 12.
military revolution at; 28, 29.

Berwick—cont.
pacification of; 98.
parliamentary election at; 12, 20.
Castle, ready to declare for the Prince of Orange; 28.
Besteney, election of; 180.
Betham, Col.; 41.
Bethell, Solicitor-General, letters of; 308.
Bethlem Hospital, a Tower prisoner removed to; 8.
Bethune, M. Phillippe de, French ambassador; 299.
Betillisden, lands of; 75.
Betts:
——, an Irishman, information against; 17.
Capt. Geo., letters of; 147.
Bever, Robert Prior of, letters of admission by; 66.
Bevington, John; 154.
Bewdley, alarm of Papist plots in; 147
Bewik, John of; 75.
Beza, Theodorus; 255.
Bibbesworth, Hugh de; 145.
Bickerstaffe, Philip, intelligence from; 28.
Bidelesden, manor of; 71.
Bigg:
Anne; 197.
John, mayor of Reading; 201.
Mabel; 197.
Richard, cordwainer; ib.
Billingsley, Col. Rupert, intelligence from; 28.
Bing, Thomas, covenant by; 295.
Bingley, Sir John; 245.
Binns, letter dated at; 46.
Birch, Mr.; 131.
Bird:
Mr., reported to attend a conventicle; 16.
Dr., schoolmaster of Reading; 184, 223, 225.
—— death of; 186.
Birkhead, Mr.; 131.
Birmingham:
reported burnt by the Irish and Papists; 28.
false alarm of Irish bands at; 29.
Biset, M., witness; 59.
Bishop:
W.; 278.
—— letters of and to; 278, 279.
Bispham, Mr.; 131.
Bisse, Mr.; 267.
Blackborne, Edmund; 108.
Blackburn, bounties on cottons of; 166.
Blackden, Robert of West Harfortte, witness; 74.
"Blackemoore" the, ship; 4.
Blackman:
John, elected to a fellowship; 189, 190.
—— petition of; 217.
Blackwell:
the Archpriest, letter to; 259, 260.
George; 264.

Blackwell—*cont.*
  George, letters of and to; 277, 278, 279, 280, 281, 282, 297, 299.
  Mr., letters to; 266, 267, 268, 269.
Blaesaw, John, letter of; 279.
Blagge :
  Col.; 219.
  —— Thomas; 188, 215.
Blagrave :
  Anth., election of; 204.
  Daniel, recorder of Reading; 218.
  —— election of; 190, 193, 223.
  —— dismissal of; 192.
  George, candidature of; 199.
  John, election of; 194, 197.
Blak, Callertone, lands in; 73.
Blake :
  Sir Francis, marriage of; 58.
  —— daughter of; *ib.*
  John; 203.
  —— mayor of Reading; 218.
  Thomas; 198.
Blakene, demesne of; 138.
Blakesly, letter dated at; 141.
Blakney, Robert, prior of Tynemouth; 75.
Blanchebuche, Rob., witness; 129.
Bland, General, proposal of; 52.
Blaney, Mr., notes taken by; 21.
Blankeford, deed dated at; 144.
Blanshard, Rich., letter of; 8.
Blantire, Abbot of; 256.
Blaston, Richard, prisoner in the Fleet; 247.
Blaunchard, Isabella, lease to; 65.
Blechingley; 244.
Blenheim, battle of; 114.
Blenvit, Bernardus de, witness; 57.
"Blewcapp," the King's racehorse beaten at Newmarket; 9.
Blida, Will., prior of, witness; 91.
Blithsnoke, lands in; 73.
Blood :
  Mr., reported to attend a conventicle; 15.
  —— sons of; *ib.*
Bluet :
  Mr.; 262, 264, 266.
  —— letters to; 263, 264, 301.
  Robert, paper by; 300.
  —— letter of; 267.
  Thomas, his mission to Rome; 296, 297.
  —— statement of; 281.
  —— letter of and to; 279, 297.
Blundell *v.* Hodgkinson, case of; 162.
Blunt, John, of Swalowfyld, will of; 170.
Blunte, Richard; 266.
Blyke, William, of Haburley, grant to; 65.
Blythman, Jasper, certificate for; 36.
Bocclouch, Col.; 41.
Bodley, Sir Thomas, life of; 287.
Boebi :
  Hugh de, witness; 90.
  Walter de, witness; *ib.*
Bokman, Capt. Martin, committed to the Tower; 6.

Bolingbroke, Lord, letter of; 136.
Bolleshouere, Magister Alanus de; grant by; 91.
Bolt :
  a jesuit emissary; 268.
  ——, released on bail; 5.
Bolton :
  (by Derby); 91.
  ——, letter of; 76.
  1st Duke of, suits relating to; 151.
  —— son of; *ib.*
  2nd Duke of, letters of; *ib.*
  —— son of; *ib.*
  Lord, letter of; 31.
Bombelles, M. de, reputed a spy; 55.
Bonavant, Edward, bewitched; 185.
Bongars, Monsr.; 305.
Boniface VIII., Pope; 232.
Bonniman, Mr.; 131.
Bonner, Bishop, letter of; 276.
Books, titles of; 137, 154, 155, 195, 202, 239, 228, 240, 283.
Bookless, John; 154.
Boovington (Berkhampstead) a pretended marriage at; 9.
Boresworth, letter dated at; 254.
Borghese :
  Cardinal; 278.
  —— letters of; 279, 280.
  —— passport signed by; 297.
Boroughbridge; 92.
Boston :
  mayor of; 32.
  members returned to Convention for; 31, 32.
  (New England), government of; 38.
  —— intelligence from; 11.
  —— Governor and Council of; *ib.*
Botham, Mr., an unlicensed curate; 156.
Bottale :
  Thomas; 69.
  Matilda, widow of; *ib.*
Botwell, Col. George; 41.
Boucher, ——, attainted; 113.
Boughton :
  letter dated at; 12.
  Henry, case of; 161.
Bouillon; 44.
Boulond, a clerk; 172.
Boulogne :
  commissioners at; 287.
  expedition to; 182.
Bourdeaux; 166.
Bourghdone, Gilbert de, sheriff, witness; 70.
Bourton-on-the-Water, vicar of, case of; 163.
Bowden Park; 22.
Bower :
  Ensign, case of; 244.
  Sir William, under sheriff; 75.
Bowes :
  Hen., letter of; 159.
  Sir William, letter to; 293.
Bowland, Eliz.; 197.
Bowton, letter dated at; 222.

Bowyer:
—; 241.
Mr., letter to; 244.
Lodowick, deposition of; 185.
—— sentence on; ib.
Robert, Keeper of the Records; 239, 240.
—; 229.
—— Clerk of Parliament; 237.
Will.; 229.
—— Keeper of the Rolls; 139.
Boydell, family of; 138.
Boye:
Thomas, of Wymundham; 62.
William, grant by; ib.
Boyer, Robert, lease from; 208.
Boyle, Hon. Richard, killed in action; 85.
Brackley:
Lord Chancellor, petition to; 130.
borough of; 140, 141.
elections to Parliament for; 141.
rectory of; 140.
manor of, court rolls of; ib.
fairs and markets of; 141.
town bull and boar of; ib.
parish of St. Peter in; ib.
beating the bounds of; ib.
woods of; 130.
Viscount. See Bridgewater, Earl of.
Brackston:
Anth.; 183.
—— deprived; 223.
Will., alderman; 193.
—— mayor of Reading; 219.
Bradbury, manor of, exchange of; 133.
Bradford:
—, charge against; 121.
Thomas of; 74.
Bradley:
Henry; 188.
—— case of; 215.
John, his bail continued; 5.
—— his discharge; ib.
Bradshaw:
Edw., letter of; 146.
James, explanation by; 32.
Brady, Dr.; 233.
Brae:
Adam; 67.
Alan, son of; ib.
Braemar Castle, letter dated at; 45.
Brakston, William, dismissal of; 191.
Bramfield, Suffolk, living of; 12.
Brampton Bryan, alarm of Papist plots at; 147.
Bramwonge, lands in; 61.
Brandenburgh:
succession to; 53.
Elector of, letter of; 301.
John George, Margravine of, letter of; ib.
—— brother of; ib.
Brandling, John, minister, charge against; 9.
Brandon:
family of; 139.
the Norfolk militia at; 100, 101.
Branton, fee farm of; 75.
Brathait, an assumed name; 262.

Braunche, Ricardus; 172.
Braxton, Edw., alderman, deprived; 201.
Bray:
lands in; 197.
master; 176.
Breedon, John, election of; 199.
Bremingham, mayor of, libel on; 161.
Brent, Sir Nath., entertainment of; 185.
Brereton:
Sir Ralph; 151.
Sir Rondulf, will of; ib.
Sir William, appointment of; 243.
—— grant to; ib.
Brest, plan of the harbour of; 39.
Bretoun (Brito), Richard, witness; 60.
Brett, a chandler, encroachments by; 290.
Breval, D., introduction by; 32.
Brewood, manor and park of; 243.
Brewster, Will.; 280.
Bridewell; 277.
Bridge, Mr.; 131.
Bridgeman:
Fras., letter of; 8.
Sir Orlando, letter of; ib.
Lord Ch. Justice, letter from; 6.
Bridges:
Sir Giles, widow of; 154.
R., report by; 41.
Thomas, examination of; 278.
Bridgewater:
Mayor of; 197.
Canal; 127.
House, report on the MSS. from; 126 et seq.
manor of; 146.
Earl of, creation of; 136, 137, 140, 141, 147, 148, 149, 154, 155, 161, 165, 166.
—— Lord Lieutenant of Bucks; 156.
—— release of; 141.
—— (1631); 142.
1st Earl of; 139.
John, 2nd Earl of, household of; 137.
3rd Earl of; 151.
Scroope, Earl of; 141.
Countess of; 136.
Duke of; 134, 141.
—— order of; 243.
Bringwood Forest; 134.
Brinkburn, William, Prior of; 74.
Brinsley, Col.; 41.
Brisbane, J., letter of; 12, 19, 20.
Bristol:
Guy Carleton, Bishop of, report by; 12.
Earl of, letter of; 10.
—— dedication to; ib.
Lord of; 271.
Recorder of; 173.
Briwecurt, Ralph de, witness; 90.
Broadoaks; 359.
Brodericke, Sir John, proposals by; 37.
Brogge, Col.; 41.
Brome, Widow, Fifth Monarchy meeting held in her house; 15.
Bromfield, lordship of; 146.

Bromley:
    Sir Henry; 123.
    Sir John; 138.
    —— daughter of; 136.
    Margaret, marriage contract of; *ib.*
    Sir Thomas, Lord Chancellor; 135, 163.
    family of; 138.
Bromptone, Ricardus; 172.
Bromrig, Mr.; 112.
Bron, Alexander, widow of, quitclaim by; 60.
Broogh, Col.; 41.
Brooke:
    ——, a herald; 288.
    Colonel Filistin; 40.
    Lord, letter of; 50.
    Ralph, York Herald; 273.
    Sir Will., manslaughter of; 134.
Brothercross, hundred of; 101.
Brougham:
    exchange of; 84.
    Castle, 85, 86, 89, 90.
Broughton;
    near Skipton; 36.
    Hugh; 255.
    —— treatise by; 258.
Broun, John, of Hawkewelle, grant by; 71.
Brouncker, Lord; 8.
Broune, Isabella, quitclaim for; 64.
Brounlo, Mr.; 243.
Brown:
    Master; 76.
    William, charges against; 49.
Browne:
    ——, chaplain; 284.
    —— examination of; 294.
    Sir Anthony, examination of; 287.
    John, election of; 32, 140.
    Major-General; 189.
    Philip, information by; 13.
    —— letters of; 19.
    —— declaration by; *ib.*
    Sir Rich., Major-General of London; 6.
Browning, John; 283.
Bruce:
    Sir Alex., of Broomhall; 30.
    E., Lord, letter of; 240.
Bruges, letter dated at; 242.
Brun:
    Hugo, witness; 90.
    Richard, of Hundington, and Gilian, his wife, grants to; 62.
    Roger, of Barkeston, grant by; *ib.*
Brunet, Sir H., warrants by; 6, 7.
Brunetti, Signor, information of mass said in his house; 17.
Brunna:
    Canons of St. Peter of, grant to; 90.
    church of; *ib.*
Brunne, Robertus de, History of Britain by; 230.
Brunswick:
    Ferdinand, Duke of, correspondence of; 50.
    Henry Julius, Duke of, letter of; 301.
    Prince of; 305.
    and Lüneburg, minister of; 20.

Brussells:
    advices from; 10.
    correspondence from; 47.
    intelligence from; 19.
    letters dated at; 11, 12, 261.
    St. Gudule's in; 304.
Brute, Walter, protestation of; 231.
Bruyn:
    family of; 138.
    Roger, of Stapelford; *ib.*
Brydale, John, letter of; 22.
Brydgeman:
    Sir John; 140.
    —— letters of; 136, 147, 148.
Bubb:
    Capt., privy to the surrender of Carlisle; 29.
    duel by; 27.
Bubzow, letter dated at; 301.
Buckbend, Rob.; 284.
Buckden, letter dated at; 240.
Buckhounds, the King's, payments for; 134.
Buckhurst, Lord; 163, 231. *See* Dorset, Earl of.
Buckingham:
    Royalist forces at; 100.
    Owen, election of; 204.
    Earl of, letters of; 135.
    Marquis of, letter to; 271, 272, 289.
    Duke of; 18, 177.
    —— letter of; 9.
    —— complaints against him; *ib.*
    —— speech by; 238.
    —— case of; 248.
    —— his treachery towards Danby; 23.
    —— impeachment of; 248.
    —— attempted murder of; 6.
    —— (1628), assassination of; 289.
    Katherine, Duchess of; 136.
Bucks:
    concealed lands in; 145.
    dedications of churches in; 152, 153.
    sessions for; 153.
    documents relating to; 145, 146.
    Fifth Monarchy men in; 151.
    militia of; 165, 166.
    visitations of Papists in; 166.
    parliamentary elections in; 146, 152, 153.
    sheriff of, accounts of; 151.
Budel, Ricardus, mayor of Reading; 172, 227.
Buelwell, Elias de, witness; 91.
Buildwas:
    Abbey; 127, 142, 143, 144.
    Abbot of; 230.
    Ranulf, Abbot of; 142.
Buisson, letters dated at; 152.
Buiteler:
    Alan lo; 69.
    Sarra, daughter of; 69.
Bukheved, Ricardus; 229.
Bulkeley:
    Richard, letter of; 148.
    Thomas, pamphlet by; 167.

Bull:
 Dr. Geo.; 155.
 Miles, letter of; 10.
 William, information by; 95.
Buller, Mrs., anecdote of; 54.
Bullmer:
 Bevis, proposals by; 180.
 —— invention by; 166.
Bullock, Wm., letter of; 109.
Bulmer, ——; 137.
Bülow, J. H., Minister for Brunswick and Lüneburg, letter of; 20.
Bulstrode v. Blagrave, case of; 218.
Bulstrode:
 Henry, gentleman usher; 200.
 Rich., steward of Reading; 192.
 —— deprived; 193.
 —— letters of; 11, 19, 20, 218.
 Thomas, letter of; 218.
Bunbury:
 Dr.; 131, 184.
Bungay, Roger, letter of; 100.
Bungey, John; 255.
Bunny, Richard, recommendation of; 122.
Buntingford, minister of; 234.
Burbage, Rich., epitaph on; 287.
Burbot:
 Edward, of Fulbecke, grant by; 67.
 William, of Hundington, bond of; ib.
Burbut:
 John, of Hundington, grant to and by; 65, 66, 67.
 Edward, son of; 67.
 Richard, of Hundington; 65, 66.
Burcester:
 bailiff's accounts at; 154.
 Sir John; 75.
Burcesture, Dame Elizabeth; ib.
Burdl, Hugo, witness; 57.
Burell, John the elder, of Berwick; 75.
Burendone, Walter de, exchange by; 67.
Burfield, manor of; 133.
Burgess, Mr., vicar, articles against; 245.
Burgh (or Burroughs:)
 Sir John, translation of a treatise by; 271.
 —— naval treatise by; 249.
Burghley; 132
 Lord; 130, 133, 134, 135, 145, 252.
 —— entertains the Queen; 123.
 —— grant to; 133.
 —— letters of and to; 122, 241, 255, 281, 283, 284, 294.
 —— speech of; 293.
 —— treatise copied for; 40. See Cecil, W.
 —— political satire by; 273.
Burgundy:
 the Archduke of; 286.
 the Archduchess of; ib.
 commercial treaties with; 246.
Burle, William, son of Roger of, quit-claim by; 60.
Burlimachi, Mr., report by; 291.
Burlington, Lady; 85.
Burnet, Mr., a very good churchman; 24.
Burnham Deepdale, lands of; 102.
Burningham, Peter, alderman; 193.

Burrelle, John, of Holtelle, grant by; 72.
Burrington, Major John; 155.
Burrish, Onslow, correspondence of; 44.
Burrowes, Colonel John; 40.
Burtdone, Rob. de, witness; 69.
Burthdune, Thomas de, witness; 68.
Burwell, letter dated at; 35.
Bury:
 John, attempted subornation of; 22.
 Thos., letter of; 32.
Bus, Racins de, witness; 57.
Bushen v. Sarsfield, case of; 163.
Butler:
 Henry; 123.
 Sir Henry; 234.
 Col. John, charges against; 10.
 Sir N., offers of service by; 32.
Butterworth, Alex., letter of; 28.
Button:
 ——; 263.
 Mr.; 267.
Bye, Thomas, election of; 180.
Bykerstathe, Richard, quitclaim by; 66.
Brylle, Robert; 176.
Byndlos, J., letter of; 32.
Byng:
 Dr. Thos.; 256.
 Tho., letter of; 283.
Byrche, John; 231.
Byrd, Nicholas, petition of; 295.
Byrde, Alan, of Newcasle; 75.
Byshop:
 William, letter of; 299.
 Dr. Will., letter of; 301.
Bythewode, John, mayor of Reading; 171.
Byttilisdene, the Priests' Lands in; 74.

C.

"C.," intelligence concerning; 24.
Cadiz, expedition to (1596); 234, 237.
Cadogan, Lord, mourning for; 125.
Caddell, Col.; 41.
Cæsar, Sir Julius; 222, 239.
Caisñ, Radulphus de, witness; 57.
Cajetan:
 Cardinal; 261.
 appointment of; 278.
 decrees of; 279.
 commission from; 264.
Calais, naval skirmish near; 95.
Caldbeck, exchange of; 84.
Caldene, grange of; 144.
Calendar, reformation in the; 282.
Callerton, lands of; 75.
Calonne, M. de, French Ambassador; 55, 56.
Calour, Will., mayor of Reading; 171.
Calthorp:
 letter dated at; 93.
 A., letter of; 94.
 C., present of tobacco from; 109.
 Capt., drowned; 110, 111.
 Sir Christopher; 113, 114, 115, 116, 118.
 —— inventory of his arms; 109.

Calthorp--*cont.*
J., called to the Bar ; 111.
James ; 107, 108, 111.
—— letters of ; 97, 115, 116, 118.
Lt.-Col. James ; 99, 100, 101, 103.
John, letter of ; 95.
Sir William ; 93, 94, 95.
—— sons and grandson of ; 93, 94.
Calverly :
—, a Jesuit priest ; 266.
Charles, election of ; 202.
Calvert, Sir George, letter to ; 288.
Cambridge :
address from the heads of houses of ; 9.
the Committee at (1644) ; 100.
University ; 111.
—— annuity from ; 137.
—— disorders in the ; 254.
Emmanuel College in ; 255.
King's College in ; 155.
St. Mary's Church in ; 234.
Queen's College in ; 8.
Peterhouse, Master and Fellows of ; 254.
Trinity College at ; 283.
Chancellor of ; 133, 254.
chancellorship of ; 32.
Vice-Chancellor of ; 133, 254.
mayor and corporation of ; 133.
plays at ; 130.
proceedings against townsmen of ; 256.
Lord Plymouth's establishment at ; 38.
letters dated at ; 12, 283.
Cambridgeshire, charitable uses in ; 139.
Camden, Marquis of, letters of ; 55.
Camera :
William de, grant to ; 70.
—— Katherine, wife of ; *ib.*
Cameron :
Dr. ; 78.
—— report of his movements ; 46.
Capt., report of his movements ; *ib.*
Campbell :
Sir James, of Auchinbeck ; 50.
Colin, of Glenure, murder of ; 45.
Lord, petition signed by ; 21.
—— letters of ; 19.
Campian :
Edmund, case of ; 163, 164.
—— letter of ; 285.
Campinet, Ric., conveyance to ; 133.
Campo, Chevalier del, letters of ; 55.
Campvere, factory at ; 47.
Canterbury :
Bancroft, Archbishop of ; 258.
Edmund, Archbishop of ; 238.
Grindal, Archbishop of, letter of ; 289.
J., Archbishop of, witness ; 168.
Matthew Parker, Archbishop of ; 258.
—— register of ; 254.
Richard, Archbishop of ; 230.
William Laud, Archbishop of ; 186.
—— benefaction by ; 186, 187.
—— petition to ; 292.
—— effigies of, at Reading ; 178.
Archbishop of ; 136, 155, 256, 289.

Canterbury—*cont.*
Archbishop of, letters of and to ; 254, 257, 293, 302.
—— license by ; 137.
—— mandate of ; 282.
—— petitions to ; 284, 295.
—— resigns the Chancellorship of Cambridge ; 32.
—— suffragans of ; 295.
—— treatise by ; 253.
Charles I. at ; 288.
Queen Henrietta Maria at ; *ib.*
Christ Church of Prior of ; 282.
Convocation of ; 258.
diocese of ; 255.
—— return of Papists in ; 14, 15.
journeys to ; 174.
Parliament at ; 172.
Prerogative Court of, disorders in ; 295, 296.
—— rules of ; 296.
Registrar of the Court of ; 300.
Vicar-General of ; 295.
Capell, Hen., letter of ; 307.
Carbery :
Lord ; 149.
—— letter of ; 148.
—— family of ; 149.
Cardiff, theatre at ; 81.
Carew :
Col. ; 40.
Sir George, negotiations by ; 286.
Monsieur ; 242.
Sir Robert, letters to ; 293.
Roger, agreement by ; 209.
Nicholas ; 171.
Carpenter :
Thomas ; 176.
—— will of ; 169.
William, of Barkeston ; 62.
—— son of, grant by ; *ib.*
Carpet, Knights of the, creation of ; 274.
Carpone ; 67.
Carleton :
grant of free chace in ; 119.
parson of ; 65.
Lord, letter of ; 184, 289.
Robert de, grant by ; 64.
—— Alicia, wife of ; *ib.*
Carlisle ; 262.
evacuated by the Papists ; 29.
grant dated at ; 119.
proposal for securing ; 27.
rising of the citizens of ; *ib.*
troops to be sent to ; 28.
letter dated at ; 29.
Lord ; 125.
—— funeral of his daughter ; 42.
Earl of, letters of ; 11, 20.
Richard, Bishop of, letter of ; 84.
Carlos, Don. *See* Plymouth, Earl of.
Carmarthen :
Lord, conference by ; 55.
—— correspondence of ; 54.
—— miscellaneous letters to ; 31-39.
Marquis of ; 166.
—— letters to ; 31, 82.

Carmarthen—*cont.*
   Marquis of, his private correspondence with Hailes; 54, 55.
   —— papers of; 53 *et seq.*
   —— patent to as plenipotentiary; 56.
   —— political position of; 53.
   —— kinswoman of; 37. *See* Leeds, Duke of.
   Marchioness of, death of her daughter; 35.
   —— letters to; 35.
   —— petition to; 36.
Carmarthenshire, sheriff of; 148.
Carnaby, Thos., letter of; 13.
Carnarvon Castle:
   ruinous condition of; 242.
   constable of; *ib.*
   lands in; 146.
Carnarvonshire, rentals in; 149.
Carr:
   Charles, committed to the Tower; 6.
   John; 75.
   Sir Robert, letter to; 251.
   Thomas, of Lilborne; 74.
Carrier, Mr., case of, 156.
Carson, vicar of; *ib.*
Carter:
   Mr.; 131.
   Will., information by; 32.
Carthagena, taken by Drake; 39.
Cartwright:
   —, deprivation of; 254.
   Thos., apprehension of; 283.
Case, Mr., reported to hold a conventicle; 15.
Casom, the bridge at pulled up; 178.
Cassett, Mauricius de, witness; 57.
Castille, marriage negotiations with; 236.
Castlehaven, Lord; 136.
Castol, Monsr., minister, letter to; 304.
Castoll, Mr. [John], treatise by; 253.
Castre:
   Thomas de; 67.
   —— son of; *ib.*
   —— grants by and to; 68, 69.
   William de, charter of; 67.
Catalonia, wasted by the French; 112.
Cater:
   Mr.; 131.
   Gerald; 108.
Catesbye, Sir William, trial of; 163, 164.
Cathcart, Earl of, Commissioner for Scotland; 46.
Catherine of Braganza, gift to; 195.
Catherine, Grand Duchess, letter of; 47.
Catour, William, mayor of Reading; 210, 227.
Caudish, W., letters of; 10.
Caufeld, manor and vill of; 73.
Caurthyn, family of; 138.
Cavalerius. *See* Chevalier.
Cave:
   Thomas, of Etal; 58.
   —— Elizabeth, wife of; *ib.*
Cavendish:
   Charles, letter of; 123.
   George; 245, 251.

Caversham (or Cawsham):
   the bridge at, to be made up; 189, 216, 220.
   to be pulled down; 178.
   letter dated at; 221.
Caverswall:
   William, Lord of; 144.
   Richard, lord of; *ib.*
Cecil (or Cecill):
   Dr., letters to; 278, 282.
   Dr. John, letter of; 299.
   John, his mission to Rome; 296, 297.
   —— petition of, for vestments; 298.
   —— letters of; 302.
   Lady Frances, marriage of; 89.
   Sir Robert, letter of; 287.
   —— letters of; 135, 297.
   Sir William, witness; 119.
   —— Lord Treasurer, ; 252, 265, 293.
   —— treatise by; 293.
   —— letters of and to; 254, 284, 285, 286.
Cellier, Mr., reflections upon ; 22.
Cetlin, Sir Robert, Royal Commissioner; 247.
Chafy, John, petition of; 292.
Chaish, Bartholomœus de, witness; 57.
Challener, Sir Tho., report by ; 280.
Chaloner, Edm., letter of; 153.
Chamberlain:
   the Lord; 78, 177.
   order of; 158.
   papers relating to the office of; 233.
   —— Major, of Bednal Green, reported to attend a conventicle; 16.
Chamberleyne, John, Farmer of Alderney; 130.
Chambers, Miles, of Grantham, inventory of the goods of; 92.
Chambers, Richard, case of; 162.
Champernoun, Sir Rich., petition of; 158.
Champion, Hugh, election of; 200.
Champney:
   Anthony, his mission to Rome; 296, 297.
   —— petition of, for vestments, 298.
Chancery; 302.
   register of writs in; 231.
   Court of; 272.
   office of cursitor in; 271.
   procedure in; 307.
   High Court of; 249.
   —— letter to; 13.
Chandos, Lord; 84, 154.
Chantelause, M., work of; 303.
Chantry rents; 291.
Chapman, Rob., letter of; 10.
Chappell, Robert, letter of; 124.
Charing Cross, George II., proclaimed at; 125.
Charlemont, the only Protestant fort left in Ulster; 5.
Charles:
   Prince; 131, 271.
   Prince of Wales, letter to; 289.

INDEX. 321

Charles —*cont.*
  Edward, Prince, information as to his plans; 50, 51, 52.
  —— description of; 76.
Charles I.; 90, 147, 188, 189, 248.
  letters of, protection by; 91.
  his attitude towards the short parliament; 98.
  at Canterbury; 288.
  charter of; 168.
  commission by; 96.
  commission to make gunpowder by; 97.
  distraint of knighthood enforced by; 96, 97.
  execution of; 132.
  estimate for the Household of; 131.
  movements of his army before Marston Moor; 100.
  proclamation by; 209.
  letters of; 215, 216, 289.
  order by; 220, 306.
  State papers of; 287.
  writ of; 274.
Charles II., 84, 85, 167, 242.
  order by; 2, 6, 7.
  warrant signed by; 8.
  at Newmarket; 9.
  his natural children; 9, 18, 37, 38.
  letter to; 11.
  at Banstead Downs; 12.
  injury to and cure of; *ib.*
  desires the Duchess of Cleveland's reclusion; 19.
  promises his pardon to Lord Danby; 21.
  petition to; 30.
  marriage of his natural daughter; 37.
  political parody, time of; 39.
  regulation for his Household; 39.
  his reception in the city; 104.
  last illness of; 105.
  charter of; 68.
  proclamation of; 178, 209.
  at Reading; 194, 195.
  warrants by; 198, 218.
  death of; 199.
  address to; *ib.*
  reign of; 238.
Charleville, letters dated at; 8.
Charlton:
  Sir Job, raised to the Bench; 104.
  Thomas; 182.
Charnock, 279, 279, 280, 281.
  letters of and to; 280, 281.
  Rob., letter of; 267.
Charrone:
  Sir Guychard de, and Isabella his wife; 67, 68, 69.
  —— the younger; 70.
  —— the elder, grant to; 67, 70.
  Stephen de, grant by; 67, 70.
Charter House, statutes of the; 270.
Chartham; 255.
Chartreuse, Greater, William, prior of; 66.

Chatch, Mr., reported to hold a conventicle; 15.
Chaulton, court roll of; 146.
Chaumberleyne, Lady; 176.
Chaunceux of Canewdon, descent of the Darcy family from; 43.
Chaunterel, John, mayor of Reading; 227.
Cheadle, lands in; 145.
Chedulle, deed dated at; 129
Chelmsford, inquest held at; 284.
Chelsea:
  lands of the Cheyne family in; 152.
  college; 37.
  Hospital; 152.
  letter dated at; 35, 306.
Chelreye, Edmundus de; 171.
Chelverlescote, Hervic, clerk of; 145.
Cherton, letter dated at; 28.
Chesham:
  letter dated at; 153.
  Bois, church of; *ib.*
Cheshire:
  crosses pulled down in; 162.
  documents relating to; 137, 151.
Cheshunt, lands in; 92.
Chesshire, Eliz., letter of; 19.
Chester:
  Bishop of; 47.
  Constable of; 144.
  County Palatine of; 239.
  Earldom of; 60, 270.
  Hugh, Earl of, royal letters to; 59.
  Matilda, Countess of; *ib.*
  Ranulf, Earl of; *ib.*
  —— —— grant by; 275.
  Lucia, Countess of; 59.
  Edward I. at; 281.
  intelligence from; 35.
  letter dated at; 34.
  muster rolls of, regiments at; 31.
  orders for the Danish regiments to go to; 33.
  papists secured at; 28.
  St. Mary-on-the-Hill in; 138.
  St. Mary's Priory at; *ib.*
  the Whitefryars at; 137.
  Mr.,reported to hold a conventicle; 15.
  —— case of; 158.
Chesterfield:
  letter dated at; 93.
  an Irish alarm at; 28, 29.
  Earl of, letter of; 11, 22, 55.
  —— (1680); 240.
Chetwyud, ——; 79.
Chevalier:
  the, his health drunk; 49.
  Raoul le, will of; 284.
Cheyne:
  Agnes, will of; 152, 153.
  Anne; 151.
  Charles; 151, 153.
  —— Lord; 151.
  —— pension to; 152.
  family of, household accounts of; 151 152.

U 24952.   X

Cheyne—*cont.*
  Francis, of Chesham Boys; 151.
  Lady Jane; 151, 153.
  her house at Chelsea; 152.
  William, Lord; 151, 152, 153.
Cheynell, Fr.; 225.
Cheynes:
  church of; 153.
  seat of; *ib.*
Chibald, Mr.; 131.
Chicheley, Archbp., charter of; 282.
Chichester:
  Bishop of; 155.
  Anthony, Bishop of, claim by; 134.
  R., Bishop of, witness; 168.
  William Reed, Bishop of; 231.
Childisbra, Reg. de, witness; 129.
Chippenham, writ for; 241.
Chipping:
  Norton, the White Hart in; 37.
  Wycomb; 156.
Chiswell, Ric., bookseller; 39.
Chitting, Hen., Chester; 225.
Cholmeley:
  Sir H., papers of; 10.
  Sir Henry, will of; 139.
  Hugh, proposals by; 38.
  family of; 138.
Cholmundeston; 137.
Christian:
  Edw., letter of; 8.
  Mr., letter of introduction for; 11.
Churchill:
  Father, sent out to Jamaica; 32.
  General, in Scotland; 46.
Cicell, Colonel, letter of; 40.
Cinque Ports, Warden of the; 239.
Clapham, Richard, letter of; 85.
Clane; 129.
Clanricarde, Lady; 85.
Clare:
  Honour of; 102.
  Earl of, proceedings of against; 271.
  Lord; 84.
  Lady, reported to attend a conventicle; 15.
  Mr., identity of; 201.
Clarencieux, King-at-Arms; 275.
Clarendon:
  writ dated at; 59.
  Edward, Earl of, maxim by; 11.
  Earl of, impeachment of; 41.
  —— Lord Chancellor; 86, 272.
  —— monumental inscription for; 241.
  Henry, Earl of, steward of Reading; 197.
Clarges, Sir Thomas; 199.
Clark:
  Col.; 41.
  John, parson, letters of; 257.
Clarke:
  Edward; 136.
  John, high sheriff of Berks, order of; 222.
  —— letter of; 216.

Claveringe:
  Sir Alan de, quitclaim to; 70.
  —— Jacoba, wife of; *ib.*
Cleche:
  Master; 176.
  Richard, election of; 179, 180, 131
  —— case of; 212.
Cleland, —; 78.
Clement:
  VIII., Pope; 261.
  —— petition to; 259.
  —— brief of; 278.
  —— brief of; 297.
Clench, Robert, petition presented by; 102.
Cleonger, letter dated at; 10.
Clerk:
  Mr., letter to; 297.
  Dr. Barth.; 295.
  Edward, letter of; 211, 213.
  Sir Edward; 212.
  Capt. Edward; 216.
  Eliz., benefaction by; 180.
  Francis, *alias* Will., letters of and to; 278, 279, 280, 281.
  John, of Nesbit, grant to; 72.
  Roger, a villein; 69.
  —— Walter, son of, a villein; *ib.*
  Will., letter of; 302.
Clerkenwell:
  Green, letter dated at; 270.
  Vicarage of; 136.
Cleveland:
  duchess of, marriage of her son Henry; 8.
  —— her proposed retirement to Port Royal; 19.
Cley, Rob., assault on; 159.
Cleydone:
  Robert, quitclaim to; 66.
  —— Margaret, wife of; *ib.*
Clifford:
  Anne, Countess of Dorset, &c.; 81, 83.
  —— miniature of; 83.
  —— birth of; 86, 87.
  —— personal appearance of; 87.
  —— horoscope of; 88.
  —— her married life; 89.
  —— her children; *ib.*
  —— her widowhood; 89, 90.
  —— secluded in London during the civil wars; 90.
  —— succeeds to the Clifford estates; *ib.*
  —— living in Westmoreland; *ib.*
  —— death of; *ib.*
  Lord Francis, death of; 87.
  family of; 81 *et seq.*
  Henry, Lord, his ambitious marriage; 89.
  Lord Robert; 87.
  Rob. de, witness; 91.
Clink, the; 278, 279, 297, 302.
Clinton:
  —, reported to attend a conventicle;15.
  Lady, reported to attend a conventicle; *ib.*
Clothall; 235.
Clunlif, lands of; 143.

Clutterbuck
—, trial of ; 162.
John, collector of subsidies ; 84.
Clutton ; 137.
family of ; 138.
Clyvedon, Thomas de, grant by ; 69.
Coal, Mr., reported to hold a conventicle ; 16.
Coals :
tax on ; 130, 291.
trade in, by sea ; 271.
Coates :
Mr., " History of Reading " by ; 207.
Thomas, alderman ; 197.
—— election of ; 199, 200.
Cobard :
Wylliam, of Wymundham ; 64.
—— John, son of, grant by ; ib.
Cobbett, Col., transported ; 3.
Cobham :
Joshua, reported to attend a conventicle ; 16.
Lord, trial of ; 270.
Cockburn, Attorney-General, letters of ; 308.
Coinage :
reform of the ; 182.
proposal for change in ; 38.
Coke :
Mr. ; 10, 97.
—— suit respecting ; 108, 109, 110, 111.
Sir Edward ; 96, 133, 135.
—— letter of ; 239.
—— speech of ; 289.
—— writing of ; 241.
—— submission of ; 302.
Lord Chief Justice ; 245.
John, sheriff of Norfolk ; 100.
Rob., letter of ; 10.
—— member for Lynn ; 9.
Thomas ; 73, 98. *See* Cooke.
Cokks, Leonard ; 177.
Colby :
William de ; 64.
—— John, son of, grant by ; ib.
Colchester :
bailiffs of, petition of ; 134.
chantries in ; ib.
letter dated at ; 306.
Cole :
family of ; 169.
Henry, prisoner in the Fleet ; 247.
Mich., petition of ; 4, 5.
Colebrooke, order dated at ; 220.
Coleman :
—, information as to ; 47.
Mr., his letters from abroad ; 17.
—— factor of ; ib.
—— of Dean's Yard, information against ; ib.
Colet, Dean, Commentary by ; 40.
Colgryme, William, of Hundington ; 62.
Colle, chaplain of the chantry of ; 172, 174.
Collet, Mr., conventicle held in his house ; 15.
College of Arms, report of the ; 135.
Colleges, marriages in ; 257.

Colleppyr, H., letter of ; 23.
Colles :
family of ; 603.
Humfrey ; ib.
Michael ; ib.
William ; ib.
Colley, chantry of ; 176.
Collingwood :
Cornet Daniel, committed to the Tower, 6.
Major Dan., M.P., letters to ; 13.
Collington :
Mr. ; 262, 267, 299.
—— letter to ; 297.
—— John, letters of and to ; 277, 278, 279, 280.
Collyweston, manor house of ; 241.
Colmer, —, information by ; 161.
Cologne :
advices from ; 10.
Elector of, subsidy to ; 44.
letter dated at ; 301.
Colrane, H., letter of ; 96.
Colston Bassett, rectory of ; 133, 135.
Colston, N., a Roman Catholic priest ; 26.
Colton, Robert, prisoner in the Fleet ; 247.
Colvyle, William of Swaledale, release by ; 73.
Colvylle, John, of Newark, power of attorney to ; 65, 66.
Colwell, Col. ; 41.
Colwelle, Alicia, of Newark, widow, grant by ; 65, 66.
Colyngbourn, dominus Johaunes ; 172.
Combe Nona, prebend of ; 237.
Comber, Dr. Thomas, letters of ; 32.
Common Pleas, Court of :
officers of ; 241.
prothonotary in ; 307.
Commons, House of ; 252.
address from ; 252.
remonstrance from ; ib.
antiquity of ; 244.
bill of penalties passed in ; 4.
Journals of the ; 228, 244.
order of, concerning Tower prisoners ; 4.
orders of ; 102, 307.
petition of ; 255.
petition to ; 292.
precedents concerning ; 41.
privileges of the ; 246.
proceedings in ; 42.
reports of proceedings in ; 19.
Speaker of ; 241.
Compositions, office of ; 302.
Comprehension Bill, argument against the ; 32.
Compton ; 84.
House, letter dated at ; 85.
Henry, killed in a duel ; 84.
John, duel with ; ib.
Robert, manslaughter of ; 134.
Connaway, Colonel ; 40.
Connock :
Richard ; 242.
—— letter of ; 240.

Connor, Dean of; 20.
Conquett; 291.
Constable:
  A., letter of; 13.
  Mr., letter to; 264.
  Robert; 229.
Contis, Col. Aland; 41.
Conventicles, particulars of, in London and Westminster; 15.
Convention, meeting of the; 31.
Convocation:
  House of; 254.
  prolocutor of Lower House of; 285.
  gravamen read in; 296.
  petitions from; 285.
  proceedings in; 252.
Conway, Lord, letters of and to; 10, 11, 19, 20, 21, 22.
Conyers:
  family of; 43.
  Father; 262.
  Lord, petition signed by; 21.
Cook, Robert the, witness; 145.
Cooke:
  Colonel; 40.
  Col. Edw., letter of; 12.
  Sir Edward, letter of; 288.
  Ed., letter of; 10.
  Francis, William Penne's servant; 7.
  John; 43.
  Sir John, Secretary of State, letter of; 32.
  Mr.; 131.
  Robert; 275.
  Thomas, tragedy by; 43. *See* Coke.
Cookson, Anthony, funeral of; 235.
Coope, Mr.; 264.
Cooper, Lady; 98.
Cooper's Company, clerk of the; 38.
Cope, Mr.; 112, 267.
Copenhagen:
  letters dated at; 8, 20.
  correspondence from; 47.
Copleston:
  Henry, case of; 158.
  John; *ib.*
Copley:
  Averey, accounts of; 121.
  Edward, letter of; 124.
  Col., information against; 37.
  G., letter of; 19.
  Sir G., letter of; 8.
  Sir Godfrey; 20.
  Lord, intelligence from; 28.
  —— letter of; 29.
Coppemor, family of; 210.
Copthall, letter dated at; 148.
Corbet:
  Miles, conveyed to the Tower; 4.
  Sir Rob., witness; 142.
Corbridge, land in; 72.
Corby; 235.
  Castle; 28.
Cordell:
  Sir William; 139.
  —— letters of; 121.
  —— his houses; *ib.*
Corfe Castle, curate of, assault on; 159.

Cork:
  protestant regiment to be raised in; 37.
  Earl of; 85.
  Countess of; 89.
Corker, Francis, discharged from the Tower; 2.
Cormerie, John de, grant by; 60.
Corn, riots caused by the monopoly of; 50.
Cornabé, Major-Gen., report of; 49.
Cornbury:
  Lord, his desertion of James II.; 23.
  —— ill received by the Prince of Orange; 26.
  —— letter of; 242.
  Edward, Lord; 202.
Cornwall:
  Chantry rents in; 291.
  charitable uses in; 139.
  Duchy of; 242, 270.
  Reginald, Earl of; 119.
  Stannaries of; 248.
  Vice-Admiral of the North of; 242.
Cornwallis:
  Sir Charles, ambassador to Spain; 271.
  —— letter of, from the Tower; 288.
  Sir Thomas; 158.
  Sir Will., charges against; *ib.*
Corporation Act; 195.
Corselawne Chace; ranger of; 134.
Cortesley, lands in; 73.
Cosin:
  Richard, covenant by; 295.
  Dr. Rich.; 253, 258.
  —— notes by; 257.
  Will.; 171.
Cottesbrooke, letter dated at; 123.
Cottington:
  Francis, Lord, petition to; 292.
  Sir Francis; 242.
  —— letter of; 243.
Cotton:
  Edw., case of; 163.
  Mr. (*alias* Turner), conventicle held by; 15.
  Sir John, letter to; 244.
  Sir R., proceedings against; 271.
  Sir Robert; 245.
  —— collection by; 238.
  —— tracts by; 48.
  —— treatise by; 248, 249, 275, 307.
  Will., case of; 163.
Cottonian MSS., catalogues of; 271.
Council:
  Orders in; 5.
  —— for discharge of Tower prisoners; 2.
Court:
  verge of the; 2.
  regulations for the; 247.
Court, Will., case of; 233.
Courtenay, Will., letter of; 13.
Courtney, Col; 41.
Courtren:
  Sir Will.; 137, 254.
  —— bonds of; 167.
  —— bankruptcy of; *ib.*
  Lady Katherine; 137, 141.

Covent Garden:
  Bedford estate in; 140.
  Sir Kenelm Digby's lodging in; 85.
  theatre in; 79. *See* London.
Coventry:
  capitulation of; 92.
  false alarm of Irish bands at; 29.
  Parliament at; 180.
  Archdeacon of; 145, 254.
  Thomas Bentham, Bishop of; 254.
  Mr., letter to; 11.
  Mr. Secretary, his intelligence from Paris; 13.
  Sir H., letters of; 9, 307.
  Thomas, Lord, petition to; 292.
  —— Lord Keeper, letter of; 241.
  Sir Tho., letters of; 136.
  Sir Will., his designs against Danby; 12.
Cowes; 54.
Cowper, Earl of, letters of; 55.
Cox:
  Dr.; 2.
  Jo.; 8.
Crakanthorppe, Christopher, witness; 84.
Cramlingtone:
  vill of; 67, 69.
  Richard de, witness; 68.
Cramond, Highland men assembled.
Cranborne, Viscount, letter of; 287.
Cranbrook, Kent; 292.
Cranfield:
  Lady Eliz., case of; 136.
  Sir Lionel; 238.
Cransesture, John of; 74.
Cranworth, Lord Chancellor, letters to; 308.
Cratele, grant of fee chase in; 119.
Craufurd, David, letter to; 24.
Craven:
  lands in; 89.
  John; 274.
  Lord; 84.
Crawlawe, manor of; 70.
Crayford, Sir Rob.; 137.
Crebillion, —; 79.
Creed:
  Esquire, reported to frequent a conventicle; 15.
  Major, transported; 4.
  Will., elected to a scholarship; 184, 225.
Creissi, Hugh de, witness; 144.
Crellius:
  young, a Socinian, information against; 17.
  —— wife of; *ib.*
Cresseuer, M., letter of; 44.
Crevequer, Symon de, grant by; 60.
Crewe:
  —; 145.
  Lord; 107, 109.
  Ranulph, Speaker of the House of Commons, warrant of; 241.
Crick, —, information against; 283.
" Cripple," Lord Suffolk's race-horse, winner at Newmarket; 9.

Crips, Mr. Capt.; 265.
Croft:
  Sir James, grant to; 133.
  —— commission to; 145.
Crofton, Zachary, clerk, discharged from the Tower; 4.
Crofts, Capt., Lieut.-Governor of Carlisle; 27.
Croke, Judge, in the Exchequer; 273.
Crokesdene, Convent of St. Mary at; 144.
Cromartie:
  Earl of, son of, attainted; 49.
  Lady, letter of; *ib.*
Crompton:
  Dr., treatise by; 254.
  Rob., letter of; 32.
Cromwell:
  Oliver, letters patent of; 41.
  Lord; 163.
  Lord General; 178.
  Lord Protector; 193.
  —— petition to; 248.
  —— proclamation of; 178.
  —— warrant by; 221.
  Sir Oliver, signature of; 242.
  Richard, proclamation of; 193.
  Thomas; 181.
Cross, Mr., reported to hold a conventicle; 16.
Crosse:
  John, letter of; 166.
  Sir Rob.; 158.
Crouch, William, prisoner in the Fleet; 247.
Crow:
  John, benefaction by; 181.
  Patricius; 26.
Crowe, Edward, petition of; 291.
Croxton, John; 230.
Croydon, letters dated at; 223.
Crusset, Will., witness; 145.
Crux, James, yeoman, petition of; 290, 291.
Cudington; 137.
Cudworth:
  Dr., of Cambridge University; 9.
  Ralph, letter of; 239, 240.
Cuffe:
  —; 22.
  Henry, letter of; 286.
Culpeper:
  Thomas, Lord, letter of; 22.
  —— colonial patent for; 10.
Cumberland:
  proposed declaration by the gentry of; 27.
  Margaret, Countess of; 81, 84, 86, 87.
  Duke of; 46, 78.
  —— his politics; 49.
  —— correspondence of; 47.
  Earls of; 81 *et seq.*
  George, 3rd Earl of; 81, 82, 83, 86, 87, 88.
  Henry, Earl of, death of; 88, 89, 90.
Cumin, John, Sire de Buchan, witness; 150.
Cuningburg', Willelmus de, witness; 57.
Cunningham, John, letter of; 32.

Cunyngham, Cudbertus, witness; 150.
Cunstable, Sir Harry; 82.
Curli, Rob. de, witness; 128.
Curry Revell, manor of; 146.
Curzon, Mr.; 123.
Cusacke, Sir Thomas, claim of succession to; 249.
Cusinton, Rich. de, grant to; 145.
Customs:
   establishment of the office of; 39, 40.
   Secretary to the Commissioners of the; 13.
Custom House:
   office of Searcher, purchase of; 13.
   salaries and fees in the; 249.
   purchase of a place in; 292.
Czartoryski, Prince Adam, letters of; 55.

D.

" D," the son of, received into the Roman Catholic Church; 24.
Dackney, Thomas, tenure of; 103.
Dacre, Gregory, Lord, Margaret, sister of, claim by; 275.
Dacres, Francis, Lord, trial of; 130.
D'Adliemar, Comte, letters of; 55.
Dalby:
   Edward, Steward of Reading; 194.
   —— letters of; 211, 219.
   John, Recorder of Reading; 200.
Dale, Will., sacrilege by; 162.
Dallison, Dr.; 257.
Dalrymple, Lord, letters of; 55.
Dalston:
   Mr.; 86-90.
   Christ., proposal by; 27.
Dalton-in-the-Giles, lands in; 73.
Daltone, John de, land of; 72.
Dalyell, Rob., petition of; 46.
Danby:
   Countess of, accident to; 21.
   —— attempts against; 22.
   —— letters of and to; 9, 10, 12, 13, 19, 22, 25, 28, 35.
   —— brothers of; 10.
   —— See Carmarthen, Marchioness of.
   Thomas, Earl of; 30, 39.
   —— appointed Lord High Treasurer; 9.
   —— candidature of his son; 12, 35.
   —— disarms the garrison of York; 27.
   —— his attitude towards the Revolution; 26.
   —— his commitment to the Tower; 21.
   —— his relations with Lord Shaftesbury; 12.
   —— his exertions for the Prince of Orange in the North; 26, 27.
   —— his installation as K.G.; 19.
   —— his journey to Leeds deferred; 29.
   —— household accounts of; 42.
   —— impeachment of; 13, 20, 21.

Danby—cont.
   Thomas, Earl of, monumental inscription of; 38.
   —— proposed as Chancellor of Cambridge; 32.
   —— secret correspondence of; 11.
   —— summoned for some great matter; 26.
   —— summoned to the Convention; 38.
   —— summons Berwick to surrender; 28.
   —— summons Hull to surrender; 27.
   —— reported treachery in his household; 11.
   —— letters and papers of; 2 et seq.
   —— letters of and to; 8 et seq., 18, 19, 21, 22, 25-30, 27, 28, 31-37, 307.
   See Carmarthen, Marquis of.
Dande:
   Rowland, conveyance to; 133.
   —— presentation to; 135.
Daneby-upon-Yore, vill of; 69.
Daniell:
   Thos.; 41.
   —— cf Grenley, witness; 90, 91.
   William, speech by; 289.
Dantzic, letter from magistrates of; 276.
Danvers:
   Col., information against; 20.
   Lady; 78.
Darcie:
   —, lands of; 134.
   T., letter to; 282.
D'Arcy:
   family of; 43.
   Sir Conyers, letter of; 9.
   Edw., monopoly granted to; 246.
   Capt. Peter, intelligence from; 45.
   W., services of unrequited; 11.
   v. Markham, case of; 162.
   Lord; 43.
   —— purchase of a Frisian horse by; 123.
   Sir John, register book of; 43.
   Robert, will of; 43.
   Sir Robert, will of; 43.
   Thos., will of; ib,
Dare, Martin, agreement by; 209.
Darell:
   John, letter of; 280.
   Philip; 217.
D'Artois, Comte de, debts of; 54.
Darwin:
   Ann; 93.
   Erasmus, verses by; 93.
   Francis, of Creskeld, report on the manuscripts of; 90.
   Robert; 91.
   —— Waring; 93.
Dashwood, Sir Samuel, letters of; 32.
Dates, —, a popish bookseller; 17.
Daucus, Hew, actor; 79.
Daunteseye, Walter; 171.
Dauntsey Church, (Wilts.), monumental inscription in; 38.

Davenport:
    Arthur; 138.
    Sir Humphrey, Lord Chief Baron, petition to; 290.
Daveys, Rich., letter of; 306.
David, Signor, a popish agent, information against; 17.
Davies:
    —, reported a dangerous person; 16.
    Mr.; 131.
Davison, Mr., report from the Tower by; 287.
Dawson, Thomas; 177.
Dayrolles, —, letter of; 44.
Day, Mr., letter of; 97.
D. B., letter of; 263.
Deane:
    Chapel of; 156.
    John, trial of, for piracy; 13.
    Rich.; 187.
Dearing, Mr.; 254.
De Cardenas, Don Alonzo, Spanish Ambassador; 241.
De Conti, Girolamo Alberti, application by; 12.
Dee, John, protection for; 220.
De Gama, Stephen Farera, sentenced to death; 135.
De Grey, Thomas, letters of; 114, 115.
Delamare:
    Robertus; 173.
    Thomas; 171.
De la Pole, family of; 139.
Delavale:
    Ann; 74.
    Anthony, witness; 74.
    Baron; 58.
    Edward; 78.
    —— marriage of; 58.
    Eustace, witness; 68.
    Sir Francis, letter to; 78.
    Sir Francis Blake, letter to; 79, 80.
    —- play by; 81.
    George, instructions to; 76.
    Guy; 74.
    —— Henry, witness; 68.
    Sir Henry, witness; 71.
    Hugo, witness; 67, 68.
    alias Horsley James, grant to; 73.
    —— pardon to; ib.
    —— Margery, wife of; 73, 75.
    —— certificate relating to; 75.
    —— letters of attorney by; 73.
    Johannes, charter of; 73, 74.
    John; 73.
    —— lease to; 75.
    —— letters to; 76, 79.
    —— senior; 74.
    Sir John; 75, 76, 77, 78.
    Sir John Hussey, 58.
    —— letters to; 80.
    —— play by; 81.
    Lady; 76, 77, 78, 81.
    Sir Robert, lease by; 70.
    —— witness; 71.
    —— ib.
    —— Margaret, wife of; ib.

Delavale—cont.
    John, son of; 71.
    Robert, grant to; 74.
    —— witness; ib.
    Sir William, lease to; 71.
    —— witness; ib.
    —— livery of sesin to; ib.
    —— Margaret, wife of; ib.
Delawarre, Isabella, Lady, process against; 241.
De Kendall, Baron, a spy; 54.
De L'Isle, Sir Warin; 171.
Denbigh; 146.
    Lord, petition signed by; 21.
Denerose, dominus Job.; 172.
Dengayn, W., letter of; 95.
Denge, manor of, lease of; 160.
Denham, Master John, an astronomer; 88.
Denison, Dr., funeral sermon by; 183.
Denmark:
    Embassy from; 82.
    English ambassador in; 8.
    King of, in England; 78.
    Prince George of; 136.
    —— Household of; 166.
    Princess Anne of, at Reading; 201.
    protestant auxiliaries from; 110.
    superstitions current in; 8.
    wars of, with Sweden; 10.
Denne:
    Roger le, witness; 57.
    —— son of; ib.
Dennis, Benjamin, reported to teach in a conventicle; 16.
Denny:
    Capt., letter of; 45.
    Sir Edward, appointment of; 270.
De Oliva, Johannes Paulus; 104.
Deptford, Navy Office at; 8.
Derby:
    Irish bands expected at; 28.
    scouts sent out from; 29.
    Earl of; 149, 150, 154.
    —— creation of; 167.
    Edward, Earl of; 153.
    —— grant to; 141.
    —— witness; 119.
    Ferdinando, Earl of; 153, 154.
    Henry, Earl of; 153.
    Thomas, Earl of; 149.
    Earls of, MSS. of; 127.
    Countess of; 130, 154.
    Alice, Countess Dowager of; 136, 149.
    Margaret, Countess of, letter of; 82.
    —— —— Francis, son of; ib.
Derbyshire, Lieutenancy of; 122.
Dereham; 118.
    Thomas, a malignant, case of; 104.
Derham:
    Elizabeth, letter of; 13.
    Sir Rich., case of; 32.
Dering, Edw., examination of; 283.
Derry:
    alternative for the relief of; 34.
    condition of refugees from; 35.
    the defence of, dramatized; 42.
    salary of Governor of; 37, 38.

Desborough, proceedings against non-jurors in; 156.
Desmond:
　Earl of, forfeiture of; 133.
　letter of; 288.
D'Espagne, Mr., Sermons preached by; 132.
D'Espernon, Duke, narrative of his residence in England; 41.
Dessau; 304, 305.
　letter dated at; 301.
Dessell, John; 155.
D'Este, —, envoy extraordinary to England; 19.
Dethek, Robert de; 91.
Dethick, William, Garter King-at-Arms; 273.
Devayn, Mrs.; 125.
Devizes, concealed lands in; 133.
Devon:
　Chantry rents in; 291.
　lands in; 146.
　concealed lands in; 145.
　Countess of; 84.
　Earl of, letter of and to; 27.
　levies in; 213.
Dewisland, hundred of; 140.
Dexter, Col. Ralph; 41.
Dickens, Col., M. Guy, correspondence of; 44.
Dierth, Willelmus clericus de, witness; 57.
Digby:
　Mr. (*alias* Long Digby), notes taken in the King's Bench by; 21.
　Sir John, ambassador to Spain; 272.
　Sir Kenelm, death of; 85.
Digges, Sir Dudley, proceedings against; 248.
Dighton:
　Christopher, letter of; 108, 110.
　Mr., bencher; 226.
Dilham, lands in; 95.
Dilhorne (Dulverne):
　parish of; 144.
　lands in; 145.
Dillon:
　Col. Cary, case of; 10.
　—— grant of lands to, in reprisal; 11.
　Mr., suspected Jacobite agent; 47.
Dilston, letter dated at; 26, 27.
Dionysius, Areop., the *Hierarchia* by; 40.
Dissington, lands of; 75.
" D. L.", letter of intelligence respecting; 24.
Docking:
　sheep-walks near; 96.
　post house at; 118.
Dodd, John, candidate for Reading; 206.
Doddington Piggott, rectory of; 67.
Doddridge, Sir John, treatise by; 250, 252, 270.
Dodington, John, committed to the Tower; 6, 7.
Dodsworth·
　Francis, letter of; 28.
　Roger; 43.

Dolman:
　Alban; 263, 267, 277.
　family of; 112.
　Sir Thomas; 112, 196.
　—— son of; 112.
Dominique, Island of; 167.
Don Carlos. *See* Plymouth, Earl of.
Doncaster; 124.
　arrest at; 52.
　measures for defending against the Irish; 28.
　sign of the " Bell " in; 230.
Dormer:
　Sir Robert, commission for; 134.
　Mr., of Peterly, Papist; 166.
Dorset:
　Anne, Countess of, prevented from going to London by her husband; 83, 84.
　See Pembroke, Countess of.
　Duke of, ambassador to Paris, letters of; 54.
　—— Carmarthen's opinion of him 54, 55.
　Earl of; 83.
　—— his extravagance; 89.
　Edw., Earl of, Lord Chamberlain; 247, 290.
　Richard, Earl of; 89.
　Robert, Earl of, death of; 89.
Dorsetshire:
　charitable uses in; 139.
　Chantry rents in; 291.
Dorthorruld, Sir David de; 150.
Douay, English College at; 280.
Doublet, John; 172.
Doughtie, Thomas, Steward of Earlshall, 139.
Douglas; 44.
　Lieut.-Gen., Master General of the Ordnance in Scotland; 25.
　Col. Will.; 41.
Doumvile, Ro., witness; 84.
Dovenachbirn, lands of; 143.
Dover:
　foreign enlistments at; 9. ·
　suffragan bishop of; 284.
Dowgle, William, of Edmonton; 160.
Downes:
　John, proceedings against; 4.
　Mr.; 131.
Downing:
　Sir George, discharged from the Tower; 8.
　Capt. John, committed to the Tower; 7.
Downs, letter dated from the; 9.
Doyle *v.* Waynman, case of; 296.
D'Oyly, Sir Will., information by; 13.
Drake:
　Sir F., plan of his voyage; 39.
　—— his expedition to the West Indies; 82.
　—— libel against; 159.
Dranefeld:
　Hugo de, witness; 57.
　—— sons of; 57.

Draper, Stephen, reported to hold a Quakers' meeting ; 15.
Drax, Francis ; 85.
Drayton Beauchamp, court rolls of ; 151.
Drayton Church, monuments in ; 153.
Drede, Edith, of Haberley ; 65.
Dresden, negotiations with Hanover at ; 55.
Drew, Laur. ; 172.
Drissotic, lands of ; 143.
Drovere, Thomas ; 172.
Drumlangrig :
   Earl and Countess of ; 23.
   Lord, letters of ; 45.
Drummond :
   James, of Bokeldie, information by ; 44.
   —— murder committed by ; 45.
   —— escape of ; 46.
   P , letter of ; 52.
Drury :
   Mr. ; 96.
   —— letter of ; 280.
   —— Rob., letter to ; 277.
   Dr. Will., treatise by ; 256.
" D. U.", letter of ; 261.
Dublin ; 109, 111.
   Abbey of, St. Mary in ; 142, 143, 144, 230.
   charter dated at ; 143.
   Dorset Street in ; 80.
   letters dated at ; 11, 241.
   Mich Boyle, Archbishop of, his salary as Chancellor ; 12.
   —— letter of ; 10.
   Provostship of Trinity College in ; 10.
   records preserved at ; 241.
   theatre at ; 77, 79, 80.
   Castle, assembly at ; 289.
   —— letter dated at ; 243.
Duckott, A., letters of ; 279, 300.
Ducke, Nich., opinion by ; 212.
Du Cross, —, letter of ; 39.
Duddelie, Sir Rob. ; 158.
Dudlesbone, deed dated at ; 142.
Dudley, Edmund, accounts of ; 132.
Duffild, Edm. ; 240.
Dumbarton, Douglas, Lord, letter of ; 20.
Dumfermline, Alexander Seton, Earl of ; 272.
Dunbar :
   Lord, his health drunk ; 49.
   Patricius, witness ; 150.
   Mr., alleged treachery of ; 11.
Dunblane :
   views of ; 42.
   Lord ; 13, 22.
   —— disarms the garrison of York ; 27.
   —— his candidature at Berwick ; 12, 13.
   —— tutor of ; 13.
Dunch, E., Deputy Lieutenant of Berks ; 216.
Dundalk :
   evacuated ; 110.
   letter dated at ; 288.
Dundas, Rob., information by ; 49.
Dundee :
   Viscount, reported victory of ; 36, 37.
   —— letter of intelligence to ; 23.

Dunkirk :
   fortifications of ; 49, 55.
   letter dated at ; 44.
   ships of, captured ; 82.
Dunrobin, farm journal at ; 154.
Dunsmore :
   Lady Audrey, letter of ; 148.
   Lord, his house in Surrey ; ib.
Dunstable Houghton, church of ; 156.
Dunster, Stephen, election of ; 180.
Durdens, near Epsom ; 241.
Durham :
   deed dated at ; 71.
   letter dated at ; 27.
   New Elvert in ; 26
   lands in ; 73.
   Bishop of, pastoral letter of ; 30.
   John Cosin, Bishop of, will of ; 303.
   Matthew Hutton, Bishop of, letter of ; 258.
   Pilkington, Bishop of, letter of ; 285.
   bishopric of ; 72, 73, 242.
   Dean of ; 49, 250.
   Whittington, Dean of ; 285.
Du Plessis :
   / Mon., letter to ; 292.
Duport, John, letter by ; 254.
Dutch ships in the Thames ; 262.
   war, account of an action in the ; 85.
Duval, Mr. ; 35.
Duxfelde, lands in ; 74.
Dyer :
   Sir James, Chief Justice ; 119, 163, 231.
   Mr. Matthew, reported to teach at a meeting house ; 16.
Dymoche, Tho., prisoner in the Fleet ; 247.
Dymock :
   Sir Edw., case of ; 161.
   —— prosecution by ; 135.
Dymmoke, John, treatise by ; 250.
Dyvelstone, Tho. de, witness ; 68.

E.

Eager, Mr., reported to hold a conventicle ; 15.
Eagle :
   Hastins, intelligence from ; 28.
   Solomon, conventicle held in his house ; 16.
" Eagle " the ship ; 3.
Earl Marshal, privilege of the ; 39.
Earlshall in Frampton, court rolls of ; 138, 139.
East Basham ; 111.
   tithes of ; 114.
   constable of ; 101.
East Coker, drawings of roofs at ; 308.
East Indian Company, advance to the Government by ; 115.
East Indies :
   affairs in the ; 44.
   French and English companies in the ; 53.
East Looe, burgess-ship of ; 19.
East Newton, letter dated at ; 37.

Easton, letter dated at; 11.
Eastwell; 308.
Eaton, Mr.; 131.
Eccles, church of; 156.
Eccleshall:
  castle of; 243.
  church, Charnes Chapel in; 162.
Ecclesiastical Courts:
  irregularities in the; 300.
  state of; 295.
Eccleston, Henry, letters of; 147.
Ede, Johannes; 173.
Eden:
  Mr., Minister to America; 53.
  —— letters of; 55.
Edes, Dr., dialogues written by; 272.
Edgeman, —; 242.
Edinburgh:
  Convention at; 31.
  the Cross in; ib.
  Danish auxiliaries intended for; 33.
  destination of Protestant fleet to; ib.
  intelligence from; 25, 31.
  letters dated at; 23, 25, 46.
  Orders in Council at; 24.
  state of; 52.
  state of parties in; 36.
  Castle, as a prison; 52.
  —— escape from; 46.
Edlin, Mrs., information by; 22.
Edlyn, Mr., charge against; 9.
Edmonds, Father, prisoner; 262.
Edmonson, Mr., 43.
Edmund, Tho.; 284, 286.
Edmunds, —, a Jesuit; 266.
Ed., T., letter of; 278.
Edward:
  I., grant of; 119.
  II., life of; 281.
  III., charter of; 168.
  —— grant of; 119.
  IV., household of; 294.
  —— letter of; 93.
  —— ordinances of; 270.
  —— Princess Cicely, mother of; ib.
  V., sumptuary laws of; 281.
  VI., charter of; 168.
  —— letter of and to; 282, 283.
  —— will of; 282.
  Prince, letters of; 48.
Edwards:
  Captain, recalled to Flanders; 241.
  Mr.; 131.
  —— schoolmaster; 194, 226.
  Tho.; 266.
  —— case of; 160.
Edwyneye, lands in; 144.
Effingham:
  Earl of, his mission to Virginia; 32.
  Lady; 135.
Egerton:
  Lady Alice; 149.
  Ellen, marriage contract of; 129, 136.
  family of; 138, 151.
  Hugh, daughter of; 136.
  John, letters of; 137.
  Sir John; 141, 147.
  Lord Chancellor; 130, 154.

Egerton—cont.
  Lord Chancellor, speech of; 294.
  —— letter of; 251.
  Lady Mary; 149.
  —— letter of; 137.
  pedigree of; ib.
  Ralph, marriage of; 137, 145.
  Sir Thomas; 156, 289.
  —— Lord Keeper, reflections against; 156, 157, 158, 159, 160.
  —— books of; 137.
  —— inventories of goods of; ib.
  —— letters of and to; 135, 136, 137.
  —— letter of; 245.
  —— MSS. of; 126.
  —— Solicitor-General; 132, 133.
  —— son of; 137.
  —— Elizabeth, wife of; ib.
  —— brief of; 303.
  —— member for Reading; 182.
Egmont, Earl of, memorial of; 167.
Eland, manor of, court rolls of; 126.
Elandshire, lands in; 72.
Eldesue, Will.; 171.
Elfmelee, manor of; 72.
Elie, Dr.; 263.
Eliot, Sir John, proceedings against; 248.
Elizabeth:
  Queen; 87, 88, 132, 236, 237.
  —— address to; 252.
  —— a plea for toleration presented to; 297.
  —— entertained by Lord Burghly; 123.
  —— at Woodstock; 300.
  —— charges against her purveyor; 160.
  —— charter of; 168.
  —— commission by; 145.
  —— confirmation of grant by; 133.
  —— grant by; 210.
  —— death of; 251, 286, 287.
  —— funeral of; 275.
  —— her marriage urged; 285.
  —— household of; 250.
  —— leases by; 156.
  —— letters of and to; 81, 150, 245, 251, 256, 286, 287, 289, 292, 293, 294.
  —— letter to; 256.
  —— license to export corn by; 95.
  —— mortgage by; 133.
  —— offices belonging to; 270.
  —— petition to, against Mary Stuart; 130.
  —— petitions to; 156, 157, 251.
  —— players of; 177, 178.
  —— physician of; 135.
  —— sale of Crown lands by; 133.
  —— speech by; 238.
  —— writs of; 258.
  Princess; 81.
  —— marriage of (1612); 287.
  —— players of; 185.
Ellerker, Jo., intelligence from; 28.
Ellesdon, Will., declaration by; 13.
Ellesmere:
  Lord; 126, 134, 159, 161, 163, 302.
  Lord Chancellor; 137, 156, 169, 275.

INDEX. 331

Ellesmere—*cont.*
   Lord Chancellor, inquisition for ; 141, 142.
   —— letters of ; 239, 286, 288.
   —— speech of ; 289.
Elliot :
   H., letters of; 55.
   John ; 141.
   —— agreement by ; 209.
   Mr., letters of ; 55.
   Tom, at Newmarket ; 9.
Ellis, ——, an Oliverian captain charged with sedition ; 12.
Ellisworth, ——, player ; 233.
Elmet, Robert, grant to ; 72.
Elsenham, manor of ; 94.
Elsynge :
   Henry ; 239, 248.
   —— treatise by ; 41.
   —— keeper of the Records ; 239, 240.
Elston :
   deeds relating to the manor of ; 90 *et seq.*
   Hall ; 93.
Elton, George, committed to the Tower ; 6.
Eltone, parish of ; 74.
Elwood *v.* Deering, case of ; 163.
Ely :
   Bishop of ; 104, 118, 155.
   Cox, Bishop of ; 255, 256, 258.
   —— a plea for temporalities by ; 296.
   —— his refusal to minister in the Queen's Chapel ; 285.
   —— injunctions by ; *ib.*
   —— on Bishop's revenues ; 296.
   —— letters of ; 254, 284, 285, 296.
   diocese of ; 255, 283, 286.
   Humphrey, narrative by ; 298.
   Dr. Humfrey, letter of ; *ib.*
   Isle of, liberties of ; 255.
   Willelmus de, witness ; 57.
Elyas :
   filius Hugonis ; 57.
   —— Letiz, daughter of ; *ib.*
Emeldone, Richard de, grant to ; 70.
Emley :
   John ; 74.
   Park, saw-mill and smithies in ; 123.
Emperor :
   the ; 55, 245.
   —— intrigue of, with Marie Antoinette ; 56.
   —— letter to ; 300.
   —— treaty with ; 19.
Eneschallen, Baron of, case of ; 233.
Enfield :
   school ; 151.
   lands in ; 92.
Engilie, Henry, of Fraynyshe, grant by ; 64.
England :
   the Admirals of, list of ; 38.
   Almoner of ; 183.
   —— claim of felon's chattels by ; 134.
   Attorney-General of ; 145, 159, 163, 202.

England—*cont.*
   Augmentation Office ; 153.
   Bank of, forgeries upon ; 50.
   case of the free shipwrights of ; 37.
   clerk of the Pipe ; 152.
   commercial relations with Austria ; 53.
   Coronation ceremony in ; 235.
   Court of General Sessions of ; 104.
   Council, of letter of the ; 133.
   Council of State of ; 218.
   Chronicles of ; 230, 231, 232.
   Earl Marshal of ; 121, 273.
   Earl Marshal's Court in ; 222.
   a fast-day appointed in ; 98.
   French spies in ; 54.
   grant of the fisheries of ; 134.
   Great Seal of ; 241.
   the King's Footman ; 176, 177.
   Lord Chamberlain of ; 13, 155.
   Lord Chancellor of; 13, 21, 198.
   Lord Chief Justice of; 13.
   Lord General of ; 99.
   Lord High Admiral of ; 252, 253.
   Lord Keeper of ; 160, 187, 213, 250.
   Lord Treasurer of ; 199, 251.
   the Northern counties of, firm for the prince ; 29.
   Parliaments held in ; 171, 172.
   Parliament of, Privileges of ; 238.
   —— proceedings in ; 235, 236, 237, 238.
   —— Speaker of the ; 167.
   peerage of ; 235, 236.
   price of grain in ; 96.
   Privy Council of ; 128, 129, 130, 136, 238.
   —— minutes of the ; 53.
   —— precedence of the ; 135.
   proclamation against duels in ; 104.
   proclamation against highwaymen in ; *ib.*
   projects relative to the revenue of ; 38.
   Quadruple Alliance of (1677) ; 19.
   Queen of ; 48.
   Queen's Advocate ; 308.
   reform of the currency in ; 112.
   return of grants made in ; 42.
   revenue of ; 42, 130.
   Secretary of State for ; 251.
   Solicitor-General of ; 145.
   sovereignty of the sea of ; 239.
   statistics relating to ; 249.
   table of weights and measures in ; 42.
   treaty with France ; 276.
   Treasurership of ; 246.
   War Office of ; 205.
   and Wales, view of the state of ; 40.
Englefield, Thomas, serjeant-at-law ; 170.
Epping Forest, conventicle held in ; 16.
Epsom, letter dated at ; 85.
Erdesdone, chaplain of ; 70.
Erichsburg, letter dated at ; 301.
Erleham, Robertus de, witness ; 57.
Ernault, Estienne, secret correspondence with, interrupted ; 25.
Erne, Will., election of ; 180.
Ernest, Archduke, letter of ; 286.

Errington:
  Rich., player; 185.
  Thomas, letter of; 26.
  John, of Levylls; 74.
Escrigg; 9.
Essex:
  Earl of; 178, 240, 272, 289.
  —— lord lieutenant of Ireland, letters of; 9, 19.
  —— arraignment of; 287.
  —— divorce of; 250.
  —— his device in the lists; 251.
  —— execution of; 290.
  —— letters of and to; 10, 11, 245, 251, 292, 307.
  —— players of; 177.
  —— speeches of; 251.
  —— verses by; 245.
  —— secretary of; 286.
  —— Lord General; 189.
  Arthur, Earl of; 92.
  Robert, Earl of, High Steward of Reading; 183.
  Robert Devereux, Earl of; 271, 272.
  Walter, Earl of, installation of; 287.
  House, purchase of; 10.
  —— disputed possession of; ib.
Est, Mr.; 131.
Estbury, John; 171.
Estirlings, engagement with; 95. Cf.
Estlein:
  Thomas de, grant by; 145.
  —— wife and son of; ib.
Eton:
  College; 109, 155.
  —— letter dated at; 243.
  Rich., Keeper of the Rolls; 139.
Eugenius IV., Pope; ib.
Eure, Sampson, letter of; 147.
Evan, Mrs.; 78.
Evans:
  George, letters of and to; 10, 13, 19.
  Rev. ——, his opinion against the Comprehension Bill; 32.
Evelyn, G., letter of; 238.
Everingham, letter dated at; 13.
Ewart, Mr., letters of; 55.
Ewing, Col. Thos.; 41.
Exchequer:
  the; 167.
  arguments in the; 246.
  forgeries in the; 156.
  payments of the; 250.
  phraseology of the; 132.
  procedure of the; 234.
  records of the; 40.
  salaries and fees in; 250.
  treatise on the; 40.
  treasury of the; 249.
  Court of; 249, 291.
  —— clerks of, petition, of; 292.
  —— proceedings in the; 97, 98.
  Chief Baron of the; 250, 290, 292.
  Baron of the; 291.
Excise:
  farmers of, at Rotherham; 7.
  office of Receiver-General of; 11.

Excise—cont.
  papers relating to; 8, 9.
Exeter:
  the Prince of Orange entrenched at; 26.
  Bishop of; 254.
  —— proposed translation of; 13.
  W. Alley, Bishop of; 283.
  Chancellor of, case of extortion by; 162.
  Countess, reported to frequent a conventicle; 15.
  diocese of, suspected persons in; 253.
  mayor of, charge of reviling the; 158.
  House, letter dated at; 241.
Eykering, grant of free chase in; 119.
Eynes, Will., case of; 161.
Eyre, John, case of; 151.

F.

F. A., petition by; 237.
Fabio, Signor, a suspected Abbot, information against; 17.
Fachel, Nicholas; 172.
Fagel, W., letter of; 44.
Fairfax:
  Lord, intelligence from; 32.
  —— his rising at York; 26.
  —— suspicious of; 37.
  —— his servant suspected; 36.
  Sir Thomas; 102.
  —— examination by; 189, 190.
  —— order by; 217, 220.
Fakenham:
  manor of; 99.
  sessions at; 100.
  array of militia at; 101, 102.
Falderley, Adam de; 68.
Falkland, Lord, daughter of, in danger; 151.
Falmouth pier; 118.
Falmouth, Earl of, killed in action; 85.
Fane:
  Sir Henry, candidature of; 199.
  —— election of; 202.
  Lord, candidate for Reading; 206.
  Lady Mary, descent of; 149.
Fanshaw:
  Henry, return by; 130.
  Sir T.; 234.
  v. Paschall, case of; 160.
Farham, John, mayor of Reading; 171, 227.
Farnese, Cardinal; 265, 266, 299.
Farnham:
  the Court at; 122.
  letter dated at; 14.
Fauconberg:
  Lord, arms to be received from; 25.
  Tho.; 249.
Fayrbairn, Mrs. Mary, letters of; 154.

Fayrechilde, William ; 67.
Feake, Mr. ; 131.
Feckenham, charter dated at ; 144.
   forest of ; 134.
Felton, George, prisoner in the Fleet ; 247.
Fenis, Sir Richard ; 132.
Fenn, Edw., petition of ; 11.
Fennel, Sir John, witness; 91.
Fenton, lands in ; *ib.*
Fenwyke:
   John de, chaplain ; 72.
   Thomas of ; 75.
Fens, the, Lords adventurers for draining : 100.
Ferguson, Mr., alleged letter by ; 42.
Fermanagh, Lord and Lady ; 152.
Fermor, Sir William, charge of extortion against ; 95.
Ferne, John, treatise against ; 289.
Ferrers, Walter, charge against ; 146.
Ferrieres, Jean de, letter of ; 277.
Ferrybridge ; 121.
   letter dated at ; 29.
Feversham, Lord, petition signed by ; 21.
Fielding :
   Capt., privy to the surrender of Carlisle ; 29.
   justice, at Bow Street, letters of ; 50.
   Mr., play by ; 81.
   Roger, appointment of; 307.
Fiennes, pedigree of ; 132.
Filius Audele, Will., witness; 144.
Filius Turchil, Ric., witness ; 129.
Fillengley :
   Ralph de; 128.
   —— William, son of ; *ib.*
Filmer :
   Sir E. ; 19.
   Sir R. ; 240.
Filsham, lands in ; 73.
Filungeleia :
   Jurdan, de, witness ; 129.
   Walter de, witness ; *ib.*
Finch :
   Lord Keeper, letters of ; 9, 12.
   —— illness of ; 98.
   Lord Chief Justice ; 248, 288.
   Sir John, charge of ; 252.
   Mr. John, speeches of; 288.
Finished ; 133.
Finnemore, William ; 183.
Finsechietti, Comte de, letter of ; 44.
First Fruits and Tenths, Court of ; 250.
Fish :
   Rev. Robert, letter of ; 33.
   a Papist agent ; 259, 261.
   examination of ; 298.
   John ; 281.
   —— letter of ; 104.
   Mr. ; 103.
   Payne ; 241.
   Robert, letters of ; 262.
   —— his mission to Rome ; 263.
Fitch, John, case of ; 166.
Fitz, H., letter to ; 282.

Fitzharding, Visc., petition of for employment ; 11.
Fitzherbert :
   Mr., letter of ; 78.
   Mrs., her relations with the Prince of Wales ; 56.
   Alleyne, letters of ; 55.
Fitzjames [Lady], reported to frequent a conventicle ; 15.
Fitz-Morris, Lord Thomas ; 273.
FitzPatrick, Colonel, his position in Ireland ; 20.
Flamville, John de, witness ; 145.
Flanders ; 203, 241.
   campaign in ; 39, 111, 112.
   emigration to ; 262.
   intelligence from ; 238.
Flecher, William and Dionisia, his wife, grant by ; 66.
Fleet :
   prison of the ; 4, 135, 185.
   committal for contempt to ; 159.
   letter written from the ; 156, 157.
   rates for commons in the ; 247.
   Warden of the ; 246, 247, 291.
Fleete :
   Jane, letter of ; 13.
   Thos., mariner, discharged from the Tower ; 5.
Fleetwood :
   —, a Jacobite agent ; 44.
   Arthur, letter of ; 9.
   Geo., proceedings against ; 4.
   Lord ; 192.
   Mr. ; 238.
   Will., reported to attend a conventicle ; 16.
Fleming, Father ; 269.
Fletcher :
   Mr. ; 263.
   Sir Geo., attitude of ; 27, 28, 29.
   Capt. John ; 3.
Fletewood, J. ; 152.
Fletwoode, Will., treatise by ; 307.
Flintshire, documents relating to ; 146.
Florence :
   indulgence dated at ; 139.
   letters dated at ; 11, 12.
Flower, Mr. ; 131.
Floyd, John, letter to ; 279.
Foliot, Henry, mayor of Reading ; 227.
Folkes, Martin, letter of ; 22.
Folyot, Richard, licensed to fortify ; 119.
Fontainebleau, letters dated from ; 19.
Fontearcada, Visconde de, note by ; 166.
Foote :
   Samuel, the actor, letters of ; 77, 78, 79.
   —— at the French play ; 79.
   —— his distinguished visitors ; 78.
   —— his sentiments for the Delaval family ; 77-79.
   —— illness of ; 78.
   —— resident at Blackheath ; *ib.*
Ford :
   letter dated at ; 13.
   Castle ; 58.

Ford—*cont.*
   Mr., motion by ; 191.
   —— minister ; 192.
   Simon, minister, stipend of ; 178.
Forde, Odenel de, marriage of ; 58.
" Foresight," the ship ; 3.
Forest of Dean ; 250.
Forester, Ricardus ; 171.
Forrest, Gabriel de la ; 166.
Forsbrook:
   township of ; 144.
   lands in ; 145.
   Robertus de ; 144.
Forster:
   Sir Humphrey ; 186.
   Mr. ; 37.
Fort St. George, news from ; 31.
Fortescue:
   John, grant to ; 133.
   Sir John ; 166.
   Rich. ; 222.
Fortese, Art., letter of ; 10.
Forthe, Rob., representation by ; 300.
Fosset, Mr., examinations of ; 49.
Foster:
   Mrs. Bridget ; 26.
   John ; 201.
   Thomas, of Eddirstone ; 74.
   Judge, certificate by ; 2.
Fotherby, —— ; 85.
Fotheringay ; 251.
   trial at ; 303.
Foulis, D. A., letter of ; 27.
Fowler :
   Dr. ; 131.
   Mr. ; 190.
   —— conventicle held by ; 212.
   —— motion by ; 191.
   —— pamphlet by ; 192.
   —— minister ; 194.
   Mary, case of ; 161.
   Richard, conspiracy against ; *ib.*
Fowch, George, petitions of ; 290, 291, 292.
Fox:
   C. J., letter of ; 55.
   H , letters of ; 44, 45, 76.
   Peter, suspected Jacobite agent ; 47.
   Sir Stephen, Paymaster-General ; 38.
Foxholes, grant of free chase in ; 119.
F. R., letter of ; 292.
Frackman, Mr., reported to hold a conventicle ; 15.
Framlingham Castle :
   keeper of ; 280.
   petition of prisoners in ; 302.
   Priests confined in ; 299.
Framlingham, Sir William de, witness ; 69.
France :
   army of, under Turenne ; 10.
   Canada Bay Company of, case of ; 166.
   conditions of peace with, laid down by Parliament ; 115.
   diplomatic relations with ; 54.
   extravagance of the Court of ; *ib.*
   hostilities with, in America ; 45.
   intelligence from ; 52, 55.

France—*cont.*
   Jacobites in ; 44, 50, 51.
   navy of ; 53.
   negotiations with ; 44.
   peace of Paris concluded with ; 207.
   —— Ryswick concluded with ; 204.
   prisoners of ; 177.
   profected commercial treaty with ; 42, 54.
   prophecy concerning ; 109.
   ravages by the army and privateers of ; 112, 117.
   relations with ; 41.
   reported invasion from ; 46, 47.
   spies of, in England ; 54.
   trade with ; 291.
   treaty with ; 265, 276.
   treaty papers relating to ; 19.
   vote for the war with ; 109.
   war with ; 206, 210.
Franceis, Rob., witness ; 128.
Francklin, Will., letter of ; 34.
Frankfort, advices from ; 10.
Franklin :
   Dr., movements of ; 54.
   Rich., letter of ; 13.
Frauncays, Will. le, witness ; 91.
Fraxnet, Roger de, witness ; 57.
Fraynesch, deed dated at ; 65.
Fraynyshe, lands in ; 64.
Frazerburgh ; 46.
Frederic, Prince, letters of ; 48, 49.
Frederick :
   Prince, tradesmen's bills of ; 52.
   —— installed as Knight of the Garter ; *ib.*
Freemasons, charge to ; 308.
Frem, Mr., letter of ; 294.
Freman :
   John, of Hundington ; 66.
   —— quitclaim to ; 65.
Frescheville :
   Lord ; 124.
   —— letter of ; 23.
   Sir T., letter of ; 9.
Frevitt :
   Drogo de, witness ; 57.
   Ralph de, witness ; *ib.*
Frodsham, lease of ; 135.
Frowde, Ph., warrant by ; 27.
Fry, Tho., letter of ; 226.
Fryer :
   Colonel ; 40.
   William, letter of ; 13.
Fryth, Charles, letter of ; 34.
" F. T.," intercepted letter of ; 36.
Fulforde, lands in ; 145.
Fulham, 185.
   letter dated at ; 78.
Fulk, Dr. ; 253.
Fulke, Will. ; 284.
Fullarton, Col. Will., letter of ; 55.
Furn', Jordanus de, witness ; 57.
Fytt, Ricardus ; 229.

G.

Gainsborough, letter dated at ; 122.
Gallow, hundred of ; 101, 103, 104.
Gamage, Will., playactor, information against; 161.
Gandye, Will., deprived ; 223.
Gardener, Henry, collector of excise ; 216.
Gardiner :
   Bishop ; 234.
   —— deprivation of ; 282.
   —— letter to ; 283.
Garland :
   Aug., proceedings against ; 4.
   Humphrey, of Gray's Inn, letter of ; 10.
Garnet :
   Father ; 268.
   —— letter of ; 259.
   alias Walley, letters of and to ; 279.
Garraway, Mr. ; 179.
Garrett, Mr., schoolmaster ; 192.
Garrhlayn, lord of ; 150.
Garrick, David, actor, letters of ; 80, 81.
Garricks, the ; 78.
Garter King-at-Arms ; 292.
   nomination of ; 39.
Garth, George, lease to ; 156.
Gascoigne :
   Leonard, case of ; 161.
   Mr. ; 43.
Gascon, Sir Bernard, letter of ; 12.
Gatehouse, the prison of ; 4, 5.
Gaunt :
   Gilbert de ; 60.
   Nycholas, mayor of Cambridge ; 133.
Gayer, Robertus ; 229.
G. D., letter of ; 293.
Gedington woods, disafforested by the Crown ; 12.
Genoa ; 290.
   letters dated at ; 12, 259.
George I. :
   address to ; 205.
   death of ; 125.
   mourning for ; *ib.*
   proceedings at the coronation of ; 228.
George II. :
   proclamation of ; 125.
   his Queen ; *ib.*
   his quarrel with the Prince of Wales ; 134.
   letter to ; 47.
   royal letters of ; 45.
   proclamation of ; 205.
George III. :
   accession of ; 206.
   anecdote of ; 48.
   education of his sons ; 47, 48.
   his new telescope ; 55.
   his relations with Hanover ; *ib.*

George III.—*cont.*
   second illness of ; 207.
   jubilee of ; 208.
   letters of ; 55.
   marriage of ; 207.
George, Mr., petition of ; 11.
Georgia, instructions for ; 304.
Gerard :
   Mr. ; 262.
   John, examination of ; 259.
   J. D., lord, letters of ; 20.
   Sir Thomas ; 135, 149, 150.
Germany ; 76.
   army in ; 47.
   intelligence from ; 45.
   treaty papers relating to ; 44.
Gerrard :
   Gilbert ; 209.
   —— lease to ; 156.
   Thomas, schoolmaster ; 191, 192.
   —— proceedings against ; 193, 194.
Gescum, Sir Adam de, sheriff, witness ; 68.
G. G., letter from ; 263.
Gibbs :
   Nath., prisoner from the Tower ; 5.
   —, of Walthamstow, reported to attend a conventicle ; 16.
Gibraltar, attempt against ; 205.
Gibson :
   Rich., report by ; 37.
   Thomas, letter of ; *ib.*
   William, in Gracechurch Street, reported to attend a conventicle ; 16.
Gifford :
   Dr., letters of ; 278.
   William, letter of ; 299.
Giffordus, Doctor ; 259.
Gilbert :
   J., information by ; 38.
   John, letter of ; 145.
   Mr. ; 136.
Gill, Joseph, elected to a scholarship ; 207.
Gilling ; 37.
Gisburne, Prior of ; 303.
Givanas, Mr. ; 110.
Glanvile :
   John ; 248.
   Serjeant, Speaker of the Short Parliament ; 98.
Glasgow, Archbishop of ; 306.
Glassachet, lands of ; 143.
Glenlus, charter dated at ; 150.
Glisson, Dr., Professor of Medicine, his salary in arrears ; 9.
Gloucester :
   Chantry rents in ; 291.
   concealed lands in ; 145.
   libel on tradesmen of ; 161.
   writ dated at ; 59.
   Bishop of ; 155, 254.
   Dr. Johnson, Bishop of ; 49.
   Robert, Bishop of, letter of ; 33, 34.
   Duke of ; 174.
   —— grant to ; 95.
   —— minstrels of ; 174.
   Humphrey, Duke of ; 238.
   Thos., Duke of, Appellant ; 271.

Gloucester—*cont.*
    Duchess of, letter of ; 136.
    Earl of, creation of ; 167.
    Castle ; 250.
Glovers, demand for a separate corporation by the ; 292.
Glyndowerduy, Griff. de, witness ; 142.
Gocelyn, Johannes ; 173.
Goddard :
    Capt., aspersions by ; 190.
    Col. Vincent ; 217.
Godfrey :
    Sir Edmund Bury, murder of ; 22, 23.
    Stephen, letter of ; 30.
Godmanchester, sale of a chantry and guild in ; 133.
Godolphin :
    Lord ; 153.
    —— letters of ; 42.
    Mr. ; 21.
    Sidney, letters of ; 20.
    Sir William, of Sparger, narrative by ; 41.
Godstow, abbey and convent of ; 140.
Goff, —, a republican refugee, in New England ; 11.
Gogh, Owayn, of Havenemund ; 142.
Golden Grove, letter dated at ; 148, 149.
Goldsmyth :
    John le, mayor of Reading ; 227.
    Rich. ; 180.
Goldwell, Mr., deputy steward ; 132.
Golthwaite, scurrilous play at ; 162.
Good Mr. Jhon., letter to ; 281.
Goodgroome, Rich., transported ; 4.
Goodman, Abraham, committed to the Tower ; 6.
Goodrick :
    Sir H., disarms the garrison of York ; 27.
    —— intelligence from ; 29, 30.
    —— letters of ; 26, 34.
Goodwin, Dr. Thomas ; 141.
Goos, Abraham, map engraved by ; 39.
Gordon :
    Duchess of, letter to ; 23.
    Lord Lewis, report of his movements ; 46.
    Sir John, letter to ; 23.
    Sir William, of Park, report of his movements ; 46.
Gorhambury, letter dated at ; 276.
Goring :
    bailiffs' accounts at ; 154.
    House, marriage solemnized at ; 8.
    George, Lord, Vice-Chamberlain ; 247.
Gosling, Mr. ; 124.
Gosnell, John, petition of ; 4, 5.
Gostwicke, William, schoolmaster ; 179, 200, 226.
Gottorp, letter dated at ; 301.
Gower :
    — ; 145.
    Sir Thos., his troop of horse ; 28.
    —— letter from ; 29.
Graeme, General, play by ; 81.

Grafton :
    Duke of, his position in the ministry ; 53.
    Mr. ; 282.
    House, King James I. and his Queen at ; 88.
Granada, woollen manufactures of ; 45.
Granby, Marquis of, letters of ; *ib.*
Grant :
    Dr. ; 131.
    —, minister of St. Dunstan's, West ; 40.
    —, treatise by ; *ib.*
Grantham :
    Protestant massacres reported at ; 28.
    Semaun, quitclaim to ; 65.
Graper :
    Adam, quitclaim to ; 70.
    —— Agnes, wife of ; *ib.*
Graun, —, *Te Deum* by ; 55.
Graves, Mr., at Limehouse, reported to attend a meetinghouse ; 16.
Gravesend ; 185.
    prisoners conveyed from ; 4.
Gravett, Will. ; 283.
Gray :
    Sir James, correspondence of ; 47.
    Sir Ralph, witness ; 72.
    Richard ; 74.
    Robert ; 72.
    Sir Thomas, of Horton, grant by ; *ib.*
    —— witness ; *ib.*
    William, release by ; *ib.*
Gray's Inn, letter dated at ; 23.
Grayes, letter dated at ; 231.
Great :
    Britain, revenues at ; 247.
    Ness, glebe of ; 156.
Greave, Mr., of Gresham College, case of ; 240.
Green :
    Mr., reputed son of Charles II. ; 9.
    Mrs., mother of Lord Plymouth ; 18.
Greene :
    John A. ; 267.
    Joshua, letter of ; 101.
    R., play by ; 132.
    —, committed to the Tower ; 7.
Greenhill, Mr., schoolmaster ; 225.
Greenwich :
    the Court at ; 137.
    lecturer at ; 136.
    letters dated at ; 96, 289.
    heath ; 88.
Greenwood, Ambrose ; 126.
Gregory XV., Pope, letter of ; 289.
Grene, Walterus atte ; 171.
Grenehill, Rich. ; 184, 185.
Grenley :
    lands in ; 90, 91.
    Evn de ; 90.
    —— Alice, daughter of, grant by ; *ib.*
    Herbert de ; *ib.*
    —— Adam, son of, witness ; *ib.*
    Hugh de ; 91.
    —— son of, grant by ; *ib.*
    Ric. de ; *ib.*
    —— Adam, son of, assignment by ; *ib.*

Grenley—cont.
Robert de; 90, 91.
—— Richard, son of, witness; 90.
—— Hugh, son of, grant to; 90.
—— John, son of; 90, 91.
William de, witness; 90.
Grenville:
Bernard, letter of; 12.
Rich.; 152.
Gresford, rectory of; 146.
Grey:
—, a woollen draper in Ratcliff, reported to attend a meeting house; 16.
F., letter of; 279.
Lord, trial of; 270.
Lady Jane, claim of; 182.
—— proclamation issued by; 294.
William; 182.
Greville, Sir Fulke, letter of; 251.
Griffenfeld, —, foreign minister, letter of; 20.
Griffin, Dr. Hugh, letter to; 259.
Griffith:
Dr.; 131.
John; 146.
Owen; 155.
Griffyn:
Ambrose, trial of; 163, 164, 165.
Jane, trial of; 163, 164, 165.
Willm., of Southladd; 163, 164.
Griffyths, Rich.; 147.
Grigg, —; 154.
Grimsby, depositions taken at; 35.
Grimsthorp:
letters dated at; 35.
Papist cavalry expected to attack; 28.
Grimston:
Will., letter to; 27.
Mr., chairman for grievances; 98.
Grindall:
Archbishop; 256.
—— letter of and to; 276, 300.
Gringley-on-the-Hill, deeds relating to the manor of; 90 et seq.
Griphus, Peter, papal nuncio, dispensation by; 137.
Gripp:
John, elected to a Fellowship; 191.
—— a scholar; 193.
Grippe, William, letter of; 213.
Grosvenor, Walter, witness; 122.
Grove, Walter, atte; 172.
Grover:
Mr.; 179.
Will., fined; 204.
Grymeston:
fortification of the mansion of; 119.
inquisitions for the hundred of; 103.
Gubaud, Margery, Prioress of Stikeswald; 60, 61, 62.
Gubione, Sir Hugh, witness; 67.
Guernsey; 177.
Book of; 129, 130.
charters relating to; 129.
conger-house built in; 130.
proceedings relating to; 129, 130.
Isle of; 289.

Guest, Ellys, player; 185.
Guildford, Parliamentary troops at; 220.
Guisborough, hospital and free school at; 303.
Gulston, Mr., knighted; 104.
Gunchetel; 60.
Gunter:
Anne, accused of possession by the devil; 135.
Brian, examination of; ib.
Gurney, Hugo de, grant by; 91.
Guthree, James, prisoner in the Fleet, petition of; 290.
Guybon:
Francis; 105.
Sir Thomas; 103, 105.
Gwyn, Mr.; 263.
Gwynne, Dr., play written by; 272.
Gybbon, John, Bluemantle, tract by; 42.

H.

" H. A.," letter signed by; 10.
Habeas corpus, prisoners brought up by; 2.
Haberley; 65.
deed dated at; 66.
Hacker:
Colonel; 92.
Col. Francis, trial of; 3.
Hacket, N., letter of; 165.
Hackney, vicar of; 284.
Hackwood, letter dated at; 151.
Haddington, battle of; 232.
Haddock, Rich., a proctor; ib.
Haddocks, Dr., letters of; 278.
Haftridge, Mr.; 131.
Haggarston, Sir Thomas, Lieut.-Governor of Berwick; 23.
Hagman Adam, grant by and to; 71, 72.
Hague:
the; 76.
—— advices from; 10, 29.
English ambassador to; 44.
letters dated at the; 9, 12, 13, 19, 20, 44, 55, 82.
Haile, Mr.; 131.
Hailes, Daniel, secretary of the Embassy in France; 54, 55.
Haines, Mr.; 131.
Hakewill:
W., argument by against Impositions; 237.
—— Record searches by; 240.
Hakluyt, Rich., work by; 234.
Haldisly, manor of; 119.
Haldisworth, Dr., murder of; 120.
Hale:
Mrs.; 78.
Serjeant, suit against; 156, 157.
—— charges against; 158, 159.
Sir Edw., case of; 41.

Hales:
　John; 234.
　—— proceedings against; 286.
Haliclande, lands in; 72.
Halifax:
　lands in; 138.
　negligence of the watch in; 120.
　Geo., 1st Marquis of; 119.
　Lord, his designs against Danby's ministry; 12.
　—— investigation by; 40.
Hall:
　Arthur, petition by; 156.
　E., letter of; 281.
　John, chaplain; 72.
　Mr.; 131, 271.
Hallewin, Jacob, regimental schoolmaster; 41.
Halliley, J., letter of; 13.
Halling, letter dated at; 241.
Halomshire; 129.
Hals, manor of; 140.
Halse, Sir Nicholas, lands of; 291.
Halsey, John, letter of; 159.
Halston, preceptory of Hospitallers at; 146.
Halton, manor of, claim to; 138.
Hulys, Edward, Keeper of the Rolls; 139.
Halywelle, lands of; 75.
Hambleton, Marquis; 243.
Hamburgh; 304.
　letter dated at; 8.
Hamelton, Col. Mimgo; 41.
Hamerden, lands in; 73.
Hamilton:
　Duke of, letters of and to; 25, 37.
　—— reports of his movements in London; 24.
　—— supports the Prince of Orange; 23.
　—— intelligence from; 34.
　—— James, committed to the Tower; 7.
Hamlin, Edw., alderman of Reading; 188.
Hammerton, a Jesuit teacher, arrested; 29.
Hammond:
　Col. Robert, High Steward of Reading; 191, 218.
　Mrs., lodging of; 26.
　Dr., opinion of; 129.
Hampden:
　George; 135.
　John, case of; 273.
　Mr.; 109.
Hampshire:
　classified return of nonconformists in; 14.
　Club; 76.
Hampton; 171.
　Court, letter dated at; 95.
　Mr.; 238, 239, 244.
　—— treatise by; 254.
Hamsey, estate of; 114.
Hamsterley, John, of Bynbroke, quitclaim by; 65.
Hanford, Philip de, deed of; 142.
Hanger, ——, a profligate companion of the Prince of Wales; 56.

Hanmer:
　Sir John, inducements to surrender Hull offered to; 27.
　Mr.; 92.
Hannah, Lady; 178.
Hanover:
　affairs of; 47.
　secret treaty by; 55.
Hansby, Ral., letter of; 26.
Hanses, C., letter of; 23.
Hanson, Mr., case of; 159.
Harald, John, mayor of Reading; 227.
Harbord:
　Sir Ch., letters of; 9.
　Will., his dispute with Lord Conway; 10.
　—— mission of; 111.
Harbotelle:
　Guichard, grant by; 74.
　John; 75.
　Thomas, agreement by; 74.
Harcostell, Mr., reported to hold a conventicle; 16.
Harcourt, Father, information against; 17.
Hardie, Mr.; 131.
Harding:
　Honora, her pension in arrear; 11.
　Queen's Advocate, letters of; 308.
Hardredeshulle:
　Will. de; 145.
Hardwicke, Lord Chancellor, correspondence of; 50, 51, 52.
Hare:
　Eliza; 117.
　Lady Elizabeth, letter of; ib.
　George, wounded at sea; ib.
　Sir Thomas, selected as candidate for Norfolk; 106, 108.
Harewech, John de, witness; 91.
Hareynge, Samson, witness; 71.
Haridance, Will., letter of; 101.
Harington:
　Sir John, epigrams by; 272, 273.
　—— letter of; 273.
Harlow, Sir Ro., sacrilege by; 147.
Harman, Sir J., letter of; 8.
Harnys, Edwd., licensed preacher; 285.
Harpur:
　family of; 138.
　Lady; 117.
　John, marriage contract of; 136.
　Will., of Ruysshall, son of; 136.
Harrington:
　James, transported; 4.
　Sir James, committed to the Tower; 3.
　John, seditious discourses of reported; 13.
　Sir John; 242.
Harris:
　Serjeant; 231.
　Sir James, letter of; 55.
Harrison:
　Col., instructions to; 220.
　Lieut., discharged from the Tower; 5.
　Mrs., case of; 192.

Harrison—*cont.*
  Thomas, deprived; 223.
  —— claim of; *ib.*
  —— of Efford, accusation against; 146.
Harrys:
  Rob., Keeper of the Rolls, ; 139.
  Rowland, Keeper of the Rolls; *ib.*
Harryson, Rich., licensed preacher; 285.
Hart, Thomas; 176.
Hartburne, Vicar of; 72.
Hartington, Marq. of (1755), letter of; 47.
Hartlaw, lands of; 75.
Hartlibb, Samuel, discharged from the Tower; 8.
Harvey, Col., transported; 3.
  D.   ; 300.
  Edm., proceedings against; 4.
  Mr.; 117.
Harwood:
  Col. Edw.; 41.
  Sarah, evil practises of; 22.
Haselrig:
  Sir Arthur, his death in the Tower; 2.
  —— son of; *ib.*
Haslam, Edw., charges against; 156.
Hassall, Jo., Dean of Norwich; 97.
Hast, Richard, letter of; 26.
Hastingleigh, Kent; 290.
Hastings:
  Lady Alice; 167.
  Sir Francis; 238.
Hatche:
  David atte; 169.
  mayor of Reading; 227.
Hatton:
  Mr.; 131.
  Sir Chr.; 84, 133, 237.
  —— letter of; 306.
  Michael, correspondence of; 47.
Haughmond:
  Thomas, Abbot of, case of; 160.
  Christopher, Abbot of, case of; *ib.*
Haughton, letter dated at: 124.
Haukes, Rev. Mr., bill against; 148.
Haverfield, letter dated at; 136.
Havering at Bower, petition from; 135.
Haversham, Lord, speech of; 115.
Havre; 54.
Haward:
  John, reported to attend a conventicle; 16.
  Rich., reported to attend a conventicle; *ib.*
Hawke, Sir Edw., letters of; 45.
Hawkewell, lands in; 71, 72.
Hawks, Master of the, privileges of; 134.
Haworth, William, suspected of murder; 120, 121.
Hay:
  John, attainted; 46.
  Thomas, charges against; *ib.*
Haydock, Lodge, letter dated at; 148.
Hayes:
  Mr., 117.
  Will., letter of; 7.

Haymarket, theatre, petition for a license for; 77, 78.
Haynes Hill; 186.
Haynes:
  ——, information by; 23.
  Major, committed to the Tower; 3.
Hayton, ——; 141.
Heacham; 103.
  Marshes; 98.
Head, Mr.; 202.
Headley:
  Martin, letter of; 20.
  —— letter of; 10.
Heale, Hen., sketch of Freemasonry by; 308.
Heath:
  ——, reported a dangerous person; 16.
  James, petition of; 307.
  Sir Robert, Attorney-General; 271.
  —— his unsuccessful candidature at Reading; 186.
  —— letters of; 243, 306.
Heburne:
  Mr., deprived; 279.
  —— letter of; 278.
Hecimere, dominus Jolaynus de; 62.
Hedle, manor and vill of; 73.
Heidelberg, letter dated at; 301.
Heland, lands in; 70.
Helmstadt, University at; 304.
Helpingham, church of; 90.
Hemmings, John, player; 233,
Hemsworth, Francis, letter of; 306.
Henchman, Mr.; 131.
Henckel, an optician; 55,
Henderson:
  Col. Fras.; 41.
  Col. Rob.; *ib.*
  Sir John, character of; 53.
Heneage:
  Mr.; 239.
  Mich., Keeper of the Rolls; 133, 139.
  Thos., Keeper of the Rolls; 133, 139.
Hengham, Magnum and Parvum; 228.
Henley; 174.
  players of; 172.
  John, vindication by; 50.
Henningham, Mr., reported to attend a conventicle; 15.
Henrietta Maria:
  crosses to France; 85.
  gift to; 184.
  letter to; 289.
Henry I., grant by; 58.
Henry II., 58, 59.
  letters of; 59.
  charter of; 143.
  charters of to Rufford Abbey; 62, 63, 119.
Henry III.:
  charters of; 168, 179.
  grant of; 119.
Henry IV.:
  charter of; 168.
  protest against; 239.
Henry VI.:
  charter of; 168.
  grant by; 129.

y 2

Henry VI. -*cont*.
   letters of and to ; 302.
   Queen of, letter of; 282.
Henry VII. :
   charter of ; 168.
   his landing at Milford Haven; 274.
   household accounts of ; 182.
Henry VIII. :
   charters of ; 168, 179.
   fines levied in the reign of ; 242.
   will of ; 282, 302.
   Mary, daughter of ; 287.
Henry:
   Prince of Wales ; 271.
   —— creation of ; 275.
   —— illness and death of; 286, 287.
   Medicus, of Hundington ; 63.
   —— Robert, son of, grant by ; 63.
Hepbourne :
   —— letters of and to ; 297, 299, 302.
   Mr. Anth.; 62, 263.
Heptonstall, manor of, Court rolls of ; 126,
   at Home ; 246.
Heralds at Arms ; 246.
Heralds :
   fees of the ; 275.
   petition of ; 292.
   painters, bill of charges of ; 19.
Herault, John, bailly of Jersey, petition
   of ; 130.
Herbert :
   Admiral ; 35.
   Edw., Solicitor-General ; 186.
   of Chirbury, Edward, Lord ; 149.
   James, petition of ; 9.
   John ; 286.
   Luke, reported to attend a conven-
    ticle ; 16.
   Lady Mary, anagram for ; 146.
   Hon. Richard ; 149.
   —— family of ; *ib*.
Herbotelle :
   Bartram ; 73.
   Johanna, wife of ; *ib*.
   Edmund de, grant to ; *ib*.
   John, grant by ; *ib*.
   —— of Haroppe ; 74.
   —— of Swaredale, release to ; 73.
   —— of Tynemouth ; *ib*.
   Ralph, grant to ; *ib*.
   Sir Ralph ; 73, 74.
   —— Isabel, daughter of ; 73.
   Rob., grant by ; *ib*.
   Sir Robert ; *ib*.
   Thomas, Chaplain, grant by ; *ib*.
   —— of Cramlingbone, release to ; *ib*.
Hereford :
   Church ritual in ; 148.
   Bishop of ; 155, 231.
Herford, lands in ; 68, 70.
   vill of ; 67.
Herierbi, Robert de, wife of ; 59, 60.
Herlesheved, Rob., witness ; 129.
Hermitage, The, in Wapping ; 16.
Herne, Benj., treasonous speeches reported
   by ; 10.
Heron:
   family of ; 58.

Heron—*cont*.
   James, at Abingdon ; 214.
   Sir John, agreement by ; 70.
   —— witness ; 72.
   William, 58.
   —— Elizabeth, daughter of ; 58.
   Sir William ; 72.
Herpefeild, Nich., prisoner in the Fleet ;
   247.
Hert, Will., election of ; 180.
Hertford :
   Assizes at ; 234.
   Earl of ; 161.
   —— letter to ; 251.
   —— proceedings against ; 286.
   —— about to entertain the Queen ; 123.
Herthella, deed relating to ; 57.
Herthill, parish register of ; 42.
Hertil Willelmus, parson of, witness ; 57.
Hervey, Alice, daughter of, quitclaim by ;
   60.
Hervye, Will. Clarencieux ; 225.
Hervnge, Adhomar, witness ; 72.
Hesilden ; 71.
Hesse :
   Landgrave of ; 305.
   Maurice, Landgrave of, letter of ; 301.
Hetone, Alan de, witness ; 71.
Heveuingham, Will., proceedings against ;
   4.
Hewit, Dr. ; 131.
Hewlett, William, prisoner in the Tower ; 2.
Hewley, John, letter of ; 35.
Hewsham, lands of ; 75.
Hewson, Dr. ; 131.
Heydon, Sir Christopher, astronomical ob-
   servations by ; 245.
Heye, lands in ; 61.
Heylin, Mr. ; 131.
Heyrun, Sir William, sheriff, witness 69.
Heywood, Will., assault on ; 159.
Hexham, lands in ; 71.
Hicham, church of ; 90.
Hickman, Dr. N. ; 152.
Hide, Mr., librarian ; 244.
Hide, Margaret, benefaction by ; 181.
Hidwyne, Robert, of Appirlee ; 72.
Higden, Ralph, *Polychronicon* by ; 230.
Higham Farrers, letter from ; 306.
High Commission, Court of :
   case in ; 156.
   marriage annulled by ; 159.
Highlands, pacification of the ; 45, 46.
Hill :
   Thomas ; 261.
   Will. ; 239.
Hilliard, information against ; 35.
Hillsborough :
   letter dated at ; 35.
   proposed relief of ; 34.
Hilton :
   lead mines at ; 145.
   manor of, exchange of ; 133.
   Sir Thomas ; 75, 76.
   Waultier, de Turbaton ; 234.
Hinchinbrook, Lady ; 125.
Hind, James, prisoner from the Tower ; 5.
Hindostan, description of ; 53.

Hinton, Gyles, alderman, resignation of ; 200.
Hobart :
    Sir Henry, Attorney-General ; 135, 239, 240.
    Sir John, letters of ; 100, 101, 102.
Hobbs, Thomas, treatise of ; 41.
Hobson :
    Kath., complaint against ; 184.
    Paul, committed to the Tower ; 6, 7.
Hogil, Thomas de, witness ; 71.
Holborne, Sir Robert, argument by ; 238.
Holcorne ; 278.
Holdene, William, quitclaim by ; 72.
Holderness :
    Countess of ; letter of ; 39.
    Earl of ; 43, 44, 45, 49.
    —— as governor of the English Princes ; 47, 48.
    —— index to his correspondence ; 53.
    —— of, letters to ; 47, 48, 52.
    papers ; 43, *et seq.*
Hole, :
    —— reported a dangerous person ; 16.
    family of ; 138.
    John, information by ; 161.
    —— will of ; 169.
Holford :
    lands in ; 70.
    deed dated at ; *ib.*
    family of ; 138.
Holkham, letters dated at ; 10.
Holland ; 37, 42.
    assistance requested from ; 111.
    English sailors enlisted by ; 9.
    fleet of, under sail for England ; 26.
    foreign correspondence from ; 53.
    intelligence from ; 112, 116.
    movements of Jacobites in ; 47.
    negotiations with ; 20.
    preparations for an expedition from ; 25.
    proposed treaty of commerce with Sweden ; 39.
    prospects of war with ; 26.
    Scotch factory in ; 47.
    Scotch troops in ; 40, 47.
    Stadtholder of ; 47.
    taxation in ; 41.
    trade with ; 291.
    (England), charitable uses in ; 139.
    Earl of ; 154, 222.
    —— High Steward of Reading ; 184, 214.
    —— license by ; 222.
    Henry, Earl of ; 250.
    Mr., discourse of the Navy by ; 40.
    John, an account of his death ; 273.
    Sir John ; 99, 106.
    Philip, discharged from the Tower ; 8.
Holles, Sir John, of Houghton ; 146.
Hollis :
    Col. ; 41.
    Francis, Lord ; 210.
    Lady, reported to frequent a conventicle ; 15.
Holmes :
    Major Robert, committed to the Tower ; 7.

Holmes—*cont.*
    Capt. Rob., committed to the Tower ; 3.
Holmewood, Edward, petition of ; 292.
Holstein, Duke of, envoy of ; 19.
Holt :
    Father ; 297.
    Jas., letter of ; 28.
    —— letter to ; 259, 260.
    Robert, M.P., his necessitous condition ; 10.
    Sir Thomas, Recorder of Reading ; 200.
Holteby, a Jesuit ; 279.
Holtelle :
    vill of ; 72.
    deed dated at ; *ib.*
Holway, Mr. ; 131.
Holyhead ; 243.
Holyrood House, letter dated at ; 24.
Holywell, documents relating to ; 146.
Home, Sir Patrick, letter of ; 25.
Honington. *See* Hundington.
Hontone, Gilbert de, grant to ; 64.
Hoogan, Sir Tho. ; 101.
Hooke, Mr. ; 131.
Hope, George, letter of ; 148.
Hopkins :
    Henry, writ of ; 291.
    M., letter of ; 10.
    Rev. Matthew, letters to ; 9, 13.
Hopkinson, Mr. ; 43.
Hopton :
    Dr. Chaplain ; 276.
    Lord ; 188, 216.
    Sir —, de, witness ; 142.
    Thomas, deed of entail by ; 74.
    William ; 93.
Hornby, Edward, letter of ; 292.
Horne :
    Mr., character of ; 159.
    Dr. Rob., instructions to ; 286.
Horsley :
    deeds dated at ; 71, 72.
    lands in ; 68, 72, 74.
    letter dated at ; 135.
    South, lands in ; 71, 72.
    —— vill of ; 69.
    West, wood of ; 72.
    Cuthbert ; 75, 76.
    alias Delaval, James ; 73.
    John, grants to ; 72.
    —— de, grants by ; 71, 72.
    —— of Ulchester ; 74.
    Richard de, sheriff, witness ; 70, 71.
    Roger ; 74.
    Thomas de, exchange by ; 69.
Horseman, —, discharged from the Tower ; 5.
Horton :
    Castle and Manor of ; 73.
    deeds dated at ; 67-70, 72, 74.
    fields of ; 67, 70, 71.
    manor of ; 67, 69, 72, 133.
    vill of ; 69, 70, 74.
    lands in ; 74.
    vicarage of ; 294.

Horton—*cont.*
    windmill of ; 74.
    Henry, son of Ralph of, quitclaim by ; 71.
    John, son of Robert the Chaplin of, quitclaim to ; 71.
    Matilda de ; 69.
    —— Richard, son of ; 69.
    —— Robert, grandson of, grant by ; 69.
    Richard de ; 68.
    Robert, son of Walter of ; 71.
    Sir Waleran de ; 68, 70.
    Waleran de ; 68, 69, 70.
    —— Radulf, son of, grant to ; 68.
    —— Isabella, daughter of ; 69.
    Col. Jere, order by ; 216.
    sheriff of ; 68.
Horwell, Colonel ; 40.
Hospitallers, order of ; 128.
Host, Capt. ; 117.
Hotham, Sir John, letter of ; 8.
Hothfield :
    letter dated at ; 85.
    Lord, manuscripts of ; 81 *et seq.*
Houghton Thobie, the King's Woodward general, letter to ; 241.
Hounesby :
    William de, quitclaim to ; 60.
    —— Margery, wife of ; *ib.*
Hoveden :
    Robertus de ; 229.
    Rogerus ; 231.
Hovell, Sir Richard ; 102.
Howard :
    Bernard, letter of ; 12, 20.
    of Effingham, Charles, Lord, order by ; 134.
    Francis, letter to ; 28.
    Henry, prosecution of ; 273.
    James, committed to the Tower ; 3.
    John, reported to attend a conventicle ; 16.
    Lord, defeated off Calais ; 95.
    Lord William ; 83.
    Mr. ; 55.
    —— surrenders Carlisle ; 29.
    Philip, committed to the Tower ; 3.
    Sir Rob., committed to the Tower ; *ib.*
    —— information concerning ; 13.
    William, discharged from the Tower ; 8.
Howbel, John, sequestration of ; 145.
Howe :
    Lord, letters of ; 55.
    Mr. ; 131.
    Sir T. G., mortgage by ; 154.
Howghtone, Sewallus, grant by ; 72.
Howlett, Nich., prebendary ; 97.
Howley, letter dated at ; 123.
Howpill Will., letter of ; 306.
Howse :
    Rob., minister, stipend of ; 178.
    Sam., alderman, deprived ; 196.
Howth ; 243.
Hoynck, Otho. ; 92.
H. P., prisoner in the Fleet ; 247.
Hudleston, Anth., proposal by ; 27.

Hudson, Mr. ; 131.
Hudson's Bay Company, case of ; 166.
Hughes :
    Mr., reported to attend a conventicle ; 16.
    S., Vicar of St. Laurence, Reading ; 226.
Hughse, Will., Treasurer of the Inner Temple, letter of ; 306.
Hulebert, Sarah, benefaction to ; 226.
Hull ; 36.
    Company of Carpenters in ; 32.
    Danish troops landed at ; *ib.*
    election of High Steward in ; 8.
    intelligence from ; 32.
    Lieut.-Governor of ; 37.
    letters dated at ; 28, 29, 37, 77.
    military revolution at ; 27.
    movements of troops at ; 26.
    negotiations for the surrender of ; 27.
    plan of the citidel of ; 39.
    Protestant fleet detained at ; 33.
    Rich., trial of ; 162.
Hulle, Thomas, of Fraynche, grant to ; 66.
Hullemoreton, manor of ; 145.
Hume, Sir Patrick, character of ; 24.
Humfrey :
    Dr. L., oration by ; 300.
    —— letter of ; 281, 285.
Humphreys :
    counterfeit title of ; 30.
    Mr. ; 131.
Hundington ; 59.
    deeds dated at ; 60 *et seq.*
    grange of ; 62.
    the Cook's well in ; 64.
    the fields of ; 63, 65.
    twene-ye-gate in ; 64.
    vill of ; 61.
    Dampdike in ; 64.
    Holmwelledale in ; 63.
    Lynestanges in ; 64.
    Nezergate in ; *ib.*
    Northesteyndal in ; *ib.*
    Oldedikes in ; *ib.*
    Mathew, son of Alan de, grants by ; 61.
    —— Nicholas, son of, grant by ; *ib.*
    Stayndale in ; 63.
    Gilbert, vicar of ; 64.
    Hamo de, quitclaim by ; 59.
    grants of land in ; 59, 60, 61, 62, 63, 64.
    Henricus, medicus de ; 64.
    —— William, son of ; *ib.*
    Nicolas, the clerk of ; *ib.*
    —— Margery, daughter of ; *ib.*
    Peter de ; 64.
    Ralph de, clerk ; *ib.*
    Richard de, chaplain, quitclaim by ; 64.
    Roger de ; 62.
    —— William, son of ; *ib.*
    —— —— Matilda, his daughter ; *ib.*
    Robert de ; 65.
    —— Walter, son of ; *ib.*
    —— —— grant by ; 63.
    Robert, "adportam anlœ" of, grants to ; 63, 64.

Hundington—*cont.*
  Robert, Alice, wife of; 64.
  —— de, quitclaim by; 65.
  William, son of Henry de, grants by; 61.
  William, vicar of, witness; 61.
Hunks, Col. Hercules, discharged from the Tower; 3.
Hunsden:
  Lord; 163.
  —— son of; 293.
Hunstanton; 93, 107, 109, 112, 114, 117, 118.
Hunt:
  John, election of; 180.
  Mr.; 131.
Hunter, Andrew, regimental chaplain; 41.
Hunthifield:
  William de, of Byrtone; 64.
  —— John, son of, grant to; *ib.*
Huntingdon; 250.
  documents dated at; 63.
  Earl of, creation of; 167.
  —— exchange by; 133.
  —— Lieutenant of the north parts; 82.
  Lucy, Countess of, letter of; 9.
  Rob., proposal by; 11.
  William, mayor of Reading; 227.
Hurst:
  church of; 169.
  John of Scotylthorpe, quitclaim by; 66.
Huss, confutation of; 155.
Hussey:
  Sir Charles, of Hunnington; 67.
  Mr. John, steward; 132.
  Robert, Esq., admitted a monk; 66.
  —— Anne, wife of; *ib.*
  Sir Thos., his interest in Lincolnshire; 28.
  —— presentation by; 67.
Hussey-Delaval:
  Sir John; 76.
  Lady; 76, 79.
Hutchins:
  Ralph, priest; 137.
  the Rev. Mr., presentation for desired; 25.
Hutchinson:
  Eliz., memorial presented by; 31.
  John, committed to the Tower; 6.
  Julius, letter of; 125.
Hutton:
  Dr., of Aynhoe; 153.
  Justice; 252.
  E., letter to; 281.
  Matthew, letter of; 253.
  Col. Will.; 41.
Huyck, Dr. Tho., instructions to; 286.
H. W.:
  information by; 16.
  companion of; *ib.*
Hyde:
  Sir Edward, letter of; 242.
  Capt. Hugh; 3.
  Lawrence, letters of 20.

Hyde—*cont.*
  Mr.; 21.
  —— expenses of his mission; 38.
  Mrs., judgment against; 243.
Hyldyard, Will., letters of; 306.
Hyll, James, letter to; 299.
Hyndford, Earl of, correspondence of; 44.
Hynynge the Parker; 67.

I.

"I. B.," letter signed by; 10.
Idzikowski, Joseph, work by; 240.
Inchbald, G., actor, letter of; 81.
Inchiquin, Lord, despatches from; 10.
Independents, intelligence respecting the conventicles of, in London; 16.
India:
  state of affairs in; 55.
  stock, fall of; 78.
Ingby, Christopher, non-juror; 156.
Inglese, Father; 95.
Ingram:
  Mr., charged with harbouring Papists horses; 25.
  Thos.; 140.
Inner Temple; 307.
  Benchers and Treasurer of the, letters to; 306.
  gift to library of; 304.
  Society of; 288.
  See also London. Temple.
Inniskilling, success by the garrison of; 35.
Ipswich; 166.
Irby, Sir Anth.; 10.
Ireland:
  affairs of; 20, 187, 239.
  arms for seized; 27.
  army for; 189.
  the army in; 37.
  bread contract for the forces in; 36.
  campaign in; 109, 110, 111.
  chieftain of; 160.
  commissariat frauds in; 36.
  complaint of grievances from; 289.
  council of; 12.
  governor of; 142, 143.
  forfeited lands in; 133.
  French spies in; 55.
  King's revenue in; 290.
  landing of troops in; 35.
  loan for suppressing the rebellion in; 30.
  newsletters from; 35.
  papers relating to; 10.
  Parliament of; 20, 289, 290.
  form of Parliaments in; 129.
  Poyning's Law in; *ib.*
  primate of; 20.
  proclamation in; 242.
  relief for the Protestants in the north of; 34.

Ireland—*cont.*
  reported invasion of Scotland from; 37.
  restoration to estates in; 242, 243.
  revenue of; 13, 41.
  rumoured invasions from; 44.
  skirmishes in; 35.
  speeches delivered in; 245.
  state of accounts in; 7.
  Strafford's government in; 99, 100.
  succours for the army in; 217.
  students from; 307.
  treasurer of; 288.
  treatise on; 250.
  troops for; 209.
  vote for the reduction of; 109.
  Lord Chancellor of; 20, 249.
  government of; 20.
  Lord Deputy of; 247, 289, 290.
  Lord Lieutenant of; 10, 307.
  —— and Council of; 242.
  Lord President of, apology of; 289.
  Lord Primate of, speech of; *ib.*
  Thomas, schoolmaster; 196, 197.
Ireton:
  Alderman, committed to the Tower; 3.
  —— transported; 4.
Irland, Sir John, Lieutenant of Man; 149.
Isaackson, Dr.; 131.
Isle of Man; 135.
  bailiff of; 150.
  captain of; *ib.*
  church of Holy Trinity in; *ib.*
  church of St. Lupus in; *ib.*
  church of St. Ninian in; *ib.*
  church of St. Runan in; *ib.*
  documents relating to; 149, 150, 151.
  lieutenant of; 149.
  plague in; 76.
Isleworth, letter dated at; 82.
Islington; 137.
Islip; 174.
Ivingho, court rolls of; 145.

J.

Jackson:
  ——, letter of; 35.
  Sir John, case of; 163.
  Edward, his house at Retford; 124.
  Francis, letter of; 307.
  Lieut. Thomas, recommendation for; 37.
  Roger; 140.
Jacob, Solomon, a convict; 50.
Jacobites:
  movements of; 46, 47.
  plots of; 44.

Jamaica:
  Admiralty proceedings at, for piracy; 13.
  departure of the English fleet for; 9.
  governor of; 10, 20.
  intelligence from; 45.
  letters dated at; 11.
  outrages by privateers of; 8.
  Romish priest sent out to; 32.
"James," the ship; 85.
James I.; 135.
  charter of; 168.
  commission by; 96.
  coronation of; 270.
  grant by; 248.
  his propositions to the Lords of the Council; 293.
  letters of and to; 81, 134, 251, 287, 288, 293, 301.
  petition to; 289.
  speech of; 252.
  State papers of; 287.
  succession of; 251.
  "the fishing project" submitted to; 246.
  warrant by; 134.
James II.; 31.
  abdication of; 42.
  birth of his children; 111.
  birth of his son; 108.
  charter of; 168.
  deserted by his followers; 23.
  grant by; 152.
  his Declarations as common as ballads; 25.
  his flight from Ireland; 111.
  news of his flight; 28.
  proclamations by; 39, 105, 111, 199, 209.
  volunteers enlisted to guard his Queen; 26.
  warrants signed by; 19.
  late King of England; 159.
  his party in Edinburgh; 36.
  charge of drinking his health; 35.
James VI., letters of and to; 287, 292, 293.
James:
  Father, of Somerset House; 17.
  Major, charge against; 10.
  Mr.; 249.
  Sir John, proposal by; 11.
  Roger; 238.
Jar, Morgan Ap., witness; 142.
Jeffereyes, Mr.; 131.
Jeffreys:
  Herb.. Commissioner of Virginia; 19.
  Sir George; 22.
  —— to be made Lord Chief Justice; 104.
  Lord Chancellor; 108.
Jemmatt:
  Mr., minister; 192.
  S., mayor of Reading, deprived; 195.
Jenkins:
  Dr., opinion by; 214.
  Sir Leoline; 219.
Jenks, case of, discussed at a club; 13.

Jennings, Robert, schoolmaster; 191, 193, 194, 226.
Jennison, Lieut.; 26.
Jerrard, Mr., schoolmaster; 226.
Jersey; 166.
  bailly of; 130.
  King's Advocate in; 240.
Jerusalem, Hospital of St. John of; 140, 249.
Jesuits, papers relating to; 248, 280, 305.
Jewell, Bishop, letter to; 281.
Jews:
  naturalization of the, resisted; 206.
  proposal for the taxation of; 38.
  proposal for treating as aliens; 35.
J. F., a song composed by; 272.
J. H., letter from; 263.
J. M., letter of; 244.
John, King:
  charter of, in Ireland; 142, 143.
  grant by; 91.
  Pipe Roll of; 241.
Johnson:
  James, his death in the Tower; 5.
  George, letter of; 22.
Johnston:
  Dr. N.; 43.
  Archibald, prisoner in the Tower; 6.
  Margaret, petition of, to live with her father in the Tower; ib.
Johnstone, —, objections to his mission to Lisbon; 53.
Jokinton, Philippus de, witness; 57.
Jones:
  —, a tailor, reported to hold a conventicle; 15, 16.
  —, information for treason against; 16.
  Cadwallader, accusations against; 167.
  Dr. Henry, letter of; 300.
  Hugh Valence, letter of; 44.
  Judge, treatise by; 252.
  Justice; 22, 272.
  Mr.; 131, 280.
  —— of Lincoln's Inn, Chairman for Privileges; 98.
  Thomas, letters to; 20.
Jowett, Jo., letter of; 9.
Joy:
  Geoffrey; 72.
  Richard, of Hundington, and Johanna his wife, will of; 65.
  —— Cecily, daughter of; ib.
  —— Alice, daughter of; ib.
  Thomas, grant to; 72.
Joynes, John, presentation of; 67.
Jubilee:
  granted by the Pope; 284.
  of George III.; 208.
Julius II., Pope, Bull of; 255.
Justice:
  Will., election of; 181.
  William, election of; 179.
Juxon, Will., letter of; 222.

K.

Karnaby, William de, witness; 71.
Karretbrennan, lands of; 143.
Katherine of Braganza, Queen, at Reading; 197.
Kaverswalle:
  Roger de; 144.
  —— Henry son of, and Mary his wife, grant by; ib.
  See Caverswall.
Kebelsworthe, manor of; 73.
Kechin, Richard, letter of; 285.
Kedewelly, David; 173.
Keene, Sir B., correspondence of; 47.
Keith, Robert, correspondence of; 44, 47, 55.
Kelly:
  —; 76.
  report by; 45.
Kelssale, Hen., election of; 180.
Kemble, Mr., actor; 81.
Kempley, manor of; 154.
Kendale, John, of Newcastle, grant by; 72.
Kendrick:
  Mr., portrait of; 206.
  John, will of; 183, 194.
Kennedy:
  Andrew, committed to the Tower; 5.
  James, letters of; 10, 12.
Kennet, the river; 169, 224.
Kenrick:
  Mr., meagre contribution by; 221.
  John, benefaction by; 202.
  Sir Will.; 197.
Kensington:
  credentials dated at; 76.
  the Council chamber at; 124.
Kent; 163.
  seaport towns of; 276.
  John, mayor of Reading; 227.
  Simon, election of; 180.
Kentish, Mr., reported to hold a conventicle; 15, 16.
Kerrill:
  Elizabeth, petition of; 292.
  John; ib.
Kestaven; 65.
Kethvie:
  Mr.; 138.
  —— Christine, wife of; ib.
Kew, document dated at; 300.
Kidderminster:
  lands and tenements in; 65, 66.
  manor of; 66.
Kidwelly, Morgan; 176.
Kiffin, Mr., conventicle held by; 16.
Kilburn, Alan de; 69.
Kildare, Earl of, claim for restoration by the kin of; 275.
Killegrew:
  Henry, committed to the Tower; 3.
  Lady; 136.

Killegrew—*cont.*
　Sir Rob., committed to the Tower; 3.
　Sir W., letters of; 9.
　Sir William; 222.
　—— proposals by; 10.
Killeshin, lands in; 152.
Killyngworth, John de, senior, lease by; 71.
Kilmaynhaune, lands of; 290.
Kinaston, Sir Edw.; 142.
King:
　Mr.; 131.
　—— his supposed "discovery"; 19.
　Mrs, actress; 77.
　Rich., elected to a Fellowship and Scholarship; 193.
　Thomas, letters of; 13, 20.
　—— reported to teach at a meeting house; 16.
Kingdon, —, intelligence from; 12.
Kingesmylle, John; 176.
Kingshill, court of the manor of; 228.
Kingsmill, Andrew, letter of; 283.
King's Bench:
　Court of; 291.
　judgments of the; 229.
　Justice of the; 250.
King's Remembrancer, office of; 246, 271.
Kingston, Duke of; 152.
Kingswood Forest, ranger of; 134.
Kinloch Moidart, brothers of; 46.
Kinsale Harbour; 20.
Kircksham, William, jun., deed by; 183.
Kirkham, George, petition of; 295.
Kirketon, grant of free chace in; 119.
Kirklees, letter dated at; 31.
Kirrie, lordship and barony of; 273.
Kirton, deeds relating to; 91.
Knaresborough, election for the convention at; 35.
Knaspole, Major, house of; 308.
Knell:
　Mr.; 131.
　Tho.; 284.
Knight:
　J., letter of; 13.
　Nathan; 202.
　—— election of; 209.
　—— re-election of; 197.
　Roger, precedency of; 222.
　Sir Ralph, letters of; 20.
　Walter, of Staple Inn; 211, 212.
　—— letter of; 219.
Knightsbridge, a suspected Roman emissary in; 17.
Knockin:
　farm house burnt at; 159.
　letter dated at; 147.
Knokyn Castle, grant dated at; 142.
Knole House; 89.
Knolles:
　Sir Fr.; 163, 210, 221.
　—— election of; 183.
　—— sen., election of; 186, 190.
　—— jun., election of; 186, 189.
　Sir Robert, project of; 275.
Knottesford; 137.

Knowles:
　——, reported to assist at a conventicle; 15.
　Admiral, conduct of; 53.
　Mr., reported to hold a conventicle; 16.
　Rob., election of; 182.
Knox, John, letters of; 277.
Knyphausen, Baron, intelligence from; 45.
Kynard, Rich., Sir, witness; 150.
Kyrk-Andrew, grant dated at; *ib.*
Kyrkeby, Joh.; 174.
Kyrkeyat:
　William, atte, of Hortone; 64.
　Gilbert, son of, quitclaim to; *ib.*

L.

Laceby, decay of tillage in; 257.
Laci, Hug de, witness; 144.
Lacy:
　John, letter of; 120, 121.
　—— of Brearley, indenture of; 126.
Laghton, vicar of; 230.
Laicles Xrofer, prisoner in the Fleet; 247.
Laiham, living of, presentation to the; 160.
Lake:
　Mr., minister; 147.
　Sir Thomas; 291.
Lakefelde, lands in; 62.
Lakin, John, licensed preacher; 285.
Lamb:
　Isaac, of Bedlam, reported to hold a conventicle; 16.
　Rev., ——, rector of Southwell; 116.
Lambard, Will.; 154.
Lambert:
　Charles; 41.
　Capt. James; 4.
　Col. John, transported; 3, 4.
　General; 92, 212.
Lambeth:
　Articles of; 256.
　lands in; *ib.*
　licenses dated at; 218.
　Church, Archbishops Court in; 271.
　See London.
Lamibyn, Henry, vicar; 169.
Lamere, Sir John, suspicious conduct of his regiment; 32.
Lancashire:
　Catholic levies in; 26.
　charges against the sheriff of; 35.
　justices of; 146.
　military movements in; 28.
Lancaster:
　sessions at; 35.
　Herald; 270.
Lane:
　John; 284.
　—— letter of; 307.

Langbaine, Gerard, letter of; 240.
Langham, Sir James, reported to frequent a conventicle; 15.
Langhorn:
—, Penn the Quaker's Counsel; 18.
Mr. Thomas, his execution; 22.
Langtoft, Peter de, the *Gesta Anglorum* by; 230.
Langurth, Mr., covering address to for Lord Danby's correspondence; 11.
Lansdowne, Lord, letters of; 22.
Lante, Mr.; 131.
Large, Tho., prisoner in the Fleet; 247.
Lascelles:
  Edmund, letter of; 93.
  Geo., of Elston, inventory of the estate of; 92.
  anecdote of; *ib.*
  military services of; 92, 93.
  Henry, service by, to Charles II.; 92.
  family of; 91, 92.
Latimer:
  Lord, elected for Knaresborough; 35.
  —— letters of and to; 9, 13, 19, 21, 26, 27, 35.
  —— order of the council for; 39.
  —— proposals for his marriage; 22.
  —— the state of his debts; 35.
  —— his father-in-law; 30.
Laud:
  Archbishop, as Licenser; 239.
  —— benefaction by; 196, 197, 226.
  —— effigy of; 196.
  —— kinsfolk of; 197, 198, 205.
  —— letters of; 223, 225.
  —— life of; 203.
  —— portrait of; 206.
  —— report concerning; 185.
Lauderdale:
  Countess of, letters of; 19, 38.
  Earl of, letters of; 19.
  Duke of, letter to; 13.
  Duchess of, letter to; *ib.*
Laurence:
  Mr., reported to preach at a meeting house; 16.
  Sir John, letter of; 306.
Lavyngtone, Thomas, mayor of Reading; 174.
Lawley, Thomas, application by; 135.
Lawson:
  Capt.; 30.
  Father; *ib.*
Law Tax, farm of the; 19.
Leathersellers:
  Company of, petition of; 292.
  Masters and Wardens of, petition to; 290.
" L. E.," intelligence concerning; 24.
Leche, Richard; 177.
Le Acator, John; 171.
Le Clerk, Thomas; *ib.*
Le Courier, specimens of the; 52.
Le Despenser, Lord; 111.
Lee:
  Francis, petition of; 4, 5.
  Geo.; 146.

Lee—*cont.*
  Henry; 122.
  Mr.; 131.
  Robt., license to; 233.
Leech, Sir Rob., discharged from the Tower; 4.
Leeds:
  an alarm of the Irish at; 28.
  letter dated at; 12.
  Duke of; 43, 124.
  —— letter to; 42.
  —— memorandum by; 55, 56.
Leeke, Gifford, letters of; 158.
Leeward Islands, Secretary in the; 36.
Le Fogelere, Joh.; 171.
Legh:
  Sir John; 274.
  letter of; 148.
Leghorn, letter dated at; 43.
Leigh, Worcestershire; 303.
Leicester:
  burglary at; 146.
  letter dated at; 276.
  St. Mary's Abbey, in the Meadows in; 140.
  —— Richard, Abbot of; *ib.*
  —— John, Abbot of; *ib.*
  Earl of; 133, 163, 164, 258.
  —— letters of and to; 135, 251, 275, 285, 297, 306.
  —— players of; 177.
Leicestershire:
  documents relating to; 146.
  Lord Lieutenant and Custos Rotulorum of; 36.
Leigh, Peter; 150.
Leighton:
  B., petition of; 35.
  Sir Ellis, letter to; 10.
  Sir Thos., mission of; 129.
Leintwardine; sacrilege at; 147.
Leipsic, correspondence from; 47.
Leirton, lands in; 91.
Leith Links, rendezvous of Scotch militia at; 24.
Leland, John, work by; 236.
Le Loke, William, of Hundington, grant to; 63.
Lemon, Thos.; 98.
Le Neve, Peter, letter of; 113.
Lenox, Duke of; 185.
Lent, order for observance of; 306.
Lenthall, John, admitted to bail; 2.
Le Politer, Ad.; 171.
Le Seirmersur, Ernaldus; 129.
Lesley:
  Bishop, discourse by; 287.
  Dr.; 131.
Leslie, Mr.; 24.
L'Estrange:
  family of; 138.
  Report on the MSS. of; 93 *et seq.*
  Sir Christopher; 104, 105, 107, 108, 109, 111.
  Edward; 105, 107, 108.
  Hamon; 114.
  Sir Hamon; 96, 98, 99, 100, 102, 103.

L'Estrange—*cont.*
　claims and charges against ; 102, 103, 104.
　petition to Parliament presented by ; 102.
　John ; 138.
　Sir John, witness ; 142.
　Lewkenor ; 118.
　Sir Nicholas ; 104, 105, 106, 108, 109, 110, 111, 112, 113, 114, 117, 118.
　—— wife of ; 112.
　—— heavy assessment of, for Land Tax ; 113.
　Roger ; 118, 142.
　Sir Roger ; 111, 112, 113, 114, 118.
　—— daughter of ; 111, 112, 118.
　—— wife of ; 112.
　—— committed to Newgate ; *ib.*
　—— Roger, son of ; 111, 112, 114.
　—— his " History of Josephus " ; 113.
　Thomas ; 117, 142.
Lesure, Mr. ; 125.
Leveing, Will., committed to the Tower ; 7.
Leveneti :
　Will., son of, witness ; 91.
　Adam ; *ib.*
　—— William, son of, grant by ; *ib.*
Lever, Thomas, treatise by ; 254.
Leveret, Adam, witness ; 90.
Leveson, John, *v.* Shepherd, case of ; 230.
Lewin, Dr., judge of the Prerogative Court ; 300.
Lewis, John, bailed ; 5.
Lewkener, Robert, Chancery suit of ; 108.
Lews, lands of ; 24.
Lewyn :
　Alice, of Hundington, grant to ; 64.
　Dr. W., letter of ; 295.
　John, of Hundington, power of attorney by ; 65.
　William, grants to ; 63.
Lewys, John, letter of ; 7.
Lexington, Lord, information against ; 35.
Ley, Roger, curate, certificate by ; 214.
Liancourt, Duke de, reputed a spy ; 55.
Libbe, Mr., certificate by ; 226.
Licenses to eat flesh ; 137.
Lichfield :
　mayor and corporation of, petition of ; 26.
　—— office of Recorder of ; 26.
　—— restoration of charter to ; 26, 125, 152.
　and Coventry, Bishop of ; 155.
Liddington, W., letter of ; 286.
Lidisdene ; 68.
Liége, letter dated at ; 44.
Lilborne, John, of ; 74.
Lilbourne :
　Col. Rob., transported ; 3.
　—— proceedings against ; 4.
Lile :
　Robert, of Falton ; 74.
　Thomas, of Newton Hall ; *ib.*
Lille, letter dated at ; 299.
Lilly, John, petition of ; 251.

Limborow, Lord, and his Lady, reported to frequent a conventicle ; 15.
" L. L.", intelligence concerning ; 24.
Lloyd :
　Dr. John ; 253.
　Dr. Will. ; 197.
　Mr. ; 131.
　Sir Marmaduke ; 140.
Lincoln ; 232.
　concealed lands in ; 145.
　deeds relating to ; 91.
　letter dated at ; 32.
　prebend in ; 237.
　Registers of ; 156.
　St. Mary of Crakepole in ; 65.
　St. Faith the Virgin in ; *ib.*
　Bishop of ; 243, 254.
　John, Bishop, of petition to ; 292.
　J. Williams, Bishop of ; 213.
　Robert, Bishop of ; 67.
　Thos. Barlow, Bishop of ; 240.
　Tho. Cooper, Bishop of, sermon preached by ; 283.
　William, Bishop of, petitions to ; 292.
　Dean of ; 32.
　Earl of, libel against ; 161.
　—— letters of ; 135.
　Eliz., Countess of, letter of ; *ib.*
　Hawisia de ; 65.
　Alice, daughter of ; *ib.*
　Henry de Lacy, Earl of, exchange by ; 144.
　Robert de ; 62, 63.
　—— Robert, son of, grant by ; 62.
　—— Hawisia, daughter of, grant to ; 63.
Lincoln's Inn ; 159.
Lincoln's Inn Fields, letter dated at ; 84.
Lincolnshire :
　address from ; 76.
　dispute relative to lands in ; 59.
　documents relating to ; 138.
　elections in ; 35.
Lindsey :
　charitable uses in ; 139.
　Earl of ; 35, 242.
　letters of ; 9, 10, 20, 22, 28, 39.
　petition signed by ; 21.
　services of, at the Coronation ; 35.
Line, ——, preacher at a conventicle ; 16.
Lingard, Will., letter of ; 134.
Linley, Col. ; 40.
" Lion ", the ship ; 82.
Lisbon :
　British Consul at ; 37.
　earthquake at ; 45.
Lisle, Lord, patronage of ; 136.
Lister :
　a Jesuit ; 277.
　Matthew, information against ; 35.
　—— petition of ; *ib.*
Little Bytham, letter dated at ; 33.
Littleton :
　letter dated at ; 161.
　Dr., Adam ; 153.
　Edw., confession of ; 146.
　Sir Edw. ; 273.

Littleton—*cont.*
Lord, anecdote of ; 48.
Lord keeper, letter of ; 136.
Liverdun, dean of ; 279.
Liveries, master of, instructions to ; 249.
Liverpool ; 44.
transport of troops from ; 32.
Lockhart, Sir Will., letter of ; 9.
Lochiel, the "late" ; 46.
Lockier :
[Lady] reported to frequent a conventicle ; 15.
Sir William, reported to frequent a conventicle ; *ib.*
Lockman, John, agent ; 142.
Lockyer, Capt. Nicholas ; 92.
Lodbroke, Simon, election of ; 180.
Loddon, the river ; 224.
Lodington, Sam., letter of ; 307.
Loke, William, of Hundington, grants by ; 64.
Lomleye, John de, grant by ; 70.
Long :
Mr. ; 262.
Rob., case of ; 160.
—— junior ; 108.
Longchamp, Hug. de, witness ; 144.
Longdedenham, rectory of ; 156.
Longford ; 37.
Longueville, Mr. Will., letter to ; 12.
London ; 27, 161, 176, 188, 199, 200, 215.
letters dated at ; 9, 25, 26, 32, 36, 41, 86, 93, 103, 108, 109, 137, 162, 238, 277, 280, 281, 292, 293.
Aldersgate Street in ; 85.
church of St. Botolph in, burial in ; 103.
conventicles held without ; 16.
American minister in ; 55.
Augustine Friars in house and chapel in ; 89.
Barbican, letter dated at the ; 147, 148.
Barbican House in ; 140.
Willoughby House in ; *ib.*
Barkly Street, in ; 35.
Battersea, Popish sisterhood in ; 17.
Baynard's Castle in ; 90.
Bedford House at ; 82, 240.
Bishop of ; 242, 263.
—— letters to ; 297, 298, 301.
—— jurisdiction of ; 296.
—— assists Princess Anne's escape ; 27.
—— letter of ; *ib.*
Grindal, Bishop of, letters of ; 281, 284, 285.
H. Compton, Bishop of ;
John Aylmer, Bishop of, letter of ; 306.
R., Bishop of, witness ; 168.
Richard, Bishop of ; 137.
—— witness ; 119.
William, Bishop of, letter of ; 242.
bishopric of ; 256.

London—*cont.*
Bishopsgate, conventicle held at Hand Alley in, 16.
Devonshire House, conventicle held at ; *ib.*
Spittlefields, conventicle held in ; *ib.*
Winford Street, in Angel Alley, conventicle held in ; *ib.*
Bishopsgate Without, conventicles held in ; *ib.*
—— Golden Arrow at ; *ib.*
Blackfriars ; 304.
Bridges Street, conventicle held in ; 15.
Bridgwater House in ; 126.
Chancellor of ; 282.
Chanon Row, Lord Wharton's house in ; 86.
Charing Cross, the King's coffee house at ; 17.
charters of ; 235, 302.
Cheapside in ; 290.
Christ Church parish, petition of ; *ib.*
Christ's Hospital in ; 195, 202.
City of, loan by ; 133.
Clarendon House in ; 86.
Clifford's Inn in ; 241.
Coleman Street, meeting of Socinians held in ; 17.
—— Bell Alley in ; 18.
Cutler's Hall, conventicle held at ; 16.
Corporation of, order by ; 182.
council at ; 230.
Covent Garden ; 290.
—— conventicles held in ; 15.
Cripplegate, Fifth Monarchy meeting held at Glovers' Hall, Beech Lane, in ; 16.
Custom House at ; 153.
destruction of papists' houses in, forbidden ; 31.
diocese of ; 295.
documents relating to ; 139.
Dorset House, reported burnt in the Fire ; 85.
Dowgate Hill, conventicle held in the Chequers' Yard at ; 16.
Downing Street ; 79.
Drury Lane ; 290.
—— priests and friars harboured in ; 17.
—— the Whitehorse in ; *ib.*
—— the Red Posts in ; *ib.*
—— the Spanish Ambassador's house in ; *ib.*
—— Will's coffee house, Russel Street, in, newsletters issued at ; 20.
East Smithfield, Star Alley, conventicles held in ; 16.
expenses of a journey to, from Reading ; 172, 174, 177.
Fauxhall, suspected sisterhood in ; 17.
Fenchurch Street, intended meeting of anarchists in ; 20.
Fetter Lane in ; 222.

London—*cont.*
  Fetter Lane, conventicle held in New Street, near ; 16.
  Fleet Street ; 39, 243.
  —— the "Three Daggers" in ; 124.
  General Post Office at ; 27.
  Gerrard Street in ; 124.
  Gray's Inn in ; 249.
  Great Russell Street, conventicle in ; 15.
  Hatton Garden, presentation to the Church of ; 25.
  Haymarket, mass said at a strongwater shop in ; 17.
  —— the Blew Balconies in ; 18.
  —— the King's Head in ; *ib.*
  Holborn, a papist bookseller in ; 22.
  —— bailiffs' accounts for ; 140.
  —— conventicles in ; 15.
  —— Duke Street, mass said in ; 17.
  —— Portugal Street, priests harboured in ; 17.
  —— Sun tavern in ; *ib.*
  —— Turnstyle in ; *ib.*
  —— St. John Baptist's Head near ; *ib.*
  —— Short's Gardens, conventicle held in ; 15.
  Hustings Court at ; 179.
  remembrancer of ; *ib.*
  Inner Temple, letter dated at ; 244.
  —— Hare's Court in ; 218.
  intelligence from ; 98, 113, 117.
  King's Street (Long Acre), mass said in ; 17.
  —— sign of St. Paul in ; *ib.*
  Lambeth, conventicle held by a ropemaker in ; 16.
  —— Marsh in ; 122.
  liberty of citizens of Reading in ; 183.
  Lincoln's Inn, church in ; 154.
  Little Suffolk Street, the Barbars Pools in ; 23.
  —— Lockey's house in ; 152.
  Lombard Street in ; 235.
  lord mayor of, letter to ; 52, 251, 294.
  —— petition to ; 290.
  Marine, *alias* Wellclose Square in ; 127.
  Middle Temple, in ; 28.
  Miles Lane in ; 226.
  Milk Street, St. Mary Magdalen in ; 254.
  Moorfields ; 5.
  Newgate ; 272.
  newsletter from ; 28.
  New Southampton Buildings, conventicle in ; 15.
  New Stairs, conventicle held near ; *ib.*
  Old Exchange, proclamation of James II. at ; 105.
  Old Southampton Buildings in ; 93.
  Pall Mall, the "King's Arms" in ; 125.
  Parliament held at ; 211.

London—*cont.*
  Phillpott Lane in, Sir Edward Osborne's house in ; 122.
  Piccadilly, conventicle held in ; 15.
  port of, office of Searcher in ; 10.
  printers of, case of the ; 232.
  proposed contract for ; 42.
  provisions ordered from ; 136.
  Pudding Lane, the Fire at ; 85.
  The Quakers' House in ; 152.
  reception of Charles II. by the city of ; 104.
  Red Lion Square in ; 136.
  Rolls Office, rights to reversions in ; 22.
  St. Alban's Street, popish books published in ; 17.
  —— sign of the Wheel in ; *ib.*
  St. Anne's Church in ; 124.
  St. Giles, the plague in ; 85.
  —— Cripplegate, in ; 233.
  St. James, Court at, letter dated from ; 121.
  St. James' Park, the cockpit in ; 90, 92.
  St. Leonard's, Shoreditch, in ; 214.
  St. Martin's-le-Grand in ; 238.
  St. Paul's Churchyard ; 39, 50.
  St. Sepulchre's Church in ; 235.
  St. Thomas' Hospital in ; 140.
  Salisbury Court, Dorset House in ; 89.
  Savoy, Duchy House in the ; 88.
  scarcity of grain in ; 96.
  Serjeants' Inn in ; 31.
  sheriffs of ; 4, 5, 251, 286.
  Sir John Oldcastle's House in ; 152.
  Smithfield, unlicensed press in ; 18.
  —— Bartholomew Court in ; *ib.*
  —— the White Bare in ; *ib.*
  Southwark, conventicles held in ; 15.
  —— Fan Street, Quaker's meeting held in ; 15.
  —— Farthing Alley, conventicle held in ; 16.
  —— Firefoot Lane, conventicle held in ; *ib.*
  —— Globe Alley, conventicle held in ; *ib.*
  —— Goat Yard, Horsey Down, conventicle held in ; *ib.*
  —— Long Lane, conventicle held in ; 15.
  —— Maid Lane, conventicle held in ; *ib.*
  —— New Lane, conventicle held in ; *ib.*
  —— St. Mary Magdalen, conventicle held in the parish of ; *ib.*
  —— St. Mary Overs, conventicle held near ; *ib.*
  —— St. Savoryes Mill, conventicle held in ; *ib.*
  —— St. Thomas' Hospital, masters and governors of, petition to ; 290.
  —— Salisbury Street, conventicle held in ; *ib.*

London—*cont.*
  Southwark, The Mayes, conventicles held in; 16, 290.
  —— Winchester Park, conventicles held in; 15.
  Spittlefields, Bell Lane in; 16.
  —— conventicles held in; *ib.*
  Stepney, meeting house in; *ib.*
  Strand, Bedford House in; 87.
  Stratford Langthorn, conventicle held at; 16.
  Stratford-le-Bow, bailiffs' accounts for; 140.
  —— Surgeon's Hall, burnt in the Fire; 85.
  Swallow Street, conventicle held in; 15.
  Tart Hall, mass said at; 17.
  Thanet House in; 85.
  the "Bear" at the Bridge foot in; *ib.*
  the great Fire in; *ib.*
  the old Exchange in; 17.
  the Plague in; 84, 85, 196, 213, 214.
  the Rolls, Sir William Cordell's house in the; 121.
  the Temple, in; 124, 241, 242.
  —— records of; 249.
  Temple Bar, the fire at; 85.
  —— proclamation of James II. at; 105.
  —— the school within; 213.
  Thames Street, "Three Cranes" in; 16.
  Tower of, Lieutenant of the. *See* Tower; 192.
  trade with Reading; 213, 215, 216, 220.
  trial of the seven Bishops in; 108, 109.
  Vere Street (Farrington), conventicle in; 15.
  visitors for the diocese of; 286.
  conventicle held in Booby Lane in; 16.
  Warwick Street, priests and monks harboured in; 17.
  —— King's Arms in; *ib.*
  Weavers' Company of; 19.
  West Ham, conventicle held in the parish of; 16.
  Whitechapel, conventicle held in; 16.
  Whitehall, proclamation of James II. at; 105.
  and Middlesex, sheriffs of; 2.
Londonderry. *See* Derry.
Lopez:
  Dr., trial of; 135.
  —— monopoly for; 133.
Lordecot, Henry, land of; 61.
Lords:
  House of, Journals of; 244.
  —— jurisdiction of; 238.
  —— petition of, for a free Parliament; 31.
  —— order by; 4, 129, 130.
  of the Council, letter of; 245.

Loudon, Lord, prisoner in the Tower; 98.
Louis XVI.; 56.
Love:
  —, reported to hold a conventicle; 16.
  Thomas, intelligence from; 28.
  Capt. Thomas, recommendation of; *ib.*
Loveday, Samuel, of Leadenhall Street, reported to hold a conventicle; 16.
Lovelace:
  Col.; 41.
  Sir Richard, Custos rotulorum; 213.
Lovell, Lord; 175.
Loving:
  Monsieur, letter to; 242.
  Will, letter to; *ib.*
Low:
  Countries; 251.
  —— Government of the; 305.
  —— Jesuit influence in; 280.
Lowe, Col. Hercules, appointment of; 9.
Lower:
  Lieut.-Col.; 219, 220.
  —— letter of; 189.
Lowther:
  letter dated at; 27.
  Abraham, of Dedford, reported to attend a conventicle; 16.
  Christopher, witness; 84.
  John, letter of; 28.
  —— and Richard, proposals by, for securing the Northern counties; 27.
  Sir John, death of, 90.
  —— services of; 29.
  Mary, witness; 84.
  Sir Wm.; 124.
Lowton; 148.
Lucas:
  Lord; 245.
  Thos., letter of; 306.
  —— restoration of; 134.
  Will.; 149.
Luci:
  Godfrey de, witness; 60.
  Ric. de, witness; 144.
Lucius III., Papal Bull of; 249.
Lucy:
  Kingsmill, letter of; 241.
  Robert, petition of; 156.
  —— *versus* Bishop of St. David's, case of; 156.
Ludlow:
  alarm of papist plots in; 147.
  Castle; *ib.*
Luke:
  Sir Samuel, letters of; 100.
  Walter, award by; 170.
Lumley:
  Lord, disarms the garrison of York; 27.
  —— his quarrel with Lord Willoughby; *ib.*
  —— letter of; *ib.*
  —— petition signed by; 21.
  Lady, reported to frequent a conventicle; 15.
Luneuburgh, duchy of; 304.

Lunne:
  Christian, petition of; ib.
  Michael, prisoner in the Tower; 6.
Lurtkoe, Henry, lands of; 62.
Lusancy, Monsieur; 17.
Luther:
  confutation of; 155.
  opinion regarding; 305.
Luxembourg, Duke of, intelligence from; 56.
Lydgate, John, "Life of St. Alban," by; 231.
Lydiard Millicent, manor of; 160.
Lydoll, Richard; 183.
Lyford, Sebastian, alderman, deprived; 201.
Lyle, Geoffrey de, grant to; 61.
Lylee, Sir Robert, sheriff, witness, 72.
Lynacre:
  Will.; 176.
  —— election of; 180.
Lynaker, ——; 173.
Lyndon, Geo., purchase of a commission by; 93.
Lyndsay, David, letter of; 25.
Lynn:
  a keelman of; 103.
  almhouses of; 102.
  charter of the borough of; 98.
  coach to; 109.
  escape of prisoners taken at; 103.
  muster of the trained bands at; 105.
  parliamentary election for; 9.
  post to; 108.
  siege of; 102, 103, 104.
  corporation of, letter of; 10.
Lynne; 112.
Lyons Inn, treasurer of; 306.
Lytiltone, Chief Justice; 174.

M.

Macdonald:
  Allan, report of his movements; 46.
  Archibald; ib.
  Æneas, report of his movements; ib.
  Colonel, case of; 159.
  —— of Barrisdale; 46.
  Donald, alias adopted by; ib.
  —— indemnity for; ib.
MacDowell, Donaldus, witness; 150.
MacGregor:
  Clan of; 44.
  James. See Drummond James.
Mackay, General, reported defeat of; 36, 37.
Mackenzie, Sir Geo., letter of; 30.
Macklin:
  Charles, actor, letters of; 79, 80.
  —— his business prospects; 79, 80.
  —— in Dublin; 80.

Macleod:
  Alexander, attainted; 50.
  John, advocate, stratagem by; ib.
  Lord, information against; 49.
  —— letter of; ib.
Macmahon, Parkyns, trial of; 50.
Madenache, Ad. de; 171.
Maddockes, R., letter of; 9.
Madgeburg; 304.
Madox, Mr.; 153.
Madrid:
  correspondence from; 47.
  letter dated at; 45.
Maguire, Cornelius, case of; 233.
Mahony, Jer., intelligence from; 26.
Mak Dovell, Uthred, witness; 150, 151.
Makugny, Col.; 41.
Maidenhead; 209.
Maidford, common rights in; 141.
Mailorsaysnek, forest of; 142.
Mainwaring:
  John, letter of; 239.
  Sir Thos., deprived; 223.
Maister, John, letter of; 278.
Major:
  Mr.; 263.
  Thomas, letters of attorney by; 71.
Malden, parliamentary election at; 20.
Malet, Robert, of Quainton; 145.
Mallony, Sir John, case of; 161.
Malmesbury, Order in Council as to; 31.
Malone, Edm., letter of; 132.
Malpas; 137.
  almshouse at; 151.
  barony of, claim to; 138.
  David de, descent from; 137.
Malta:
  Knights of; 265, 266.
  Order of; 265.
Malton, Lord; 125.
Mamesfelde, Roger de, clerk, grant to and by; 61.
Manchester; 233.
  bounties on linens of; 166.
  letter dated at; 145.
  Earl of; 217.
  —— Lord General; 101, 104.
  Lady, reported to attend a conventicle; 15.
  Lord, order of; 243.
Maners, Robert, of Etal, witness; 72.
Manger; Mr.; 253.
Mann, Mr., plan of Reading by; 207.
Mannering, Dr., case of; 98.
Manning:
  Dr., Henry, case of; 162.
  Mathew, letter of; 104.
Mannington, Lady, play introduced at Court by; 79.
Mansell, Sir Robert, monopoly of making glass to; 91.
Mansfield:
  manor of; 146.
  "Crown Inn" at; 124.
  Count; 183.
  Lord; 45.
  —— anecdote of; 48.

Manton, Mr., reported to hold a conventicle; 15.
Manwaring, —; 249.
Manwayring, Roger, proceedings against; 245.
Manwood:
  Chief Baron; 163.
  Roger, letters of; 306.
  Sir Roger; 250.
Maplested, Much, letter dated at;
Mar, Earl of, political character of; 30.
Marcelline, John, petition of; 160.
March, Lord, play by; 81.
Marcha:
  Galfridus de, witness; 91.
  —— Thorold, brother of; ib.
Margate; 116.
Marham, Johannes, junior; 173.
Marie Antoinette, Queen, statement relative to; 56.
Mariot:
  Peter, of Huntingtone, grants by and to; 61, 62, 63.
  —— Robert, son of; 61, 62.
  —— Matthew, son of, and Margery his wife, grants by; 63.
Marischal:
  Earl; 44.
Markar, Petrus; 229.
Markbam, Thos.; 122.
Marle, battle of; 10.
Marlborough:
  Duke of; 126.
  —— returns to England; 116.
  Earl of; 85.
  —— letters of; 11, 19.
Marlow; 187.
Maronites, Prince of the; 205.
Marrett, Mr.; 240.
Marriage, licenses for; 295.
Marseilles, Lazaret at; 55.
Marshal, John, Earl; 274.
Marshalsea, prison of; 269.
Marsham, Sir John, letter of; 241.
Marten, Richard, petition of; 292.
Martin:
  V., Pope; 302.
  Henry, proceedings against; 4.
  Sir Henry; 248.
  —— report by; 291.
  —— petition to; 290.
  Richard; 251.
Marton, deeds relating to; 91.
Martyn, Edw., letters of; 148.
Mary:
  Queen, proclamation by; 182.
  —— marriage of; ib.
  of Modena, at Reading; 200.
  II., Queen, notification to; 57.
  Princess; 276.
  Queen of Scots, household of; 303.
  —— proceedings against; 251, 303.
  See Scotland, Queen of.
Marvell, Andrew, sermon by; 285.
Maseres, M. S.; 304.

Mason:
  Mr.; 131.
  —— petition of; 11.
  Henry; 241.
  Sir Rich., entertains the King; 12.
Massareene, Earl of, statement by; 56.
Massey, family of; 138.
Massie, Richard, conveyance to; 137.
Massy, Willielmus; 229.
Masterson, Rob.; 41.
Mather, Increase, memorial presented by; 31.
Mathewe, John, amenity to; 94.
Mathew, Sir Toby, report concerning; 185.
Mauduit:
  Johannes, land of; 68.
  William; 69.
  —— Isabella, daughter of; ib.
Maulunel:
  Robert; 62.
  —— Henry, son of, grant to; 62.
Maulyverer, Mr., Lord Dunblane's tutor, letter to; 13.
Maxwell, —; 99.
May:
  Joseph, election of; 201, 202.
  Thomas, schoolmaster; 200, 226.
Maydenhede; 174.
Maydenhythe; 171, 174.
Mayds Morton, letter dated at; 166.
Maydwell, Sam., letter of; 10.
Mayllorsays, manor of; 154.
Maynard:
  Lord, petition signed by; 21.
  John; 237.
  Thomas, petition of; 37.
  W., letter of; 11.
Mayne:
  intelligence from; 251.
  Simon, deceased in the Tower; 3.
  proceedings against; 4.
Maynesforth, John, vicar; 208.
Maynwaringe:
  Thos., letter of; 210.
  Sir Thomas, letter of; 215, 216.
Mayo:
  —, reported to hold a conventicle; 15.
  Mr., reported to hold a conventicle; 16.
Mayott:
  Mary; 197.
  Sarah; 198.
Mead:
  Mr., his meeting house in Stepney; 16.
  Will., of Cornhill, reported to attend a conventicle; ib.
Meadowe, Sir Philip, treatise by; 10, 11.
Mecklenburg, Charles, Duke of, letter of; 301.
Mediterranean, naval expedition to the; 40.
Meere, John, sentence on; 160.
Meklyden, hermitage of St. Ninian in; 74.
Melfort:
  Earl of, his blind confidence in Scotch loyalists; 23.
  —— letter to; 23.
  —— secretary of; 25.
Melshbourne, letter dated at; 137.

Melton, of Ashton, family of ; 43.
Mendham, John, saddler; 118.
Mendip, forest of ; 239.
Mennes, Sir Jo. ; 8.
Mennill, family of; 43.
Méon, Jean ; 58.
Merchant-Tailors, Company of, petition to ; 292.
Merdeffen, lands in ; 70..
Meredith :
 Mr., Sir W. Temple's secretary, letter of ; 13.
 Roger, letter of ; 20.
Merioneth ; 140, 146.
 sheriff of, petition for exemption of the ; 136.
Merrick :
 John, elected to a scholarship; 205.
 Robert, faculty for pluralities, grant to; 294.
Mershe, John, letter of ; 306.
Merton, monastery of, library of the ; 231.
Mertone, Walter de ; 231.
Mewe, Dr. Peter, gift by ; 196.
Mexborough, Lord and Lady; 78.
M. I., letter of; 259.
Michelburne, Col. John, petition of ; 37, 38.
Michell ; 263, 264.
 Sir Francis, degradation of; 275.
Micklethwaite, Dr., complaints of ; 288.
Miclebric, Adam de, witness; 57.
Midford, R., letter of ; 27.
Midgley, right of common in ; 126.
Middleborough ; 293.
Middlesex :
 concealed lands in ; 145.
 petition from ; 240.
 sheriffs of ; 251.
 Earl of, committed to the Tower ; 6, 222.
Middle Temple :
 preferments in the ; 111.
 society of ; 288.
Middleton :
 bailiff's accounts at ; 154.
 letter dated at ; 28.
 Anne, petition of; 4.
 Earl of ; 105.
 ―― receives the custody of Argyll ; 2.
 Peter, at Killvinton, letter of intelligence to ; 25.
 T.; 8.
 Thos., prisoner in the Gatehouse ; 4.
 Mr. ; 36, 301.
Mildmay :
 Henry, sentence on; 4.
 Sir Walter; 145, 163.
Milford Haven, landing of Henry VII. at ; 274.
Militia, debates relative to ; 42.
Mille, Will., enquiry concerning ; 160.
Millington, Gilb., proceedings against ; 4.
Milne, William, witness ; 72.
Milton :
 (Kent) rights of oyster fishing in ; 9.
 Christopher ; 209.
Milward, Stephen, information against ; 161.

Minshall, Mr., at Bourton, Papist ; 166.
Mint :
 Armoury of the, fees and salaries in the ; 250.
 office of Master of the ; 20.
Missop, ―, plays produced by ; 79.
Mitcham, "Monster" seen at ; 282.
Mitchell, Andrew, foreign correspondence of; 47.
Mitforde :
 Alexander ; 75.
 John de : 71.
 ―― Margaret, daughter of ; ib.
 Robert of ; 75.
 ―― daughter of ; ib.
 Robert de, grant to ; 68.
Mitforth :
 Bartram ; 160.
 ―― Jane, widow of, petition by ; ib.
Mochrun, lord of ; 150.
Modbury :
 parishioners of, petition by ; 158.
 church of ; ib.
Modyford, Sir Tho., case of ; 8.
Moffet, Mr.; 131.
Mogge, Will. ; 176.
Mold, documents relating to ; 146.
Monk, General ; 37, 92, 212.
Monmouth :
 concealed lands in ; 145.
 Duke of, attainted ; 199.
 ―― order signed by ; 11.
 ―― petition to ; 197.
 ―― the King's affection for him ; 9.
Monmouthshire ; 140.
 charitable uses in ; 139.
Monouse, Sir Humphrey, letter of ; 22.
Monopolies, attacked by Parliament ; 98.
Monson :
 John, petition by ; 11.
 ―― petition of ; 290.
Mont, St. André, plan of the camp at ; 39.
Montagu, ― ; 79.
Montague :
 Mr., letters to ; 19.
 Sir Henry, Lord Chief Justice ; 289.
 R., letters of ; 19.
Moor Park, lands at ; 92.
Moore, Joseph, player ; 185.
 Lieut.-Govr. of Jamaica ; 45.
 Mr. ; 131.
 Thomas, letter to ; 277.
Mordant, John, prisoner in the Fleet ; 247.
Mordaunt, Henry, letter of ; 99.
More :
 Lady Catherine, reported to attend a conventicle ; 15.
 Rich., election of ; 180, 181.
 Thomas, letter to ; 268.
 Sir Thomas, life of ; 275.
 ―― work by ; 238.
Morefelde :
 manor of ; 74.
 deed dated at ; ib.
Morell, ― ; 108.
Morewood ; 111.

INDEX. 355

Morgan:
  Colonel; 40.
  Mrs.; 179.
  Anthony, appointment of; 241.
  Sir Henry, allegations against; 13.
  brother-in-law of; 32.
Morice, Sir Will., warrants by; 2, 3, 5, 6.
Moris, Robertus; 172.
Morland:
  Sir S., letter of; 20.
  —— petition of;
Morle, lands in; 73.
Morley. See Agbrigg.
Mornay, Ph. de, Sieur de Plessis; 35.
Morocco:
  envoy to; 76.
  King of, letter of; 288.
Morre, Fraunces; 235.
Morrell, Hugh, petition of; 291.
Morrice, James, commentary by; 40.
Morris:
  Capt., his company; 190.
  Mr.; 131.
Morton; 137.
  church of; 90.
  grant of free chace in; 119.
  lead mines at; 145.
  Guy de; ib.
  Hen. de; ib.
  Mr.; 131.
Morys, Robertus, mayor of Reading; 174.
Moryson, Francis, Commissioner of Virginia; 19.
Morzania, Sir Andrew de, witness; 150.
Mosely, Will., certificate for; 214.
Motte, Peter de la, petition of; 290.
Mounson:
  William, Lord; 4.
  —— sentence on; ib.
Mount:
  Alexander, Earl of, letter of; 35.
  Hugh, Earl of, bond of; 11.
Mountagu:
  Edw. Lord, letter of; 12.
  Marquis of; 75.
Mountjoy:
  Lord; 286.
  —— letter of; 251.
Mount Morris, Lord; 49.
  —— speech of; 293.
Moyer, Sam., committed to the Tower; 3.
Moyl, ——, witness; 142.
Mullins, Mr.; 291.
Multon, Richard de; 69.
Mumby, court rolls of; 139.
Munchausen, Baron, letter of; 44.
Munro, Alex., letters of; 55.
Munster:
  letters dated at; 45.
  Presidency, Court of; 8.
  settlement of; 133.
  treaty of; 234.
Murlegan, lands of; 143.
Murphy, ——, an actor; 78.

Murray:
  Earl of, son of; 135.
  Duncan, attestation by; 150.
  James, report by; 304.
  "Little," reported to frequent a conventicle; 15.
  William, Solicitor-General, examination of; 49.
Murton:
  Anthony, mortgagee; 75.
  Lenert, of Berwick; ib.
Muscamp:
  Robert de, grant to; 58.
  coheiresses of; ib.
Musgrave:
  Sir Christ., attitude of; 27, 28, 29.
  —— receives the surrender of Carlisle; 29.
  Sir Philip; 84, 86.
Mush:
  John, his mission to Rome 296, 297.
  —— letters of and to; 263, 264, 268, 278, 279, 302.
Muskerry, Lord, killed in action; 85.
Mussipont; 263.
Myddelton:
  Sir Hugh, suit against; 156, 157.
  Sir Thos., letter of; 148.
Myldmey, Henry, letters of; 100, 102.
Myller, ——, letter of; 98.
Mynatt, Th., clerk of court; 165.
Myryman, Thomas; 177.

N.

Nacklin, Mr. Robert, in Dalby, reported to attend a meeting house; 16.
Nailer, James, petition of; 39.
Nairne, Mr. James, letter of; 49.
Nang, P., letter to; 282.
Naples; 265.
  letters dated at; 266, 269.
  English prisoners at; 270.
Naseby, battle of; 92.
Nash:
  Tho., letter of; 306.
  —— obscene poems by; 272.
  —— play by; 132.
Naunton, Robert, case of; 158.
Navarre, King of, letter of; 292.
Navy:
  Commissioners of the; 8.
  debate on the state of the; 115.
  discourse concerning the; 42.
  papers relating to the; 7.
  state of the; 40.
  report on the state of the; 131.
  report on the dockyards of the; 8.
Navy office; 11.
Naylor:
  Rev. Fermor; 155.
  Thos.; 126.

z 2

Neale:
    George, letter of; 12.
    —— brother of; *ib.*
    Thos., letter of; 20.
    —— the Mastership of the Mint for; 20.
Neckar:
    M., character of; 55.
    —— his controversy with Caloune; *ib.*
Negus, Francis, letter of; 105, 107.
Neitherthorpe, letter dated at; 36.
Nelson, Mr.; 263.
Nerbona, Stephen de, grant by; 128.
Nest, Mr., conventicle held by; 15.
Nethercott, Charles, letter of; 77.
Netherlands:
    intended export of corn to; 95, 96.
    proposals for peace in the; 296.
Neusum:
    Geoffrey de; 68.
    —— Richard, son of; *ib.*
    Simon de, grants to and by; *ib.*
Nevill:
    A.; 135.
    Hen., election of; 193.
    —— committed to the Tower; 6.
    Sir Henry; 286.
Neville:
    Edward, descent of; 149.
    Col. Richard, high sheriff of Reading; 223.
    Sir Christ., letter to; 32.
Nevyll:
    Anth., conveyance to; 133.
    John, letter of; 120, 121.
New, Esquire, reported to attend a conventicle; 15.
Newark:
    letter dated at; 82.
    Protestant massacres reported at; 28.
Newbery, John, bookseller; 50.
Newborne Church, inventory of; 75.
Newbury; 171.
    sessions at; 213.
Newcastle; 92.
    corporate seal of; 72.
    deeds dated at; 70.
    foreign trade with; 291.
    lease of coal mines near; 70.
    letter dated at; 10.
    mayor of; 62.
    petition of, for a free Parliament; 27.
    Pilgrim Street in; 73.
    the Sand Hill in; 72.
    House, letter dated at; 126.
    -on-Tyne, pleas held at; 233.
    Duke of; 46, 51, 100, 124, 126.
    —— calls out the militia of Yorkshire; 26.
    —— characters of his children; 22.
    —— correspondence of; 43, 44, 45, 47.
    —— his regiment of foot; 26.
    —— intended seizure of; 30.
    —— letters of and to; 20, 22, 27.
    —— notes by; 26.
    —— petition signed by; 21.
    H., Duke of, letter of and to; 12.
    Duchess of; 13.

Newcomen:
    George, intelligence from; 35.
    Mr.; 131.
    Th., sermons by; 235.
    Sir Thomas, conditions granted to; 37.
Newel, Sam., memorial presented by; 31.
New England:
    intelligence from; 167.
    governor of; *ib.*
    memorial of the Dissenters in; 31.
New Forest; 11.
    condition of the; 9.
    return of the deer in; 14.
    salary of warden of the; 12
Newfoundland:
    list of fishing vessels to; 8.
    state of the revenue of; 38.
Newgate; 52, 159.
Newhall House; 92.
Newhaven, Viscount; 151.
Newington, letters dated at; 123.
Newman:
    John; 214.
    head burgess of Reading; 221.
Newmarket; 308.
    Charles II. at; 104.
    letters dated at; 9, 13.
    racing at; 13.
    the Court at; 9.
    William III. at; 109.
Newminster, John, Abbot of; 74.
Newport:
    Lord; 84.
    Pagnell, letter dated at; 100.
    royalist advance on; *ib.*
Newry, burnt by the Papists; 35.
Newshame, manor of; 73.
Newsome:
    deed dated at; 71.
    lands in; *ib.*
Newton:
    Mr.; 131.
    Thomas; 185.
New York, governor of; 166.
Nicholas:
    Christin, mayor of Reading; 176.
    —— Master of the Guild of Reading; 227.
    Mr.; 279.
    IV., Pope, Bull of; 150.
    Secretary; 210.
    Sir Edw., order by; 2.
    —— warrant by; 2, 3.
Nicholls, Francis, commission to; 26.
Nichols, ——, of Wansted, reported to attend a conventicle; 16.
Nimeguen, peace of; 20, 41.
Nivernois, Duke de; 54.
Noel, Edw., letter of; 11.
Nonsuche, the Court at; 135.
Norays:
    Henry de, of Clawurtt; 90.
    —— Alex., son of, grant by; *ib.*

Norfolk :
  address to James II. from ; 106.
  Commission of the Peace in ; 107.
  Commissions of Array for ;. 99, 100, 101.
  Commissioners for charitable uses in ; 96.
  —— for compounding in ; 104.
  —— for compositions of knighthood in ; 97.
  —— for taxation in ; 103.
  compositions for knighthood in ; 96, 97.
  county affairs of ; 11, 12.
  direction for parliamentary elections in ; 105, 106.
  high constables of ; 97, 99.
  justices of ; 100, 107, 108.
  Lord Lieutenant of ; 99, 105, 106.
  Deputy Lieutenants of; 100, 105, 106, 107.
  muster master of ; 99.
  petition from the county of ; 101, 102.
  the committee for; 101, 102, 103.
  repeal of the Test Act in ; 107.
  sheriff of ; 100.
  trained bands of ; 99–105.
  militia of ; 105, 106.
  Dean and Chapter of, forfeited lands of ; 103.
  Duke of ; 35, 303.
  —— attitude of ; 107.
  —— Earl Marshal ; 38.
  —— letters of and to ; 94, 105, 106, 107, 108.
Norham :
  county of ; 75.
  lands in ; 72.
Norice :
  Dr. ; 263.
  D. ; 262.
Normavell, John, vicar of Sandal ; 120.
Norreis, Master ; 176.
Norrens, Henry ; 91.
Norreys, Lord, petition signed by ; 21.
Norris ; 263.
  Lord ; 163.
  —— letters of ; 287, 288.
  Henry, Lord, grant by ; 133.
  —— —— Margery, wife of ; *ib.*
Norrys, Tho., letter of ; 306.
North :
  council of the ; 120, 121.
  Lord Deputy of ; 293.
  —— ; 266, 283.
  —— Chief Justice ; 21, 22.
  Roger, Lord ; 274.
Northall ; 87.
Northallerton, intelligence through the postmaster of ; 25.
Northampton :
  county of ; 241.
  Papist cavalry reported at ; 28.
  Parliament at ; 172.
  Countess of ; 89.
  Countess of, death and funeral of ; 84.
  Earl of ; 239.

Northampton—*cont.*
  —— Constable of the Tower ; 12.
  —— creation of ; 167.
  —— counterfeit name of ; 30.
  —— letters of and to ; 10, 20, 84, 85, 251.
  Will. de Bohun, Earl of, witness ; 168.
Northamptonshire, documents relating to ; 40.
North Crawley, letter dated at ; 166.
North Dissingtone, lands in ; 73.
North End, letter dated at ; 78.
Northey, Sir Edward, counsel for Earl Danby, letter of ; 22.
North Greenhoe, chief constables of ; 100, 104.
  —— hundred of ; 101.
Northop, documents relating to ; 146.
North Shields, theatre at ; 81.
Northumberland ; 257.
  deeds relating to ; 67 *et seq*, 75.
  intelligence from ; 36.
  rebellion in ; 126.
  sheriffs of ; 74.
  Countess of, letter of ; 19.
  Duke of, letter to ; 284.
  —— play by ; 81.
  —— rebellion of ; 182.
  Duchess of ; 76.
  Lady ; 77.
Northumberland House, letter dated at ; 76.
Northumbria, documents relating to ; 58.
North Wales, rumoured invasion of ; 44.
Northwold, manor of ; 103.
Northwood, Barningham, letter dated at ; 306.
Northy, William, of Old Ford, reported to attend a meeting house ; 16.
Norton :
  Baron, removed to the King's Bench ; 104.
  John, reported to hold a Quaker's meeting ; 15, 16.
  Mr. ; 131.
  —— opinion of ; 129.
  Robertus de ; 57.
  Tho., letter of ; 254, 283.
Norwich ; 45, 94.
  attitude of the magistrates of ; 114.
  conventicle of non-jurors in ; *ib.*
  Christ Church in ; 97.
  Church lands of ; 270.
  Exchequer payments at ; 250.
  letter dated at ; 99.
  muster of the trained bands at ; 105.
  restoration of the Cathedral in ; 97.
  sessions at ; 100.
  visitors to diocese of ; 286.
  Bishop of ; 95, 96, 107, 113, 155.
  —— dispossessed ; 114.
  —— expected death of ; 13.
  —— letter to ; 277.
  John Parkhurst, Bishop of ; 271.
  Castle, letter dated at ; 106.
  —— Grand Jury Chamber at ; *ib.*
  Col. Sir John ; 92.

Norwich—*cont.*
Dean and Chapter of; 97.
See of, expenses in; 271.
Norys, John; 175.
Nottingham:
intended meeting of the Protestant peers at; 30.
letters dated at; 27.
loyalty of; 126.
troops sent to; *ib.*
Earl of; 273, 289.
—— his pension in arrear; 13.
—— letters of; 13, 35.
Charles, Earl of; 253.
H. Finch, Earl of, Lord Chancellor, treatise by; 307.
Lord, letter of; 25.
Notts:
Deputy Lieutenants of; 124, 126.
documents relating to; 146.
Nottinghamshire:
Lord Lieutenancy of; 122.
Lord Lieutenant of; 124.
possessions of Rufford Abbey in; 119.
riots in; 50.
"N. P.":
letter of warning by; 11.
Noy:
Sir William, Attorney-General; 272.
—— opinion by; 212.
—— letter of; 141.
Nugent, Hon. Will.; 37.
Nutfield, letter dated at; 238.
Nyxe:
Thomas, of Lobthorpe, quit-claim to; 66.
—— Katherine, wife of; *ib.*

O.

Oakham; 92.
Oakhampton, election at; 13.
Oakley Park, ranger of; 134.
Oates, Titus; 104.
Oaths, administrations of; 307.
Oatlands, the Court at; 123, 148.
O'Brien, Lord, letter of; 23.
Octavius, papal Nuncio, letter of; 261.
Odiham; 186.
Ofchinche; 278.
Offarell:
Irriell, petition of; 160.
Boye; *ib.*
Oggel:
Gilbert de, witness; 68.
Roger de, witness; *ib.*
Ogilvie:
Lord, attempted arrest of; 46.

Ogilvie—*cont.*
—— French regiment of; *ib.*
—— his Scotch regiment in Holland; 47.
Ogle:
Ewyn, Lord of; 74.
Ralph, Lord, witness; 73.
Luke, letter of; 12.
Colonel; 40.
Earl of, letter of; 10.
Lord, letters of; 8, 9.
Lady. *See* Newcastle, Duchess of.
William of; 74.
Ohio, fighting on the; 45.
Okeham, John, commissioner; 224.
Okey, John, conveyed to the Tower; 4.
Olab, King of the Isles; 150.
Oldcorns, Mr., proposal by; 280.
Olivekrans, Joh. Paulin, Swedish plenipotentiary; 20.
Oliver, Richard, a dangerous prisoner; 6.
Onyon, Matthew; 141.
Orange Mal, conventicle held in the house of; 15.
Orange:
Prince of; 20, 202.
—— about to visit England; 19.
—— address to; 76.
—— counterfeit name of; 30.
—— dedication to; 240.
—— expected landing of; 25.
—— fortifies Exeter; 26.
—— instruments signed by; 31.
—— marching towards Reading; 27.
—— summons to Convention signed by; 38.
—— letters of and to; 9, 10, 11, 19, 20, 44.
Orde, William de, release to; 72.
Ordnance:
office of, order from the; 25.
—— fees and salaries in the; 250.
Orkney, Lord; 114.
Orme, Robert, treatises by; 53.
Ormond:
Duke of; 22.
—— present to; 179.
—— his health drunk; 49.
—— his life threatened; 8.
—— letter of; 307.
—— lord-lieutenant of Ireland, letters of; 20.
Earl of; letter to; 228.
—— reported to be planning Danby's overthrow; 12.
Orpyd, John, election of; 180.
Orrery, Earl of, letters of; 8, 9, 10, 11.
Orwell, Lord, play by; 81.
Osborne:
Charles; 8.
—— indebtedness of; 35.
—— letters of; 12, 19, 20, 26, 36.
Sir Edward; 122.
John, a loan by; 291.
Peter, treatise by; 40.
Robert, letter of; 95.
Sir Thomas, grant to; 8, 41.
—— Treasurer of the Navy; 8.

Osborne—*cont.*
　Sir Thomas, sworn of the Privy Council; 8.
　Lady, letters to; 7.
　Lady Bridget, letter to; 9.
　Lady Marthe, proposed marriage of; 12.
Osgoodcross, subsidy roll for; 120.
Osnaburgh:
　bishopric of; 48.
　Bishop of; 52.
Ossory, Earl of, letters of; 20.
Oswestry, hundred of; 140.
Otter-hounds, the King's under keeper of; 292.
Ougel, John of Freynish, grant by; 62.
Ourd, Edw., letter of; 10.
Ovenden, manor of, court rolls of; 126.
Overbury, Sir Nich., letter of; 148.
Overton:
　Col. Rob., prisoner in the Tower; 3, 6.
　Rob. de, witness; 129.
Ovyngham, parish of; 74.
Ovyngtone, William, bond by; 73.
Owen:
　—, a New England Minister; 11.
　David, witness; 122.
　Hugh, letter of; 148.
　John, of Wotton, forced loan from; 211.
　Lewis; 136.
Owthorpe, letter dated at; 125.
Oxford; 27, 173, 178.
　bishopric of; 135.
　Charles I. at; 216.
　All Souls College at, charter of; 282.
　—— warden of; 225.
　Christ Church College in; 124, 155.
　—— Dean of; 155.
　—— irregularities in; 258.
　—— Proctor for; 285.
　Downing College in; 208.
　Magdalen College in; 140, 141.
　—— fellows of, letter of; 267.
　Magdalen Hall in; 213.
　New College in; 242, 272.
　Oriel College in; 217.
　Pembroke College in; 207.
　Queen's College, letter dated at; 244.
　St. John's College in; 183, 184, 189. 193, 197, 198, 204, 205, 206, 207, 213, 217, 225, 226.
　—— president and fellows of; 222, 223, 225.
　University College in; 218, 241.
　Council of War at; 220, 222.
　orders dated at; 220.
　diocese of; 255.
　document dated at; 91.
　election of town clerk in; 57.
　license dated at; 119.
　letter dated at; 240, 283.
　mayor and corporation of; 31.
　order dated at; 215.
　royalist forces at; 100.
　treasonable libel uttered at; 52.
　University of; 256, 302.
　vacant bishopric of; 155.

Oxford—*cont.*
　Vice-Chancellor of; 225.
　—— and Mayor of; 52.
　Earl of; 95.
　—— case of; 155.
　—— letters of; 42, 43.
　Lord, petition signed by; 21.
　Dukes of; 42, 43.
Oxfordshire, grant of lands in; 133.

P.

Paddon:
　Mr.; 240.
　Will., certificate by; 191.
Page:
　Mr.; 197.
　—— indictment against; 50.
　Will., schoolmaster, of Reading; 186, 189, 191, 223, 225.
　—— suit by; 194, 195.
Paget:
　Lord; 259.
　—— Will.; 146.
Paggnam, Colonel; 40.
Palatinate, affairs of; 301.
Palatine:
　Frederick, Elector; 301, 305.
　—— marriage of; 287.
　Counties; 250.
Palgrave:
　J., letter of; 306.
　Mr., reader in the Temple; 306.
Palmer:
　Chas., project by; 38.
　John; 225.
　Sir Tho., case of; 162.
Panton, Colonel; 40.
Papists, intelligence respecting, in London; 17.
Parcho, Abbot and Convent of, grant to; 91.
Parent, Ricardus, witness; 57.
Parham:
　letter dated at; 10.
　Nic., letter of; 114.
Paris:
　ambassador to; 40.
　foreign correspondence dated at; 44.
　intelligence from; 13, 19, 20, 47, 298.
　letters dated at; 9, 10, 11, 12, 13, 19, 20, 298.
　news from; 76.
　theological faculty at; 280.
　the stage in; 79.
　work published at; 235.
　Edw., certificate by; 191.
Parkelathe, grant of fee chace in; 119.
Parker:
　—, letter of; 260.
　Abr., intelligence from; 35.
　Archbishop, letters of and to; 281, 283, 284, 285.
　John, petitions of; 4, 290.
　Sir Tho.; 117.

Parkinson:
 Edmund; 230.
 John, letters of; 240.
Parliament:
 Act of pains and penalties passed by; 4.
 army of the; 101, 189.
 Lord General of the; 189.
 assessments by the; ib.
 election of a Speaker in; 98.
 the Short, report of proceedings in; ib.
 the Long, report of proceedings in; 99, 100.
 grant of subsidies by; 84.
 office of Clerk in; 248.
 ordinance of, for levying the militia; 101, 102.
 petition to; 101.
 petition from; 130.
 proceedings in; 229.
 report of proceedings in; 38, 109, 110, 114, 115, 116.
 prorogation of; 76.
 public bills in; 246.
 proceedings in; ib.
 letter to; 288.
 Secretary of lower House of; ib.
 Serjeant-at-Arms of lower House of; ib.
Parr, Mr.; 179.
Parrell, D., letter of; 35.
Parry, Sir Thomas, ambassador to France; 287.
Parsons:
 ——, his interview with the Pope; 299.
 ——, movements of; 297.
 Father; 261, 264, 268.
 —— letters of; 259, 260, 264, 269, 278, 279, 280.
 Mr., reported to hold a conventicle; 15.
Pate, Hercy, assignment of a monopoly to; 91, 92.
Paterby:
 Eudo de, clerk, release by; 69.
 —— grant by; 70.
Patricius, filius comitis Patricii, witness; 57.
Paulett, Sir A., letter to; 245.
Paul's Cross, sermon preached at; 283.
Pawley, Richard; 218.
Pawling, Robt., expulsion of; 31.
Payne:
 ——, elected to a scholarship; 204.
 Captain, a companion of the Prince of Wales; 56.
 Ricardus, goldsmith; 175.
Peacock, Sam., letter to; 13.
Peake, Francis; 121.
Pears, Col.; 41.
Pearson, Mr.; 285.
Peck, Edw., letter of; 242.
Peddar:
 Capt.; 159.
 Toby, letter of; 97.
 —— case of; 103.
Peel Castle; 149.

Peele, Mr., vicar of Wollaston; 142.
Peers, subscriptions by; 84.
Peirson, Stephen, forfeiture of; 119.
Pelham, Henry, letter of; 44.
Pell, Valentine; 108.
Pembroke:
 Earl of; 222.
 —— marriage of his daughter; 121.
 Wm., Earl of, epitaph on; 237.
 —— witness; 119.
 Countess of; 81, 82, 84, 85, 86.
 —— complaints against her tenants; ib.
 —— her law suits; 84, 86, 88, 89, 90.
 —— her houses in Westmoreland and Craven; 85.
 —— memoirs of; 86—.
 —— subscription to the Crown by; 84.
 —— daughter of, death of; ib.
 —— her death; 244.
 —— religious poems by; 272, 273.
 and Montgomery, Earl of, death of; 87.
 Philip, Earl of, death of; 89.
Pembrokeshire; 140.
Pen, Will., in Hampshire, reported to attend a conventicle; 16.
Penbrugg, Rogerus; 171.
Pendennis, letter dated at; 242.
Penne, William, prisoner in the Tower; 7.
Pennington:
 Isaac, his death in the Tower; 3.
 —— proceedings against; 4.
 Thomas, proposal by; 35.
Penrith, Confirmation at; 84.
Penshurst, rector of; 929.
Pepys:
 S.; 8, 37.
 Samuel, statement by, relative to Tangier; 14.
Percee, J., letter of; 282.
Percy:
 Dr., letter of; 76.
 Lord Algernon; ib.
Perkyns, Willielmus; 173.
Perne, Dr. Andrew, letters of; 283, 284.
Pernecote, Will., election of; 180.
Perneys:
 Robert, grant by; 170.
 —— Alice, wife of; ib.
Pers, John, of London, election of; 180.
Persens, Will., letters of; 301.
Perth, Earl of, letter of; 23.
Peryam, Judge Will., letter of; 306.
Perys, Frere, of St. Faith's, letter of; 95.
Pesecod, family of; 138.
Peter, Simon; 174.
Peterborough:
 vacant bishopric of; 155.
 Bishop of; 22.
 William, Bishop of; ib.
 Earl of, committed to the Tower; 30.
 —— affront offered to; 4.
 —— petition of; 37.
Peters, Mr.; 184.

Peterson, Dr. Will., case of; 163.
Petraponte:
    Ricardus de, witness; 57.
    Symon de, witness; *ib.*
Petre:
    Lord, petition of; 104, 105.
    Robert, charge against; 156.
    Sir William, Royal Commissioner; 247.
Pett:
    Robert; 265.
    —— brother of; *ib.*
Pettitt, Thos., Recorder of Reading; 201.
Petyt:
    book of; 241.
    W.; 239, 240, 249.
    —— manuscript collection of; 233, 235, 236.
    —— letters of and to; 241, 242, 244.
Pexall, Ralph, Keeper of the Rolls; 139.
Peyton:
    John; 268.
    —— petition of; 35.
    Sir John; 36.
Phaire, Col. Rob., bailed; 2.
Philadelphia, return of Franklin to; 54.
Philip:
    II., body guard of; 304.
    and Mary; 120, 121.
    —— book written against; 121.
Philipot, John, Rougedragon; 225.
Phillipps:
    Francis; 272.
    John, discharged from the Tower; 5.
Phipps, Constantine; 197.
Phleak, Phelim, proceedings against; 289.
Piccioli Giulio, letter to; 279.
Pickering:
    Rich.; 284.
    Eyre of, observations on the; 307.
Piggasse, Mr.; 131.
Pile, Francis, Deputy Lieutenant of Berks; 216.
Pilgrim, Rich., transferred to the Gatehouse; 5.
Pim, Esquire, reported to frequent a conventicle; 15.
Pipe:
    Office; 8.
    Roll, preserved at Dublin; 241.
Pippard, Peter, a suspected Jacobite; 44.
Pitfield, Justice, of Hogsden, informations against Nonconformists before him; 17.
Pits, Mr. Arthur, banishment of; 298.
Pitsligo, Lord, movements of; 46.
Pitt, William, letters of; 45, 53, 54.
Pittes, Arthur, letter of; 279.
Pityngtone, Tho. de, clerk; 72.
Pius V., Bull of; 281.
Plaistow, conventicle held in; 16.
Plandon, Andr., licensed preacher; 285.
Plate, Peter; 152.
Plater, —, released on bail; 5.
Playing cards, monopoly of; 246.
Plessys:
    John de, grant by; 70.
    —— Richard, son of; *ib.*
Plombières, letters dated at; 152.

Plowden, Edmund, commissioner; 224.
Plumsted, Clement, reported to attend a conventicle; 16.
Plymouth; 50.
    Drake's voyage from; 39.
    English sailors poisoned at; 110.
    seizure of a prize-ship at; 9.
    Earl of, natural son of Charles II., his defective training; 18.
    —— allowance to; 38.
    —— letters of; 9, 10, 11, 19.
    Lady, letter of; 25.
Pococke:
    Edward, letter of; 240.
    Thomas, schoolmaster, 189, 190, 191, 225.
Poke, Thomas, elected to a scholarship; 197.
Poland:
    mission to; 38.
    Stephen, King of, letter of; 256.
    King of, letter of Minister of; 245.
Pole, Cardinal, letter of; 300.
Pomfret:
    measures for defending against the Irish; 28.
    Jesuit school at; 29.
    letter dated at; 122.
Pomponne, Arnauld de, letter of; 19.
Pondicherry, capture of; 54.
Pont a Mousson, Lorraine, letter dated at; 298.
Pontefract; 124.
    letter dated at; 120.
    Castle, keepership of; 122.
    Lady; 125. *See* Pomfret.
Poole:
    Arthur; 265.
    —— prisoner in the Fleet; 247.
Pope:
    the, declared a foreign enemy; 163, 164.
    —— reported communication with; 185.
    Sir Thomas; 286.
    —— and Lady; 121.
Popejoy, Mr.; 131.
Popham:
    Sir John; 135.
    —— letters of; 288, 306.
Popish Plot, the; 21, 39, 104, 105.
Pordage:
    Dr. John, stipend of; 189.
    —— pamphlet by; 192.
Porkerle, manor and vill of; 73.
Porter:
    Sir Charles, letter to; 28.
    John, committed to the Tower; 3.
Portland, Earl of, killed in action; 85.
Portman, John, transported; 4.
Portmirnoch, lands of; 143.
Portmore, letter dated at; 20.
Port Royal; 19.
Portsmouth; 171.
    charter dated at; 179.
    Drake's return to; 39.

Portsmouth—*cont.*
   letter dated at; 32.
   prize-ship at; 82.
   Duchess of, her jewels redeemed by the King; 13.
Portugal:
   ambassador of; 166.
   envoy to; 76.
   funeral of the Queen Mother of; 39.
Potter:
   Mr.; 267.
   Vinc., proceedings against; 4.
Potts, J.; 102.
Poultney, Sir William, sued for not proceeding against Nonconformists; 17.
Pound, —; 266.
Powis:
   Lord; 22.
   Lady, reflections upon; *ib.*
Powterell, Walter, trial of; 163, 164.
Poynter, Rev. James, resignation of scholarship by; 206.
Prat:
   John, of Hundington; 65.
   —— of Retford, witness; 90.
   Ralph, of Gronlay, grant by; 91.
   Walter, grant to; 90.
Pratt, Charles, letter of; 13.
Prayer Book:
   objections to the; 294.
   subscription to; 284.
Presbyterians, intelligence respecting conventicles of, in London; 16.
Prestbury; 137.
Presthope:
   Philip de; 142.
   —— Constance, widow of; *ib.*
Preston:
   Castle and manor of; 73.
   Lord, commission countersigned by; 26.
   —— suspicions of; 37.
   John, senior, of Mile End, reported to attend a meeting house; 16.
   —— junior, of Mile End, reported to attend a meeting house; *ib.*
   Sir Christopher de, arrest of; 129.
Pretender, the; 44.
Price:
   —, information against; 17.
   George; 185.
Prickett, George, letters of; 35.
Pride, Sir Thomas; 192.
Primrose, Sir Archibald; 240.
Prince, Edward, town clerk of Oxford; 57.
"Prince Magnus," letter signed by; 25.
Prinknesh, letter dated at; 136.
Privateers, papers relating to; 166.
Privy Council:
   lords of, petition to; 290.
   letters of the; 306.
   remonstrance to; 307.
Probate, valuators for; 295.
Prohibitions; 302.
   papers relating to; 156.

Proude (or Prut), John, election of; 180.
Provision, documents relating to; 236.
"Provoked Husband," the play; 77.
Prowght, John, election of; 180.
Prussia:
   foreign correspondence from; 53.
   Hanoverian treaty with; 55.
   King of, royal letters of; 45.
   Prince Henry of, hostility of; 54.
Prydeaux, Thomas, of Orcharton; 158.
Prynne:
   W.; 238.
   —— law arguments by; 232.
   —— reading by; 249.
Psalms, metrical version of; 307.
Puckering:
   H., letter of; 10.
   Sir John, Lord Keeper; 127, 160.
   —— letters of; 137, 306.
Puleston, George, letter of; 148.
Pullen, Dr.; 131.
Pultney, Lord; 78.
Punchardon:
   Rob. de, agreement by; 70.
   —— Cecily, wife of; 71.
Punig, Adam de, witness; 57.
Purbeck:
   Lord Lieutenant of; 39.
   proceedings against Papists in; *ib.*
   Viscount, letter of; 35.
   —— family of; *ib.*
Purcell, Edw., removed from the Tower; 8.
Puritans:
   a memorial from; 252.
   catechism against the; 254.
Purmat, Gilbert, of Great Hall, grant by; 60.
Purseglove, Robert, letters patent to; 303.
Pychelesthorne, rental of; 145.
Pykeringe, Christ., witness; 84.
Pylesgate, deed dated at; 72.
Pymme, Mr., speech of; 98.
Pymond, Edmund; 230.
Pynder, John le, grant to; 63.
Pyrton,—, letter to; 306.

Q.

Quakers:
   intelligence respecting the meeting houses, &c. of, in London; 16.
   position of the; 34.
Quebec:
   state of, report on the; 304.
   governor of; *ib.*
Queenborough, parliamentary election at; 20.
Queensbury:
   Duke of, his jealousy of Hamilton; 23.
   Duchess of, supposed letter of; *ib.*

Quelpington:
  Osbert de; 68.
  —— Nicholas, son of, grant by; *ib.*
  —— Matilda, daughter of; *ib.*
Quelymtone:
  Osbert de, grant by; 71.
  —— Matilda, daughter of; *ib.*
Quérouaille, Louise de, birth of her son; 9.
Quiberon Bay, letters dated from; 45.
Quin, Mr.; 131.
Quintin, Mr. Rich., reported to attend a conventicle; 16.

R.

Rabell, Mons., his healing waters; 12.
Radcliffe, Hon. Francis, levies for his troop; 27.
Radley, letter dated at; 137.
Radnorshire, elections in; 35.
Raleigh:
  Sir Walter; 246.
  —— "Apollogie" by; 234.
  —— commission for; 134.
  —— discourse by; 271.
  —— his monopoly of wines; 132.
  —— letters of; 245, 251, 288.
  —— naval treatise by; 252.
  —— trial of; *ib.*
Ramsden, Mr., a parson; 284.
Ramsey:
  Abbey, foundation charter of; 235.
  Church of Holy Trinity in; 120.
  John, offer made by, to procure a place; 13.
  —— letters of; 12, 13, 22.
  Sir John; 134.
Randolph:
  Ed., articles by; 38.
  —— letter of; 11.
Rands, Thomas, case of; 159.
Ranelagh:
  Lord, case of; 20.
  —— Treasurer of Ireland, letter of; 19.
  —— his disputes with the Council of Ireland; 12.
  —— letter of; 307.
Rasswell, Mr., reported to hold a conventicle; 15.
Rastell, Thomas, letter of; 35.
Rastold, Master; 175.
Ratclif, Sir George, proceedings against; 99.
Ratcliffe:
  Lieut.-Col. Thomas, letter to; 26.
  T. M., letter of; 279.
Ratenham, lands of; 143.
Ratisbon, Diet of; 245.
Ravenscroft, Mr. James; *ib.*
Rawson, Rev. Jos., letter of; 136.

Rawsthorn, Edw., letters of; 145.
Rawtenstall, manor of, court rolls of; 126.
Rayer, Will., proposal of, for the excise; 8.
Raymes, John, grant to; 72.
Raymond, John, election of; 181.
Raynham; 107.
Raynold, Johannes; 175.
Reackes, Mr.; 131.
Read, Reade:
  Mr., illness of; 123.
  —— letter to; 243.
  Compton, elected to a scholarship; 197.
  Hannah, in New England; 98.
  Susan; *ib.*
  Thomas, letter of; 243.
Reading:
  report of the MSS. of; 167.
  catalogue of the MSS. of; 196.
  "History of"; 207.
  heraldic arms of; 225.
  order dated at; 220.
  aspersion on the town of; 189, 190.
  Earl of; 176.
  apprentices of; 186.
  cloths of; 214, 215.
  weavers of; 168.
  coblers of; 218.
  lottery in; 186.
  law business relating to; 174, 175.
  payment of burgess-money in; 176, 177.
  hearth money in; 218.
  trade companies of; 224.
  provisions bought in; 176.
  regulation of trade in; 214, 219.
  puritan party in; 218.
  the common beam in; 175, 208.
  disputes in the town council of; 193.
  clothiers and dyers of; 182, 184, 188.
  deeds relating to; 168, 169, 170.
  case of witchcraft in; 185.
  great frost in; 178.
  the plague in; 183, 186, 190, 196, 209, 213.
  Dutch prisoners at; 218.
  excise levied in; 216.
  coach-hire to Oxford from; 205.
  rates of water-carriage from, to London; 210.
  town charities of; 184, 185.
  common chest of; 179.
  market tolls in; 190.
  burgesses of; 169, 170.
  contributions to the Parliament from; 189, 216, 217.
  Court of Record at; 208.
  unlawful subsidy (1626), assessed on; 184.
  lighting of; 192.
  Register of the Acts of; 179.
  liberty of the burgesses in London; 182, 183.
  fire-engines of; 179, 195, 196.
  dearness of corn in; 206, 207.
  inoculation in; 207.
  provisions for the Justices at; 203, 204.

Reading—*cont.*
 payment of Chepingavell in; 175, 176, 180.
 publication of libels in; 208.
 Court leet of; 210.
 sale of tobacco in; 185.
 players at; 185, 210.
 Mulberry plants for; 212.
 perambulation of; 193, 200.
 ship-money in; 186.
 contributions to the Royalist forces in; 216, 219, 220.
 Corporation Act in; 195.
 jurisdiction of the Bishop of Salisbury in; 205.
 petition for peace by; 187.
 plan of; 207.
 fairs in; 198, 199.
 loans to the Crown by; 187, 188, 189, 195, 196, 215.
 prices of fish at; 171, 172, 176.
 wages of members of Parliament for; 171, 172, 177.
 the poor-rates in; 209.
 benevolence paid by; 178.
 defence of; 188, 189, 223.
 accounts of the common chest of; 171, 172.
 during the civil wars; 187-190, 215-220, 225.
 the Restoration in; 194, 195, 211.
 the Revolution in; 202.
 rejoicing for the peace of Ryswick at; 204.
 rope dancers expelled from; 190.
 disorderly persons in; 214.
 unlawful games in; 212.
 payments to wrestlers at; 173.
 to archers at; 173.
 to minstrels at; 171, 172, 173, 174.
 to players at; 172, 173, 174, 177, 178.
 town musicians of; 183.
 reform of alehouses in; 222.
 swan-mark of; 181.
 game of swans in; 176.
 assessments for taxes in; 209, 210.
 proceedings by *quo warranto* against; 209, 210.
 compositions for Knighthood in; 184, 214.
 the King's Evil in; 186.
 assize of arms in; 170, 171.
 charities of; 211.
 benefactions to; 180, 209.
 Regulations and Ordinances of; 224.
 High Steward of; 181, 183, 184, 191, 192, 193, 194, 195, 197, 199, 200, 207, 212, 217, 218, 221, 222.
 constables of; 173.
 serjeants of; 190.
 bell-man of; 192.
 cripple-carrier of; 195, 203.
 governor of; 178, 187, 188.
 recorder of; 200, 201, 204, 205.
 oaths of the corporation officers of; 182.
 town clerk of; 201, 217, 219.

Reading—*cont.*
 resignations in the Town Council of; 188.
 admission of burgesses for; 181.
 mayors of; 168, 169, 170, 171, 172, 173, 174, 175, 176, 178, 179, 181, 185, 191, 192, 193, 194, 195, 196, 197, 198, 199, 200, 201, 202, 214, 217, 218, 226, 227.
 —— election of; 200.
 —— salary of; 203.
 aldermen of; 187, 200, 201, 202.
 dismissal of alderman of; 189.
 aldermen deprived in; 201, 202.
 chamberlain of; 211.
 sub-chamberlain of; *ib.*
 swanherd of; 177.
 chief fireman of; 196.
 seneschal of the Gild of; 210.
 Prior of; 211.
 Princess Amelia at; 205.
 —— Anne at; 201.
 Queen Anne proclaimed at; 204.
 Charles I. at; 184, 215, 220.
 Charles II. at; 195, 211, 218.
 Cromwell at; 178.
 Edward VI. at; 182.
 George II. proclaimed at; 205.
 George III. proclaimed at; 206.
 James II. at; 200.
 —— proclaimed in; 199.
 Catharine of Braganza at; 197, 200.
 Mary of Modena, at 200.
 Philip and Mary at; 182.
 William III. at; 202, 203.
 Duke of York at; 198.
 the Lord Chancellor at; *ib.*
 Greenland in; 215.
 the Abbey Mill in; 224.
 the Hallowed Brook in; 183, 224.
 Gardener's Crosse in; 176, 177.
 Jerard's Cross in; 177.
 le Flexchepynge in; 174.
 the Forbery in; 198.
 the Forlorne Hope in; 202.
 Abbey of; 178.
 order dated at; 223.
 and Convent of; 170.
 Abbot of; 168, 169, 172, 174, 180, 181, 210, 211, 212.
 All Hallow's Chapel in; 177.
 parish of St. Giles in; 191.
 ——, rector of St. Giles of; 168.
 Grey Friars Church in; 181.
 ——, Church of St. Laurence in; 169, 174, 178, 189, 203, 205, 208, 209, 226.
 St. Mary's Church in; 173, 183, 191.
 rectory of St. Mary of; 168.
 conventicles in; 212, 219.
 Archiepiscopal visitation at; 185.
 Episcopal visitation at, 205.
 charters of; 168, 201, 202, 205, 208, new charter for; 186, 192, 193, 196.
 confirmation of the charter of; 178, 179.
 articles of the charter of; 182.
 surrender of the charter of; 190, 219.

Reading—*cont.*
  expenses of confirming the charter of; 172.
  town hall of; 192.
  the town hall not to be let for entertainments; 203, 205, 210.
  Guildhall of; 171, 173, 174, 175.
  Council Chamber of; 178.
  Broad Street in, shambles in; 219.
  Castle Street in; 175.
  High Street in; 168, 176.
  Orte Lane in; 195, 200.
  the hospital in; 182.
  the comptor of; 178, 188.
  la Pyndfold in; 174.
  house of correction in; 182, 214, 225.
  cucking stool in; 191.
  le Pyllory in; 174, 185.
  the stokks in; 174.
  the High Cross in; 173.
  Leeche, almshouse in; 222.
  Portmannesbrok, meadow in; 169.
  the Bere Inn at; 175, 176, 178, 200.
  Le Belle Inn at; 173, 176, 177.
  the George Inn at; 177.
  the "Golden Bear" in; 205.
  the Shipp Inn at; 179.
  corporate seal of; 197, 227.
  the corporation mace of; 178, 180, 181, 190, 191, 194, 207, 211.
  musters at; 175, 177, 181, 182, 183, 184, 187, 190, 209, 210, 213, 216, 222, 223.
  troops quartered in; 197, 209, 212, 220, 221.
  spoliations by soldiers in; 216, 217.
  the Free School of; 182, 184, 185, 186, 189, 190, 191, 192, 193, 194, 195, 196, 197, 206, 207, 218, 222, 223, 225, 226.
  Blue School, boys of; 206.
  —— payments to scholars in; 193.
  —— schoolmaster of; 221.
  parliamentary elections at; 180, 181, 182, 186, 189, 190, 192, 197, 199, 209, 221.
  return of Members of Parliament for; 173.
  elections by ballot at; 205.
  municipal elections in; 211.
Reason, Mr., reported to assist at a conventicle; 15.
R. B., letter of; 279.
R. [or P.] B., letter of; 278.
"R. C.," letter of; 251, 261.
Rebyll, Margaret, marriage of; 187.
Records:
  keeper of the; 239, 240.
  clerk of the; 239.
  fees for searching remitted; *ib.*
Recusants:
  return of, in several dioceses; 155.
  proceedings against; 238.
  compositions for; 242.
Reddriff, —, reported to hold a conventicle; 16.

Rede:
  John, bailed; 2.
  Will., election of; 180.
Redhod:
  Ralph, of Hundington; 62.
  —— Avicia, daughter of, quitclaim by; *ib.*
  —— Christiana, widow of, quitclaim by; *ib.*
Redmore, battle of; 274.
Reede, F. de, letters of; 9, 12.
Reeve, Mr., schoolmaster; 226.
Reeves:
  Mr.; 131.
  —— schoolmaster; 191.
Regent, the Prince, address to; 208.
Reide, Johannes, grant to; 74.
Religious houses, valuation of lands of the; 250.
Remyngtone, John, letters of attorney by; 71.
Renalow, Lady, reported to frequent a conventicle; 15.
Renniger, Dr.; 237.
Requests:
  the Court of; 275.
  Master of the; 134, 154, 231.
Reresby, Sir John, governor of York, taken prisoner; 27.
Retford:
  lands in; 91.
  deeds dated at; 90, 91.
  Helias de, clerk, witness; 90.
  East; 124.
Revell, Russell; 166.
Revels:
  children of the; 233.
  master of the, plays licensed by; 185.
Revesby, Abbot of; 62, 64.
Reygate, Sir John de; 64.
Reynakyns, —, charge against; 95.
Reynolds:
  John, case of; 233.
  Dr.; 258.
  Dr. Edw., Vice-Chancellor of Oxford; 225.
  Sir Carey; 123.
  R. F., letter from; 263.
  R. G., paper addressed to; 297.
Rheims; 277.
Rhine, French successes on the; 112.
Rhodes, —, recommendation of; 36.
Rhuddlan, documents relating to; 146.
Ricnelt:
  John, limner; 186.
  —— distiller; *ib.*
Rich:
  Jeremiah, a shorthand writer; 195.
  Thos., election of; 194.
  Sir Thos., portrait of; 206.
  Sir Will., candidature of; 199.
  —— election of; 202.
  Lady, letter of; 251.
  Miss Mary, play by; 81.
Richard II., 271.
  charter of; 168.
Richard III., pardon by; 73.

Richards, John, of Burghfield; 208.
Riche:
　Edm., Archbishop, life of; 276.
　Hatton, duel with; 84.
Richenildtorp, grant of land in; 57.
Richier, Mr., case of; 167.
Richardson:
　Ferd., grant of office to; 135.
　John, declaration of; 22.
　—— clerk; 73.
　Sir Thomas, funeral of his wife; 103.
Richmond:
　letter dated at; 121.
　office of feodary of; 132.
　honour of, survey of; 139.
　bailiff of; 69.
　(Yorks) parliamentary election at; 45.
　Duke of, (1680); 240.
　—— challenge sent to; 6.
　—— letters of; 55.
Richō, Willelmus cocus, witness; 57.
Rickmersworth, manor of, court-rolls of; 132.
Riddlesworth, manor of; 94.
Rider, Will., letter of; 20.
Ridley:
　family of; 138.
　Mr.; 131.
Rievaulx:
　Abbey of; 230.
　Ailred, Abbot of; 231.
　—— history by; 240.
Rigby:
　Mr.; 25.
　—— Master of Requests; 231.
Riggs:
　Edw., prisoner from the Tower; 5.
　—— discharged by *Habeus Corpus*; ib.
Riperes, Hug'iz de, witness; 57.
Ripon:
　reported to be fired by the Irish; 29.
　Dean of, proposal by; 39.
Risby, letter dated at; 32.
Rivers, Earl; 270.
Rixton, Eliz., prioress of St. Mary at Chester; 138.
Roach, Miss; 78.
Robartes:
　Foulke, prebendary; 97.
　R., letter of; 12.
Robert:
　(Rupert) Prince; 215, 216.
　son of John the Tanner, witness; 90, 91.
　the Smith of Hundington,grant to; 62.
　—— Emma, wife of; ib.
Roberts:
　Lord; 84.
　Mr., letter to; 85.
　—— John, safe conduct for; 27.
　Thos., discharged from the Tower; 5.
Robertson:
　Colonel Adrian, pay of his regiment; 40.
　E. R. G.; 307.

Robinson; 262.
　Sir John, Lieutenant of the Tower; 2–7.
　—— alleged neglect of his duties at the Tower; 12.
　Sir Thomas, correspondence of; 47.
　Richard, treatise by 303.
　Will., high sheriff of Yorkshire; 36.
Robottom, —, released on bail; 5.
Robson, Mr.; 239.
Roche:
　Lord, claim of; 163.
　Reginald, Abbot of, witness; 91.
Rochester:
　See of; 255.
　Bishop of, his resignation as Ecclesiastical Commissioner; 30.
　Thomas Trilleck, Bishop of; 231.
　Dean of; 84, 185.
　Lord, grants to; 134.
　—— letter of; 251.
　Viscount; 273.
Rochford:
　Earl of, letter of; 44.
　—— correspondence of; 47.
Rockall, Mr.; 131.
Rodney, Sir George, *felo de se*; 134.
Roe, Owen, his death in the Tower; 3.
Rogers:
　Eliz., letter of; 36.
　Henry, letter to, intercepted; 37.
　Rich., consecration of; 284.
Rogerson, John, of Branxton; 72.
Rohaghe, grant of free chace in; 119.
Roke, lands in 73.
Rokeby:
　Ralph, Master of the Requests; 154.
　—— letters of; 306.
　Thomas, certificate by; 36.
Rolf, Nich., petition of; 307.
Rolles:
　Mr.; 212.
　letter dated at; 240.
Rolls:
　chapel of the; 238.
　Keeper of the; 133.
　—— ——, in the Tower; 139.
　Master of the; 139, 157.
　—— —— papers relating to the office of; 19.
Rolt, Robert, letter of; 306.
Romare, William, Earl of, letter of; 59.
Rome:
　Appeals to; 239.
　English College at; 301.
　constitutions of the; 302.
　English students in; 269.
　letters dated at; 153, 260, 278, 301.
Rook, Admiral; 112.
Rookeby, Jacob, letter of; 27.
Rookwood, Col.; 41.
Roos:
　Lord, letters of; 19.
　Lady; 93, 95.
　—— Katherine; 9.
Ropere, Henry, mayor of Reading; 227.
Roschild, treaty of; 10.

INDEX. 367

Rose:
  Castle, letter dated at; 84.
  Mr., a Flemish pervert, information against; 17.
Ross, John Leslie, Bishop of; 234.
Roswell, Mr., reported to hold a conventicle; 15.
Rothel, Edward I. at; 231.
Rotheram:
  farmers of the Excise at; 7.
  grant of free chace in; 119.
Rotterdam; 29.
  Jacobite agents in; 47.
  troops embarked at; 24.
Rou, Roman de; 58.
Rouen:
  merchants of; 291.
  price of coals at; ib.
Rouge Croix; 292.
Rouquillos, Don Carlos, letter of; 19.
Rowds, Chantry of, sale of; 133.
Rowe, Owen, proceedings against; 4.
Rowlandson, Mr.; 131.
"Royal Sovereign," the ship; 118.
Royse, John, of Henley, lease to; 208.
Royston, the Court at; 156.
Ruabon, court rolls of; 146.
Rudyard, Sir Benjamin, motion by; 98.
Rudyng, John, lease to; 140.
Rufford; 124, 125.
  grant of free chase in; 119.
  Abbey, Report on the MSS. at; 119 et seq.
  —— chartulary of; 119.
  —— grant of free warren to; ib.
  Abbot of, license to; ib.
Rumsey, Walter, letter of; 148.
Rupe, Reginald, Abbot of, witness; 91.
Rupert:
  Prince; 100, 147.
  —— at Banstead Downs; 12.
Ruscel, William, mayor of Reading; 169, 227.
Rush:
  Sir John; 206.
  Mountague, elected to a scholarship; ib.
  —— resignation of scholarship by; 207.
Rushe, case of; 244.
Rushen:
  Castle; 149.
  John, reported to attend a conventicle; 16.
Rushworth, John, letters of; 20.
Russell:
  —, "the funeral monger"; 42.
  Jeremiah, petition of; 36.
  Mr.; 101.
  —— counterfeit name of; 30.
Russia:
  diplomatic relations with; 55.
  Navy of; 43.
  treaty papers relating to; 44.
  Empress of; 44.
  —— request for a telescope by; 55.
Ruthen, Lord; 178.

Rutland:
  county of; 241.
  Earls of, as Lieutenants of Notts; 122.
  Earl of, letters of; 19, 22.
  —— petition signed by; 21.
  —— refusal of office by; 86.
  Henry, Earl of, witness; 119.
  Countess of, letters of; 22.
Ruvigny, M. de, his mission to England; 19.
Ryby, Margaret; 65.
Rycot, letters dated at; 13, 31.
Rydale, John de, witness; 68.
Rye:
  —; 141.
  John, transported; 4.
  House Plot; 198.
Ryevallis, Liber Sanctæ Mariæ de; 229.
Ryhil:
  Sir Thomas de; 69.
  —— Isabella, wife of; 70.
  —— Michael, son of; 69.
  —— Guischard, son of; ib.

S.

Sacheverell, Dr. Henry, case of; 117, 118.
Sackville:
  Edward; 89.
  Lord George, correspondence of; 45.
  Lady Isabella; 89, 90.
  Lady Margaret; 83.
  Sir Richard; 236.
  Lord Richard; 89.
  Rob., letter of; 306.
  House, letter dated at; ib.
  See Dorset, Earl of.
Sadleir:
  Mrs. Anne, of Standon; 234, 235.
  Ralph; 234.
  Sir Ralph, his mission to Scotland; 235.
  —— case of; 236.
  Sir Thomas, funeral of; 235.
Sadler, Mr.; 131.
St. Alban's:
  mayor of, wife of the; 274.
  Francis, Visc., proceedings in Parliament against him; 247.
  and Clanrickard, Ulick, Earl of, restoration of; 242, 243.
St. Andrews:
  Presbytery of; 49.
  Professor of Divinity at; ib.
St. Augustines, taken by Drake; 39.
St. Cloud, purchase of; 54.
St. Davids, Bishop of, case of; 156.
St. Domingo, taken by Drake; 39, 82.
St. Dunstan's in the West, church of; 40.
St. Eustatia, French claims on; 54.
Sainte Foy, —, letter of; 55.

St. George:
  Sir Oliver; 42.
  ― letter to; 35.
  ― proposal by; 36.
  Sir Henry, MSS. of; 273.
  Richard, Norroy King-at-Arms; *ib.*
St. Germain's, proclamation dated at; 111.
St. Ives; 242.
  curate of, case of; 233.
St. Jago, taken by Drake; 39.
St. James, expulsion of Prince Frederic from; 134.
St. John:
  island of; 167.
  Countess of; 137.
  Mr.; 273.
  Sir Alex.; 162.
  Lady Arbella, letter of; 137.
St. Katherine, John, Prior of, near Lincoln; 66.
St. Lawrence, Gulf of; 167.
St. Marc, M. de, a French informer; 55.
St. Martins in the Fields, Bedford estate in; 140.
St. Paul, Bedford estate in; *ib.*
St. Paul's Cathedral, documents relating to; *ib.*
St. Petersburg, royal letter dated at; 47.
St. Pierre:
  family of; 138.
  Vrian de; *ib.*
  Sir John de; *ib.*
St. Werburgh's, grant to; 275.
Salinas, Don Bernardo de, letters of; 19.
Salisbury; 50.
  charges of a journey to; 183.
  chartulary of; 231.
  Bishop of; 155, 174, 176, 202, 205, 225.
  ― gift to; 195.
  Seth Ward, Bishop of; 18. *See* Sarum.
  Earl of, committed to the Tower; 30.
  Robert, Earl of; 176, 293.
  Earl of, creation of; 167.
  ― letter of; 239.
  ― treatise by; 252.
  ― warrants of; 89, 241.
  ― apology for; 251.
  ― letter of; 258.
  Countess of, letter to; 19.
  Lord, letters of; *ib.*
  House, letter dated at; 243.
Salmon, Col. Edw., transported; 4.
Salop, lands in; 146.
Salt, prerogative concerning; 98.
Salter, Thomas, letter of; 19.
Saltergate; 63.
Salusburie, Sir Robert, inventory of; 146.
Salway, Major Rich. committed to the Tower; 6.
Salwyn, ―, suspected Jacobite agent; 52.
Samlesbury, Lower Hall at; 29.
Samon, Colonel, committed to the Tower; 3.
Sample, William, parish clerk; 191.
Sampson, Dr. Tho., letter of; 281.

Sandal:
  church of; 156.
  ― inventory of goods in; 119, 120.
  John de, grant to; 119.
Sanders:
  Mr.; 221.
  Peter, indictment against; 121.
Sanderson:
  Dr.; 113.
  Mr.; 131.
  William, treatise by; 272.
Sandes, Master; 176.
Sandylandes, Sir James; 134.
Sandys, Bishop, letters of and to; 284.
Sandwich, Earl of, funeral of; 9.
Sanford, Rich., victualler, discharged from the Tower; 5.
Sansom, John, letter of; 20.
Saquevyle:
  Sir Thomas; 94.
  ― son of, and Dame Isabel, his widow; *ib.*
Sare, Richard, letters of; 112, 114.
Sarsfield, General Richard, repulsed at Inniskilling; 35.
Sartore, Thomas; 284.
Sarum, diocese of, return of Dissenters in; 18.
Saucheverel:
  Ralph, witness; 91.
  Robert de; *ib.*
Saumur, letter dated at; 11.
Saunders:
  John, election of; 183.
  ― letter of; 211.
  ― warrant against; 130.
  T., letters of; 109, 110, 111.
Savage:
  Edward, George, Patrick, suspected Jacobites; 44.
  Willielmus; 229.
Savigny:
  Abbey of; 142.
  Rich., Abbot of, witness; *ib.*
  Arrand, Prior of, witness; *ib.*
  Geoffrey, subprior of, witness; *ib.*
  Chapter of; *ib.*
  cellarers of; *ib.*
  Robert, master of the novices of; *b.*
  infirmarer of; *ib.*
  porter of; *ib.*
  Unfridus, monk of; *ib.*
Savile:
  Mr., case of; 122.
  Madam, of Methley; 124, 125.
  Augustus William, report on the MSS. of; 119 *et seq.*
  Edward; 121.
  ― marriage settlement of; 119.
  ― revenues of; 121.
  George; 123, 124.
  ― of Wakefield, collector of subsidies; 120.
  Sir George; 78, 119, 124, 125, 126.
  ― candidature of; 125.
  ― affairs of; 123.
  ― indenture of; 126.

INDEX.   369

Savile—*cont.*
Sir George, letters of; 122, 123.
—— surety to a bond; 122.
—— of Heath; 121.
Gertrude, letter of; 125.
Sir Henry; 120, 122.
John, of Howley; 121.
Sir John; 123.
—— Baron of the Exchequer; 123.
Lady; 148.
Thos., Viscount, case of; 163.
Savill, Hugh, witness: 120.
Savoy; 271.
Hospital of the; 160.
Sawnders, John, his punishment for slander; 182.
Saxony, Christian II., Duke of, letter of; 301.
Saye, Edward, Lord; 132.
Scarborough:
movements of troops at; 27.
secured for the Prince of Orange; *ib.*
Scarisbeck, Humfrey; 149.
Scarlet, John; 284.
Scarsdale [Lady], reported to frequent a conventicle; 15.
Scelingon, church of; 90.
Schelton, Col., 41.
Schiken, Symon, son of John of Little Hall, grant to; 60.
Schleswig Holstein:
Christian Albrecht, Duke of, letter of; 19.
John Adolphus, Duke of, letter of; 301.
Schomberg:
Duke of, in Ireland; 109.
Marshal, letters of, and to; 36.
—— in confinement; 36.
Schot, Col.; 41.
Schwartzenberg, letter dated at; 301.
Scilly Isles, mines in; 209.
Sclater, Dr., vicar of Clerkenwell; 136.
Scory, Bishop, letter of; 282.
Scot:
Hugh, grant by; 60.
—— wife of; *ib.*
Richard, of Newcastle, lease to; 70.
Walterus, witness; 68.
Scotch battalion at Hull; 26.
Scotland, Alexander II., King of; 150.
Alexander III., King of; *ib.*
Mary, Queen of; 234, 235, 237, 286.
—— —— petition for her execution; 130.
—— —— ambassador to; 293.
a regiment for; 35.
commissioner of; 20.
deputation to the King from the Council of; 25.
disaffection to James II. in; 23.
excerpts of records relating to; 231, 233.
information against Jacobites in; 51, 52.
intended expedition to; 110.
intercepted letters for; 30.
Lord Advocate of; 49.
Lord Chancellor of; 272.

Scotland—*cont.*
Lord Justice, clerk of; 45.
Lord Register of; 240.
Parliament of; 239.
plot in; 114.
progress of the Revolution in; 23, 24.
restraint on corn imported from removed; 12.
safe conduct for nobility of; 27.
scandalous newsletters from; 36, 37.
Secretary of; 286.
—— letter of; 251.
rumoured invasion of; 44.
Union with; 115, 116.
warden of the East Marches against; 293.
Scott:
Cuthbert, prisoner in the Fleet; 247.
Thomas, grant to; 73.
Scotus, Adam, witness; 90.
Scragge:
Robert, of Sumerby; 62.
—— John, son of, grant by; *ib.*
Scrope, Esquire, reported to frequent a conventicle; 15.
Sculthorpe, manor of; 103.
Seaforth, Earl of, opinion respecting; 24.
Seager, William; 292.
Seakes:
Francis; 188.
—— appointment of; 220.
—— case of; 215.
Seals, notices of; 25, 58, 60, 61, 62, 63, 64, 126, 129, 138, 141, 142, 144, 149, 168, 227, 243.
Seamor, Sir Edw., charge against; 38.
Seaton, grant of a fair at; 41.
Seckendorff, Monsieur, works by; 53.
Secker, —, anecdote of; 48.
Seddon, Mr.; 131.
Sedgemoor:
battle of; 179.
Inclosure Bill for; 136.
Sedgwick, George; 85.
Seghill, lands in; 71.
Scisdon, poll book of; 145.
Sekford, Thomas, Master of the Requests; 134.
Selby; 124.
Percivall, lease to; 74.
Seldon:
John, proceedings against; 271.
—— treatises by; 237, 240, 248.
Seleby:
Adam de, witness; 68, 69.
Sir Adam de, witness; 67, 68.
Selham, Ricardus; 172.
Sellers, John, prisoner from the Tower; 5.
Selvan:
Osbertus; 57.
Ralph, charter of; *ib.*
—— seal of; 58.
Selwyn, Mr., banker, of Paris; 79.
Sempringham:
Thomas, prior of; 66.
—— privileges of the Order of; *ib.*
Senndye, Arthur, designs by; 130.
Sens, Jacobite agent at; 50, 51.

U 24952.   A A

Seraphin, Monsieur; 302.
Seringapatam; 55.
Serjeants-at-Arms, services of; 246.
Serocold, Lieut. William, proposals by; 38.
Seton:
   lands of; 75.
   Delavale; 58, 73.
   —— disputed possession of; 75.
   —— Chantry of Our Lady in; 74.
Sewers, Commissioners of; 256.
Seymer:
   Sir Francis, speech of; 98.
   (Lady), reported to frequent a conventicle; 15.
Seymour, Sir Francis; 274.
Seyver, Dr. Henry; 282.
Shad Tame, conventicle held in the house of; 15.
Shaddesden, Sir Will. de, witness; 91.
Shaftesbury:
   Earl of, association of; 219.
   —— his jealousy of Coventry; 12.
   —— his sentiments towards Lord Danby; ib.
   —— information obtained by his servant; 11.
   —— information respecting his party; 13.
   —— letter of; 241.
   —— speech of; 42.
Shale, John, letter of; 20.
Shales, John, commissary for Ireland; 36.
Shandoys, Lord, duel of; 84.
Sharp, Rob., declaration of; 284.
Sharpe, —, wife of; 160.
Shaw:
   Mr.; 131.
   Sir John; 11.
Shawe:
   Eliz., petition of; 160.
   John, a founder; 196.
Shawdene; 74.
Sheffield; 121, 123, 305.
   manor of; 133.
   intelligence from; 29.
   Lodge; 122.
Shelburne:
   Lord, anecdote of; 48.
   —— letter of; 207.
Sheldon, Richard, letter of; 36.
Shelfe, manor of, controlls of; 126.
Shelford; 146.
Shepperd, Nicholas; 254.
Shore:
   Sir Henry, estimate by; 36.
   —— letter of; 12.
   —— treatise by; 42.
Sheridan, Thomas, letters of; 20.
Sherland, Edw., suit against; 156, 157.
Shiningfield, lands at; 208.
Shipdam, letters dated at; 101.
Ship-money; 248.
   arguments in the case of; 273.
   attacked in Parliament; 98.
   case of; 246, 248.
   levy of; 272.

Shippy, —, of Wansted, reported to attend a conventicle; 16.
Ships, names of; 296.
Shirburne, Joseph, a creditor of the Crown; 13.
Shirley, Sir Thomas, grant to; 248.
Shoote, Mr., sermon by; 235.
Short, Francis, Junr. of Darchett, pardon to; 134.
Shottone, chapel of; 70.
Shovell:
   Sir Cloudesley, accident on his ship; 111.
   —— letter of; 70.
Shrewsbury:
   letters dated at; 35, 159.
   pleas held at; 233.
   Earl of; 164, 121, 122, 123.
   —— charge of poisoning; 160.
   —— counterfeit name of; 30.
   —— letter to; 35.
   —— summons to; 36.
   Earls of, at Rufford Abbey; 119 et seq.
   Francis, Earl of; 119, 120, 121.
   —— marriage of his daughter; 119.
   —— and of his son; 121.
   Gilbert, Earl of, Earl Marshal: 121.
   Countess of; 123.
   Elizabeth, Countess of, bond of; 122.
   Lord, letter to; 34.
   Mary, Countess of, letter of; 83.
Shropshire:
   church ritual in; 148.
   documents relating to; 127, 142–4.
   riots in; 50.
Sichestan, grant of a loft in; 60.
Sicily, King of, service of; 265.
Sicklemore, Jo., letter of; 267.
Sidney, Sir Philip, letter of 289. See Sydney.
Sighalle:
   deed dated at; 71.
   manor of; ib.
Sigismund, John, letter of; 301.
Simonds, —; 98.
Simone, Signor, in the Haymarket, information against; 17.
Singleton:
   Mr.; 196.
   Thomas, schoolmaster; 194.
Six Clerks, right of appointment of the; 19.
Skeffington, Will.; 146.
Skelton, Mr., proposed as governor to Lord Plymouth; 18.
Skinner, Thomas, reprimand of; 190.
Skippon, Mr. Will.; 162.
Skipton, parish church of; 87.
Skipton Castle; 84, 85, 86, 87, 90.
Skirack, arms of Papists seized in; 20.
Skirbech, court rolls of; 139.
Skircote, manor of, court rolls of; 126.
Skoryare, William; 227.
Skye, Isle of, indulgence to the inhabitants of; 52.
Skynner, Vincent, articles against; 156.
Skyrack, subsidy roll for; 120.

Slaney, Lord; 273.
Slaton, Mr., reported to hold a conventicle; 15, 16.
Sleaford, meeting of gentry at, for the Prince of Orange; 28.
Slezer:
   J., his march to Edinburgh; 25.
   John, " Theatrum Scotiæ " by; 42.
Slingsby:
   Col; 41.
   Sir Rob., discourse on the Navy by; 40.
Smalborough, lands in; 95.
Smalculd, letter dated at; 301.
Smalebroke, Thomas, case of; 161.
Smallwood:
   Matthew, letter of; 10.
   Mr., recommendation for; 12.
Smalman, Geo., letter of; 141.
Smelt, Mr., tutor in the Royal Family; 47, 48.
Smith:
   Master; 176.
   Mr.; 131.
   Consul, correspondence of; 47.
   Cornet, proceedings against; 203.
   Henry, proceedings against; 4.
   Jane; 197.
   Nath., letter of; 55.
   John; 203.
   —— letter to; 267.
   Thos., a place requested for; 13.
   Sir T., letters of; 283, 294.
   —— protest of; 286.
   Mr. Secretary, letter of; 294.
Smithdon, hundred of; 101.
Smithfield, brawling in; 9.
Smyrna Fleet, captured by the French; 112.
Smyth:
   Richard, election of; 181.
   Tho.; 172, 176.
   —— mayor of Reading; 227.
Snellinge, Charles, petition of; 291.
Snettisham, timber cast up at; 100.
Snigge, Baron; 239.
Soames, Dr.; 131.
Socinians, meetings held by; 17, 18.
Sodor:
   John, Bishop of; 150.
   Mark, Bishop of; ib.
   Nicholas, Bishop of; ib.
   Simon, Bishop of; ib.
   Thos., Bishop of; 138.
Somerby, field of; 64.
Somerscales, Robt., letter of; 122.
Somerset:
   Chantry rents in; 291.
   concealed lands in; 145.-
   Duke of, letter of; 95, 276.
   Earl of, proceedings against; 248, 271.
   Frances Carr, Countess of, arraignment of; 245.
   Lord Protector, proclamation by; 239.

Somerset House; 85.
   mass said at; 17.
Somersham, petition of copyholders of; 158.
Sompner, Mr.; 131.
Songs, Protestant; 305.
Soothill; 121.
   letters dated at; 120.
Sotherne, Robert, of Doram, chaplain; 73.
Sotherton, Thomas, letter of; 103.
Soudleia, land in; 145.
Southampton:
   the cloth trade at; 213.
   Earl of, arraignment of; 287.
   —— examination of; 245.
   —— letter of; 218.
   —— release of; 293.
   Lord; 84.
Southcott, John, letter of; 10.
Southeron, Robert, of Durham, clerk; 73.
South Sea Bubble, petition relating to; 205.
South Stoke, enclosure of commons in; 192.
Southwell:
   letter dated at; 125.
   Robert, petition of; 251.
   Sir Rob., grant by; 139.
   —— letters of; 8, 36.
Southworth:
   Christ.; 266.
   —— examination of; 268.
Spain; 250.
   ambassador of, audience of; 148, 241.
   ambassador to; 287.
   depredations against in the West Indies; 8.
   embassy to; 11.
   English College in; 269.
   influence of the Jesuits in; 280.
   King of; 265, 286, 297.
   peace of Paris concluded with; 207.
   proposed commercial treaty with; 54.
   relations with; 82, 131.
   St. Lucas in; 82.
   spies from; 263.
   state of the war in; 115.
   succession to the dominions of; 112.
   the Infanta of, plot in favour of; 266.
   treaty with; 19, 56, 265.
Spalding, manor of; 242.
Sparkes, Mr.; 131.
Sparrow, Ralph, of Ipswich, petition of; 166.
Sparwecester; 69.
Speenhamland; 193.
Spelhorne, lands in; 61.
Spelman:
   Sir Henry, works by; 239.
   —— the Glossary by; 244.
Spelsbury, manor of; 240.
Spendlone, Jo., prebendary; 97.
Spicer, Rev. John, schoolmaster; 206, 207, 226.
Spira, Frances, "Relation" of; 235.
Spitalfields; 45.
Spittle, Hospital of, master of the; 159.

Spofford ; 284.
Sponge, John, discharged from the Tower ; 5.
Sprigg, Serjeant, discharged from the Tower; ib.
Spygournel, Richard ; 142.
Squier, John, vicar, certificate by ; 214.
Squire, Mr. ; 131.
Stafford :
 priory of St. Thomas without; 144.
 —, charge against ; 121.
 Colonel of the Queen's volunteers; 26.
 Lord, information of mass said at his house; 17.
 —— warrant by ; 146.
 Marq. of; 132.
 Sir James de; 144.
 Ralph, Earl of ; ib.
 Ralph de, steward, witness ; 168.
 Thomas, commissioner ; 224.
Staffordshire :
 allowance to the Clerk of the Peace for; 10.
 charitable uses in ; 139.
 documents relating to ; 144, 145, 146.
 glass making in ; 91, 92.
 parliamentary election in; 145.
 petition of the Members of Parliament for ; 10.
Staincross, subsidy roll for ; 120.
Staines, vicarage of; 294.
Stainland, manor of, court rolls of; 126.
Stamford, letter dated at; 85.
Standon ; 234, 235.
Stanesfelde, Jamys, bailiff of Halifax ; 120.
Stanhope :
 Dame Margaret, deed of sale by ; 146.
 Sir Jo. ; 157.
 Sir Tho., charges against ; 122.
 —— of Shelford ; 146.
 Lady, as an actress; 78, 80.
Stanley :
 —, a merchant reported to frequent a conventicle ; 15.
 —— family of ; 139.
 Henry, inquisition for ; 146.
 Sir John, grant of Man to ; 149.
 Rand ; 149, 150.
 Robert ; 159.
 Thos., letter of ; 147.
 —— Lord ; 138.
 William ; 74.
Stannee, W., letter of ; 282.
Stansfeild, Luke ; 126.
Stantun :
 Letitia de, grant by ; 144.
 —— William, son of ; ib.
Stapeley, parson of; 288.
Stapilton, Bryan, 95.
Staple Inn, letter dated at ; ib.
Stapylton, Sir Miles, attack upon ; 29.
Star Chamber :
 the ; 133, 256.
 Bill of penalties in ; 272.
 cases in the ; 135, 159, 160, 239.
 assault on a messenger of the ; 159.
 citation before the ; 271.

Star Chamber— cont.
 judges in the ; 294.
 practises of the ; 246.
 proceedings in ; 283, 286.
 reports of cases in the ; 231.
 Secretary in the ; 287.
 sentence of ; 185.
 speeches in the ; 246, 248.
 attacked by Parliament ; 98.
 Court of, treatise on ; 275, 302.
Starkey :
 George ; 190.
 Ra. ; 238.
States General of the United Provinces ; 287.
 ambassador of ; 19.
 Army List of the (1607) ; 40.
 letter from the ; 19.
 treaty with ; ib.
Staunciall, John, election of; 181.
Staunton, Walter de, mayor of Reading; 227.
Steinford, Helyas de, witness ; 57.
Stendahl, letter dated at ; 301.
" Stephens : "
 alias the Earl of Shrewsbury ; 30.
 Edward, case of, the election of; 232.
 Joel, mayor of Reading ; 211.
 —— deprived ; 193.
 Tho., alderman, deprived ; 201.
 Mr., 131.
Stepkins, Mr. Peter, rogueries of ; 38.
Steppey, Sir John, letters of ; 55.
Steuart, Francis, commission for ; 135.
Stevens, Joel ; 178.
Stewky, living of ; 107.
Stiklaw :
 lands in ; 68, 69, 70.
 William de, grants by ; 68, 69.
 —— Roger, son of; 69. See Stykelaw.
Stikeswold :
 brethren of ; 61.
 prioress and convent of ; 63.
 Eva, prioress of ; grant by ; 62.
 nuns of ; ib.
 Roger de ; 60.
 —— son of ; ib.
 —— mother of ; ib.
 charter dated at ; 65. See Stixwold, Stykeswald.
Stileman, Robert ; 100, 102.
Still, John, letter of ; 283.
Stivechala :
 grant of lands in ; 128.
 Ric. clericus de ; 129.
Stivers, ——, in Southwark, a shorthand writer ; 23.
Stixwold :
 convent of, charters relating to ; 58, 59, 60, 61.
 prioress of, rent payable to ; 64.
 lands of ; 67.
 See Stykeswald, Stikeswold.
Stockdale, Rob., letter of ; 9.
Stock Exchange, abuses of the; 45.
Stockholm :
 intelligence from; 10
 letter dated at ; 20.

INDEX. 373

Stockild, letter dated at ; 37.
Stoke :
    battle of ; 274.
    Goldington, manor of ; 249.
    under Hambdon, Somerset ; 292.
Stokes :
    Dr., letter to ; 243.
    Philip, sieur de ; 145.
Stokwell ; 274.
Stondcyle meadow ; 60.
Stone, Andrew, letter of ; 44.
Stony, John ; 154.
Store, Edward, clerk ; 74.
Storour, Sir Edward, chaplain ; *ib.*
Stote :
    Richard, letter of ; 19.
    Sir Richard, letters of; 12.
Stoughton :
    Adrian, letter of ; 306.
    Francis, letter of ; *ib.*
Stourbridge fair, confirmation of ; 133.
Stow, Col. Lennog ; 41.
Stowe, church of ; 90.
Stowell, —, indictment against ; 121.
Strafford, subsidy roll for ; 120.
Strafford :
    Earl of, declaration against ; 248.
    —— his necessitous condition ; 11.
    —— illness of ; 98.
    —— letters of ; 9, 10.
    —— impeachment of; 41, 99, 100, 244.
Straford, Walter, intelligence from ; 151.
Strange, Dr. Alexander, sermons by ; 234.
Strasbourg, Egon Franç, Prince of ; 19.
Straunge, Henry, Lord, agreement by ; 132.
Streatley, bailiffs' account at ; 154.
Stredleg, Sir Hugh de, witness ; 91.
Street, T., requests the dignity of Serjeant-at-law ; 9.
Stretton :
    lands in ; 91.
    case of, ritual at ; 148.
Strickland, Sir Wm. ; 125.
Strigoil, Ric. de, witness ; 144.
Strip, John, petition of ; 213.
Strode :
    Charles, letter of ; 9.
    Will., candidate for Reading ; 206.
Strother, Tho., witness ; 72.
Struggell, John ; 187.
Stuart, Lady Arabella, death of ; 83.
Stubbs, Francis, prisoner from the Tower ; 5.
Sturbrige, fair at ; 261.
Sturley, Henry, assault by ; 159.
Sturmins, Johannes, formula of; 253, 255.
Stuteville, Will. de, witness ; 144.
Stutgardt, letter dated at ; 301.
Stutsky :
    Mrs., information against ; 17.
    her foolish husband ; *ib.*
Stybbynge, John ; 284.
Stykelawe :
    vill of ; 67, 68.
    Ralph de ; 68.
    —— Henry, son of, grant by ; *ib.*
    Richard de; 68.
    —— Thomas, son of, quitclaim by ; *ib.*

Stykelawe—
    Richard de, chaplain, grant by ; 67.
    See Stikelaw.
Stykeswald :
    master and convent of ; 61, 62.
    Sir Robert, vicar of ; 60.
    Sir Theobalde de, witness; 60. *See*
    Stikeswold, Stixwold.
Style :
    Philip, certificate by ; 141.
    Will., petition of ; 307.
Styward, Dr., letter in favour of ; .283.
Suethorpe, Walterus de, witness ; 68.
Suffolk :
    Earl of, creation of ; 167.
    —— judgment on ; 246.
    —— wife of ; *ib.*
    Duke of, letter of ; 94, 95.
    Henry, Duke of ; attainder of ; 132.
    Duchess of, letter to ; 284.
Sulhampstead, manor of ; 133.
Sunart, Jacobites concealed at ; 46.
Sunderland :
    Earl of ; 107, 108.
    —— letters of ; 19.
    Lord ; 21.
Sunnynges, players of ; 173.
" Surprise," the Privateer ; 118.
Surrey :
    charitable uses in ; 139.
    classified return of Nonconformists in ; 14, 15.
    direction for parliamentary election, in ; 106.
    militia of, inspected by the King ; 12.
    sheriff of ; 134.
Sussex :
    lands in ; 73.
    concealed lands in ; 145.
    Earl of ; 163, 164.
    petition of ; 37.
    Anne, Countess of, letter of ; 20.
    Lord, petition signed by ; 21.
Sutherland :
    history of the family of ; 154.
    Alan, thane of ; *ib.*
Sutton ; 88.
    Valence, vicar of ; 229.
    -Super-Trent, lands in ; 73.
Sutton's Hospital, nomination for ; 292.
Swaffam, post to ; 111.
Swakecliffe, Oxon., letter dated at ; 37.
Swallow, Robert, discharged from the Tower ; 5.
Swallowfyld, Church of All Saints in ; 170.
Swan, Mr. ; 131.
Swanton Morley ; 114.
Sweden :
    ambassador of, neglects to salute the English flag ; 3.
    anticipated hostilities with ; 49.
    King of, alleged plot against ; 10
    —— hostility of ; 54.
    King elect of ; 286.

Sweden—cont.
  proposed treaty of commerce with Holland; 39.
  ships of, to join the English fleet; 111.
  wars of, with Denmark; 10.
Swynburne, Thomas, grant to; 73.
Swynne:
  lands in; ib.
  Henry, marriage contract by; ib.
  —— Henry, son of; ib.
Syckes, William; 74.
Sydney:
  Lord, letters of; 55.
  Lady; 98.
  Mr., appointment of; 242.
  —— counterfeit name of; 30.
  Sir Henry, letters and speeches of; 245.
Sylvius, Sir Gabriel, letters of; 9, 12.
Symes, a constable; 185.
Symmonds, Mr.; 131.
Syndelsham, players of; 173.
Sypsay, Church of St. Margaret in; 139.
Syward, Thomas; 171.

T.

Taaf, —; 79.
Tadcaster, document dated at; 26.
Tailboys, Rich., letter of; 306.
Tailour:
  Francis, letter of; 268.
  —— wife of; 268, 269.
Talbot:
  Edw., case of; 160.
  George; 274.
  —— Lord, witness; 119.
  Gilbert, Lord; 149.
  Lady Mary, marriage settlement of; 119.
  Sir John, Lieutenant of Ireland; 129.
  Rich., committed to the Tower; 7.
  Thomas; 254.
  Lord; 120.
Tallibolyon, account roll of; 149.
Tanckred:
  Chr., letter of; 36.
  —— of Whixley, information by; 25.
Tanfield:
  Sir Laurence; 240.
  —— petition to; 292.
Tangier:
  estimate for the mole at; 38.
  governorship of; 11.
  letter dated at; 12.
  papers relating to; 10.
  pay of the garrison of; 14.
  state of; 239.
Tankard, Capt.; 29.
Tankersley:
  manor of; 119.
  hunting at; 120.

Tarbet, Lord, intelligence from; 36.
Tarporley, hermitage at; 137.
Tarressi, Signor, a popish agent, information against; 17.
Tasburgh:
  Bem¹; 108.
  Thomas, letter of; 306.
Tate, Francis, treatise by; 287, 293.
Tawke, Ricardus, goldsmith; 175.
Taylor:
  Christopher, of Waltham Abbey, reported to attend a conventicle; 16.
  Jeremy; 152.
  John, letter of; 114.
  John B. D., exactions of; 290.
  Thomas; 291.
  —— letter of; 211.
  Will., of Barking, conventicle held in the house of; 16.
  Lieut.-Col., monument to; 208.
Teame, the river; 147.
Tedmans, Mr., reported to hold a conventicle; 15.
Tefford', Adam, clericus de, witness; 57.
Tempest:
  Capt.; 28.
  Col. John, letter of; 36.
  —— sons of, ib.
  Edward; 261.
  Madam, letter to, intercepted; 36.
  Rowland, letter of; 26.
Temple:
  Order of the; 128, 249.
  account of the organ in; 308.
  letter dated from; 226.
  master of, grievances of; 288.
  gardens; 306.
  hall, installation in; 289.
  Inner, report on the MSS. of; 227 et seq. See London.
  —, discharged from the Tower; 5.
  James, proceedings against; 4.
  Jo., letter of; 20.
  Peter, proceedings against; 4.
  Sir William, letters of and to; 9, 10, 12, 19, 20.
  —— secretary of; 13.
  v. Ayleworth, case of; 163.
Templeman:
  Robert, of Hortone, grant by; 67, 69.
  —— Michel, son of; 69.
  Sir Richard; ib.
Terell:
  Francis, jun., alderman; 202, 198.
  Richard, Esq., petition of; 246.
Test Act; 42.
Teuw, manor of; 240.
Tewkesbury; 238.
  case of the borough of; 232.
Thackham:
  Mr., schoolmaster; 196.
  Thomas, mayor of Reading; 215, 216.
Thames:
  a process server ducked in; 159.
  deodand for a boat wrecked in; 183.

Thanet :
    Earl of ; 84.
    —— letter of ; 85.
    —— petition signed by ; 21.
    —— death of ; 85.
    Earls of ; 81 *et seq.*
    Margaret, Countess of, letter of ; 85, 86, 89.
" The John's Adventure," ship; 13.
Theobalds, lands at ; 92.
Thetford :
    assizes at ; 107.
    the Norfolk militia at ; 100.
Thewles, Mr. ; 264.
Thomas :
    R., letter of ; 9.
    Rob., letter of ; 12.
    Sir Rob., letter to ; 10.
Thompson :
    Edward, intelligence from ; 36.
    Henry, letter of ; 7.
    Mr. ; 131.
Thomson, John, discharged from the Tower ; 2.
Thorach ; 250.
Thoresby, Peter de, witness ; 69.
Thornhagh, St. Andrew, letter of ; 126.
Thornhill :
    letter dated at ; 122, 123.
    manor of, court rolls of ; 126.
    records at ; *ib.*
    Church, presentation to ; 124.
Thornton, Alice, letter of ; 37.
Thorold, Natt. ; 93.
Thorpedale, land in ; 63.
Thorton, Tho., proctor ; 285.
Throckmorton, Rob., letter of ; 166.
Thurland, Edw., prisoner in the Fleet ; 247.
Thurleby, Thos., deed by ; 133.
Thurlow, Lord Chancellor, letters of ; 55.
Thurman, Mr. ; 131.
Thurot, Admiral of France ; 47.
Thursby :
    W., letters of ; 107, 108, 111, 112.
    —— wife of, character of ; 112.
Thurstan, Samuel, election of ; 57.
Thurston, Margaret, petitions of ; 292.
Thynne :
    Francis, treatise on Knighthood by ; 270.
    H., letter of ; 307.
Tichborn, Rob., proceedings against ; 4.
Tichbourne :
    ——, the Regicide, insecurely confined in the Tower ; 12.
    transported ; 4.
Ticonderoga, capture of ; 45.
Till, Mr. ; 261.
Tilley :
    Ann, clandestine betrothal of ; 160.
    George, abduction of his daughter ; *ib.*
Tipper :
    Rob. ; 222.
    Will. ; 239.
Tippo Saib, English policy towards ; 55.
Tirconry, reported to attend a conventicle ; 15.

Tisdall, Mich., letter of ; 241.
Tithes ; 254.
    exemptions from ; 258.
    payment of ; *ib.*
Titley :
    Mr., correspondence of ; 47.
    Walter, letter of ; 44.
Tokesford, grant of free chace in ; 119.
Toledo, Cardinal ; 263.
Tolonne, British fleet at ; 76.
Tomas, filius Hugonis, witness ; 57.
Tompson, Sir Henry, letter to ; 9.
Tomyowe, Richard, of London ; 208.
Toug, Thos., prisoner from the Tower ; 5.
Topclif, William de, parson, grant to ; 65.
Topcliffe, Mr. ; 277.
Topclyffe, Richard, letter of ; 122.
Topham, Dr. John ; 20.
Topsham, embarkation of arms at ; 36.
Torbay, reported landing of the French at ; 111.
Torp :
    Willelmus, parson of, witness ; 57.
    —— Helias, brother of ; *ib.*
    grant of lands in ; 62.
Torrington, Earl of, letters of ; 55, 92.
Totness, Archdeacon of ; 163.
Tounson, Robart, sermon by ; 235.
Tourneure, Tym., letter of ; 148.
Tourville, M., introduction of ; 32.
Towcotts, Roger ; 176.
Tower :
    the ; 52, 245.
    goldsmiths' money secured in, from the fire ; 85.
    Keeper of the Rolls in the ; 139.
    letter dated at the ; 36.
    Lieut. of the ; 22, 263.
    —— order of ; 5.
    prisoners in the ; 8.
    records in the ; 241.
    valuation of ordnance in ; 250.
    warrants, 1-7. *See* Loudon.
    Rob. ; 284.
Townley, Mr., of Carr ; 43.
Townshend :
    Mr., letter of ; 78.
    Roger ; 107, 108.
    Lord ; 106, 107, 108, 109, 111.
    —— his mission to Holland ; 116.
Towton, letter dated at ; 26.
Trade :
    Board of ; 166.
    Council of ; 7.
Trapeston, church of ; 90.
Travers :
    John, confession of ; 254.
    Sam., care of ; 163.
    Mr., recommendation of ; 306.
Treasury, records of the ; 39, 40.
Trensham, Dr. George ; 267.
Trent, ——, a Jacobite agent ; 44.
Tresame, Lewis, letter of ; 306.
Tresham, Sir Thomas, trial of ; 163, 164.
Treswell :
    a herald ; 288.
    Rob. ; 241.
Trevanion *v.* Vivian, case of ; 163.

Trevor :
  John, letters of ; 55.
  Sir John, letter of ; 12.
  Sir Thomas ; 291.
Trevors [Lady], reported to frequent a conventicle ; 15.
Trewe:
  William, of Huntington ; 64.
  —— Emma, widow of ; *ib.*
Trewike, Adam de ; 68.
Trewyke, John de, witness ; *ib.*
Trice, Jasper, conveyance to ; 133.
Tripp, John, son of, at college ; 191.
Troke, Robert, clerk, grant to ; 64.
Trott, John, trial of ; 162.
Trumbull, Dr. ; 22.
Trussell, Sir Will., exchange by ; 138.
Trym, document dated at ; 129.
Tuer, Thomas ; 197.
Tufton :
  family of ; 81 *et seq.*
  Thomas, his election to Parliament ; 86.
Turenne, Marshal, at Marle ; 10.
Turin, correspondence from ; 47.
Turkelyn, account roll of ; 149.
Turkey, aid solicited for ; 245.
Turner :
  a papist bookseller, information against ; 17, 22.
  —— released on bail ; 5.
  Mr., conventicle held by ; 15.
  Christopher, precedency ; 222.
  Mr. Francis ; 304.
  Richard, lease from ; 208.
  Thomas, burgess of Reading ; *ib.*
  Will., deprived ; 223.
  ——, *alias* Cotton, conventicle held by ; 15.
Turnor, Edmund ; 220.
Turpin :
  Richard, land of ; 62.
  Will., reported to attend a conventicle ; 16.
Turpyn, John, power of attorney to ; 71.
Tuscany, Grand Duke of ; 38.
Tutevill, Mr. ; 131.
Tweedmouth, deed dated at ; 75.
Twistleton, Philip, released from the Tower ; 5.
Twittenham ; 107, 108.
Tyborne, prisoners conveyed to ; 4.
Tyler :
  Rich., prisoner from the Tower ; 5.
  —— discharged by *Habeas Corpus* ; *ib.*
Tyndall, John, letter of ; 135.
Tyne, the river ; 70.
Tynemouth :
  parish and vicar of ; *ib.*
  garrison of ; 28.
  prior of ; 75.
  John, prior of ; 74.
  Castle, plan for reducing ; 28.
  —— summoned to surrender ; 29.
Tynners, the, case of ; 248.
Tynoco, Emanuel, Louys, trial of ; 135.
Typoots, Paul, notary ; 284.

Tyreswelle :
  Henry of ; 91.
  —— Robert, son of, and Alice Hirdman, his wife, grant by ; *ib.*
Tyrone, Earl of, grant to ; 133.
Tyrrell, J., letter of ; 240.
Tyrringtoft, vill of ; 68.

U.

Uffington, near Stamford, letter dated at ; 32.
Uleken, A., minister for Sleswig Holstein, letter of ; 20.
Ulecotes, Philip de, grant to ; 91.
Ulrich, letter of ; 300.
Underwood :
  [Justice], willing to proceed against Nonconformists ; 17.
  Stephen, list of the Pipe Rolls by ; 152.
  William, bond to ; 73.
Unframville, Robert de ; 70.
Unthanke, town and manor of ; 75.
Uphton, manor of ; 133.
Uppermore, reported Jacobite victory at ; 36, 37.
Upton, Roman remains discovered at ; 116.
Usher, Mrs., actress ; 77
Utie, Dr. ; 131.
Utrecht ; 49.
  peace of ; 49, 118.
Uuellebec. *See* Wellebec.
Uvedale, Dr. Rob. ; 151.

V.

Vachel :
  John, grant to ; 169.
  Tanfield ; 186, 187, 189, 190.
  —— Deputy Lieutenant of Berks ; 216.
  Thomas ; 197.
  —— election of ; 181.
  family of ; 169.
  Willielmus ; 173.
Vale Royal, Abbot of ; 138.
Valette, Duke of. *See* D'Espernon, Duke.
Vall, Mr. ; 37.
Valladolid, English college at ; 297.
Valpy, Mr., schoolmaster ; 207.
Vanderhaghen, Mr. ; 206.
Vane, Sir Henry, transported ; 3.
Van Heele, Peter, letter of ; 304.

Vanitia ; 76.
Van Reede, —, letter to ; 9.
Vau Wyngaarter suspected Jacobite agent ; 47.
Varney :
    George, letter of ; 217.
    Greville, letter to ; 251.
Vaughan :
    Edward, trial of ; 162.
    letters of ; 9, 10, 11.
    Rich. Will., indictment against ; 50.
    Sir R. ; 162.
Vaus, Agnes de, grant by ; 68.
Vaux, Lord, trial of ; 163, 164.
Vavasour, Sir Walter, letter to ; 26.
Veer, Col. John ; 41.
Venables, family of ; 138.
Venice ; 279.
    correspondence from ; 47.
    epigram by a senator of ; 11.
    reversion of the embassy to ; 53.
Verdon, Bertram de, witness ; 128.
Vere :
    Colonel Edw. ; 40.
    Colonel Horatio, his service in Holland ; 40.
    Sir F., *Commentaries* by ; 234.
Vergennes :
    M. de ; 55.
    —— anecdotes of ; 54, 56.
    —— character of ; 54.
Verney, Will., letter of ; 219.
Vernon, Mr., reported treasonable toasts drunk at his table ; 49.
Vestments, petition for use of ; 298.
Veterani, General, defeated by the Turks ; 112.
Vienna :
    correspondence from ; 47.
    foreign correspondence dated at ; 44.
Villa Hermosa, Duque de, letter of ; 19.
Villars, Edward, of Loughborough, grant by ; 66, 67.
Villeins, conveyance of ; 68, 69.
Villeroy ;
    Marshal ; 112.
    M. ; 282.
Villers, Col., promises by ; 37.
Villiers :
    Capt. ; 28.
    —— dismissed from Tynemouth Castle ; 30.
    Col. ; 36.
    —— complaints against his regiment ; 36, 37.
    Lieut.-Govr. of Tynemouth ; 28.
    Sir Henry, attitude of ; 29.
Vimiera, battle of ; 208.
Vincent :
    Augustin ; 292.
    Mr., conventicle held in his house ; 16.
    —— the elder, reported to hold a conventicle ; 16.
Viner, Sir Robert ; 22.

Vineter :
    Thomas le ; 169.
    —— daughters of, grant by ; *ib.*
Virginia :
    bachelors of, address by ; 166.
    commissioners of, petitions from ; 19.
    governor of ; 10.
    lottery for the succour of ; 211
    writ for the Assembly of ; 14.
    Swans point, Jame's River in ; 19.
Vivian, Sir Francis, governor of Mawes Castle, oppressions by ; 163.
Voltaire, tragedy by ; 79.
Vontoissein, —, letter of ; 33.
Vyck, Lewes de, Queen's Attorney in Guernsey ; 130.
Vyner, Sir Rob., letter of ; 9, 12, 20.

W.

Waard, Sir John, recovery against ; 69.
Wac :
    Baldwin, confirmation of grant by ; 90.
    Hugh, grant by ; *ib.*
Wacelin :
    Johannes, grant to ; 57.
    Ricardus, witness ; *ib.*
    Robertus, witness ; *ib.*
Waddon, Mr., schoolmaster ; 225.
Wade :
    — ; 78, 79.
    General, in Scotland ; 46.
    John, of Systone, lease by ; 65.
    Mr. ; 263.
Wadisworth, Richard ; 126.
Wadsworth :
    freeholders of, grant to ; 126.
    manor of, court rolls of ; *ib.*
Wake, Thomas, de Lydel, witness ; 168.
Wakefield :
    letter dated at ; 29.
    mills, lease of ; 123.
    workhouse at ; 52.
Walcot, Capt. Thomas, arrested ; 8.
Waldegrave :
    family of ; 127.
    Lady (1794) ; *ib.*
Waldenses, the, confutation of ; 155.
Wales ; 280.
    clerk of the Crown in ; 135.
    Council of ; 120.
    conquest of ; 231.
    contributions levied in ; 140.
    documents relating to ; 146, 147.
    jurisdiction of the Council of ; 41.
    Lord President of the Council of ; 147.
    sacrileges in ; *ib.*
    sheriffs and escheators in ; 136, 148, 149.
    statistics relating to ; 249.
    marches of ; 252.

Wales—cont.
  marches of, forest deer in the; 134.
  —— jurisdiction of the; 147.
  Edward, Prince of (1254); 236.
  Henry, Prince of; 234, 240, 249.
  —— —— death of; 251.
  —— —— players of; 178.
  —/ —— gift to; 184.
  —— —— revenues and debts of; 242.
  Prince of, clerk to the Council of the; ib.
  —— lands assigned to the; ib.
  —— (1638) birth of; 108, 179.
  —— (1773) character of; 47, 48, 56.
  —— letters of; 48.
  —— tradesmen's bills of; 52.
  —— installed as Knight of the Garter; ib.
  —— and Princess of (1737), in disgrace; 134.
  Principality of; 270.
Walker:
  Edw.; 5, 8, 220.
  John; 74, 284.
  Obadiah; 244.
  —— letters of; 241.
  Stuart, duel with; 84.
  Thomas; 222, 225.
  —— exhibition granted to; 213.
  —— of Scotylthorpe, quitclaim by; 66.
  Sir William, reported to attend a conventicle; 15.
  —— wife of; ib.
Walkinshaw, Mr., of Scotstown, a Jacobite agent; 51, 52.
Wall, General, correspondence of; 47.
Waller:
  Mr., statement of accounts by; 36.
  Robert, letters of; 37.
  Wooding, petition of; 292.
  Sir Hardres, proceedings against; 4.
  —— transported; 3.
Walley, Father, a Jesuit; 269, 277. *See* Garnet.
Wallingford; 173, 196, 210.
  garrison of; 219.
  fortifications of; 188, 216.
  liberties of the honour of; 141.
  lieut.-governor of; 189.
  W., Earl of, letter of; 214.
  —— high steward of Reading; 221.
Wallis:
  William, charge of witchcraft against; 185.
  —— Edith, wife of; ib.
Wallop:
  Sir Henry, letter of; 288.
  Rob., sentence on; 4.
Walmesley, Will., certificate for; 29.
Walpole
  barony of; 45.
  opinion as to; 266.
  H.; 45.
  Mr.; 107, 113.
  Robert; 108.
  Sir Robert, letters of and to; 43, 55.
Walsh, Sir Robert, letter of; 19.

Walsingham:
  Sir Francis; 133, 255, 259.
  —— ambassador to France; 271.
  —— letters of; 135, 306.
  —— petition to 134.
Walter, E., letter of; 306.
Walters, Rob., committed to the Tower; 6, 7.
Walton, John, petition of; 292.
Wansted, conventicle held in; 16.
Warburton, Peter, letter of; 146.
Ward:
  Dean, Provost of Trinity College, Dublin; 10.
  John, of Hundington, grant to; 65, 66.
  Sir Patience, letter of; 12.
  Richard; 169.
  —— junior, commissioner; 224.
  —— of Hundington, grant to; 65, 66.
  William, of Bedlington; 74.
  —— of Cowpen; ib.
  —— Member of Parliament; 171.
  —— mayor of Reading; 169, 227.
  —— of Hundington, grant to; 65, 66.
Wardour, Madame, letter to; 10.
Wardoure, Chidiock, clerk of the Pells; 156.
Wardrobe, the; 250.
Wards:
  master of, instructions to; 249.
  and Liveries, Court of, fees and salaries in; 250.
  —— master of the, instructions to; 234.
Warenne:
  Earl of; 103.
  Comes de; 57.
  Isabel Comitissa de; ib.
  Reginaldus de; ib.
  Willelmus de; ib.
Warham, Archbishop, register of; 255.
Warmestray, Dr.; 131.
Warnabe, land in; 59.
Warram, Mr. Robert; 265.
Warrington; 92.
Warriston, Lord, prisoner in the Tower; 5.
Warwick:
  concealed lands in; 145.
  House, letter dated at; 82.
  Countess of; 87, 88.
  Ambrose, Earl of, death of; 87.
  Richard, Earl of; 274.
  Robert, Earl of, naval instructions from; 252.
  Theo. de Beauchamp, Earl of, witness; 168.
  Countess of, her property restored; 95.
  Sir P., letter of; 7.
  Mr.; 263.
Warwickshire:
  documents relating to; 145.
  riots in; 49.
Washington, Lawrence, grant of office to; 130.
Waspa, Baldwin de, witness; 90.
Waterford, manuscripts of the Marchioness; 58 *et seq.*

Waterhouse, Tho., petition of; 37.
Waters, Capt., case of; 240, 244.
Watford, manor of, court rolls of; 132.
Wathous, rector of; 69.
Watkis, John; 239.
Watlington:
   Park, letter dated at; 79.
   Mr., chamberlain; 203.
Watson:
   Mr.; 268, 269.
   —— letter to; 302.
   —— mayor of Berwick; 13.
   —— reported to hold a conventicle; 16.
   W., imprisonment of; 277.
   —— letters of; 306.
   William, letters of and to; 298, 299, 300.
Watton, letter dated at; 66.
Wauf, Walterus, witness; 150.
Way, Rich., sale by; 169.
Wayt, Thos., proceedings against; 4.
Webb:
   Daniel, restoration at; 223.
   David, elected to a scholarship; 197, 198.
Weddalle, Edward; 73.
Welbeck, letter dated at; 27, 123.
Wellebec:
   Adam, Abbot of, witness; 57.
   John, prior of, witness; ib.
   Richard, Abbot of, witness; 91.
Weller, Samuel, elected to a scholarship; 204.
Welles, Ricardus; 229.
Wells:
   Cathedral Church of; 237.
   profane plays and sports at; 161.
   recorder of; ib.
   mayor of, information against; ib.
   Mr.; 217, 218.
Wendie, Mr. Thomas; 256.
Wennevall, Willelmus de, witness; 57.
Wentworth:
   Elizabeth; 93.
   Henry; ib.
   Lord, letter of; 243.
   —— Lord Deputy of Ireland; 247, 289.
   Lord W., letter of; 306.
   Peter, proceedings against; 239.
   —— speech by; 238.
   Sir Thos., letter of; 8.
   —— late member for Yorkshire; 125.
West:
   Abell, petition of; 4.
   Sir Thos., letter of; 306.
West Basham, tithes of; 114.
Westby, letter dated at; 35.
Westcote, Abell, petition of; 5.
Westdeeping, church of; 90.
West Derham, letter dated at; 13.
Westham, conventicle held in; 16.
Westhidwene:
   deed dated at; 72.
   lands in; ib.
   manor of; ib.

Westhorp, letter dated at; 94.
West Indies, Drake's expedition to; 39.
Westmerland, Robert; 189.
Westminster:
   the Great Almry in, conventicle in; 15.
   the Little Almry in, Quakers' meeting in; ib.
   charter dated at; 119.
   church of; 42.
   concord dated at; 169.
   documents dated at; 84, 94.
   Long Ditch, conventicle in; 15.
   order dated at; 218.
   Parliament at; 172, 180.
   Pipe office at; 152.
   Statute of (1275); 40.
   treasuries of; 246.
   Tuttle Street, Fifth Monarch meeting in; 15.
   Hall, preparations for a trial in; 39.
Westmoreland:
   documents relating to; 145.
   proposed declaration by the gentry of; 27.
   Lord; 111.
Weston:
   lands in; 91.
   letter dated at; 166.
   Sir Richard, negotiations by; 286.
   ——; 222.
   of Lovaine; 258.
Westone, Mr.; 177.
Westronich, manor of; 102.
Wethermere; 68.
Wettenhall:
   family of; 138.
   William, will of; ib.
   —— Isabel, wife of; ib.
Weybridge, drawings of roofs at; 308.
Weymans, J. & T., Merchants of Rotterdam; 29.
Whalley, ——, of Notts., case of; 121.
Wharncliff, hunting at; 120.
Wharton Park, swine in; 85.
Wharton:
   Philip, Earl of; 87.
   his house in London; 86.
   letter of; 95.
   Lord, family of; 15.
   —— reported to frequent a conventicle; ib.
   —— reported dead of the plague; 85.
   —— speech of; 115.
   William, prisoner in the Fleet; 247.
Wheathamstead, advowson of; 243.
Wheler, Will, letter of; 37.
Whetley, John de, vicar of Tynemouth; 70.
Whitaker, Will.; 133.
Whitchester:
   John de; 70.
   —— Eda, wife of; ib.
White, J., letter of; 126.
   Mr. W.; 265.
   Rich., committed to the Tower; 6.
   Thomas, petition of; 292.
   Sir Thos., portrait of; 206.
Whitefriars; 85, 306.

Whitehall ; 112, 185, 293.
 conference at ; 98.
 James II. proclaimed at ; 199.
 letters dated at ; 26, 105, 108, 114, 222, 258.
 the Board at ; 97.
 the Court at ; 247.
 warrant dated at ; 221.
 William III. at ; 203.
Whitcheved, Alan, lease by ; 71.
Whitelocke, B. ; 102, 191, 192, 197, 218, 226.
 Sir James, justice ; 214.
 Sir John, justice ; 213.
Whitepan, Rich., of Little Eastcheap, reported to attend a conventicle ; 16.
Whitfield :
 John, deposition of ; 130.
 Archbishop ; 256, 300.
 —— petitions to ; 255, 276, 284, 294.
 John, letter of ; 283.
 —— letters of and to ; 254, 255.
Whitgreve, William, pedigree of ; 138.
Whithern :
 Priory of, grants to ; 150.
 Register of ; *ib.*
Whiting, J., of Lincoln's Inn, letter of ; 103.
Whitlaythe, tithes in ; 75.
Whitley Park, sale of ; 210.
Whitly, movements of troops at ; 27.
Whitney, vicar of ; 245.
Whittington, William ; 250.
Whittlewood, forest of ; 141.
Whitworth, Mr., British envoy to Poland ; 53.
Whyte, Rowland, letter of ; 148.
Whytyng, John, letter of ; 98.
Wiborne, examination of ; 283.
Wickliffe :
 John ; 282.
 —— confutation of ; 155.
Widdrington, E. :
 letter of ; 10.
 Eliz., letter of ; 13.
 Lord, governor of Berwick ; 28.
 dismissed from Berwick ; 29.
 W., letter of ; 10.
Wigarus Camerarius, witness ; 57.
Wigfall, William, petition of ; 4.
Wigmore, the Cross of destroyed ; 147.
Wild, Dr. ; 131.
Wilde, John, of Ancaster, lease by ; 65.
Wildeman :
 John, committed to the Tower ; 3.
 —— transported ; 4.
Wilder, Mr., trial of ; 179.
Wildman :
 Major ; 42.
 John, information by ; 37.
Wiles, Alan, Matthew son of, grant by ; 61.
Wilgebi, lands in ; 60.
Wilkes, Col. ; 92.
Wilkinson, —, actor ; 77.
Willey, Anne, suit of ; 154.
William I. ; 230.

William III. ; 35, 36, 43, 179.
 assassination plot against ; 112.
 charge of swearing at him ; 35.
 letter to ; 33.
 movements of ; 110, 111.
 plan of the camp of ; 39.
 warrant by ; 134.
William IV., charter of ; 168.
William & Mary, coronation of ; 37, 38.
William :
 Prince, letters of ; 48.
 —— tradesmen's bills of ; 52.
William, John, election of ; 180, 181.
Williams :
 Mr. ; 131, 141.
 —— sermon preached by ; 132.
 Mrs. ; 103.
 Sir Charles Hanbury, letter of ; 44.
 —— correspondence of ; 47.
 Sir John ; 176, 177.
 Will., suit of ; 241.
 —— play writer, information against ; 161.
Williamson :
 Mr. Secretary ; 22.
 —— letters to ; 12, 13.
Willis, Browne, of Whaddon Hall, letters of ; 152, 153.
Willmer :
 Mr. ; 215.
 Edw., town clerk of Reading ; 219.
Willoughby :
 Lord ; 286, 288.
 —— his servant killed ; 287.
 —— letters to ; 31, 35,
 —— struck by Lord Lumley ; 27.
 Jo., letter of ; 20.
 P., letter of ; 82.
 D'Eresby, Lord, letter to ; 29, 32.
Wills, probate of ; 295.
Wilmott, William, town clerk of Reading ; 217.
Wilson :
 —, intercepted letter of ; 36.
 Mr. ; 131.
 Thos., letter of ; 11.
 Wilton, letter dated at ; 276.
 —— House ; 89, 90.
Wilts :
 claim to lands in ; 154.
 concealed lands in ; 145.
Win, Major, reported to frequent a conventicle ; 15.
Winch, Mr. Rich. ; 183.
Winchelsea, Earl of, letters of ; 10, 11.
Winchester ; 157, 217.
 Dean and Chapter of ; 146.
 Parliament at ; 180.
 trials at ; 270.
 Bishop of, letter to ; 277.
 George Morley, Bishop of, letter of ; 14.
 Peter, Bishop of, case of ; 238.
 Thos. Cooper, Bishop of ; 256.
 Marquis of ; 95.
 —— his designs against Danby's ministry ; 12.
 —— letter of ; *ib.*
 Lord, his misconduct at school ; 151.

Wincott, Mr. ; 257.
Windebank :
  Sir Fr. ; 96, 185, 240, 241.
  —— gift to ; 186.
  —— house of ; ib.
  —— letters of and to ; 225, 243.
  Thomas, letters of ; 135.
  Sir Thos. ; 241.
Windham :
  Mr. ; 107, 108.
  —— son of ; 108.
  —— wife of; 107, 108.
Windsor ; 18.
  commission dated at ; 224.
  Council at ; 148.
  installation of the Garter at ; 19.
  letter dated at ; 21.
  price of a dinner at ; 176.
  William III. at ; 203.
  Castle, letter dated at ; 221, 276.
  Park ; 198.
Wine, importation of ; 130.
Wingate, Edw., lease to ; 156.
Winn, Sir Rowland, examination by ; 52.
Winnike ; 134.
Winter, Salvator, a mountebank, information against ; 17.
Wirethes, William de le, conveyance to ; 62.
Wirksworth :
  regulations for mines at ; 41.
  vicar of, charges against ; 156.
Wirtemberg :
  Duke of, letter of ; 301.
  —— his arrival at Hull ; 33.
  Ferd. Guill., Duke of, letter of ; ib.
  Louis Frederick, Prince of, letter of ; 301.
Wisbeach ; 202, 263.
  Castle, keeper of ; 266.
  —— High Constable of ; ib.
  —— prisoners in ; 267.
Wise :
  Mr., schoolmaster ; 207.
  Mrs., letter to ; 13.
  Rob., of Middleton Cheney ; 141.
  W., schoolmaster ; 190, 226.
  Sir Andrew ; 265, 266.
Wiseman :
  Mr., letter to ; 259.
  Rich., letter of ; 11.
  Sir William ; 259.
Wiston ; 248.
Witcherley, Mr. ; 131.
Witherington :
  Mr., speech of ; 293.
  Sir Thomas, speech of ; ib.
Withers, Geo., committed to the Tower for libel ; 4.
Wittemberg, feeling in ; 305.
Wivell, J., letter of ; 13.
Wrigton, Robert de, witness ; 91.
Woburn, Lord Wharton's house at ; 85.
Wodehouse :
  Edmund ; 108.
  —— Robert de, son of ; 61.
  —— Marjoria, wife of ; ib.

Wodman :
  John, grant to ; 71.
  —— mason, grant by ; ib.
  —— the elder ; 72.
  —— the younger ; 71.
Wodrington or Woddryngtone :
  John de, daughter of ; ib.
  John, livery of seisin to ; 73.
  John of, sheriff ; 74.
  Rob., grant to ; ib.
  William, under sheriff ; ib.
Woffington, Mrs. ; 79.
Wogan, Tho., proceedings against ; 4.
Wokyngham :
  players of ; 172, 173.
  archers of ; 173.
Wollaston :
  manor of ; 141, 142.
  quern keepers in ; 142.
  William, commissioner ; 224.
Wolley, Sir John ; 137.
Wolseley, Capt., movements of ; 28.
Wolsey :
  Cardinal, life of ; 245.
  Sir Rich., letters of ; 152.
Wolters, Richard, intelligence from ; 47.
Wolveseye, Daniel ; 210.
Wonere, Rich. de, witness ; 142.
Wood :
  Anthony ; 244, 273.
  Edw., letter of ; 10, 20.
  John, judgment upon ; 160.
  Justice, of Wapping ; 17.
  Rich., vicar of Brackley ; 140.
  Rob., new Almanac of ; 39.
Woodbridge, license to found an almshouse at ; 134.
Woodcock, Sir Tho., baptismal fees paid by ; 249.
Woodhall Hatfield ; 234.
Woodley ; 249.
Woodman, Mr. William, a Jesuit ; 22.
Woodney, Col. Oliver ; 41.
Woodstock :
  order dated at ; 219.
  Queen Elizabeth at ; 300.
  the Privy Council at ; 213.
Woodward, Edward, elected to a fellowship ; 191.
Wooler, lordship of, grant of ; 58.
Woolley, Ezekiel, reported to attend a conventicle ; 16.
Worcester ; 217.
  battle of ; 92, 178.
  assizes at ; 233.
  E. ; 222.
  John Tiptofte, Earl of, orders for precedence by ; 274.
  Roger, Bishop of ; 230.
Workington, arms for Ireland seized at ; 27.
Worksop ; 123, 126.
Worouzow :
  M., Russian ambassador ; 55.
  —— letters of ; ib.

Worsley; 248.
  manor of; 151.
  Thomas, a recusant; 233.
"Worster" Park, Royal visit to; 12.
Worthington, Mr.; 259.
Wortland [Lady], reported to attend a conventicle; 15.
Wotefoures; 63.
Wotter, Sir, a friar; 266.
Wotton:
  letter dated at; 22.
  Mr., house of; 124.
  Will., elected to scholarship; 198.
Woym, Mrs.; 78.
Wraie, Sir Will., suit against; 159.
Wrath, Col.; 41.
Wrattesley, Richard; 177.
Wray:
  Lord, letter of; 306.
  Chief Justice; 163.
Wren:
  Sir Christopher, application of; 39.
  —— conveyance to; 140.
  —— dial and clock made by; 308.
  —— letter of; 243.
Wrexham, court rolls of; 146.
Wrey:
  Sir Bourchier; 154, 155.
  Lady Florence; 155.
Wright:
  —, warrant issued against; 297.
  Alice, petition of; 290.
  John, letters of; 13, 278.
  Thomas, prisoner in Argeere; 290.
Wrighte:
  G., clerk of the Crown; 228.
  William, of Sugbroke, quitclaim by; 66.
  —— Margaret, wife of; ib.
Wroth, Lady; 148.
Wrothe, Thomas, letter of; 306.
Wrottesley, —; 145.
Wroughton, Mr., Consul General at St. Petersburg; 47.
Wuddowes, Colonel Henry; 40.
Wuntona, Robt. de, witness; 91.
Wyat, Sir Thomas, charges against; 276.
Wyatt, Tho., certificate by; 191.
Wyburne, Mr. Anthony, letter to; 277.
Wyche, —, letter of; 307.
Wycliffe, Rob., witness; 73.
Wycombe, Ricardus; 172.
Wyges, a Jesuit priest; 266.
Wykham, Oliver, intercepted letter of; 37.
Wyldman, John; 202.
Wylde:
  Mr.; 190.
  John; 102.
Wylkyns, Will., lease to; 140.
Wymundham, deed dated at; 64.
Wynbusch, a lawyer; 174.
Wyndham:
  Sir Charles; 151.
  Thos., petition of; 10.
Wyngfelde:
  Sir John, marriage contract by; 93.
  —— daughter of; ib.

Wynkepyry, sequestration of; 145.
Wynter, Col.; 40.
Wyre, John; 230.
Wyse, Robert, grants to; 71.
Wyseman, Rich., letter of; 9.
Wytham:
  letter dated at; 13.
  Capt., overpowered by the militia; 25.
  —— his dangerous position at York; 26.
  Mrs., letter to; ib.
Wythefeld, lands in; 64.
Wythere, John of Barstone, grant to; 66.
Wythiforde, Edward, of Kyderminster, grant by; ib.
Wytney, rectory of; 135.

Y.

Yale:
  Lordship of; 146.
  Dr. Tho.; 295.
Yarmouth:
  Earl of; 107.
  —— letters of; 9, 11.
  Countess of, letter of; 38.
  Lord, letter of; 13.
  —— petition signed by; 21.
  Viscount, letter to; 13.
Yate, Tho., paper by; 300.
Yatele, players of; 173.
Yeates, Mr., chaplain; 147.
Yelverton, Charles, case of; 158.
Yeomans, Sir Robert, complaint by; 12.
Yerne; 95.
Yong, James; 284.
York; 88, 121, 123.
  account for a journey to; 124.
  address by the corporation of; 30.
  arms delivered at; 25.
  Charles I. at; 293.
  concealed lands in; 145.
  documents relating to; 57.
  election at; 35, 36, 37.
  election for the Convention at; 35.
  letters dated at; 26, 27, 28, 29, 30, 32, 34, 35, 36, 37, 306.
  license dated at; 119.
  manor of; 30, 32.
  —— letter dated at; 9.
  mayor and corporation of; 7.
  —— recommendation by; 37.
  military revolution at; 26, 27.
  mutiny of the militia at; 25.
  returns of troops at; 31.
  Round Tower in; 241.
  Scotch letters taken at; 23, 25.
  theatricals at; 77.
  Garden, mass said at; 17.
  Archbishop of; 47, 251.
  Dean of; 253.
  James, Duke of; 22, 77, 85, 104.
  —— creation of; 275.

ork—*cont.*
  James, Duke of, inquiry concerning; 241.
  —— his flag-ship in action; 85.
  —— his picture; 92.
  —— his yatcht; 4.
  —— naval report to; 8.
  —— Lord High Admiral; 38.
  Duchess of, information against her factor; 17.
  Duke of (1769), precedence of; 47.
Yorke:
  George; 135.
  Gen. Joseph, letters of; 44.
  Sir John, and his wife, libel by; 162.
  Sir Will., member of Convention for Boston; 31, 32.
Yorkshire:
  Custos Rotulorum for the East Riding of; 8.
  deeds relating to; 56, 57.
  deputy lieutenants of; 25, 28.
  enclosures destroyed in; 161.
  excise of; 37.
  high sheriff of; 36, 37.
  lands in; 73.
  letters intercepted in; 25, 36.
  list of towns in; 41.

Yorkshire—*cont.*
  petition of the gentry of; 248.
  militia of; 36.
  —— report on the; 20.
  —— to be assembled; 26.
  Papists in; 25.
  Papists horses seized in; 36.
  possessions of Rufford Abbey in; 119.
  precautions against Papists in; 37.
  projects for the Revolution in; 30.
  selection of a candidate for; 125.
  "the black box" taken in; 25.
  the Revolution begun in; 26.
Young:
  Joseph, information by; 19.
  v. Broughton, case of; 162.
  Younge, Edw., prebendary; 97.

Z.

Zinzan, Sir Sigismund, case of; 159.

www.ingramcontent.com/pod-product-compliance
Lightning Source LLC
Chambersburg PA
CBHW022333230426
43664CB00040B/478